Kawasaki 454LTD/LTD450 Vulcan 500 and Ninja 250

Service and Repair Manual

by Alan Ahlstrand

Models covered

EN450 (454LTD/LTD450) 454 cc. 1985 thru 1990
EN500 (Vulcan 500) 498 cc. 1990 thru 2007
EX250 (Ninja 250, GPX250R, GPZ250R) 248 cc. 1986 thru 2007

2053-3U6-2

© Haynes North America, Inc. 2002, 2007, 2016
With permission from J.H. Haynes & Co. Ltd.

A book in the **Haynes Service and Repair Manual Series**

ABCDE
FGHI

All rights reserved. No part of this book may be reproduced or transmitted in any form or by any means, electronic or mechanical, including photocopying, recording or by any information storage or retrieval system, without permission in writing from the copyright holder.

ISBN-10: **1-62092-234-7**
ISBN-13: **978-1-62092-234-7**

Library of Congress Control Number: 2007926030

Printed in Malaysia

Haynes Publishing
Sparkford, Nr Yeovil, Somerset BA22 7JJ, England

Haynes North America, Inc
859 Lawrence Drive, Newbury Park, California 91320, USA
www.haynes.com

16-272

Contents

LIVING WITH YOUR KAWASAKI

Introduction

Kawasaki - The Green Meanies	Page	0•4
Acknowledgements	Page	0•7
About this manual	Page	0•7
Identification numbers	Page	0•8
Buying spare parts	Page	0•10
Safety first!	Page	0•11

Daily (pre-ride) checks

Engine/transmission oil level check	Page	0•12
Coolant level check	Page	0•13
Brake fluid level checks	Page	0•14
Suspension, steering and final drive checks	Page	0•15
Legal and safety checks	Page	0•15
Tire checks	Page	0•16

MAINTENANCE

Routine maintenance and servicing

Specifications	Page	1•1
Recommended lubricants and fluids	Page	1•2
Component locations	Page	1•4
Maintenance schedule	Page	1•8
Maintenance procedures	Page	1•10

Contents

REPAIRS AND OVERHAUL

Engine, transmission and associated systems

Engine, clutch and transmission	Page	2•1
Cooling system	Page	3•1
Fuel and exhaust systems	Page	4•1
Ignition system	Page	5•1

Chassis and bodywork components

Steering	Page	6•1
Suspension	Page	6•9
Final drive	Page	6•12
Brakes	Page	7•1
Wheels	Page	7•11
Tires	Page	7•15
Frame and bodywork	Page	8•1

Electrical system
Page 9•1

Wiring diagrams
Page 9•23

REFERENCE

Dimensions and Weights	Page	REF•1
Tools and Workshop Tips	Page	REF•4
Conversion Factors	Page	REF•22
Motorcycle chemicals and lubricants	Page	REF•23
Storage	Page	REF•24
Troubleshooting	Page	REF•27
Troubleshooting equipment	Page	REF•36
Technical terms explained	Page	REF•43

Index
Page REF•51

Introduction

Kawasaki
The Green Meanies

by Julian Ryder

Kawasaki Heavy Industries

Kawasaki is a company of contradictions. It is the smallest of the big four Japanese manufacturers but the biggest company, it was the last of the four to make and market motorcycles yet it owns the oldest name in the Japanese industry, and it was the first to set up a factory in the USA. Kawasaki Heavy Industries, of which the motorcycle operation is but a small component, is a massive company with its heritage firmly in the old heavy industries like shipbuilding and railways; nowadays it is as much involved in aerospace as in motorcycles.

In fact it may be because of this that Kawasaki's motorcycles have always been quirky, you get the impression that they are designed by a small group of enthusiasts who are given an admirably free hand. More realistically, it may be that Kawasaki's designers have experience with techniques and materials from other engineering disciplines. Either way, Kawasaki have managed to be the factory who surprise us more than the rest. Quite often, they do this by totally ignoring a market segment the others are scrabbling over, but more often they hit us with pure, undiluted performance.

The origins of the company, and its name, go back to 1878 when Shozo Kawasaki set up a dockyard in Tokyo. By the late 1930s, the company was making its own steel in massive steelworks and manufacturing railway locos and rolling stock. In the run up to war, the Kawasaki Aircraft Company was set up in 1937 and it was this arm of the now giant operation that would look to motorcycle engine manufacture in post-war Japan.

They bought their high-technology experience to bear first on engines which were sold on to a number of manufacturers as original equipment. Both two- and four-stroke units were made, a 58 cc and 148 cc OHC unit. One of the customer companies was Meihatsu Heavy Industries, another company within the Kawasaki group, which in 1961 was shaken up and renamed Kawasaki Auto Sales. At the same time, the Akashi factory which was to be Kawasaki's main production facility until the Kobe earthquake of 1995, was opened. Shortly afterwards, Kawasaki took over the ailing Meguro company, Japan's oldest motorcycle maker, thus instantly obtaining a range of bigger bikes which were marketed as Kawasaki-Meguros. The following year, the first bike to be made and sold as a Kawasaki was produced, a 125cc single called the B8 and in 1963 a motocross version, the B8M appeared.

The three cylinder two-stroke 750 H2

Introduction

Model development

Kawasaki's first appearance on a road-race circuit came in 1965 with a batch of disc-valve 125 twins. They were no match for the opposition from Japan in the shape of Suzuki and Yamaha or for the fading force of the factory MZs from East Germany. Only after the other Japanese factories had pulled out of the class did Kawasaki win, with British rider Dave Simmonds becoming World 125 GP Champion in 1969 on a bike that looked astonishingly similar to the original racer. That same year Kawasaki reorganized once again, this time merging three companies to form Kawasaki Heavy Industries. One of the new organization's objectives was to take motorcycle production forward and exploit markets outside Japan.

KHI achieved that target immediately and set out their stall for the future with the astonishing and frightening H1. This three-cylinder air-cooled 500 cc two-stroke was arguably the first modern pure performance bike to hit the market. It hypnotized a whole generation of motorcyclists who'd never before encountered such a ferocious, wheelie inducing power band or such shattering straight-line speed allied to questionable handling. And as for the 750 cc version ...

The triples perfectly suited the late '60s, fitting in well with the student demonstrations of 1968 and the anti-establishment ethos of the Summer of Love. Unfortunately, the oil crisis would put an end to the thirsty strokers but Kawasaki had another high-performance ace up their corporate sleeve. Or rather they thought they did.

The 1968 Tokyo Show saw probably the single most significant new motorcycle ever made unveiled: the Honda CB750. At Kawasaki it caused a major shock, for they also had a 750 cc four, code-named New York Steak, almost ready to roll and it was a double, rather than single, overhead cam motor. Bravely, they took the decision to go ahead – but with the motor taken out to 900 cc. The result was the Z1, unveiled at the 1972 Cologne Show. It was a bike straight out of the same mould as the H1, scare stories spread about unmanageable power, dubious straight-line stability and frightening handling, none of which stopped the sales graph rocketing upwards and led to the coining of the term 'superbike'. While rising fuel prices cut short development of the big two-strokes, the Z1 went on to found a dynasty, indeed its genes can still be detected in Kawasaki's latest products like the ZZ-R1100 (Ninja ZX-11).

This is another characteristic of the way Kawasaki operates. Models quite often have very long lives, or gradually evolve. There is no major difference between that first Z1 and the air-cooled GPz range. Add water-cooling and you have the GPZ900, which in turn metamorphosed into the GPZ1000RX and then the ZX-10 and the ZZ-R1100. Indeed, the last three models share the same 58mm

The first Superbike, Kawasaki's 900 cc Z1

One of the two-stroke engined KH and KE range - the KE100B

0•6 Introduction

stroke. The bikes are obviously very different but it's difficult to put your finger on exactly why.

Other models have remained effectively untouched for over a decade: the KH and KE single-cylinder air-cooled two-stroke learner bikes, the GT550 and 750 shaft-drive hacks favored by big city despatch riders and the GPz305 being prime examples. It's only when they step outside the performance field that Kawasakis seems less sure. Their first factory customs were dire, you simply got the impression that the team that designed them didn't have their heart in the job. Only when the Classic range appeared in 1995 did they get it right.

Racing success

Kawasaki also have a more focused approach to racing than the other factories. The policy has always been to race the road bikes and with just a couple of exceptions that's what they've done. Even Simmonds' championship winner bore a strong resemblance to the twins they were selling in the late '60s and racing versions of the 500 and 750 cc triples were also sold as over-the-counter racers, the H1R and H2R. The 500 was in the forefront of the two-stroke assault on MV Agusta but wasn't a Grand Prix winner. It was the 750 that made the impact and carried the factory's image in F750 racing against the Suzuki triples and Yamaha fours.

The factory's decision to use green, usually regarded as an unlucky color in sport, meant its bikes and personnel stood out and the phrase 'Green Meanies' fitted them perfectly. The Z1 motor soon became a full 1000 cc and powered Kawasaki's assault in F1 racing, notably in endurance which Kawasaki saw as being most closely related to its road bikes.

That didn't stop them dominating 250 and 350 cc GPs with a tandem twin two-stroke in the late '70s and early '80s, but

The GT750 - a favorite hack for despatch riders

their path-breaking monocoque 500 while a race winner never won a world title. When Superbike arrived, Kawasaki's road 750s weren't as track-friendly as the opposition's out-and-out race replicas. This makes Scott Russell's World title on the ZXR750 in 1993 even more praiseworthy, for the homologation bike, the ZXR750RR, was much heavier and much more of a road bike than the Italian and Japanese competition. The fact that Russell's title remains the only Superbike world crown won by an across-the-frame four is testament to both bike and rider.

After the ZXR came the ZX-7R and the ZX-9R, a new generation of supersportsters that managed to be useable on the road as well as the track. The 750 version stuck with carburetors while the rest of the Superbike pack went on to fuel injection, something which still gives Kawasaki's racers a few more problems to deal with than their opposition. Getting a ZX-7RR Superbike to work perfectly means getting knife-edge set-up precisely right. A fraction either way and the bike goes from competitive to unrideable.

The first ZX-9R was greeted with less than overwhelming reviews mainly due to its bulk, but when the C1 model arrived for '98 after a serious weight-loss program the big Kawasaki was truly a match for the then king of the hill, the FireBlade. Sales figures reflected the revised opinions of the road-testers, but a year later the Yamaha R1 arrived to re-arrange the parameters by which cutting edge sportsters are judged. But if you don't spend all your biking time at track days, the big Kawasaki is at least as good a road bike as the competition., especially if you're big, tall, or in the habit of carrying a passenger from time to time.

The company's Supersport 600 contenders have, like the bigger bikes, been more sports-tourers than race-replicas, yet they too have been competitive on the track. Indeed, the

The high-performance ZXR750

flagship bike, the ZZ-R1100, is most definitely a sports tourer capable of carrying two people and their luggage at high speed in comfort all day and then doing it again the next day. Try that on one of the race replicas and you'll be in need of a course of treatment from a chiropractor.

Through doing it their way Kawasaki developed a brand loyalty for their performance bikes that kept the Z1's derivatives in production until the mid-'80s and turned the bike into a classic in its model life. You could even argue that the Z1 lives on in the shape of the 1100 Zephyr's GPz1100-derived motor. And that's another Kawasaki invention, the retro bike. But when you look at what many commentators refer to as the retro boom, especially in Japan, you find that it is no such thing. It is the Zephyr boom. Just another example of Japan's most surprising motorcycle manufacturer getting it right again.

The Ninja ZX-7R ZX750P model

The Kawasaki LTD, Vulcan 500 and EX250

EN450/500

Kawasaki's entry into the lightweight cruiser market came with the introduction of the EN450 (known as the 454 LTD in the US and the LTD 450 in other markets). Its successor, the EN500 (Vulcan 500) was introduced in 1990 (both bikes were sold during the 1990 model year).

The engine was a liquid cooled, two-cylinder four-stroke with double overhead camshafts driven by chain from the center of the crankshaft. Four valves per cylinder were operated by forked rocker arms located on the underside of each camshaft. The crankcases were two-piece, split horizontally, with a separate cylinder block. A balancer shaft, gear-driven off the crankshaft, was located in the front of the crankcase.

Drive was transmitted to the six-speed gearbox by chain through a cable-operated, five-spring multi-plate clutch, and to the rear wheel by a cogged belt and sprockets (EN450 and EN500 A models) or by a drive chain and sprockets (EN500 C models).

Fuel was drawn into the engine via two 34 mm constant vacuum Keihin carburettors. Kawasaki's Clean Air System, initially only fitted to US market models, reduced the level of unburned hydrocarbons in the exhaust gases. The exhaust system was a two-into-two design with a crossover pipe.

The chassis comprised a square-section, steel duplex cradle frame with a box-section swingarm. Front suspension was by conventional, non-adjustable telescopic forks and rear suspension was by twin shock absorbers with spring pre-load adjustment only.

Braking was by one single-piston disc brake at the front and a drum brake at the rear.

The Kawasaki Clean Air System was fitted to all market models in 2001.

EX250

The EX250 (Ninja 250R in the US; GPZ250R or GPX250R in other markets) was introduced in 1986.

The engine and transmission unit was a liquid cooled, two-cylinder four-stroke similar to that of the EN450/500. A two-into-two exhaust system with crossover pipe was fitted.

The frame was a diamond design, constructed from round-section tubular steel, and rear suspension was by a single shock absorber and Kawasaki's Uni-Trak rising rate progressive linkage.

Braking on 1986 and 1987 models was by one single-piston disc brake at front and rear. 1988 and later models used a single, two-piston disc brake at front and rear.

Styled as a sport bike, the EX250 was fitted with a fairing (including a belly pan on 1988 and later models), clip-on handlebars and individual speedometer and tachometer units.

Acknowledgements

Our thanks to Bike World, Sunnyvale California, for supplying the motorcycles used for the EN500 photographs and to Joe Ortiz, who did the mechanical work and suggested many of the photographs.

Thanks also to Grand Prix, Santa Clara, California, for supplying the motorcycle used for the EX250 photographs, to Mark Zeuger, service manager, for fitting the project into his shop's busy schedule, and to Craig Wardner, service technician, for doing the mechanical work and supplying valuable technical information. The introduction "Kawasaki - the Green Meanies" was written by Julian Ryder, with additional information on the EN450/500 and EX250 models by Alan Ahlstrand.

About this manual

The aim of this manual is to help you get the best value from your motorcycle. It can do so in several ways. It can help you decide what work must be done, even if you choose to have it done by a dealer; it provides information and procedures for routine maintenance and servicing; and it offers diagnostic and repair procedures to follow when trouble occurs.

We hope you use the manual to tackle the work yourself. For many simpler jobs, doing it yourself may be quicker than arranging an appointment to get the motorcycle into a dealer and making the trips to leave it and pick it up. More importantly, a lot of money can be saved by avoiding the expense the shop must pass on to you to cover its labor and overhead costs. An added benefit is the sense of satisfaction and accomplishment that you feel after doing the job yourself.

References to the left or right side of the motorcycle assume you are sitting on the seat, facing forward.

We take great pride in the accuracy of information given in this manual, but motorcycle manufacturers make alterations and design changes during the production run of a particular motorcycle of which they do not inform us. No liability can be accepted by the authors or publishers for loss, damage or injury caused by any errors in, or omissions from, the information given.

0•8 Identification numbers

Engine and frame numbers

The frame serial number is stamped into the right side of the steering head. The engine number is stamped into the right side of the crankcase and is visible from the right side of the machine. Both of these numbers should be recorded and kept in a safe place so they can be given to law enforcement officials in the event of a theft.

The frame serial number and engine serial number should also be kept in a handy place (such as with your driver's license) so they are always available when purchasing or ordering parts for your machine.

The model code (e.g. EN500-C9) can be determined from the frame serial numbers in the accompanying table.

EN450/500

Year	Model Code	Frame number range	Engine number range
1985	EN450 A1	US JKAENGA1-FA000001 to 013000 UK EN450A-000001 to 013000	EN450EA-000001 to 013000 EN450AE-000001 to 012000
1986	EN450 A2	US JKAENGA1-GA013001 to 028000 UK EN450A-013001 to 028000	ENG450AE-013001 to 028000 EN450A-012001 to 026000
1987	EN450 A3	US JKAENGA1-HA028001 to O32000 UK EN450A-028001 to 032000	EN450EA-028001 to 030300 EN450A-026001 to 030300
1988	EN450 A4	US JKAENGA1-JA032001 to 035300 UK EN450A-030301-on	EN450A-032001 to 033000 EN450A-030301-on
1989	EN450 A5	US JKAENGA1-KA035301-on UK EN450A-035301-on	EN450A-033301-on EN450A-033301-on
1990	EN450 A6	US JKAENGA1-LA040001-on UK model not imported	EN450AE-033301-on
1990	EN500 A1	US JKAENVA1-LA000001 to 007000 UK EN500A-000001-on	EX500-008186 to 010200/011051 to 015050 EN500AE-018001-on
1991	EN500 A2	US JKAENVA1-MA007001 to 0081851/ 010201 to 011050/015051 to 025000 UK EN500A1 continued	EX500AE-018001-on
1992	EN500 A3	JKAENVA1-NA025001 to O45000 UK EN500A-025001-on	EX500AE-018001-on EN500AE-018000-on
1993	EN500 A4	US JKAEXNA1-PA045001 UK EN500A3 continued	EN500AE-018000-on

Identification numbers

The following table is a breakdown of 1994 and later initial frame numbers by model and year of production:

Year	Model	Initial frame number
1994	EN500-A5	JKAENVA1-RA090001 or EN500A-080001
1995	EN500-A6	JKAENVA1-SA090001 or EN500A-090001
1996	EN500-A7	JKAENVA1-TA090001 or EN500A-100001
1996	EN500-C1	JKAENVC1-TA000001 or EN500C-000001
1997	EN500-C2	JKAENVC1-TA005001 or EN500C-005001
1998	Not available	
1999	EN500-C4	JKAENVC1-XA156001 or JKAEN500ACA-156001
2000	EN500-C5	JKAENVC1-YA164001 or JKAEN500ACA-164001
2001	EN500-C6	JKAENVC1-1A168001 or JKAEN500ACA-168001
2002	EN500-C7	JKAENVC1-2A173001 or JKAEN500ACA-173001
2003	EN500-C8	JKAENVC1-3A180001 or JKAEN500ACA-180001
2004	EN500-C9	JKAENVC1-4A185001
2005	EN500-C10	JKAENVC1-5A189001
2006	EN500-C6F	JKAENVC1-6A196001
2007	EN500-C7F	JKAENVC1-7A204001

EX250

Year	Model	Initial frame number
1986	EX250-E1	JKAEXME1-GA000001 or EX250E-000001
1987	EX250-E2	JKAEXME1-HA006201 or EX250E-000001
1988	EX250-F2	JKAEXMF1-JA000001, JKAEXMF1-JA008946, EX250-F000001 or EX250F-008946
1989	EX250-F3	JKAEXMF1-KA004604, JKAEXMF1-JA008946, EX250-F000001 or EX250F-008946
1990	EX250-F4	JKAEXMF1-LA014001
1992	EX250-F6	JKAEXMF1-KA004604, JKAEXMF1-JA008946, EX250-F000001 or EX250F-008946
1993	EX250-F7	JKAEXMF1-PA030001
1994	EX250-F8	JKAEXMF1-RA038001 or EX250F-038001
1995	EX250-F9	JKAEXMF1-SA044001 or EX250F-044001
1996	EX250-F10	JKAEXMF1-TA049001 or EX250F-049001
1997	EX250-F11	JKAEXMF1-VA052001 or EX250F-052001
2000	EX250-F14	JKAEXMF1-YA069001
2001	EX250-F15	JKAEXMF1-1A077001
2002	EX250-F16	JKAEXMF1-2A086001
2003	EX250-F17	JKAEXMF1-3A096001
2004	EX250-F18	JKAEXMF1-4DA00001
2005	EX250-F19	JKAEXMF1-5DA07709
2006	EX250-F6F	JKAEXMF1-6DA16601
2007	EX250-F7F	JKAEXMF1-7DA27401

Identification numbers

Buying spare parts

Once you have found all the identification numbers, record them for reference when buying parts. Since the manufacturers change specifications, parts and vendors (companies that manufacture various components on the machine), providing the ID numbers is the only way to be reasonably sure that you are buying the correct parts.

Whenever possible, take the worn part to the dealer so direct comparison with the new component can be made. Along the trail from the manufacturer to the parts shelf, there are numerous places that the part can end up with the wrong number or be listed incorrectly.

The two places to purchase new parts for your motorcycle – the accessory store and the franchised dealer – differ in the type of parts they carry. While dealers can obtain virtually every part for your motorcycle, the accessory dealer is usually limited to normal high wear items such as shock absorbers, tune-up parts, various engine gaskets, cables, chains, brake parts, etc. Rarely will an accessory outlet have major suspension components, cylinders, transmission gears, or cases.

Used parts can be obtained for considerably less than new ones, but you can't always be sure of what you're getting. Once again, take your worn part to the salvage yard for direct comparison.

Whether buying new, used or rebuilt parts, the best course is to deal directly with someone who specializes in parts for your particular make.

The engine number is stamped in the top of the crankcase on the right-hand side of the engine (EX250 shown)

The frame number is stamped in the right-hand side of the steering head (EX250 shown)

Safety first! 0•11

Professional mechanics are trained in safe working procedures. However enthusiastic you may be about getting on with the job at hand, take the time to ensure that your safety is not put at risk. A moment's lack of attention can result in an accident, as can failure to observe simple precautions.

There will always be new ways of having accidents, and the following is not a comprehensive list of all dangers; it is intended rather to make you aware of the risks and to encourage a safe approach to all work you carry out on your bike.

Asbestos

● Certain friction, insulating, sealing and other products - such as brake pads, clutch linings, gaskets, etc. - contain asbestos. Extreme care must be taken to avoid inhalation of dust from such products since it is hazardous to health. If in doubt, assume that they do contain asbestos.

Fire

● Remember at all times that gasoline is highly flammable. Never smoke or have any kind of naked flame around, when working on the vehicle. But the risk does not end there - a spark caused by an electrical short-circuit, by two metal surfaces contacting each other, by careless use of tools, or even by static electricity built up in your body under certain conditions, can ignite gasoline vapor, which in a confined space is highly explosive. Never use gasoline as a cleaning solvent. Use an approved safety solvent.

● Always disconnect the battery ground terminal before working on any part of the fuel or electrical system, and never risk spilling fuel on to a hot engine or exhaust.

● It is recommended that a fire extinguisher of a type suitable for fuel and electrical fires is kept handy in the garage or workplace at all times. Never try to extinguish a fuel or electrical fire with water.

Fumes

● Certain fumes are highly toxic and can quickly cause unconsciousness and even death if inhaled to any extent. Gasoline vapor comes into this category, as do the vapors from certain solvents such as trichloro-ethylene. Any draining or pouring of such volatile fluids should be done in a well ventilated area.

● When using cleaning fluids and solvents, read the instructions carefully. Never use materials from unmarked containers - they may give off poisonous vapors.

● Never run the engine of a motor vehicle in an enclosed space such as a garage. Exhaust fumes contain carbon monoxide which is extremely poisonous; if you need to run the engine, always do so in the open air or at least have the rear of the vehicle outside the workplace.

The battery

● Never cause a spark, or allow a naked light near the vehicle's battery. It will normally be giving off a certain amount of hydrogen gas, which is highly explosive.

● Always disconnect the battery ground terminal before working on the fuel or electrical systems (except where noted).

● If possible, loosen the filler plugs or cover when charging the battery from an external source. Do not charge at an excessive rate or the battery may burst.

● Take care when topping up, cleaning or carrying the battery. The acid electrolyte, even when diluted, is very corrosive and should not be allowed to contact the eyes or skin. Always wear rubber gloves and goggles or a face shield. If you ever need to prepare electrolyte yourself, always add the acid slowly to the water; never add the water to the acid.

Electricity

● When using an electric power tool, inspection light etc., always ensure that the appliance is correctly connected to its plug and that, where necessary, it is properly grounded. Do not use such appliances in damp conditions and, again, beware of creating a spark or applying excessive heat in the vicinity of fuel or fuel vapor. Also ensure that the appliances meet national safety standards.

● A severe electric shock can result from touching certain parts of the electrical system, such as the spark plug wires (HT leads), when the engine is running or being cranked, particularly if components are damp or the insulation is defective. Where an electronic ignition system is used, the secondary (HT) voltage is much higher and could prove fatal.

Remember...

✗ **Don't** start the engine without first ascertaining that the transmission is in neutral.

✗ **Don't** suddenly remove the pressure cap from a hot cooling system - cover it with a cloth and release the pressure gradually first, or you may get scalded by escaping coolant.

✗ **Don't** attempt to drain oil until you are sure it has cooled sufficiently to avoid scalding you.

✗ **Don't** grasp any part of the engine or exhaust system without first ascertaining that it is cool enough not to burn you.

✗ **Don't** allow brake fluid or antifreeze to contact the machine's paintwork or plastic components.

✗ **Don't** siphon toxic liquids such as fuel, hydraulic fluid or antifreeze by mouth, or allow them to remain on your skin.

✗ **Don't** inhale dust - it may be injurious to health (see Asbestos heading).

✗ **Don't** allow any spilled oil or grease to remain on the floor - wipe it up right away, before someone slips on it.

✗ **Don't** use ill-fitting wrenches or other tools which may slip and cause injury.

✗ **Don't** lift a heavy component which may be beyond your capability - get assistance.

✗ **Don't** rush to finish a job or take unverified short cuts.

✗ **Don't** allow children or animals in or around an unattended vehicle.

✗ **Don't** inflate a tire above the recommended pressure. Apart from overstressing the carcass, in extreme cases the tire may blow off forcibly.

✔ **Do** ensure that the machine is supported securely at all times. This is especially important when the machine is blocked up to aid wheel or fork removal.

✔ **Do** take care when attempting to loosen a stubborn nut or bolt. It is generally better to pull on a wrench, rather than push, so that if you slip, you fall away from the machine rather than onto it.

✔ **Do** wear eye protection when using power tools such as drill, sander, bench grinder etc.

✔ **Do** use a barrier cream on your hands prior to undertaking dirty jobs - it will protect your skin from infection as well as making the dirt easier to remove afterwards; but make sure your hands aren't left slippery. Note that long-term contact with used engine oil can be a health hazard.

✔ **Do** keep loose clothing (cuffs, ties etc. and long hair) well out of the way of moving mechanical parts.

✔ **Do** remove rings, wristwatch etc., before working on the vehicle - especially the electrical system.

✔ **Do** keep your work area tidy - it is only too easy to fall over articles left lying around.

✔ **Do** exercise caution when compressing springs for removal or installation. Ensure that the tension is applied and released in a controlled manner, using suitable tools which preclude the possibility of the spring escaping violently.

✔ **Do** ensure that any lifting tackle used has a safe working load rating adequate for the job.

✔ **Do** get someone to check periodically that all is well, when working alone on the vehicle.

✔ **Do** carry out work in a logical sequence and check that everything is correctly assembled and tightened afterwards.

✔ **Do** remember that your vehicle's safety affects that of yourself and others. If in doubt on any point, get professional advice.

● If in spite of following these precautions, you are unfortunate enough to injure yourself, seek medical attention as soon as possible.

0•12 Daily (pre-ride) checks

1 Engine/transmission oil level check

Before you start:

✔ Start the engine and allow it to reach normal operating temperature.

Caution: Do not run the engine in an enclosed space such as a garage or workshop.

✔ Stop the engine and support the motor-cycle on its sidestand. Allow it to stand undisturbed for a few minutes to allow the oil level to stabilize. Make sure the motorcycle is on level ground.

✔ The oil level is viewed through the window in the clutch cover on the right-hand side of the engine. Wipe the glass clean before inspection to make the check easier.

Bike care:

● If you have to add oil frequently, you should check whether you have any oil leaks. If there is no sign of oil leakage from the joints and gaskets the engine could be burning oil (see *Troubleshooting*).

The correct oil

● Modern, high-revving engines place great demands on their oil. It is very important that the correct oil for your bike is used.
● Always top up with a good quality oil of the specified type and viscosity and do not overfill the engine.

Oil type	
Through 2000	API grade SE, SF or SG
2001 and later	API grade SE, SF or SG, or API grade SH, SJ or SL meeting JASO MA standard
Oil viscosity	
In cold climates	SAE 10W-40 or 10W-50
In warm climates	SAE 20W-40 or 20W-50

1 With the motorcycle held vertical, check the oil level in the window at the bottom of the clutch cover (arrow). The level should be between the upper and lower level marks. If it's low, unscrew the oil filler cap (upper arrow) and add oil. This is the EN450/500 oil window

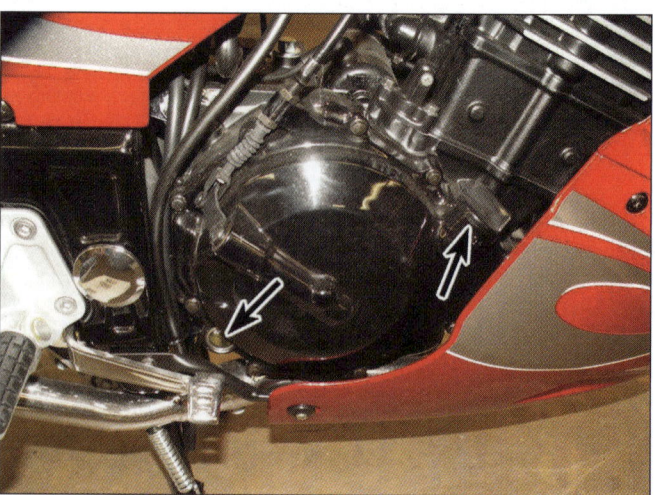

2 The EX250 oil level is checked in the same way - if the oil level is not between the lines in the window (lower arrow), remove the filler cap (upper arrow) to add oil

Daily (pre-ride) checks 0•13

2 Coolant level check

> ⚠ **Warning: DO NOT remove the filler neck pressure cap to add coolant. Topping up is done via the coolant reservoir tank filler. DO NOT leave open containers of coolant about, as it is poisonous.**

Before you start:

✔ Make sure you have a supply of coolant available (a mixture of 50% distilled water and 50% corrosion inhibited ethylene glycol anti-freeze is needed).
✔ Always check the coolant level when the engine is cold.
Caution: Do not run the engine in an enclosed space such as a garage or workshop.
✔ Ensure the motorcycle is held vertical while checking the coolant level. Make sure the motorcycle is on level ground.

Bike care:

● Use only the specified coolant mixture. It is important that anti-freeze is used in the system all year round, and not just in the winter. Do not top the system up using only water, as the system will become too diluted.
● Do not overfill the reservoir tank. If the coolant is significantly above the F (full) level line at any time, the surplus should be siphoned or drained off to prevent the possibility of it being expelled out of the overflow hose.
● If the coolant level falls steadily, check the system for leaks (see Chapter 1). If no leaks are found and the level continues to fall, it is recommended that the machine is taken to a Kawasaki dealer for a pressure test.

1 The coolant reservoir on EN450 and early EN500 models can be checked through the access hole in the right side cover. With the motorcycle on its centerstand or held upright, the coolant level should be between the lines on the side of the reservoir. If it's low, unscrew the cap, add coolant to bring the level to the upper level line, then tighten the cap securely

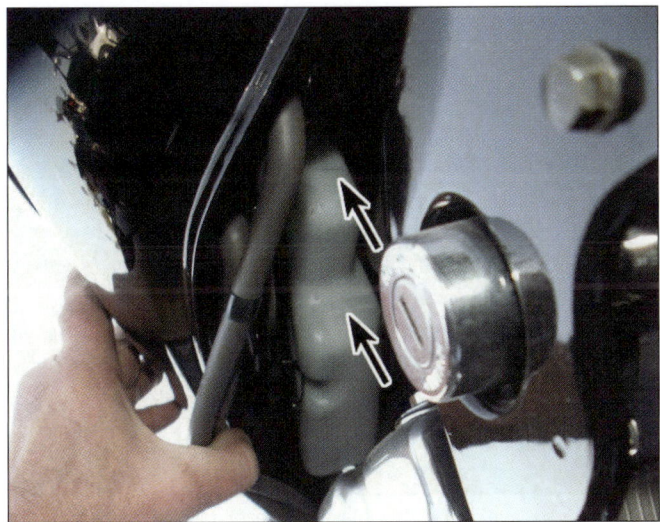

2 The coolant reservoir on later EN500 models is behind the right side cover. The level lines are visible at the front of the cover (arrows). To remove the cap and add coolant, you'll need to remove the side cover (see Chapter 8). Add coolant to bring the level to the upper level line, then tighten the cap securely

3 You'll need to remove the seat and left side cover for access to the EX250 coolant reservoir (see Chapter 8). With the motorcycle held upright, the coolant level should be between the lines on the side of the reservoir. If it's low, unscrew the cap, add coolant to bring the level to the upper level line, then tighten the cap securely

Daily (pre-ride) checks

3 Brake fluid level check

The rear brake fluid level check only applies to EX250 models.

> **Warning:** Hydraulic fluid can harm your eyes and damage painted surfaces, so use extreme caution when handling and pouring it and cover surrounding surfaces with rag. Do not use fluid that has been standing open for some time, as it absorbs moisture from the air which can cause a dangerous loss of braking effectiveness.

Before you start:

✔ Ensure the motorcycle is held vertical while checking the levels. Make sure the motorcycle is on level ground.

✔ Make sure you have the correct hydraulic fluid. DOT 4 is recommended. Never reuse old fluid.

✔ Wrap a rag around the reservoir being worked on to ensure that any spillage does not come into contact with painted surfaces.

Bike care:

● The fluid in the front and rear brake master cylinder reservoirs will drop slightly as the brake pads wear down.

● If any fluid reservoir requires repeated topping-up this is an indication of a hydraulic leak somewhere in the system, which should be investigated immediately.

● Check for signs of fluid leakage from the hydraulic hoses and components – if found, rectify immediately.

● Check the operation of both brakes before taking the machine on the road; if there is evidence of air in the system (spongy feel to lever on all models or pedal on EX250 models), it must be bled as described in Chapter 7.

1 With the front brake fluid reservoir as level as possible, check that the fluid level is above the LOWER level line on the inspection window. If the level is low on a round reservoir like this one, remove the reservoir screws (arrows), lift off the cover and add the specified fluid to bring the level up to the upper level line cast on the inside of the reservoir

2 The fluid level on rectangular front reservoirs is checked in the same way (the fluid level should be above the LOWER level line on the inspection window). If the level is low, remove the reservoir screws (arrows), lift off the cover and add the specified fluid to bring the level up to the upper level line cast on the inside of the reservoir

Daily (pre-ride) checks

3 The rear brake fluid reservoir on EX250 models is translucent and the fluid level can be seen through the plastic. If it's low, unscrew the cap and add the specified fluid to bring the level up between the lines

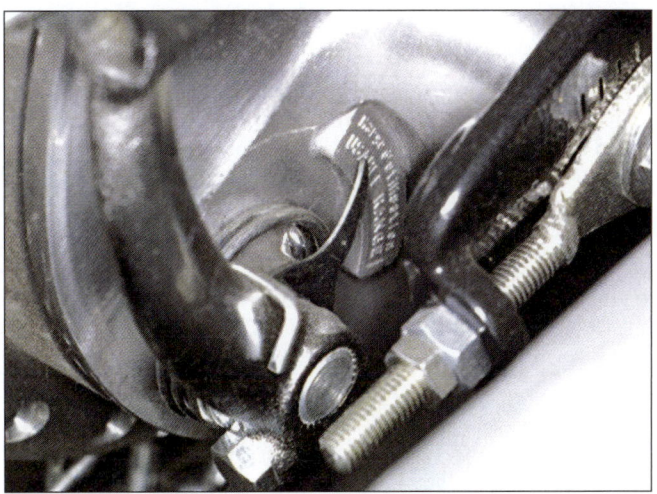

4 If the motorcycle has rear drum brakes (EN450/500 models), check lining wear. Press the brake pedal and note the position of the wear indicator pointer. If it's past the USABLE RANGE area cast on the brake drum, it's time for new brake shoes (see Chapter 7)

4 Suspension, steering and final drive checks

Suspension and Steering:
● Check that the front and rear suspension operate smoothly without binding.
● Check that the suspension is adjusted as required.
● Check that the steering moves smoothly from lock-to-lock.

Final drive:
● On chain drive models, check the drive chain slack isn't excessive and adjust it if necessary (see Chapter 1).
● On chain drive models, lubricate the chain if it looks dry (see Chapter 1).

● On belt drive models, inspect the belt and sprockets for wear or damage (see Chapter 1).

5 Legal and safety checks

Lighting and signalling:
● Take a minute to check that the headlight, tail light, brake light, instrument lights and turn signals all work correctly.
● Check that the horn sounds when the switch is operated.
● A working speedometer graduated in mph is a statutory requirement in the UK.

Safety:
● Check that the throttle grip rotates smoothly and snaps shut when released, in all steering positions. Also check for the correct amount of freeplay (see Chapter 1).
● Check that the engine shuts off when the kill switch is operated.
● Check that sidestand return spring holds the stand securely up when retracted.

Fuel:
● This may seem obvious, but check that you have enough fuel to complete your journey. If you notice signs of fuel leakage – rectify the cause immediately.
● Ensure you use the correct grade unleaded fuel – see Chapter 4 Specifications.

0•16 Daily (pre-ride) checks

6 Tire checks

The correct pressures:
● The tires must be checked when **cold**, not immediately after riding. Note that low tire pressures may cause the tire to slip on the rim or come off. High tire pressures will cause abnormal tread wear and unsafe handling.
● Use an accurate pressure gauge.
● Proper air pressure will increase tire life and provide maximum stability and ride comfort.

Tire care:
● Check the tires carefully for cuts, tears, embedded nails or other sharp objects and excessive wear. Operation of the motorcycle with excessively worn tires is extremely hazardous, as traction and handling are directly affected.
● Check the condition of the tire valve and ensure the dust cap is in place.
● Pick out any stones or nails which may have become embedded in the tire tread. If left, they will eventually penetrate through the casing and cause a puncture.

● If tire damage is apparent, or unexplained loss of pressure is experienced, seek the advice of a tire fitting specialist without delay.

Tire tread depth:
● Kawasaki recommends a minimum of 1 mm on the front tire. The minimum on the rear tire is 2 mm, or 3 mm if the motorcycle is ridden at speeds over 80 mph.
● Many tires now incorporate wear indicators in the tread. Identify the triangular pointer or 'TWI' mark on the tire sidewall to locate the indicator bar and replace the tire if the tread has worn down to the bar.

Tire pressures

Front	28 psi (1.9 Bars)
Rear (EN450/500)	
US, Canada and South Africa	
Up to 215 lbs (97.5 kg) load	28 psi (1.9 Bars)
Above 215 lbs (97.5 kg) load	32 psi (1.9 Bars)
Others	28 psi (1.9 Bars)
Rear (1986 and 1987 EX250)	32 psi (1.9 Bars)
Rear (1988 and later EX250)	
US, Canada and South Africa	
Up to 215 lbs (97.5 kg) load	28 psi (1.9 Bars)
Above 215 lbs (97.5 kg) load	32 psi (1.9 Bars)
Others	28 psi (1.9 Bars)

1 Check the tire pressures when the tires are **cold** and keep them properly inflated

2 Measure tread depth at the center of the tire using a tread depth gauge

3 Tire tread wear indicator bar and its location marking (usually either an arrow, a triangle or the letters TWI) on the sidewall (arrowed)

Chapter 1
Routine maintenance and servicing

Contents

Air filter element – servicing	21
Air suction valves – check	4
Battery electrolyte level/specific gravity – check	15
Brake caliper and master cylinder – overhaul	32
Brake fluid – replacement	27
Brake hose(s) – replacement	34
Brake pads and shoe linings – wear check	11
Brake pedal position and play – check and adjustment (drum brakes)	12
Brake system – general check	10
Carburetor synchronization – check and adjustment	6
Clutch – check and adjustment	8
Coolant – replacement	30
Cooling system – check	24
Cylinder compression – check	See Chapter 2C
Drive chain – lubrication	1
Drive chain and sprockets – wear check	9
Drivebelt chain – check and adjustment	2
Engine oil/filter – change	20
Evaporative emission control system (California models only) – check	7
Exhaust system – check	25
Fasteners – check	26
Fork oil – replacement	31
Fuel hoses – replacement	33
Fuel system – check and filter cleaning	22
Idle speed – check and adjustment	5
Lubrication – general	13
Rear brake cam – lubrication (drum brakes)	29
Rear suspension – lubrication	23
Spark plugs – clean and regap	3
Steering head bearings – check and adjustment	16
Steering head bearings – lubrication	28
Suspension – check	17
Throttle and choke operation/grip freeplay – check and adjustment	18
Valve clearances – check and adjustment	19
Wheels and tires – general check	14

Degrees of difficulty

Easy, suitable for novice with little experience		**Fairly easy,** suitable for beginner with some experience		**Fairly difficult,** suitable for competent DIY mechanic		**Difficult,** suitable for experienced DIY mechanic	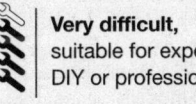	**Very difficult,** suitable for expert DIY or professional	

Specifications

Note: *A certain amount of maintenance data is included on decals stuck to the underside of the seat, on the inside of the right-hand side cover or on the drive chain guard.*

Engine
Spark plug type
    EN450/500 models (US and Canada) .... NGK D9EA or ND X27ES-U
    EN450/500 models (UK) .... NGK DR8ES or ND X27ESR-U
    EX250 models .... NGK DR9EA or ND X27ESR-U
Spark plug gap .... 0.6 to 0.7 mm (0.024 to 0.028 inch)

1•2 Routine maintenance and servicing

Specifications (continued)

Engine idle speed
- EN450/500 models (except California) .... 1200 ± 50 rpm
- EN450/500 California models .... 1300 ± 50 rpm
- EX250 models (except California) .... 1300 ± 50 rpm
- EX250 models (California) .... 1200 ± 50 rpm

Valve clearances (COLD engine)
- EN450/500
  - Intake .... 0.13 to 0.18 mm (0.005 to 0.007 inch)
  - Exhaust .... 0.18 to 0.23 mm (0.007 to 0.009 inch)
- EX250
  - Intake .... 0.08 to 0.13 mm (0.003 to 0.005 inch)
  - Exhaust .... 0.11 to 0.16 mm (0.004 to 0.006 inch)

Carburetor synchronization (vacuum difference
between cylinders) .... Less than 2 cm (0.391 inch) Hg
Cylinder numbering (from left side to right side of bike) .... 1 – 2

Chassis

Brake pad minimum thickness .... 1.0 mm (0.04 in)
Brake shoe lining minimum thickness .... 2.5 mm (0.10 in)
Brake pedal position below the top of the footrest
- EN450/500 models .... 50 to 60 mm (2 to 2-5/16 inches)
- EX250 models .... Approximately 40 mm (1-5/8 inches)

Freeplay adjustments
- Throttle grip .... 2 to 3 mm (0.08 to 0.12 inch)
- Clutch lever (gap between lever and lever bracket
  when freeplay is taken up) .... 2 to 3 mm (0.08 to 0.12 inch)
- Rear brake pedal (EN450/500 models) .... 20 to 30 mm (0.8 to 1.2 inch)
- Choke lever (if equipped) .... 2 to 3 mm (0.08 to 0.12 inch)

Drive belt (EN450/500 models)
- Slack (at 4/5 kg/9.9 lbs pressure)
  - EN450 models .... 8.5 to 18.5 mm (0.33 to 0.73 inch)
  - EN500 models .... 6.0 to 12.5 mm (0.24 to 0.49 inch)

Drive chain
- Slack
  - Standard .... 35 to 40 mm (1.38 to 1.57 in)
  - Service limit .... 45 mm (1.77 in)
- 20-link length .... 323 mm (12.73 in) maximum

Battery electrolyte specific gravity .... 1.280 at 20°C (68°F)
Tire pressures and tread depth .... see Daily (pre-ride) checks

Torque specifications

Oil drain plug
- EN450/500 .... 29 Nm (22 ft-lbs)
- EX250 .... 20 Nm (174 in-lbs)

Oil filter
- EN450/500 .... 17 Nm (150 in-lbs)
- EX250 .... 20 Nm (174 in-lbs)

Coolant drain bolt(s)
- EN450/500 models .... 12 Nm (104 inch-lbs)
- EX250 models .... 8 Nm (69 inch-lbs)

Spark plugs
- EN450/500 models .... 14 Nm (120 inch-lbs)
- EX250 models .... 13 Nm (113 inch-lbs)

Valve cover bolts .... See Chapter 2

Recommended lubricants and fluids

Engine/transmission oil type .... API grade SJ, SL or higher (without moly additives) meeting the JASO MA standard

Engine/transmission oil viscosity
- In cold climates – up to 15°C (60°F) .... SAE 10W40 or 10W50
- In warm climates – above 5°C (40°F) .... SAE 20W40 or 20W50

Engine/transmission oil capacity
- EN450/500 models
  - Oil change only .... 2.8 liters (3.0 US qt, 4.9 Imp pt)
  - Oil and filter change .... 3.0 liters (3.2 US qt, 5.3 Imp pt)
  - Engine dry (after overhaul) .... 3.4 liters (3.6 US qt, 6.0 Imp pt)

Routine maintenance and servicing 1•3

EX250 models	
Oil change only	1.5 liters (1.6 US qt, 2.6 Imp pt)
Oil and filter change	1.9 liters (2.0 US qt, 3.3 Imp pt)
Engine dry (after overhaul)	Not specified
Coolant type	50/50 mixture of ethylene glycol based antifreeze and soft water
Capacity – total	
EN450/500 models	1.4 liters (1.5 US qt, 2.5 Imp pt)
EX250 models	1.0 liters (1.6 US qt, 1.8 Imp pt)
Brake fluid	DOT 4
Fork oil type	SAE 10W20 - fork oil
Fork oil capacity – EN450 models	
At oil change	Approx. 300 cc
Dry fill (after overhaul)	355 ± 2.5 cc
Fork oil capacity – EN500 models	
At oil change	Approx. 330 cc
Dry fill (after overhaul)	385 ± 2.5 cc
Fork oil capacity – EX250 models	
At oil change	Approx. 170 cc
Dry fill (after overhaul)	202 ± 2.5 cc
Fork oil level*	
EN450 models	162 ± 2 mm (6.38 ± 0.08 in)
EN500 models	128 ± 2 mm (5.04 ± 0.08 in)
EX250 models	226 ± 2 mm (4.65 ± 0.08 in)
Drive chain	SAE 90 oil or aerosol chain lubricant suitable for O-ring chains
Wheel bearings	Medium weight, lithium-based multi-purpose grease
Swingarm and Uni-Trak pivot bearings	Medium weight, lithium-based multi-purpose grease
Cables and lever pivots	Chain and cable lubricant or 10W30 motor oil
Sidestand/centerstand pivots	Medium-weight, lithium-based multi-purpose grease
Brake pedal/shift pedal pivots	Chain and cable lubricant or 10W30 motor oil
Throttle grip	Multi-purpose grease or dry film lubricant

Measured from the top of the fork tube with the fork compressed and the spring removed

1•4 Routine maintenance and servicing

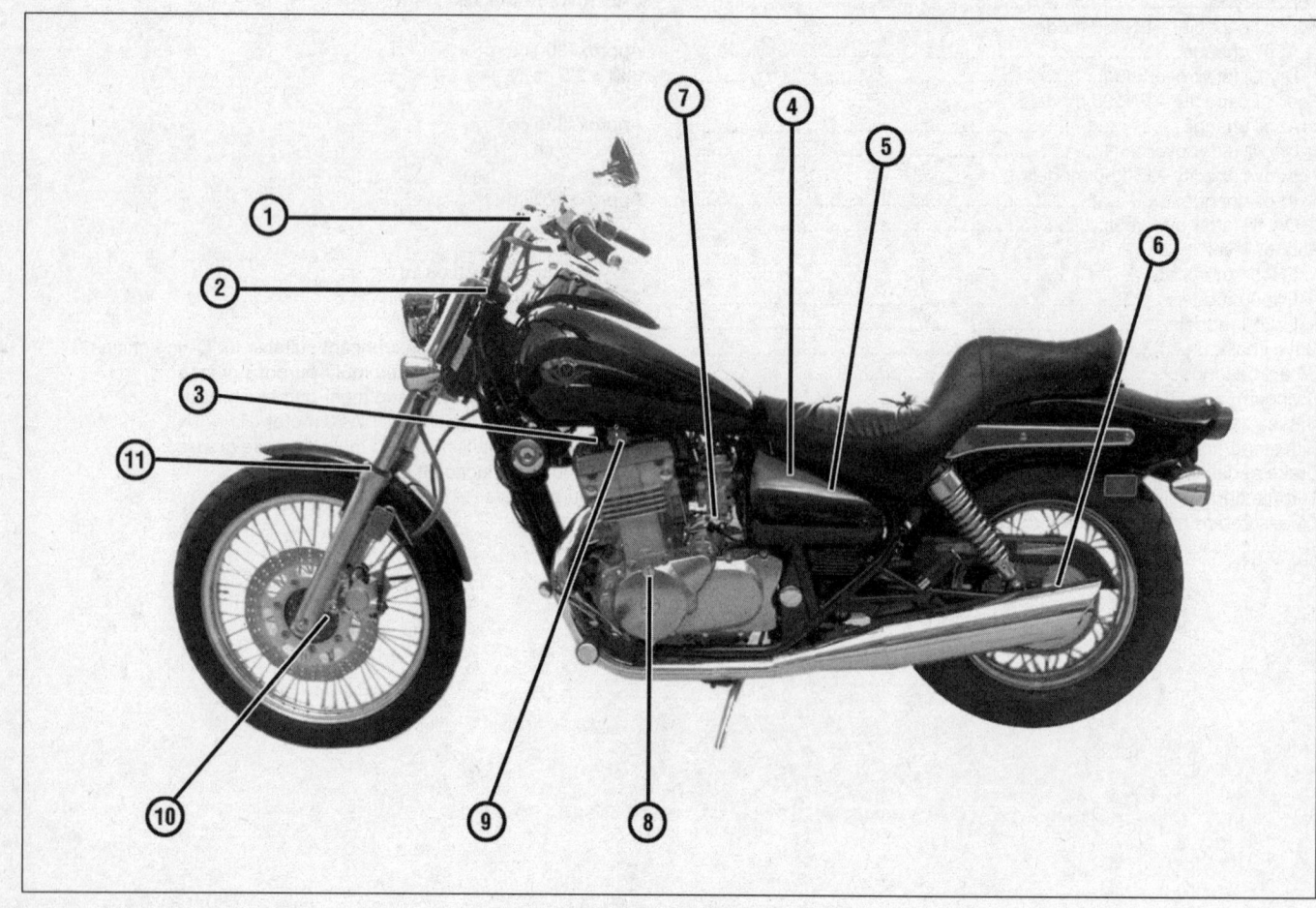

Maintenance points - EN450/500 models

1. Clutch cable adjuster
2. Steering head bearings
3. Left spark plug
4. Air filter
5. Battery
6. Drive chain or belt adjusters
7. Idle speed adjuster (throttle stop screw)
8. Timing hole cover
9. Fuel tap
10. Front fork drain plug
11. Fork oil seal

Routine maintenance and servicing 1•5

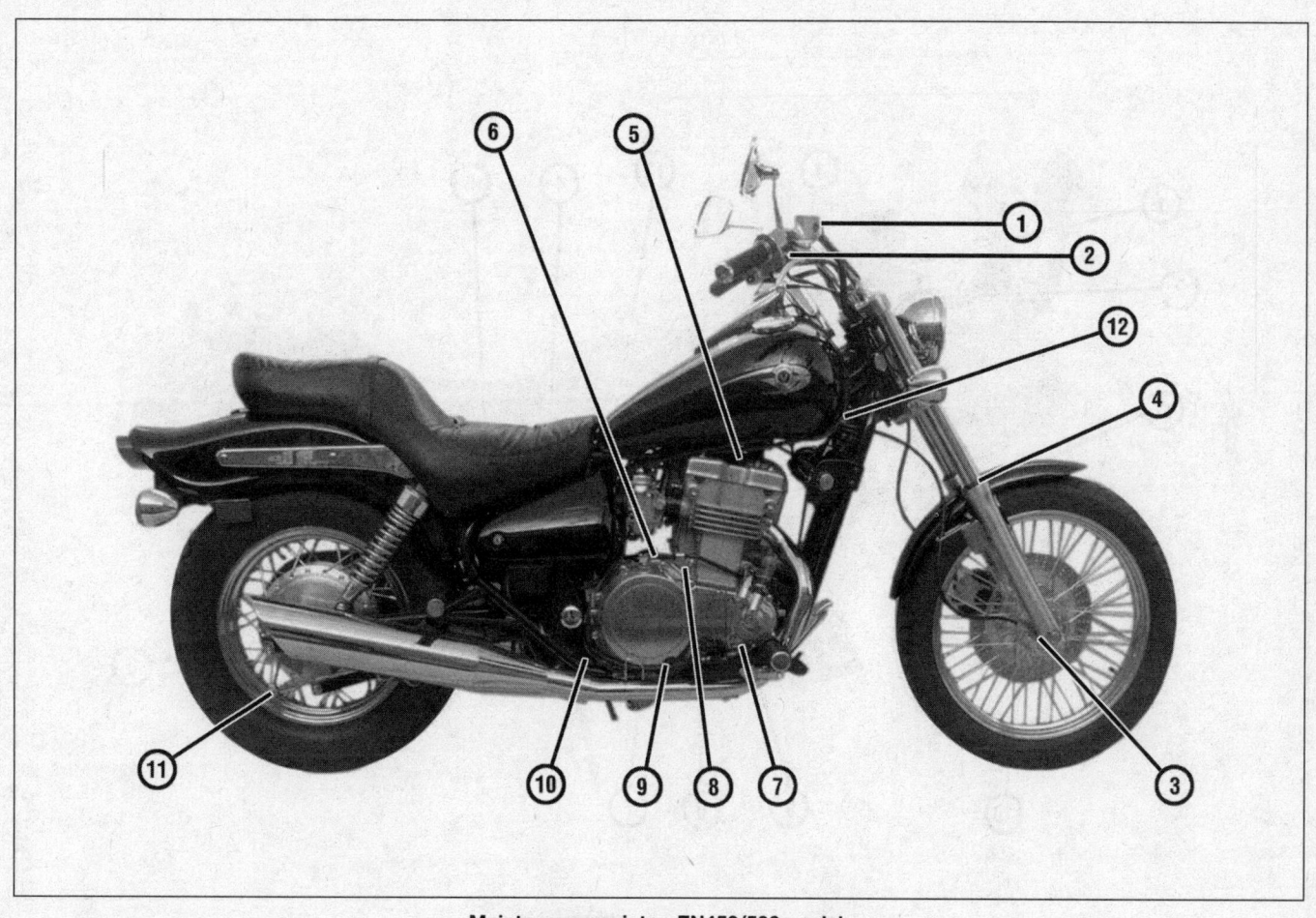

Maintenance points - EN450/500 models

1 Front brake master cylinder reservoir
2 Throttle cable adjuster
3 Fork drain plug
4 Fork oil seal
5 Right spark plug
6 Lower clutch adjuster
7 Coolant drain plug
8 Oil filler plug
9 Oil level window
10 Rear brake light switch
11 Rear brake adjuster
12 Coolant reservoir

1•6 Routine maintenance and servicing

Maintenance points - EX250 models

1 Clutch cable adjuster
2 Steering head bearings
3 Left spark plug
4 Air filter
5 Battery
6 Drive chain adjusters
7 Idle speed adjuster (throttle stop screw)
8 Timing hole cover
9 Fuel tap
10 Front fork drain plug
11 Fork oil seal
12 Coolant reservoir

Routine maintenance and servicing 1•7

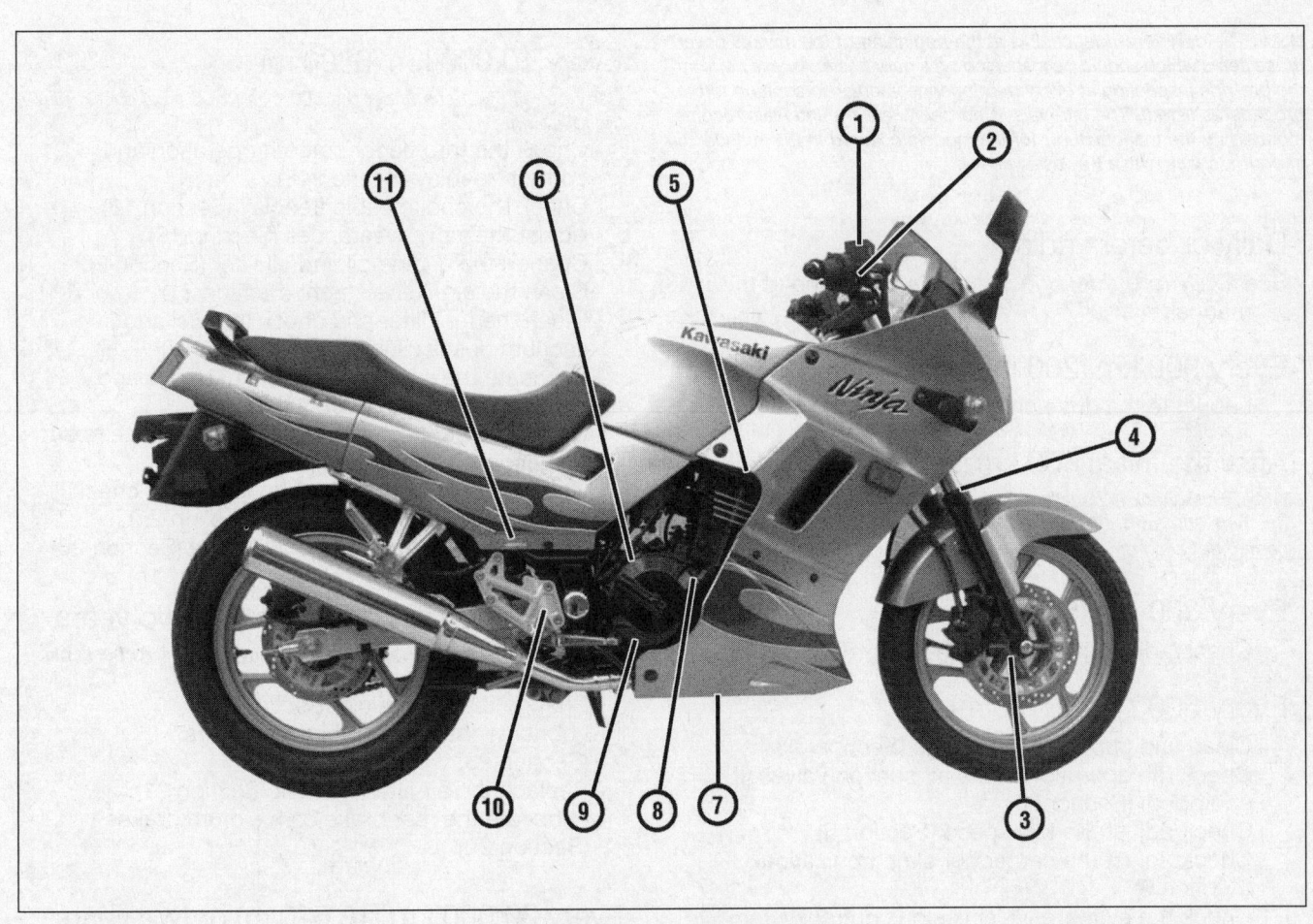

Maintenance points - EX250 models

1. Front brake master cylinder reservoir
2. Throttle cable adjuster
3. Fork drain plug
4. Fork oil seal
5. Right spark plug
6. Lower clutch adjuster
7. Coolant drain plug
8. Oil filler plug
9. Oil level window
10. Rear brake light switch
11. Rear brake fluid reservoir

Routine maintenance intervals

US and Canadian models

Note: *The daily (pre-ride) checks at the beginning of the manual cover those items which should be inspected on a daily basis. Always perform the pre-ride inspection at every maintenance interval (in addition to the procedures listed). The intervals listed below are the intervals recommended by the manufacturer for the models covered in this manual. If in doubt, check with a Kawasaki dealer.*

Daily or before riding
See 'Daily (pre-ride) checks' at the beginning of this manual.

Every 300 km (200 m)
- [ ] Lubricate the drive chain (Section 1)

After the initial 800 km (500 m)
Note: *This check is usually performed by a Kawasaki dealer after the first 800 km (500 m) from new. Thereafter, maintenance is carried out according to the following intervals of the schedule.*

Every 800 km (500 m)
- [ ] Check/adjust the drive chain slack (Section 2)

Every 5000 km (3100 m)
- [ ] Clean and gap the spark plugs (Section 3)
- [ ] Check the operation of the air suction valves (if equipped) (Section 4)
- [ ] Check/adjust the idle speed (Section 5)
- [ ] Check/adjust the carburetor synchronization (Section 6)
- [ ] Check the evaporative emission control system (California models) (Section 7)
- [ ] Check/adjust the clutch freeplay (Section 8)
- [ ] Check the drive chain and sprockets for wear (Section 9)
- [ ] Check the brake system (Section 10)
- [ ] Check the brake pads and shoe linings (Section 11)
- [ ] Check/adjust the brake pedal position – drum brake (Section 12)
- [ ] Lubricate all cables (Section 13)
- [ ] Lubricate the clutch and brake lever pivots (Section 13)
- [ ] Lubricate the gearchange/brake lever pivots and the sidestand/centerstand pivots (Section 13)
- [ ] Check the tires and wheels (Section 14)
- [ ] Check the battery electrolyte level (Section 15)
- [ ] Check the steering head bearings for freeplay (Section 16)
- [ ] Check the suspension (Section 17)
- [ ] Check the fuel hoses (Section 22)

Every 10,000 km (6200 m)
Carry out all the items under the 5000 km (3100 mile) check, plus the following:
- [ ] Check the throttle for smooth operation and correct freeplay (Section 18)
- [ ] Check the choke cable freeplay (Section 18)
- [ ] Adjust the valve clearances (Section 19)
- [ ] Change the engine oil and oil filter (Section 20)
- [ ] Clean the air filter element (Section 21)
- [ ] Clean the fuel filter and check the fuel and vacuum hoses (Section 22)
- [ ] Lubricate the swingarm needle bearings and Uni-trak linkage (Section 23)
- [ ] Check the cooling system for leaks and the hose condition (Section 24)
- [ ] Check the exhaust system for leaks and check the tightness of the fasteners (Section 25)
- [ ] Check the tightness of the fasteners (Section 26)

Every 20,000 km (12,420 m) or two years
Carry out all the items under the 10,000 km (6200 mile) check, plus the following:
- [ ] Change the brake fluid (Section 27)
- [ ] Lubricate the steering head bearings (Section 28)
- [ ] Replace the air filter element (Section 21)
- [ ] Lubricate the rear brake cam – drum brakes (Section 29)

Every 30,000 km (18,630 m) or two years
Carry out all the items under the 10,000 km (6200 mile) check, plus the following:
- [ ] Change the coolant (Section 30)
- [ ] Change the fork oil (Section 31)

Every two years
- [ ] Overhaul the brake caliper(s) and master cylinder(s) (Section 32)

Every four years
- [ ] Replace the fuel hoses (Section 33)
- [ ] Replace the hydraulic brake hose(s) (Section 34)

Non-scheduled maintenance
- [ ] Cylinder compression check (Chapter 2C)

All except US and Canadian models

Note: *The daily (pre-ride) checks at the beginning of the manual cover those items which should be inspected on a daily basis. Always perform the pre-ride inspection at every maintenance interval (in addition to the procedures listed). The intervals listed below are the intervals recommended by the manufacturer for the models covered in this manual. If in doubt, check with a Kawasaki dealer.*

Daily or before riding
See *'Daily (pre-ride) checks'* at the beginning of this manual.

Every 600 km (400 m)
☐ Lubricate the drive chain (Section 1)

After the initial 1000 km (600 m)
Note: *This check is usually performed by a Kawasaki dealer after the first 1000 km (600 m) from new. Thereafter, maintenance is carried out according to the following intervals of the schedule.*

Every 1000 km (600 m)
☐ Check/adjust the drive chain slack (Section 2)

Every 6000 km (3700 m)
☐ Clean and gap the spark plugs (Section 3)
☐ Check the operation of the air suction valves (if equipped) (Section 4)
☐ Change the engine oil (Section 20)
☐ Check/adjust the clutch freeplay (Section 8)
☐ Check the drive chain and sprockets for wear (Section 9)
☐ Check the brake system (Section 10)
☐ Check the brake pads and shoe linings (Section 11)
☐ Check/adjust the brake pedal position – drum brake (Section 12)
☐ Check the steering head bearings for freeplay (Section 16)
☐ Check the tires and wheels (Section 14)
☐ Check the battery electrolyte level (Section 15)
☐ Check the fuel hoses (Section 22)

Every 12,000 km (7400 m)
Carry out all the items under the 6000 km (3700 m) check, plus the following:
☐ Adjust the valve clearances (Section 19)
☐ Clean/inspect the air filter element (Section 21)
☐ Check the throttle for smooth operation and correct freeplay (Section 18)
☐ Check the choke cable freeplay (Section 18)
☐ Check/adjust the idle speed (Section 5)
☐ Check/adjust the carburetor synchronization (Section 6)
☐ Change the engine oil and oil filter (Section 20)
☐ Check the suspension (Section 17)
☐ Lubricate the swingarm needle bearings and Uni-trak linkage (Section 23)
☐ Lubricate all cables (Section 13)
☐ Lubricate the clutch and brake lever pivots (Section 13)
☐ Lubricate the gearchange/brake lever pivots and the sidestand/centerstand pivots (Section 13)
☐ Check the exhaust system for leaks and check the tightness of the fasteners (Section 25)
☐ Check the tightness of the fasteners (Section 26)
☐ Check the evaporative emission control system (California models) (Section 7)
☐ Clean the fuel filter and check the fuel and vacuum hoses (Section 22)
☐ Check the cooling system for leaks and the hose condition (Section 24)

Every 24,000 km (14,900 m) – or every two years
Carry out all the items under the 12,000 km (7400 m) check, plus the following:
☐ Change the coolant (Section 30)
☐ Change the brake fluid (Section 27)
☐ Lubricate the steering head bearings (Section 28)
☐ Change the fork oil (Section 31)

Every four years
☐ Overhaul the brake caliper(s) and master cylinder(s) (Section 32)

Non-scheduled maintenance
☐ Lubricate the rear brake cam – ER drum brake (Section 29)
☐ Replace the fuel hoses (Section 33)
☐ Replace the hydraulic brake hose(s) (Section 34)
☐ Cylinder compression check (Chapter 2C)

1•10 Routine maintenance and servicing

1.2 Spray the lubricant onto the inside of the chain so that it will spread outward when the chain moves

2.4 Push up on the bottom run of the belt or chain and measure how far it deflects - if it's not within the specified limits, adjust the belt or chain

Deciding where to start or plug into the routine maintenance schedule depends on several factors. If you have a motorcycle whose warranty has recently expired, and if it has been maintained according to the warranty standards, you may want to pick up routine maintenance as it coincides with the next mileage or calendar interval. If you have owned the machine for some time but have never performed any maintenance on it, then you may want to start at the nearest interval and include some additional procedures to ensure that nothing important is overlooked. If you have just had a major engine overhaul, then you may want to start the maintenance routine from the beginning. If you have a used machine and have no knowledge of its history or maintenance record, you may desire to combine all the checks into one large service initially and then settle into the maintenance schedule prescribed.

The Sections which outline the inspection and maintenance procedures are written as step-by-step comprehensive guides to the performance of the work. They explain in detail each of the routine inspections and maintenance procedures on the check list. References to additional information in applicable Chapters is also included and should not be overlooked.

Before beginning any maintenance or repair, the machine should be cleaned thoroughly, especially around the oil filter, spark plugs, cylinder head covers, side covers, carburetors, etc. Cleaning will help ensure that dirt does not contaminate the engine and will allow you to detect wear and damage that could otherwise easily go unnoticed.

Maintenance information is printed on decals under the seat or under the right-hand side cover and on the chain guard. If the information on the decals differs from that included here, use the information on the decal.

1 Drive chain (EX250 models) – lubrication

Note 1: *If the chain is extremely dirty, it should be removed and cleaned before it's lubricated (see Chapter 6).*
Note 2: *Belt drive models do not require periodic lubrication. The drive belt should be kept clean and dry.*

1 The best time to lubricate the chain is after the motorcycle has been ridden. When the chain is warm, the lubricant will penetrate the joints between the side plates, pins, bushings and rollers to provide lubrication of the internal load bearing areas.

2 Use a good quality aerosol chain lubricant (marked as being suitable for O-ring chains) and apply it to the area where the side plates overlap – not the middle of the rollers **(see illustration)**. With the bike on its centerstand, hold the plastic nozzle near the edge of the chain and turn the wheel by hand as the lubricant sprays out - repeat the procedure on the inside edge of the chain.

3 After applying the lubricant, let it soak in a few minutes before wiping off any excess.

2 Drive belt/chain and sprockets - check and adjustment

1 A drive belt is used on 1985 through 1996 (A7) EN450/500 models. 1996 C1 and later EN450/500 models, as well as all EX250 models, use a drive chain.

Check

2 A neglected drive belt or chain won't last long and can quickly damage the sprockets. Routine adjustment and inspection isn't difficult and will ensure maximum service life.

3 To check the belt or chain, place the bike on the centerstand and shift the transmission into Neutral. Make sure the ignition switch is OFF.

4 Push up on the bottom run of the chain or belt and measure the slack midway between the two sprockets **(see illustration)**, then compare your measurements to the value listed in this Chapter's Specifications. As wear occurs, the belt or chain will actually stretch, which means adjustment by removing some of the slack is needed. **Note:** *Repeat the slack measurement at several different points along the length of the belt or chain.*

5 Remove the belt or chain guard (it's held in place by two bolts).

Belt drive models

6 Check the entire length of the belt for damaged or worn teeth, fraying or cracks. Replace the belt if any of these conditions are visible.

> **Warning:** *If the belt is worn past the nylon facing material, replace it immediately or it may cause an accident.*

Note: *If the belt is in need of replacement, also check the sprockets as described below - they may also be worn.*

Chain drive models

7 Since the chain will rarely wear evenly, rotate the rear wheel so that the chain can be checked along its entire length. In some cases where lubrication has been neglected, corrosion and pitting may cause the links to bind and kink, which effectively shortens the chain's length. If the chain is tight between sprockets, rusty or kinked, or if any of the pins are loose or rollers damaged, it's time for a new chain. If you find a tight area, mark it with felt pen or paint, and repeat the slack measurement after the bike has been ridden. If the chain is still tight in the same area, it may be damaged or worn. Because a tight or kinked chain can damage the transmission output shaft bearing, it's a good idea to replace it.

Routine maintenance and servicing 1•11

2.8a On belt drive models, check the sprocket teeth (arrow) for wear (rear sprocket shown)

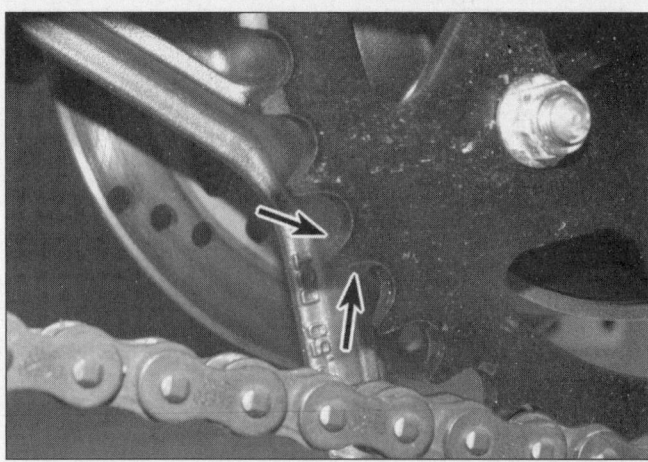

2.8b On chain drive models, check for wear on either side of the sprocket teeth (arrows)

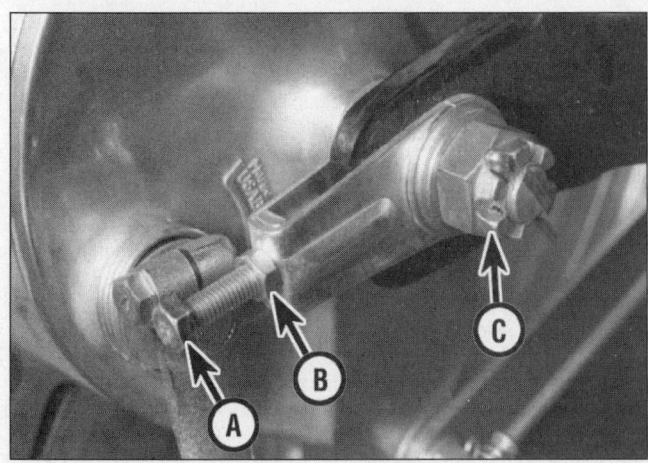

2.11a Loosen the torque link nut (drum brakes) and axle nut, then loosen the locknut and back-off the bolt (belt drive and EX250 chain drive) . . .

A Adjuster bolt
B Adjuster locknut
C Axle nut

2.11b . . . and EN500 chain drive

A Adjuster nut
B Adjuster locknut
C Axle nut

All models

8 Remove the shift lever and engine sprocket cover (see Chapter 6). Check the teeth on the engine sprocket and rear sprocket for wear **(see illustrations)**. On belt drive models, refer to Chapter 6 for the pulley diameter and tooth height measurement procedures if the sprockets appear to be worn excessively.

Adjustment

9 Rotate the rear wheel until the belt or chain is positioned with the least amount of slack present.

10 On EN450/500 models, remove the cotter pin (if equipped) for the torque link nut on the rear brake panel and loosen the nut.

11 Loosen and back-off the locknuts on the adjuster bolts or nuts **(see illustrations)**.

12 Remove the cotter pin and loosen the axle nut **(see illustration 2.11a or 2.11b)**.

13 Turn the axle adjusting bolts or nuts on both sides of the swingarm until the proper belt or chain tension is obtained (get the adjuster on the belt or chain side close, then set the adjuster on the opposite side). Be sure to turn the adjusting bolts or nuts evenly to keep the rear wheel in alignment. If the adjusting bolts or nuts reach the end of their travel, the belt or chain is excessively worn and should be replaced with a new one (see Chapter 6).

14 When the belt or chain has the correct amount of slack, make sure the marks on the adjusters correspond to the same relative marks on each side of the swingarm **(see illustration)**.

15 On EN450/500 models, tighten the axle nut snugly, then apply the rear brake firmly to center the shoes. On all models, tighten the axle to the torque listed in the Chapter 7 Specifications, then recheck the belt or chain slack and readjust if necessary. Once the slack is correctly set, install a new cotter pin. If necessary, turn the nut an additional amount to line up the cotter pin hole with the

2.14 When the adjuster bolts are set evenly, the adjuster marks (arrow) on both sides should line up with the same marks in the swingarm, but don't rely completely on this; make a visual check of sprocket alignment as well

1•12 Routine maintenance and servicing

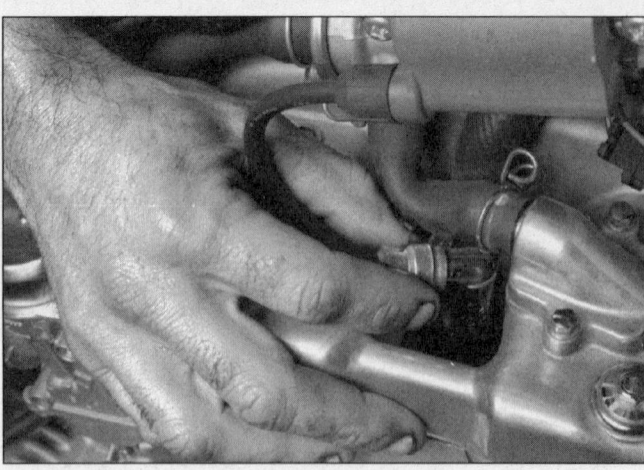

3.2a On EN450/500 models, rotate the spark plug caps back and forth to loosen them . . .

3.2b . . . and on EX250 models, pull the caps up and forward . . .

castellations in the nut - don't loosen the nut to do this.
16 Tighten the adjuster locknuts (and the torque link nut on EN450/500 models) securely.

HAYNES HiNT *The marks on the swingarm and chain adjusters are a guide to correct wheel alignment. To check wheel alignment refer to Chapter 7.*

3 Spark plugs – clean and regap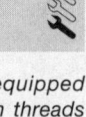

Note: *These motorcycles are equipped with spark plugs that have 12 mm threads and an 18 mm wrench hex. Make sure your spark plug socket is the correct size before attempting to remove the plugs. A suitable tool should be included in the bike's tool kit.*

1 Remove the fuel tank (see Chapter 4). If you're working on a 1986 or 1987 EX250, remove the knee grip covers (see Chapter 8).
2 Disconnect the spark plug caps from the spark plugs **(see illustrations)**. If available, use compressed air to blow any accumulated debris from around the spark plugs. Remove the plugs **(see illustration)**.
3 Inspect the electrodes for wear. Both the center and side electrodes should have square edges and the side electrode should be of uniform thickness. Look for excessive deposits and evidence of a cracked or chipped insulator around the center electrode. Compare your spark plugs to the color spark plug reading chart on the inside rear cover. Check the threads, the washer and the ceramic insulator body for cracks and other damage.
4 If the electrodes are not excessively worn, and if the deposits can be easily removed with a wire brush, the plugs can be regapped and reused (if no cracks or chips are visible in the insulator). If in doubt concerning the condition of the plugs, replace them, as the expense is minimal.
5 Cleaning spark plugs by sandblasting is permitted, provided you clean the plugs with a high flash-point solvent afterwards.
6 Before installing new plugs, make sure they are the correct type and heat range. Check the gap between the electrodes, as they are not preset. For best results, use a wire-type gauge rather than a flat gauge to check the gap **(see illustration)**. If the gap must be adjusted, bend the side electrode only and be very careful not to chip or crack the insulator nose **(see illustration)**. Make sure the washer is in place before installing each plug.
7 Since the cylinder head is made of aluminum, which is soft and easily damaged, thread the plugs into the heads by hand. Slip a short length of hose over the end of the plug to use as a tool to thread it into place **(see illustration)**. The hose will grip the plug well enough to turn it, but will start to slip if the plug begins to cross-thread in the hole – this will prevent damaged threads and the accompanying repair costs
8 Once the plugs are finger tight, the job can be finished with a socket. If a torque wrench is available, tighten the spark plugs to the torque listed in this Chapter's Specifications. If you do not have a torque wrench,

3.2c . . . then pull them off the plugs and check them for brittleness or cracking

3.2d Use an extension and a deep socket (preferably one with a rubber insert to protect the plug) to remove the spark plugs; a magnet can be used to lift the plugs out of the head once they're loose

Routine maintenance and servicing 1•13

3.6a Spark plug manufacturers recommend using a wire type gauge when checking the gap - if the wire doesn't slide between the electrodes with a slight drag, adjustment is required

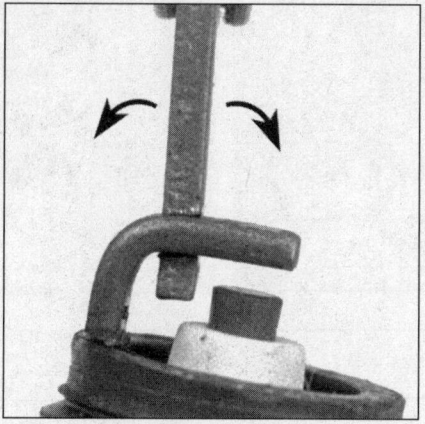

3.6b To change the gap, bend the side electrode only, as indicated by the arrows, and be very careful not to crack or chip the ceramic insulator surrounding the center electrode

3.7 A length of rubber hose will save time and prevent damaged threads when installing the spark plugs

tighten the plugs finger tight (until the washers bottom on the cylinder head) then use a wrench to tighten them an additional 1/4 turn. Regardless of the method used, do not over-tighten them.
9 Reconnect the spark plug caps.
10 Install the fuel tank (see Chapter 4). If you're working on a 1986 or 1987 EX250, install the knee grip covers.

HAYNES HINT *Stripped plug threads in the cylinder head can be repaired with a thread insert - see 'Tools and workshop tips' in the Reference section.*

4 Air suction valves – check

1 The air suction valves, installed on US EN450/500 models, are one-way check valves that allow fresh air to flow into the exhaust ports. The suction developed by the exhaust pulses pulls the air from the air cleaner, through a hose to the air switching valve, through a pair of hoses and a pair of reed valves, and finally into the exhaust ports. The introduction of fresh air helps ignite any fuel that may not have been burned by the normal combustion process.
2 Remove the fuel tank (see Chapter 4).
3 Disconnect the hoses from the air suction valves **(see illustration)**. Remove the bolts **(see illustration)** and lift off the covers.
4 Check the valves for cracks, warping, burning or other damage. Check the area where the reeds contact the valve holder for scratches, separation and grooves. If any of these conditions are found, replace the valve.
5 Wash the valves with solvent if carbon has accumulated between the reed and the valve holder.
6 Installation of the valves is the reverse of removal. Be sure to use a new gasket.

5 Idle speed – check and adjustment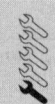

1 The idle speed should be checked and adjusted after the carburetors are synchronized and when it is obviously too high or too low. Before adjusting the idle speed, make sure the valve clearances and spark plug gaps are correct.

⚠ *Warning: Turn the handlebars back-and-forth and see if the idle speed changes as this is done. If it does, the accelerator cable may not be adjusted correctly, or it may be worn out. Be sure to correct this problem before proceeding.*

2 The engine should be at normal operating temperature, which is usually reached after 10 to 15 minutes of stop and go riding. Place the motorcycle on the centerstand with the transmission in neutral and the engine idling.

4.3a Squeeze the spring clip (arrow), slide it back along the hose and detach the hose from the air suction valve

4.3b Unbolt the air suction valve from the valve cover to inspect it

1•14 Routine maintenance and servicing

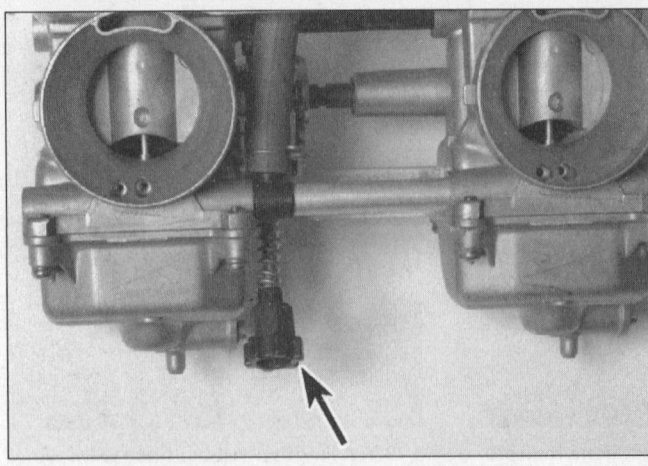

5.3a Turn the idle speed adjusting screw (arrow) in or out until the correct idle speed is obtained (carburetors removed from engine for clarity) - here's the EN450/500 ...

5.3b ... and this is the EX250

3 Turn the throttle stop screw until the idle speed listed in this Chapter's Specifications is obtained. The throttle stop screw is located on the left-hand side of the bike next to the carburetor (see illustrations).
4 Snap the throttle open and shut a few times, then recheck the idle speed. If necessary, repeat the adjustment procedure.
5 If a smooth, steady idle can't be achieved, the fuel/air mixture may be incorrect. Refer to Chapter 4 for additional carburetor information.

6 Carburetor synchronization – check and adjustment

Warning: *Gasoline (petrol) is extremely flammable, so take extra precautions when you work on any part of the fuel system. Don't smoke or allow open flames or bare light bulbs near the work area, and don't work in a garage where a gas-type appliance (such as a water heater or clothes dryer) is present. Since gasoline is carcinogenic, wear nitrile gloves when there's a possibility of being exposed to fuel. If you spill any fuel on your skin, rinse it off immediately with soap and water. When you perform any kind of work on the fuel system, wear safety glasses and have a fire extinguisher suitable for a class B type fire (flammable liquids) on hand.*

Warning: *Take great care not to burn your hand on the hot engine unit when accessing the gauge take-off points on the intake manifolds. Do not allow exhaust gases to build up in the work area; either perform the check outside or use an exhaust gas extraction system.*

1 Carburetor synchronization is simply the process of adjusting the carburetors so they pass the same amount of fuel/air mixture to each cylinder. This is done by measuring the vacuum produced in each cylinder. Carburetors that are out of synchronization will result in decreased fuel mileage, increased engine temperature, less than ideal throttle response and higher vibration levels.

2 To properly synchronize the carburetors, you will need a set of two vacuum gauges or calibrated tubes (manometer) to indicate engine vacuum. **Note:** *Because of the nature of the synchronization procedure and the need for special instruments, most owners leave the task to a Kawasaki dealer.*
3 Start the engine and let it run until it reaches normal operating temperature, then shut it off.
4 Remove the fuel tank (see Chapter 4).
5 Detach the vacuum hoses or caps from the fitting on the front of each carburetor body (see illustration), then hook up the vacuum gauge set or the manometer according to the manufacturer's instructions. Make sure there are no leaks in the set-up, as false readings will result.
6 Disconnect the fuel delivery pipe to the carburetors and in its place, connect a longer length of pipe to a remote fuel tank. Have an assistant hold the remote fuel tank out of the way, but in such a position that fuel can still be delivered and access to the carburetors is unobstructed.
7 Start the engine and make sure the idle speed is correct.

6.5 Disconnect the vacuum line from each carburetor (arrow)

6.9 Turn this screw to synchronize the carburetors (carburetors removed from engine for clarity)

Routine maintenance and servicing 1•15

7.2 Evaporative emission control system components (EX250 shown)

A Charcoal canister   B Liquid-vapor separator

7.6a To remove the components, disconnect the hoses (arrows) from the bottom of the separator as well as the hose from the top . . .

8 The vacuum readings for both of the cylinders should be the same, or at least within the tolerance listed in this Chapter's Specifications. If the vacuum readings vary, adjust as necessary.
9 To perform the adjustment, synchronize the carburetors by turning the butterfly valve adjusting screw, as needed, until the vacuum is identical or nearly identical for both cylinders **(see illustration)**. **Note:** *Do not press down on the screw while adjusting it or a false reading will be obtained.*
10 When the adjustment is complete, recheck the vacuum readings and idle speed, then stop the engine. Remove the vacuum gauge or manometer and attach the hoses or caps to the fittings on the carburetors. **Note:** *Do not forget to reconnect the vacuum line to the T-fitting before reinstalling the fuel tank.*
11 Reinstall the fuel tank and seat.

7 Evaporative emission control system (California models only) – check

> ⚠ **Warning:** *Gasoline is extremely flammable, so take extra precautions when you work on any part of the fuel or emission control system. See the Warning in Section 6.*

1 This system, installed on California models to conform to stringent emission control standards, routes fuel vapors from the fuel system into the engine to be burned, instead of letting them evaporate into the atmosphere. When the engine isn't running, vapors are stored in a carbon canister.

Hoses
2 To begin the inspection of the system, remove the seat and fuel tank (see Chapters 4 and 8 if necessary). Inspect the hoses from the fuel tank, carburetors and liquid/vapor separator to the canister for cracking, kinks or other signs of deterioration **(see illustration)**.

Liquid/vapor separator test
3 Disconnect the breather hose from the separator and inject about 20 cc of gasoline into the fitting with a syringe.
4 Disconnect the fuel return hose from the tank and place the end of the hose in a container level with the top of the tank.
5 Start the engine and let it idle. If the fuel comes out of the hose, the separator is good; if not, replace it.

Component inspection
6 Label and disconnect the hoses, then remove the separator and canister from the machine. **Note:** *For system inspection, it's easiest to remove the separator, canister, fuel tank bracket and air suction switching valve as a unit* **(see illustrations)**.
7 Check the separator closely for cracks or other signs of damage. If these are found,

replace it **(see illustration)**.
8 Inspect the canister for cracks or other signs of damage. Tip the canister so the nozzles point down. If fuel runs out of the canister, the liquid/vapor separator is probably bad – check it as described above. The fuel inside the canister has probably caused damage, so it would be a good idea to replace it also.

8 Clutch – check and adjustment

1 Correct clutch freeplay is necessary to ensure proper clutch operation and reasonable clutch service life. Freeplay normally changes because of cable stretch and clutch wear, so it should be checked and adjusted periodically.
2 Clutch cable freeplay is checked at the lever on the handlebar. Slowly pull in on the lever until resistance is felt, then note how far the lever has moved away from its bracket at

7.6b . . . and remove the mounting screws (arrows) (EN450/500 shown; the EX250 screws are beneath the bracket) . . .

7.6c . . . and take the assembly off of the motorcycle

1•16 Routine maintenance and servicing

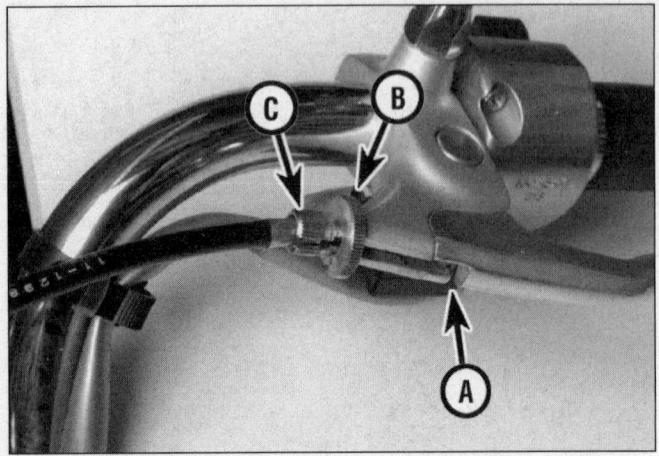

8.2 Check clutch freeplay between the lever and bracket; make the initial adjustment at the lever

- A Check freeplay here
- B Lockwheel
- C Adjuster

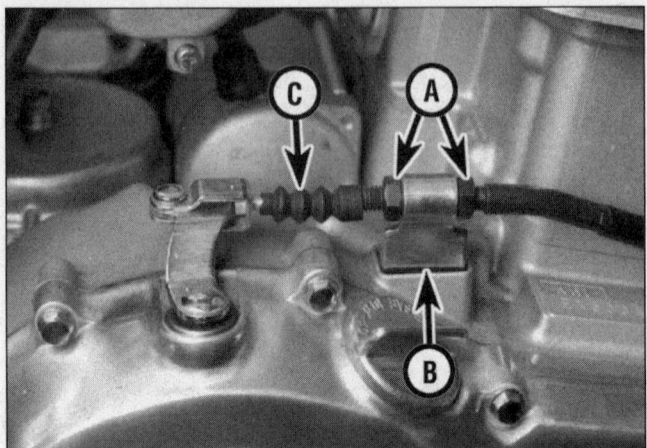

8.4a Details of the lower end of the clutch cable (EN450/500)

- A Adjusting nuts
- B Bracket
- C Dust cover

the pivot end **(see illustration)**. Compare this distance with the value listed in this Chapter's Specifications. Too little freeplay may result in the clutch not engaging completely. If there is too much freeplay, the clutch might not release fully.

3 Freeplay adjustments can be made at the clutch lever by loosening the lockwheel and turning the adjuster until the desired freeplay is obtained. Always retighten the lockwheel once the adjustment is complete. If the lever adjuster reaches the end of its travel, try adjusting the cable at its bracket on the engine as described below.

4 Loosen the adjusting nuts at the lower end of the cable completely **(see illustrations)**.

5 Loosen the knurled lockwheel at the clutch lever and turn the adjuster in or out to expose approximately 5 or 6 mm of threads between the adjuster and the lockwheel.

6 Pull the clutch cable tight to remove all slack, then tighten the adjusting nuts against the bracket at the lower end of the cable.

7 Turn the adjuster at the clutch lever until the correct freeplay is obtained, then tighten the lockwheel.

8 If freeplay still can't be adjusted to within the specified range, the cable is probably stretched and should be replaced with a new one, or the clutch may be worn out (see Chapter 2).

9 Once the cable is adjusted properly, turn the numbered adjusting wheel (span adjuster) to position the clutch lever a comfortable distance from the handlebar.

9 Drive chain and sprockets (chain drive models) – wear check

1 Remove the chain guard (it's held on by two bolts). Check the entire length of the chain for damaged rollers, loose links and pins. Hang a 20 lb (9 kg) weight on the bottom run of the chain and measure the length of 20 links (21 pins) along the top run. Rotate the wheel and repeat this check at several places on the chain, since it may wear unevenly. Compare your measurements with the maximum 20-link length listed in this Chapter's Specifications. If any of your measurements exceed the maximum, replace the chain.

HAYNES HINT *Never install a new chain on old sprockets, and never use the old chain if you install new sprockets – replace the chain and sprockets as a set.*

2 Remove the engine sprocket cover (see Chapter 6). Check the teeth on the engine sprocket and the rear sprocket for wear as described in Section 2.

10 Brake system – general check

1 A routine general check of the brakes will ensure that any problems are discovered and remedied before the rider's safety is jeopardized.

2 Check the brake lever and pedal for loose connections, excessive play, bends, and other damage. Replace any damaged parts (see Chapter 7).

3 Make sure all brake fasteners are tight. Check the brake pads and shoe linings for wear (see Section 11) and make sure the fluid level in the reservoir(s) is correct (see *Daily (pre-ride) checks*). Look for leaks at the hose connections and check for cracks in the hoses. If the lever is spongy, bleed the brakes as described in Chapter 7.

4 Make sure the brake light operates when the brake lever is depressed. The front

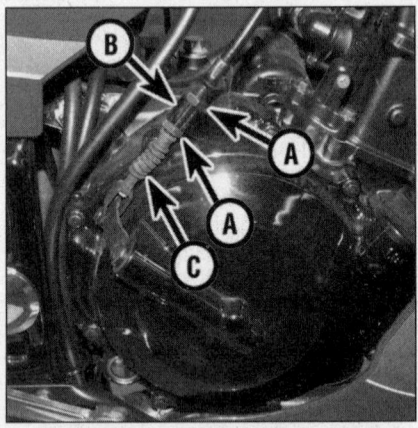

8.4b Details of the lower end of the clutch cable (EX250)

- A Adjusting nuts
- B Bracket
- C Dust cover

brake light switch is not adjustable. If it fails to operate properly, replace it (see Chapter 9).

5 Make sure the brake light is activated when the rear brake pedal is depressed approximately 15 mm (0.6 inch) on EN450/500 models, and 10 mm (0.4 inch) on EX250 models.

6 If adjustment is necessary, hold the switch and turn the adjusting nut on the switch body **(see illustrations)** until the brake light is activated when required. Turning the switch out will cause the brake light to come on sooner, while turning it in will cause it to come on later. If the switch doesn't operate the brake lights, check it as described in Chapter 9.

Routine maintenance and servicing 1•17

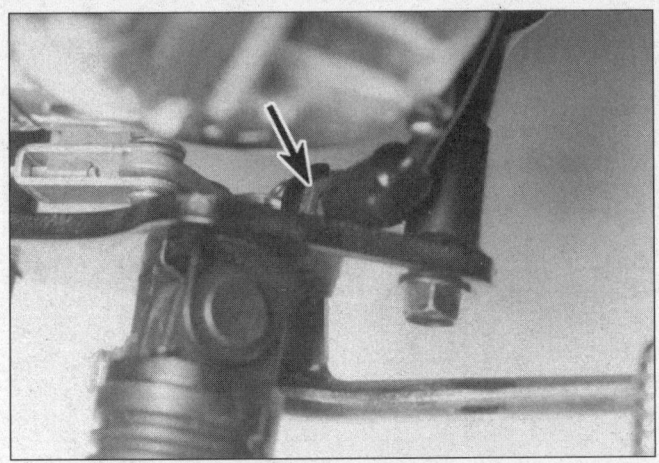
10.6a To adjust the rear brake light switch, hold the switch body and turn the locknut (arrow) - here's the EN450/500 . . .

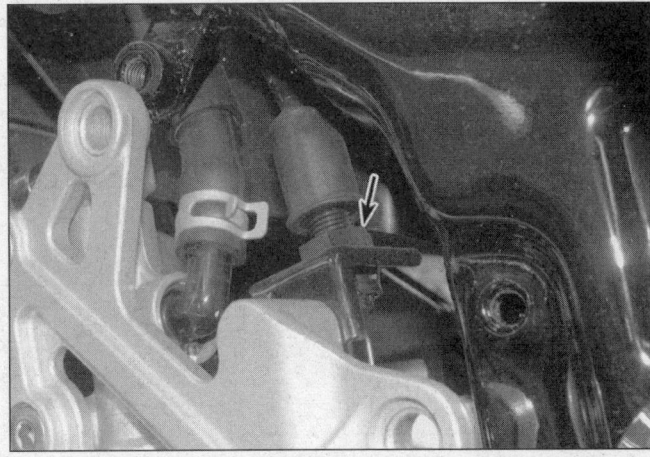
10.6b . . . and this is the EX250 (switch bracket removed for clarity)

11 Brake pads and shoe linings – wear check

1 The brake pads (disc brakes) and shoe linings (drum brakes) should be checked at the recommended intervals and replaced when worn beyond the limit listed in this Chapter's Specifications.

Brake pads

2 On early models with single-piston brake calipers, remove the caliper without disconnecting the brake hose so you can see clearly into the front of the caliper (see Chapter 7) **(see illustration)**.
3 On later models, brake pad wear can be checked without removing the brake caliper **(see illustration)**.
4 The brake pads should have at least the specified minimum amount of lining material remaining on the metal backing plate **(see illustration)**. If the pads are dirty or if you are in doubt as to the amount of friction material remaining, remove them for inspection (see Chapter 7) and measure the thickness of the friction material.
5 If the pads are worn excessively, they must be replaced (see Chapter 7).

Brake shoe linings

6 To check the rear brake linings, press the brake pedal firmly and look at the indicator on the brake drum **(see illustration)**. If the pointer is beyond the Usable Range scale, replace the brake shoes (see Chapter 7).

12 Brake pedal position and play – check and adjustment (drum brakes)

1 Rear brake pedal position is largely a matter of personal preference. Locate the pedal so that the rear brake can be engaged quickly and easily without excessive foot movement. The recommended factory set-

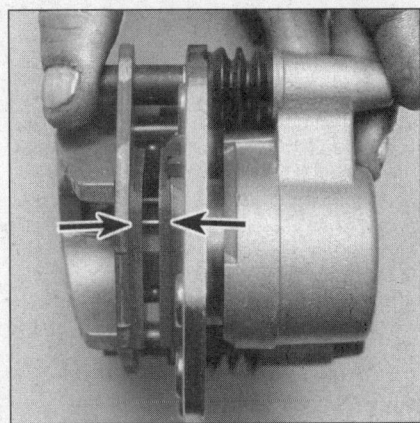
11.2 On single-piston models, look into the front of the caliper to check the brake pads for wear (arrows)

ting is listed in this Chapter's Specifications and is expressed as the difference in height between the brake pedal tip (when at rest) and the top of the footrest rubber.

11.3 On dual-piston calipers, look into the rear side of the caliper - when the friction material is worn to the wear line (arrow), it's time for new pads

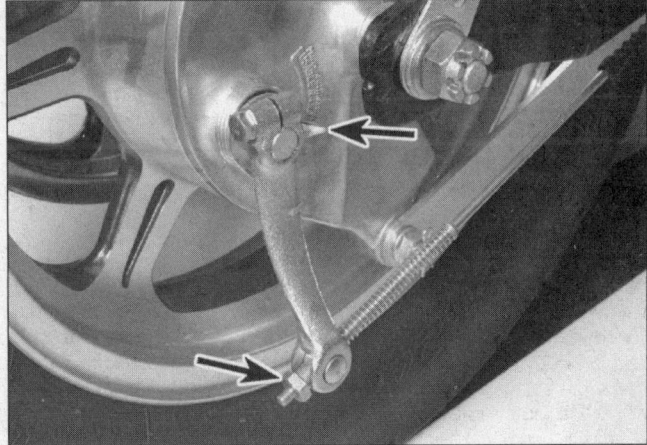
11.6 If the pointer (upper arrow) goes past the Usable Range indicator toward the rear of the bike, the linings are worn and must be replaced; the adjuster (lower arrow) is used to set brake pedal freeplay

1•18 Routine maintenance and servicing

12.2 To adjust the brake pedal position, loosen the locknut (arrow) and turn the adjusting bolt

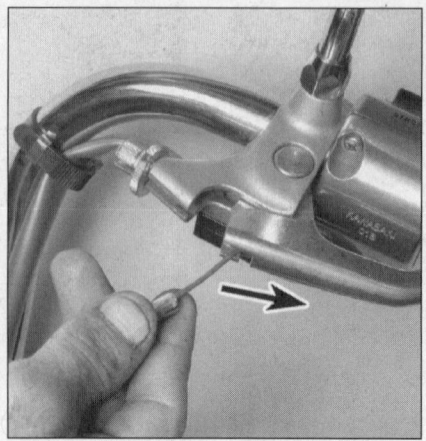

13.3a To disconnect the clutch cable, line up the slots in the bracket, lockwheel and adjuster, then turn the cable in the direction of the arrow and slide it downward through the slots

13.3b Lubricating a cable with a pressure lube adapter (make sure the tool seats around the inner cable)

2 To adjust the position of the pedal, loosen the locknut on the adjusting bolt, turn the bolt to set the pedal position and tighten the locknut **(see illustration)**.
3 With the pedal position adjusted correctly, check freeplay. Apply the rear brake and compare the pedal travel with that listed in this Chapter's Specifications.
4 To adjust the freeplay, turn the adjuster at the rear end of the brake rod **(see illustration 11.6)**.
5 If necessary, adjust the brake light switch (see Section 10).

13 Lubrication – general

1 Since the controls, cables and various other components of a motorcycle are exposed to the elements, they should be lubricated periodically to ensure safe and trouble-free operation.
2 The footrests, clutch and brake lever, brake pedal, shift pedal and side and centerstand pivots should be lubricated frequently. In order for the lubricant to be applied where it will do the most good, the component should be disassembled. However, if chain and cable lubricant is being used, it can be applied to the pivot joint gaps and will usually work its way into the areas where friction occurs. If motor oil or light grease is being used, apply it sparingly as it may attract dirt (which could cause the controls to bind or wear at an accelerated rate).
3 The clutch cable should be separated from the handlebar lever and bracket before it is lubricated **(see illustration)**. This is a convenient time to inspect the bushing at the end of the cable. The cable should be treated with motor oil or a commercially available cable lubricant which is specially formulated for use on motorcycle control cables. Cable oiler clamps for pressure lubricating the cables with spray can lubricants are available and ensure that the cable is lubricated along its entire length **(see illustration)**. If motor oil is being used, tape a funnel-shaped piece of heavy paper or plastic to the end of the cable, then pour oil into the funnel and suspend the end of the cable upright. Leave it until the oil runs down into the cable and out the other end. When attaching the cable to the lever, be sure to lubricate the barrel-shaped fitting at the end with high-temperature grease.
4 To lubricate the throttle and choke cables, disconnect the cable(s) at the lower end, then lubricate the cable with a pressure lube adapter **(see illustration 13.3b)**. See Chapter 4 for the choke cable removal procedure.
5 Refer to Chapter 9, Section 16 and remove the speedometer cable. Lubricate the inner cable, taking care not to lubricate the upper few inches of the cable as the lubricant may travel up into the instrument head.

14 Wheels and tires – general check

1 Routine tire and wheel checks should be made with the realization that your safety depends to a great extent on their condition.

Wheels

2 The cast wheels used on some models are virtually maintenance free, but they should be kept clean and checked periodically for cracks and other damage. Never attempt to repair damaged cast wheels; they must be replaced. Check the valve rubber for signs of damage or deterioration and have it replaced if necessary. Also, make sure the valve stem cap is in place and tight.
3 The wheel bearings will wear over a period of time and result in handling problems. Place the motorcycle on its centerstand and take the weight off the front wheel. Check for any play in the bearings by pushing and pulling the wheel against the hub. Also rotate the wheel and check that it rotates smoothly.
4 If any play is detected in the hub, or if the wheel does not rotate smoothly (and this is not due to brake drag), the wheel bearings must be replaced (see Chapter 7).

Wire wheels

5 On models with wire wheels, periodically check the spokes for damage, breakage or corrosion. A broken or bent spoke must be replaced with a new one immediately because the load taken by it will be

14.5 Check the tension of the spokes periodically, but don't overtighten them

Routine maintenance and servicing 1•19

15.3 Remove the junction box bracket (arrow) and lift the junction box to uncover the battery

15.5 ALWAYS disconnect the negative cable (with minus mark) before the positive cable (with plus mark) and connect it after the positive cable to prevent sparks which could cause a battery explosion

transferred to adjacent spokes, which may in turn fail. Loose spokes should be tightened with a special spoke wrench to avoid damaging the spoke nipple, but be careful not to overtighten them and distort the rim **(see illustration)**.

6 If you suspect that any of the spokes are incorrectly tensioned, tap each one with a spoke wrench and note the sound produced. Properly tensioned spokes with make a sharp pinging sound, loose ones will make a lower pitch or dull sound, and overtightened spokes will make a higher-pitched sound. Unevenly tensioned spokes will promote rim misalignment - check the wheel runout and alignment (see Chapter 7) and seek the help of a wheel building expert if this is suspected.

7 Check the wheel bearings as described in Steps 3 and 4.

Tires

8 Refer to *Daily (pre-ride) checks*.

15 Battery electrolyte level/ specific gravity – check

Warning: Be extremely careful when handling or working around the battery. The electrolyte is very caustic and an explosive gas (hydrogen) is given off when the battery is charging.

Note: *Parts of this section apply to fillable batteries, installed as original equipment on all EN450/500 models and 1994 and earlier EX250 models. The maintenance-free batteries used on 1995 and later EX250 models do not require periodic checks of the electrolyte level.*

Level check

1 Remove the seat (see Chapter 8).
2 Where necessary for access, remove the fuel tank and bracket (see Chapter 4).
3 On EN450 models, remove its bolts and lift off the igniter, then release the battery holder bracket. On EN500 models, unbolt the junction box bracket and lift it off together with the junction box and battery cover **(see illustration)**. Note the position of the carburetor vent tube and battery vent tube.
4 It may be possible to view the battery level marks without disconnecting its leads and lifting it out of its box. The electrolyte level is visible through the translucent battery case – it should be between the Upper and Lower level marks.
5 To remove the battery, remove the bolts securing the battery cables to the battery terminals (remove the negative cable first, positive cable last) **(see illustration)**. Pull the battery straight up to remove it, having first disconnected the vent tube from its side.
6 To top up the battery, remove the cell caps and fill each cell to the upper level mark with distilled water. Do not use tap water (except in an emergency), and do not overfill. If the level is within the marks on the case, additional water is not necessary. Refit the cell caps and mop up any water spills.

 *The cell holes are quite small, so it may help to use a clean plastic squeeze bottle with a small spout to add the water.*

7 Slip the battery back into its holder and reconnect the vent tube, making sure that it is not pinched at any point **(see illustration)**. Reconnect the cables to the battery, attaching the positive cable first and the negative cable last; install the plastic cap over the positive terminal. Install the junction box bracket. Ensure that the end of the carburetor tube is well away from the air intake before installing the seat.

Specific gravity check

8 A specific gravity check measures the state of charge of the battery. If the specific gravity is low, the battery is not fully charged. This may be due to corroded battery terminals, a dirty battery case, a malfunctioning charging system, or loose or corroded wiring connections. On the other hand, it may be that the battery is worn out, especially if the machine is old, or that infrequent use of the motorcycle prevents normal charging from taking place.
9 You will need a battery hydrometer to measure specific gravity and the battery must be removed from the bike and cell caps removed as described above.
10 Refer to *Checking battery specific gravity* in the *Fault Finding Equipment* section of *Reference* at the end of this manual. Specific gravity should be 1.280 at 20°C (68°F) in a good condition charged battery.

15.7 The clear plastic vent tube supplied with the battery fits inside the motorcycle's drain tube (arrow) when the battery is installed

1•20 Routine maintenance and servicing

16.6 Loosen the lower pinch bolt on each fork (arrow)

16.7 Loosen the steering stem bolt (arrow), but don't remove it or the stem will slip down

16 Steering head bearings – check and adjustment

1 EN450/500 motorcycles are equipped with tapered roller steering head bearings. EX250 models are equipped with ball-and-cone type steering head bearings. Steering head bearings can become dented, rough or loose during normal use of the machine and in extreme cases can cause steering wobble.

Check

2 To check the bearings, place the motorcycle on the centerstand and block the machine so the front wheel is in the air.
3 Point the wheel straight ahead and slowly move the handlebars from side-to-side. Dents or roughness in the bearing races will be felt and the bars will not move smoothly.
4 Next, grasp the fork legs and try to move the wheel forward and backward. Any looseness in the steering head bearings will be felt. If play is felt in the bearings, adjust the steering head as follows:

Adjustment

5 Remove the fuel tank to provide easier access (see Chapter 4). If you're working on an EX250, remove the fairing panels as well (see Chapter 8).
6 Loosen the fork lower pinch bolts **(see illustration)**. This allows the necessary vertical movement of the steering stem in relation to the fork tubes.
7 Loosen (DO NOT remove) the steering stem bolt **(see illustration)**.
8 Use a spanner wrench (C-spanner) to loosen the bearing adjuster nut **(see illustration)**.
9 Carefully tighten the bearing adjuster nut until the steering head is tight but does not bind when the forks are turned from side-to-side. The object is to set the adjuster nut so that the bearings are under a very light loading, just enough to remove any freeplay.

16.8 Use a spanner wrench like this one to loosen or tighten the steering stem locknuts (upper triple clamp removed for clarity)

Caution: Take great care not to apply excessive pressure because this will cause premature failure of the bearings.

10 Retighten the steering stem bolt and the fork pinch bolts, in that order, to the torque values listed in the Chapter 6 Specifications.
11 Recheck the steering head bearings for play as described above. If necessary, repeat the adjustment procedure. Reinstall all parts previously removed.
12 Refer to Chapter 6 for steering head bearing lubrication and replacement procedures.

17 Suspension – check

1 The suspension components must be maintained in top operating condition to ensure rider safety. Loose, worn or damaged suspension parts decrease the bike's stability and control.
2 While standing alongside the motorcycle, lock the front brake and push on the han-

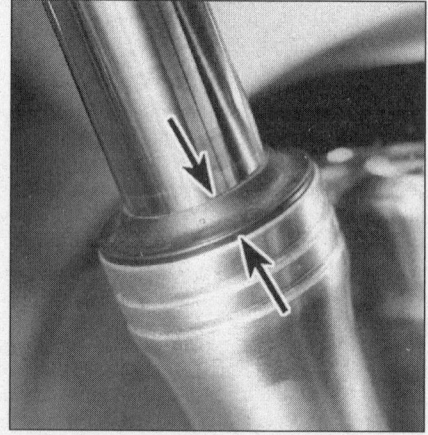

17.3 Check above and below the fork seals (arrows) for signs of oil leakage

dlebars to compress the forks several times. See if they move up-and-down smoothly without binding. If binding is felt, the forks should be disassembled and inspected as described in Chapter 6.
3 Carefully inspect the area around the fork seals for any signs of oil leakage **(see illustration)**. If leakage is evident, the seals must be replaced as described in Chapter 6.
4 Check the tightness of all suspension nuts and bolts to be sure none have worked loose.
5 Inspect the rear shock absorber(s) for fluid leakage and tightness of the mounting nuts. If leakage is found, the shock(s) should be replaced.
6 Set the bike on its centerstand. Grab the swingarm on each side, just ahead of the axle. Rock the swingarm from side to side – there should be no discernible movement at the rear. If there's a little movement or a slight clicking can be heard, make sure the pivot shaft nuts are tight. If the pivot nuts are tight but movement is still noticeable, the swingarm will have to be removed and the bearings replaced as described in Chapter 6.
7 Inspect the tightness of the rear suspension nuts and bolts.

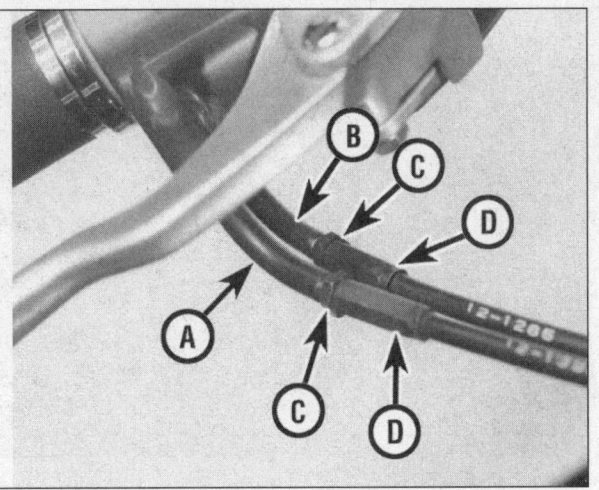

Routine maintenance and servicing 1•21

18.4 On EN450/500 models, loosen the accelerator or decelerator cable locknut and turn the adjusting nut to obtain the correct throttle freeplay

A   Accelerator cable (toward front of bike)
B   Decelerator cable (toward rear of bike)
C   Locknuts
D   Adjusting nuts

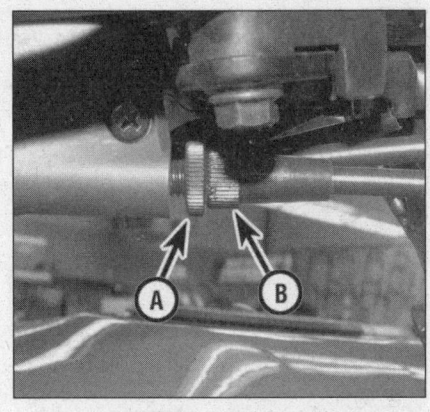

18.7 On EX250 models, loosen the accelerator cable lockwheel and turn the adjuster to obtain the correct throttle freeplay

A   Lockwheel   B   Adjuster

18 Throttle and choke operation/grip freeplay – check and adjustment

Throttle freeplay check

1   With the engine stopped, make sure the throttle grip rotates easily from fully closed to fully open with the front wheel turned at various angles. The grip should return automatically from fully open to fully closed when released. If the throttle sticks, check the throttle cables for cracks or kinks in the housings. Also, make sure the inner cables are clean and well-lubricated.
2   Check for a small amount of freeplay at the grip and compare the freeplay to the value listed in this Chapter's Specifications.

Throttle cable adjustment

Note: *These motorcycles use two throttle cables – an accelerator cable and a decelerator cable.*

3   Freeplay adjustments can be made at the throttle end of the cable.

EN450/500

4   Loosen the locknuts on both throttle cable adjusters **(see illustration)**. Turn the adjusters all the way in, causing the maximum amount of play at the throttle grip.
5   With the throttle grip in the closed position (have an assistant hold it there if necessary), back out the adjuster on the decelerator cable until all of the clearance between the cable bracket and stopper is eliminated. At this point, tighten the locknut on the decelerator cable.
6   Back out the adjuster on the accelerator cable to obtain the throttle grip freeplay listed in this Chapter's Specifications, then tighten the locknut.

EX250

7   Loosen the lockwheel on the cable where it leaves the handlebar **(see illustration)**. Turn the adjuster until the desired freeplay is obtained, then retighten the lockwheel.

All models

8   If the cables can't be adjusted at the grip end, adjust them at the lower ends. To do this on an EN450/500, first remove the fuel tank (see Chapter 4). On an EX250, remove the right knee grip pad (see Chapter 7).
9   Fully back off the upper adjuster nut towards the cable ferrule on each cable, then screw the lower adjuster nut up the thread (see illustrations). This will create a large amount of freeplay at the throttle grip.
10   Make sure the throttle grip is in the fully closed position.
11   Working on the decelerator cable first, back off the lower adjuster nut, then thread the upper nut down the thread until the inner cable just becomes tight; tighten both nuts against the bracket.
12   Back off the accelerator cable lower nut and thread the upper nut down the thread until the desired freeplay is obtained at the throttle grip, then tighten both nuts against the bracket.
13   Make sure the throttle linkage lever contacts the throttle stop screw when the throttle grip is in the closed throttle position.

18.9a Throttle cable adjusters at the carburetors (EN450/500)

A   Accelerator cable adjuster   C   Locknuts
B   Decelerator cable adjuster

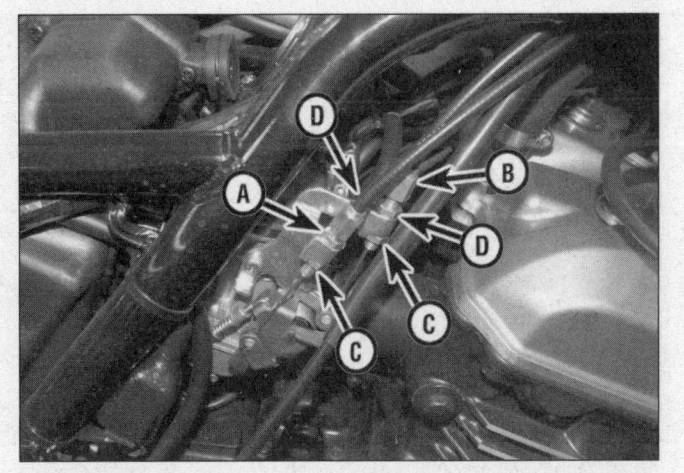

18.9b Throttle cable adjusters at the carburetors (EX250)

A   Accelerator cable   C   Lower adjusting nuts
B   Decelerator cable   D   Upper adjusting nuts

1•22 Routine maintenance and servicing

18.14 Check freeplay of the choke lever at the handlebar (EN450 and EX250 models)

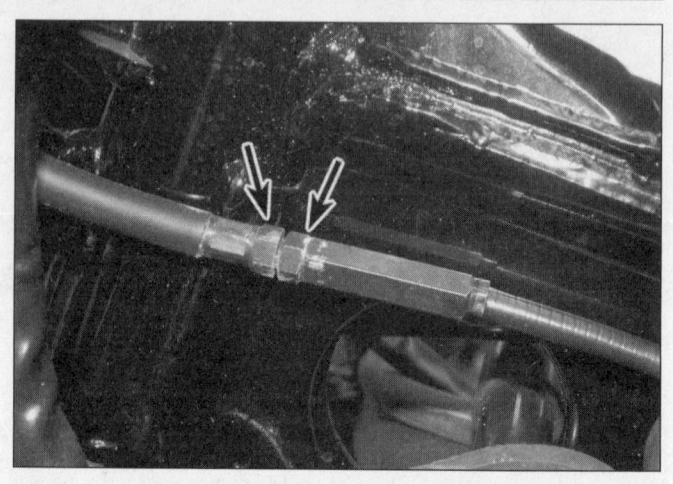

18.15 Loosen the locknut (left arrow) and turn the adjuster (right arrow) to adjust choke freeplay

⚠️ *Warning: Turn the handlebars all the way through their travel with the engine idling. Idle speed should not change. If it does, the cables may be routed incorrectly. Correct this condition before riding the bike.*

Choke cable check

EN450 and EX250 models

14 There should be a small amount of freeplay at the choke lever **(see illustration)**. Observe the choke plunger end on the carburetors and very slowly operate the choke lever on the handlebar until the choke linkage shaft contacts the plunger. Using a ruler, measure the distance when the choke lever is in this position to its OFF position. Compare with the value listed in this Chapter's Specifications.

15 If freeplay is incorrect, locate the cable adjuster at the handlebar on EN450 models or inside the left-hand side of the fairing on EX250 models **(see illustration)**. Loosen the locknut, turn the adjusting nut to set freeplay and tighten the locknut.

EN500 models

16 Inspect the choke handle and plunger **(see illustration)**. The choke should pull out easily and stay out by itself. If it doesn't, check the plunger bushing for wear and damage and replace as necessary.

19 Valve clearances – check and adjustment

1 The engine must be completely cool for this maintenance procedure, so let the machine sit overnight before beginning.
2 Disconnect the cable from the negative terminal of the battery (see Section 15).
3 On all models, refer to Chapter 4 and remove the fuel tank. On California models, remove the EVAP canister, then reinstall the forward canister bolt (the one that supports the coolant tube). This will prevent the tube from being pulled out of position when the radiator is moved forward. If you're working on an EX250, drain the cooling system (see Section 30). Remove the upper fairing and right ignition coil (see Chapters 8 and 5). If you need to adjust the valves on a 1986 or 1987 EX250, you'll also need to remove the upper engine mounting brackets (together with the ignition coils) (see Chapters 2 and 5).

HAYNES HiNT *To keep from having to remove the radiator and fan on EX250 models, loosen the radiator upper mounting bolts and remove the lower mounting bolts and position the lower end of the radiator forward with a block of wood. This provides access to the No. 2 left exhaust valve adjuster.*

4 Remove the valve cover (see Chapter 2).
5 Remove the covers from the crankshaft rotation bolt and timing inspection holes **(see illustrations)**.

18.16 On EN500 models, make sure the choke plunger lever moves freely and the bushing (arrow) is in good condition

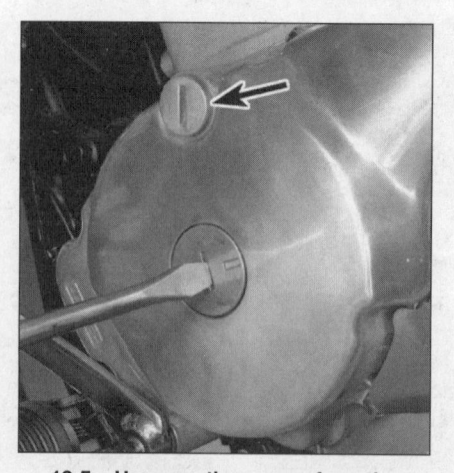

19.5a Unscrew the covers from the crankshaft rotation bolt and timing window (arrow) - inspect the cover O-rings and replace them if they're worn or damaged . . .

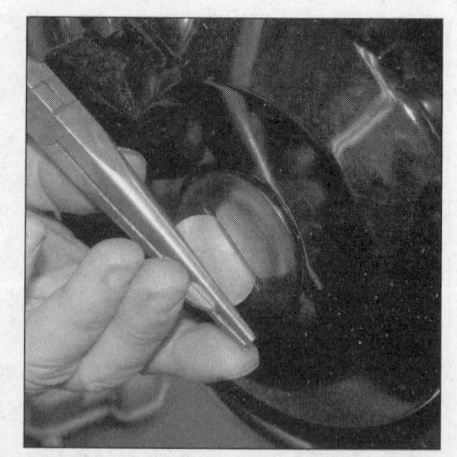

19.5b . . . a coin and pliers will prevent damage to the slots if you don't have a screwdriver wide enough

Routine maintenance and servicing 1•23

19.6a Turn the crankshaft clockwise with a socket . . .

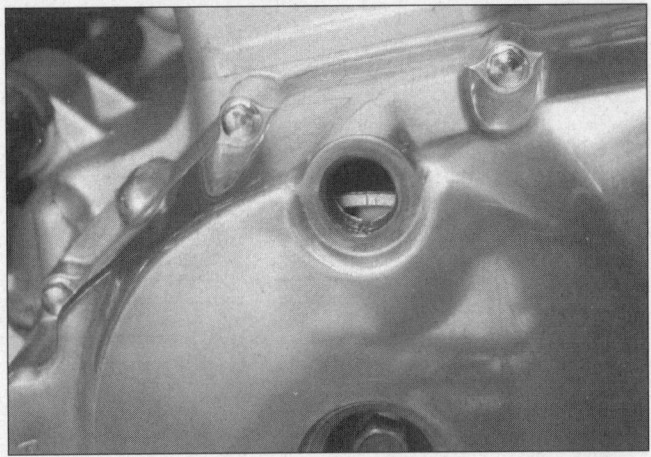

19.6b . . . until the T mark on the rotor aligns with the timing notch (EN450/500) . . .

TOOL TiP *A coin and a pair of pliers will work to unscrew the timing hole covers without damage if you don't have a screwdriver with a blade wide enough.*

6 Position the no. 1 piston (on the left-hand side of the engine) at Top Dead Center (TDC) on the compression stroke. Do this by turning the crankshaft clockwise, with a socket placed on the crankshaft bolt, until the T mark (EN450/500) or 1T mark (EX250) on the rotor is aligned with the timing mark on the crankcase **(see illustrations)**. Now, check the position of the no. 1 cylinder cam lobes – they should be pointing upward (EN450/500) or outward (EX250) **(see illustrations)**. If the cam lobes aren't pointing upward (EN450/500) or outward (EX250), rotate the crankshaft one complete turn and realign the marks. Piston no. 1 is now at TDC compression.

HAYNES HiNT *The crankshaft may tend to rotate out of the correct position due to the weight of the crankshaft throws. To* hold the crankshaft in the correct position for valve adjustment, place a ratchet or breaker bar on the crankshaft bolt and tie it to the bike (see illustration).

19.6c . . . or the 1T mark aligns with the pointer (EX250) . . .

19.6d . . . and the no. 1 cam lobes point upward (EN450/500) . . .

7 With the engine in this position, all of the valves for cylinder no. 1 can be checked.

8 Start with the no. 1 intake valve clearance. Insert a feeler gauge of the thick-

19.6e . . . or away from each other (EX250) (arrows)

19.6f To hold the engine in the correct position for valve adjustment, secure it with a socket and breaker bar, tied to the bike

1•24 Routine maintenance and servicing

19.8a For the most accurate measurement on EN450/500 models, use a pair of feeler gauges - because each rocker arm operates two valves, adjusting one valve affects the setting of the other one

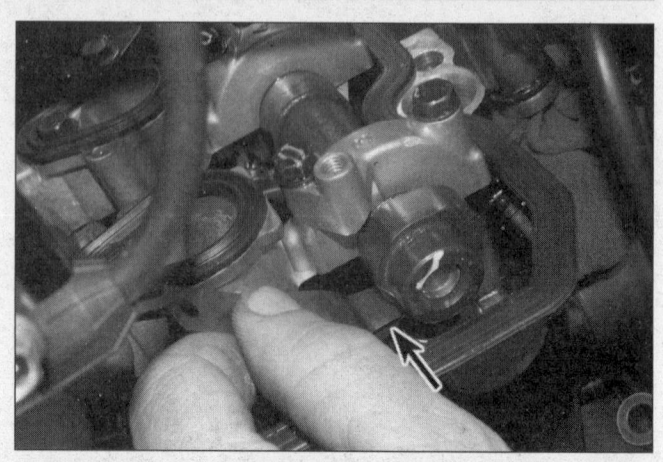

19.8b EX250 rocker arms each operate one valve, so a single feeler gauge (arrow) can be used

ness listed in this Chapter's Specifications between each valve stem and adjuster screw **(see illustrations)**. Pull it out slowly – you should feel a slight drag. If there's no drag, the clearance is too loose. If there's a heavy drag, the clearance is too tight. **Note:** *Ideally, valve clearances should be measured with go/no-go feeler gauges.*

9 If the clearance is incorrect, loosen the adjuster screw locknut and turn the adjuster screw in or out, as needed. A small flat-bladed screwdriver and slim open-end wrench can be used to adjust the valves, although access is limited. Alternatively, an aftermarket valve adjusting tool can be used **(see illustrations)**.

10 Hold the adjuster screw with a screwdriver (or the special tool) to keep it from turning and tighten the locknut. Recheck the clearance to make sure it hasn't changed.

11 Now adjust the no. 1 exhaust valves, following the same procedure you used for the intake valves. Make sure to use the correct size feeler gauge – the clearance differs for the exhaust valves.

12 Rotate the crankshaft clockwise to align

19.9a A special valve adjusting tool will help with the limited access - the socket **(A)** loosens and tightens the locknut while the screwdriver **(B)** turns the adjusting screw (this is the EN450/500 tool) . . .

the C mark (EN450/500) or 2T mark (EX250) on the rotor with the timing mark on the crankcase, which will position piston no. 2

19.9b . . . and here's the version used with the EX250

at TDC compression **(see illustration)**. The cam lobes for no. 2 cylinder should now point upward (EN450/500) or outward (EX250) **(see illustrations)**.

13 Adjust all four valves on cylinder no. 2 as previously described.

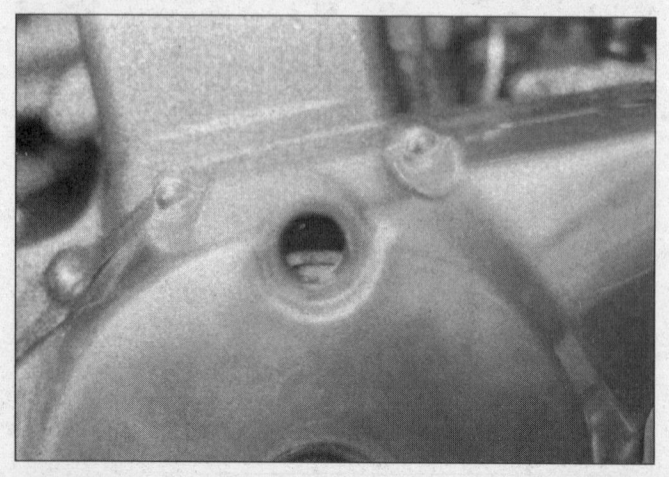

19.12a Turn the crankshaft until the C mark (EN450/500) or 2T mark (EX250) aligns with the timing notch . . .

19.12b . . . and the no. 2 cam lobes point upward (EN450/500) . . .

Routine maintenance and servicing 1•25

19.12c ... or away from each other (EX250), then adjust the valves for the no. 2 cylinder

20.4 Remove the engine oil drain plug (arrow) (EN450/500)

14 Install the valve cover and all of the components that had to be removed to get it off.
15 Install all components removed for access and reconnect the cable to the negative terminal of the battery.

20 Engine oil/filter – change

Note: *For some models the oil and filter replacement intervals are separate; if you're changing the oil only, ignore the filter information.*

1 Consistent routine oil and filter changes are the single most important maintenance procedure you can perform on a motorcycle. The oil not only lubricates the internal parts of the engine, transmission and clutch, but it also acts as a coolant, a cleaner, a sealant, and a protectant. Because of these demands, the oil takes a terrific amount of abuse and should be replaced often with new oil of the recommended grade and type.

HAYNES HiNT *Saving a little money on the difference in cost between a good oil and a cheap oil won't pay off if the engine is damaged.*

2 Before changing the oil and filter, warm up the engine so the oil will drain easily. Be careful when draining the oil, as the exhaust pipes, the engine, and the oil itself can cause severe burns. If the oil filter is being replaced on 1988 and later EX250 models you are advised to remove the lower fairing (see Chapter 8).
3 Put the motorcycle on the centerstand over a clean drain pan. Remove the oil filler cap to vent the crankcase and act as a reminder that there is no oil in the engine.

EN450/500 models
4 Remove the drain plug from the sump **(see illustration)** and allow the oil to drain into the pan. Discard the sealing washer on the drain plug; it should be replaced whenever the plug is removed.

5 As the oil is draining, remove the oil filter **(see illustrations)**. If additional maintenance is planned for this time period, check or service another component while the oil is allowed to drain completely.
6 Wipe any remaining oil off the filter sealing area of the crankcase.
7 Check the condition of the drain plug threads.
8 Coat the gasket on a new filter with clean engine oil. Install the filter and tighten it to the amount listed in this Chapter's Specifications.
9 Slip a new sealing washer over the drain plug, then install and tighten the plug. Tighten the drain plug to the torque listed in this Chapter's Specifications. Avoid overtightening, as damage to the engine case will result.

EX250 models
10 Remove the drain plug from the sump **(see illustration)** and allow the oil to drain into the pan. Discard the sealing washer on the drain plug; it should be replaced whenever the plug is removed.

20.5a Remove the oil filter with a filter wrench or a special socket; the special socket is best, since it allows the filter to be tightened accurately with a torque wrench (EN450/500)

20.5b Let the oil drain completely from the drain plug and filter openings (EN450/500)

20.10 Unscrew the oil drain plug (right arrow) and loosen the filter bolt (left arrow) . . .

1•26 Routine maintenance and servicing

20.11a . . . some oil will drain from the filter cover, even if the engine has been drained . . .

20.11b . . . once the filter oil has drained, remove it all the way

11 As the oil is draining, remove the oil filter **(see illustrations)**. If additional maintenance is planned for this time period, check or service another component while the oil is allowed to drain completely.

12 Remove the inner cover from the oil filter **(see illustration)**. Remove the filter element from the bypass valve, twisting it as you do so to ease removal.

13 Remove the washer and spring from the bypass valve, then remove the outer cover and small O-ring. Remove the large O-ring from the cover.

14 If the relief valve holes are clogged or if the valve rattles when you shake it, refer to Chapter 2 for disassembly and inspection procedures. Test by blowing air through it **(see illustration)**. This is especially important if there has been debris inside the engine (clutch or bearing material, etc.).

15 Coat new O-rings with clean engine oil. Assemble the filter by reversing Steps 12 and 13.

Caution: *Be sure to reinstall the washer between the spring and filter cartridge to prevent damage to the rubber gasket. If you can't find the washer, it may be stuck to the old filter cartridge.*

16 Install the filter and drain bolt and tighten them to the torque listed in this Chapter's Specifications. Avoid overtightening, as damage to the engine case will result.

All models

HAYNES HiNT *Before refilling the engine, check the old oil carefully. If the oil was drained into a clean pan, small pieces of metal or other material can be easily detected. If the oil is very metallic colored, then the engine is experiencing wear from break-in (new engine) or from insufficient lubrication. If there are flakes or chips of metal in the oil, then something is drastically wrong internally and the engine will have to be disassembled for inspection and repair. If there are pieces of fiber-like material in the oil, the clutch is experiencing excessive wear and should be checked.*

17 Refill the crankcase to the proper level with the recommended oil and install the filler cap. Start the engine and let it run for two or three minutes. Shut it off, wait a few minutes, then check the oil level as described in Daily (pre-ride) checks, and top up if necessary. Check that there are no oil leaks around the drain plug and filter.

18 The old oil drained from the engine cannot be reused in its present state and should be disposed of. Check with your parts store, disposal facility or environmental agency to see whether they will accept the oil for recycling. Don't pour used oil into drains or onto the ground. After the oil has cooled, it can be drained into a suitable container (capped plastic jugs, topped bottles, etc.) for transport to a disposal site.

21 Air filter element – servicing

EN450 models

1 Remove both side covers (see Chapter 8).

2 Unhook the spring, remove the cap and take out the filter element on one side of the bike.

3 Repeat Step 2 on the other side of the bike.

20.12 Oil filter details (EX250)

1 *Small O-ring*
2 *Relief valve/bolt*
3 *Outer cover*
4 *Large O-ring*
5 *Spring*
6 *Washer*
7 *Filter element*
8 *Inner cover*

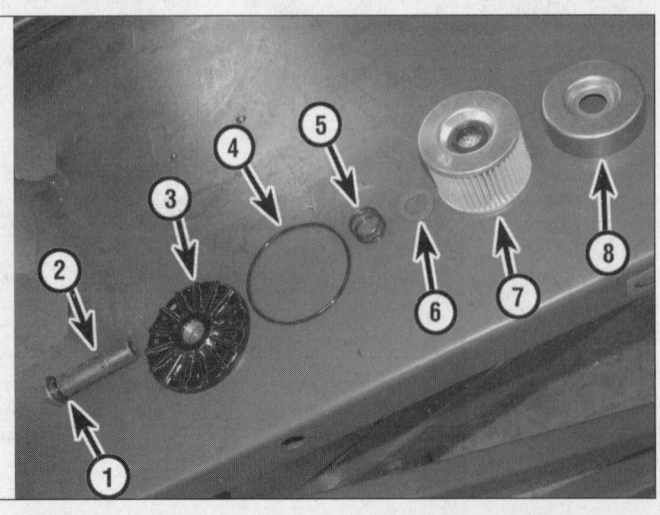

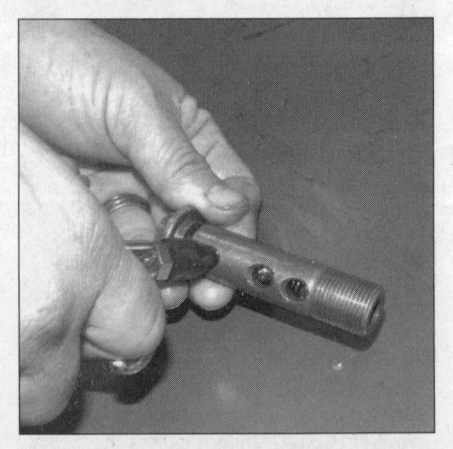

20.14 Check the relief valve for clogging by blowing compressed air through it

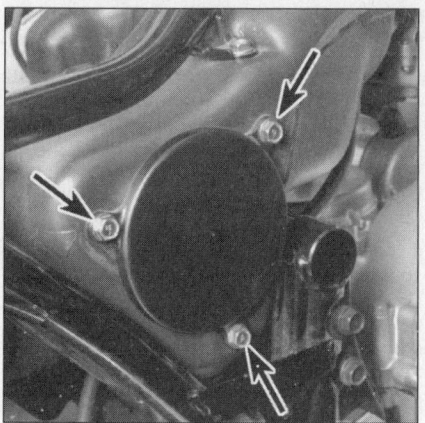

Routine maintenance and servicing 1•27

21.8a Remove three bolts (arrows), take off the cover...

21.8b ...and pull out the filter element

21.8c Filter element details (EN500 models)

4 Wipe out the housing with a clean rag, then stuff a rag into each opening to keep out foreign material.

5 Check the element and its foam gasket for tears or other damage. Replace the element if it's damaged.

6 Tap the element on a hard surface to remove the dirt. Finish cleaning by blowing compressed air from the inside of the element to the outside.

EN500 models

Through 1996

7 Remove the right side cover (see Chapter 8).

8 Remove three bolts, lift off the air filter cover and remove the air filter element **(see illustrations)**.

1997 and later

9 Remove the left side cover (see Chapter 8).

10 Disconnect the alternator electrical connector and remove the starter relay (see Chapter 9).

11 Unbolt the case from the air cleaner housing. Remove the retainer and element.

12 Wipe out the housing with a clean rag,

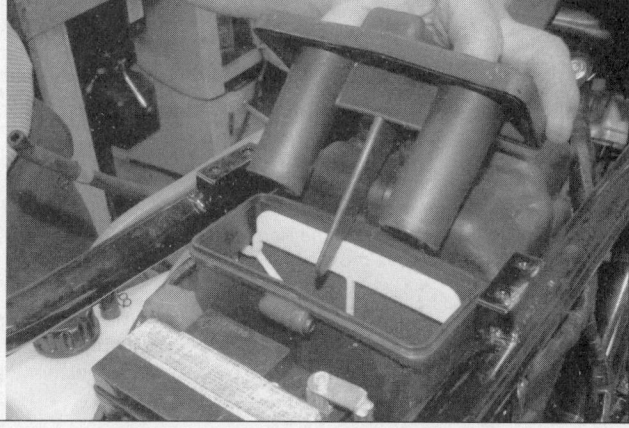

21.16a Remove the retaining band and lift off the cover...

then place a clean rag in the air box opening to keep out dirt.

All years

13 Clean the element with solvent. If compressed air is available, use it to clean the element by blowing from the inside out (from the mesh side toward the foam side). If the foam is extremely dirty or torn, replace the element with a new one.

14 Soak the element in clean SAE 30 engine oil. Squeeze as much oil as possible out of the element, then squeeze the element inside a clean rag to remove more oil.

EX250 models

15 Remove the seat (see Chapter 8).

16 Remove the housing retaining strap. Lift off the housing cover and remove the element holder, then separate the element from the holder **(see illustrations)**. Wipe out the housing with a clean rag.

21.16b ...then lift out the foam element and check the wire screen for clogging

21.16c The foam element fits between the wire screen and the plastic support

22.8 The fuel tap is secured to the tank by two screws

17 Clean the element with solvent. If compressed air is available, use it to clean the element by blowing from the inside out (from the mesh side toward the foam side). If the foam is extremely dirty or torn, replace the element.
18 Soak the element in clean SAE 30 engine oil. Squeeze as much oil as possible out of the element, then squeeze the element inside a clean rag to remove more oil.

All models

19 Reinstall the filter by reversing the removal procedure. Make sure the element is seated properly in the filter housing before installing the cover.
20 Reinstall all components removed for access.

22 Fuel system – check and filter cleaning

Warning: *Gasoline (petrol) is extremely flammable, so take extra precautions when you work on any part of the fuel system. Don't smoke or allow open flames or bare light bulbs near the work area, and don't work in a garage where a gas-type appliance (such as a water heater or clothes dryer) is present. If you spill any fuel on your skin, rinse it off immediately with soap and water. When you perform any kind of work on the fuel system, wear safety glasses and have a fire extinguisher suitable for a class B type fire (flammable liquids) on hand.*

1 Check the fuel tank, the fuel tap, the fuel hoses and the carburetors for leaks and evidence of damage.
2 If carburetor gaskets are leaking, the carburetors should be disassembled and rebuilt by referring to Chapter 4.
3 If the fuel tap is leaking, tightening the screws may help. If leakage persists, the tap should be disassembled and repaired or replaced.
4 If the fuel hoses are cracked or otherwise deteriorated, replace them.
5 Check the vacuum hose connected to the fuel tap. If it is cracked or otherwise damaged, replace it.
6 The fuel filter may become clogged and should be removed and cleaned periodically. In order to clean the filter, the fuel tank must be drained. On all models the fuel filter is integral with the fuel tap.
7 Remove the fuel tank (see Chapter 4). Drain the fuel into an approved fuel container.
8 Loosen and remove the screws that attach the fuel tap to the tank **(see illustration)**. Remove the tap and filter.
9 Clean the filter with solvent and blow it dry with compressed air. If the filter is torn or otherwise damaged, replace the entire fuel tap.
10 Install the tank. Refill the tank and check carefully that there are no leaks.

23 Rear suspension – lubrication

Refer to Chapter 6 and dismantle the swingarm (and Uni-trak linkage on EX250 models) for lubrication of the needle roller bearings.

24 Cooling system – check

Warning: *The engine must be cool before beginning this procedure.*

Note: *Refer to Daily (pre-ride) checks and check the coolant level before performing this check.*

1 The entire cooling system should be checked carefully at the recommended intervals. Look for evidence of leaks, check the condition of the coolant, check the radiator for clogged fins and damage and make sure the fan operates when required.
2 Remove the fuel tank (Chapter 4).
3 Examine each of the rubber coolant hoses along its entire length. Look for cracks, abrasions and other damage. Squeeze each hose at various points. They should feel firm, yet pliable, and return to their original shape when released. If they are dried out or hard, replace them.
4 Check for evidence of leaks at each cooling system joint. Tighten the hose clamps carefully to prevent future leaks.
5 Check the radiator for evidence of leaks and other damage. If leaks are noted, remove the radiator (refer to Chapter 3) and have it professionally repaired.

HAYNES HiNT *Leaks in the radiator leave telltale scale deposits or coolant stains on the outside of the core below the leak*

Caution: *Do not use a liquid leak stopping compound to try to repair leaks.*

6 Check the radiator fins for mud, dirt and insects, which may impede the flow of air through the radiator. If the fins are dirty, force water or low pressure compressed air through the fins from the backside. If the fins are bent or distorted, straighten them carefully with a screwdriver.
7 Remove the pressure cap by turning it counterclockwise (anticlockwise) until it reaches a stop. If you hear a hissing sound (indicating there is still pressure in the system), wait until it stops. Now, press down on the cap with the palm of your hand and continue turning the cap counterclockwise until it can be removed **(see illustrations)**. Check the condition of the coolant in the system. If it is rust colored or if accumulations of scale are visible, drain, flush and refill the system with new coolant. Check the cap gaskets for cracks and other damage. Have the cap tested by a dealer service department or replace it. Install the cap by turning it clockwise until it reaches the first stop, then push down on the cap and continue turning until it can turn no further.
8 Check the antifreeze content of the coolant with an antifreeze hydrometer **(see illustration)**. Sometimes coolant may look like it's in good condition, but might be too weak to offer adequate protection. If the hydrometer indicates a weak mixture, drain, flush and refill the cooling system (see Section 30).
9 Start the engine and let it reach normal operating temperature, then check for leaks again. As the coolant temperature increases, the fan should come on automatically and the temperature should begin to drop. If it does not, refer to Chapter 3 and check the fan and fan circuit carefully.
10 If the coolant level is consistently low, and no evidence of leaks can be found, have the entire system pressure checked by a dealer service department or radiator shop.
11 On models equipped with a carburetor warmer system, check that the filter is not blocked.

25 Exhaust system – check

1 Periodically check all of the exhaust system joints for leaks and loose fasteners. The lower fairing (1988 and later EX250 models) will have to be removed to do this properly (see Chapter 8). If tightening the clamp bolts

Routine maintenance and servicing 1•29

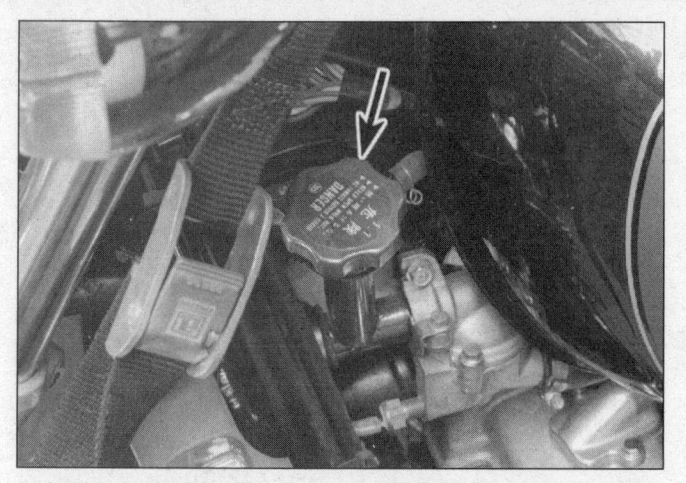

24.7a The cooling system pressure cap (arrow) is located on the left side of the bike (EN450/500) . . .

24.7b . . . and inside the fairing on EX250 models

fails to stop any leaks, replace the gaskets (a procedure which requires disassembly of the system).

2 The exhaust pipe flange nuts at the cylinder heads are especially prone to loosening, which could cause damage to the head. Check them frequently and keep them tight.

26 Fasteners – check

1 Since vibration of the machine tends to loosen fasteners, all nuts, bolts, screws, etc. should be periodically checked for proper tightness.
2 Pay particular attention to the following:
Spark plugs
Engine oil drain plug
Shift pedal
Footrests, sidestand and centerstand
Engine mounting bolts
Front fork pinch bolts
Rear shock absorber mounting bolts
Uni-trak linkage bolts (EX250 models)
Front axle and clamp bolt
Rear axle nut

3 If a torque wrench is available, use it along with the torque specifications at the beginning of this, or other, Chapters.

27 Brake fluid – replacement

1 The brake fluid should be replaced at the prescribed interval or whenever a master cylinder or caliper overhaul is carried out.
2 Refer to the brake bleeding section in Chapter 7, noting that all old fluid must be pumped from the fluid reservoir and hydraulic line before filling with new fluid.

HAYNES HiNT *Old brake fluid is invariably much darker in color than new fluid, making it easier to see when old fluid has been expelled from the system.*

28 Steering head bearings – lubrication

1 Refer to Chapter 6 and remove the steering stem/lower triple clamp from the frame headstock. There is no need to remove the lower bearing race from the stem or to remove the bearing outer races from the headstock; remove all old grease, check them for wear and apply new grease before reassembly.
2 If the bearings show signs of wear replace them; replace the top and bottom bearing sets at the same time.

29 Rear brake cam – lubrication (drum brakes)

1 Refer to Chapter 7 and remove the brake cam from the brake panel. Remove all traces of old grease from the surface of the

24.7c Release all pressure from the cooling system, then slowly remove the cap

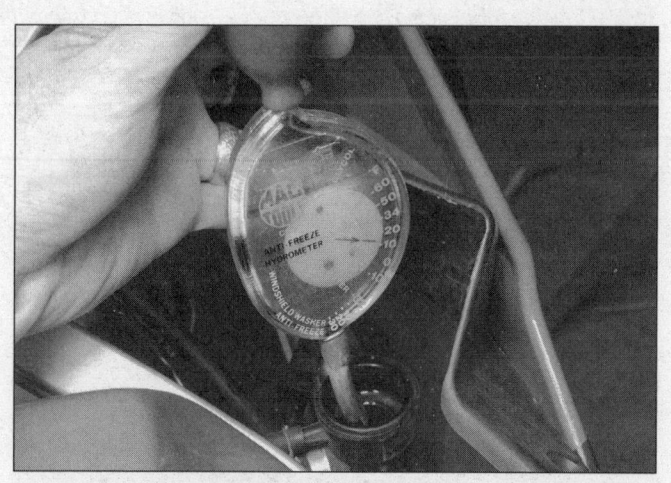

24.8 An antifreeze hydrometer is helpful in determining the condition of the coolant

1•30 Routine maintenance and servicing

30.2a The coolant drain bolt is located in the bottom of the water pump cover. Here's the EN450/500 . . .

30.2b . . . and this is the EX250 (arrow)

cam and its hole in the brake panel. Apply a smear of high melting-point grease to the two bearing surfaces of the cam and the operating flat on its end. Also apply a smear of high melting-point grease to the brake shoe pivot on the brake panel and the spring hooks where they engage the holes in the brake shoes.

2 Assemble the brake cam and shoes in the brake panel as described in Chapter 7.

Caution: Do not apply too much grease, otherwise there is a risk of it contaminating the brake shoe linings.

30 Coolant – replacement

Warning: Allow the engine to cool completely before performing this maintenance operation. Also, don't allow antifreeze to come into contact with your skin or painted surfaces of the motorcycle. Rinse off spills immediately with plenty of water. Antifreeze is highly toxic if ingested. Never leave antifreeze lying around in an open container or in puddles on the floor; children and pets are attracted by its sweet smell and may drink it. Check with local authorities (councils) about disposing of used antifreeze. Many communities have collection centers which will see that antifreeze is disposed of safely. Antifreeze is also combustible, so don't store or use it near open flames.

Draining

1 On EN500 C models, remove the instrument cluster (see Chapter 9). On EX250 models, remove the upper and lower fairings (see Chapter 8).

2 Place a large, clean drain pan under the right-hand side of the engine (EN450/500) or the left side (EX250). Remove the drain bolt from the bottom of the water pump cover **(see illustrations)** and allow the coolant to drain into the pan.

HAYNES HiNT *It's a good idea to leave the radiator cap tightly secured until the drain pan is in position, then loosen the cap. That way, coolant will dribble out slowly when the drain bolt is removed, allowing you to get the drain bolt out* of the way. Once the pressure cap is removed, the coolant will rush out with considerable force, so position the drain pan accordingly. Remove the pressure cap completely to ensure that all of the coolant can drain.

3 With the drain pan in position, remove the pressure cap **(see illustration 24.7a or 24.7b)**. Be prepared to move the drain pan, since the direction of coolant flow will change as the coolant drains **(see illustration)**.

4 If you're working on an EX250, remove the cylinder drain bolt **(see illustration)** and allow the coolant to drain from it.

5 Drain the coolant reservoir. Refer to Chapter 3 for the reservoir removal procedure. Wash the reservoir out with water.

Flushing

6 Flush the system with clean tap water by inserting a garden hose in the radiator filler neck. Allow the water to run through the system until it is clear when it exits the drain bolt hole. If the radiator is extremely corroded, remove it by referring to Chapter 3 and have it cleaned by a professional.

7 Check the drain bolt gasket(s). Replace if necessary.

30.3 Coolant will spurt out at first, so have the drain pan ready

30.4 On EX250 models, remove the cylinder drain bolt (arrow)

Routine maintenance and servicing 1•31

30.14 Fill the cooling system up to the bottom of the reservoir tank hose union (arrow)

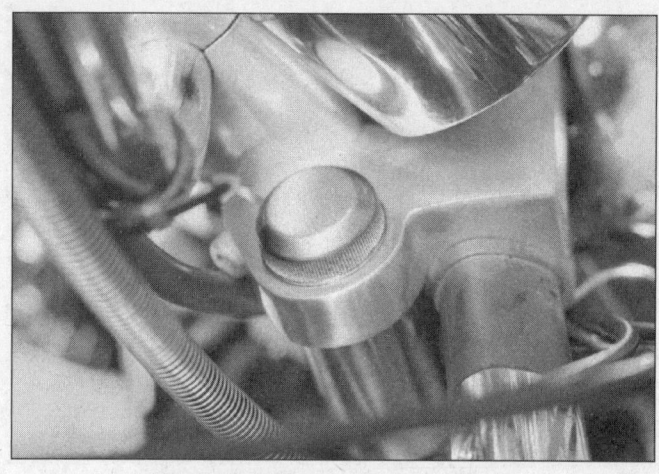

31.3 Pull off the fork cap (if equipped)

8 Clean the hole, then install the drain bolt and tighten it to the torque listed in this Chapter's Specifications.
9 Fill the cooling system with clean water mixed with a flushing compound. Make sure the flushing compound is compatible with aluminum components, and follow the manufacturer's instructions carefully.
10 Start the engine and allow it to reach normal operating temperature. Let it run for about ten minutes.
11 Stop the engine. Let the machine cool for a while, then cover the pressure cap with a heavy rag and turn it counterclockwise to the first stop, releasing any pressure that may be present in the system. Once the hissing stops, push down on the cap and remove it completely.
12 Drain the system once again and reinstall the drain bolt(s).
13 Fill the system with clean water, then repeat Steps 10, 11 and 12.

Refilling

14 Fill the system with the proper coolant mixture (see this Chapter's Specifications); pour the coolant in slowly to avoid trapping air in the system. When the system is full (all the way up to the bottom of the reservoir tank hose union in the radiator cap filler neck) **(see illustration)**, fully install the cap and start the engine. Allow the engine to reach normal operating temperature, then shut it off.
15 Let the engine cool down, cover the radiator cap with a heavy rag and loosen it to the first stop to allow any pressure in the system to bleed off before the cap is removed completely. Recheck the coolant level in the radiator filler neck. If it's low, add more coolant until it reaches the bottom of the reservoir tank hose union.
16 Leave the pressure cap off and start the engine. Let it idle and observe the coolant in the filler neck. When no more air bubbles can be seen in the coolant the system is bled of air. Stop the engine, top up the coolant if necessary and refit the pressure cap.
17 Fill the reservoir tank with coolant up to the correct level (see *Daily (pre-ride) checks*). Check that there are no coolant leaks and install any components removed for access.
18 Do not dispose of the old coolant by pouring it down a drain. Instead, pour it into a heavy plastic container, cap it tightly and take it to an authorized disposal site or a service station.

31 Fork oil – replacement

1 If you're working on an EX250, remove the lower fairing (if equipped) and the handlebar (see Chapters 8 and 6).
2 Place the motorcycle on the centerstand and position a jack with a block of wood on the jack head under the engine.
3 If you're working on a 1985 through 1988 EN450 model, bleed off the air pressure through the air valve at the top of the fork. On all models, remove the cap from the top of the fork **(see illustration)**.
4 Push the top plug downward against spring pressure with a Phillips screwdriver or similar tool, remove the retaining ring and release the spring pressure **(see illustrations)**.

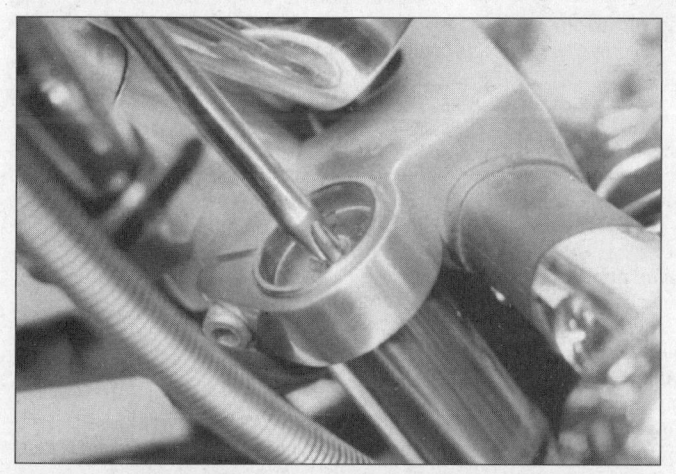

31.4a Push down on the fork cap plug and remove the retaining ring (EN500 model shown; others similar) . . .

31.4b . . . once the retaining ring is removed, release the spring pressure

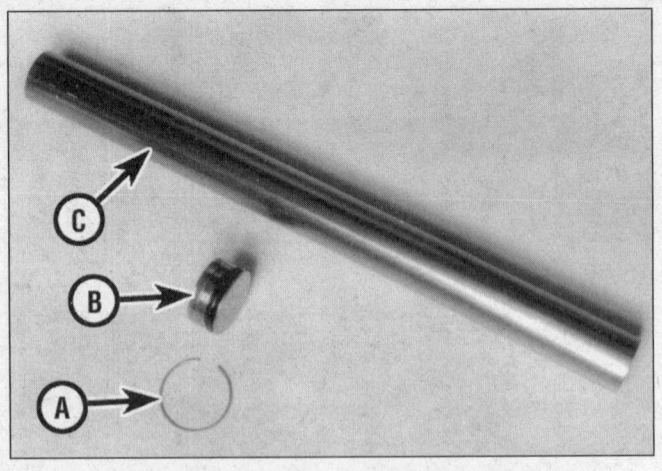

1•32 Routine maintenance and servicing

31.5 Remove the fork cap plug and lift out the spacer

- A Retaining ring
- B Fork cap plug and O-ring
- C Spacer

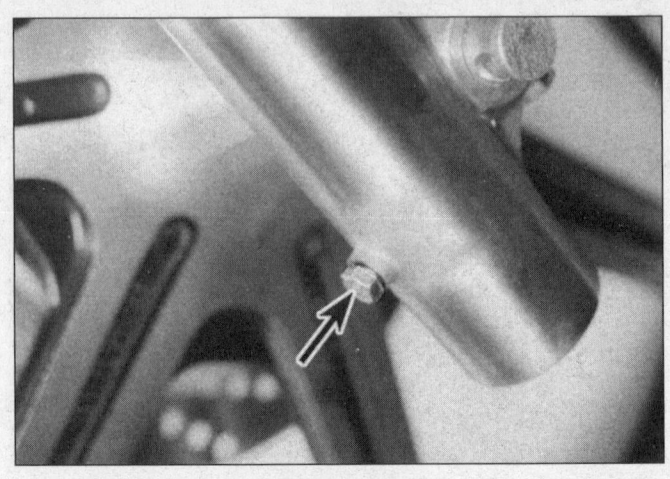

31.7 There's a fork drain screw at the bottom of each fork leg (arrow)

5 Lift out the top plug, O-ring and spacer **(see illustration)**.
6 Lift out the fork spring.
7 Place a drain pan under the fork leg and remove the drain screw **(see illustration)**.

⚠ **Warning: Do not allow the fork oil to contact the brake disc, pads or tire. If it does, clean the disc with brake system cleaner, wipe off the tire, and replace the pads before riding the motorcycle. Make up a cardboard chute to direct oil away from the disc and tire.**

8 After most of the oil has drained, slowly compress and release the forks to pump out the remaining oil. An assistant will most likely be required to do this procedure.
9 Check the drain screw gasket for damage and replace it if necessary. Clean the threads of the drain screw with solvent and let it dry, then install the screw and gasket, tightening it securely.
10 Pour the type and amount of fork oil listed in this Chapter's Specifications, into the fork tube through the opening at the top **(see illustration)**.

HAYNES HiNT *Remove the jack from under the engine and slowly pump the forks a few times to purge the air from the upper and lower chambers.*

11 Fully compress the front forks (you may need an assistant to do this). Insert a stiff tape measure into the fork tube and measure the distance from the oil to the top of the fork tube. Compare your measurement to the value listed in this Chapter's Specifications. Drain or add oil, as necessary, until the level is correct.
12 Check the O-ring on the top plug, then coat it with a thin layer of multi-purpose grease. Install the fork spring with its tapered end facing downwards. Install the top plug, push it down against the spring pressure, install the retaining ring and slowly release

the top plug.
13 Tighten the fork tube pinch bolts to the torque listed in the Chapter 6 Specifications. Install the handlebar, tightening the bolts to the torque listed in the Chapter 6 Specifications.
14 Repeat the procedure to the other fork. Note that it is essential that the oil quantity and level is identical in each fork.
15 Install all components removed for access.

32 Brake caliper and master cylinder – overhaul

Hydraulic seals will deteriorate over a period of time and lose their effectiveness, leading to sticking operation, fluid loss, or allowing the ingress of dirt. Refer to Chapter 7 and dismantle the components for seal replacement.

33 Fuel hoses – replacement

⚠ **Warning: Gasoline (petrol) is extremely flammable, so take extra precautions when you work on any part of the fuel system. Don't smoke or allow open flames or bare light bulbs near the work area, and don't work in a garage where a gas-type appliance (such as a water heater or clothes dryer) is present. Since gasoline is carcinogenic, wear nitrile gloves when there's a possibility of being exposed to fuel, and, if you spill any fuel on your skin, rinse it off immediately with soap and water. When you perform any kind of work on the fuel system, wear safety glasses and have a fire**

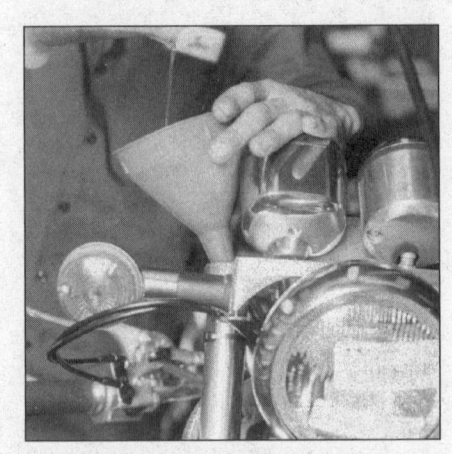

31.10 Use a funnel to pour oil into the fork

extinguisher suitable for a Class B type fire (flammable liquids) on hand.

1 Remove the fuel tank (see Chapter 4). Disconnect the fuel hoses from the fuel tank and/or tap and from the carburetors, noting the routing of each hose and where it connects (see Chapter 4 if required). It is advisable to make a sketch of the various hoses before removing them to ensure they are correctly installed.
2 Secure each new hose to its unions using new clamps. Run the engine and check that there are no leaks before taking the machine out on the road.

34 Brake hose(s) – replacement

1 The hydraulic hoses will in time deteriorate with age and should be replaced regardless of their apparent condition. Refer to Chapter 7.

Chapter 2 Part A
Engine, clutch and transmission - EN450/500 models

Contents

Balancer shaft - removal and installation	18
Camshaft chain tensioner - removal and installation	7
Camshafts, rocker arm shafts and rocker arms - removal, inspection and installation	8
Clutch - removal and installation	14
Clutch cable - replacement	15
Crankcase - disassembly and reassembly	17
Cylinder block - removal and installation	10
Cylinder head - removal and installation	9
Engine - removal and installation	5
External shift mechanism - removal, inspection and installation	16
General information	1
Major engine repair - general note	4
Oil pan - removal and installation	11
Oil pressure relief valve - removal, inspection and installation	13
Oil pump - removal and installation	12
Operations possible with the engine in the frame	2
Operations requiring engine removal	3
Primary chain, camshaft chain and guides - removal, inspection and installation	19
Shift drum and forks - removal, inspection and installation	22
Transmission shafts - disassembly and reassembly	21
Transmission shafts - removal and installation	20
Valve cover - removal and installation	6

Degrees of difficulty

Easy, suitable for novice with little experience	**Fairly easy,** suitable for beginner with some experience	**Fairly difficult,** suitable for competent DIY mechanic	**Difficult,** suitable for experienced DIY mechanic	**Very difficult,** suitable for expert DIY or professional

Specifications

General
Bore
    EN450 models .... 72.0 mm (2.834 inches)
    EN500 models .... 74.0 mm (2.913 inches)
Stroke .... 58.0 mm (2.283 inches)
Displacement
    EN450 models .... 454 cc
    EN500 models .... 498 cc
Compression ratio
    EN450 models .... 10.7 : 1
    EN500 models
        Except California .... 10.8 : 1
        California .... 10.7 : 1

2A•2 Engine, clutch and transmission - EN450/500 models

Torque specifications

Valve cover bolts	9.8 Nm (87 in-lbs)
Camshaft bearing cap bolts	12 Nm (104 in-lbs)
Camshaft sprocket bolts	15 Nm (132 in-lbs)*
Rocker arm shafts	
1985 through 1996 (A7)	51 Nm (38 ft-lbs)
1996 (C1) and later	39 Nm (29 ft-lbs)
Oil pipe bolts (on cylinder head top surface)	Not specified
Camshaft chain tensioner cap	4.9 Nm (43 in-lbs)
Camshaft chain tensioner mounting bolts	8.8 Nm (78 in-lbs)
Cylinder head bolts	
6 mm bolts	9.8 Nm (87 in-lbs)
10 mm bolts	51 Nm (38 ft-lbs)
Crankcase bolts	
6 mm bolts	12 Nm (104 in-lbs)
8 mm bolts	27 Nm (20 ft-lbs)
Connecting rod nuts	36 Nm (27 ft-lbs)
Primary chain guide bolts	8.8 Nm (78 in-lbs)*
Clutch cover bolts	
1985 through 1996 (A7)	Not specified
1996 (C1) and later	11 Nm (95 in-lbs)
Clutch cover baffle bolts (1996 C1 and later)	9.8 Nm (87 in-lbs)*
Clutch spring bolts	9.3 Nm (82 in-lbs)
Clutch hub nut	130 Nm (98 ft-lbs)
Oil pump bolts	Not specified*
Oil pan bolts	12 Nm (104 in-lbs)
Oil pipe-to-cylinder head union bolts	12 Nm (104 in-lbs)
Oil pipe-to-crankcase union bolts	
Left front corner of case	
Through 1996 (A7)	20 Nm (174 in-lbs)
1996 (C1) and later	7.8 Nm (69 in-lbs)
Left side of case (upper bolt)	7.8 Nm (69 in-lbs)
Left side of case (lower bolt)	12 Nm (104 in-lbs)
Bottom of case (inside oil pan)	12 Nm (104 in-lbs)
Right rear corner of engine	7.8 Nm (69 in-lbs)
Cylinder head "Y" line to case	20 Nm (174 in-lbs)
Oil pressure relief valve-to-oil pan	15 Nm (132 in-lbs)*
Oil passage plugs	
Allen head	Not specified*
Hex head	
EN450 models	17 Nm (150 in-lbs)
EN500 models (through 1996 A7)	23 Nm (16.5 ft-lbs)
EN500 models (1996 C1 and later)	18 Nm (156 in-lbs)
Shift drum bearing retainer bolts	Not specified*

*Apply non-hardening thread locking agent to the threads.

Engine, clutch and transmission - EN450/500 models 2A•3

1 General information

The engine/transmission unit is a water-cooled, in-line, parallel twin. The valves are operated by double overhead camshafts which are chain driven off the crankshaft. The engine/transmission assembly is constructed from aluminum alloy. The crankcase is divided horizontally.

The crankcase incorporates a wet sump, pressure-fed lubrication system which uses a gear-driven, dual-rotor oil pump, an oil filter and by-pass valve assembly, a relief valve and an oil pressure switch. Also contained in the crankcase is the balancer shaft and the starter motor clutch.

Power from the crankshaft is routed to the transmission via the clutch, which is of the wet, multi-plate type and is chain-driven off the crankshaft. The transmission is a six-speed, constant-mesh unit.

2 Operations possible with the engine in the frame

The components and assemblies listed below can be removed without having to remove the engine from the frame. If, however, a number of areas require attention at the same time, removal of the engine is recommended.

Gearshift mechanism external components
Water pump
Starter motor
Alternator
Clutch assembly (except housing)
Oil pan and pressure relief valve
Valve cover, camshafts and rocker arms
Cam chain tensioner
Cylinder head
Cylinder block and pistons

3 Operations requiring engine removal

It is necessary to remove the engine/transmission assembly from the frame and separate the crankcase halves to gain access to the following components:

Clutch housing
Crankshaft, connecting rods and bearings
Transmission shafts
Shift drum and forks
Balancer shaft
Starter motor clutch
Camshaft chain
Primary chain
Oil pump

4 Major engine repair - general note

1 It is not always easy to determine when or if an engine should be completely overhauled, as a number of factors must be considered.
2 High mileage is not necessarily an indication that an overhaul is needed, while low mileage, on the other hand, does not preclude the need for an overhaul. Frequency of servicing is probably the single most important consideration. An engine that has regular and frequent oil and filter changes, as well as other required maintenance, will most likely give many miles of reliable service. Conversely, a neglected engine, or one which has not been broken in properly, may require an overhaul very early in its life.
3 Exhaust smoke and excessive oil consumption are both indications that piston rings and/or valve guides are in need of attention. Make sure oil leaks are not responsible before deciding that the rings and guides are bad. Refer to Chapter 2C and perform a cylinder compression check to determine for certain the nature and extent of the work required.
4 If the engine is making obvious knocking or rumbling noises, the connecting rod and/or main bearings are probably at fault.
5 Loss of power, rough running, excessive valve train noise and high fuel consumption rates may also point to the need for an overhaul, especially if they are all present at the same time. If a complete tune-up does not remedy the situation, major mechanical work is the only solution.
6 An engine overhaul generally involves restoring the internal parts to the specifications of a new engine. During an overhaul the piston rings are replaced and the cylinder walls are bored and/or honed. If a rebore is done, then new pistons are also required. The main and connecting rod bearings are generally replaced with new ones and, if necessary, the crankshaft is also replaced. Generally the valves are serviced as well, since they are usually in less than perfect condition at this point. While the engine is being overhauled, other components such as the carburetors and the starter motor can be rebuilt also. The end result should be a like-new engine that will give as many trouble free miles as the original.
7 Before beginning the engine overhaul, read through all of the related procedures to familiarize yourself with the scope and requirements of the job. Overhauling an engine is not all that difficult, but it is time consuming. Plan on the motorcycle being tied up for a minimum of two weeks. Check on the availability of parts and make sure that any necessary special tools, equipment and supplies are obtained in advance.
8 Most work can be done with typical shop hand tools, although a number of precision measuring tools are required for inspecting parts to determine if they must be replaced. Often a dealer service department or motorcycle repair shop will handle the inspection of parts and offer advice concerning reconditioning and replacement. As a general rule, time is the primary cost of an overhaul so it doesn't pay to install worn or substandard parts.
9 As a final note, to ensure maximum life and minimum trouble from a rebuilt engine, everything must be assembled with care in a spotlessly clean environment.

5 Engine - removal and installation

⚠ *Engine removal and installation should be done with the aid of an assistant to avoid damage or injury that could occur if the engine is dropped. A hydraulic floor jack should be used to support and lower the engine if possible (they can be rented at low cost).*

Removal

1 Set the bike on its centerstand (if equipped) and disconnect the battery (negative cable first).
2 Remove the seat (see Chapter 8) and the fuel tank (see Chapter 4).
3 Remove the side covers (see Chapter 8).
4 Drain the coolant and the engine oil (see Chapter 1).
5 Remove the air filter housing (see Chapter 4).
6 On US models remove the air suction valves and the vacuum switching valve (see Chapter 1).
7 Remove the carburetors (see Chapter 4) and plug the intake openings with rags.
8 Remove the radiator, radiator hoses and coolant tubes (see Chapter 3).
9 Remove the ignition coils and brackets (see Chapter 5).
10 Remove the exhaust system (see Chapter 4).
11 Remove the shift pedal (see Section 16).
12 Remove the engine sprocket cover, unbolt the engine sprocket and detach the sprocket and belt from the engine (see Chapter 6).
13 Disconnect the lower end of the clutch cable from the lever and remove the cable bracket (see Chapter 1).
14 Mark and disconnect the wires from the oil pressure switch, neutral switch and the starter motor. Unplug the brake light switch, alternator, sidestand and pickup coil electrical connectors (see Chapters 5 and 9).
15 Support the engine with a floor jack and a wood block.
16 With the engine supported, remove the upper rear mounting bolts, lower rear mount-

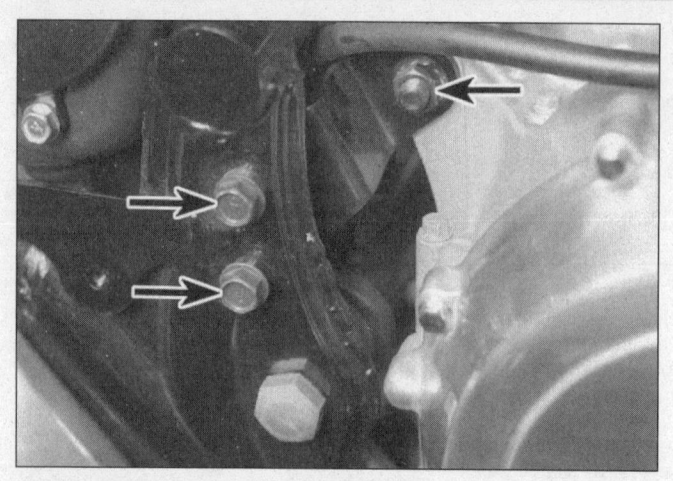

2A•4 Engine, clutch and transmission - EN450/500 models

5.16a With the engine securely supported, remove the mounting bolts at the upper rear...

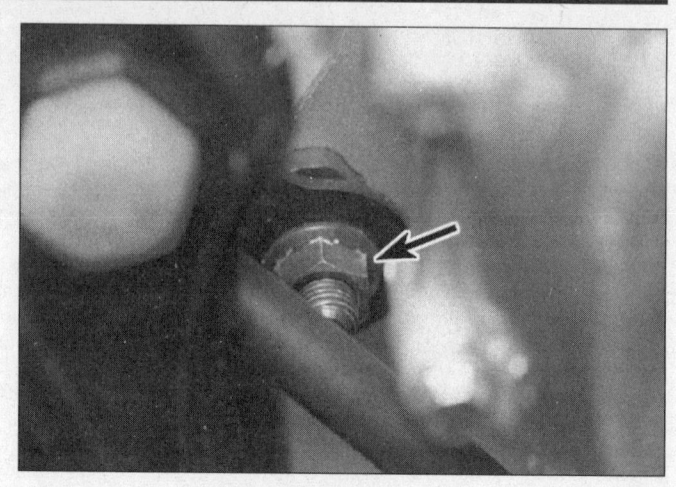

5.16b ...at the lower rear...

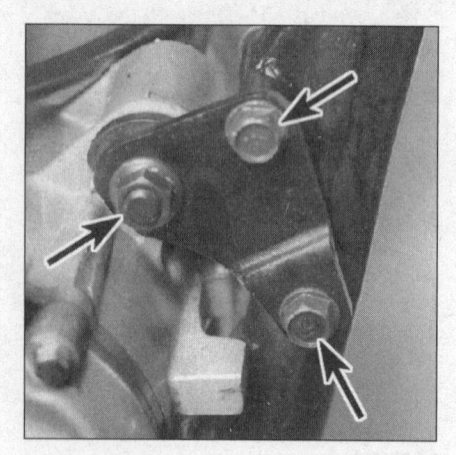

5.16c ...and at the front

ing bolts and front mounting bolts **(see illustrations)**.

17 Make sure no wires or hoses are still attached to the engine assembly.

18 Slowly and carefully lower the engine assembly away from the bike, then guide it out the right side.

Installation

19 Installation is the reverse of removal. Note the following points:
   a) Don't tighten any of the engine mounting bolts until they all have been installed.
   b) Use new gaskets at all exhaust pipe connections.
   c) Tighten the engine mounting bolts and frame downtube bolts securely.
   d) Adjust the drive chain/belt, rear brake, throttle cables, choke cable (if equipped) and clutch cable following the procedures in Chapter 1.

6 Valve cover - removal and installation

Note: *The valve cover can be removed with the engine in the frame. If the engine has been removed, ignore the steps which don't apply.*

Removal

1 Set the bike on its centerstand (if equipped).

2 Drain the engine coolant and remove the reservoir tank (see Chapters 1 and 3).

3 Remove the fuel tank (see Chapter 4).

4 Remove the side covers (see Chapter 8). Disconnect the coolant tubes (see Chapter 3).

5 On US models, remove the air suction valves and the vacuum switching valve (see Chapter 1).

6 If necessary for removal access, remove the ignition coils and their brackets, along with the spark plug wires (see Chapter 5).

7 Remove the valve cover bolts **(see illustration)**.

8 Lift the cover off the cylinder head **(see illustration)**. If it's stuck, don't attempt to pry it off - tap around the sides with a plastic hammer to dislodge it. **Note:** *Pay attention to the locating dowels as you remove the cover - if they fall into the engine, major disassembly may be required to get them out.*

Installation

9 Remove the locating dowels from the valve cover **(see illustration)**. Peel the rubber gasket from the cover. If it's cracked, hardened, has soft spots or shows signs of

6.7 Remove the valve cover bolts (arrow)

6.8 Lift the cover off the engine - if it's stuck, tap gently on the side with a soft faced hammer; don't pry the cover loose

Engine, clutch and transmission - EN450/500 models 2A•5

6.9 Be careful not to lose the locating dowels (arrows) or let them fall into the engine

6.11a Be sure the gasket seats securely in the groove (arrow)

general deterioration, replace it with a new one.
10 Clean the mating surfaces of the cylinder head and the valve cover with lacquer thinner, acetone or brake system cleaner. Apply a thin film of RTV sealant to the half-circle cutouts on each side of the head.
11 Install the gasket to the cover. Make sure it fits completely into the cover groove **(see illustration)**. Apply a small amount of silicone sealer to the corners of the half-circle portions of the gasket **(see illustration)**.
12 Position the cover on the cylinder head, making sure the gasket doesn't slip out of place.
13 Check the rubber seals on the valve cover bolts, replacing them if necessary. Install the bolts, tightening them evenly to the torque listed in this Chapter's Specifications.
14 The remainder of installation is the reverse of removal. Fill the cooling system with the recommended type and amount of coolant (see Chapter 1).

7 Camshaft chain tensioner - removal and installation

Removal

Caution: Once you start to remove the tensioner bolts, you must remove the tensioner all the way and reset it before tightening the bolts. The tensioner extends and locks in place, so if you loosen the bolts part way and then retighten them, the tensioner or cam chain will be damaged.

1 Loosen the tensioner cap bolt while the tensioner is still installed **(see illustration)**.
2 Remove the tensioner mounting bolts and take it off the engine.

Caution: Don't turn the engine with the tensioner removed or damage may occur.

3 Remove the tensioner cap bolt and O-ring.

Installation

4 Check the O-ring on the tensioner body for cracks or hardening. It's a good idea to replace this O-ring whenever the tensioner cap is removed.

Original tensioner

5 Place the tensioner mounting bolts where you can reach them with one hand while the other hand holds the tensioner in position in Step 7.
6 Press the end of the rod that contacts the chain into the tensioner body. At the same time, turn the other end of the rod clockwise with a screwdriver until the rod protrudes about 3/8-inch (10 mm) from the tensioner body.

Caution: Don't turn the rod counterclockwise (anticlockwise) or it may separate from the tensioner. If this happens it can't be reassembled.

7 Place the tensioner in position on the engine. Push it firmly against the engine, remove the screwdriver, and install the mounting bolts finger-tight.

Caution: If the tensioner moves away from the engine before you tighten the bolts, the rod will extend too far. If this happens (or you think it might have happened), remove the tensioner and repeat Step 6, then continue with Step 7.

6.11b Apply a small amount of silicone sealant to the corners of the half-circle portions of the gasket (arrows)

7.1 Loosen the tensioner cap bolt (A) while the tensioner is still on the engine, then remove the mounting bolts (B)

2A•6 Engine, clutch and transmission - EN450/500 models

7.9 New tensioners come with a keeper (arrow) to hold the rod in position for installation; add the keeper to your tool collection for the next time you need to remove and install the tensioner

8.2a Position the EX mark on the exhaust camshaft even with the cylinder head surface and the sprocket punch mark up (arrows) . . .

8.2b . . . the IN mark on the intake camshaft should also be even with the head surface and the sprocket punch mark should be up (arrows) . . .

8 Tighten the mounting bolts to the torque listed in this Chapter's Specifications.

New tensioner
9 New tensioners come with a keeper that fits in the tensioner rod slot and holds the rod in the correct position for installation (see illustration).
10 Place the tensioner on the engine. Install the mounting bolts and tighten them to the torque listed in this Chapter's Specifications.
11 Pull the keeper out with needle nosed pliers.

HAYNES HiNT *Save the keeper and place it in your toolbox for future use. You can use it to hold the tensioner rod in position next time you install the tensioner, leaving both hands free.*

Original or new tensioner
12 Install the tensioner cap and O-ring. Tighten the cap to the torque listed in this Chapter's Specifications.

8 Camshafts, rocker arm shafts and rocker arms - removal, inspection and installation

Note: *This procedure can be performed with the engine in the frame.*

Camshafts
Removal
1 Remove the valve cover (see Section 6).
2 Turn the engine to position no. 2 cylinder at TDC compression (see Chapter 1 - *Valve clearances - check and adjustment*). When the engine is positioned correctly, the EX mark on the exhaust camshaft and the IN mark on the intake camshaft will align with the cylinder head top surface (see illustrations). To ease reassembly, mark the sprockets and chain with a felt pen (see illustration).
3 Remove the camshaft chain tensioner (see Section 7).

4 Remove the upper chain guide (see illustration).
5 Remove the bolts and lift the oil pipes and O-rings from the cylinder head (see illustration).
6 Unscrew the bearing cap bolts for one of the camshafts, a little at a time, until they are all loose, then unscrew the bearing cap bolts for the other camshaft.

Caution: If the bearing cap bolts aren't loosened evenly, the camshaft may bind.

Remove the bolts and lift off the bearing caps. Note the letters on the bearing caps which correspond to those on the cylinder head (see illustration). When you reinstall the caps, be sure to install them in the correct positions.
7 Pull up on the camshaft chain and carefully guide the camshaft out (see illustration). With the chain still held taut, remove the other camshaft. Look for marks on the camshafts (see illustration). The intake camshaft should have an IN mark and the exhaust camshaft should have an EX mark.

8.2c . . . once the camshafts are positioned correctly, mark across the chain and sprocket with a felt pen to ease reassembly

8.4 The center four camshaft bearing cap bolts also secure the chain guide; its arrow points toward the front of the engine

Engine, clutch and transmission - EN450/500 models 2A•7

8.5 Remove the oil pipe bolts (arrows) and lift the oil lines and O-rings out of the engine

8.6 The camshaft bearing caps have letter marks to indicate position; the caps must be reinstalled in the correct locations to prevent camshaft seizure

If you can't find these marks, label the camshafts to ensure they are installed in their original locations. **Note:** *Don't remove the sprockets from the camshafts unless absolutely necessary.*

8   While the camshafts are out, don't allow the chain to go slack - there's a protrusion inside the crankcase that's designed to keep the chain from falling off the sprocket on the crankshaft **(see illustration)**, but if it's worn, the chain may fall off and bind between the crankshaft and case, which could damage these components. Wire the chain to another component to prevent it from dropping down. Also, cover the top of the cylinder head with a rag to prevent foreign objects from falling into the engine. Refer to Chapter 2C for inspection procedures.

Installation

9   If you removed the sprockets, be sure to install them correctly; they're identical, with each sprocket having bolt holes for the exhaust and intake camshafts. The intake camshaft sprocket uses the bolt holes

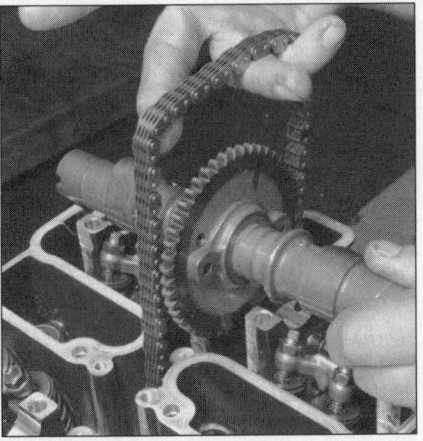

8.7a Lift the camshafts out of the head and disengage them from the chain

8.7b The camshafts are identified by IN or EX markings

labeled IN; the exhaust camshaft sprocket uses the bolt holes labeled EX **(see illustration)**.

10   Make sure the bearing surfaces in the cylinder head and the bearing caps are clean, then apply a light coat of engine

8.8 This protrusion in the bottom of the engine case is designed to prevent the cam chain from falling out of mesh with the crankshaft sprocket, but to be safe, tie the chain up so it can't drop down

8.9 Each sprocket has two sets of bolt holes; those labeled EX are used for the exhaust camshaft, while those labeled IN are used for the intake camshaft

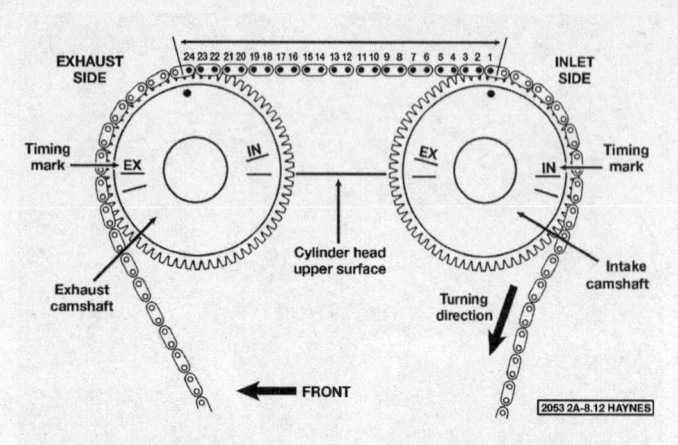

2A•8 Engine, clutch and transmission - EN450/500 models

8.12 With no slack in the camshaft chain, there should be 24 link pins present between the punch marks on the cam sprockets

8.13a Make sure the bearing cap dowels are in position

assembly lube or moly-based grease to each of them.

11 Apply a coat of moly-based grease to the camshaft lobes and bearing surfaces. Make sure the camshaft bearing journals are clean, then lay the camshafts in the cylinder head (do not mix them up), ensuring the marks on the cam sprockets are aligned properly **(see illustrations 8.2a, 8.2b and 8.2c)**.

12 Make sure the crankshaft mark is still positioned at TDC compression for cylinder no. 2 and the camshaft marks are still aligned properly, then mesh the chain with the camshaft sprockets. Count the number of chain link pins between the punch marks **(see illustration)**. There should be no slack in the chain between the two sprockets.

13 Make sure the camshaft dowels are in place **(see illustration)**. Carefully set the bearing caps in place (arrows pointing toward the front of the engine and in their proper positions) **(see illustration 8.6)** and install the bolts. Tighten them in the recommended sequence **(see illustration)**, to the torque listed in this Chapter's Specifications.

14 Insert your finger or a wood dowel into the cam chain tensioner hole and apply pressure to the cam chain. Check the timing marks to make sure they are aligned (see Step 3) and there are still the correct number of link pins between the punch marks on the cam sprockets. If necessary, change the position of the sprocket(s) on the chain to bring all of the marks into alignment.

Caution: If the marks are not aligned exactly as described, the valve timing will be incorrect and the valves may contact the pistons, causing extensive damage to the engine.

15 Install the tensioner as described in Section 7.

16 Adjust the valve clearances (see Chapter 1).

17 Turn the engine with a socket on the crankshaft rotation bolt. If you feel a sudden increase in resistance, stop turning. The valves may be hitting the pistons due to incorrect assembly. Find the problem and fix it before turning the engine any further, or serious damage may occur.

18 The remainder of installation is the reverse of removal.

Rocker arm shafts and rocker arms

Removal

19 Remove the camshafts following the procedure given above. Be sure to keep tension on the camshaft chain.

20 Unscrew one rocker shaft from the cylinder head and pull it out **(see illustrations)**.

21 Remove the rocker arms and springs **(see illustration)**.

22 Repeat the above Steps to remove the other rocker arm shafts and rocker arms. Keep all of the parts in order so they can be reinstalled in their original locations.

23 Refer to Chapter 2C for inspection procedures.

Installation

24 Position a rocker arm and spring in the cylinder head, with the spring toward the center of the cylinder head **(see illustration)**.

25 Lubricate the rocker arm shaft with engine oil and slide it into the cylinder head and through the rocker arm and spring. Tighten it to the torque listed in this Chapter's Specifications.

26 Repeat Steps 24 and 25 to install the remaining rocker arms and shafts.

27 Install the camshafts following the procedure described earlier in this Section.

9 Cylinder head - removal and installation

Caution: The engine must be completely cool before beginning this procedure, or the cylinder head may become warped.

Note: This procedure can be performed with the engine in the frame. If the engine has been removed, ignore the steps which don't apply.

8.13b Camshaft bearing cap tightening sequence (the center four bolts also secure the chain guide) - tighten the no. 1 and no. 2 bolts evenly to specifications first, then tighten the others in numerical order

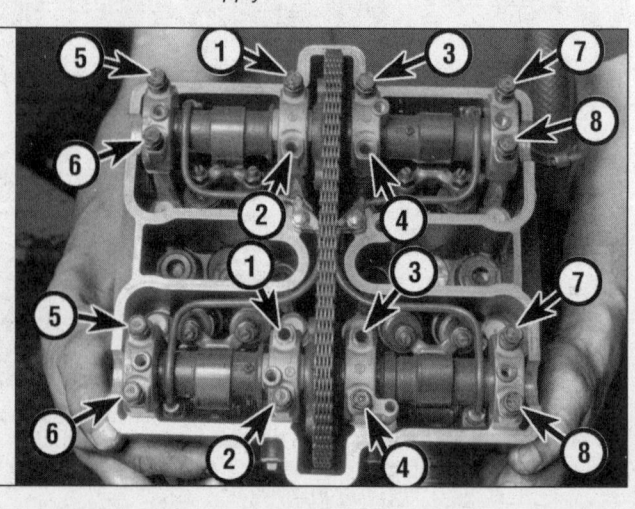

Engine, clutch and transmission - EN450/500 models 2A•9

8.20a Insert an Allen wrench into the rocker shaft head (a bit like this one is necessary for tightening the plug to specifications) . . .

8.20b . . . unscrew the shaft and pull it out

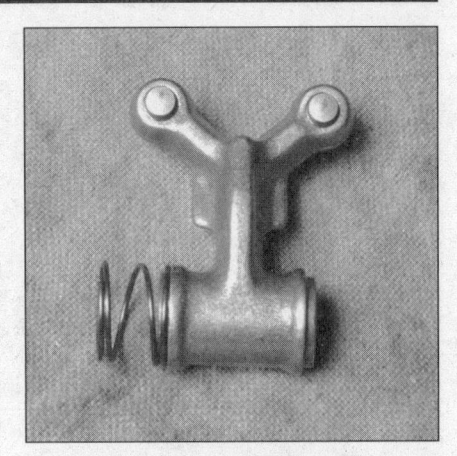

8.21 Remove the rocker arms and springs

8.24 The rocker arm springs (arrow) go between the rocker arm and the center of the head

9.6 Remove the oil pipe banjo bolts

Removal

1 Set the bike on its centerstand (if equipped).
2 Remove the valve cover (see Section 6).
3 Remove the exhaust system (see Chapter 4).
4 Remove the cam chain tensioner (see Section 7).
5 Remove the camshafts (see Section 8).
6 Remove the oil pipe banjo bolts and washers from the rear of the cylinder head **(see illustration)**.
7 Remove the small cylinder block-to-cylinder head bolts and the main oil pipe mounting bolt **(see illustrations)**.
8 Loosen the cylinder head bolts, a little

9.7a Remove one small head-to-block bolt (upper arrow), the oil pipe mounting bolt (lower arrow) . . .

9.7b . . . and one small head-to-block bolt located inside the head

2A•10 Engine, clutch and transmission - EN450/500 models

9.8a Use a deep socket to remove the head bolts

9.8b Head bolt TIGHTENING sequence - the arrow points to the front of the engine

9.9 Lift the head off the cylinder block

9.10 Remove the old gasket

at a time, using the reverse order of the tightening sequence **(see illustrations)**.

9   Pull the cylinder head off the cylinder block **(see illustration)**. If the head is stuck, tap upward against the rocker shaft heads with a rubber mallet to jar it loose, or use two wooden dowels inserted into the intake or exhaust ports to lever the head off. Don't attempt to pry the head off by inserting a screwdriver between the head and the cylinder block - you'll damage the sealing surfaces.

10   Lift the head gasket off the cylinder block **(see illustration)**.

11   Stuff a clean rag into the cam chain tunnel to prevent the entry of debris.

12   Locate the two dowel pins to make sure they haven't fallen into the engine. If they are in the head, put them in their holes in the cylinder block.

13   Check the cylinder head gasket and the mating surfaces on the cylinder head and block for signs of leakage, which could indicate warpage. Refer to Chapter 2C and check the flatness of the cylinder head.

14   Clean all traces of old gasket material from the cylinder head and block. Be careful not to let any of the gasket material fall into the crankcase, the cylinder bores or the water passages.

Installation

15   Lay the new gasket in place on the cylinder block. Make sure the UP mark on the gasket is positioned on the right-hand side of the engine **(see illustration)**. Never reuse the

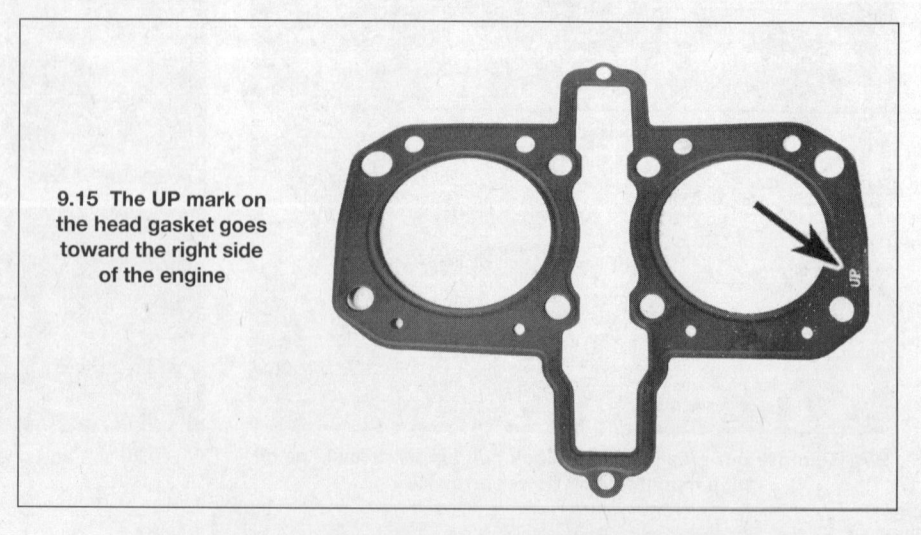

9.15 The UP mark on the head gasket goes toward the right side of the engine

old gasket and don't use any type of gasket sealant.

16 Carefully lower the cylinder head over the studs. It is helpful to have an assistant support the camshaft chain with a piece of wire so it doesn't fall and become kinked or detached from the crankshaft. When the head is resting against the cylinder block, wire the cam chain to another component to keep tension on it.

17 Install the head bolts. Using the proper sequence (see illustration 9.8b), tighten the bolts to approximately half of the torque listed in this Chapter's Specifications.

18 Using the same sequence, tighten the bolts to the full torque listed in this Chapter's Specifications.

19 Install the small cylinder block-to-cylinder head bolts, tightening them to the torque listed in this Chapter's Specifications.

20 Install the oil line mounting and banjo bolts. Use new washers on the banjo bolts (see illustration).

21 Install the camshafts (see Section 8) and adjust the valves (see Chapter 1). Install all components removed for access.

22 Change the engine oil and refill the cooling system (see Chapter 1).

10 Cylinder block - removal and installation

Removal

1 Following the procedure given in Section 9, remove the cylinder head. Make sure the crankshaft is positioned at Top Dead Center (TDC) for cylinder no. 2.

2 Remove the water pump together with the water pipe (see Chapter 3).

3 Remove the oil pipe mounting bolt (see illustration).

4 Lift out the camshaft chain rear guide (see illustration).

5 Lift the cylinder block straight up to remove it (see illustration). If it's stuck, tap around its perimeter with a soft-faced hammer. Don't attempt to pry between the block and the crankcase, as you will ruin the sealing surfaces. As you lift, note the location of the dowel pins. Be careful not to let these drop into the engine.

6 Stuff clean shop towels around the pistons (see illustration) and remove the gasket and all traces of old gasket material from the surfaces of the cylinder block and the cylinder head.

7 Refer to Chapter 2C for inspection procedures.

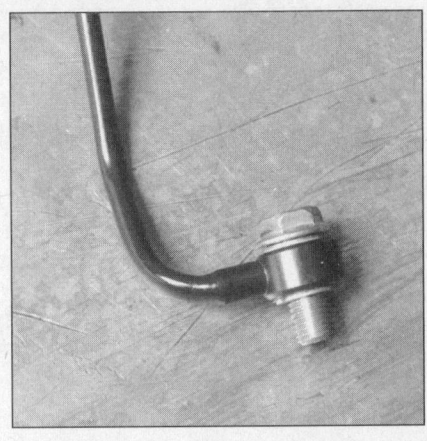

9.20 There's a washer on each side of the oil line banjo bolt fittings - replace them whenever the banjo bolts are removed

10.3 If you haven't already done so for cylinder head removal, remove the oil pipe mounting bolt

10.4 Lift the rear cam chain guide out of the engine (cylinder block removed for clarity)

10.5 Lift the cylinder block up and off the crankcase and pistons; don't lose the dowels (arrows)

10.6 Place rags under the pistons to protect them and keep debris out of the crankcase

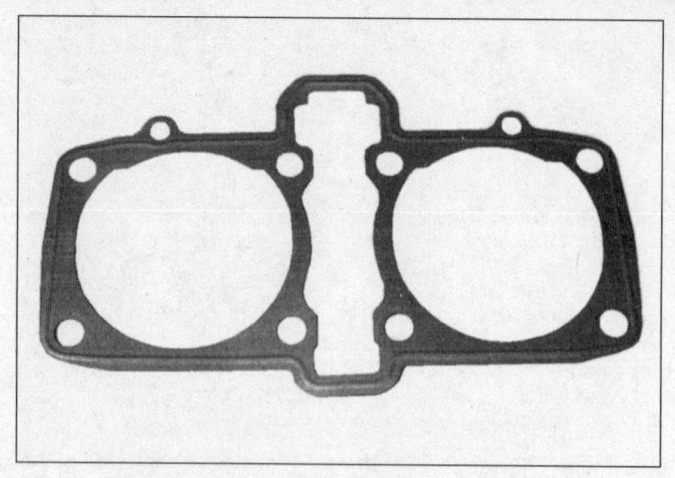

2A•12 Engine, clutch and transmission - EN450/500 models

10.9 Install the base gasket with the ridge upward

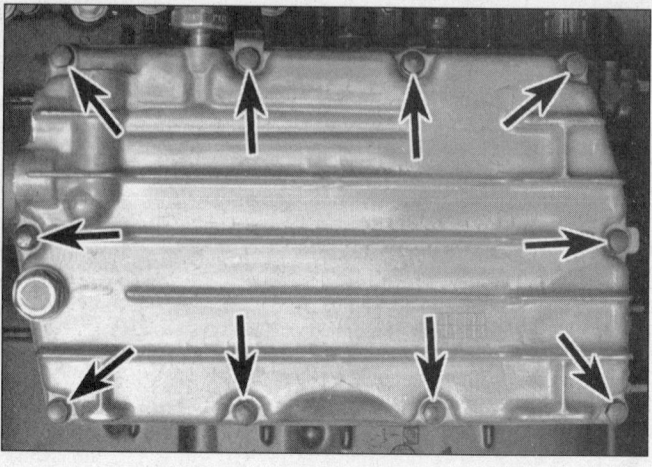

11.5a Remove the oil pan bolts (arrows)

Installation

8 Lubricate the cylinder bores with plenty of clean engine oil. Apply a thin film of moly-based grease to the piston skirts.

9 Install the dowel pins, then place a new cylinder base gasket on the crankcase with the ridge in the gasket upward **(see illustration)**. Some gaskets also have an arrow, which must point to the front of the engine.

10 Slowly rotate the crankshaft until both of the pistons are at the same level. Slide lengths of welding rod or pieces of a straightened-out coat hanger under the pistons, on both sides of the connecting rods. This will help keep the pistons level as the cylinder block is lowered onto them.

11 Attach two piston ring compressors to the pistons and compress the piston rings. Large hose clamps can be used instead - just make sure they don't scratch the pistons, and don't tighten them too much.

12 Install the cylinder block over the pistons and carefully lower it down until the piston crowns fit into the cylinder liners. While doing this, pull the camshaft chain up, using a hooked tool or a piece of coat hanger. Push down on the cylinder block, making sure the pistons don't get cocked sideways, until the bottoms of the cylinder liners slide down past the piston rings. A wood or plastic hammer handle can be used to gently tap the block down, but don't use too much force or the pistons will be damaged.

13 Remove the piston ring compressors or hose clamps, being careful not to scratch the pistons. Remove the rods from under the pistons, then reset the engine to TDC for cylinder number 2.

14 Install the cam chain rear guide **(see illustration 10.4)**.

15 The remainder of installation is the reverse of removal.

11 Oil pan - removal and installation

Note: *The oil pan can be removed with the engine in the frame.*

Removal

1 Set the bike on its centerstand (if equipped).

2 Drain the engine oil and remove the oil filter (see Chapter 1).

3 Remove the exhaust system (see Chapter 4).

4 Remove the small screw and disconnect the wire from the oil pressure switch (see Chapter 9).

5 Remove the oil pan bolts and detach the pan from the crankcase **(see illustrations)**.

6 Remove all traces of old gasket material from the mating surfaces of the oil pan and crankcase.

Installation

7 Check the small O-rings in the oil passages in the crankcase and the large O-ring around the oil filter hole (in the pan) for cracking and general deterioration **(see illustration)**. Replace them if necessary. The flat side of the O-rings must face the crankcase.

8 Position a new gasket on the oil pan. A thin film of RTV sealant can be used to hold the gasket in place. Install the oil pan and bolts, tightening the bolts to the torque listed in this Chapter's Specifications, using a criss-cross pattern.

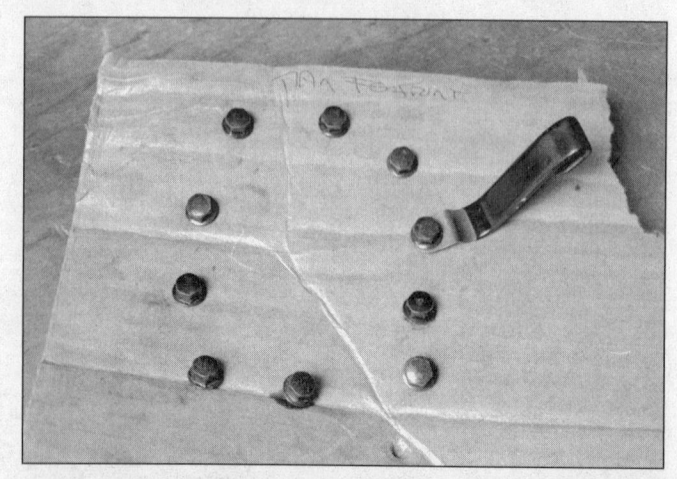

11.5b Place the bolts in a holder, such as a piece of cardboard with holes punched in it - the bolt that goes next to the oil pressure switch also secures a wiring harness retainer

11.7 Make sure the O-rings are in position (arrows); the three O-rings to the left have a flat side, which goes upward (against the crankcase and away from the oil pan)

Engine, clutch and transmission - EN450/500 models 2A•13

12.2 Unbolt the pickup from the pump so you can inspect the O-ring - use non-permanent thread locking agent on the bolt threads during assembly

12.3 Remove the snap-ring and the pump drive gear

12.4 Remove the pump mounting bolts

12.5 Lift out the pump and its oil pipe; if necessary, unbolt the pipe from the pump and remove them separately

9 The remainder of installation is the reverse of removal. Install a new filter and fill the crankcase with oil (see Chapter 1), then run the engine and check for leaks.

12 Oil pump - removal and installation

Note: *Oil pump removal requires that the engine be removed and the crankcase disassembled.*

Removal

1 Remove the engine and disassemble the crankcase (see Sections 5 and 17).
2 Remove the oil pump pickup tube from the pump so you can inspect the O-ring **(see illustration)**.
3 Remove the snap-ring and detach the oil pump gear from the shaft **(see illustration)**.
4 Remove the pump mounting bolts **(see illustration)**.
5 Remove the pump and its oil pipe **(see illustration)**.
6 Refer to Chapter 2C for inspection procedures.

Installation

7 Installation is the reverse of removal, with the following additions:

a) *Make sure the pickup O-ring is in place.*
b) *Use non-permanent thread locking agent on the pickup mounting screws and the oil pump mounting bolts.*
c) *Install the drive gear with its recessed side away from the pump (see illustration).*

12.7 The recessed side of the drive gear faces away from the oil pump - the snap-ring fits into the recess

2A•14 Engine, clutch and transmission - EN450/500 models

13.2 Location of the oil pressure relief valve (arrow)

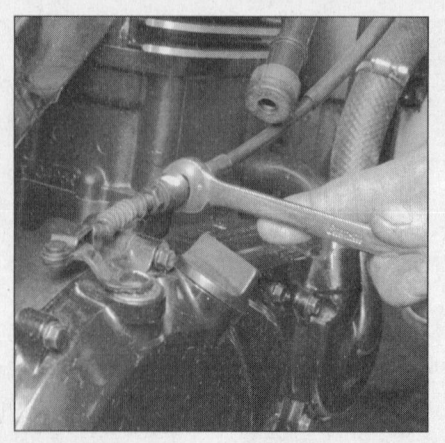

14.3 Loosen the forward clutch cable nut to create slack

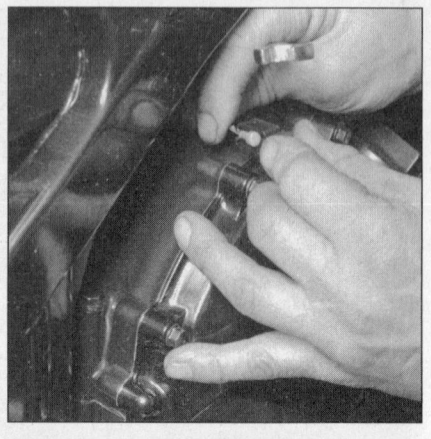

14.4 Disengage the end of the cable from the release lever

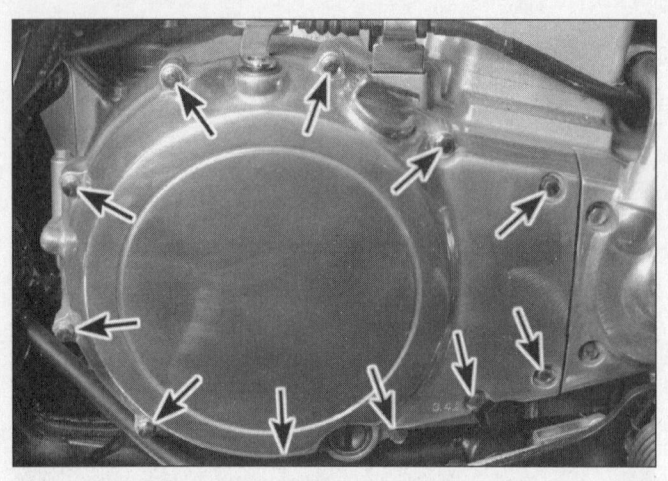

14.5a Remove the clutch cover bolts (arrows) . . .

14.5b . . . take the cover off (tap it gently with a soft-faced hammer if it's stuck) . . .

14.5c . . . and note the location of the cover dowel

13 Oil pressure relief valve - removal, inspection and installation

Removal
1 Remove the oil pan (see Section 11).
2 Unscrew the relief valve from the oil pan **(see illustration)**.

Inspection
3 Clean the valve with solvent and dry it, using compressed air if available.
4 Using a wood or plastic tool, depress the steel ball inside the valve and see if it moves smoothly. Make sure it returns to its seat completely. If it doesn't, replace it with a new one (don't attempt to disassemble and repair it).

Installation
5 Apply a non-permanent thread locking compound to the threads of the valve and install it into the oil pan, tightening it to the torque listed in this Chapter's Specifications.

6 The remainder of installation is the reverse of removal.

14 Clutch - removal and installation

Note: *The clutch (except the housing) can be removed with the engine in the frame. Removal of the housing requires that the engine be removed and the crankcase disassembled.*

Removal
1 Set the bike on its centerstand (if equipped).
2 Drain the engine oil (see Chapter 1).
3 Completely loosen the forward adjustment nut on the clutch cable at its bracket on the clutch cover **(see illustration)**.
4 Pull the cable out of the bracket, then detach the cable end from the lever **(see illustration)**.
5 Remove the clutch cover bolts and take the cover off together with the release lever **(see illustrations)**. If the cover is stuck, tap around its perimeter with a soft-face hammer. 1996 and later C models (C1 and later) have a baffle inside the cover. It need not be removed for normal clutch service. If you do remove it, note that the bolts are secured with thread locking agent and may be difficult to remove.

Engine, clutch and transmission - EN450/500 models 2A•15

14.6a Loosen the spring bolts in a criss-cross pattern . . .

14.6b . . . when spring tension is released, remove the bolts, springs and the spring plate

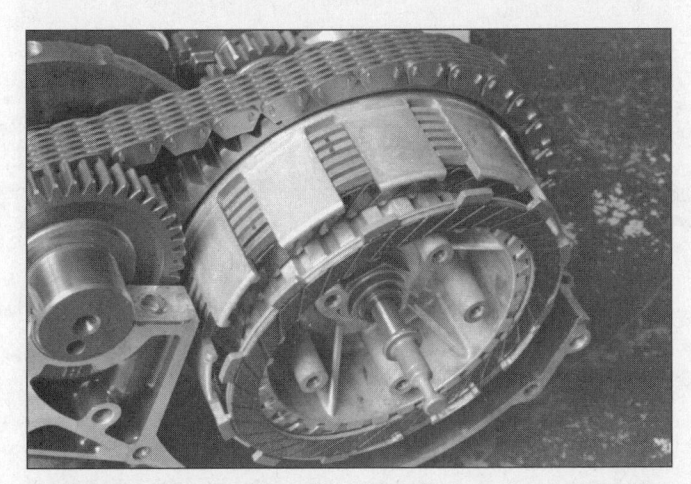

14.7 Remove the clutch pushrod from the hub, then remove the friction plates and metal plates - note the direction of the grooves in the friction plates; they must be reinstalled the same way

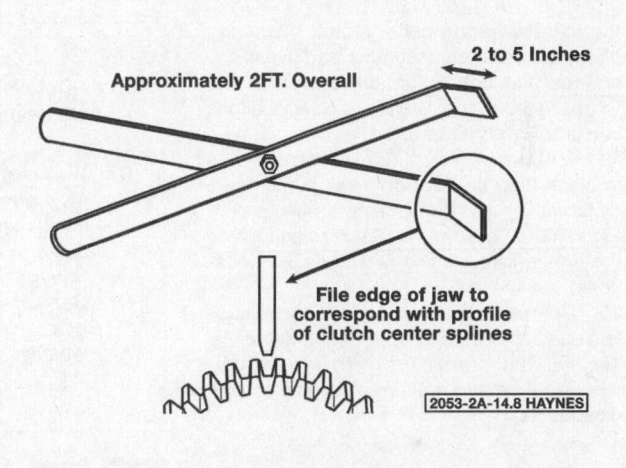

14.8 You can make your own clutch holding tool out of steel strap

6 Loosen the clutch spring bolts in a criss-cross pattern **(see illustration)**. To prevent the assembly from turning, thread one of the cover mounting bolts into the case and wedge a screwdriver between the bolt and the clutch housing. Remove the clutch springs, spring plate and bearing **(see illustration)**.
7 Note the direction of the radial grooves in the friction plate, then remove the pushrod, friction plates and steel plates from the clutch housing **(see illustration)**.
8 Remove the clutch hub nut, using a special holding tool (Kawasaki tool no. 57001-305 or 1243 or an equivalent tool available from an aftermarket tool supplier) to prevent the clutch housing from turning. An alternative to this tool can be fabricated from some steel strap, bent at the ends and bolted together in the middle **(see illustration)**. The nut is self-locking, so discard it and replace it with a new one during installation.
9 Remove the washer, clutch hub and thrust washer **(see illustration)**.
10 Refer to Chapter 2C for inspection procedures.

Installation

11 Install the clutch housing thrust washer and the clutch hub. Install a new hub nut and tighten it to the torque listed in this Chapter's Specifications. Use the technique described in Step 8 to prevent the hub from turning.

12 Coat the clutch friction plates with engine oil. Install the clutch plates, starting with a friction plate and alternating them. There are seven friction plates and six steel plates. Be sure the radial grooves in the friction plates are pointed in the correct direction **(see illustration 14.7)**.
13 Lubricate the pushrod and install it

14.9 Remove the nut and washer, then remove the clutch hub and thrust washer

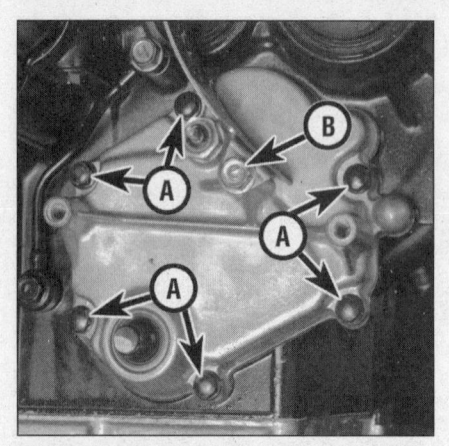

2A•16 Engine, clutch and transmission - EN450/500 models

16.9 Remove the cover bolts (A) - the larger bolt (B) secures the bottom end of the drive belt guard on belt drive models

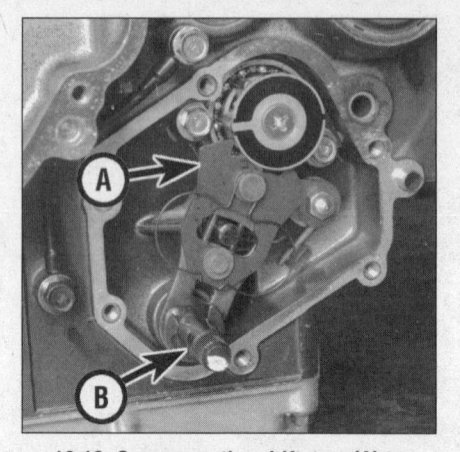

16.10 Compress the shift arm (A) to disengage it from the shift cam, and slide the shift shaft (B) out of the casing

16.11a Remove the nut (A) and detach the washer, gear positioning lever, spring and washer. Note the return spring pin (B)

16.11b Details of the gear positioning lever

- A Nut
- B Washer (the collar fits inside the gear positioning lever hole)
- C Spring
- D Gear positioning lever
- E Washer

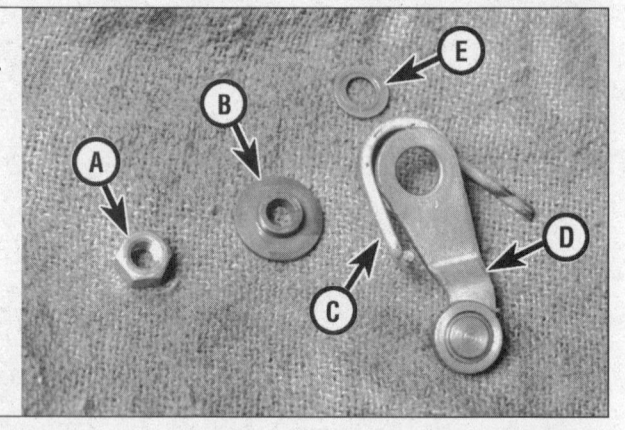

through the spring plate. Mount the spring plate to the clutch assembly and install the springs and bolts, tightening them to the torque listed in this Chapter's Specifications in a criss-cross pattern.

14 Make sure the clutch cover dowel is in place (see illustration 14.5c). Install the clutch cover and bolts, using a new gasket. Tighten the bolts, in a criss-cross pattern, to the torque listed in this Chapter's Specifications.

15 Connect the clutch cable to the release lever and adjust the freeplay (see Chapter 1).

16 Fill the crankcase with the recommended type and amount of engine oil (see Chapter 1).

15 Clutch cable - replacement

1 Disconnect the upper end of the clutch cable from the lever (see Chapter 1).
2 Disconnect the clutch cable from the release lever (see Section 14).
3 Before removing the cable from the bike, tape the lower end of the new cable to the upper end of the old cable. Slowly pull the lower end of the old cable out, guiding the new cable down into position. Using this method will ensure the cable is routed correctly.
4 Lubricate the cable (see Chapter 1). Reconnect the ends of the cable by reversing the removal procedure, then adjust the cable following the procedure given in Chapter 1.

16 External shift mechanism - removal, inspection and installation

Note: *The external shift mechanism can be removed with the engine in the frame.*

Shift lever and pedal

1 Set the bike on its centerstand.
2 Remove the shift pedal bolt. Take the shift pedal off the shaft.
3 Remove the shift linkage bolts.
4 To ease installation, make alignment marks on the shift lever shafts and the shift levers. Remove the snap-rings and pull the shift levers off the shafts.
5 Installation is the reverse of removal. The shift linkage rod should be at 90-degrees to the shift levers. Adjust as needed with the nuts on the linkage rod. When correctly adjusted, the linkage rod should be at 90-degree angles to the two shift levers.

Shift mechanism

Removal

6 Remove the shift pedal and linkage (Steps 1 through 4).
7 Remove the drive belt, engine pulley and belt guard (see Chapter 6).
8 Disconnect the electrical connector from the neutral switch (see Chapter 9).
9 Remove the shift mechanism cover bolts and remove the cover (see illustration).
10 Compress the shift mechanism arm against the spring tension to disengage it from the shift drum cam (see illustration). Slide the shift mechanism out of the casing.
11 Remove the nut from the gear positioning lever. Remove the locating washer, lever, spring and washer (see illustrations).
12 Refer to Chapter 2C for inspection procedures.

Installation

13 Assemble the positioning lever components (see illustration 16.11b) and install on the casing. The shift drum should be in neutral so that the positioning lever roller locates in the neutral detent. Ensure that the leg of the return spring is correctly located against the casing web (see illustration 16.11a).
14 Slide the external shift mechanism into place, compressing the shift arm against the spring to clear the shift drum. Make sure the springs are positioned correctly.
15 Apply high-temperature grease to the lip of the seal. Wrap the splines of the shift shaft with electrical tape, so the splines won't damage the seal as the cover is installed.
16 Install a new gasket on the casing. Carefully guide the cover into place and install the screws, tightening them securely.
17 Install the engine pulley, drive belt and engine pulley cover (see Chapter 6).
18 Install and adjust the shift pedal and linkage (see Steps 1 through 5).

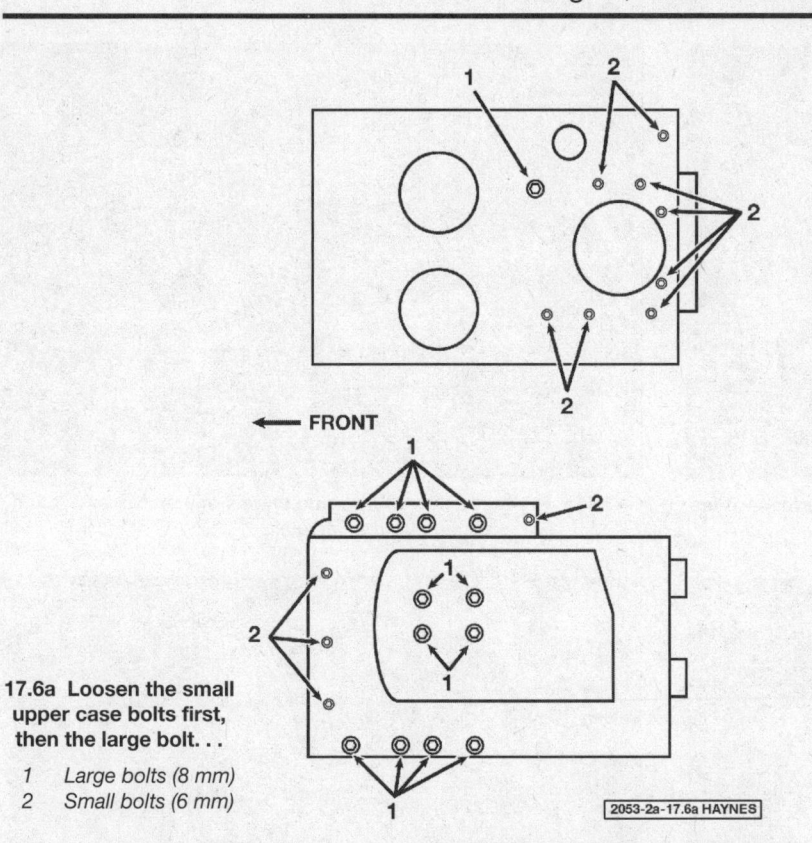

Engine, clutch and transmission - EN450/500 models 2A•17

17.6a Loosen the small upper case bolts first, then the large bolt...

1 Large bolts (8 mm)
2 Small bolts (6 mm)

17.6b ... and place them in order in a holder (a piece of cardboard with holes punched in it works well)

17.9a Remove the mounting bolt and lift out the outer oil pipe

19 Check the engine oil level and add some, if necessary (see Chapter 1).

17 Crankcase - disassembly and reassembly

1 To examine and repair or replace the crankshaft, connecting rods, bearings, clutch housing, transmission components, oil pump, balancer and starter motor clutch, the crankcase must be split into two parts.
2 Remove the engine from the motorcycle (see Section 5). Remove the clutch cover (see Section 14) and the external shift mechanism (see Section 16).
3 Remove the water pump and coolant pipe (on the cylinder block) (see Chapter 3).
4 Remove the alternator cover (see Chapter 9).

Disassembly

5 If the crankcase is being separated to remove the crankshaft, remove the alternator rotor and the stator (see Chapter 9), cylinder head, cylinder block and pistons (see Sections 9 and 10 and Chapter 2C). Remove the clutch if you are separating the crankcase halves to disassemble the transmission main drive shaft (see Section 14).
6 Remove the small upper crankcase half bolts, then the single large bolt **(see illustrations)**.
7 Turn the engine upside-down and remove the oil filter (see Chapter 1, if necessary).
8 Remove the oil pan (see Section 11) and retrieve the O-rings from the oil passages.
9 Remove the oil pump outer pipe and main oil pipe connecting bolt **(see illustrations)**.

17.9b Remove the main oil pipe connecting bolt on the side of the case (arrow)...

17.9c ... and one in the oil pan (upper arrow), then disconnect the oil pipe from the engine (lower arrow)

2A•18 Engine, clutch and transmission - EN450/500 models

17.10 The tightening sequence numbers for the large lower case bolts are cast into the case (arrows)

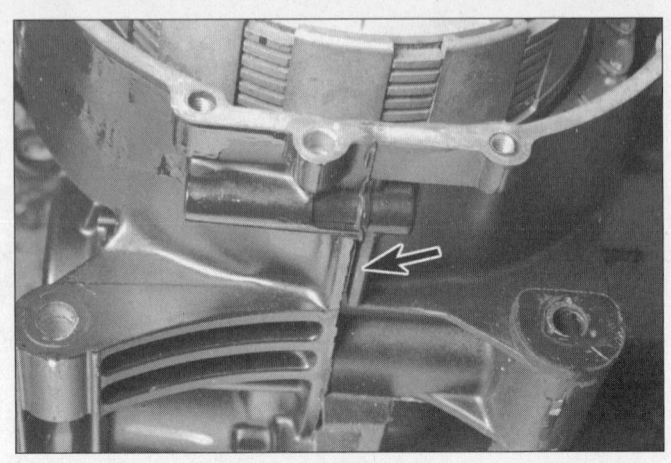

17.11a Pry only at the pry points; there's one on the end of the case (arrow) . . .

17.11b . . . one on the clutch side (arrow) . . .

17.11c . . . and one on the alternator side (arrow)

10 Remove the small lower crankcase half bolts, then the large bolts **(see illustration 17.6a and the accompanying illustration)**.
11 Carefully pry the crankcase apart. Pry ONLY in the areas indicated **(see illustrations)**.
12 Separate the crankcase halves **(see illustration)**.
13 Refer to Sections 18 through 22 and Chapter 2C for information on the internal components of the crankcase.

Reassembly

14 Remove all traces of sealant from the crankcase mating surfaces. Be careful not to let any fall into the case as this is done.
15 Check to make sure the two dowel pins are in place in their holes in the mating surface of the upper crankcase half **(see illustrations)**. Pour some engine oil over the transmission gears, the crankshaft main bearings and the shift drum. Don't get any oil on the crankcase mating surface.
16 Apply a thin, even bead of Kawasaki

17.12 Lift the lower case half off the upper case half

17.15a Note the location of the case dowels (arrow) . . .

17.15b . . . there's one in each end of the case

17.16 Spread a thin layer of gasket sealant on the mating surfaces, but don't place it too close to the bearings

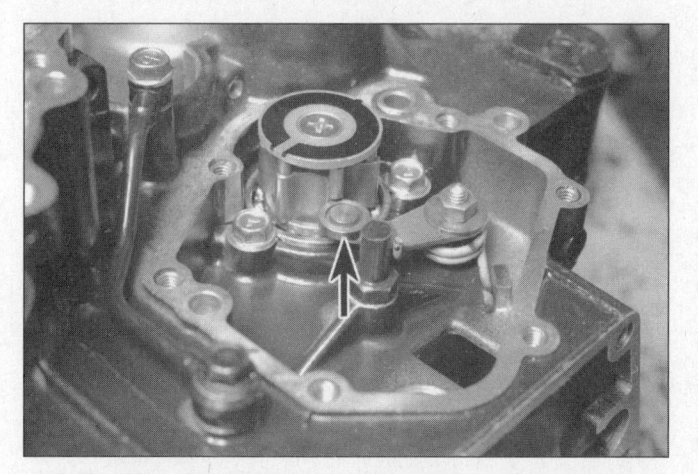

17.17a When the shift drum is in neutral, the gear positioning lever fits into the slot in the shift cam (arrow)

17.17b The shift forks should be in the Neutral position . . .

Bond sealant (part no. 56019-120) to the crankcase mating surfaces **(see illustration)**.

Caution: Don't apply an excessive amount of sealant, and don't apply it next to the bearing inserts, as it will ooze out when the case halves are assembled and may obstruct oil passages and prevent the bearings from seating.

17 Check the position of the shift drum, shift forks and transmission shafts - make sure they're in the neutral position **(see illustrations)**.

18 Carefully assemble the crankcase halves. While doing this, make sure the shift forks fit into their gear grooves, and guide the breather tube into its hole in the lower crankcase half **(see illustration)**.

19 Install the lower crankcase half bolts

17.17c . . . and so should the fork slots in the gears (arrows) - while you're checking the gears, take a good look to make sure nothing is in the case that doesn't belong there

17.18 Be sure both ends of the breather tube fit into their holes when the cases are assembled (transmission output shaft removed for clarity)

2A•20 Engine, clutch and transmission - EN450/500 models

18.2 Correct alignment of the marks on the balancer gear and crankshaft gear is essential to prevent severe engine vibration

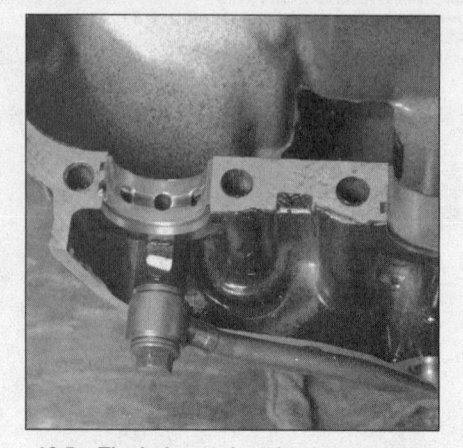

18.5a The balancer bearing inserts near the external oil line have oil grooves...

18.5b ...while the inserts at the opposite end of the balancer are smooth

and tighten them so they are just snug.
20 In two steps, tighten the larger bolts (8 mm), in the indicated sequence, to the torque listed in this Chapter's Specifications **(see illustration 17.6a)**.
21 Install the smaller (6 mm) bolts in the lower crankcase half, tightening them to the torque listed in this Chapter's Specifications.
22 Install the main oil connecting pipe **(see illustration 17.9b)**. Use new O-rings coated lightly with engine oil.
23 Apply engine oil to both ends of the oil pump outer pipe, then install the ends in their holes **(see illustration 17.9a)**. Apply non-permanent thread locking compound to the bolt that secures the outer pipe.
24 Install the oil pan (see Section 11).
25 Turn the case over and install the upper crankcase half bolts. Tighten the large (8 mm bolt) first, then tighten the others in the indicated sequence to the torque listed in this Chapter's Specifications **(see illustration 17.6a)**.
26 Turn the main drive shaft and the output shaft to make sure they turn freely. Also make sure the crankshaft turns freely.
27 The remainder of installation is the reverse of removal, with the following additions:
a) Once the external shift linkage is installed, shift the transmission through all the gear positions and back to Neutral. Because the positive neutral finder locks out second gear when the output shaft isn't spinning, you'll have to spin the output shaft to shift into second through sixth gears.
b) After the engine is installed, be sure to refill the engine oil and coolant.

18 Balancer shaft - removal and installation

Removal

1 Split the crankcase (see Section 17).
2 If you're only planning to remove the balancer (not the crankshaft), turn the crankshaft until the marks on the balancer and crankshaft gears are aligned **(see illustration)**.
3 Lift the balancer shaft and gear out of the crankcase.
4 Refer to Chapter 2C for inspection and bearing selection procedures.

Installation

5 Clean the bearing saddles in the case halves, then install the bearing inserts in their webs in the case **(see illustrations)**. The bearing insert next to the oil line has an oil groove. When installing the bearings, use your hands only - don't tap them into place with a hammer.
6 Lubricate the bearing inserts with engine assembly lube or moly-based grease.
7 Carefully lay the balancer in the bearings. Be sure the " - " mark on the balancer gear aligns with the "0" mark on the crankshaft gear **(see illustration 18.2)**. Incorrect alignment will cause severe engine vibration.
8 The remainder of installation is the reverse of the removal steps.

19 Primary chain, camshaft chain and guides - removal, inspection and installation

Removal

Primary chain and camshaft chain

1 Remove the engine (see Section 5).
2 Separate the crankcase halves (see Section 17).
3 Remove the crankshaft (see Chapter 2C).
4 Remove the chains from the crankshaft.

Chain guides

5 The cam chain front guide can be lifted from the cylinder block after the head has been removed (see Section 9).
6 The cam chain rear guide is fastened to the crankcase with a retaining pin and lock-pin **(see illustrations)**. Pull out the lock-pin

19.6a Remove this lock-pin if you plan to remove the cam chain guide - DO NOT forget to reinstall it, or the chain guide retaining pin could slide out and damage the crankshaft while it's spinning...

19.6b ...after removing the crankshaft, pull out the retaining pin and remove the cam chain guide

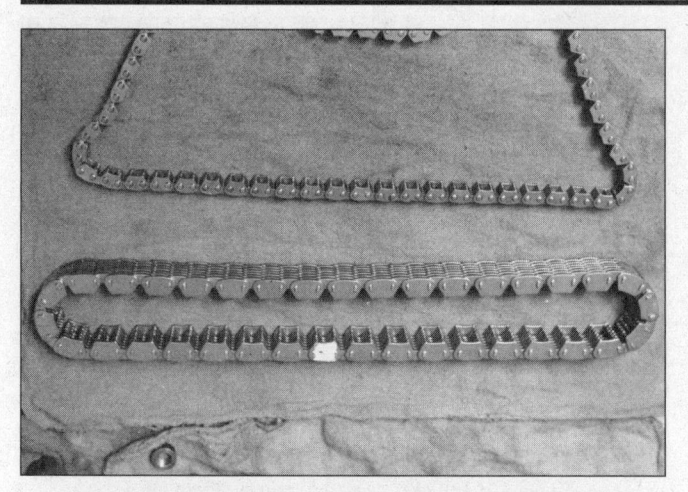

Engine, clutch and transmission - EN450/500 models 2A•21

19.9 When checking the camshaft chain or primary chain, measure the length of twenty links and compare to the length listed in this Chapter's Specifications

19.12 Check both primary chain guides for wear (the lower one is shown here) and replace them if necessary

and push the retaining pin out, then lift out the chain guide.

7 The primary chain guide in the lower case half is secured by a bolt.

8 The primary chain guide in the upper case half is secured by two bolts.

Inspection

Primary chain and camshaft chain

9 The primary and camshaft chains are checked in a similar manner. Pull the chain tight to eliminate all slack and measure the length of twenty links, pin-to-pin **(see illustration)**. Compare your findings to this Chapter's Specifications.

10 Also check the chains for binding and obvious damage.

11 If the twenty-link length is not as specified, or there is visible damage, replace the chain.

Chain guides

12 Check the guides for deep grooves, cracking and other obvious damage, replacing them if necessary **(see illustration)**.

Installation

13 Installation of these components is the reverse of the removal procedure. When installing the primary chain guides, apply a non-hardening thread locking compound to the threads of the bolts. Tighten the bolts to the torque listed in this Chapter's Specifications. Apply engine oil to the faces of the guides and to the chains.

20 Transmission shafts - removal and installation

Removal

1 Remove the engine and clutch, then separate the case halves (see Sections 5, 14 and 17).

2 Before removing either shaft, check the backlash of each set of gears. To do this, mount a dial indicator with the plunger of the indicator touching a tooth on one of the gears, then move the gear back and forth within its freeplay, holding its companion gear stationary. Check each set of gears, recording the measurements, and compare the results to this Chapter's Specifications. If the backlash between any pair of gears exceeds the limit, replace both gears (see Section 21).

3 The output shaft can simply be lifted out of the upper half of the case **(see illustration)**. The main drive shaft **(see illustration)** is removed together with the clutch housing (see Chapter 2C). If they are stuck, use a soft-face hammer and gently tap on the bearings on the ends of the shafts to free them.

4 Refer to Section 21 for information pertaining to transmission shaft service and Section 22 for information pertaining to the shift drum and forks.

20.3a The output shaft (arrow) can simply be lifted out ...

20.3b ... the main drive shaft is removed together with the clutch housing

2A•22 Engine, clutch and transmission - EN450/500 models

20.5 At each end of the shafts there's a set pin for the small bearing and a set ring for the large bearing

20.6a The hole in the small bearing (arrow) . . .

20.6b . . . must fit over the set pin (lower arrow) - the groove in the large bearing must fit over the set ring (upper arrow) . . .

20.6c . . . if the bearings are correctly installed, they will fit into their saddles with no gap between the bearing and case

Installation

5 Check to make sure the set pins and rings are present in the upper case half, where the shaft bearings seat **(see illustration)**.
6 Carefully lower each shaft into place. The holes in the needle bearing outer races must engage with the set pins, and the grooves in the ball bearing outer races must engage with the set rings **(see illustrations)**.
7 The remainder of installation is the reverse of removal.

21 Transmission shafts - disassembly and reassembly

HAYNES HINT *When disassembling the transmission shafts, place the parts on a long rod or thread a wire through them to keep them in order and facing the proper direction.*

1 Remove the shafts from the case (see Section 20).

Main drive shaft
Disassembly
2 All of the main drive shaft parts slide off the shaft except first gear, which is integral with the shaft, and the ball bearing, which is a press fit.
3 Each freewheeling gear is secured with a toothed washer and snap-ring. Use snap-ring pliers to remove the snap-rings.

Caution: There are two sizes of snap-ring, with only a small difference between them. Be sure to keep the snap rings in their original locations and to replace them with ones of the same size.

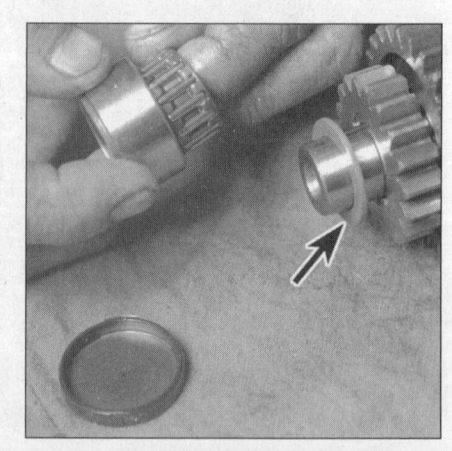

21.4a Remove the bearing plug . . .

21.4b . . . the outer bearing, inner bearing and spacer (arrow) . . .

Engine, clutch and transmission - EN450/500 models 2A•23

21.4c ... slide off second gear...

21.4d ... remove the snap-ring and toothed washer, then slide off sixth gear...

21.4e ... slide off the sixth gear bushing and toothed washer - on assembly, align the oil holes in bushing and shaft...

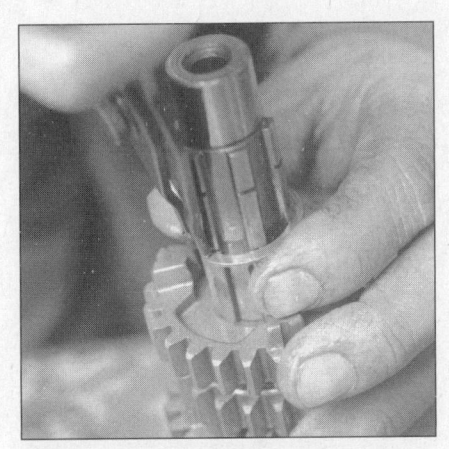

21.4f ... then remove the snap-ring...

21.4g ... slide the third-fourth gear cluster off the shaft...

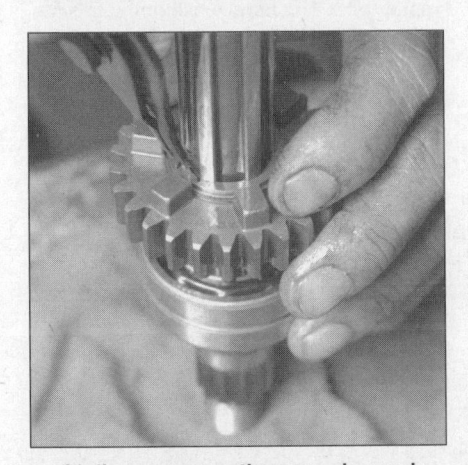

21.4h ... remove the snap-ring and toothed washer...

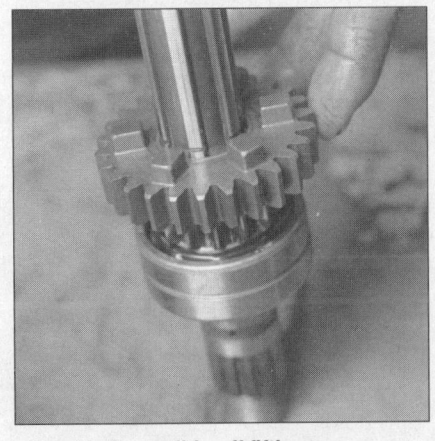

21.4i ... slide off fifth gear...

21.4j ... and the fifth gear bushing (if equipped) - on assembly, align the oil holes in bushing and shaft

4 To disassemble the main drive shaft, refer to the accompanying photographs **(see illustrations)**. Refer to Chapter 2C for inspection procedures.

Reassembly

5 During reassembly, always use new snap-rings and align the opening of the ring with a spline groove.

6 To reassemble the main drive shaft, reverse the disassembly process.

7 Check the assembled main drive shaft to make sure all parts are installed correctly.

Output shaft

Disassembly

8 All of the output shaft parts slide off the shaft except the ball bearing, which is a press fit. Fifth gear is secured to the shaft by three steel balls, installed in channels in the

2A•24 Engine, clutch and transmission - EN450/500 models

21.10a Pull off the bearing outer race . . .

21.10b . . . the bearing and spacer (arrows)

21.10c Slide first gear off the shaft

21.10d The next gear on the output shaft is fifth gear . . .

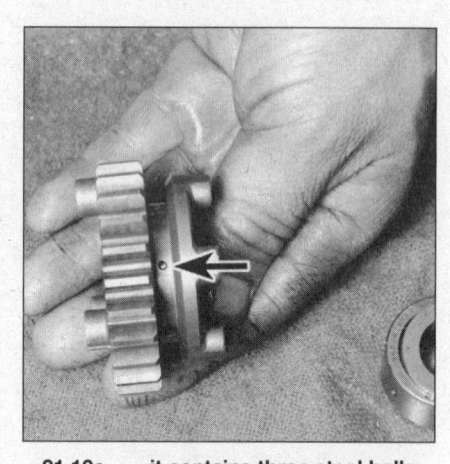

21.10e . . . it contains three steel balls (arrow) that will prevent the gear from being removed unless they're flung outward by centrifugal force . . .

21.10f . . . to disengage them from these slots (arrow) - to do so, spin the shaft rapidly with one hand while trying to slide the gear off with the other; it may take several tries, but the gear will come off with light hand pressure once the balls are spun outward

gear, which must be spun outward by centrifugal force. To do this, spin the shaft with one hand, and at the same time, lift the gear with the other hand. This may take several tries.

9 Each freewheeling gear is secured with a toothed washer and snap-ring. Use snap-ring pliers to remove the snap-rings.

10 To disassemble the output shaft, refer to the accompanying illustrations **(see illustrations)**.

21.10g Remove the snap-ring and toothed washer, then slide third gear off the shaft . . .

21.10h . . . this will expose the bushing shared by third and fourth gears . . .

Engine, clutch and transmission - EN450/500 models 2A•25

21.10i ... slide off the bushing and fourth gear

21.10j Remove the toothed washer, then the snap-ring ...

21.10k ... and slide sixth gear off the shaft

21.10l Remove the snap-ring ...

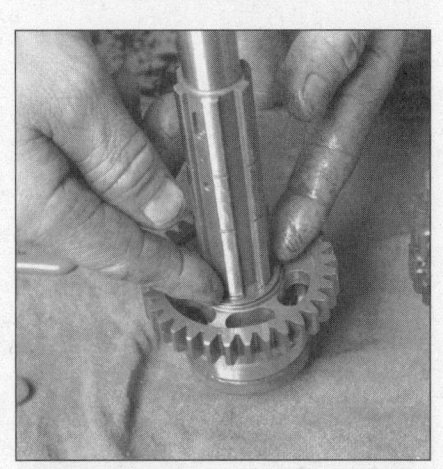

21.10m ... and the toothed washer ...

21.10n ... and slide second gear off the shaft

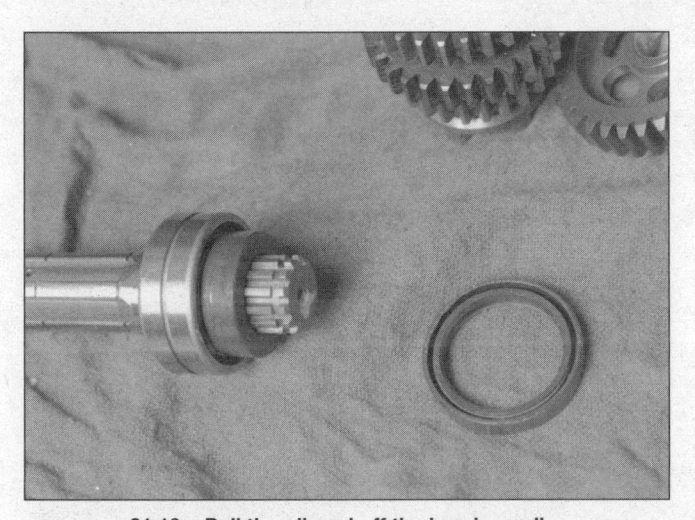

21.10o Pull the oil seal off the bearing collar

21.10p If the bearing is worn or damaged, place it in a bearing splitter, press it off the shaft and press a new one on (or have the job done by a motorcycle dealer)

Reassembly

11 Reassembly is basically the reverse of the disassembly procedure, but take note of the following points:
 a) Always use new snap-rings and align the opening of the ring with a spline groove.
 b) When installing the bushing for third and fourth gear, align the oil hole in the bushing with the hole in the shaft.
 c) When installing fifth gear, don't use grease to hold the balls in place - to do so would impair the positive neutral finder mechanism. Just set the balls in their holes (the holes that they can't pass through), keep the gear in a verti-

2A•26 Engine, clutch and transmission - EN450/500 models

22.2a Note the positions of the shift forks on the rod, then slide out the rod and remove the forks

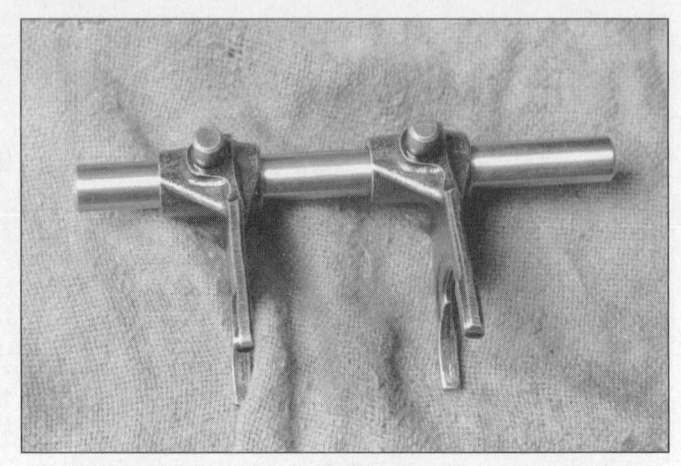

22.2b It's a good idea to reassemble the forks to the rod temporarily so you don't forget how they go

cal position and carefully set it on the shaft (engine oil will help keep them in place). The spline grooves that contain the holes with the balls must be aligned with the slots in the shaft spline grooves.

d) Lubricate the components with engine oil before assembling them.

22 Shift drum and forks - removal, inspection and installation

Removal

1 Remove the engine and separate the crankcase halves (see Sections 5 and 17).
2 Support the shift forks and pull the shift rod out **(see illustrations)**.
3 Remove the shift drum bearing retaining bolts **(see illustration)**.
4 Remove the cotter pin and pull out the guide pin **(see illustration)**.
5 Pull the shift drum out of the case far enough to remove the third/fourth shift fork **(see illustration)**, then slide the shift drum out of the case **(see illustration)**.

22.3 Remove the shift drum bearing retainer bolts (arrows)

Installation

6 Installation is the reverse of removal, noting the following points:
a) Install the shift drum part-way into the case and install the third/fourth shift fork (the long end goes onto the drum first).

22.4 Remove the cotter pin (split pin) and guide pin (arrows) . . .

b) Be sure to use a new cotter pin and install it correctly **(see illustration 22.4)**.
c) Lubricate all parts with engine oil before installing them.
d) Apply a non-permanent locking agent to the threads of the bearing retainer bolts and tighten them securely.

22.5a . . . and slide the shift drum out of the fork and case

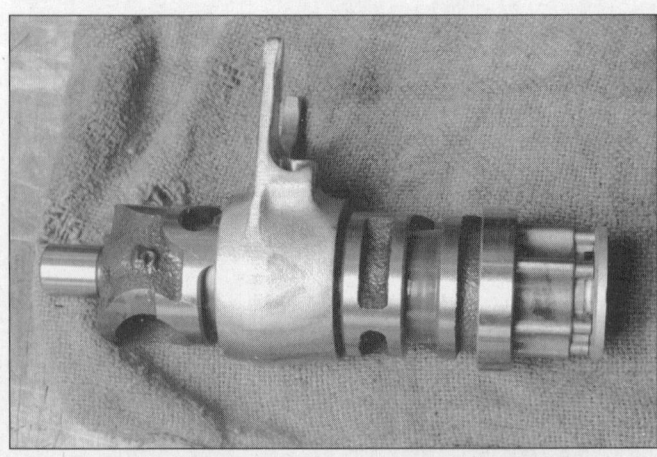

22.5b Reassemble the shift fork to the drum

Chapter 2 Part B
Engine, clutch and transmission - EX250 models

Contents

Balancer shaft and gears - removal and installation	17
Camshaft chain and guides - removal, inspection and installation	18
Camshaft chain tensioner - removal and installation	7
Camshafts, rocker arm shafts and rocker arms - removal, inspection and installation	8
Clutch - removal and installation	13
Clutch cable - replacement	14
Crankcase - disassembly and reassembly	16
Cylinder block - removal and installation	10
Cylinder head - removal and installation	9
Engine - removal and installation	5
External shift mechanism - removal, inspection and installation	15
General information	1
Major engine repair - general note	4
Oil pressure relief valve - removal, inspection and installation	12
Oil pump - removal and installation	11
Operations possible with the engine in the frame	2
Operations requiring engine removal	3
Shift drum and forks - removal, inspection and installation	21
Transmission shafts - disassembly and reassembly	20
Transmission shafts - removal and installation	19
Valve cover - removal and installation	6

Degrees of difficulty

Easy, suitable for novice with little experience & **Fairly easy,** suitable for beginner with some experience & **Fairly difficult,** suitable for competent DIY mechanic & **Difficult,** suitable for experienced DIY mechanic & **Very difficult,** suitable for expert DIY or professional

Specifications

General
Bore	62.0 mm (2.44 inches)
Stroke	41.2 mm (1.622 inches)
Displacement	248 cc
Compression ratio	12.0:1

Torque specifications
Valve cover bolts	9.8 Nm (87 in-lbs)
Camshaft bearing cap bolts	12 Nm (104 in-lbs)
Camshaft sprocket bolts	15 Nm (132 in-lbs)*
Camshaft chain tensioner mounting bolts	Not specified*
Camshaft chain rear guide bolts	
Upper	25 Nm (18 ft-lbs)
Lower	27 Nm (20 ft-lbs)
Cylinder head bolts	
Underside bolt	12 Nm (104 in-lbs)
Upper bolts	25 Nm (18 ft-lbs)

Torque specifications (continued)

Crankcase bolts	
6 mm bolts	12 Nm (104 in-lbs)
8 mm bolts	27 Nm (20 ft-lbs)
Connecting rod nuts	27 Nm (20 ft-lbs)
Clutch cover bolts	Not specified
Clutch cover baffle bolts (US models)	9.8 Nm (87 in-lbs)*
Clutch spring bolts	8.8 Nm (78 in-lbs)
Clutch hub nut	130 Nm (98 ft-lbs)
Oil pump bolts	Not specified*
Oil pipe-to-cylinder head union bolts	12 Nm (104 in-lbs)
Oil hose-to-crankcase union bolts	20 Nm (174 in-lbs)
Oil pressure relief valve-to-crankcase	15 Nm (132 in-lbs)*
Oil passage plug to lower crankcase half	15 Nm (132 in-lbs)*
Shift drum bearing retainer bolts	Not specified*
Shift drum positioning bolt	25 Nm (18 ft-lbs)
Shift drum pin plate Allen bolt	Not specified*
Return spring pin	20 Nm (174 in-lbs)*

*Apply non-hardening thread locking agent to the threads.

1 General information

The engine/transmission unit is a water-cooled, in-line, parallel twin. The valves are operated by double overhead camshafts which are chain driven off the crankshaft. The engine/transmission assembly is constructed from aluminum alloy. The crankcase is divided horizontally.

The crankcase incorporates a wet sump, pressure-fed lubrication system which uses a gear-driven, dual-rotor oil pump, an oil filter and by-pass valve assembly, a relief valve and an oil pressure switch. Also contained in the crankcase is the balancer shaft.

Power from the crankshaft is routed to the transmission via the clutch, which is of the wet, multi-plate type and is chain-driven off the crankshaft. The transmission is a six-speed, constant-mesh unit.

2 Operations possible with the engine in the frame

The components and assemblies listed below can be removed without having to remove the engine from the frame. If, however, a number of areas require attention at the same time, removal of the engine is recommended.

    Gearshift mechanism external components
    Water pump
    Starter motor
    Alternator
    Starter motor clutch
    Clutch assembly
    Oil pump and pressure relief valve
    Valve cover, camshafts and rocker arms
    Cam chain tensioner
    Cylinder head
    Cylinder block and pistons

3 Operations requiring engine removal

It is necessary to remove the engine/transmission assembly from the frame and separate the crankcase halves to gain access to the following components:

    Crankshaft, connecting rods and bearings
    Transmission shafts
    Shift drum and forks
    Balancer shaft
    Camshaft chain
    Primary chain

4 Major engine repair - general note

1   It is not always easy to determine when or if an engine should be completely overhauled, as a number of factors must be considered.

2   High mileage is not necessarily an indication that an overhaul is needed, while low mileage, on the other hand, does not preclude the need for an overhaul. Frequency of servicing is probably the single most important consideration. An engine that has regular and frequent oil and filter changes, as well as other required maintenance, will most likely give many miles of reliable service. Conversely, a neglected engine, or one which has not been broken in properly, may require an overhaul very early in its life.

3   Exhaust smoke and excessive oil consumption are both indications that piston rings and/or valve guides are in need of attention. Make sure oil leaks are not responsible before deciding that the rings and guides are bad. Refer to Chapter 2C and perform a cylinder compression check to determine for certain the nature and extent of the work required.

4   If the engine is making obvious knocking or rumbling noises, the connecting rod and/or main bearings are probably at fault.

Engine, clutch and transmission - EX250 models 2B•3

5.13a With the engine securely supported, remove the mounting bolts at the front . . .

5.13b . . . and at the upper and lower rear (arrows)

5 Loss of power, rough running, excessive valve train noise and high fuel consumption rates may also point to the need for an overhaul, especially if they are all present at the same time. If a complete tune-up does not remedy the situation, major mechanical work is the only solution.

6 An engine overhaul generally involves restoring the internal parts to the specifications of a new engine. During an overhaul the piston rings are replaced and the cylinder walls are bored and/or honed. If a rebore is done, then new pistons are also required. The main and connecting rod bearings are generally replaced with new ones and, if necessary, the crankshaft is also replaced. Generally the valves are serviced as well, since they are usually in less than perfect condition at this point. While the engine is being overhauled, other components such as the carburetors and the starter motor can be rebuilt also. The end result should be a like-new engine that will give as many trouble free miles as the original.

7 Before beginning the engine overhaul, read through all of the related procedures to familiarize yourself with the scope and requirements of the job. Overhauling an engine is not all that difficult, but it is time consuming. Plan on the motorcycle being tied up for a minimum of two weeks. Check on the availability of parts and make sure that any necessary special tools, equipment and supplies are obtained in advance.

8 Most work can be done with typical shop hand tools, although a number of precision measuring tools are required for inspecting parts to determine if they must be replaced. Often a dealer service department or motorcycle repair shop will handle the inspection of parts and offer advice concerning reconditioning and replacement. As a general rule, time is the primary cost of an overhaul so it doesn't pay to install worn or substandard parts.

9 As a final note, to ensure maximum life and minimum trouble from a rebuilt engine, everything must be assembled with care in a spotlessly clean environment.

5 Engine - removal and installation

⚠ *Engine removal and installation should be done with the aid of an assistant to avoid damage or injury that could occur if the engine is dropped. A hydraulic floor jack should be used to support and lower the engine if possible (they can be rented at low cost).*

Removal

1 Set the bike on its centerstand (if equipped) and disconnect the battery (negative cable first).

2 Remove the seat, side covers, knee grip covers (1986 and 1987 models), fuel tank and fairing (see Chapters 4 and 8).

3 Remove the fuel tank (see Chapter 4).

4 Drain the coolant and the engine oil (see Chapter 1).

5 Loosen the clamps that secure the carburetors to the intake manifold (see Chapter 4). Secure the carburetors to the air filter housing with wire or tape so they won't fall out when the engine is removed. Disconnect the throttle and choke cables from the carburetors.

6 Mark and disconnect the wires from the oil pressure switch, neutral switch and the starter motor. Unplug the brake light switch, alternator, sidestand, ignition coil and pickup coil electrical connectors (see Chapters 5 and 9).

7 Remove the radiator, radiator hoses and coolant tubes (see Chapter 3).

8 Remove the ignition coils, together with both of the upper engine mounting brackets (see Chapter 5).

9 Remove the exhaust system (see Chapter 4).

10 Remove the drive chain sprocket from the engine (see Chapter 6).

11 Disconnect the lower end of the clutch cable from the lever and remove the cable bracket (see Chapter 1).

12 Support the engine with a floor jack and a wood block.

13 With the engine supported, remove the engine mounting through-bolts **(see illustrations)**.

14 Make sure no wires or hoses are still attached to the engine assembly.

15 Slowly and carefully lower the engine assembly away from the bike.

Installation

16 Installation is the reverse of removal. Note the following points:

a) *Don't tighten any of the engine mounting bolts until they all have been installed.*
b) *Use new gaskets at all exhaust pipe connections.*
c) *Tighten the engine mounting bolts and frame downtube bolts.*
d) *Adjust the drive chain, throttle and choke cables and clutch cable following the procedures in Chapter 1.*

6 Valve cover - removal and installation

Note: *The valve cover can be removed with the engine in the frame. If the engine has been removed, ignore the steps which don't apply.*

Removal

1 Set the bike on its centerstand (if equipped).

2 Drain the engine coolant and disconnect the coolant tube next to the valve cover (see Chapters 1 and 3).

3 Remove the seat and, on 1986 and 1987

2B•4 Engine, clutch and transmission - EX250 models

6.6 Remove the valve cover bolts, washers and seals (arrows)

6.7 Lift the cover off the engine - if it's stuck, tap gently on the side with a soft faced hammer; don't pry the cover loose

models, the knee grip covers (see Chapter 8).

4 Remove the fuel tank (see Chapter 4).

5 Remove the ignition coils, along with the spark plug wires (see Chapter 5).

6 Remove the valve cover bolts **(see illustration)**.

7 Lift the cover off the cylinder head **(see illustration)**. If it's stuck, don't attempt to pry it off - tap around the sides with a plastic hammer to dislodge it.

Installation

8 Peel the rubber gasket and spark plug hole seals from the cover or cylinder head **(see illustration)**. If they're cracked, hardened, have soft spots or shows signs of general deterioration, replace them with new ones.

9 Clean the mating surfaces of the cylinder head and the valve cover with lacquer thinner, acetone or brake system cleaner. Apply a thin film of RTV sealant to the half-circle cutouts on each side of the head.

10 Install the gasket to the cover. Make sure it fits completely into the cover groove. Apply a small amount of silicone sealer to the corners of the half-circle portions of the gasket.

11 Position the cover on the cylinder head, making sure the gasket doesn't slip out of place.

12 Check the rubber seals on the valve cover bolts, replacing them if necessary. Install the bolts, tightening them evenly to the torque listed in this Chapter's Specifications.

13 The remainder of installation is the reverse of removal. Fill the cooling system with the recommended type and amount of coolant (see Chapter 1).

7 Camshaft chain tensioner - removal, disassembly, assembly and installation

Removal

Caution: Once you start to remove the tensioner bolts, you must remove the tensioner all the way and reset it before tightening the bolts. The tensioner extends and locks in place, so if you loosen the bolts part way and then retighten them, the tensioner or cam chain will be damaged.

1 Remove the tensioner mounting bolts and take it off the engine **(see illustration)**.

Caution: Don't turn the engine with the tensioner removed or damage may occur.

Disassembly

2 Remove the ball retainer and spring **(see illustration)**.

3 Remove the pushrod lock screw and pull the pushrod out of the tensioner body.

4 Remove the tensioner spring.

5 Check the O-ring on the tensioner body for cracks or hardening. It's a good idea to replace this O-ring whenever the tensioner is removed.

Reassembly

6 Place the tensioner spring in the pushrod. Install the spring and pushrod in the

6.8 Remove the gasket and spark plug well seals

7.1 Loosen the tensioner lockscrew (upper arrow) while the tensioner is still on the engine, then remove the mounting bolts (lower arrows)

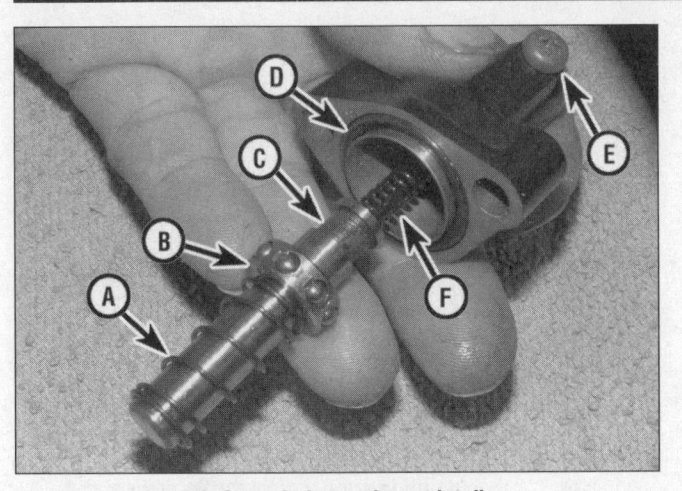

Engine, clutch and transmission - EX250 models 2B•5

7.2 Cam chain tensioner details

A Spring
B Ball retainer
C Pushrod
D O-ring
E Lock screw
F Tensioner spring

7.6 Press the pushrod and its spring into the tensioner body, then tighten the lockscrew into the pushrod groove to secure it

tensioner body, press the pushrod all the way in and secure it with the lock screw **(see illustration)**.

7 Install the ball and retainer on the pushrod, then install the ball and retainer spring.

Installation

8 Make sure the tensioner piston is pressed all the way into the body and secured in that position with the lock screw.
9 Install a new O-ring on the tensioner body.
10 Place the tensioner in position on the engine and install the mounting bolts. Tighten the mounting bolts to the torque listed in this Chapter's Specifications.
11 Loosen the lockscrew about 2 mm (3/32 inch) to let the tensioner pushrod extend, then tighten the lock screw.

8 Camshafts, rocker arm shafts and rocker arms - removal, inspection and installation

Note: *This procedure can be performed with the engine in the frame.*

Camshafts
Removal

1 Remove the valve cover (see Section 6).
2 Turn the engine to position no. 2 cylinder at TDC compression (see Chapter 1 - *Valve clearances - check and adjustment*). When the engine is positioned correctly, the EX mark on the exhaust camshaft and the IN mark on the intake camshaft will align with the cylinder head top surface **(see illustration)**. To ease reassembly, mark the sprockets and chain with a felt pen.
3 Remove the camshaft chain tensioner (see Section 7).
4 Remove the upper chain guide **(see illustration)**.
5 Unscrew the bearing cap bolts for one of the camshafts, a little at a time, until they are all loose, then unscrew the bearing cap bolts for the other camshaft.

Caution: If the bearing cap bolts aren't loosened evenly, the camshaft may bind.

8.2 Position the EX and IN marks on the camshafts even with the cylinder head surface (arrows)

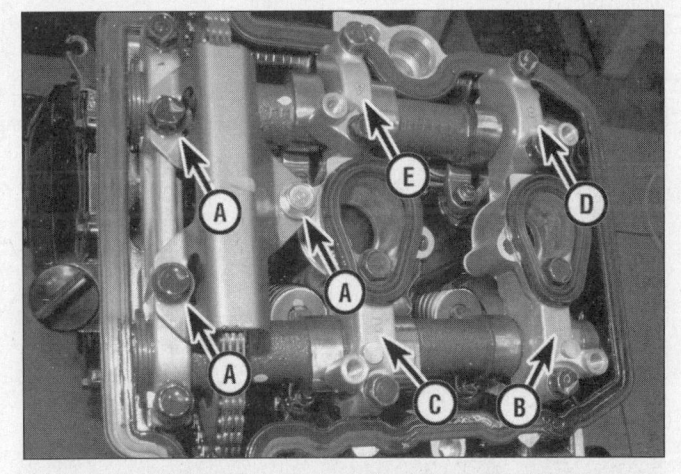

8.4 Upper chain guide and bearing cap details

A Chain guide bolts
B No. 1 bearing cap mark
C No. 2 bearing cap mark
D No. 3 bearing cap mark
E No. 4 bearing cap mark

8.5a Remove the front cap bolts, noting their different lengths ...

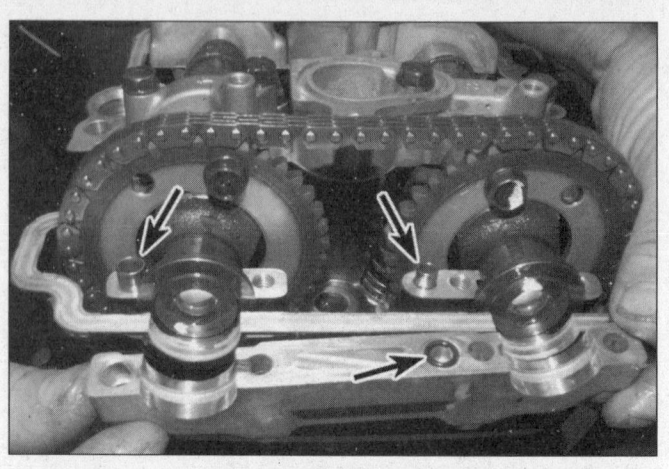

8.5b ... then lift off the cap and locate its dowels and O-ring (arrows) ...

Remove the bolts, noting their different lengths (see illustration), and lift off the bearing caps, then remove their dowels and O-rings (see illustrations). Note the numbers on the bearing caps which give the cap locations (see illustration 8.4). When you reinstall the caps, be sure to install them in the correct positions.

6 Pull up on the camshaft chain and carefully guide the camshaft out. With the chain still held taut, remove the other camshaft. Look for marks on the camshafts. The intake camshaft should have an IN mark and the exhaust camshaft should have an EX mark. If you can't find these marks, label the camshafts to ensure they are installed in their original locations. **Note:** *Don't remove the sprockets from the camshafts unless absolutely necessary.*

7 Stuff clean rags into the cam chain tunnel to keep dirt and small parts from falling in.

8 Number the rocker arms with felt pen so they can be returned to their original positions (see illustration). Lift off the rocker arms and pivot bases.

9 While the camshafts are out, don't allow the chain to go slack - there's a protrusion inside the crankcase that's designed to keep the chain from falling off the sprocket on the crankshaft, but if it's worn, the chain may fall off and bind between the crankshaft and case, which could damage these components. Wire the chain to another component to prevent it from dropping down. Also, cover the top of the cylinder head with a rag to prevent foreign objects from falling into the engine.

10 Refer to Chapter 2C for inspection procedures.

Installation

11 If you removed the sprockets, be sure to install them correctly; they're identical, with each sprocket having bolt holes for the exhaust and intake camshafts. The intake camshaft sprocket uses the bolt holes labeled IN; the exhaust camshaft sprocket uses the bolt holes labeled EX (see illustration).

12 Install the rocker arm pivot bases in the cylinder head. Apply a light coat of engine assembly lube or moly-based grease to each of them, then install the rocker arms.

13 Make sure the bearing surfaces in the cylinder head and the bearing caps are clean, then apply a light coat of engine assembly lube or moly-based grease to each of them.

14 Apply a coat of moly-based grease to the camshaft lobes and bearing surfaces. Make sure the camshaft bearing journals are clean, then lay the camshafts in the cylinder head (do not mix them up), ensuring the marks on the cam sprockets are aligned properly.

15 Make sure the crankshaft mark is still positioned at TDC compression for cylinder no. 2 and the camshaft marks are still aligned properly, then mesh the chain with the camshaft sprockets. Count the number of chain link pins between the EX mark on the exhaust camshaft and the IN mark on the intake camshaft (see illustration). There should be no slack in the chain between the two sprockets.

16 Make sure the camshaft dowels and O-rings are in place (see illustrations 8.5b, 8.5c and 8.5d). Carefully set the bearing caps in place (arrows pointing toward the front of the engine and in their proper positions) (see illustration 8.4) and install the bolts. Tighten them in the recommended sequence (see illustration), to the torque listed in this Chapter's Specifications.

17 Insert your finger or a wood dowel into the cam chain tensioner hole and apply pressure to the cam chain. Check the timing marks to make sure they are aligned (see Step 3) and there are still the correct number of link pins between the EX and IN marks on the cam sprockets. If necessary, change the

8.5c ... the small caps have dowels (arrows) ...

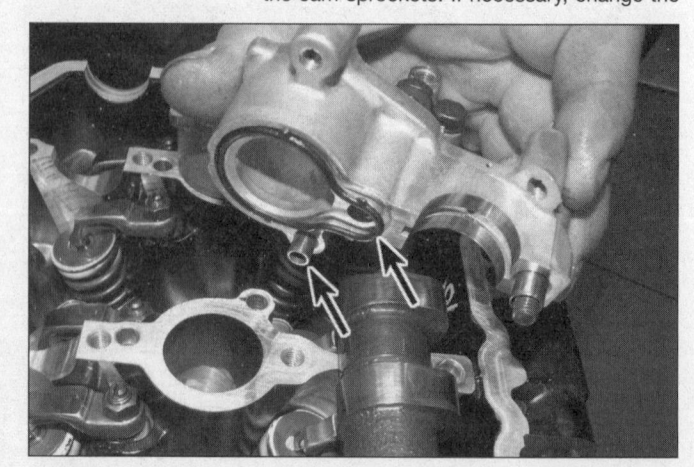

8.5d ... and the center caps have dowels and O-rings (arrows)

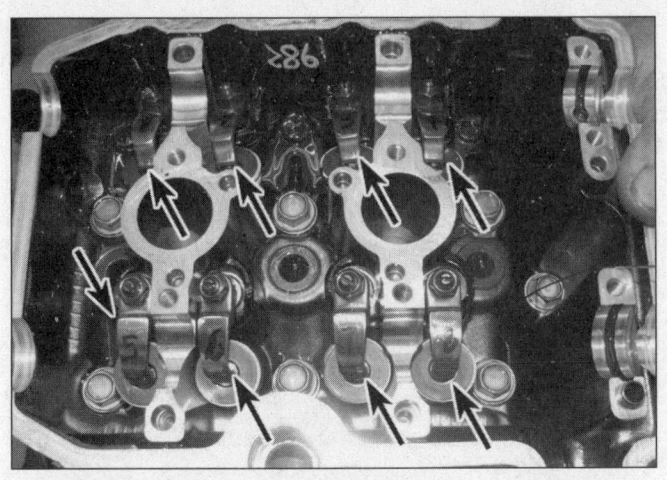

Engine, clutch and transmission - EX250 models 2B•7

8.8a Number the rocker arms (arrows) with felt pen, then lift them off . . .

8.8b . . . and remove the pivot bases (arrows)

8.11 Each sprocket has two sets of bolt holes; those labeled EX are used for the exhaust camshaft, while those labeled IN are used for the intake camshaft

position of the sprocket(s) on the chain to bring all of the marks into alignment.

Caution: If the marks are not aligned exactly as described, the valve timing will be incorrect and the valves may contact the pistons, causing extensive damage to the engine.

18 Install the tensioner as described in Section 7.
19 Adjust the valve clearances (see Chapter 1).
20 Turn the engine with a socket on the crankshaft rotation bolt. If you feel a sudden increase in resistance, stop turning. The valves may be hitting the pistons due to incorrect assembly. Find the problem and fix it before turning the engine any further, or serious damage may occur.
21 The remainder of installation is the reverse of removal.

9 Cylinder head - removal and installation

Caution: The engine must be completely cool before beginning this procedure, or the cylinder head may become warped.

Note: *This procedure can be performed with the engine in the frame. If the engine has been removed, ignore the steps which don't apply.*

Removal

1 Set the bike on its centerstand (if equipped).
2 Remove the valve cover (see Section 6).
3 Remove the exhaust system (see Chapter 4).
4 Remove the cam chain tensioner (see Section 7).
5 Remove the camshafts and rocker arms (see Section 8).
6 Remove the thermostat housing (see Chapter 3).
7 Remove the ignition coils, together with the engine mounting brackets (see Section 5).
8 Remove the front cam chain guide (see Section 18).
10 Loosen the clamps that secure the carburetors to the intake manifold (see Chapter 4). Secure the carburetors to the air filter housing with wire or tape so they won't fall out when the cylinder head is removed.

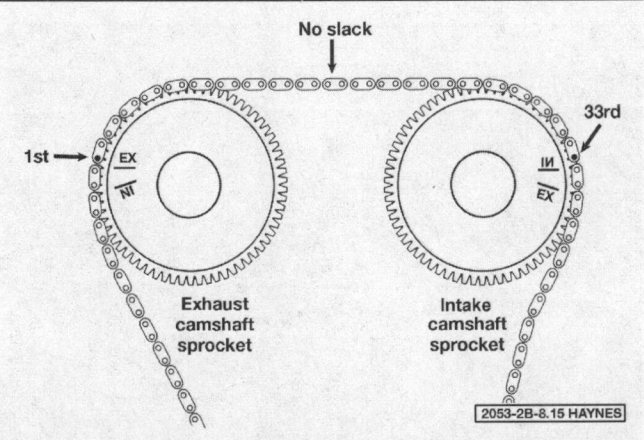

8.15 With no slack in the camshaft chain, there should be 33 link pins present between the EX and IN marks on the cam sprockets

8.16 Camshaft bolt TIGHTENING sequence

2B•8 Engine, clutch and transmission - EX250 models

9.11 Remove one bolt from the underside of the cylinder head (arrow)

9.12 Cylinder head bolt TIGHTENING sequence - bolt no. 8 (hidden) is on the underside

11 Remove the bolt that secures the cylinder block to the underside of the head **(see illustration)**.
12 Loosen the cylinder head bolts, a little at a time, using the reverse order of the tightening sequence **(see illustration)**.
13 Pull the cylinder head off the cylinder block **(see illustration)**. If the head is stuck, tap upward with a rubber mallet to jar it loose, or use two wooden dowels inserted into the intake or exhaust ports to lever the head off. Don't attempt to pry the head off by inserting a screwdriver between the head and the cylinder block - you'll damage the sealing surfaces.
14 Lift the head gasket off the cylinder block **(see illustration 9.13)**.
15 Stuff a clean rag into the cam chain tunnel to prevent the entry of debris.
16 Locate the two dowel pins to make sure they haven't fallen into the engine. If they are in the head, put them in their holes in the cylinder block.
17 Check the cylinder head gasket and the mating surfaces on the cylinder head and block for signs of leakage, which could indicate warpage. Refer to Chapter 2C and check the flatness of the cylinder head.
18 Clean all traces of old gasket material from the cylinder head and block. Be careful not to let any of the gasket material fall into the crankcase, the cylinder bores or the water passages.

Installation

19 Lay the new gasket in place on the cylinder block. Never reuse the old gasket and don't use any type of gasket sealant.
20 Carefully lower the cylinder head over the studs. It is helpful to have an assistant support the camshaft chain with a piece of wire so it doesn't fall and become kinked or detached from the crankshaft. When the head is resting against the cylinder block, wire the cam chain to another component to keep tension on it.
21 Install the head bolts. Using the proper sequence **(see illustration 9.12)**, tighten the bolts to approximately half of the torque listed in this Chapter's Specifications.
22 Using the same sequence, tighten the bolts to the full torque listed in this Chapter's Specifications.
23 Install the front cam chain guide (see Section 18).
24 Install the camshafts (see Section 8) and adjust the valves (see Chapter 1). Install all components removed for access.
25 Change the engine oil and refill the cooling system (see Chapter 1).

10 Cylinder block - removal and installation

Removal

1 Following the procedure given in Section 9, remove the cylinder head. Make sure the crankshaft is positioned at Top Dead Center (TDC) for cylinder no. 2. Remove the pivot bolt for the rear cam chain guide (see Section 18).
2 Unbolt the coolant tube from the water pump and remove the tube (see Chapter 3).
3 Remove the carburetors (see Chapter 4).
4 Lift the cylinder block straight up to remove it **(see illustration)**. If it's stuck, tap around its perimeter with a soft-faced hammer. Don't attempt to pry between the block and the crankcase, as you will ruin the sealing surfaces. As you lift, note the location of the dowel pins. Be careful not to let these drop into the engine.
5 Stuff clean shop towels around the pis-

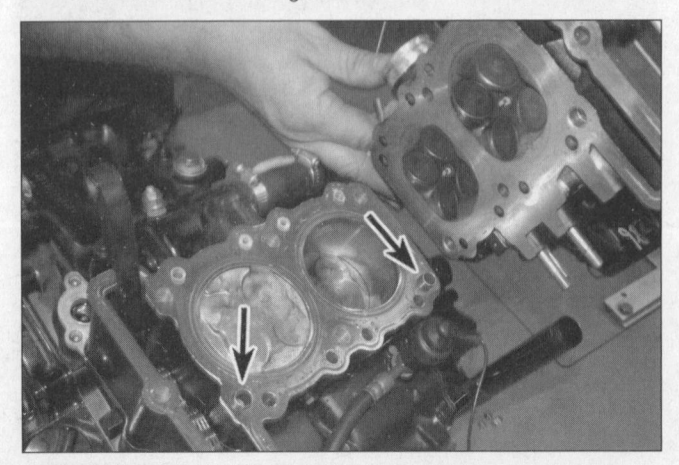

9.13 Lift the head off, remove the gasket and locate the dowels (arrows)

10.4 Lift the cylinder off, remove the gasket and locate the dowels (arrows)

Engine, clutch and transmission - EX250 models 2B•9

11.2 Remove the snap-ring and oil pump drive gear

11.3a It will be easier to loosen the cover screws while the pump is still bolted to the engine

tons and remove the gasket and all traces of old gasket material from the surfaces of the cylinder block and the cylinder head.
6 If necessary, remove the thermostat and coolant hose from the cylinder (see Chapter 3).
7 Refer to Chapter 2C for inspection procedures.

Installation

8 Lubricate the cylinder bores with plenty of clean engine oil. Apply a thin film of moly-based grease to the piston skirts.
9 Install the dowel pins (see illustration 10.4), then place a new cylinder base gasket on the crankcase with the ridge in the gasket upward.
10 Slowly rotate the crankshaft until both of the pistons are at the same level. Slide lengths of welding rod or pieces of a straightened-out coat hanger under the pistons, on both sides of the connecting rods. This will help keep the pistons level as the cylinder block is lowered onto them.
11 Attach two piston ring compressors to the pistons and compress the piston rings. Large hose clamps can be used instead - just make sure they don't scratch the pis-

tons, and don't tighten them too much.
12 Install the cylinder block over the pistons and carefully lower it down until the piston crowns fit into the cylinder liners. While doing this, pull the camshaft chain up, using a hooked tool or a piece of coat hanger. Push down on the cylinder block, making sure the pistons don't get cocked sideways, until the bottoms of the cylinder liners slide down past the piston rings. A wood or plastic hammer handle can be used to gently tap the block down, but don't use too much force or the pistons will be damaged.
13 Remove the piston ring compressors or hose clamps, being careful not to scratch the pistons. Remove the rods from under the pistons, then reset the engine to TDC for cylinder number 2
14 The remainder of installation is the reverse of removal.

11 Oil pump - removal and installation

Note: *The oil pump can be removed with the engine in the frame.*

Removal

1 Remove the clutch (see Section 13).
2 Remove the snap-ring and take the drive gear off the pump (see illustration).
3 If you're planning to disassemble the pump, loosen its cover screws while the pump is still bolted to the engine (see illustration). Remove the pump mounting bolts and take the pump off the engine, together with its dowels and O-rings (see illustrations).
4 Refer to Chapter 2C for inspection procedures.

Installation

5 Installation is the reverse of removal, with the following additions:
   a) Use new O-rings and make sure the dowels are installed.
   b) Make sure the oil pump drive shaft engages the water pump shaft (see illustration).
   c) Use non-permanent thread locking agent on the oil pump mounting bolts.
   d) Use a new snap-ring on the drive gear.

11.3b Remove the mounting bolts (arrows) . . .

11.3c . . . and take the pump off - on installation, use new O-rings and make sure the dowels are in place . . .

11.5 . . . and align the tab on the oil pump shaft (arrow) with the slot in the water pump

2B•10 Engine, clutch and transmission - EX250 models

12.2 Unscrew the oil pressure relief valve (arrow)

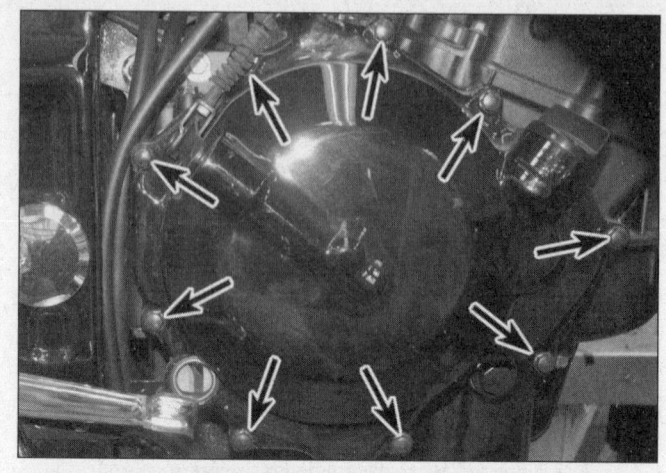

13.5a Remove the clutch cover bolts (arrows) . . .

13.5b . . . locate the dowels (A) and remove the spring plate bolts (B), the springs beneath them and the spring plate

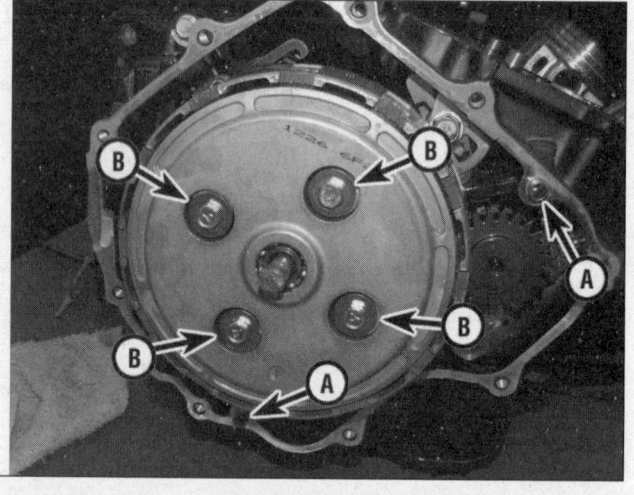

12 Oil pressure relief valve - removal, inspection and installation

Removal
1　Remove the clutch (see Section 13).
2　Unscrew the relief valve from the crankcase **(see illustration)**.

Inspection
3　Clean the valve with solvent and dry it, using compressed air if available.
4　Using a wood or plastic tool, depress the steel ball inside the valve and see if it moves smoothly. Make sure it returns to its seat completely. If it doesn't, replace it with a new one (don't attempt to disassemble and repair it).

Installation
5　Apply a non-permanent thread locking compound to the threads of the valve and install it, tightening it to the torque listed in this Chapter's Specifications.
6　The remainder of installation is the reverse of removal.

13 Clutch - removal and installation

Note: *The clutch can be removed with the engine in the frame.*

Removal
1　Set the bike on its centerstand (if equipped).
2　Drain the engine oil (see Chapter 1).
3　Completely loosen the forward adjustment nut on the clutch cable at its bracket on the clutch cover **(see illustration 8.4b in Chapter 1)**.
4　Pull the cable out of the bracket, then detach the cable end from the lever on the engine.
5　Remove the clutch cover bolts and take the cover off together with the release lever **(see illustrations)**. If the cover is stuck, tap around its perimeter with a soft-face hammer. California models have a baffle inside the cover. It need not be removed for normal clutch service. If you do remove it, note that the bolts are secured with thread locking agent and may be difficult to remove.
6　Loosen the clutch spring bolts in a criss-cross pattern **(see illustration 13.5b)**. To prevent the assembly from turning, thread one of the cover mounting bolts into the case and wedge a screwdriver between the bolt and the clutch housing. Remove the clutch springs, spring plate and bearing.
7　Note the direction of the radial grooves in the friction plate, then remove the pushrod, friction plates and steel plates from the clutch housing **(see illustrations)**.
8　Remove the clutch hub nut, using a special holding tool (Kawasaki tool no. 57001-305 or 1243 or an equivalent tool available from an aftermarket tool supplier) to prevent the clutch housing from turning. An alternative to this tool can be fabricated from some steel strap, bent at the ends and bolted together in the middle **(see illustration 14.8 in Chapter 2A)**. The nut is self-locking, so discard it and replace it with a new one during installation.
9　Remove the washer, clutch hub and clutch housing **(see illustration)**.
10　Refer to Chapter 2C for inspection procedures.

Installation
11　Lubricate the bearings and friction surfaces with clean engine oil, then install the clutch housing and the clutch hub. Install the washer and a new hub nut and tighten it to the torque listed in this Chapter's Specifications. Use the technique described in Step 8 to prevent the hub from turning.
12　Coat the clutch friction plates with engine oil. Install the clutch plates, starting with a friction plate and alternating them. There are five friction plates and four steel plates. Be sure the radial grooves in the friction plates are pointed in the correct direction **(see illustration 13.7a)**.
13　Lubricate the pushrod and install it through the spring plate. Mount the spring plate to the clutch assembly and install the springs and bolts, tightening them to the torque listed in this Chapter's Specifications in a criss-cross pattern.

Engine, clutch and transmission - EX250 models 2B•11

13.7a Remove the clutch nut and washer (A) and note the direction of the friction plate grooves (B) . . .

13.7b . . . then slide the clutch plates and hub off

13.9a Slide the clutch housing off . . .

13.9b . . . then remove the bearing, collar and thrust washer (arrows)

14 Make sure the clutch cover dowels are in place **(see illustration 13.5b)**. Install the clutch cover and bolts, using a new gasket. Tighten the bolts, in a criss-cross pattern, to the torque listed in this Chapter's Specifications.
15 Connect the clutch cable to the release lever and adjust the freeplay (see Chapter 1).
16 Fill the crankcase with the recommended type and amount of engine oil (see Chapter 1).

14 Clutch cable - replacement

1 Disconnect the upper end of the clutch cable from the lever (see Chapter 1).
2 Disconnect the clutch cable from the release lever.
3 Before removing the cable from the bike, tape the lower end of the new cable to the upper end of the old cable. Slowly pull the lower end of the old cable out, guiding the new cable down into position. Using this method will ensure the cable is routed correctly.
4 Lubricate the cable (see Chapter 1). Reconnect the ends of the cable by reversing the removal procedure, then adjust the cable following the procedure given in Chapter 1.

15 External shift mechanism - removal, inspection and installation

Note: *The external shift mechanism can be removed with the engine in the frame.*

Shift lever and pedal
1 Set the bike on its centerstand.
2 Remove the shift pedal bolt and linkage lever bolt **(see illustration)**.
3 To ease installation, make alignment marks on the shift lever shafts and the shift levers. Pull the shift levers off the shafts.
4 Installation is the reverse of removal. The shift linkage rod should be at 90-degrees

15.2 Make an alignment mark on the shaft (left arrow), then remove the pinch bolt completely and unscrew the pedal bolt (right arrow)

to the shift levers. Adjust as needed with the nuts on the linkage rod **(see illustration)**.

2B•12 Engine, clutch and transmission - EX250 models

15.4 Loosen the locknuts (arrows) and turn the rod to adjust the linkage

15.7a Here's the assembled external shift linkage

Shift mechanism

Removal

5 Remove the shift pedal and linkage (Steps 1 through 3).
6 Remove the clutch (see Section 13).
7 Pull the overshift limiter and shift mechanism arm away from the shift drum, then slide the shift shaft out of the crankcase **(see illustrations)**.
8 If necessary, unscrew the Allen bolt from the end of the shift drum and remove the pin plate and shift drum pins **(see illustration)**.
9 Refer to Chapter 2C for shift mechanism inspection procedures. If the shift shaft seal is worn or damaged, pry it out and press in a new one with a socket or seal driver **(see illustration)**.

Installation

10 If the shift drum pins and plate were removed, reinstall them. Use non-permanent thread locking agent on the Allen bolt and tighten it securely, but don't overtighten it and strip the threads.
11 Make sure the return spring is correctly positioned on the shift shaft **(see illustra-**

15.7b Spread the overshift limiter (upper arrow) and shift mechanism arm (lower arrow) away from the shift drum pins . . .

15.7c . . . and slide the shift shaft out of the case

tion). Slide the shift shaft into place, pulling back the overshift limiter and shift mechanism arm to clear the shift drum. Make sure the return spring ends are positioned on each side of the return spring pin **(see illustration 15.7a)**. Release the overshift limiter and shift mechanism arm and engage them with the shift drum pins.
12 Install the clutch (see Section 13).
13 Install and adjust the shift pedal and linkage (see Steps 1 through 4).
14 Check the engine oil level and add some, if necessary (see Chapter 1).

15.8 Remove the Allen bolt (arrow) to remove the pin plate and pins from the shift drum

15.9 Replace the shift shaft seal if it has been leaking

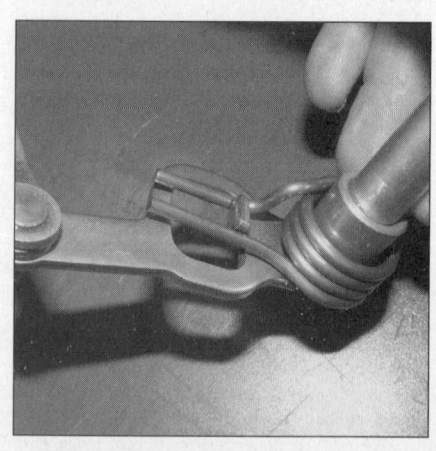

15.11 The return spring fits on the shaft like this

Engine, clutch and transmission - EX250 models 2B•13

16.7a Remove the oil line bolt (right arrow) - the other two connections (left arrows) are held in place by O-rings . . .

16.7b . . . and make sure the bolt's oil passage (arrow) is clear

16.7c Pull off the oil line and replace the O-rings

16.12 Use new copper washers on each side of the oil hose fittings (arrows)

16 Crankcase - disassembly and reassembly

1 To examine and repair or replace the crankshaft, connecting rods, bearings, clutch housing and balancer, the crankcase must be split into two parts.
2 Remove the engine from the motorcycle (see Section 5).
3 Remove the external shift mechanism (see Section 15).
4 Remove the water pump and coolant tube and hose (see Chapter 3).
5 Remove the starter motor and starter reduction gear (see Chapter 9).
6 Remove the oil pump (see Section 11).
7 Remove the external oil tube **(see illustrations)**. Note: *Remove the following components only if the crankshaft is to be removed.*
8 Remove the valve cover, camshaft chain tensioner and camshafts (see Sections 6, 7 and 8).
9 Remove the cylinder head and cylinder block (see Sections 9 and 10).

10 Remove the pistons (see Chapter 2C).
11 Remove the alternator rotor (see Chapter 9).
12 Remove the external oil hose **(see illustration)**.
13 Remove the oil pressure switch and neutral switch (see Chapter 9).
14 Remove the neutral positioning bolt, sealing washer, spring and pin **(see illustration)**.
15 Remove the clutch and external shift mechanism (see Sections 13 and 15).

16.14a Unscrew the neutral positioning bolt . . .

16.14b . . . and remove the washer, spring and plunger

2B•14 Engine, clutch and transmission - EX250 models

16.17 Here are the crankcase upper bolts (arrows) - bolt A has a copper washer and is longer than the others

16.19a Place the crankcase on blocks so it won't rest on the connecting rods

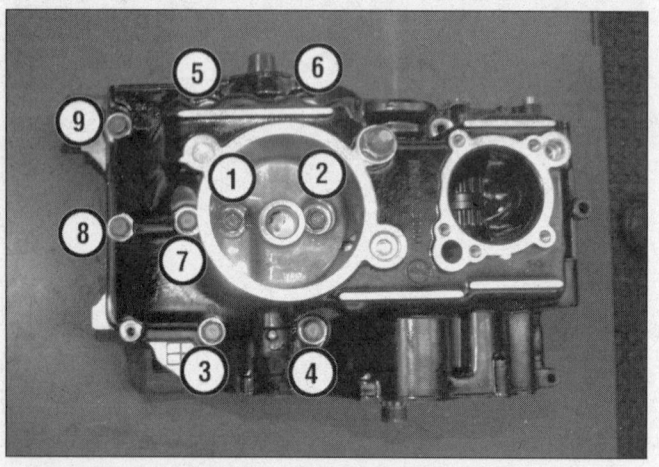

16.19b Here's the TIGHTENING sequence for the 8 mm crankcase bolts (bolts 8 and 9 are longer)

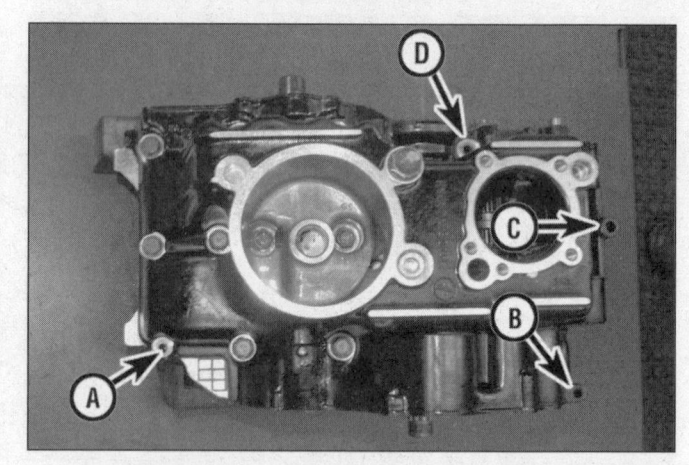

16.19c After tightening the 8 mm bolts, tighten the 6 mm bolts evenly

- A M6 X 38 mm
- B M6 X 60 mm
- C M6 X 135 mm
- D M6 X 85 mm (with copper washer)

16 Unbolt the cam chain guide lever and remove its components as an assembly (see Section 18).

17 Loosen the upper crankcase bolts in a criss-cross pattern, then remove them **(see illustration)**.

18 Remove the oil filter and strainer screen (see Chapter 1).

19 Place the lower crankcase on blocks so it doesn't rest on the connecting rods **(see illustration)**. Loosen the lower crankcase bolts in a criss-cross pattern, then remove them **(see illustration)**.

20 Carefully pry the crankcase apart. Pry ONLY in the pry points around the crankcase seam.

21 Separate the crankcase halves **(see illustration)**.

22 Refer to Sections 17 through 21 and Chapter 2C for information on the internal components of the crankcase.

Reassembly

23 Remove all traces of sealant from the crankcase mating surfaces. Be careful not to let any fall into the case as this is done.

24 Check to make sure the two dowel pins are in place in their holes in the mating surface of the upper crankcase half **(see illustration 16.21)**. Pour some engine oil over the transmission gears, the crankshaft main bearings and the shift drum. Don't get any oil on the crankcase mating surface.

25 Apply a thin, even bead of Kawasaki Bond sealant (part no. 56019-120) to the crankcase mating surfaces.

Caution: Don't apply an excessive amount of sealant, and don't apply it next to the bearing inserts, as it will ooze out when the case halves are assembled and may obstruct oil passages and prevent the bearings from seating.

26 Check the position of the shift drum, shift forks and transmission shafts - make sure they're in the neutral position (see Section 21).

16.21 Lift off the lower crankcase half and locate the dowels (arrows)

Engine, clutch and transmission - EX250 models 2B•15

17.2 Be sure the marks on the balancer gear and crankshaft gear are lined up (arrows)

17.3 The balancer shaft (arrow) rides in two bearings in the crankcase

27 Carefully assemble the crankcase halves. While doing this, make sure the shift forks fit into their gear grooves.

28 Install the lower crankcase half bolts and tighten them so they are just snug.

29 In two steps, tighten the larger bolts (8 mm), in sequence, to the torque listed in this Chapter's Specifications **(see illustration 16.19b)**. Once these are tightened, tighten the smaller bolts (6 mm) evenly to the specified torque.

30 Turn the main drive shaft and the output shaft to make sure they turn freely. Also make sure the crankshaft turns freely.

31 The remainder of installation is the reverse of removal, with the following additions:
 a) Once the external shift linkage is installed, shift the transmission through all the gear positions and back to Neutral. Because the positive neutral finder locks out second gear when the output shaft isn't spinning, you'll have to spin the output shaft to shift into second through sixth gears.
 b) After the engine is installed, be sure to refill the engine oil and coolant.

17 Balancer shaft and gears - removal and installation

Removal

1 Split the crankcase (see Section 16).

2 If you're only planning to remove the balancer (not the crankshaft), turn the crankshaft until the marks on the balancer and crankshaft gears are aligned **(see illustration)**.

3 Lift the balancer shaft and gear out of the crankcase **(see illustration)**.

4 Refer to Chapter 2C for inspection and bearing selection procedures.

Installation

5 Clean the bearing saddles in the case halves, then install the bearing inserts in their webs in the case (see Chapter 2C). When installing the bearings, use your hands only - don't tap them into place with a hammer.

6 Lubricate the bearing inserts with engine assembly lube or moly-based grease.

7 Carefully lay the balancer in the bearings. Be sure the timing marks on the balancer gear and crankshaft gear align **(see illustration 17.2)**. Incorrect alignment will cause severe engine vibration.

8 The remainder of installation is the reverse of the removal steps.

18 Camshaft chain and guides - removal, inspection and installation

Removal

Camshaft chain

1 Remove the engine (see Section 5).

2 Separate the crankcase halves (see Section 16).

3 Remove the crankshaft (see Chapter 2C).

4 Remove the chain from the crankshaft **(see illustration)**.

Chain guides

5 The cam chain front (exhaust side) guide can be lifted from the cylinder block after the camshafts have been removed **(see illustration)**.

18.4 The crankshaft must be lifted partway out of its bearings to get the timing chain off

18.5 Here are the exhaust side cam chain guide (left arrow) and intake side guide (right arrow)

2B•16 Engine, clutch and transmission - EX250 models

18.6a The upper end of the intake side guide is secured by this pivot - use a new O-ring on installation

18.6b To detach the lower end, remove the pivot bolt (arrow)...

6 The cam chain rear (intake side) guide is fastened to the cylinder head with a pivot bolt and to the crankcase through a linkage. Remove the bolts and take the guide out of the engine **(see illustrations)**.
7 Refer to Chapter 2C for inspection procedures.

Installation
8 Installation of these components is the reverse of the removal procedure. Apply engine oil to the faces of the guides and to the chain.

18.6c ... be sure to reinstall the collar on the pivot bolt - the wide side (arrow) goes toward the engine

19 Transmission shafts - removal and installation

Removal
1 Remove the engine and clutch, then separate the case halves (see Sections 5, 13 and 16).
2 Before removing either shaft, check the backlash of each set of gears. To do this, mount a dial indicator with the plunger of the indicator touching a tooth on one of the gears, then move the gear back and forth within its freeplay, holding its companion gear stationary. Check each set of gears, recording the measurements, and compare the results to the Chapter 2C Specifications. If the backlash between any pair of gears exceeds the limit, replace both gears (see Chapter 2C).
3 The transmission shafts can simply be lifted out of the upper half of the case **(see illustration)**. If they are stuck, use a soft-face hammer and gently tap on the bearings on the ends of the shafts to free them.
4 Refer to Section 20 and Chapter 2C for information pertaining to transmission shaft

19.3a The transmission shafts mesh like this when installed

19.3b Lift out the output shaft, noting the location of its dowel and set ring (arrows)...

Engine, clutch and transmission - EX250 models 2B•17

19.3c ... then lift out the drive shaft, also noting the location of its dowel and set ring (arrows)

19.5 The shift forks and drum are installed in the case like this - note the locations of the dowels and set rings (arrows)

service and Section 21 for information pertaining to the shift drum and forks.

Installation

5 Check to make sure the set pins and rings are present in the upper case half, where the shaft bearings seat **(see illustration)**.
6 Carefully lower each shaft into place. The holes in the needle bearing outer races must engage with the set pins, and the grooves in the ball bearing outer races must engage with the set rings **(see illustrations 19.3a and 19.3b)**.
7 The remainder of installation is the reverse of removal.

20 Transmission shafts - disassembly and reassembly

HAYNES HiNT *When disassembling the transmission shafts, place the parts on a long rod or thread a wire through them*

to keep them in order and facing the proper direction.

1 Remove the shafts from the case (see Section 19).
2 The transmission gears and shafts on these models are basically the same as on the EN450/500. Refer to Chapter 2A for disassembly and reassembly procedures.
3 Refer to Chapter 2C for inspection procedures.

21 Shift drum and forks - removal, inspection and installation

Removal

1 Remove the engine and separate the crankcase halves (see Sections 5 and 16).
2 Remove the shift drum bearing retaining bolts **(see illustration)**.
3 Support the shift forks and pull the shift rods out **(see illustrations)**.
4 Remove the neutral positioning bolt

21.2 Remove the shift fork retainer - on installation, it engages the slot in the fork shaft (arrow) . . .

(see illustrations 16.14a and 16.14b).
5 Pull the shift drum out of the case far enough to remove the shift cam snap-ring

21.3a Note the identifying marks on the forks (arrows) . . .

21.3b . . . then pull out the fork rods and remove the forks - note the locations of the retainer slot and circlip (arrows)

2B•18 Engine, clutch and transmission - EX250 models

21.5a Remove the snap-ring (arrow) from the shift cam . . .

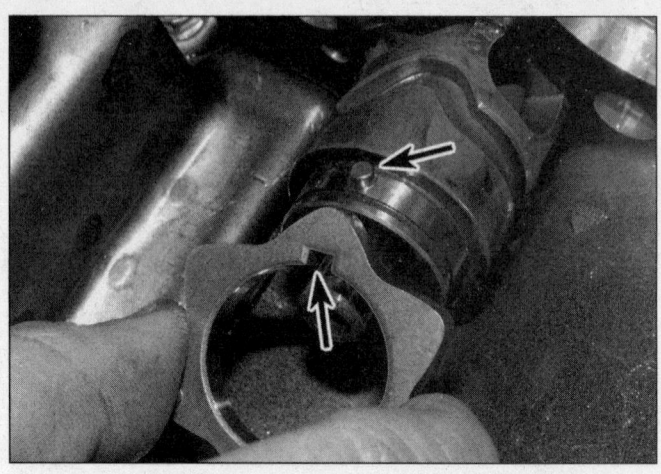

21.5b . . . and remove the shift cam from the shift drum - on installation, align the notch with the pin (arrow)

and shift cam **(see illustrations)**, then lift the shift drum out of the case.

Installation

6 Installation is the reverse of removal, noting the following points:

a) *Install the shift drum part-way into the case and install the shift cam and snap-ring, facing the raised boss on the shift cam away from the shift drum and aligning the notch in the shift cam with the pin on the shift drum* **(see illustration 21.5a)**.

b) *Lubricate all parts with engine oil before installing them.*

c) *Apply a non-permanent locking agent to the threads of the bearing retainer bolts and tighten them securely.*

Chapter 2 Part C
General engine overhaul procedures

Contents

Balancer shaft - inspection	18	External shift mechanism - inspection	13
Camshaft and rocker arms - inspection	6	General information	1
Clutch - inspection	12	Initial start-up after overhaul	22
Clutch housing, crankshaft and main bearings - removal, inspection, main bearing selection and installation	16	Main and connecting rod bearings - general note	15
		Major engine repair - general note	2
Connecting rods and bearings - removal, inspection, bearing selection and installation	17	Oil pressure check	4
		Piston rings - installation	11
Crankcase components - inspection and servicing	14	Pistons - removal, inspection and installation	10
Cylinder block - inspection	9	Primary chain, camshaft chain and guides - inspection	19
Cylinder compression - check	3	Recommended break-in procedure	23
Cylinder head and valves - disassembly, inspection and reassembly	17	Shift drum and forks - inspection	21
		Transmission gears and shafts - inspection	20
Engine disassembly and reassembly - general information	5	Valves/valve seats/valve guides - servicing	7

Degrees of difficulty

Easy, suitable for novice with little experience

Fairly easy, suitable for beginner with some experience

Fairly difficult, suitable for competent DIY mechanic

Difficult, suitable for experienced DIY mechanic

Very difficult, suitable for expert DIY or professional

Specifications

EN450/500 models

Camshaft and rocker arms
Lobe height (intake and exhaust)
  1985 through 1996
    Standard .... 35.635 to 35.761 mm (1.403 to 1.408 inch)
    Minimum .... 35.55 mm (1.40 inch)
  1997 and later
    Standard .... 35.419 to 35.527 mm (1.394 to 1.398 inch)
    Minimum .... 35.32 mm (1.390 inch)
Bearing oil clearance
  Standard .... 0.030 to 0.071 mm (0.001 to 0.003 inch)
  Maximum .... 0.16 mm (0.006 inch)
Journal diameter
  Standard .... 24.950 to 24.970 mm (0.982 to 0.983 inch)
  Minimum .... 24.92 mm (0.981 inch)
Camshaft runout
  Standard .... 0.03 mm (0.001 inch) or less
  Maximum .... 0.1 mm (0.003 inch)
Camshaft chain 20-link length (maximum) .... 128.9 mm (5-5/64 inches)
Rocker arm inside diameter
  Standard .... 12.50 to 12.518 mm (0.492 to 0.493 inch)
  Maximum .... 12.55 mm (0.494 inch)
Rocker shaft diameter
  Standard .... 12.466 to 12.484 mm (0.490 to 0.491 inch)
  Minimum .... 12.44 mm (0.489 inch)

Cylinder head, valves and valve springs

Cylinder head warpage limit .... 0.05 mm (0.002 inch)
Valve stem bend limit .... 0.05 mm (0.002 inch)
Valve stem diameter
   Standard
      Intake .... 5.475 to 5.490 mm (0.2155 to 0.216 inch)
      Exhaust .... 5.455 to 5.470 mm (0.2147 to 0.215 inch)
   Minimum
      Intake .... 5.46 mm (0.2149 inch)
      Exhaust .... 5.44 mm (0.2141 inch)
Valve head thickness
   Standard
      Intake .... 0.5 mm (0.020 inch)
      Exhaust .... 1.0 mm (0.039 inch)
   Minimum
      Intake .... 0.25 mm (0.010 inch)
      Exhaust .... 0.7 mm (0.027 inch)
Valve guide inside diameter (intake and exhaust)
   Standard .... 5.50 to 5.512 mm (0.2165 to 0.2170 inch)
   Maximum .... 5.58 mm (0.2196 inch)
Valve seat width (intake and exhaust) .... 0.5 to 1.0 mm (0.020 to 0.040 in)
Valve spring free length
   Standard
      Inner .... 36.3 mm (1.429 inch)
      Outer .... 40.4 mm (1.59 inch)
   Minimum
      Inner .... 35 mm (1.378 inch)
      Outer .... 39 mm (1.535 inch)

Cylinder block

Bore diameter
   Standard
      EN450 models .... 72.494 to 72.506 mm (2.8540 to 2.8545 inches)
      EN500 models .... 74.0 to 74.012 mm (2.9133 to 2.9138 inches)
   Maximum
      EN450 models .... 72.6 mm (2.858 inches)
      EN500 models .... 74.11 mm (2.9177 inches)
Taper limit .... 0.05 mm (0.002 inch)
Out-of-round limit .... 0.05 mm (0.002 inch)

Pistons

Piston diameter
   Standard .... 73.942 to 73.957 mm (2.9111 to 2.9116 inches)
   Minimum .... 73.79 mm (2.905 inches)
Piston-to-cylinder clearance
   Standard .... 0.044 to 0.070 mm (0.0017 to 0.0027 inch)
   Maximum .... 0.17 mm (0.0066 inch)
Oversize pistons and rings .... + 0.5 mm (+0.020 inch) (one oversize only)
Ring side clearance
   Standard
      Top .... 0.03 to 0.07 mm (0.0017 to 0.0027 inch)
      Second .... 0.02 to 0.06 mm (0.0007 to 0.0023 inch)
   Maximum
      Top .... 0.17 mm (0.0066 inch)
      Second .... 0.16 mm (0.0062 inch)
Ring groove width
   Standard
      Top .... 0.82 to 0.84 mm (0.032 to 0.033 inch)
      Second .... 1.01 to 1.03 mm (0.039 to 0.040 inch)
      Oil .... 2.01 to 2.03 mm (0.079 to 0.080 inch)
   Maximum
      Top .... 0.92 mm (0.036 inch)
      Second .... 1.12 mm (0.044 inch)
      Oil .... 2.11 mm (0.083 inch)
Ring thickness (top and second)
   Standard .... 0.77 to 0.79 mm (0.030 to 0.031 inch)
   Minimum .... 0.7 mm (0.027 inch)

Ring end gap
  Standard
    Top and second .... 0.2 to 0.35 mm (0.008 to 0.013 inch)
    Oil .... 0.2 to 0.7 mm (0.008 to 0.027 inch)
  Maximum
    Top and second .... 0.7 mm (0.027 inch)
    Oil .... 1.0 mm (0.039 inch)

Crankshaft and bearings
Main bearing oil clearance
  Standard .... 0.020 to 0.044 mm (0.0008 to 0.0017 inch)
  Maximum .... 0.08 mm (0.003 inch)
Main bearing journal diameter
  No mark on crank throw .... 35.984 to 35.992 mm (1.4166 to 1.4170 inch)
  "1" mark on crank throw .... 35.993 to 36.000 mm (1.4170 to 1.4173 inch)
Main bearing bore diameter
  No mark on case .... 39.009 to 30.016 mm (1.5357 to 1.5360 inch)
  "0" mark on case .... 39.000 to 39.008 mm (1.5354 to 1.5357 inch)
Crankshaft endplay
  Standard .... 0.05 to 0.25 mm (0.002 to 0.010 inch)
  Maximum .... 0.4 mm (0.016 inch)
Crankshaft runout limit .... 0.05 mm (0.002 inch)
Connecting rod side clearance
  Standard .... 0.13 to 0.33 mm (0.005 to 0.013 inch)
  Maximum .... 0.5 mm (0.019 inch)
Connecting rod bearing oil clearance
  Standard
    Through 1996 (A7) .... 0.036 to 0.066 mm (0.0016 to 0.0025 inch)
    1996 (C1) and later .... 0.043 to 0.073 mm (0.0017 to 0.0029 inch)
  Maximum .... 0.1 mm (0.004 inch)
Connecting rod big-end bore diameter
  No mark on side of rod .... 41.00 to 41.008 mm (1.6141 to 1.6144 inch)
  "0" mark on side of rod .... 41.009 to 41.016 mm (1.6145 to 1.6148 inch)
Connecting rod journal (crank pin) diameter
  No mark on crank throw .... 37.984 to 37.994 mm (1.4954 to 1.4958 inch)
  "0" mark on crank throw .... 37.995 to 38.000 mm (1.4958 to 1.4960 inch)
Connecting rod bend and twist, maximum .... 0.2 mm (0.008 inch) per 100 mm (3.94 inches)
Primary chain 20-link length (maximum) .... 193.4 mm (7-39/64 inches)

Oil pump and relief valve
Oil pressure (warm) .... 2.8 to 3.3 Bars (40 to 48 psi) @ 4000 rpm
Relief valve opening pressure .... 4.3 to 5.9 Bars (63 to 85 psi)
Oil pump clearances
  Outer rotor to body
    Standard .... 0.15 to 0.23 mm (0.006 to 0.009 inch)
    Wear limit .... 0.3 mm (0.012 inch)
  Inner rotor to outer rotor .... Less than 0.2 mm (0.008 inch)

Balancer shaft
Balancer shaft bearing oil clearance
  Standard .... 0.02 to 0.05 mm (0.0008 to 0.0019 inch)
  Maximum .... 0.09 mm (0.0035 inch)
Balancer shaft journal diameter
  No mark on balancer .... 27.987 to 27.993 mm (1.1018 to 1.1020 inch)
  "0" mark on balancer .... 27.994 to 28.00 mm (1.1021 to 1.1023 inch)
Balancer shaft bearing bore diameter
  No mark on case .... 30.014 to 31.025 mm (1.2210 to 1.2214 inch)
  "0" mark on case.. .... 31.000 to 31.013 mm (1.2204 to 1.2210 inch)

Clutch
Spring free length
  Standard .... 34.2 mm (1.346 inch)
  Minimum .... 33.1 mm (1.303 inch)
Friction plate thickness
  Standard .... 2.9 to 3.1 mm (0.114 to 0.122 inch)
  Minimum .... 2.75 mm (0.108 inch)
Friction and steel plate warpage
  Standard .... 0.2 mm (0.008 inch)
  Limit .... 0.3 mm (0.012 inch)

Transmission

Primary drive reduction ratio:
    EN450 models.. 2.952 : 1 (62/21T)
    EN500 models.. 2.652 : 1 (61/23T)
Gear ratios:
    1st gear... 2.571 : 1 (36/14T)
    2nd gear.. 1.777 : 1 (32/18T)
    3rd gear... 1.380 : 1 (29/21T)
    4th gear... 1.125 : 1 (27/24T)
    5th gear... 0.961 : 1 (25/26T)
    6th gear... 0.851 : 1 (23/27T)
Final drive reduction ratio... 2.720 : 1 (68/25T)
Gear backlash
    Standard... 0.02 to 0.19 mm (0.0008 to 0.0074 inch)
    Maximum.. 0.23 mm (0.009 inch)
Shift fork groove width
    Standard... 5.05 to 5.15 mm (0.199 to 0.202 inch)
    Maximum.. 5.3 mm (0.208 inch)
Shift fork ear thickness
    Standard... 4.9 to 5.0 mm (0.193 to 0.197 inch)
    Minimum.. 4.8 mm (0.189 inch)
Shift fork guide pin diameter
    Standard... 7.9 to 8.0 mm (0.311 to 0.315 inch)
    Minimum.. 7.8 mm (0.307 inch)
Shift drum groove width
    Standard... 8.05 to 8.2 mm (0.317 to 0.323 inch)
    Maximum.. 8.3 mm (0.326 inch)

EX250 models

Camshaft and rocker arms

Lobe height (intake and exhaust)
    1986 and 1987
        Standard... 32.229 to 32.370 mm (1.269 to 1.274 inch)
        Minimum.. 32.13 mm (1.265 inch)
    1988 and later
        Standard... 30.53 to 31.67 mm (1.202 to 1.247 inch)
        Minimum.. 30.43 mm (1.198 inch)
Journal diameter
    Standard... 23.950 to 23.970 mm (0.943 to 0.944 inch)
    Maximum.. 23.92 mm (0.942 inch)
Bearing inside diameter
    Standard... 24.000 to 24.021 mm (0.945 to 0.946 inch)
    Minimum.. 24.08 mm (0.948 inch)
Camshaft runout
    Standard... 0.02 mm (0.0008 inch) or less
    Maximum.. 0.1 mm (0.003 inch)
Camshaft chain 20-link length (maximum).. 128.9 mm (5.075 inches)

Cylinder head, valves and valve springs

Cylinder head warpage limit... 0.05 mm (0.002 inch)
Valve stem bend limit .... 0.05 mm (0.002 inch)
Valve stem diameter
    Standard
        Intake... 4.975 to 4.990 mm (0.1958 to 0.1964 inch)
        Exhaust.. 5.455 to 5.470 mm (0.2147 to 0.215 inch)
    Minimum
        Intake... 4.96 mm (0.195 inch)
        Exhaust.. 4.94 mm (0.194 inch)
Valve head thickness
    Standard
        Intake... 0.65 mm (0.026 inch)
        Exhaust
            1986 and 1987... 0.8 mm (0.031 inch)
            1988 and later .... 0.7 mm (0.028 inch)
    Minimum
        Intake... 0.3 mm (0.012 inch)

    Exhaust
        1986 and 1987 .... 0.4 mm (0.016 inch)
        1988 and later .... 0.5 mm (0.020 inch)
Valve guide inside diameter (intake and exhaust)
    Standard .... 5.00 to 5.012 mm (0.196 to 0.197 inch)
    Maximum .... 5.08 mm (0.2196 inch)
Valve seat width (intake and exhaust) .... 0.5 to 1.0 mm (0.020 to 0.040 in)
Valve spring free length
    1986 and 1987
        Standard
            Inner .... 31.8 mm (1.251 inch)
            Outer .... 36.4 mm (1.433 inch)
        Minimum
            Inner .... 30.1 mm (1.185 inch)
            Outer .... 34.9 mm (1.374 inch)
    1988 and later
        Standard
            Inner .... 30.7 mm (1.209 inch)
            Outer .... 35.0 mm (1.378 inch)
        Minimum
            Inner .... 29.1 mm (1.146 inch)
            Outer .... 33.4 mm (1.315 inch)

Cylinder block
Bore diameter
    Standard .... 62.000 to 62.012 mm (2.4409 to 2.4414 inches)
    Maximum .... 62.10 mm (2.4448 inches)
Taper limit .... 0.05 mm (0.002 inch)
Out-of-round limit .... 0.05 mm (0.002 inch)

Pistons
Piston diameter
    Standard .... 61.942 to 61.957 mm (2.4386 to 2.4392 inches)
    Minimum .... 61.80 mm (2.433 inches)
Piston-to-cylinder clearance
    Standard .... 0.044 to 0.070 mm (0.0017 to 0.0027 inch)
    Maximum .... Not specified
Oversize pistons and rings .... + 0.5 mm (+0.020 inch) (one oversize only)
Ring side clearance (1986 and 1987)
    Standard (top and second) .... 0.02 to 0.06 mm (0.0007 to 0.0023 inch)
    Maximum (top and second) .... 0.16 mm (0.0062 inch)
Ring side clearance (1988 and later)
    Standard
        Top .... 0.03 to 0.07 mm (0.0017 to 0.0027 inch)
        Second .... 0.02 to 0.06 mm (0.0007 to 0.0023 inch)
    Maximum
        Top .... 0.17 mm (0.0066 inch)
        Second .... 0.16 mm (0.0062 inch)
Ring groove width (1986 and 1987)
    Standard
        Top and second .... 0.81 to 0.83 mm (0.031 to 0.032 inch)
        Oil .... 2.01 to 2.03 mm (0.079 to 0.080 inch)
    Maximum
        Top and second .... 0.91 mm (0.035 inch)
        Oil .... 2.11 mm (0.083 inch)
Ring groove width (1988 and later)
    Standard
        Top .... 0.82 to 0.84 mm (0.032 to 0.033 inch)
        Second .... 1.01 to 1.03 mm (0.039 to 0.040 inch)
        Oil .... 2.01 to 2.03 mm (0.079 to 0.080 inch)
    Maximum
        Top .... 0.92 mm (0.036 inch)
        Second .... 1.12 mm (0.044 inch)
        Oil .... 2.11 mm (0.083 inch)
Ring thickness (top and second)
    Standard .... 0.77 to 0.79 mm (0.030 to 0.031 inch)
    Minimum .... 0.7 mm (0.027 inch)

Pistons (continued)

Ring end gap
  Standard
    Top and second .... 0.30 to 0.45 mm (0.012 to 0.018 inch)
    Oil
      1986 and 1987 .... 0.2 to 0.8 mm (0.008 to 0.031 inch)
      1988 and later .... Not specified
  Maximum
    Top and second .... 0.7 mm (0.027 inch)
    Oil
      1986 and 1987 .... 1.10 mm (0.043 inch)
      1988 and later .... Not specified

Crankshaft and bearings

Main bearing oil clearance
  Standard .... 0.014 to 0.038 mm (0.0006 to 0.0015 inch)
  Maximum .... 0.08 mm (0.003 inch)
Main bearing journal diameter
  No mark on crank throw .... 29.984 to 29.992 mm (1.1807 to 1.1808 inch)
  "1" mark on crank throw .... 29.993 to 30.000 mm (1.1808 to 1.1811 inch)
Main bearing bore diameter
  No mark on case .... 33.009 to 33.016 mm (1.2995 to 1.2998 inch)
  "0" mark on case .... 33.000 to 33.008 mm (1.2992 to 1.2995 inch)
Crankshaft endplay
  Standard .... 0.05 to 0.20 mm (0.002 to 0.008 inch)
  Maximum .... 0.4 mm (0.016 inch)
Crankshaft runout limit .... 0.05 mm (0.002 inch)
Connecting rod side clearance
  Standard .... 0.13 to 0.38 mm (0.005 to 0.015 inch)
  Maximum .... 0.5 mm (0.019 inch)
Connecting rod bearing oil clearance
  Standard .... 0.031 to 0.059 mm (0.0012 to 0.0023 inch)
  Maximum .... 0.1 mm (0.004 inch)
Connecting rod big-end bore diameter
  No mark on side of rod .... 36.00 to 36.008 mm (1.417 to 1.418 inch)
  "0" mark on side of rod .... 36.009 to 36.016 mm (1.4176 to 1.4179 inch)
Connecting rod journal (crank pin) diameter
  No mark on crank throw .... 32.984 to 32.992 mm (1.2985 to 1.2989 inch)
  "0" mark on crank throw .... 32.993 to 33.000 mm (1.2989 to 1.2992 inch)
Connecting rod bend and twist, maximum .... 0.2 mm (0.008 inch) per 100 mm (3.94 inches)

Oil pump and relief valve

Oil pressure (warm) .... 3.43 Bars (49.8 psi) @ 4000 rpm
Relief valve opening pressure .... Not specified
Oil pump clearances .... Not specified

Balancer shaft

Balancer shaft bearing oil clearance
  Standard .... 0.020 to 0.044 mm (0.0008 to 0.0017 inch)
  Maximum .... 0.08 mm (0.0031 inch)
Balancer shaft journal diameter
  No mark on balancer .... 25.984 to 26.000 mm (1.0229 to 1.0236 inch)
  "0" mark on balancer .... 25.993 to 26.00 mm (1.0233 to 1.0236 inch)
Balancer shaft bearing bore diameter
  No mark on case .... 29.000 to 29.008 mm (1.1417 to 1.1420 inch)
  "0" mark on case.. .... 29.009 to 29.016 mm (1.1421 to 1.1423 inch)

Clutch

Spring free length
  Standard .... 32.6 mm (1.283 inch)
  Minimum .... 31.7 mm (1.248 inch)
Friction plate thickness
  Standard .... 2.9 to 3.1 mm (0.114 to 0.122 inch)
  Minimum .... 2.8 mm (0.110 inch)
Friction and steel plate warpage
  Standard .... 0.2 mm (0.008 inch)
  Limit .... 0.3 mm (0.012 inch)

Transmission

Gear backlash
- Standard .... 0.0 to 0.17 mm (0.0 to 0.0066 inch)
- Maximum .... 0.25 mm (0.010 inch)

Shift fork groove width
- Standard .... 5.05 to 5.15 mm (0.199 to 0.202 inch)
- Maximum .... 5.3 mm (0.208 inch)

Shift fork ear thickness
- Standard .... 4.9 to 5.0 mm (0.193 to 0.197 inch)
- Minimum .... 4.8 mm (0.189 inch)

Shift fork guide pin diameter
- Standard .... 5.9 to 6.0 mm (0.232 to 0.236 inch)
- Minimum .... 5.8 mm (0.228 inch)

Shift drum groove width
- Standard .... 6.05 to 6.2 mm (0.238 to 0.244 inch)
- Maximum .... 6.3 mm (0.248 inch)

1 General information

Included in this portion of Chapter 2 are general inspection and overhaul procedures. The information includes advice concerning preparation for an overhaul and the purchase of replacement parts, as well as inspection procedures which will tell you if a part must be reconditioned or replaced.

The Specifications included in this Part are only those necessary for the inspection and overhaul procedures which follow. Refer to earlier parts of Chapter 2 for additional Specifications.

2 Major engine repair - general note

1 It is not always easy to determine when or if an engine should be completely overhauled, as a number of factors must be considered.

2 High mileage is not necessarily an indication that an overhaul is needed, while low mileage, on the other hand, does not preclude the need for an overhaul. Frequency of servicing is probably the single most important consideration. An engine that has regular and frequent oil and filter changes, as well as other required maintenance, will most likely give many miles of reliable service. Conversely, a neglected engine, or one which has not been broken in properly, may require an overhaul very early in its life.

3 Exhaust smoke and excessive oil consumption are both indications that piston rings and/or valve guides are in need of attention. Make sure oil leaks are not responsible before deciding that the rings and guides are bad. Refer to Section 3 and perform a cylinder compression check to determine for certain the nature and extent of the work required.

4 If the engine is making obvious knocking or rumbling noises, the connecting rod and/or main bearings are probably at fault.

5 Loss of power, rough running, excessive valve train noise and high fuel consumption rates may also point to the need for an overhaul, especially if they are all present at the same time. If a complete tune-up does not remedy the situation, major mechanical work is the only solution.

6 An engine overhaul generally involves restoring the internal parts to the specifications of a new engine. During an overhaul the piston rings are replaced and the cylinder walls are bored and/or honed. If a rebore is done, then a new piston is also required. Crankshaft, connecting rod and balancer bearings are usually replaced, with thicker inserts if necessary to restore bearing clearances to specified limits. Generally the valves are serviced as well, since they are usually in less than perfect condition at this point. While the engine is being overhauled, other components such as the carburetor and the starter motor can be rebuilt also. The end result should be a like-new engine that will give as many trouble-free miles as the original.

7 Before beginning the engine overhaul, read through all of the related procedures to familiarize yourself with the scope and requirements of the job. Overhauling an engine is not all that difficult, but it is time consuming. Plan on the vehicle being tied up for a minimum of two (2) weeks. Check on the availability of parts and make sure that any necessary special tools, equipment and supplies are obtained in advance.

8 Most work can be done with typical shop hand tools, although a number of precision measuring tools are required for inspecting parts to determine if they must be replaced. Use of precision measuring equipment is described in the *Tools and Workshop Tips* section at the end of this manual. Often a dealer service department or repair shop will handle the inspection of parts and offer advice concerning reconditioning and replacement. As a general rule, time is the primary cost of an overhaul so it doesn't pay to install worn or substandard parts.

9 As a final note, to ensure maximum life and minimum trouble from a rebuilt engine, everything must be assembled with care in a spotlessly clean environment.

3 Cylinder compression - check

Refer to illustration 3.5

1 Among other things, poor engine performance may be caused by leaking valves, incorrect valve clearances, a leaking head gasket, or worn pistons, rings and/or cylinder walls. A cylinder compression check will help pinpoint these conditions and can also indicate the presence of excessive carbon deposits in the cylinder heads.

2 The only tools required are a compression gauge and a spark plug wrench. Depending on the outcome of the initial test, a squirt-type oil can may also be needed.

3 Run the engine until it reaches normal operating temperature. Place the motorcycle on the centerstand, remove the fuel tank,

2C•8 General engine overhaul procedures

3.5 A compression gauge with a threaded fitting for the spark plug holes is preferred over the type that requires hand pressure to maintain a seal

4.2a To check the oil pressure, remove the plug (arrow) and connect an oil pressure gauge using the proper adapter (EN450/500) . . .

4.2b . . . and here's the EX250 check point

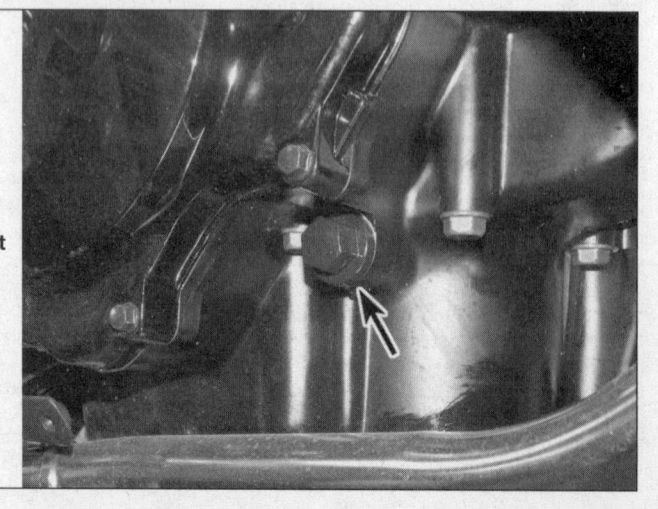

then remove the spark plugs (see Chapter 1, if necessary). Work carefully - don't strip the spark plug hole threads and don't burn your hands.

4 Disable the ignition by unplugging the primary wires from the coils (see Chapter 5). Be sure to mark the locations of the wires before detaching them.

5 Install the compression gauge in one of the spark plug holes **(see illustration)**. Hold or block the throttle wide open.

6 Crank the engine over a minimum of four or five revolutions (or until the gauge reading stops increasing) and observe the initial movement of the compression gauge needle as well as the final total gauge reading. Repeat the procedure for the other cylinder and compare the results to the value listed in this Chapter's Specifications.

7 If the compression in both cylinders built up quickly and evenly to the specified amount, you can assume the engine upper end is in reasonably good mechanical condition. Worn or sticking piston rings and worn cylinders will produce very little initial movement of the gauge needle, but compression will tend to build up gradually as the engine spins over. Valve and valve seat leakage, or head gasket leakage, is indicated by low initial compression which does not tend to build up.

8 To further confirm your findings, add a small amount of engine oil to each cylinder by inserting the nozzle of a squirt-type oil can through the spark plug holes. The oil will tend to seal the piston rings if they are leaking. Repeat the test for the other cylinder.

9 If the compression increases significantly after the addition of the oil, the piston rings and/or cylinders are definitely worn. If the compression does not increase, the pressure is leaking past the valves or the head gasket. Leakage past the valves may be due to insufficient valve clearances, burned, warped or cracked valves or valve seats, or valves that are hanging up in the guides.

10 If compression readings are considerably higher than specified, the combustion chambers are probably coated with excessive carbon deposits. It is possible (but not very likely) for carbon deposits to raise the compression enough to compensate for the effects of leakage past rings or valves. Remove the cylinder head and carefully decarbonize the combustion chambers (see Chapter 2A or 2B).

4 Oil pressure check

Warning: If the oil passage plug is removed when the engine is hot, hot oil will drain out - wait until the engine is cold before beginning this check (it must be cold to perform the relief valve opening pressure check, anyway).

1 Remove the right footpeg (see Chapter 8).

2 Remove the plug at the bottom of the crankcase on the right-hand side and install an oil pressure gauge **(see illustrations)**.

3 Start the engine and watch the gauge while varying the engine rpm. The pressure should stay within the relief valve opening pressure listed in this Chapter's Specifications. If the pressure is too high, the relief valve is stuck closed. To check it, see Chapter 2A or 2B.

4 If the pressure is lower than the standard, either the relief valve is stuck open, the oil pump is faulty, or there is other engine damage. Begin diagnosis by checking the relief valve (see chapter 2A or 2B), then the oil pump. If those items check out okay, chances are the bearing oil clearances are excessive and the engine needs to be overhauled.

5 If the pressure reading is in the desired range, allow the engine to warm up to normal operating temperature and check the pressure again, at the specified engine rpm. Compare your findings with this Chapter's Specifications.

6 If the pressure is significantly lower than specified, check the relief valve and the oil pump.

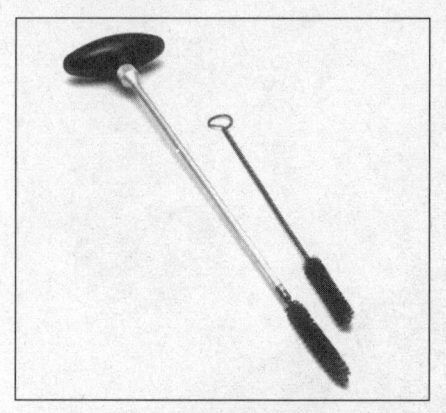

General engine overhaul procedures 2C•9

5.2 A selection of brushes is required for cleaning holes and passages in the engine components

5.3 An engine stand can be made from short lengths of 2 x 4 lumber and lag bolts or nails

5 Engine disassembly and reassembly - general information

1 Before disassembling the engine, clean the exterior with a degreaser and rinse it with water. A clean engine will make the job easier and prevent the possibility of getting dirt into the internal areas of the engine.

2 In addition to the precision measuring tools mentioned earlier, you will need a torque wrench, a valve spring compressor, oil gallery brushes (see illustration), a piston ring removal and installation tool, a piston ring compressor, a pin-type spanner wrench and a clutch holder tool (which is described in Chapter 2A). Some new, clean engine oil of the correct grade and type, some engine assembly lube (or moly-based grease), a tube of Kawasaki Bond liquid gasket (part no. 92104-1003) or equivalent, and a tube of RTV (silicone) sealant will also be required. Although it may not be considered a tool, some Plastigage (type HPG-1) should also be obtained to use for checking bearing oil clearances. Note: *Plastigage use is described in the* Tools and Workshop Tips *section at the end of this manual.*

3 An engine support stand made from short lengths of 2 x 4's bolted together will facilitate the disassembly and reassembly procedures (see illustration). The perimeter of the mount should be just big enough to accommodate the engine oil pan. If you have an automotive-type engine stand, an adapter plate can be made from a piece of plate, some angle iron and some nuts and bolts.

4 When disassembling the engine, keep "mated" parts together (including gears, cylinders, pistons, etc. that have been in contact with each other during engine operation). These "mated" parts must be reused or replaced as an assembly.

5 Engine/transmission disassembly should be done in the following general order with reference to the appropriate Sections.

Remove the cylinder head
Remove the cylinder block
Remove the pistons
Remove the clutch
Remove the oil pan
Remove the external shift mechanism
Remove the alternator rotor/stator coils and starter clutch (see Chapter 9)
Separate the crankcase halves
Remove the crankshaft and connecting rods
Remove the balancer shaft and gears
Remove the transmission shafts/gears
Remove the shift drum/forks

6 Reassembly is accomplished by reversing the general disassembly sequence.

6 Camshaft and rocker arms - inspection

HAYNES HiNT *Before replacing camshafts or the cylinder head and bearing caps because of damage, check with local machine shops specializing in motorcycle engine work. In the case of the camshafts, it may be possible for cam lobes to be welded, reground and hardened, at a cost far lower than that of a new camshaft. If the bearing surfaces in the cylinder head are damaged, it may be possible for them to be bored out to accept bearing inserts. Due to the cost of a new cylinder head it is recommended that all options be explored before condemning it as trash!*

Camshafts

1 Inspect the cam bearing surfaces of the head and the bearing caps. Look for score marks, deep scratches and evidence of spalling (a pitted appearance).

2 Check the camshaft lobes for heat discoloration (blue appearance), score marks, chipped areas, flat spots and spalling (see illustration). Measure the height of each lobe with a micrometer (see illustration) and compare the results to the minimum lobe height listed in this Chapter's Specifications. If damage is noted or wear is excessive, the camshaft must be replaced.

3 Next, check the camshaft bearing oil clearances with Plastigage, referring to the *Tools and Workshop Tips* section at the end of this manual. Clean the camshafts, the bearing surfaces in the cylinder head and the bearing caps with a clean, lint-free cloth, then lay the cams in place in the cylinder head, with the cam timing marks positioned correctly for camshaft installation (see Chapter 2A or 2B). Engage the cam chain with the cam gears, so the camshafts don't turn as the bearing caps are tightened.

4 Cut eight strips of Plastigage (type HPG-1) and lay one piece on each bearing

6.2a Check the lobes of the camshaft for wear - here's a good example of damage which will require replacement (or repair) of the camshaft

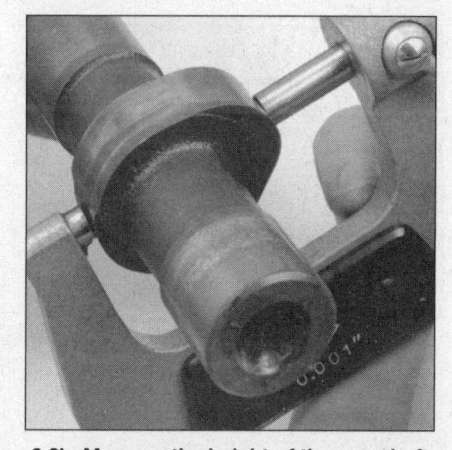

6.2b Measure the height of the camshaft lobes with a micrometer

2C•10 General engine overhaul procedures

6.7 Measure the cam bearing journals with a micrometer

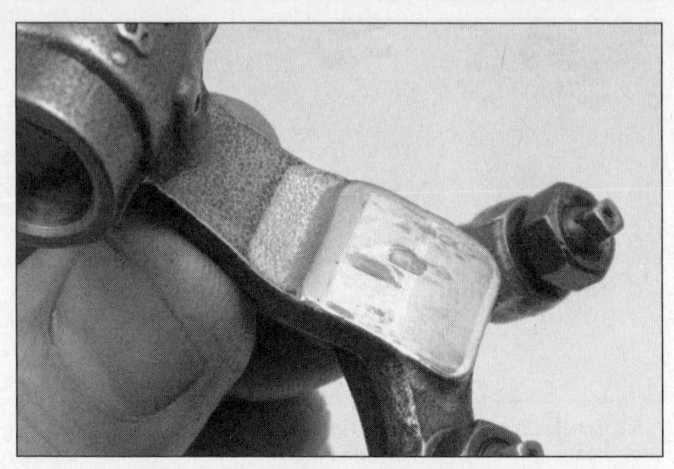

6.11 Inspect the rocker arms, especially the faces that contact the cam lobes, for wear

journal, parallel with the camshaft centerline.
5   Install the camshaft bearing caps, referring to Chapter 2A or 2B for the correct sequence and tightening torque.
6   Now unscrew the bearing cap bolts, a little at a time, and carefully lift off the bearing caps.
7   Refer to the *Tools and Workshop Tips* section at the end of this manual for instructions on how to read the bearing clearance when using Plastigage. Compare the results to this Chapter's Specifications. If the oil clearance is greater than specified, measure the diameter of the cam bearing journal with a micrometer **(see illustration)**. If the journal diameter is less than the specified limit, replace the camshaft with a new one and recheck the clearance. If the clearance is still too great, replace the cylinder head and bearing caps with new parts (see the Haynes Hint that precedes Step 1). Remove all traces of Plastigage from the components without scratching their surfaces.
8   Except in cases of oil starvation, the camshaft chain wears very little. If the chain has stretched excessively, which makes it difficult to maintain proper tension, replace it with a new one (see Chapter 2A or 2B).

9   Check the sprockets for wear, cracks and other damage, replacing them if necessary. If the sprockets are worn, the chain is also worn, and also the sprocket on the crankshaft (which can only be remedied by replacing the crankshaft). If wear this severe is apparent, the entire engine should be disassembled for inspection.
10   Check the chain guides for wear or damage. If they are worn or damaged, the chain is worn out or improperly adjusted. Refer to Chapter 2A or 2B for guide replacement procedures.

Rocker arms

11   Clean all of the rocker arm components with solvent and dry them off. Blow through the oil passages in the rocker arms with compressed air, if available. Inspect the rocker arm faces for pits, spalling, score marks and rough spots **(see illustration)**. If the faces of the rocker arms are damaged, the rocker arms and the camshafts should be replaced as a set.
12   Check the adjusting screws for wear or damage. If you're working on an EN450/500, check the rocker arm-to-shaft contact areas as well. Look for cracks in each rocker arm.

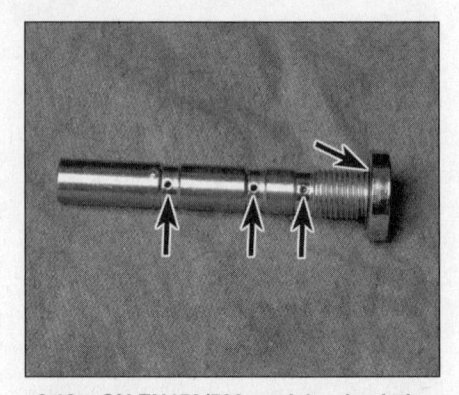

6.12a ON EN450/500 models, check the rocker shaft for wear, make sure the oil holes (lower arrows) are clear and inspect the O-ring under the head (upper arrow); it's a good idea to replace the O-ring whenever the shaft is removed

Measure the diameter of the rocker arm shafts, in the area where the rocker arms ride, and compare the results with this Chapter's Specifications. Also measure the inside diameter of the rocker arms **(see illustrations)** and compare the results with this

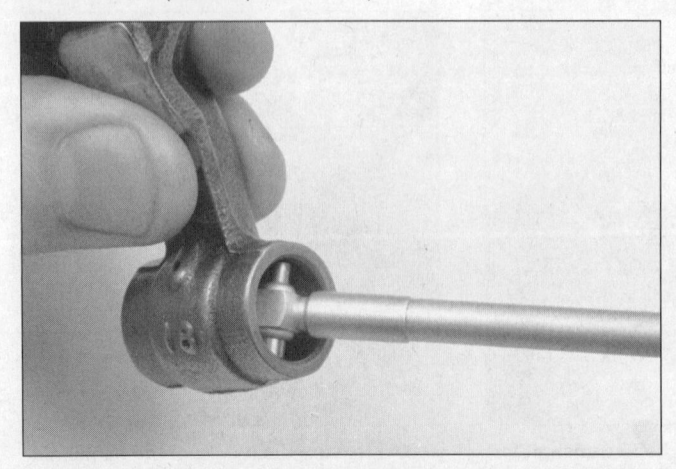

6.12b Measure the inside diameter of the rocker arm - in this case a telescoping gauge is expanded against the bore of the rocker arm, then locked ...

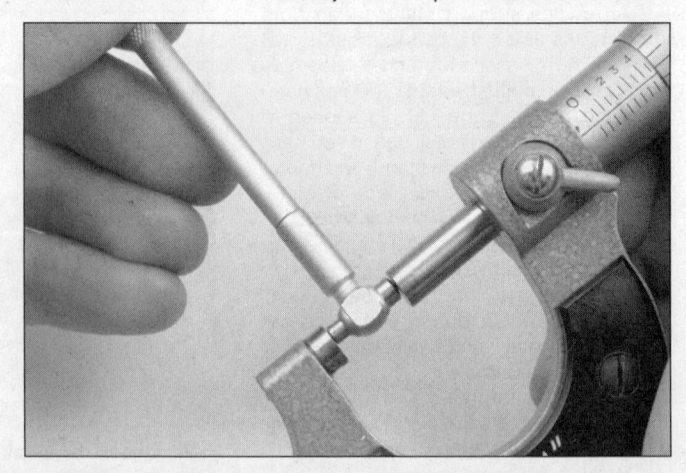

6.12c ... and a micrometer is used to measure the gauge

General engine overhaul procedures 2C•11

8.7a Compress the valve springs with a valve spring compressor

8.7b Remove the valve keepers/collets with needle-nose pliers or tweezers

Chapter's Specifications. If either the shaft or the rocker arms are worn beyond the specified limits, replace them as a set.

13 If you're working on an EN450/500, replace the O-ring under the head of the rocker arm shaft.

7 Valves/valve seats/valve guides - servicing

1 Because of the complex nature of this job and the special tools and equipment required, servicing of the valves, the valve seats and the valve guides (commonly known as a valve job) is best left to a professional.

2 The home mechanic can, however, remove and disassemble the head, do the initial cleaning and inspection, then reassemble and deliver the head to a dealer service department or properly equipped motorcycle repair shop for the actual valve servicing. Refer to Section 8 for those procedures.

3 The dealer service department will remove the valves and springs, recondition or replace the valves and valve seats, replace the valve guides, check and replace the valve springs, spring retainers and keepers (as necessary), replace the valve seals with new ones and reassemble the valve components.

4 After the valve job has been performed, the head will be in like-new condition. When the head is returned, be sure to clean it again very thoroughly before installation on the engine to remove any metal particles or abrasive grit that may still be present from the valve service operations. Use compressed air, if available, to blow out all the holes and passages.

8 Cylinder head and valves - disassembly, inspection and reassembly

1 As mentioned in the previous Section, valve servicing and valve guide replacement should be left to a dealer service department or motorcycle repair shop. However, disassembly, cleaning and inspection of the valves and related components can be done (if the necessary special tools are available) by the home mechanic. This way no expense is incurred if the inspection reveals that service work is not required at this time.

2 To properly disassemble the valve components without the risk of damaging them, a valve spring compressor is absolutely necessary. This special tool can usually be rented/hired, but if it's not available, have a dealer service department or motorcycle repair shop handle the entire process of disassembly, inspection, service or repair (if required) and reassembly of the valves.

Disassembly

3 Remove the rocker arm shafts and rocker arms (see Chapter 2A or 2B). Store the components in such a way that they can be returned to their original locations without getting mixed up (labeled plastic bags work well).

4 Before the valves are removed, scrape away any traces of gasket material from the head gasket sealing surface. Work slowly and do not nick or gouge the soft aluminum of the head.

HAYNES HINT *Instructions for using gasket remover can be found in the Tool and Workshop Tips section at the end of the manual.*

5 Carefully scrape all carbon deposits out of the combustion chamber area. A hand held wire brush or a piece of fine emery cloth can be used once the majority of deposits have been scraped away. Do not use a wire brush mounted in a drill motor, or one with extremely stiff bristles, as the head material is soft and may be eroded away or scratched by the wire brush.

6 Before proceeding, arrange to label and store the valves along with their related components so they can be kept separate and reinstalled in the same valve guides they are removed from (again, plastic bags work well for this).

7 Compress the valve spring on the first valve with a spring compressor, then remove the keepers/collets (see illustrations) and the retainer from the valve assembly. Do not compress the springs any more than is absolutely necessary. Carefully release the valve spring compressor and remove the springs and the valve from the head. If the valve binds in the guide (won't pull through), push it back into the head and deburr the area around the keeper/collet groove with a very fine file or whetstone.

8 Repeat the procedure for the remaining valves. Remember to keep the parts for each valve together so they can be reinstalled in the same location.

9 Once the valves have been removed and labeled, pull off the valve stem seals with pliers and discard them (the old seals should never be reused), then remove the spring seats.

10 Next, clean the cylinder head with solvent and dry it thoroughly. Compressed air will speed the drying process and ensure that all holes and recessed areas are clean.

11 Clean all of the valve springs, keepers/collets, retainers and spring seats with solvent and dry them thoroughly. Do the parts from one valve at a time so that no mixing of parts between valves occurs.

12 Scrape off any deposits that may have formed on the valve, then use a motorized wire brush to remove deposits from the valve heads and stems. Again, make sure the valves do not get mixed up.

Inspection

13 Inspect the head very carefully for cracks and other damage. If cracks are found, a new head will be required. Check the cam bearing surfaces for wear and evidence of seizure. Check the camshafts and rocker arms for wear as well (see Section 6).

14 Using a precision straightedge and a feeler gauge, check the head gasket mating surface for warpage. Lay the straightedge lengthwise, across the head and diagonally (corner-to-corner), intersecting the head bolt holes, and try to slip a 0.002 in (0.05 mm) feeler gauge under it, on either side of each

2C•12 General engine overhaul procedures

8.14 Lay a precision straightedge across the cylinder head and try to slide a feeler gauge of the specified thickness (equal to the maximum allowable warpage) under it

8.15 Measuring the valve seat width

combustion chamber **(see illustration)**. If the feeler gauge can be inserted between the head and the straightedge, the head is warped and must either be machined or, if warpage is excessive, replaced with a new one.

15 Examine the valve seats in each of the combustion chambers. If they are pitted, cracked or burned, the head will require valve service that is beyond the scope of the home mechanic. Measure the valve seat width **(see illustration)** and compare it to this Chapter's Specifications. If it is not within the specified range, or if it varies around its circumference, valve service work is required.

16 Clean the valve guides to remove any carbon buildup, then measure the inside diameters of the guides (at both ends and the center of the guide) with a small hole gauge and a 0-to-1-inch micrometer **(see illustrations)**. If the guides exceed the maximum value given in the Chapter's Specifications, they must be replaced. The guides are measured at the ends and at the center to determine if they are worn in a bell-mouth pattern (more wear at the ends). If they are, guide replacement is an absolute must.

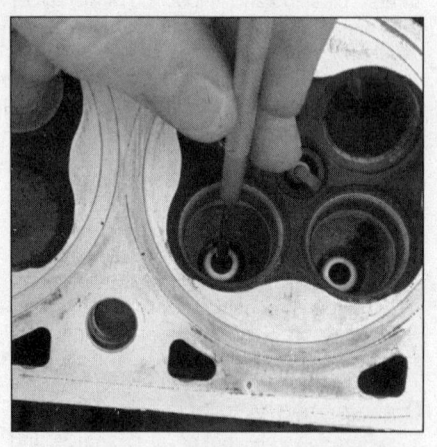

8.16a Insert a small hole gauge into the valve guide and expand it so there's a slight drag when it's pulled out

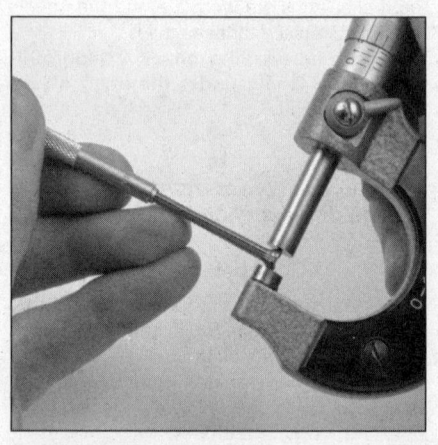

8.16b Measure the small hole gauge with a micrometer

17 Carefully inspect each valve face for cracks, pits and burned spots. Check the valve stem and the keeper/collet groove area for cracks **(see illustration)**. Rotate the valve and check for any obvious indication that it is bent. Check the end of the stem for pitting and excessive wear. The presence of any of the above conditions indicates the need for valve servicing.

18 Measure the valve stem diameter and replace if it exceeds the minimum value listed in this Chapter's Specifications **(see illustration)**. Also check the valve stem for bending.

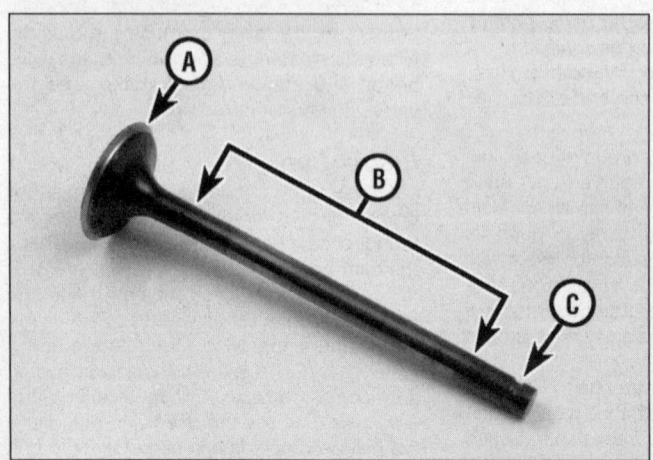

8.17 Check the valve face (A), stem (B) and keeper groove (C) for signs of wear and damage

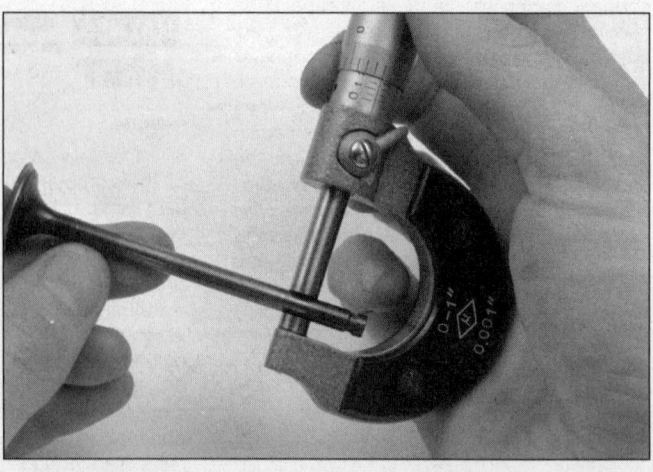

8.18 Measure the valve stem diameter with a micrometer

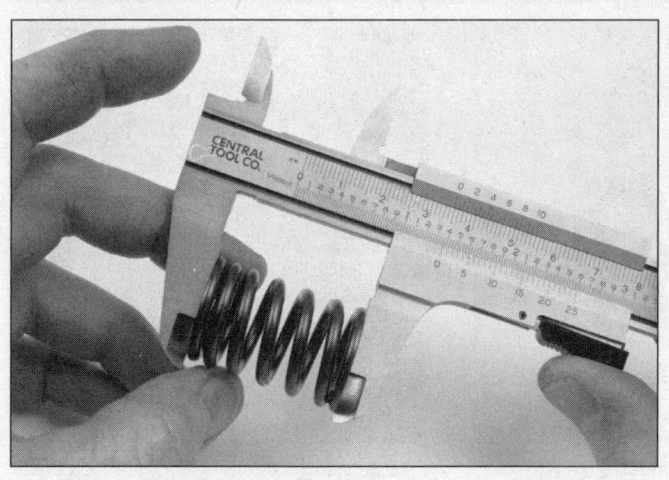

General engine overhaul procedures 2C•13

8.19a Measure the free length of the valve springs

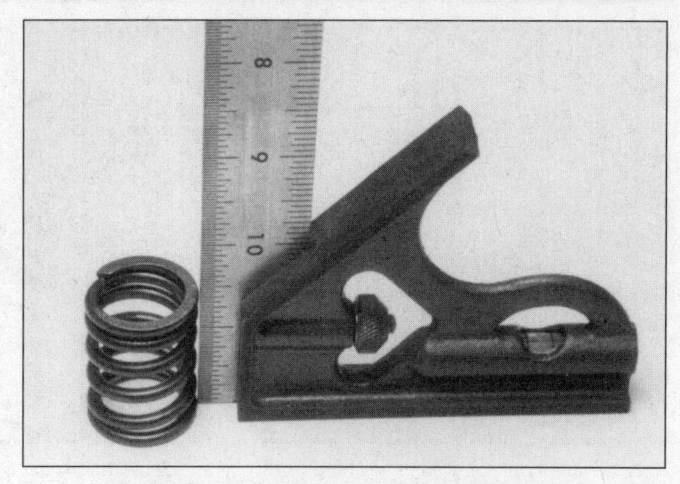

8.19b Check the valve springs for squareness

Set the valve in a V-block with a dial indicator touching the middle of the stem. Rotate the valve and note the reading on the gauge. If the stem runout exceeds the value listed in this Chapter's Specifications, replace the valve.

19   Check the end of each valve spring for wear and pitting. Measure the free length **(see illustration)** and compare it to this Chapter's Specifications. Any springs that are shorter than specified have sagged and should not be reused. Stand the spring on a flat surface and check it for squareness **(see illustration)**.

20   Check the spring retainers and keepers/collets for obvious wear and cracks. Any questionable parts should not be reused, as extensive damage will occur in the event of failure during engine operation.

21   If the inspection indicates that no service work is required, the valve components can be reinstalled in the head.

Reassembly

22   Before installing the valves in the head, they should be lapped to ensure a positive seal between the valves and seats. This procedure requires fine valve lapping compound (available at auto parts stores) and a valve lapping tool. If a lapping tool is not available, a piece of rubber or plastic hose can be slipped over the valve stem (after the valve has been installed in the guide) and used to turn the valve.

23   Apply a small amount of fine lapping compound to the valve face **(see illustration)**, then slip the valve into the guide. **Note:** *Make sure the valve is installed in the correct guide and be careful not to get any lapping compound on the valve stem.*

24   Attach the lapping tool (or hose) to the valve and rotate the tool between the palms of your hands. Use a back-and-forth motion rather than a circular motion **(see illustration)**. Lift the valve off the seat and turn it at regular intervals to distribute the lapping compound properly. Continue the lapping procedure until the valve face and seat contact area is of uniform width and unbroken around the entire circumference of the valve face and seat **(see illustrations)**.

25   Carefully remove the valve from the guide and wipe off all traces of lapping compound. Use solvent to clean the valve and wipe the seat area thoroughly with a solvent soaked cloth. Repeat the procedure for the remaining valves.

26   Lay the spring seats in place in the cylinder head, then install new valve stem seals on each of the guides. Use an appropriate

8.23 Apply the lapping compound very sparingly, in small dabs, to the valve face only

8.24a A hose, pushed over the end of the valve, can be used to turn the valve back and forth

8.24b After lapping, the valve face should exhibit a uniform, unbroken contact pattern (arrow) . . .

8.24c . . . and the seat should be the specified width (arrow) with a smooth, unbroken appearance

2C•14 General engine overhaul procedures

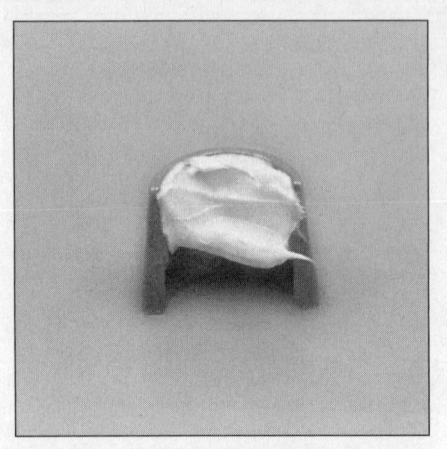

8.27 A small dab of grease will help hold the collets in place on the valve spring while the valve is released

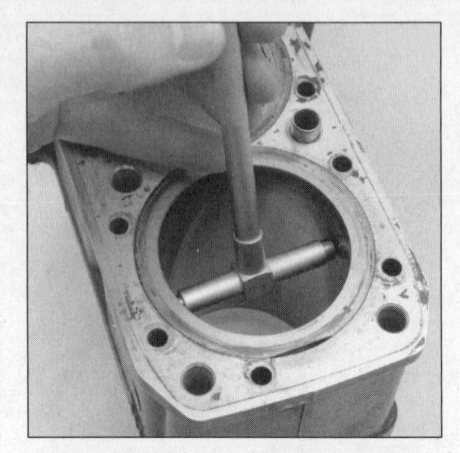

9.2 Measure the cylinder bore with a telescoping gauge (then measure the gauge with a micrometer)

10.3 Using a sharp scribe, scratch the cylinder numbers into the piston crowns - also note the arrow, which must point to the front

size deep socket to push the seals into place until they are properly seated. Don't twist or cock them, or they will not seal properly against the valve stems. Also, don't remove them again or they will be damaged.

27 Coat the valve stems with assembly lube or moly-based grease, then install one of them into its guide. Next, install the spring seats, springs and retainers, compress the springs and install the keepers/collets. **Note:** *Install the springs with the tightly wound coils at the bottom (next to the spring seat).* When compressing the springs with the valve spring compressor, depress them only as far as is absolutely necessary to slip the keepers/collets into place. Apply a small amount of grease to the keepers/collets **(see illustration)** to help hold them in place as the pressure is released from the springs. Make certain that the keepers/collets are securely locked in their retaining grooves.

28 Support the cylinder head on blocks so the valves can't contact the workbench top, then very gently tap each of the valve stems with a soft-faced hammer. This will help seat the keepers/collets in their grooves.

29 Once all of the valves have been installed in the head, check for proper valve sealing by pouring a small amount of solvent into each of the valve ports. If the solvent leaks past the valve(s) into the combustion chamber area, disassemble the valve(s) and repeat the lapping procedure, then reinstall the valve(s) and repeat the check. Repeat the procedure until a satisfactory seal is obtained.

9 Cylinder block - inspection

Caution: *Don't attempt to separate the liners from the cylinder block.*

1 Check the cylinder walls carefully for scratches and score marks.

2 Using the appropriate precision measuring tools, check each cylinder's diameter near the top, center and bottom of the cylinder bore, parallel to the crankshaft axis **(see illustration)**. Next, measure each cylinder's diameter at the same three locations across the crankshaft axis. Compare the results to this Chapter's Specifications. If the cylinder walls are tapered, out-of-round, worn beyond the specified limits, or badly scuffed or scored, have them rebored and honed by a dealer service department or a motorcycle repair shop. If a rebore is done, oversize pistons and rings will be required as well. **Note:** *Kawasaki supplies pistons in one oversize only - +0.020 inch (+0.5 mm).*

3 As an alternative, if the precision measuring tools are not available, a dealer service department or motorcycle repair shop will make the measurements and offer advice concerning servicing of the cylinders.

4 If they are in reasonably good condition and not worn to the outside of the limits, and if the piston-to-cylinder clearances can be maintained properly (see Section 10), then the cylinders do not have to be rebored; honing is all that is necessary.

5 To perform the honing operation you will need the proper size flexible hone with fine stones, or a "bottle brush" type hone, plenty of light oil or honing oil, some shop towels and an electric drill motor. Hold the cylinder block in a vise (cushioned with soft jaws or wood blocks) when performing the honing operation. Mount the hone in the drill motor, compress the stones and slip the hone into the cylinder. Lubricate the cylinder thoroughly, turn on the drill and move the hone up and down in the cylinder at a pace which will produce a fine crosshatch pattern on the cylinder wall with the crosshatch lines intersecting at approximately a 60-degree angle. Be sure to use plenty of lubricant and do not take off any more material than is absolutely necessary to produce the desired effect. Do not withdraw the hone from the cylinder while it is running. Instead, shut off the drill and continue moving the hone up and down in the cylinder until it comes to a complete stop, then compress the stones and withdraw the hone. Wipe the oil out of the cylinder and repeat the procedure on the remaining cylinder. Remember, do not remove too much material from the cylinder wall. If you do not have the tools, or do not desire to perform the honing operation, a dealer service department or motorcycle repair shop will generally do it for a reasonable fee.

6 Next, the cylinders must be thoroughly washed with warm soapy water to remove all traces of the abrasive grit produced during the honing operation. Be sure to run a brush through the bolt holes and flush them with running water. After rinsing, dry the cylinders thoroughly and apply a coat of light, rust-preventative oil to all machined surfaces.

10 Pistons - removal, inspection and installation

1 The pistons are attached to the connecting rods with piston pins that are a slip fit in the pistons and rods.

2 Before removing the pistons from the rods, stuff a clean shop towel into each crankcase hole, around the connecting rods. This will prevent the circlips from falling into the crankcase if they are inadvertently dropped.

Removal

3 Using a sharp scribe, scratch the number of each piston into its crown. Each piston should also have an arrow pointing toward the front of the engine **(see illustration)**. If not, scribe an arrow into the piston crown before removal. Support the first piston, grasp the circlip with needle-nose pliers and remove it from the groove. If the pin won't come out, fabricate a piston pin removal tool from threaded stock (stud), nuts, washers and a piece of pipe.

General engine overhaul procedures 2C•15

10.6 Remove the piston rings with a ring removal and installation tool

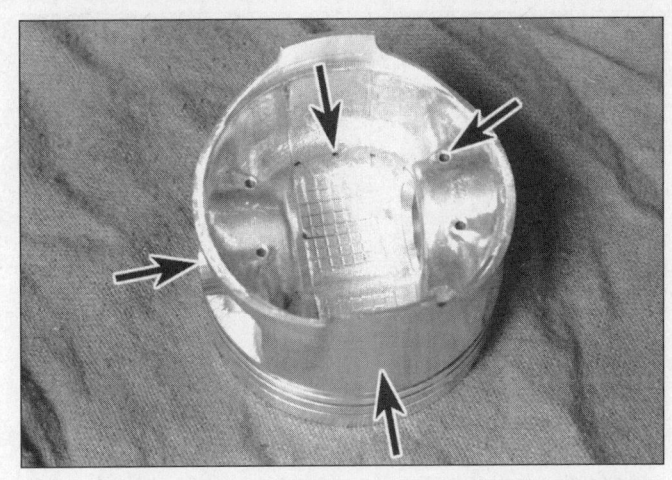

10.11 Check the piston pin bore and the piston skirt for wear, and make sure the internal holes are clear (arrows)

4 Push the piston pin out from the opposite end to free the piston from the rod. You may have to deburr the area around the groove to enable the pin to slide out (use a triangular file for this procedure). Repeat the procedure for the other piston.

Inspection

5 Before the inspection process can be carried out, the pistons must be cleaned and the old piston rings removed.

6 Using a piston ring installation tool, carefully remove the rings from the pistons **(see illustration)**. Do not nick or gouge the pistons in the process.

7 Scrape all traces of carbon from the tops of the pistons. A hand-held wire brush or a piece of fine emery cloth can be used once most of the deposits have been scraped away. Do not, under any circumstances, use a wire brush mounted in a drill motor to remove deposits from the pistons; the piston material is soft and will be eroded away by the wire brush.

8 Use a piston ring groove cleaning tool to remove any carbon deposits from the ring grooves. If a tool is not available, a piece broken off the old ring will do the job. Be very careful to remove only the carbon deposits. Do not remove any metal and do not nick or gouge the sides of the ring grooves.

9 Once the deposits have been removed, clean the pistons with solvent and dry them thoroughly. Make sure the oil return holes below the oil ring grooves are clear.

10 If the pistons are not damaged or worn excessively and if the cylinders are not rebored, new pistons will not be necessary. Normal piston wear appears as even, vertical wear on the thrust surfaces of the piston and slight looseness of the top ring in its groove. New piston rings, on the other hand, should always be used when an engine is rebuilt.

11 Carefully inspect each piston for cracks around the skirt, at the pin bosses and at the ring lands **(see illustration)**.

12 Look for scoring and scuffing on the thrust faces of the skirt, holes in the piston crown and burned areas at the edge of the crown. If the skirt is scored or scuffed, the engine may have been suffering from overheating and/or abnormal combustion, which caused excessively high operating temperatures. The oil pump and cooling system should be checked thoroughly. A hole in the piston crown, an extreme to be sure, is an indication that abnormal combustion (pre-ignition) was occurring. Burned areas at the edge of the piston crown are usually evidence of spark knock (detonation). If any of the above problems exist, the causes must be corrected or the damage will occur again.

13 Measure the piston ring-to-groove clearance by laying a new piston ring in the ring groove and slipping a feeler gauge in beside it **(see illustration)**. Check the clearance at three or four locations around the groove. Be sure to use the correct ring for each groove; they are different. If the clearance is greater than specified, new pistons will have to be used when the engine is reassembled.

14 Check the piston-to-bore clearance by measuring the bore (see Section 9) and the piston diameter. Make sure that the pistons and cylinders are correctly matched. Measure the piston across the skirt on the thrust faces at a 90-degree angle to the piston pin, about 1/2-inch (13 mm) up from the bottom of the skirt **(see illustration)**. Subtract the piston diameter from the bore diameter to obtain the clearance. If it is greater than specified,

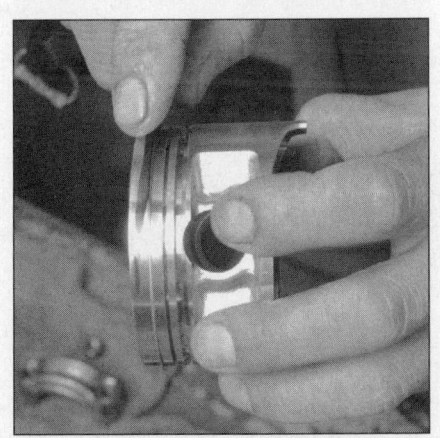

10.13 Measure the piston ring-to-groove clearance with a feeler gauge

10.14a Measure the piston diameter with a micrometer

10.14b If you don't have a micrometer, piston clearance, out-of-round and cylinder taper can be measured with a piece of feeler gauge stock

2C•16 General engine overhaul procedures

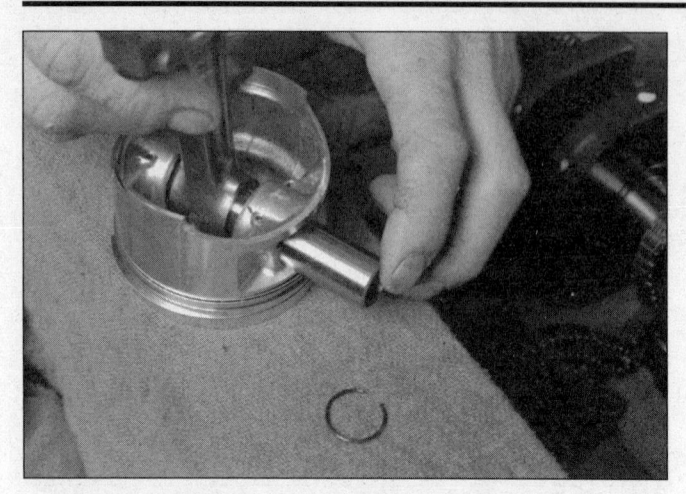

10.15 Slip the pin into the piston and try to wiggle it back-and-forth; if it's loose, replace the piston and pin

11.3a Square the ring in the bore by turning the piston upside down and tapping on the ring . . .

the cylinders will have to be rebored and new oversized pistons and rings installed. If the appropriate precision measuring tools are not available, the piston-to-cylinder clearances can be obtained, though not quite as accurately, using feeler gauge stock. Feeler gauge stock comes in 12-inch lengths and various thicknesses and is generally available at auto parts stores. To check the clearance, select a 0.002 in (0.07 mm) feeler gauge and slip it into the cylinder along with the appropriate piston **(see illustration)**. The cylinder should be upside down and the piston must be positioned exactly as it normally would be. Place the feeler gauge between the piston and cylinder on one of the thrust faces (90-degrees to the piston pin bore). The piston should slip through the cylinder (with the feeler gauge in place) with moderate pressure. If it falls through, or slides through easily, the clearance is excessive and a new piston will be required. If the piston binds at the lower end of the cylinder and is loose toward the top, the cylinder is tapered, and if tight spots are encountered as the feeler gauge is placed at different points around the cylinder, the cylinder is out-of-round. Repeat the procedure for the remaining piston and cylinder. Be sure to have the cylinders and pistons checked by a dealer service department or a motorcycle repair shop to confirm your findings before purchasing new parts.

15   Apply clean engine oil to the pin, insert it into the piston and check for freeplay by rocking the pin back-and-forth **(see illustration)**. If the pin is loose, new pistons and pins must be installed.

16   Refer to Section 11 and install the rings on the pistons.

Installation

17   Install the pistons in their original locations with the arrows pointing to the front of the engine. Lubricate the pins and the rod bores with clean engine oil. Install new circlips in the grooves in the inner sides of the pistons (don't reuse the old circlips). Push the pins into position from the opposite side and install new circlips. Compress the circlips only enough for them to fit in the piston. Make sure the clips are properly seated in the grooves.

11 Piston rings - installation

1   Before installing the new piston rings, the ring end gaps must be checked.
2   Lay out the pistons and the new ring sets so the rings will be matched with the same piston and cylinder during the end gap measurement procedure and engine assembly.
3   Insert the top (No. 1) ring into the bottom of the first cylinder and square it up with the cylinder walls by pushing it in with the top of the piston **(see illustration)**. The ring should be about one inch above the bottom edge of the cylinder. To measure the end gap, slip a feeler gauge between the ends of the ring **(see illustration)** and compare the measurement to the Specifications.
4   If the gap is larger or smaller than specified, double check to make sure that you have the correct rings before proceeding.
5   If the gap is too small, it must be enlarged or the ring ends may come in con-

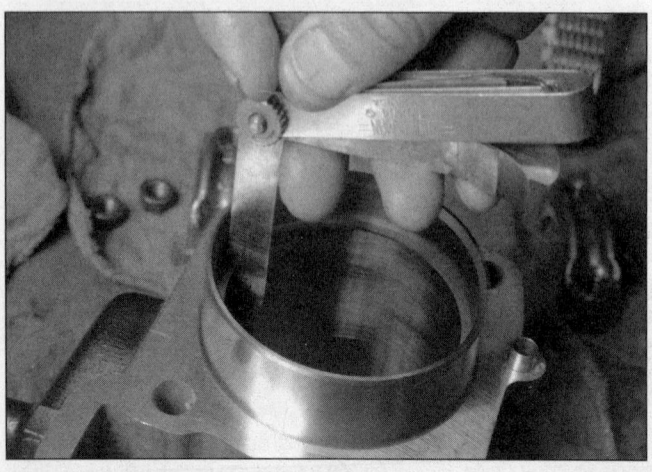

11.3b . . . then check the piston ring end gap with a feeler gauge

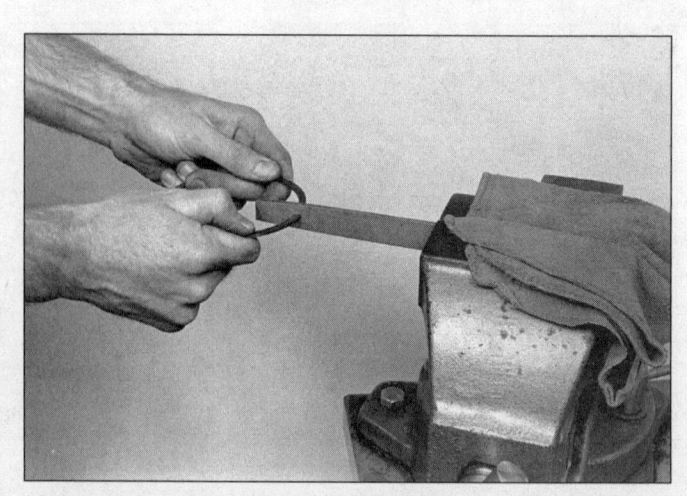

11.5 If the end gap is too small, clamp a file in a vise and file the ring ends (from the outside in only) to enlarge the gap slightly

General engine overhaul procedures 2C•17

11.9a Installing the oil ring expander - make sure the ends don't overlap

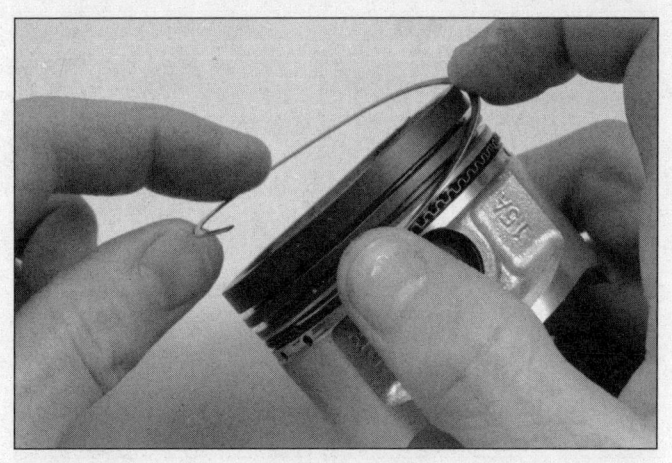

11.9b Installing an oil ring side rail - don't use a ring installation tool to do this

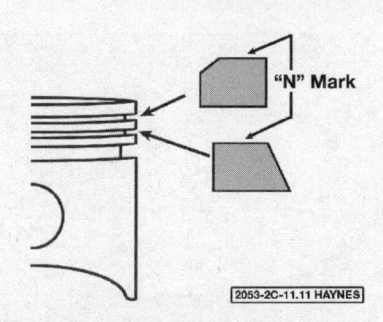

11.11 Don't confuse the top ring with the second (middle) compression ring

tact with each other during engine operation, which can cause serious damage. The end gap can be increased by filing the ring ends very carefully with a fine file **(see illustration)**. When performing this operation, file only from the outside in.

6 Excess end gap is not critical unless it is greater than 0.040 in (1 mm). Again, double check to make sure you have the correct rings for your engine.

7 Repeat the procedure for each ring that will be installed in the first cylinder and for each ring in the remaining cylinder. Remember to keep the rings, pistons and cylinders matched up.

8 Once the ring end gaps have been checked/corrected, the rings can be installed on the pistons.

9 The oil control ring (lowest on the piston) is installed first. It is composed of three separate components. Slip the expander into the groove, then install the upper side rail **(see illustrations)**. Do not use a piston ring installation tool on the oil ring side rails as they may be damaged. Instead, place one end of the side rail into the groove between the spacer expander and the ring land. Hold it firmly in place and slide a finger around the piston while pushing the rail into the groove. Next, install the lower side rail in the same manner.

10 After the three oil ring components have been installed, check to make sure that both the upper and lower side rails can be turned smoothly in the ring groove.

11 Install the no. 2 (middle) ring next. It can be readily distinguished from the top ring by its cross-section shape **(see illustration)**. Do not mix the top and middle rings.

12 To avoid breaking the ring, use a piston ring installation tool and make sure that the identification mark is facing up **(see illustration)**. Fit the ring into the middle groove on the piston. Do not expand the ring any more than is necessary to slide it into place.

13 Finally, install the no. 1 (top) ring in the same manner. Make sure the identifying mark is facing up.

14 Repeat the procedure for the remaining piston and rings. Be very careful not to confuse the no. 1 and no. 2 rings.

15 Once the rings have been properly installed, stagger the end gaps, including those of the oil ring side rails **(see illustration)**.

12 Clutch - inspection

1 Examine the splines on both the inside and the outside of the clutch hub **(see illustration)**. If any wear is evident, replace the hub with a new one.

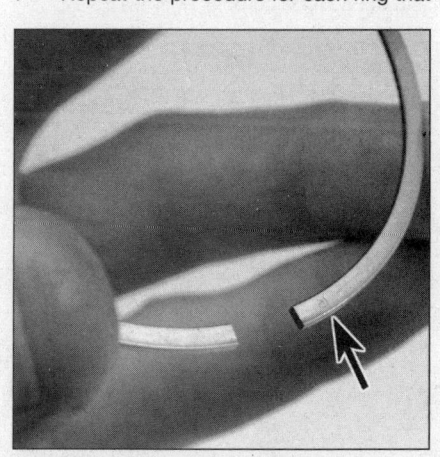

11.12 Make sure the marks on the rings (arrow) face up when the rings are installed on the pistons

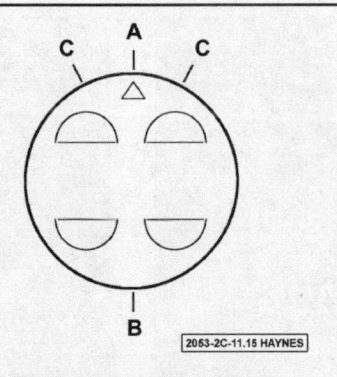

11.15 Piston ring end gap positions

A Top compression ring
B Second compression ring and oil ring expander
C Oil ring side rail (30-40 degrees from "A")

12.1 Check the clutch hub splines (arrows) for wear and distortion

2C•18 General engine overhaul procedures

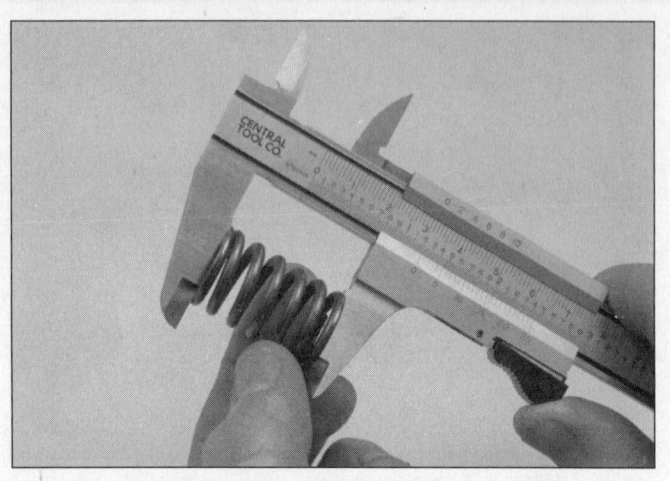

12.2 Measure the clutch spring free length

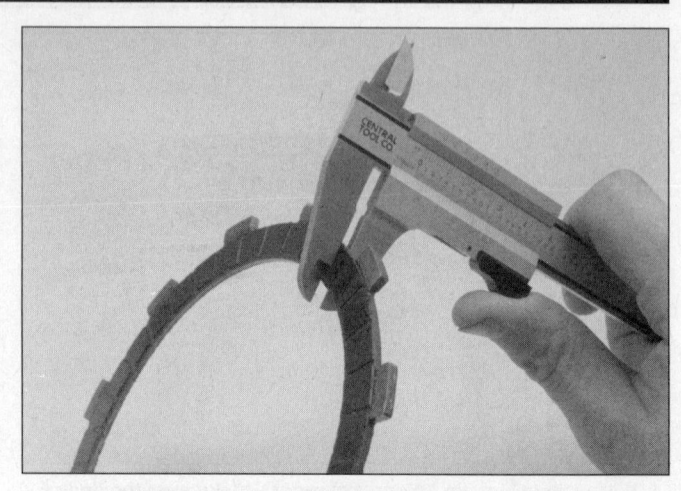

12.3 Measure the thickness of the friction plates

2 Measure the free length of the clutch springs **(see illustration)** and compare the results to this Chapter's Specifications. If the springs have sagged, or if cracks are noted, replace them with new ones as a set.

3 If the lining material of the friction plates smells burnt or if it is glazed, new parts are required. If the metal clutch plates are scored or discolored, they must be replaced with new ones. Measure the thickness of each friction plate **(see illustration)** and compare the results to this Chapter's Specifications. Replace the friction plates as a set if they are near the wear limit.

4 Lay all metal and friction plates, one at a time, on a perfectly flat surface (such as a piece of plate glass) and check for warpage by trying to slip a 0.012-inch (0.3 mm) feeler gauge between the flat surface and the plate **(see illustration)**. Do this at several places around the plate's circumference. If the feeler gauge can be slipped under the plate, it is warped and should be replaced with a new one.

5 Check the tabs on the friction plates for excessive wear and mushroomed edges. They can be cleaned up with a file if the deformation is not severe.

6 Check the edges of the slots in the clutch housing for indentations made by the friction plate tabs **(see illustration)**. If the indentations are deep they can prevent clutch release, so the housing should be replaced with a new one. If the indentations can be removed easily with a file, the life of the housing can be prolonged to an extent.

7 Check the clutch spring plate for wear and damage and make sure the pushrod is not bent (roll it on a perfectly flat surface or use V-blocks and a dial indicator). Check the fit of the pushrod in the spring plate bearing **(see illustration)**. Check the bearing for wear or damage. Replace the pushrod and bearing if they're worn.

8 Clean all traces of old gasket material from the clutch cover. If the release shaft seal has been leaking, it can be replaced by removing the positioning bolt on the outside of the housing (early models) and pulling out the shaft. The seal can then be pried out and a new one driven in, using a hammer and a socket with an outside diameter slightly smaller than that of the seal. Be careful when installing the release shaft not to damage the new oil seal. Note that there should be a gap of 1-to-3 mm (0.04-to-0.12 inch) between the release shaft arm and the top of the casing, and that, with the cable attached, an angle of 80-to-90 degrees is formed between arm and cable. On early models, secure the shaft with the positioning bolt.

12.4 Check all plates for warpage

12.6 Check the slots on the clutch housing for indentations

12.7 Check the pushrod and the bearing in the spring plate for wear and damage

General engine overhaul procedures 2C•19

14.2a On EN450/500 models, remove the oil line from the left front corner of the case . . .

14.2b . . . the line farther back along the left side . . .

14.2c . . . and the oil passage plug so all the lines and passages can be cleaned

4 Make sure the return spring pin isn't loose. If it is, unscrew it, apply a non-permanent locking compound to the threads, then reinstall the pin and tighten it securely.
5 Check the condition of the seal in the cover. If it has been leaking, drive it out with a hammer and punch. Drive a new seal in with a socket.

14 Crankcase components - inspection and servicing

1 After the crankcases have been separated and the crankshaft, shift drum and forks and transmission components removed, the crankcases should be cleaned thoroughly with new solvent and dried with compressed air.
2 Remove any oil pipes or hoses that haven't already been removed. All oil passages and pipes should be blown out with compressed air **(see illustrations)**.
3 Remove the breather body **(see illustrations)**. Inspect its O-ring; it's a good idea to install a new one.

13 External shift mechanism - inspection

1 Check the shift shaft for bends and damage to the splines. If the shaft is bent, you can attempt to straighten it, but if the splines are damaged it will have to be replaced.

2 Check the condition of the gear positioning lever and spring, pin plate and shift drum cam. Replace them if they are cracked or distorted.
3 Check the shift mechanism arm for cracks, distortion and wear. If any of these conditions are found, replace the shift mechanism.

14.3a The EN450/500 breather body is secured by the center bolt (arrow) . . .

14.3b . . . and the EX250 breather body is secured by these bolts (arrows)

2C•20 General engine overhaul procedures

14.4 Small burrs can be removed from the gasket surfaces with a fine sharpening stone

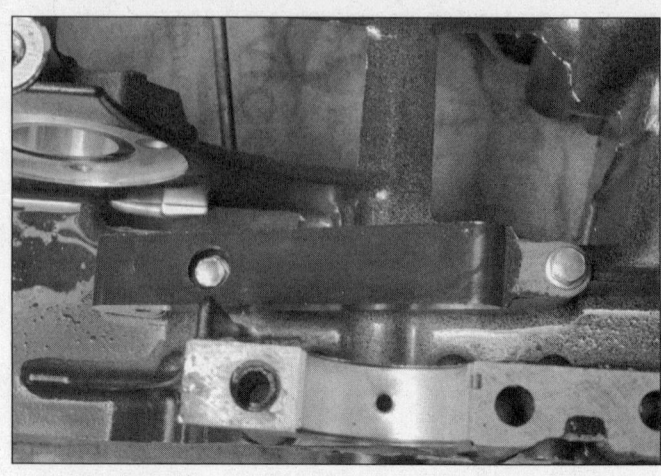

14.5 On EN450/500 models, check both primary chain guides for wear (the lower one is shown here) and replace them if necessary

4   All traces of old gasket sealant should be removed from the mating surfaces. Minor damage to the surfaces can be cleaned up with a fine sharpening stone **(see illustration)**.

Caution: *Be very careful not to nick or gouge the crankcase mating surfaces or leaks will result. Check both crankcase sections very carefully for cracks and other damage.*

5   If you're working on an EN450/500, check the primary chain guides for wear - one is in the upper case half and the other is in the lower case half **(see illustration)**. If they appear to be worn excessively, replace them.

6   On EN450/500 models, check the front cam chain guide for wear. If it's worn, remove it (see Chapter 2A).

7   On EX250 models, check the cam chain guides for wear. Replace them if problems can be seen (see Chapter 2B).

8   If any damage is found that can't be repaired, replace the crankcase halves as a set.

15 Main and connecting rod bearings - general note

1   Even though main and connecting rod bearings are generally replaced with new ones during the engine overhaul, the old bearings should be retained for close examination as they may reveal valuable information about the condition of the engine.

2   Bearing failure occurs mainly because of lack of lubrication, the presence of dirt or other foreign particles, overloading the engine and/or corrosion. Regardless of the cause of bearing failure, it must be corrected before the engine is reassembled to prevent it from happening again.

3   When examining the bearings, remove the main bearings from the case halves and the rod bearings from the connecting rods and caps and lay them out on a clean surface in the same general position as their location on the crankshaft journals. This will enable you to match any noted bearing problems with the corresponding side of the crankshaft journal.

4   Dirt and other foreign particles get into the engine in a variety of ways. It may be left in the engine during assembly or it may pass through filters or breathers. It may get into the oil and from there into the bearings. Metal chips from machining operations and normal engine wear are often present. Abrasives are sometimes left in engine components after reconditioning operations such as cylinder honing, especially when parts are not thoroughly cleaned using the proper cleaning methods. Whatever the source, these foreign objects often end up imbedded in the soft bearing material and are easily recognized. Large particles will not imbed in the bearing and will score or gouge the bearing and journal. The best prevention for this cause of bearing failure is to clean all parts thoroughly and keep everything spotlessly clean during engine reassembly. Frequent and regular oil and filter changes are also recommended.

5   Lack of lubrication or lubrication breakdown has a number of interrelated causes. Excessive heat (which thins the oil), overloading (which squeezes the oil from the bearing face) and oil leakage or throw off (from excessive bearing clearances, worn oil pump or high engine speeds) all contribute to lubrication breakdown. Blocked oil passages will also starve a bearing and destroy it. When lack of lubrication is the cause of bearing failure, the bearing material is wiped or extruded from the steel backing of the bearing. Temperatures may increase to the point where the steel backing and the journal turn blue from overheating.

6   Riding habits can have a definite effect on bearing life. Full throttle low speed operation, or lugging (laboring) the engine, puts very high loads on bearings, which tend to squeeze out the oil film. These loads cause the bearings to flex, which produces fine cracks in the bearing face (fatigue failure). Eventually the bearing material will loosen in pieces and tear away from the steel backing. Short trip riding leads to corrosion of bearings, as insufficient engine heat is produced to drive off the condensed water and corrosive gases produced. These products collect in the engine oil, forming acid and sludge. As the oil is carried to the engine bearings, the acid attacks and corrodes the bearing material.

7   Incorrect bearing installation during engine assembly will lead to bearing failure as well. Tight fitting bearings which leave insufficient bearing oil clearances result in oil starvation. Dirt or foreign particles trapped behind a bearing insert result in high spots on the bearing which lead to failure.

8   To avoid bearing problems, clean all parts thoroughly before reassembly, double check all bearing clearance measurements and lubricate the new bearings with engine assembly lube or moly-based grease during installation.

16 Clutch housing, crankshaft and main bearings - removal, inspection, main bearing selection and installation

Note: *The clutch housing removal procedures in this section apply to EN450/500 models only. The clutch housing on EX250 models can be removed without splitting the crankcase. Refer to Chapter 2B for procedures.*

Clutch housing removal

1   If you haven't already done so, remove all clutch components except the housing (see Chapter 2A).

2   Slide the clutch housing back and forth on the shaft within the limits allowed by the primary chain to expose the inner bearing

General engine overhaul procedures 2C•21

16.2 Slip the clutch housing back-and-forth to expose the inner bearing sleeve (arrow), then pull it out (EN450/500)

16.3a Lift the clutch housing and transmission main drive shaft (EN450/500) . . .

sleeve **(see illustration)**. Pull the sleeve out.
3 Lift the transmission main drive shaft and clutch housing from the case **(see illustration)**. Slip the transmission shaft out of the clutch housing and disengage the housing from the primary chain **(see illustration)**.

Crankshaft removal
4 If you haven't already done so, remove the connecting rod caps (see Section 17).
5 Before removing the crankshaft check the endplay. This can be done with a dial indicator mounted in-line with the crankshaft, or feeler gauges inserted between the crankshaft and no. 2 crankcase main journal **(see illustration)**. Compare your findings with this Chapter's Specifications. If the endplay is excessive, the case halves must be replaced.
6 Lift the crankshaft out, together with the cam chain (and primary chain on EN450/500 models) and set them on a clean surface **(see illustration)**.
7 The main bearing inserts can be removed from their saddles by pushing their centers to the side, then lifting them out **(see illustration)**. Keep the bearing inserts in order. The main bearing oil clearance should be checked, however, before removing the inserts (see Step 13).

16.3b . . . and disengage the housing from the primary chain (EN450/500)

16.5 Measure the endplay with a feeler gauge inserted between the no. 2 crank journal and the case web - if the endplay isn't as listed in this Chapter's Specifications, the case halves must be replaced

16.6 The EN450/500 crankshaft, primary chain and cam chain - the EX250 is similar, but doesn't use a primary chain

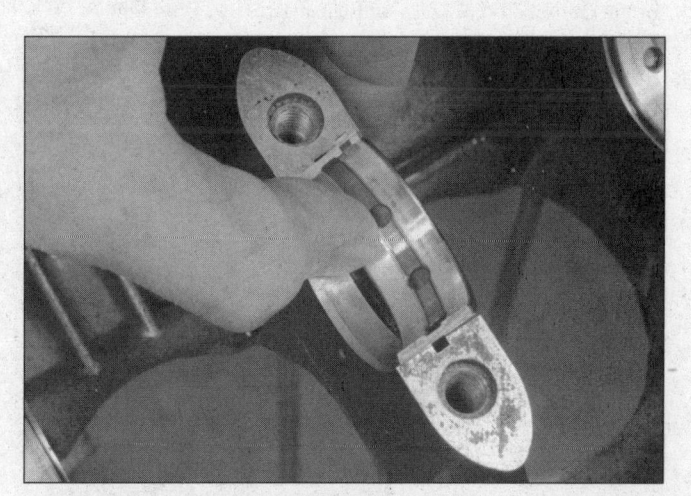

16.7 To remove a main bearing insert, push it sideways and lift it out

2C•22 General engine overhaul procedures

16.8 Inspect the bearing in the center of the clutch housing - replace the clutch housing if it's worn or damaged

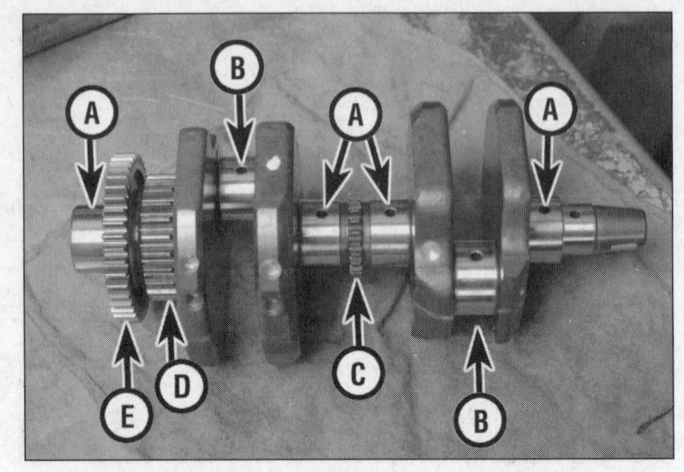

16.10 Inspect the crankshaft at the following points:

A Main bearing journals (EN450/500 shown)	C Cam chain gear
	D Primary chain gear
B Connecting rod journals	E Balancer gear

Inspection

8 Check the clutch housing bearing for wear or damage **(see illustration)**. Replace the clutch housing if necessary. Also inspect the slots in the housing (see Section 12).

9 If you haven't already done so, mark and remove the connecting rods from the crankshaft (see Section 17).

10 Clean the crankshaft with solvent, using a rifle-cleaning brush to scrub out the oil passages. If available, blow the crank dry with compressed air. Check the main and connecting rod journals for uneven wear, scoring and pits **(see illustration)**. Rub a copper coin across the journal several times - if a journal picks up copper from the coin, it's too rough. Replace the crankshaft.

11 Check the balancer gear, camshaft chain gear and primary chain gear on the crankshaft for chipped teeth and other wear. If any undesirable conditions are found, replace the crankshaft. Check the chains as described in Section 19. Check the rest of the crankshaft for cracks and other damage. It should be magnafluxed to reveal hidden cracks - a dealer service department or motorcycle machine shop will handle the procedure.

12 Set the crankshaft on V-blocks and check the runout with a dial indicator touching one of the center main journals, comparing your findings with this Chapter's Specifications. If the runout exceeds the limit, replace the crank.

Main bearing selection

13 To check the main bearing oil clearance, clean off the bearing inserts (and reinstall them, if they've been removed from the case) and lower the crankshaft into the upper half of the case. Cut pieces of Plastigage (type HPG-1) and lay them on the crankshaft main journals, parallel with the journal axis **(see illustration)** (four pieces for EN450/500 models; three pieces for EX250 models).

14 Very carefully, guide the lower case half down onto the upper case half. Install the large (8 mm) bolts and tighten them, using the recommended sequence, to the torque listed in the Chapter 2A or 2B Specifications. Don't rotate the crankshaft!

15 Now, remove the bolts and carefully lift the lower case half off. Compare the width of the crushed Plastigage on each journal to the scale printed on the Plastigage envelope to obtain the main bearing oil clearance **(see illustration)**. Write down your findings, then remove all traces of Plastigage from the journals, using your fingernail or the edge of a credit card.

16 If the oil clearance falls into the specified range, no bearing replacement is required (provided they are in good shape). If the clearance is more than the standard range, but within the service limit, replace the bearing inserts with inserts that have blue paint marks **(see illustration)**, then check the oil clearance once again (these are the thickest bearing inserts, and may be thick enough to bring bearing clearance within the specified range). Always replace all of the inserts at the same time.

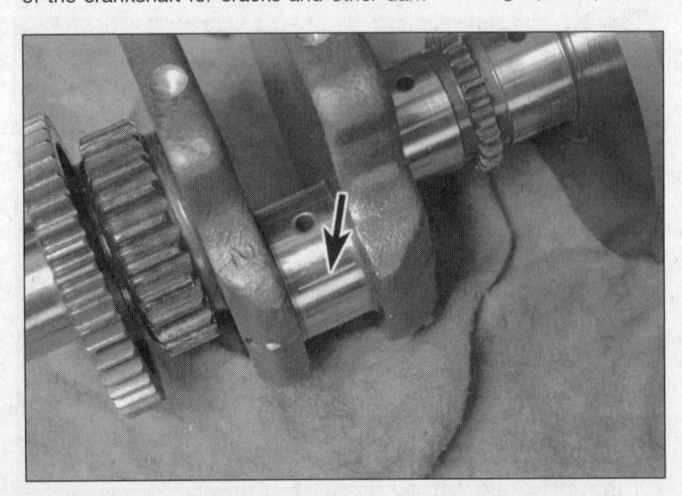

16.13 Lay the Plastigage strips (arrow) on the journals, parallel to the crankshaft centerline

16.15 Measuring the width of the crushed Plastigage (be sure to use the correct scale - standard and metric are included)

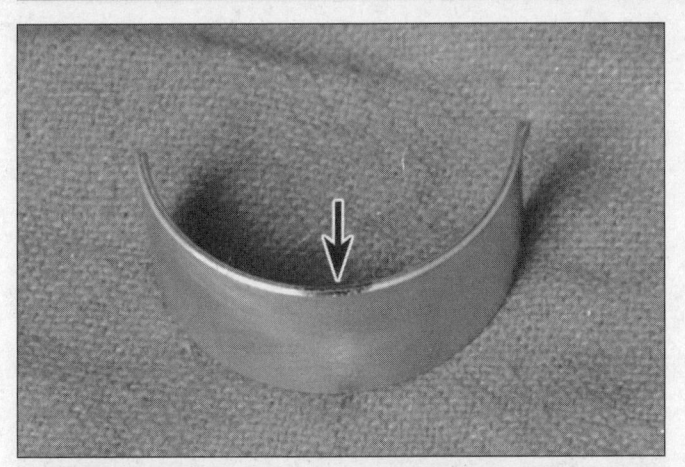

General engine overhaul procedures 2C•23

16.16 Bearing thicknesses are identified by color codes on the sides of the bearings

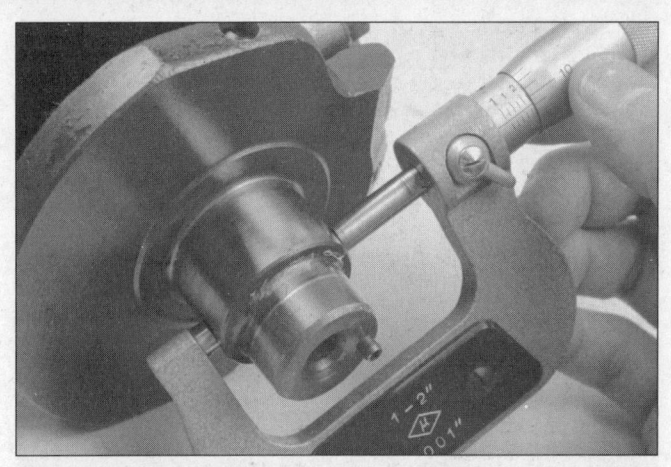

16.18 Measure the diameter of each crankshaft journal at several points to detect taper and out-of-round conditions

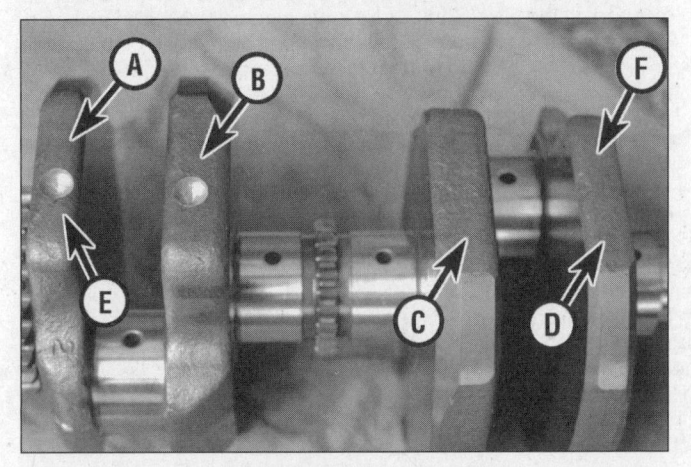

16.20 EN450/500 crankshaft mark locations (this crankshaft has no marks) (EX250 similar)

- A   No. 1 main bearing journal mark
- B   No. 2 main bearing journal mark
- C   No. 3 main bearing journal mark
- D   No. 4 main bearing journal mark
- E   No. 1 connecting rod journal mark
- F   No. 2 connecting rod journal mark

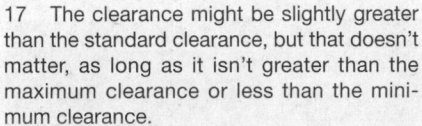

16.21a EN450/500 crankcase mark locations

- A   No. 1 main bearing bore mark
- B   No. 2 main bearing bore mark
- C   No. 3 main bearing bore mark
- D   No. 4 main bearing bore mark

17 The clearance might be slightly greater than the standard clearance, but that doesn't matter, as long as it isn't greater than the maximum clearance or less than the minimum clearance.

18 If the clearance is greater than the service limit listed in this Chapter's Specifications, measure the diameter of the crankshaft journals with a micrometer **(see illustration)** and compare your findings with this Chapter's Specifications. Also, by measuring the diameter at a number of points around each journal's circumference, you'll be able to determine whether or not the journal is out-of-round. Take the measurement at each end of the journal, near the crank throws, to determine if the journal is tapered.

19 If any crank journal has worn down past the service limit, replace the crankshaft.

20 If the diameters of the journals aren't less than the service limit but differ from the original markings on the crankshaft **(see illustration)**, apply new marks with a hammer and punch.

If the journal measures within the "no mark" range listed in the Specifications, don't make any marks on the crank (there shouldn't be any marks there, anyway).

If the journal measures within the "1" mark range listed in the Specifications, make a "1" mark on the crank in the area indicated (if it's not already there).

21 Remove the main bearing inserts and assemble the case halves (see Chapter 2A or 2B). Using a telescoping gauge and a micrometer, measure the diameters of the main bearing bores, then compare the measurements with the marks on the upper case half **(see illustrations)**. Compare the bore measurements with those listed in this Chapter's Specifications. Also compare the bore measurements to the marks on the crankcase to find out whether the marks are accurate.

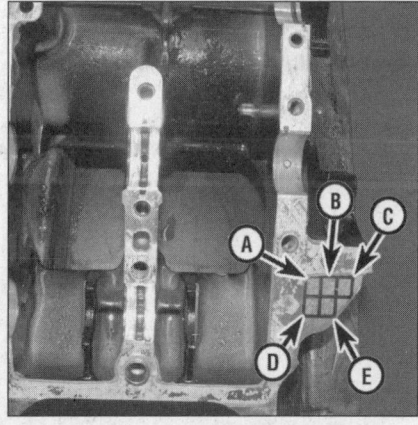

16.21b EX250 crankcase mark locations

- A   No. 1 main bearing bore mark
- B   No. 2 main bearing bore mark
- C   No. 3 main bearing bore mark
- D   Left balancer bearing bore mark
- E   Right balancer bearing bore mark

2C•24 General engine overhaul procedures

16.23 Make sure the tabs in the bearing inserts (arrows) fit into the notches in the web; the center two main bearings (EN450/500) or center main bearing (EX250) have oil grooves

16.27 Before you install the crankshaft on an EN450/500, check to be sure the cam chain guide retainer pin (lower arrow) is pushed all the way in and its lock-pin (upper arrow) is in place - if the connecting rods are installed, put pieces of hose on the studs to protect the crankshaft

22 Using the marks on the crank and the marks on the case, determine the bearing sizes as follows:

a) O mark on case, 1 mark on crankshaft - Brown
b) No mark on case or crankshaft - Blue
c) O mark on case, no mark on crankshaft - Black
c) No mark on case, 1 mark on crankshaft - Black

Installation

23 Separate the case halves once again. Clean the bearing saddles in the case halves, then install the bearing inserts in their webs in the case (see illustration). On EN450/500 models, the center two bearing inserts have oil grooves. On EX250 models, the inserts for the single center bearing have oil grooves. When installing the bearings, use your hands only - don't tap them into place with a hammer.

24 Lubricate the bearing inserts with engine assembly lube or moly-based grease.
25 You can install the connecting rods on the crankshaft at this point if the top end was removed from the engine (see Section 17).
26 On EN450/500 models, loop the camshaft chain and the primary chain over the crankshaft and lay them onto their gears.
27 On EN450/500 models, check to make sure the cam chain guide retaining pin and lock-pin are in position. If the connecting rods are in the engine, place pieces of hose over the studs to protect the crankshaft (see illustration).
28 Carefully lower the crankshaft into place. If the connecting rods are in the engine, guide them onto the crankshaft journals.
29 Assemble the case halves (see Chapter 2A or 2B) and check to make sure the crankshaft and the transmission shafts turn freely.
30 If you're working on an EN450/500, install the oil pump drive gear and clutch housing. The pin in the gear must engage the notch in the housing (see illustration). The beveled side of the clutch housing thrust washer faces the ball bearing on the transmission main drive shaft (see illustration).

17 Connecting rods and bearings - removal, inspection, bearing selection and installation

Removal

1 Before removing the connecting rods from the crankshaft, measure the side clearance of each rod with a feeler gauge (see illustration). If the clearance on any rod is greater than that listed in this Chapter's Specifications, that rod will have to be replaced with a new one.

16.30a The pin in the oil pump drive gear must engage the notch in the clutch housing (arrows) ...

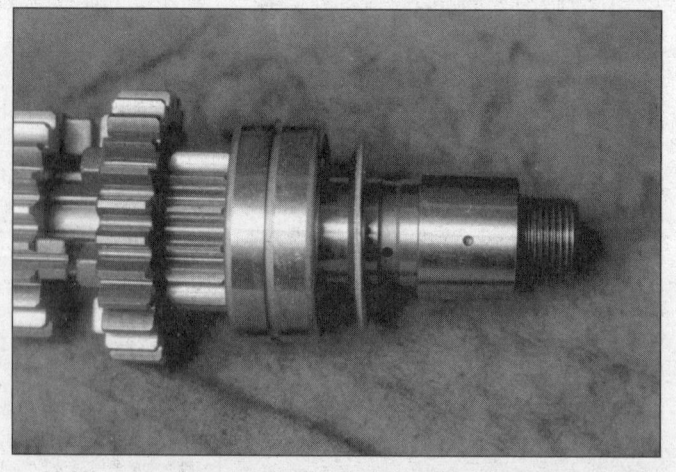

16.30b ... and the beveled side of the clutch housing thrust washer must face toward the ball bearing on the transmission main drive shaft

General engine overhaul procedures 2C•25

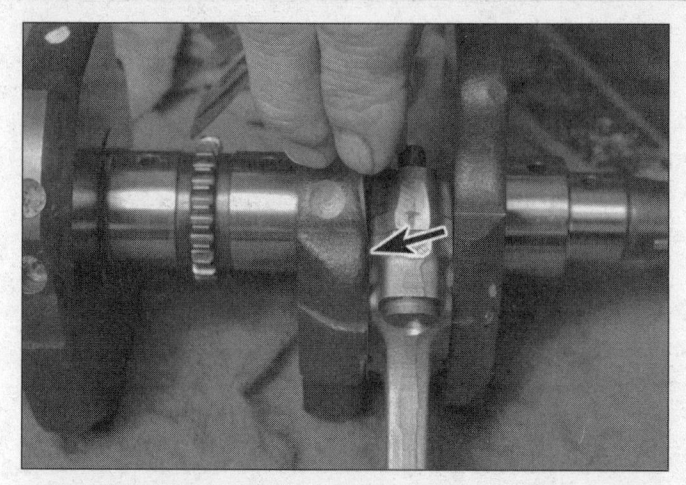

17.1 Slip a feeler gauge blade between the connecting rod and crankshaft throw (arrow) to check connecting rod side clearance

17.2 Make number marks (arrows) on the connecting rod and cap so they can be reassembled in their original positions, and note the relationship of the connecting rod to the crankshaft - the letter mark across the rod and cap indicates the connecting rod weight grade

17.3a Remove the connecting rod nuts (arrows) . . .

17.3b . . . and take the cap off the studs

2 Using a center punch, mark the position of each rod and cap, relative to its position on the crankshaft (see illustration).
3 Unscrew the bearing cap nuts, separate the cap from the rod, then detach the rod from the crankshaft (see illustrations). If the cap is stuck, tap on the ends of the rod bolts with a soft face hammer to free them.
4 Separate the bearing inserts from the rods and caps, keeping them in order so they can be reinstalled in their original locations. Wash the parts in solvent and dry them with compressed air, if available.

Inspection

5 Check the connecting rods for cracks and other obvious damage. Lubricate the piston pin for each rod, install it in the proper rod and check for play (see illustration). If it is loose, replace the connecting rod and/or the pin.
6 Examine the connecting rod bearing inserts. If they are scored, badly scuffed or appear to have been seized, new bearings must be installed. Always replace the bearings in the connecting rods as a set. If they are badly damaged, check the corresponding crankshaft journal. Evidence of extreme heat, such as discoloration, indicates that lubrication failure has occurred. Be sure to thoroughly check the oil pump and pressure relief valve as well as all oil holes and passages before reassembling the engine.
7 Have the rods checked for twist and bending at a dealer service department or other motorcycle repair shop.

Bearing selection

8 If the bearings and journals appear to be in good condition, check the oil clearances as follows:
9 Start with the rod for the number one cylinder. Wipe the bearing inserts and the connecting rod and cap clean, using a lint-free cloth.
10 Install the bearing inserts in the connecting rod and cap. Make sure the tab on the bearing engages with the notch in the rod or cap.

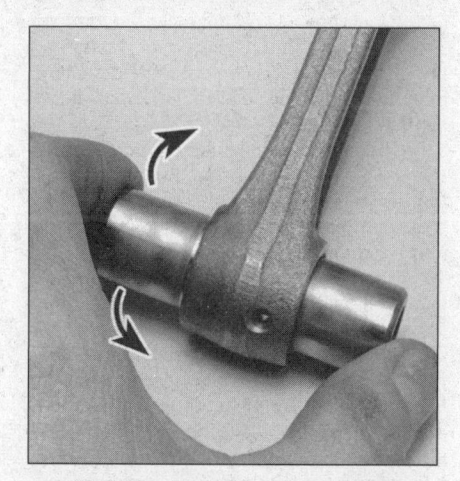

17.5 Checking the piston pin and connecting rod bore for wear

11 Wipe off the connecting rod journal with a lint-free cloth. Lay a strip of Plastigage (type HPG-1) across the top of the journal,

2C•26 General engine overhaul procedures

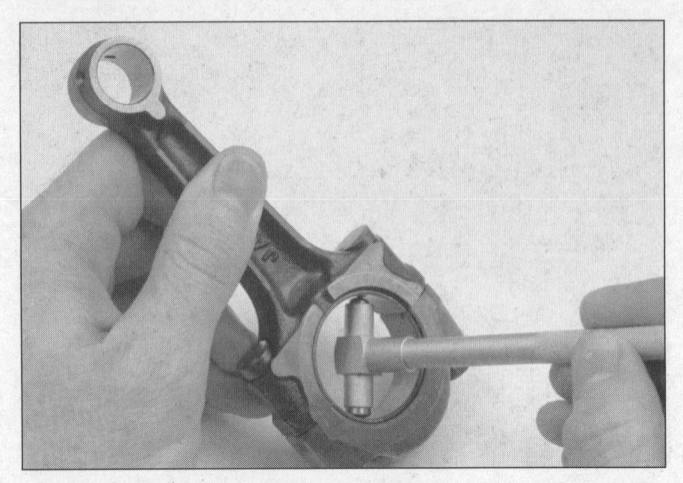

17.20a Assemble the connecting rod and measure the diameter of the bore with a telescoping gauge - then measure the gauge with a micrometer

17.20b There's a letter that indicates weight grade on each connecting rod (arrow); a "0" or the absence of a "0" around the letter can be used to select the correct bearing inserts

parallel with the journal axis **(see illustration 16.13)**.

12 Position the connecting rod on the bottom of the journal, then install the rod cap and nuts. Tighten the nuts to the torque listed in this Chapter's Specifications, but don't allow the connecting rod to rotate at all.

13 Unscrew the nuts and remove the connecting rod and cap from the journal, being very careful not to disturb the Plastigage. Compare the width of the crushed Plastigage to the scale printed in the Plastigage envelope **(see illustration 16.15)** to determine the bearing oil clearance.

14 If the clearance is within the range listed in this Chapter's Specifications and the bearings are in perfect condition, they can be reused. If the clearance is beyond the standard range, but within the service limit, replace the bearing inserts with inserts that have blue paint marks, then check the oil clearance once again (these are the thickest bearing inserts, and may be thick enough to bring bearing clearance with the specified range). Always replace all of the inserts at the same time.

15 The clearance might be slightly greater than the standard clearance, but that doesn't matter, as long as it isn't greater than the maximum clearance or less than the minimum clearance.

16 If the clearance is greater than the service limit listed in this Chapter's Specifications, measure the diameter of the connecting rod journal with a micrometer and compare your findings with this Chapter's Specifications. Also, by measuring the diameter at a number of points around the journal's circumference, you'll be able to determine whether or not the journal is out-of-round. Take the measurement at each end of the journal to determine if the journal is tapered.

17 If any journal has worn down past the service limit, replace the crankshaft.

18 If the diameter of the journal isn't less than the service limit but differs from the original markings on the crankshaft **(see illustration 16.20)**, apply new marks with a hammer and punch.

If the journal measures within the "no mark" range listed in this Chapter's Specifications, don't make any marks on the crank (there shouldn't be one there anyway).

If the journal measures within the "0" mark range listed in this Chapter's Specifications, make a "0" mark on the crank in the area indicated (if not already there).

19 Remove the bearing inserts from the connecting rod and cap, then assemble the cap to the rod. Tighten the nuts to the torque listed in this Chapter's Specifications.

20 Using a telescoping gauge and a micrometer, measure the inside diameter of the connecting rod **(see illustration)**. The mark on the connecting rod (if any) should coincide with the measurement, but if it doesn't, make a new mark **(see illustration)**.

If the inside diameter measures within the "no mark" range listed in this Chapter's Specifications, don't make any mark on the rod (there shouldn't be one there anyway).

If the inside diameter measures within the "0" mark range, make a "0" mark on the rod (it should already be there).

21 Select the correct connecting rod bearing inserts as follows:

a) *No mark on connecting rod or crankpin - Black*
b) *O mark on connecting rod or crankpin - Black*
c) *O mark on connecting rod, no mark on crankpin - Blue*
d) *No mark on connecting rod, O mark on crankpin - Brown*

22 Repeat the bearing selection procedure for the remaining connecting rod.

Installation

23 Wipe off the bearing inserts, connecting rods and caps. Install the inserts into the rods and caps, using your hands only, making sure the tabs on the inserts engage with the notches in the rods and caps. When all the inserts are installed, lubricate them with engine assembly lube or moly-based grease. Don't get any lubricant on the mating surfaces of the rod or cap.

24 Assemble each connecting rod to its proper journal, making sure the previously applied matchmarks correspond to each other and the arrow casting on the piston points to the front of the engine **(see illustration 11.15)**. Also, the letter present at the rod/cap seam on one side of the connecting rod is a weight mark. If new rods are being installed, they should both have the same letter on them to minimize vibration.

25 When you're sure the rods are positioned correctly, tighten the nuts to the torque listed in this Chapter's Specifications.

26 Turn the rods on the crankshaft. If any of them feel tight, tap on the bottom of the connecting rod caps with a hammer - this should relieve stress and free them up. If it doesn't, recheck the bearing clearance.

27 As a final step, recheck the connecting rod side clearances (see Step 1). If the clearances aren't correct, find out why before proceeding with engine assembly.

18 Balancer shaft - inspection

1 Check the shaft and gear for wear and damage. Make sure the springs inside the gear are not broken. Replace the balancer shaft if you find any undesirable conditions.

2 Check the bearings for wear and for damage such as grooves, nicks or small bits of foreign material stuck in their surfaces. Replace them if they aren't in perfect condition.

Bearing selection

3 To check the balancer bearing oil clearance, clean off the bearing inserts (and rein-

General engine overhaul procedures 2C•27

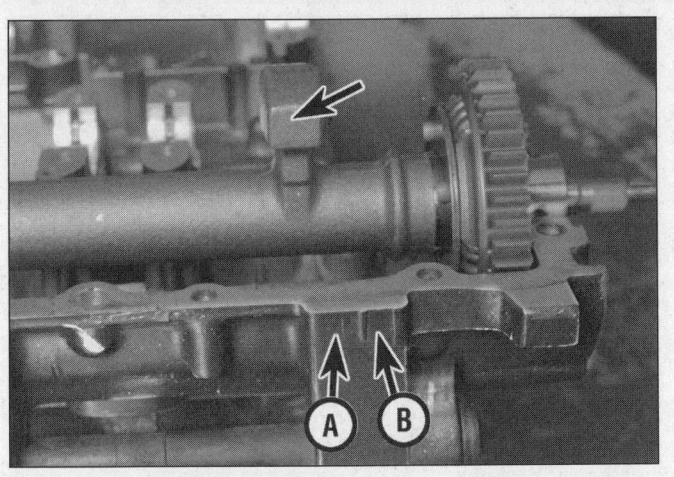

18.10 There's a journal diameter mark (or no mark, as on this balancer) on each balancer weight; there's also a size mark for each bearing bore on the case (EN450/500)

A Left bearing bore size mark
B Right bearing bore size mark

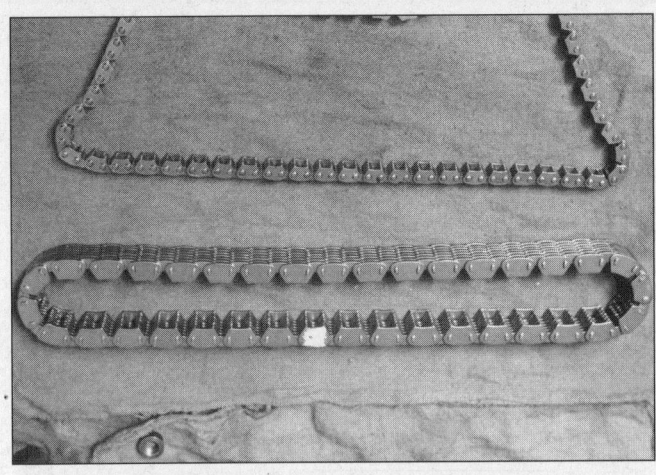

19.2 When checking the camshaft chain or the primary chain, measure the length of twenty links and compare to the length listed in this Chapter's Specifications

stall them, if they've been removed from the case) and lower the balancer shaft into the upper half of the case. Cut two pieces of Plastigage (type HPG-1) and lay them on the balancer journals, parallel with the journal axis.

4 Very carefully, guide the lower case half down onto the upper case half. Install the large (8 mm) bolts and tighten them, using the recommended sequence, to the torque listed in this Chapter's Specifications (see Chapter 2A or 2B). Don't rotate the balancer!

5 Now, remove the bolts and carefully lift the lower case half off. Compare the width of the crushed Plastigage on each journal to the scale printed on the Plastigage envelope to obtain the balancer bearing oil clearance. Write down your findings, then remove all traces of Plastigage from the journals, using your fingernail or the edge of a credit card.

6 If the oil clearance falls into the specified range, no bearing replacement is required (provided they are in good shape). If the clearance is more than the standard range, but within the service limit, replace the bearing inserts with inserts that have blue paint marks **(see illustration 16.16)**, then check the oil clearance once again (these are the thickest bearing inserts, and may be thick enough to bring bearing clearance within the specified range). Always replace all of the inserts at the same time.

7 The clearance might be slightly greater than the standard clearance, but that doesn't matter, as long as it isn't greater than the maximum clearance or less than the minimum clearance.

8 If the clearance is greater than the service limit listed in this Chapter's Specifications, measure the diameter of the balancer journals with a micrometer and compare your findings with this Chapter's Specifications. Also, by measuring the diameter at a number of points around each journal's circum-

ference, you'll be able to determine whether or not the journal is out-of-round. Take the measurement at each end of the journal to determine if the journal is tapered.

9 If either balancer journal has worn down past the service limit, replace the balancer shaft.

10 If the diameters of the journals aren't less than the service limit but differ from the original markings on the balancer shaft **(see illustration)**, apply new marks with a hammer and punch.

If the journal measures within the "no mark" range listed in the Specifications, don't make any marks on the balancer (there shouldn't be any marks there, anyway).

If the journal measures within the "0" mark range listed in the Specifications, make a "0" mark on the balancer in the area indicated (if it's not already there).

11 Remove the balancer bearing inserts and assemble the case halves (see Chapter 2A or 2B). Using a telescoping gauge and a micrometer, measure the diameters of the balancer bearing bores, then compare the measurements with the marks on the upper case half **(see illustration 16.21b or 18.10)**. Compare the bore measurements with those listed in this Chapter's Specifications. Also compare the bore measurements to the marks on the crankcase to find out whether the marks are accurate.

12 Using the marks on the crank and the marks on the case, determine the bearing sizes required as follows:

a) O mark on crankcase, O mark on balancer shaft - Brown
b) No mark on crankcase or balancer shaft - Blue
c) O mark on crankcase, no mark on balancer shaft - Black
d) No mark on crankcase, O mark on balancer shaft - Black

19 Primary chain, camshaft chain and guides - inspection

1 A primary chain is used on EN450/400 models.

Chains

2 The primary chain and camshaft chains are checked in a similar manner. Pull the chain tight to eliminate all slack and measure the length of twenty links, pin-to-pin **(see illustration)**. Compare your findings to this Chapter's Specifications.

3 Also check the chains for binding and obvious damage.

4 If the twenty-link length is not as specified, or there is visible damage, replace the chain.

Chain guides

5 Check the guides for deep grooves, cracking and other obvious damage, replacing them if necessary.

20 Transmission gears and shafts - inspection

Main drive shaft

1 Wash all of the components in clean solvent and dry them off. Rotate the ball bearing on the shaft, feeling for tightness, rough spots and excessive looseness and listening for noises. If any of these conditions are found, replace the bearing. This will require the use of a hydraulic press or a bearing puller setup. If you don't have access to these tools, take the shaft and bearing to a Kawasaki dealer or other motorcycle repair

2C•28 General engine overhaul procedures

20.4 If the gear dogs and dog holes (arrows) show signs of excessive wear, replace the gears as a set

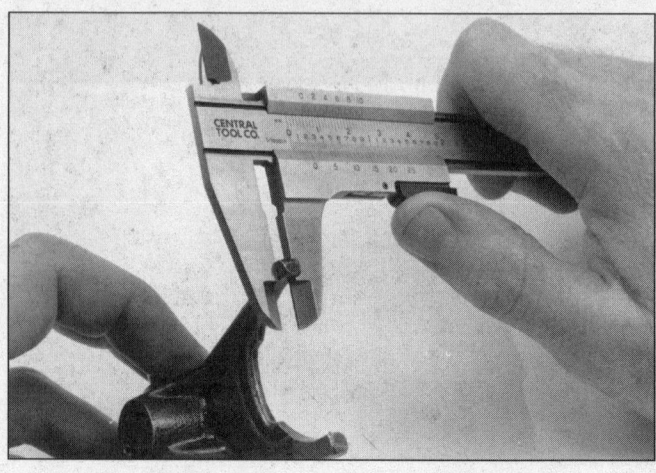

21.2 Measure the thickness of the shift fork ears

shop and have them press the old bearing off the shaft and install the new one.

2 Measure the shift fork groove between third and fourth gears. If the groove width exceeds the figure listed in this Chapter's Specifications, replace the third/fourth gear assembly, and also check the third/fourth gear shift fork (see Section 21).

3 Check the gear teeth for cracking and other obvious damage. Check the sixth gear bushing and the surface in the inner diameter of sixth gear (and the fifth gear bushing, if equipped) for scoring or heat discoloration. If the gear or bushing is damaged, replace it.

4 Inspect the dogs and the dog holes in the gears for excessive wear **(see illustration)**. Replace the paired gears as a set if necessary.

5 Check the needle bearing and outer race for wear or heat discoloration and replace them if necessary.

Output shaft

6 Refer to Steps 1 through 5 for the inspection procedures. They are the same, except that when checking the shift fork groove width you'll be checking it on fifth gear and sixth gear.

21 Shift drum and forks - inspection

1 Check the edges of the grooves in the drum for signs of excessive wear. Measure the widths of the grooves and compare your findings to this Chapter's Specifications. Check the cam and bearing on the end of the shift drum for wear and damage. If undesirable conditions are found, remove the end-plate screw and replace the cam and bearing.

2 Check the shift forks for distortion and wear, especially at the fork ears. Measure the thickness of the fork ears and compare your findings with this Chapter's Specifications **(see illustration)**. If they are discolored or severely worn they are probably bent. If damage or wear is evident, check the shift fork groove in the corresponding gear as well. Inspect the guide pins and the shaft bore for excessive wear and distortion and replace any defective parts with new ones.

3 Check the shift fork rod for evidence of wear, galling and other damage. Make sure the shift forks move smoothly on the rod. If the shafts are worn or bent, replace them with new ones.

22 Initial start-up after overhaul

Note: *Make sure the cooling system is checked carefully (especially the coolant level) before starting and running the engine.*

1 Make sure the engine oil level is correct, then remove the spark plugs from the engine. Place the engine STOP switch in the Off position and unplug the primary (low tension) wires from the coil.

2 Turn on the key switch and crank the engine over with the starter until the oil pressure indicator light goes off (which indicates that oil pressure exists). Reinstall the spark plugs, connect the wires and turn the switch to On. **Note (EN450/500 models only):** *If the oil pressure light won't go out, remove the oil filter (see Chapter 1). Hold the filter with the open end upright and pour oil into the center hole until the filter is full. Let the oil settle, then top it off again (you may need to do this twice). Reinstall the filter (a small amount of oil may leak out when you install it).*

3 Make sure there is fuel in the tank, then turn the fuel tap to the On position and operate the choke.

4 Start the engine and allow it to run at a moderately fast idle until it reaches operating temperature.

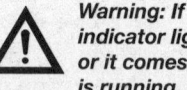

⚠ **Warning:** *If the oil pressure indicator light doesn't go off, or it comes on while the engine is running, stop the engine immediately.*

5 Check carefully for oil leaks and make sure the transmission and controls, especially the brakes, function properly before road testing the machine. Refer to Section 23 for the recommended break-in procedure.

6 Upon completion of the road test, and after the engine has cooled down completely, recheck the valve clearances (see Chapter 1).

23 Recommended break-in procedure

1 Any rebuilt engine needs time to break-in, even if parts have been installed in their original locations. For this reason, treat the machine gently for the first few miles to make sure oil has circulated throughout the engine and any new parts installed have started to seat.

2 Even greater care is necessary if the engine has been rebored or a new crankshaft has been installed. In the case of a rebore, the engine will have to be broken in as if the machine were new. This means greater use of the transmission and a restraining hand on the throttle until at least 500 miles (800 km) have been covered. There's no point in keeping to any set speed limit - the main idea is to keep from lugging (laboring) the engine and to gradually increase performance until the 500 mile (800 km) mark is reached. These recommendations can be lessened to an extent when only a new crankshaft is installed. Experience is the best guide, since it's easy to tell when an engine is running freely.

3 If a lubrication failure is suspected, stop the engine immediately and try to find the cause. If an engine is run without oil, even for a short period of time, severe damage will occur.

Chapter 3
Cooling system

Contents

Coolant level check .... See Chapter 1
Coolant reservoir - removal and installation 3
Coolant temperature gauge/light and sender unit - check
 and replacement 5
Coolant tubes - removal and installation 9
Cooling fan and thermostatic switch - check
 and replacement 4

Cooling system check .... See Chapter 1
Cooling system draining, flushing and refilling .... See Chapter 1
General information 1
Radiator - removal and installation 7
Radiator cap - check 2
Thermostat and housing - removal, check and installation 6
Water pump - check, removal, inspection and installation 8

Degrees of difficulty

Easy, suitable for novice with little experience	**Fairly easy,** suitable for beginner with some experience	**Fairly difficult,** suitable for competent DIY mechanic	**Difficult,** suitable for experienced DIY mechanic	**Very difficult,** suitable for expert DIY or professional

Specifications

General
Coolant type and mixture ratio .... See Chapter 1
Coolant capacity .... See Chapter 1
Radiator cap pressure rating .... 1.0 to 1.2 Bars (14 to 18 psi)
Thermostat rating
 EN450/500
  Opening temperature .... 69.5 to 72.5-degrees C (157 to 163-degrees F)
  Valve travel (when fully open) .... Not less than 8 mm (5/16-inch)
 EX250
  Opening temperature .... 63.5 to 66.5-degrees C (146 to 152-degrees F)
  Valve travel (when fully open) .... Not less than 6 mm (1/4-inch)

Torque specifications
Thermostatic fan switch-to-radiator
 Single-wire switch .... 7.4 Nm (65 in-lbs)
 Two-wire switch .... 18 Nm (156 in-lbs)
Coolant temperature sender unit-to-thermostat housing
 EN450, EN500 C and EX250 models .... 7.8 Nm (69 in-lbs)
 EN500 A models .... 7.4 Nm (65 in-lbs)

3•2 Cooling system

3.3a The reservoir tank is secured by two bolts (arrows) - here's the EN450/500 . . .

3.3b . . . and here's the EX250 reservoir tank

1 General information

1 The models covered by this manual are equipped with a liquid cooling system which utilizes a water/antifreeze mixture to carry away excess heat produced during the combustion process. The cylinders are surrounded by water jackets, through which the coolant is circulated by the water pump. The pump is mounted to the right side of the crankcase and is driven by the balancer shaft. The coolant passes up through a flexible hose and a coolant pipe, which distributes water around the cylinders. It flows through the water passages in the cylinder head, through a pair of tubes and hoses and into the thermostat housing. The hot coolant then flows down into the radiator (which is mounted on the frame downtubes to take advantage of maximum air flow), where it is cooled by the passing air, through another hose and back to the water pump, where the cycle is repeated. UK models include a coolant filter and temperature control valve.

2 An electric fan, mounted behind the radiator and automatically controlled by a thermostatic switch, provides a flow of cooling air through the radiator when the motorcycle is not moving. Under certain conditions, the fan may come on even after the engine is stopped, and the ignition switch is off, and may run for several minutes.

3 The coolant temperature sending unit, threaded into the thermostat housing, senses the temperature of the coolant and controls the coolant temperature gauge or light on the instrument cluster.

4 The entire system is sealed and pressurized. The pressure is controlled by a valve which is part of the radiator cap. By pressurizing the coolant, the boiling point is raised, which prevents premature boiling of the coolant. An overflow hose, connected between the radiator and reservoir tank, directs coolant to the tank when the radiator cap valve is opened by excessive pressure. The coolant is automatically siphoned back to the radiator as the engine cools.

5 Many cooling system inspection and service procedures are considered part of routine maintenance and are included in Chapter 1.

⚠ **Warning 1: Do not allow antifreeze to come in contact with your skin or painted surfaces of the motorcycle.** Rinse off spills immediately with plenty of water. Antifreeze is highly toxic if ingested. Never leave antifreeze lying around in an open container or in puddles on the floor; children and pets are attracted by its sweet smell and may drink it. Check with local authorities about disposing of used antifreeze. Many communities have collection centers which will see that antifreeze is disposed of safely.

⚠ **Warning 2: Do not remove the pressure cap from the thermostat housing when the engine and radiator are hot.** Scalding hot coolant and steam may be blown out under pressure, which could cause serious injury. When the engine has cooled, place a thick rag, like a towel, over the radiator cap; slowly rotate the cap counterclockwise (anticlockwise) to the first stop. This procedure allows any residual pressure to escape. When the steam has stopped escaping, press down on the cap while turning counterclockwise (anticlockwise) and remove it.

2 Radiator cap - check

If problems such as overheating and loss of coolant occur, check the entire system as described in Chapter 1. The radiator cap opening pressure should be checked by a dealer service department or service station equipped with the special tester required to do the job. If the cap is defective, replace it with a new one.

3 Coolant reservoir - removal and installation

1 If you're working on an EN450/500, remove the right side cover. If you're working on an EX250, remove the left side cover and, on 1986 and 1987 models, the left knee grip cover (see Chapter 8).
2 Disconnect the coolant hoses from the reservoir and catch any escaped coolant in a container.
3 Unbolt the reservoir from the bracket and take it out **(see illustrations)**.
4 Installation is the reverse of the removal steps.

4 Cooling fan and thermostatic switch - check and replacement

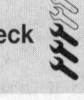

Check

1 If the engine is overheating and the cooling fan isn't coming on, first check the fuses (see Chapter 9). If the fuse is blown, check the fan circuit for a short to ground/earth (see the Wiring diagrams at the end of this book). If the fuses are all good, unplug the fan electrical connector **(see illustrations)**. Using two jumper wires, apply battery voltage to the terminals in the fan motor side of the electrical connector. If the fan doesn't work, replace the motor.
2 If the fan does come on, the problem lies in the thermostatic fan switch, the junction block, or the wiring that connects the components. Remove the jumper wires and reconnect the electrical connector to the fan.

Cooling system 3•3

4.1a Cooling fan switch (early EN450/500 models)

4.1b Cooling fan switch (later EN500 models)

a) If you're working on an early EN450/500 model (with a single-wire fan switch harness), unplug the electrical connector to the fan switch, attach a jumper wire to the harness side of the connector and ground/earth the other end of the jumper wire. If the fan comes on, the circuit to the motor is good, and the thermostatic fan switch is defective (see Step 10).

b) If you're working on a later model (with a double-wire fan switch connector), unplug the connector. Connect the terminals in the harness side of the connector together with a jumper wire. If the fan comes on, the circuit to the motor is good and the switch is defective.

3 If you're working on a single-wire model and the fan still doesn't work, find the fan relay (located under the seat on the electrical components plate - it has two white wires, a blue wire, and a yellow/blue wire attached to it) and place your hand on it. Repeatedly touch the jumper wire to ground/earth as detailed in Step 2 - if you hear/feel clicking inside the relay, the relay is proved good and the fault must lie in the wiring from the relay to the fan motor. If no clicking is heard in the relay, the fault lies in the wiring from the thermostatic fan switch to the relay. If all wiring checks out OK, the fan relay is likely to be the problem and should be replaced.

4 If you're working on a 2-wire model and the fan still doesn't work, check the wiring back to the main fuse (later 450 models) or junction box fuse (EN500 and EX250 models).

Replacement
Fan motor

⚠ **Warning: The engine must be completely cool before beginning this procedure.**

5 Disconnect the cable from the negative terminal of the battery and remove the radiator (see Section 7).

6 Remove the three bolts securing the fan bracket to the radiator **(see illustration)**. On early EN450, note which bolt secures the fan motor ground wire (EN450/500) or fan switch ground wire (EX250). Separate the fan and bracket from the radiator.

4.1c Cooling fan switch (EX250 models)

7 **Note:** *Steps 7 and 8 apply to EN450/500 models only. The fan, motor and shroud on EX250 models are sold as a complete assembly.* Remove the nut that retains the blades to the fan motor shaft **(see illustration)** and remove the fan blade assembly from the motor.

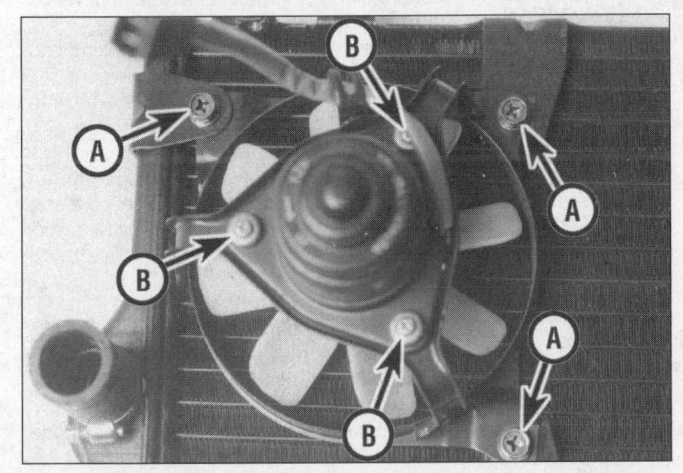

4.6 Remove the fan bracket-to-radiator bolts and separate the fan from the radiator (EN450/500 shown; others similar)

A Bracket-to-radiator bolts
B Fan motor-to-bracket screws

4.7 The EN450/500 fan blade assembly is retained to the motor shaft by a single nut (arrow)

3•4 Cooling system

5.4a The coolant temperature sender (arrow) is located at the bottom of the thermostat housing - here's the EN450/500 . . .

5.4b . . . and here's the EX250

8 Remove the screws that attach the fan motor to the bracket **(see illustration 4.6)** and detach the motor from the bracket.
9 Installation is the reverse of the removal steps.

Thermostatic fan switch

⚠️ *Warning: The engine must be completely cool before beginning this procedure.*

10 If you're working on an early EN450/500 model with a single-wire fan switch harness, don't place Teflon tape or silicone sealer on the switch threads. If you're working on a model with a two-wire fan switch harness, prepare the new switch by wrapping the new threads with Teflon tape or by coating the threads with RTV sealant.
11 Unscrew the switch from the radiator **(see illustration 4.1a, 4.1b or 4.1c)**. Be prepared for coolant spillage.
12 Quickly install the new switch, tightening it to the torque listed in this Chapter's Specifications.
13 Connect the electrical connector to the switch. Check, and if necessary, add coolant to the system (see Chapter 1).

5 Coolant temperature gauge/light and sender unit - check and replacement

Check

1 These motorcycles may be equipped with a coolant temperature gauge or a warning light.
2 If the engine has been overheating but the coolant temperature gauge hasn't been indicating a hotter than normal condition (or the warning light hasn't been coming on), begin with a check of the coolant level (see Chapter 1). If it's low, add the recommended type of coolant and be sure to locate the source of the leak.

3 Remove the seat and the fuel tank (see Chapters 8 and 4).
4 Locate the coolant temperature sender unit, which is screwed into the thermostat housing **(see illustrations)**. Disconnect the electrical connector from the sender unit and turn the ignition key to the Run position (don't crank the engine over).
  a) If you're working on a model with a temperature gauge, the gauge should read Cold.
  b) If you're working on a model with a warning light, the light should stay out.
5 With the ignition key still in the Run position, connect one end of a jumper wire to the sender unit wire and connect the other end of the jumper wire to ground. The needle on the temperature gauge should swing over to the Hot mark or the warning light should come on.

Caution: If the motorcycle has a gauge, don't ground the wire any longer than necessary or the gauge may be damaged.

6 If the gauge or light passes both of these tests but doesn't operate correctly under normal riding conditions, the temperature sender unit is defective and must be replaced.
7 If the gauge or light didn't respond to the tests properly, either the wire to the gauge is bad, the gauge itself is defective or the bulb is burned out.

Replacement

Sender unit

⚠️ *Warning: The engine must be completely cool before beginning this procedure.*

8 Unscrew the sender unit from the thermostat housing (be prepared for coolant spillage) and quickly install the new unit, tightening to the torque listed in this Chapter's Specifications.
9 Connect the electrical connector to the sender unit. Check, and if necessary, add coolant to the system (see Chapter 1).

Coolant temperature gauge or bulb

10 Refer to Chapter 9 for the coolant temperature gauge or bulb replacement procedure.

6 Thermostat and housing - removal, check and installation

⚠️ *Warning: The engine must be completely cool before beginning this procedure.*

Removal

1 If the thermostat is functioning properly, the coolant temperature gauge should rise to the normal operating temperature quickly and stay there, only rising above the normal position occasionally when the engine gets abnormally hot. If the engine does not reach normal operating temperature quickly, or if it overheats, the thermostat should be removed and checked, or replaced with a new one.
2 Refer to Chapter 1 and drain the cooling system.
3 Remove the seat and fuel tank (see Chapters 8 and 4). If you're working on an EN450/500, remove the left side cover. If you're working on an EX250, remove the fairings.

EN450/500 models

4 Disconnect the hoses and temperature sensor connector from the thermostat housing **(see illustration 5.4a and the accompanying illustration)**.
5 Loosen the clamp on the filler neck hose and unbolt the thermostat housing from the frame **(see illustration)**. Work the filler neck free of the hose and remove the thermostat housing.
6 Remove the thermostat housing cover **(see illustration)**.

Cooling system 3•5

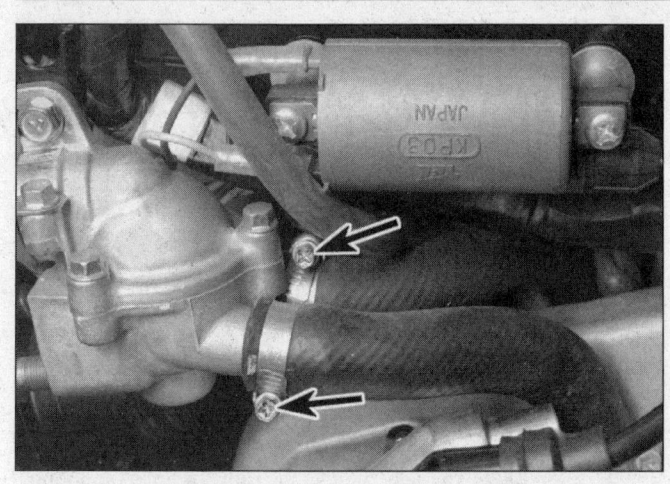

6.4 Loosen the clamps (arrows) and disconnect the hoses from the thermostat housing (EN450/500)

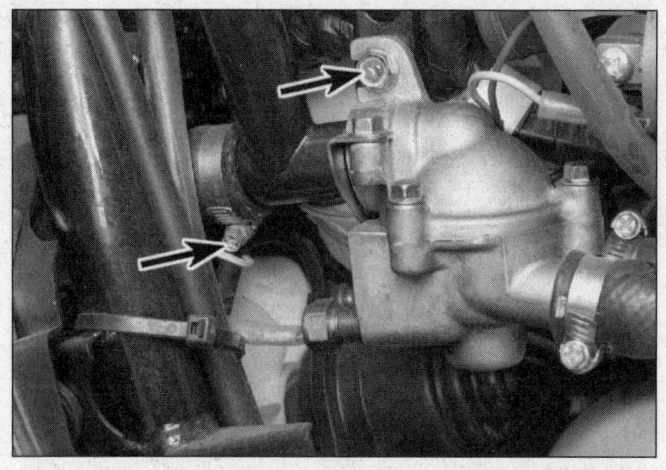

6.5 Loosen the hose clamp (lower arrow); unbolt the housing from the frame (upper arrow), then disconnect the filler neck from the hose and take the housing out (EN450/500)

EX250 models

7 Disconnect the hoses and temperature sensor wire from the thermostat housing **(see illustration 5.4b)**. Unbolt the thermostat housing and lift it out, noting that one of its bolts secures a ground wire.
8 Unbolt the thermostat housing cover and lift it off **(see illustration)**.

All models

9 Note the position of the relief hole, then lift out the thermostat **(see illustrations)**.
10 Check the cover O-ring and replace it if its condition is in doubt. It's a good idea to replace the O-ring as a matter of course.

Check

11 Remove any coolant deposits, then visually check the thermostat for corrosion, cracks and other damage. If it was open when it was removed, the thermostat is defective.
12 To check the thermostat operation, submerge it in a container of water along with a

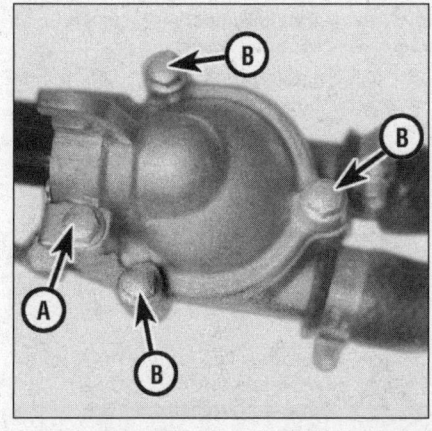

6.6 Remove the thermostat housing bolts (B); the forward bolt (A) secures the filler neck retaining bracket (EN450/500)

thermometer. The thermostat should be suspended so it does not touch the sides of the container.

6.8 Here are the EX250 thermostat housing bolts

⚠ *Warning: Antifreeze is poisonous. Do not use a cooking pan to test the thermostat.*

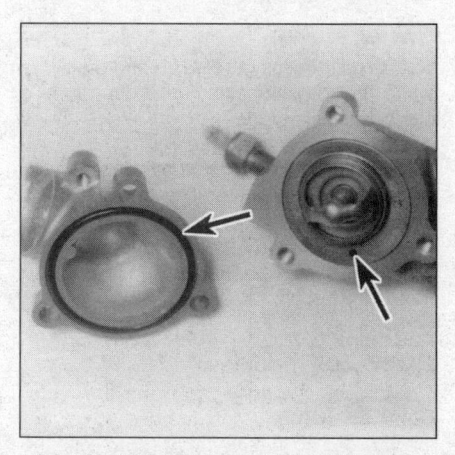

6.9a Note the position of the relief hole (right arrow); the O-ring (left arrow) should be replaced whenever the thermostat is replaced - here's the EN450/500 . . .

6.9b . . . and here's the EX250 (arrow)

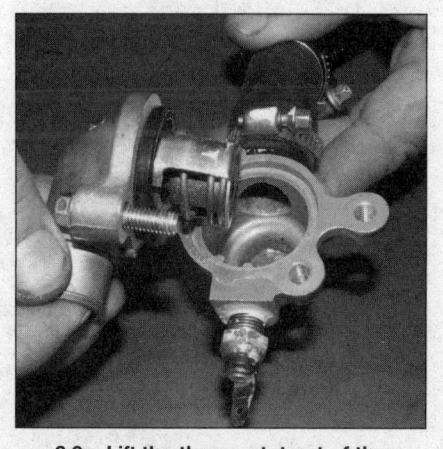

6.9c Lift the thermostat out of the housing (EX250)

3•6 Cooling system

7.6a On EN450/500 models, remove the radiator mounting bolts (arrow) from each side of the radiator . . .

7.6b . . . on EX250 models, remove the radiator grille mounting bolts (left arrows) and the radiator mounting bolts from the top front (left side of radiator shown)

13 Gradually heat the water in the container with a hot plate or stove and check the temperature when the thermostat first starts to open.
14 Compare the opening temperature to the values listed in this Chapter's Specifications.
15 Continue heating the water until the valve is fully open.
16 Measure how far the thermostat valve has opened and compare to the value listed in this Chapter's Specifications.
17 If these specifications are not met, or if the thermostat doesn't open while the water is heated, replace it with a new one.

Installation

18 Install the thermostat into the housing with the relief hole positioned correctly **(see illustration 6.9a or 6.9b)**.
19 Install a new O-ring in the groove in the thermostat cover.
20 Place the cover on the housing and install the bolts, tightening them securely.

CAUTION: On EX250 models, be careful not to let the wiring harness rub on the thermostat housing bolt. If it does, it can wear through due to movement caused by turning the handlebars, which will cause electrical problems.

21 The remainder of installation is the reverse of the removal steps. Fill the cooling system with the recommended coolant (see Chapter 1).

7 Radiator - removal and installation

Warning: The engine must be completely cool before beginning this procedure.

1 Set the bike on its centerstand (if equipped).
2 If you're working on an EX250, remove the fairing and fuel tank (see Chapters 8 and 4). Unbolt the grille from the radiator.
3 Remove the fan shroud from the radiator. Drain the cooling system (see Chapter 1).
4 Disconnect the fan motor connector. Disconnect the ground wire for the fan switch (if equipped).
5 Loosen the radiator hose clamps. Work the hoses free from the fittings, taking care not to damage the fittings in the process.
6 Remove the radiator mounting bolts **(see illustrations)**. Take the radiator out.
7 Inspect the mounting bushings. Replace them if they're cracked or deteriorated.
8 Installation is the reverse of the removal steps, with the following additions:
 a) Don't forget to connect the fan switch ground wire (if equipped).
 b) Fill the cooling system with the recommended coolant (see Chapter 1).

8 Water pump - check, removal, inspection and installation

Warning: The engine must be completely cool before beginning this procedure.

Check

1 Visually check the area around the water pump for coolant leaks. Try to determine if the leak is simply the result of a loose hose clamp or deteriorated hose.
2 Set the bike on its centerstand (if equipped). If you're working on an EX250, remove the shift linkage lever and engine sprocket cover (see Chapters 2A and 6).
3 Drain the engine coolant following the procedure in Chapter 1.

EN450/500 models

4 Loosen the hose clamp on the water pump cover fitting and remove the water pump cover bolts **(see illustration)**. Pull the cover away from the engine, separating the coolant pipe from the cylinder block as you do so.
5 Try to wiggle the pump impeller back-

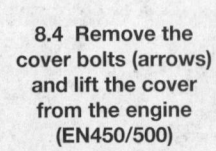

8.4 Remove the cover bolts (arrows) and lift the cover from the engine (EN450/500)

Cooling system 3•7

8.5 If you can wiggle the impeller or pull it in-and-out, the pump is defective (EN450/500)

8.11 Turn the impeller clockwise to remove it from the shaft (EN450/500)

and-forth and in-and-out **(see illustration)**. If you can feel movement, the water pump must be replaced.

6 Check the impeller blades for corrosion. If they are heavily corroded, replace the water pump and flush the system thoroughly (it would also be a good idea to check the internal condition of the radiator).

7 If the cause of the leak was just a defective cover gasket, remove the old gasket and install a new one.

Removal

8 Drain the coolant and remove the cover (if it hasn't already been removed).
9 Drain the engine oil (see Chapter 1).

EN450/500 models

10 Remove the water pump cover as described above.
11 Shift the transmission into first gear and, with the rear tire in firm contact with the floor, press the brake pedal to keep the engine from turning. Unscrew the impeller in a clockwise direction and take it off the shaft **(see illustration)**.

12 Take the water pump housing and gasket off the engine.
13 Turn the water pump shaft clockwise to remove it (if necessary).
14 Remove the gasket from the water pump housing and pry out the oil seal **(see illustration)**.

EX250 models

15 If necessary, remove the water pump cover **(see illustration)**. **Note:** *The water pump can be removed without removing the cover. However, it will be easier to unbolt the cover while the pump is still attached to the engine.*
16 Remove the water pump mounting bolts and pull it out of the engine **(see illustration)**.

Inspection

17 If you haven't already done so on an EX250 model, remove the water pump cover as described above. Check all parts for wear and damage and replace the pump if problems are found.
18 If the mechanical seal needs to be

8.14 Pry the oil seal out of the housing (EN450/500)

replaced on an EN450/500, have it pressed out and a new one pressed in by a Kawasaki dealer. The water pump on EX250 models is sold as an assembly, so it must be replaced with a new one if the mechanical seal is defective.

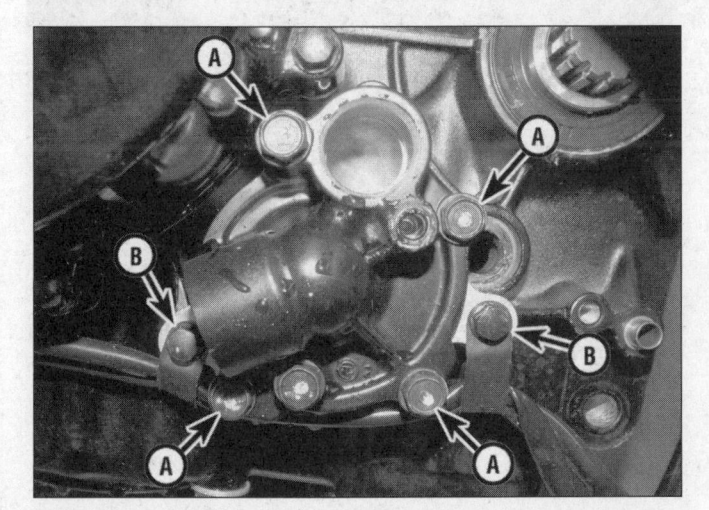

8.15a Water pump cover bolts (A) and mounting bolts (B) (EX250)

8.15b Pull the pump out of the engine - use a new O-ring on installation (EX250)

3•8 Cooling system

8.19 Install a new oil seal and gasket (EN450/500)

8.20 Position the housing on the engine, install a new gasket and the dowels (arrows); turn the impeller counter-clockwise to install it on the shaft (EN450/500)

Installation

EN450/500 models

19 Install a new oil seal and gasket on the back side of the pump housing **(see illustration)**.
20 Install the pump housing on the engine. Install the dowels (if they were removed), the shaft (if removed), a new cover gasket and the impeller **(see illustration)**. Turn the impeller counterclockwise to tighten it.
21 Install the pump cover bolts. The lower right bolt is the only one with a washer **(see illustration)**.

EX250 models

22 Install a new O-ring on the pump body **(see illustration 8.15b)**. Coat it with engine oil.
23 Align the slot in the water pump drive shaft with the tab on the oil pump shaft. Slide the water pump into the engine and tighten the mounting bolts.

24 Install the water pump cover (if it was removed), using a new gasket.

9 Coolant tubes - removal and installation

Warning: *The engine must be completely cool for this procedure.*

1 Remove the seat and fuel tank (see Chapter 4).
2 Remove the screws that secure the tubes to the engine. **Note:** *These screws may be very tight. Be sure to use the correct size screwdriver bit. It's a good idea to replace any Phillips screws with Allen screws that can be removed more easily in the future.*
3 Pull the tubes out of the engine **(see illustrations)**.

8.21 The lower right cover bolt (arrow) is the only one with a washer (EN450/500)

9.3a Pull the tubes out of the cylinder head and remove the O-rings with a pointed tool (EN450/500)

9.3b Here are the EX250 coolant tubes at the water pump (arrows)

Cooling system 3•9

9.3c The lower tube runs to this hose at the radiator (EX250) . . .

9.3d . . . the upper tube runs to this hose and fitting at the back of the engine . . .

9.3e . . . use a new O-ring if you remove the fitting

9.3f This fitting and hose run from the cylinder head to the thermostat housing (EX250)

HAYNES HiNT *The tubes will be easier to pull out if you spray a little penetrating oil into the joint where the tube enters the engine. This will break up any corrosion and free the O-ring.*

4 Remove the O-ring from each tube with a pointed tool. Lightly coat new O-rings with high-temperature grease and install them on the tubes.

5 If the tubes are being removed to provide access for other work, suspend them from the handlebars with their ends up.

6 Installation is the reverse of the removal steps.

Notes

Chapter 4
Fuel and exhaust systems

Contents

Air switching valve (US EN450/500 models) - operational test....	12
Carburetor overhaul - general information	5
Carburetors - disassembly, cleaning and inspection	7
Carburetors - reassembly and fuel level adjustment...................	8
Carburetors - removal and installation	6
Choke cable (EN450 and EX250 models) - removal, installation and adjustment..	10
Exhaust system - removal and installation.................................	11
Fuel system - check and filter cleaning........................	See Chapter 1
Fuel tank - cleaning and repair..	3
Fuel tank - removal and installation	2
Fuel tap - removal and installation	See Chapter 1
General information...	1
Idle fuel/air mixture adjustment - general information.................	4
Idle speed - check and adjustment	See Chapter 1
Throttle cables - removal, installation and adjustment	9
Throttle operation/grip freeplay - check and adjustment	See Chapter 1

Degrees of difficulty

Easy, suitable for novice with little experience	**Fairly easy,** suitable for beginner with some experience	**Fairly difficult,** suitable for competent DIY mechanic	**Difficult,** suitable for experienced DIY mechanic	**Very difficult,** suitable for expert DIY or professional

Specifications

EN450/500 models

General

Fuel tank capacity	See *Dimensions and weights* in the Reference Section near the end of this manual
Fuel grade	Unleaded or low-lead (subject to local regulations), minimum octane rating 91 RON
Idle speed..	See Chapter 1
Carburetor type	
Through 1996...	Keihin CVK34 (2)
1997 and later	Keihin CVK32 (2)

4•2 Fuel and exhaust systems

Jet sizes
Main jet
  EN 450 models
    US and Canada except US high altitude............................ 125
    US high altitude.. 122
    UK.. 112
  EN500 models (through 1996 A7)
    US and Canada
      Left carburetor... 112
      Right carburetor.. 115
    UK.. 105
  EN500 models (1996 and later, C1-on)................................... 102
Main air jet.. 100
Jet needle
  EN450 models
    US.. N31D
    UK and Canada.. N31E
  EN500 models (through 1996 A7)
    US and Canada.. N60Q
    UK
      Left carburetor... N60T
      Right carburetor.. N60S
  EN500 models (1996 and later, C1-on)
    C1
      Austria, Switzerland, US... N2WE
      UK, France, Italy, Netherlands, Germany, Europe,
        Greece, Sweden, Norway, Spain, Canada.................. N2WD
    C2 through C4
      Austria, Switzerland, Germany, US, Canada.............. N2WE
      UK, France, Italy, Netherlands, Europe, Greece,
        Sweden, Norway, Spain, Korea.................................. N2WD
    C5 and later.. N2WE
Pilot jet
  Except US high altitude, 1985 through 1990........................ 35
  US high altitude, 1985 through 1990..................................... 32
Pilot air jet.. 150
Pilot screw setting
  EN450 models
    US.. Preset
    Except US... 1-3/4 turns out
  EN500 models... 2 turns out
Starter jet
  1985 through 1996 A7.. 45
  1996 C1 and later... 48

Float
Height.. 17 mm (0.669 inch)

Fuel level
EN450 models... -0.5 mm (-0.020 inch)
EN500 models... 0.5 +/- 1 mm (0.020 +/- 0.040 inch)

Air switching valve
Closing vacuum.. 430 to 490 mm Hg (17 to 19 inches Hg)

EX250 models

General
Fuel tank capacity.. See *Dimensions and weights* in the Reference Section near the end of this manual
Fuel grade... Unleaded or low-lead (subject to local regulations), minimum octane rating 91 RON
Idle speed... See Chapter 1
Carburetor type
  1986 and 1987... Keihin CVK32 (2)
  1988 and later.. Keihin CVK30 (2)

Fuel and exhaust systems 4•3

Jet sizes

1986 and 1987
   Main jet
      Except California models.. 110
      California models... 108
   Main air jet 100
   Jet needle
      Left... N52H
      Right N52I
   Pilot jet 35
   Pilot air jet 90
   Pilot screw setting.. 2-1/2 turns out
   Starter jet 52

1988 and later
   Main jet
      US 102
      Except US... 105
   Main air jet 100
   Jet needle N16I
   Needle jet 6
   Pilot jet
      US 35
      Except US... 38
   Pilot air jet 90
   Pilot screw setting
      US (including California) .... Not specified
      Except US... 2 turns out
   Starter jet 52

Float
Height... 17 mm (0.669 inch)

Fuel level
1986 and 1987 .... -0.5 mm (-0.020 inch)
1988 and later .... -0.5 mm (-0.020 inch) to + 1.5 mm 0.060 inch)

1 General information

The fuel system consists of the fuel tank, the fuel tap and filter, the carburetors and the connecting lines, hoses and control cables.

The carburetors used on these motorcycles are two constant vacuum Keihins with butterfly-type throttle valves. For cold starting, an enrichment circuit is actuated either by a cable and the choke lever mounted on the left handlebar (EN450 models and EX250 models), or by a hand-control on the left carburetor (EN500 models).

The exhaust system is a twin pipe design with a crossover pipe.

Some of the fuel system service procedures are considered routine maintenance items and for that reason are included in Chapter 1.

2 Fuel tank - removal and installation

Warning: *Gasoline (petrol) is extremely flammable, so take extra precautions when you work on any part of the fuel system. Don't smoke or allow open flames or bare light bulbs near the work area, and don't work in a garage where a gas-type appliance (such as a water heater or clothes dryer) is present. Since gasoline is carcinogenic, wear nitrile gloves and if you spill any fuel on your skin, rinse it off immediately with soap and water. When you perform any kind of work on the fuel system, wear safety glasses and have a fire extinguisher suitable for a Class B type fire (flammable liquids) on hand.*

1 The fuel tank is held in place at the forward end by two cups, one on each side of the tank, which slide over two rubber dampers on the frame. The rear of the tank is fastened to a bracket by one or two bolts and rubber insulators (depending on model), which fit through a flange projecting from the tank.

2 Remove the seat and disconnect the cable from the negative terminal of the battery. On 1986 and 1987 EX250 models, remove the knee grip covers (see Chapter 8). On all EX250 models, remove the fairing-to-tank screws.

4•4 Fuel and exhaust systems

2.3a Fuel tank mounting bolts and lines - EX250 (EN450/500 models use a single bolt)

2.3b On EX250 models, disconnect the vacuum line and fuel line from the tap (arrows)

3 On EX250 models, mark and disconnect the breather hose and, on California models, the evaporative emission control system hoses from the tank **(see illustration)**. Disconnect the fuel hose and vacuum hose from the fuel tap **(see illustration)**.

⚠️ *Warning: There may be fuel present in the evaporative hose (marked with a red dot). Cover the hose with a rag to prevent it spraying.*

4 Remove the bolt(s) securing the rear of the tank to the bracket **(see illustration 2.3a)**.
5 On EX250 models, remove the tank-to-fairing bolts on each side (with collars) (see Chapter 8).
6 On EX450/500 models, turn the fuel tap to the On or Reserve position, lift the rear of the tank up, slide back the hose clamps and push the fuel and vacuum lines **(see illustrations)** off the fittings.
7 Slide the tank to the rear to disengage the front of the tank from the rubber dampers, then carefully lift the tank away from the machine.
8 Before installing the tank, check the condition of the rubber mounting dampers and the hoses on the underside of the tank - if they're hardened, cracked, or show any other signs of deterioration, replace them.
9 When replacing the tank, reverse the above procedure. If you're working on an EX250, install the tank-to-fairing bolts before installing the bolts at the rear of the tank. Make sure the tank seats properly and does not pinch any control cables or wires. If difficulty is encountered when trying to slide the tank cups onto the dampers, a small amount of light oil should be used to lubricate them.

3 Fuel tank - cleaning and repair

1 All repairs to the fuel tank should be carried out by a professional who has experience in this critical and potentially dangerous work. Even after cleaning and flushing of the fuel system, explosive fumes can remain and ignite during repair of the tank.
2 If the fuel tank is removed from the vehicle, it should not be placed in an area where sparks or open flames could ignite the fumes coming out of the tank. Be especially careful inside garages where a gas-type appliance is located, because it could cause an explosion.

4 Idle fuel/air mixture adjustment - general information

1 Due to the increased emphasis on controlling motorcycle exhaust emissions, certain governmental regulations have been formulated which directly affect the carburetion of this machine. In order to comply with the regulations, the carburetors on some models have a metal sealing plug pressed into the hole over the pilot screw (which controls the idle fuel/air mixture) on each carburetor, so they can't be tampered with. These should only be removed in the event of a complete carburetor overhaul, and even then the screws should be returned to their original settings. The pilot screws on other models are accessible, but the use of an exhaust gas analyzer is the only accurate way to adjust the idle fuel/air mixture and be sure the machine doesn't exceed the emissions regulations.

2.6a The EN450/500 fuel line (arrow) and vent lines . . .

2.6b . . . are attached to fittings on the tank (arrows)

Fuel and exhaust systems 4•5

6.10 Label and disconnect the vacuum lines (arrow)

6.11a Pull the spring bands back from the air cleaner housing...

2 If the engine runs extremely rough at idle or continually stalls, and if a carburetor overhaul does not cure the problem, take the motorcycle to a Kawasaki dealer service department or other repair shop equipped with an exhaust gas analyzer. They will be able to properly adjust the idle fuel/air mixture to achieve a smooth idle and restore low speed performance.

5 Carburetor overhaul - general information

1 Poor engine performance, hesitation, hard starting, stalling, flooding and backfiring are all signs that major carburetor maintenance may be required.
2 Keep in mind that many so-called carburetor problems are really not carburetor problems at all, but mechanical problems within the engine or malfunctions within the ignition system. Try to establish for certain that the carburetors are in need of a major overhaul before beginning.
3 Check the fuel tap filter, the fuel lines, the tank cap vent, the intake manifold hose clamps, the vacuum hoses, the air filter element, the cylinder compression, the spark plugs, the air suction system (US models only) and the carburetor synchronization before assuming that a carburetor overhaul is required. Also make sure that the end of the carburetor vent tube is not placed near the air intake. This will cause fuel starvation, resulting in poor performance above 3,500 rpm and a maximum engine speed of 5,000 rpm.
4 Most carburetor problems are caused by dirt particles, varnish and other deposits which build up in and block the fuel and air passages. Also, in time, gaskets and O-rings shrink or deteriorate and cause fuel and air leaks which lead to poor performance.
5 When the carburetor is overhauled, it is generally disassembled completely and the parts are cleaned thoroughly with a carburetor cleaning solvent and dried with filtered, unlubricated compressed air. The fuel and air passages are also blown through with compressed air to force out any dirt that may have been loosened but not removed by the solvent. Once the cleaning process is complete, the carburetor is reassembled using new gaskets, O-rings and, generally, a new inlet needle valve and seat.
6 Before disassembling the carburetors, make sure you have a carburetor rebuild kit (which will include all necessary O-rings and other parts), some carburetor cleaner, a supply of rags, some means of blowing out the carburetor passages and a clean place to work. It is recommended that only one carburetor be overhauled at a time to avoid mixing up parts.

6 Carburetors - removal and installation

⚠️ *Warning: Gasoline (petrol) is extremely flammable, so take extra precautions when you work on any part of the fuel system. Don't smoke or allow open flames or bare light bulbs near the work area, and don't work in a garage where a gas-type appliance is present (such as a water heater or clothes dryer). Since gasoline is carcinogenic, wear nitrile gloves and if you spill any fuel on your skin, rinse it off immediately with soap and water. When you perform any kind of work on the fuel system, wear safety glasses and have a fire extinguisher suitable for a class B type fire (flammable liquids) on hand.*

Removal

1 Remove the seat and fuel tank (see Chapter 8 and Section 2).

EN450/500 models

2 If you're working on a US EN450/500 model, remove the vacuum switching valve for the air suction system (see Chapter 1).
3 On EN450 models, disconnect the choke cable from the carburetor assembly (see Section 10).
4 Loosen the locknuts on the throttle cable adjusters at the handlebar and turn the adjusters in all the way to create the maximum amount of slack in the cables.

6.11b ... then separate the air inlet ducts from the air box and place a piece of tape (arrow) over the air box openings

EX250 models

5 Remove the knee grip covers (1986 and 1987 models only) and side covers from both sides of the bike. Remove the rear fender (see Chapter 8).
6 Remove the battery (see Chapter 1).
7 Unbolt the air box.
8 Remove the coolant reservoir (see Chapter 3).
9 Unbolt the rear brake master cylinder reservoir and secure it out of the way. The brake line can be left connected.

All models

10 Mark and disconnect the vacuum hoses from the carburetors **(see illustration)**.
11 Slide the spring bands on the air inlet ducts away from the carburetors **(see illustration)**. Separate the air intake ducts from the air box by pulling the air box rearward, or else push the ducts into the air box, then attach a piece of duct tape across the air box openings **(see illustration)**.

4•6 Fuel and exhaust systems

6.12a Loosen the clamps on the intake manifold tubes

6.12b On EX250 models, remove the left manifold tube . . .

12 Loosen the clamp screws on the intake manifolds (the rubber tubes that connect the carburetors to the engine) **(see illustration)**. If you're working on an EX250, remove the left manifold from the engine **(see illustrations)**.
13 Pull the carburetor assembly clear of the air box tubes. Raise the assembly up far enough to disconnect the throttle cables (and choke cable if equipped), then remove the carburetors from the machine.
14 After the carburetors have been removed, stuff clean rags into the intake manifold tubes to prevent the entry of dirt or other objects.

Installation

15 Position the assembly over the intake manifold tubes. Lightly lubricate the ends of the throttle cables with multi-purpose grease and attach them to the throttle pulley. Make sure the accelerator and decelerator cables are in their proper positions.
16 Tilt the front of the assembly down and insert the fronts of the carburetors into the intake manifold tubes. Push the assembly forward and tighten the clamps.
17 Make sure the ducts from the air filter box are seated properly, then slide the spring bands into position.
18 Connect the choke cable to the assembly and adjust it (see Section 10).
19 The remainder of installation is the reverse of the removal steps, with the following additions:
a) Be sure the carburetor vent tube isn't pinched. If you're working on an EN450/500, don't place the end of the vent tube near the air intake (see illustration) or fuel starvation will occur, resulting in poor performance above 3,500 rpm and failure to rev past 5,000 rpm.
b) Adjust the throttle grip freeplay (see Chapter 1).
c) Check for fuel leaks.
d) Check and, if necessary, adjust the idle speed and carburetor synchronization (see Chapter 1).

7 Carburetors - disassembly, cleaning and inspection

⚠ *Warning: Gasoline (petrol) is extremely flammable, so take extra precautions when you work on any part of the fuel system. Don't smoke or allow open flames or bare light bulbs near the work area, and don't work in a garage where a gas-type appliance is present (such as a water heater or clothes dryer). Since gasoline is carcinogenic, wear nitrile gloves and if you spill any fuel on your skin, rinse it off immediately with soap and water. When you perform any kind of work on the fuel system, wear safety glasses and have a fire extinguisher suitable for a class B type fire (flammable liquids) on hand.*

Disassembly

1 Remove the carburetors from the

6.12c . . . the tube is labeled CARB on the carburetor side and HEAD on the cylinder head side

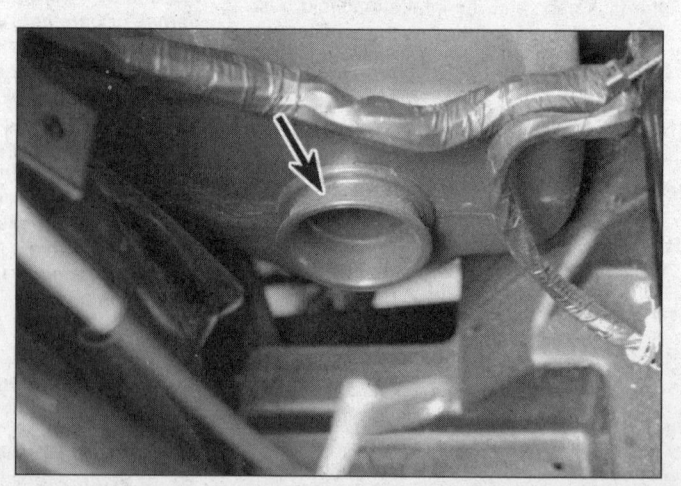

6.19 On EN450/500 models, be careful not to place the end of the carburetor vent tube near the air intake (arrow); this will cause fuel starvation

Fuel and exhaust systems 4•7

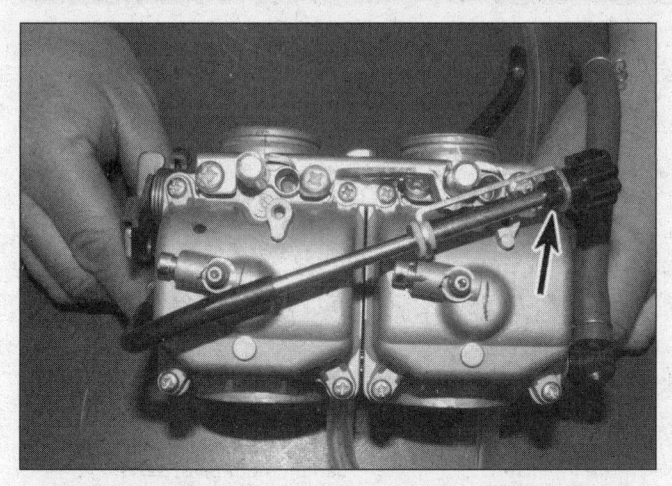

7.2a Remove the idle speed screw assembly (EX250 shown)

7.2b On the back side of the carburetor assembly, remove the screws (lower arrows) that secure the lower mounting bracket and detach the upper bracket (upper arrow)

machine as described in Section 6. Set the assembly on a clean working surface. **Note:** *Unless the O-rings on the fuel and vent fittings between the carburetors are leaking, don't detach the carburetors from their mounting brackets. Also, work on one carburetor at a time to avoid getting parts mixed up.*

2   If the carburetors must be separated from each other (during a complete overhaul, for example) remove the idle adjusting screw assembly **(see illustration)**, being careful not to lose the spring and washer on the end of the screw. Disconnect the fuel hoses. Remove the choke lever spring and choke lever (EN450/500 models) by removing the screw and plastic washers (two washers, one on each side of the lever), then remove the screws securing the upper and lower mounting plates to the carburetors **(see illustrations)**. Mark the position of each carburetor and gently separate them, noting how the throttle linkage is connected, and being careful not to lose any springs or fuel and vent fittings that are present between the carburetors.

7.2c On the front side of the carburetor assembly, remove two screws (arrows) from each carburetor and detach the bracket

3   Remove the four screws securing the top cover to the carburetor body **(see illustration)**. Lift the cover off and remove the piston spring.

4   Peel the diaphragm away from its groove in the carburetor body, being careful not to tear it. Lift out the diaphragm/piston assembly **(see illustration)**.

7.3 Each carburetor top cover is secured by four screws (arrows); one screw also secures the choke cable bracket (if equipped)

7.4 Remove the diaphragm/piston assembly from the carburetor body

4•8 Fuel and exhaust systems

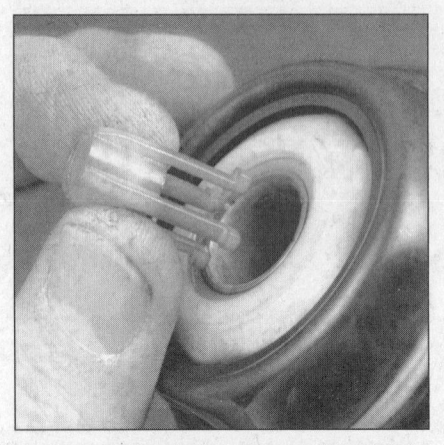

7.5a Remove the vacuum piston spring seat from the piston

7.5b Remove the needle from the piston

7.7 Push the float pivot pin out, then remove the float and valve needle assembly

7.8 Unscrew the main jet from the needle jet holder

7.9 Unscrew the needle jet holder/air bleed pipe

5 Remove the piston spring seat and separate the needle from the piston **(see illustrations)**.
6 Remove the four screws retaining the float bowl to the carburetor body, then detach the bowl.
7 Push the float pivot pin out and detach the float (and fuel inlet valve needle) from the carburetor body **(see illustration)**. Detach the valve needle from the float.
8 Unscrew the main jet from the needle jet holder **(see illustration)**.
9 Unscrew the needle jet holder/air bleed pipe **(see illustration)**.

10 Using a wood or plastic tool, push the needle jet out of the carburetor body **(see illustration)**.
11 Using a small, flat-bladed screwdriver, remove the pilot jet **(see illustration)**.
12 The pilot (idle mixture) screw is located in the bottom of the carburetor body **(see**

7.10 Working from the top of the carburetor, push the needle jet out with a wood or plastic tool

7.11 Unscrew the pilot jet

Fuel and exhaust systems 4•9

7.12a Location of the pilot screw (arrow)

7.12b One way to remove the sealing plug is to drill a very small hole above it (left arrow), then reach into the hole with a hooked tool and push out the plug (right arrow)

illustration). On US models, this screw is hidden behind a plug which will have to be removed if the screw is to be taken out. The usual way to do this is to drill a hole in the plug, then pry it out. To avoid the risk of drilling into the screw, you can also drill a very small hole above the plug, then insert a hooked tool into the hole and push the plug out **(see illustration)**. On all models, turn the pilot screw in, counting the number of turns until it bottoms lightly. Record that number for use when installing the screw. Now remove the pilot screw along with its spring, washer and O-ring.

13 The choke plunger can be removed by unscrewing the nut that retains it to the carburetor body, if the carburetors have been separated from each other (see Step 2).

Cleaning

Caution: Use only a carburetor cleaning solution that is safe for use with plastic parts (be sure to read the label on the container).

14 Submerge the metal components in the carburetor cleaner for approximately thirty minutes (or longer, if the directions recommend it).

15 After the carburetor has soaked long enough for the cleaner to loosen and dissolve most of the varnish and other deposits, use a brush to remove the stubborn deposits. Clean it again, then dry it with compressed air. Blow out all of the fuel and air passages in the main and upper body.

Caution: Never clean the jets or passages with a piece of wire or a drill bit, as they will be enlarged, causing the fuel and air metering rates to be upset.

Inspection

16 Check the operation of the choke plunger. If it doesn't move smoothly, replace it, along with the return spring.

17 Check the tapered portion of the pilot screw for wear or damage **(see illustration)**. Replace the pilot screw if necessary.

18 Check the carburetor body, float bowl and top cover for cracks, distorted sealing surfaces and other damage. If any defects are found, replace the faulty component, although replacement of the entire carburetor will probably be necessary (check with your parts supplier for the availability of separate components).

19 Check the diaphragm for splits, holes and general deterioration. Holding it up to a light will help to reveal problems of this nature.

20 Insert the vacuum piston in the carburetor body and see that it moves up-and-down smoothly. Check the surface of the piston for wear. If it's worn excessively or doesn't move smoothly in the bore, replace the carburetor.

21 Check the jet needle for straightness by rolling it on a flat surface (such as a piece of glass). Replace it if it's bent or if the tip is worn.

22 Check the tip of the fuel inlet valve needle. If it has grooves or scratches in it, it must be replaced. Push in on the rod in the other end of the needle, then release it - if it doesn't spring back, replace the valve needle.

23 Check the O-rings on the float bowl and the drain plug (in the float bowl). Replace them if they're damaged.

24 Operate the throttle shaft to make sure the throttle butterfly valve opens and closes smoothly. If it doesn't, replace the carburetor.

25 Check the floats for damage. This will usually be apparent by the presence of fuel inside one of the floats. If the floats are damaged, they must be replaced.

8 Carburetors - reassembly and fuel level adjustment

Caution: When installing the jets, be careful not to over-tighten them - they're made of soft material and can strip or shear easily.

Note: When reassembling the carburetors, be sure to use the new O-rings and gaskets.

Reassembly

1 If the choke plunger was removed, install it in its bore, followed by its spring and nut. Tighten the nut securely and install the cap.

2 Install the pilot screw (if removed) along with its spring, washer and O-ring, turning it in until it seats lightly. Now, turn the screw out the number of turns that was previously

7.17 Check the tapered portion of the pilot screw (A) for wear or damage

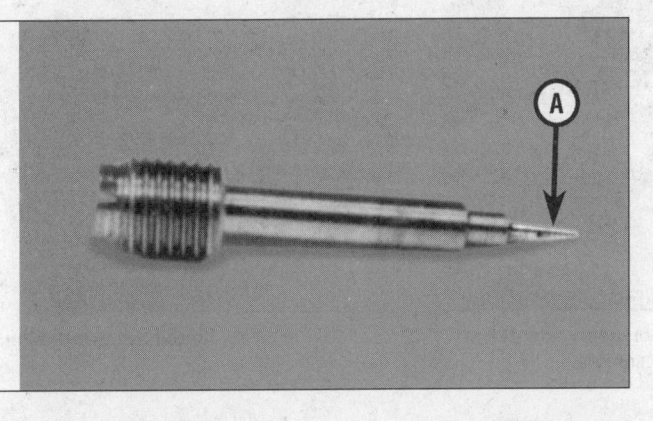

4•10 Fuel and exhaust systems

recorded. If you're working on a US model, install a new metal plug in the hole over the screw. Apply a little bonding agent around the circumference of the plug after it has been seated.

3   Install the pilot jet, tightening it securely.
4   Turn the carburetor body upside-down and install the needle jet into its hole, small diameter first **(see illustration)**.
5   Install the needle jet holder/air bleed pipe, tightening it securely.
6   Install the main jet into the needle jet holder/air bleed pipe, tightening it securely.
7   Drop the jet needle down into its hole in the vacuum piston and install the spring seat over the needle. Make sure the spring seat doesn't cover the hole at the bottom of the vacuum piston - reposition it if necessary.
8   Install the diaphragm/vacuum piston assembly into the carburetor body. Lower the spring into the piston. Seat the bead of the diaphragm into the groove in the top of the carburetor body, making sure the diaphragm isn't distorted or kinked **(see illustration)**. This isn't always an easy task. If the diaphragm seems too large in diameter and doesn't want to seat in the groove, place the top cover over the carburetor diaphragm, insert your finger into the throat of the carburetor and push up on the vacuum piston. Push down gently on the top cover - it should drop into place, indicating the diaphragm has seated in its groove.
9   Install the top cover, tightening the screws securely. If you're working on the right-hand carburetor, don't forget to install the choke cable bracket (if equipped) on the corner.
10 Invert the carburetor. Attach the fuel inlet valve needle to the float. Set the float into position in the carburetor, making sure the valve needle seats correctly. Install the float pivot pin. To check the float height, hold the carburetor so the float hangs down, then tilt it back until the valve needle is just seated (the rod in the end of the valve shouldn't be compressed). Measure the distance from the carburetor body to the top of the float and compare your measurement to the float height listed in this Chapter's Specifications. If it isn't as specified, carefully bend the tang that contacts the valve needle up or down until the float height is correct.
11 Install the O-ring into the groove in the float bowl. Place the float bowl on the carburetor and install the screws, tightening them securely.
12 If the carburetors were separated, install new O-rings on the fuel and vent fittings. Lubricate the O-rings on the fittings with a light film of oil and install them into their respective holes, making sure they seat completely.
13 Position the coil springs between the carburetors, gently push the carburetors together, then make sure the throttle linkages are correctly engaged. Check the fuel and vent fittings to make sure they engage properly also.
14 Install the upper and lower mounting plates and install the screws, but don't tighten them completely yet. Set the carburetors on a sheet of glass, then align them with a straightedge placed along the edges of the bores. When the centerlines of the carburetors are both in horizontal and vertical alignment, tighten the mounting plate screws securely.

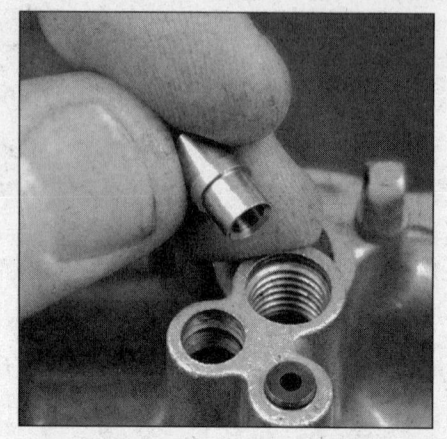

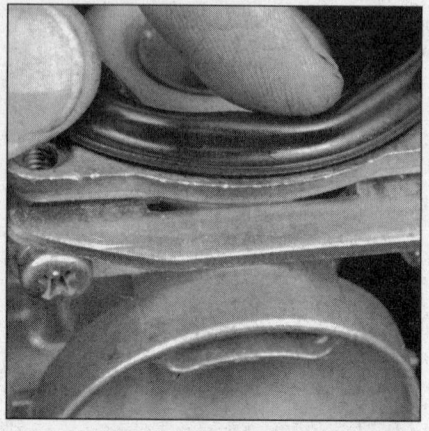

8.4 Install the needle jet, small diameter end first

8.8 Make sure the bead of the vacuum diaphragm seats in its groove, and that the diaphragm isn't distorted

15 Install the choke lever (if equipped), making sure it engages correctly with both choke plungers. Position a plastic washer on each side of the choke lever **(see illustration)** and install the screws, tightening them securely. Install the lever return spring, then make sure the choke mechanism operates smoothly.
16 Install the throttle linkage springs **(see illustration)**. Visually synchronize the throttle butterfly valves, turning the adjusting screws on the throttle linkage, if necessary, to equalize the clearance between the butterfly valve and throttle bore of each carburetor. Check to ensure the throttle operates smoothly.

Fuel level adjustment

⚠ *Warning: Gasoline (petrol) is extremely flammable, so take extra precautions when you work on any part of the fuel system. Don't smoke or allow open flames or bare light bulbs near the work area, and don't work in a garage where a gas-type appliance is present (such as a water heater or clothes dryer). Since gasoline is carcinogenic, wear nitrile gloves and if you spill any fuel on your*

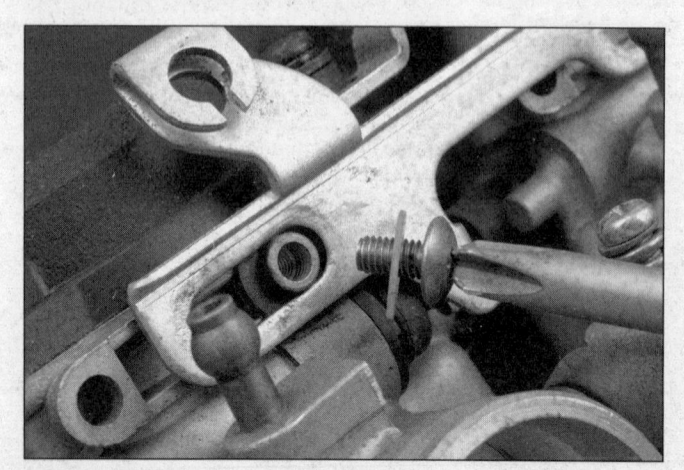

8.15 Make sure to install a plastic washer on each side of the choke lever when installing the screws

8.16 Install the throttle linkage springs

Fuel and exhaust systems 4•11

8.18 Checking the fuel level in a carburetor - the level (left arrow) should be within the specified distance of the carburetor body's low point (right arrow)

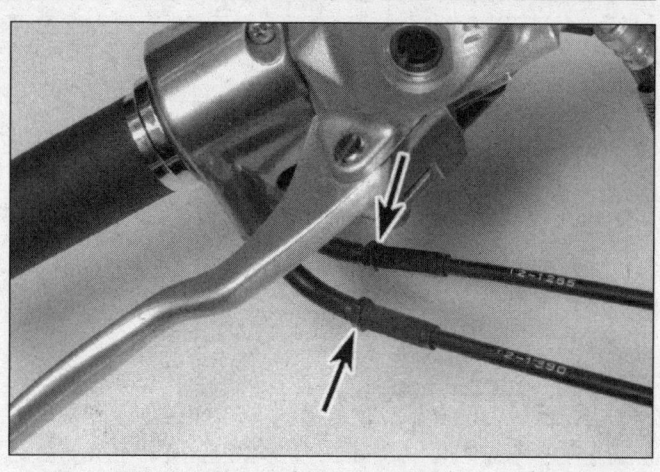

9.2 On EN450/500 models, loosen the locknuts (arrows) on the throttle cable adjusters, then turn the adjusters to create maximum slack in the cables

skin, rinse it off immediately with soap and water. When you perform any kind of work on the fuel system, wear safety glasses and have a fire extinguisher suitable for a class B type fire (flammable liquids) on hand.

17 Lightly clamp the carburetor assembly in the jaws of a vise. Make sure the vise jaws are lined with wood. Set an auxiliary fuel tank next to the vise, but at an elevation that is higher than the carburetors (resting on a box, for example). Connect a hose from the fuel tank to the fuel inlet fitting on the carburetor assembly.
18 Attach Kawasaki service tool no. 57001-1017 to the drain fitting on the bottom of one of the carburetor float bowls (both will be checked) **(see illustration)**. This is a clear plastic tube graduated in millimeters. An alternative is to use a length of clear plastic tubing and an accurate ruler. Hold the graduated tube (or the free end of the clear plastic tube) against the carburetor body, as shown in the accompanying illustration. If the Kawasaki tool is being used, raise the zero mark to a point several millimeters above the bottom edge of the carburetor main body. If a piece of clear plastic tubing is being used, make a mark on the tubing at a point several millimeters above the bottom edge of the carburetor main body.
19 Unscrew the drain screw at the bottom of the float bowl a couple of turns, then let fuel flow into the tube. Wait for the fuel level to stabilize, then slowly lower the tube until the zero mark is level with the bottom edge of the carburetor body. **Note:** *Don't lower the zero mark below the bottom edge of the carburetor then bring it back up - the reading won't be accurate.*
20 Measure the distance between the mark and top of the fuel level in the tube or gauge. This distance is the fuel level - write it down on a piece of paper, screw in the drain screw, close off the fuel supply, then move on to the next carburetor and check it the same way.
21 Compare your fuel level readings to the value listed in this Chapter's Specifications. If the fuel level in either carburetor is not correct, remove the float bowl and bend the tang up or down (see Step 10), as necessary, then recheck the fuel level. **Note:** *Bending the tang up increases the float height and lowers the fuel level - bending it down decreases the float height and raises the fuel level.*
22 After the fuel level for each carburetor has been adjusted, install the carburetor assembly (see Section 6).

9 Throttle cables - removal, installation and adjustment

Removal

EN450/500 models

1 Remove the fuel tank (see Section 2).
2 If you're working on an EN450/500, loosen the locknuts on the accelerator cable and decelerator cable at the handlebar and screw the cable adjusters in to create as much slack as possible **(see illustration)**.
3 Remove the cable retaining plate screw at the handlebar **(see illustration)**.

All models

4 Remove the cable/switch housing screws and detach the housing from the handlebar **(see illustration)**.

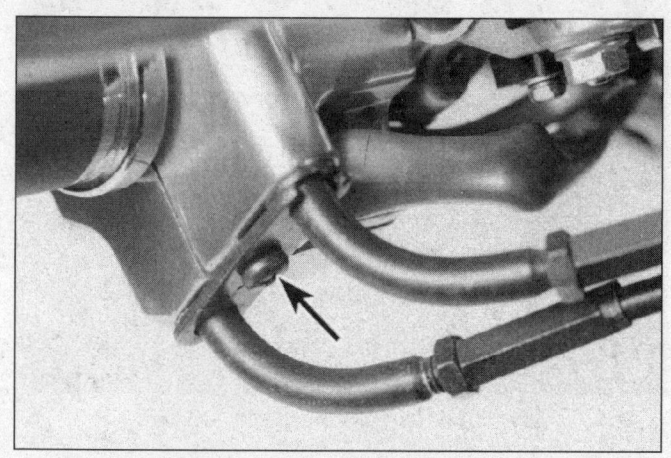

9.3 On EN450/500 models, remove the cable retaining plate screw (arrow)

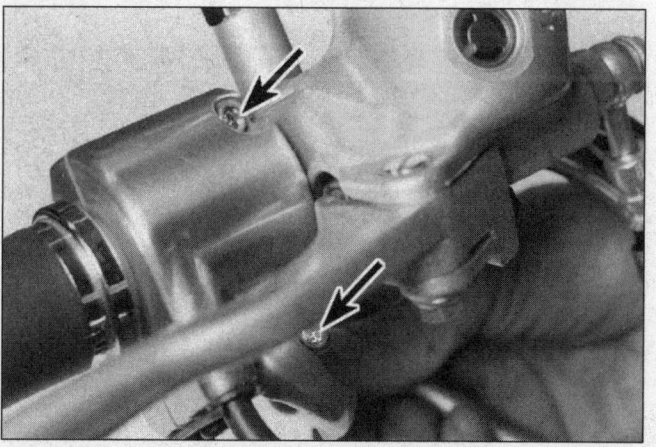

9.4 Remove the screws (arrows) and detach the cable/switch housing from the handlebar

4•12 Fuel and exhaust systems

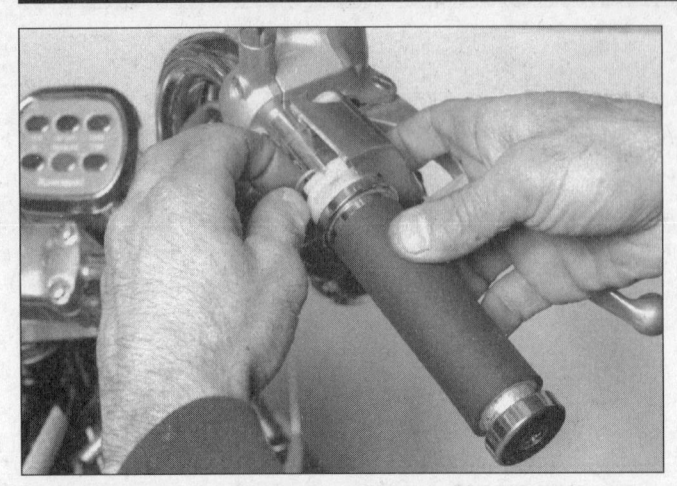

9.5a Lift the inner decelerator cable out of its groove, align it with the slots in the throttle pulley and slip the cable end out of the pulley ...

9.5b ... then do the same thing with the accelerator cable

5 Detach the cables from the cable/switch housing, then lift them out of their grooves in the throttle pulley, align the cables with the pulley slots and slip the cable ends out of the throttle pulley **(see illustrations)**.
6 Detach the decelerator and accelerator cables from the throttle pulley at the carburetor assembly **(see illustrations)**.
7 Remove the cables, noting how they are routed.

Installation

8 Route the cables into place. Make sure they don't interfere with any other components and aren't kinked or bent sharply.
9 Lubricate the end of the accelerator cable with multi-purpose grease and connect it to the throttle pulley at the carburetor. Pass the inner cable through the slot in the bracket, then seat the cable housing in the bracket.
10 Repeat the previous step to connect the decelerator cable.

11 Connect the cables to the throttle grip pulley and position them in their slots.
12 Install the cable/switch housing and tighten its screws securely.

Adjustment

13 Follow the procedure outlined in Chapter 1, *Throttle operation/grip freeplay - check and adjustment*, to adjust the cables.
14 Turn the handlebars back and forth to make sure the cables don't cause the steering to bind.
15 Operate the throttle and check the cable action. The cables should move freely and the throttle pulley at the carburetor should move back and forth in response to both acceleration and deceleration. If the cables don't operate properly, find and fix the problem before you put the fuel tank back on.
16 Install the fuel tank.
17 Start the engine. With the engine idling, turn the handlebars all the way to the left and right while listening for changes in idle speed.

If idle speed increases as the handlebars turn, the cables are improperly routed. This is dangerous. Find the problem and fix it before riding the bike.

10 Choke cable (EN450 and EX250 models) - removal, installation and adjustment

Removal

1 Remove the seat and fuel tank (see Section 2).
2 Pull the choke cable casing away from its mounting bracket at the carburetor and pass the inner cable through the opening in the bracket. Detach the cable end from the choke lever by the right-hand carburetor **(see illustration)**.
3 Remove the screws securing the choke cable/switch housing halves to the left handlebar. Pull the front half of the housing off

9.6a At the carburetors, loosen the adjuster on each cable (arrows), then align the cables with the slots in the throttle pulley and slip them out - here are the EN450/500 adjusters ...

9.6b ... and here are the EX250 adjusters

Fuel and exhaust systems 4•13

10.2 Slip the choke cable out of the bracket, then turn the cable to align it with the lever slot and slip it out of the lever

10.3 Turn the cable to align it with the handlebar lever slot and slip it out of the lever

11.4 Remove the nuts and holders from the cylinder head studs

11.5 Loosen the crossover clamp

and separate the choke cable from the lever **(see illustration)**.

4 Remove the cable, noting how it's routed.

Installation

5 Route the cable into position. Connect the upper end of the cable to the choke lever. Place the housing up against the handlebar, making sure the housing halves align correctly with each other and the handlebar. Install the screws, tightening them securely.

6 Connect the lower end of the cable to the choke lever. Pull back on the cable casing and connect it to the bracket on the right-hand carburetor.

Adjustment

7 Refer to Chapter 1 for cable adjustment procedures.

8 Install the fuel tank and all of the other components that were previously removed.

11 Exhaust system - removal and installation

1 If you're working on an EN450/500, remove the side covers (see Chapter 8). If you're working on an EX250, remove the fairing (see Chapter 8).

2 Drain the coolant (see Chapter 1).

3 Remove the radiator (see Chapter 3).

4 Remove the nuts that secure the exhaust pipe holders to the cylinder head, then remove the holders **(see illustration)**.

5 Loosen the clamp that secures the crossover pipe **(see illustration)**.

6 If you plan to separate the mufflers from the pipes, loosen the clamps **(see illustration)**.

11.6 Loosen the muffler clamps if you plan to separate the mufflers from the pipes

4•14 Fuel and exhaust systems

11.7 Remove the muffler mounting bolts at the rear footpegs (arrow)

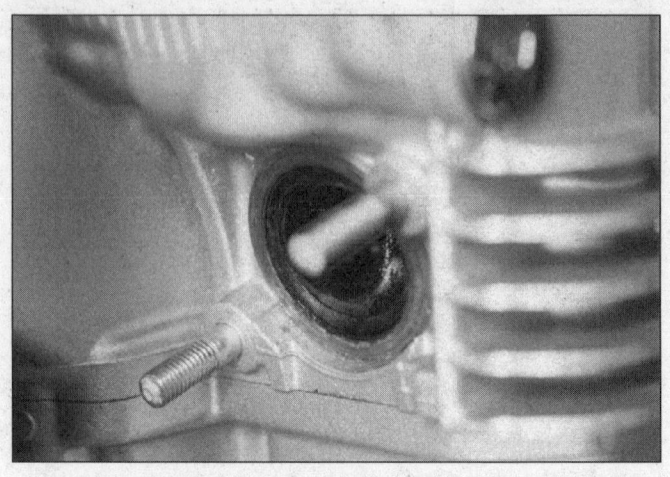

11.9a The gaskets at the cylinder head should be replaced whenever the pipes are removed

7   Remove the muffler mounting bolts at the footpeg brackets **(see illustration)**.
8   Pull the exhaust system forward, separate the right side pipe from the left side pipe and remove the system from the machine.
9   Remove the gaskets from the cylinder head and crossover pipe **(see illustrations)**.
10 Installation is the reverse of removal, with the following additions:
   a) Install new gaskets at the cylinder head. Replace the crossover clamp gasket if it's damaged.
   b) On EN450/500 models, be sure the holders overlap correctly **(see illustration)**.

HAYNES HiNT *On EX250 models, tape the collar halves together with masking tape to ease installation. The tape will burn off when the engine is run.*

12 Air switching valve (US EN450/500 models) - operational test

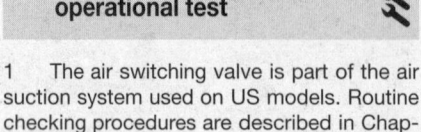

1   The air switching valve is part of the air suction system used on US models. Routine checking procedures are described in Chapter 1. If you suspect the valve has failed (for example, if the bike runs poorly at low speed or backfires during deceleration), test it as follows:
2   Remove the valve and its hoses from the motorcycle (see Chapter 1).
3   Connect a vacuum gauge to one end of the vacuum line that branches out from the T-fitting. Connect a vacuum pump to the other end.
4   Try to blow air into the large air hose. It should flow easily when there's no vacuum applied to the vacuum line.
5   Operate the vacuum pump and raise vacuum to the value listed in this Chapter's

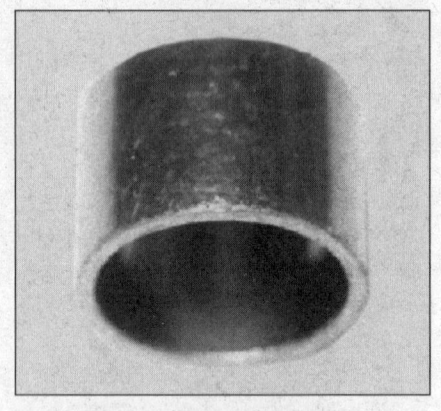

11.9b The crossover clamp gasket should be replaced if it's damaged or deteriorated

Specifications. The valve should close, making it impossible to blow air into the hose.
6   If the valve doesn't perform as described, replace it.

11.9c EX250 models also use this gasket where the pipes join the exhaust ports

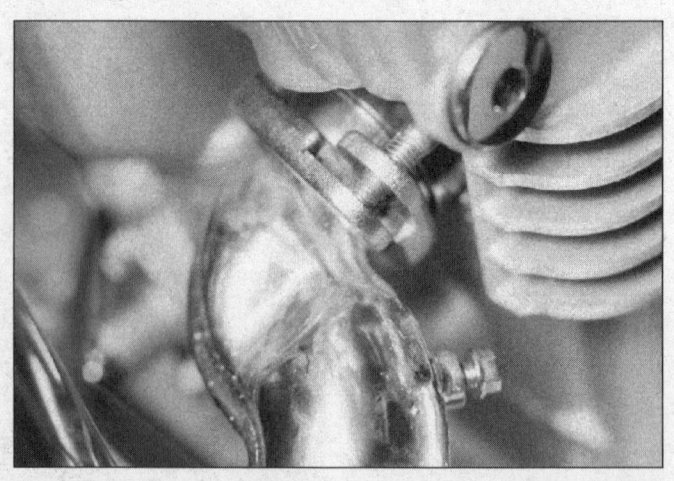

11.10 The holder halves are notched so they form a flush surface when assembled correctly

Chapter 5
Ignition system

Contents

General information	1	Ignition system - check	2
IC igniter - removal, check and installation	5	Ignition (main) switch and key lock cylinder - check, removal and installation	See Chapter 9
Ignition coils - check, removal and installation	3	Pickup coils - check, removal and installation	4
Ignition stop switch - check, removal and installation	See Chapter 9	Spark plug replacement	See Chapter 1

Degrees of difficulty

Easy, suitable for novice with little experience ⊁ **Fairly easy,** suitable for beginner with some experience ⊁ **Fairly difficult,** suitable for competent DIY mechanic ⊁ **Difficult,** suitable for experienced DIY mechanic ⊁ **Very difficult,** suitable for expert DIY or professional ⊁

Specifications

Ignition coil
Primary resistance
   EN450 models.. 2.1 to 3.2 ohms
   EN500 models.. 2.2 to 3.5 ohms
   EX250 models
      1986 and 1987... 2.1 to 3.2 ohms
      1988 and later... 2.2 to 3.5 ohms
Secondary resistance.. 10,000 to 16,000 ohms
Arcing distance.. 7 mm (1/4 in) or more
Pickup coil resistance
   EN450/500... 400 to 490 ohms
   EX250
      1986 and 1987... 400 to 490 ohms
      1988 and later... 100 to 150 ohms
Ignition timing.. Not adjustable

5•2 Ignition system

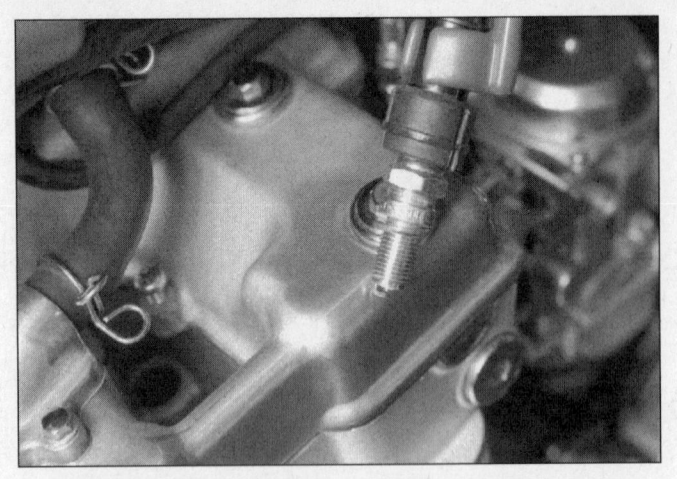

2.3 With the wire attached, ground a spark plug to the engine and operate the starter - bright blue sparks should be visible

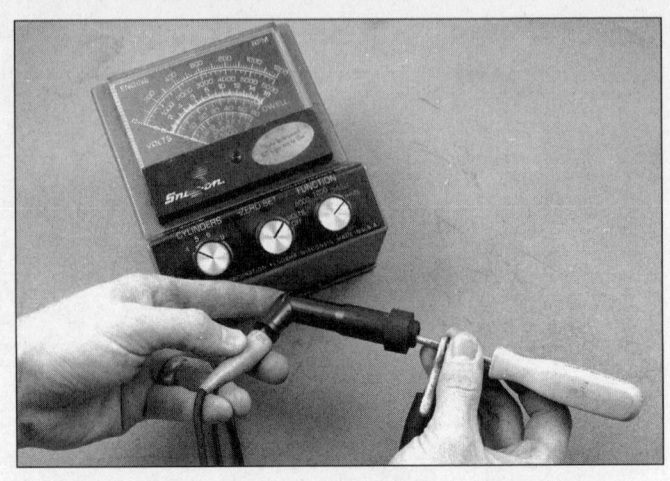

2.5 Unscrew the spark plug caps from the plug wires and measure their resistance with an ohmmeter

1 General information

This motorcycle is equipped with a battery operated, fully transistorized, breakerless ignition system. The system consists of the following components:

Pickup coils
IC igniter unit
Battery and fuse
Ignition coils
Spark plugs
Stop and main (key) switches
Primary and secondary circuit wiring

The transistorized ignition system functions on the same principle as a breaker point DC ignition system with the pickup unit and igniter performing the tasks previously associated with the breaker points and mechanical advance system. As a result, adjustment and maintenance of ignition components is eliminated (with the exception of spark plug replacement).

Because of their nature, the individual ignition system components can be checked but not repaired. If ignition system troubles occur, and the faulty component can be isolated, the only cure for the problem is to replace the part with a new one. Keep in mind that most electrical parts, once purchased, can't be returned. To avoid unnecessary expense, make very sure the faulty component has been positively identified before buying a replacement part.

2 Ignition system - check

> **Warning: Because of the very high voltage generated by the ignition system, extreme care should be taken to avoid electrical shock when these checks are performed.**

1 If the ignition system is the suspected cause of poor engine performance or failure to start, a number of checks can be made to isolate the problem.
2 Make sure the ignition stop switch is in the Run or On position.

Engine will not start

3 Disconnect one of the spark plug wires, connect the wire to a spare spark plug and lay the plug on the engine with the threads contacting the engine. If it's necessary to hold the spark plug, use an insulated tool **(see illustration)**. Crank the engine over and make sure a well-defined, blue spark occurs between the spark plug electrodes.

> **Warning: DO NOT remove one of the spark plugs from the engine to perform this check - atomized fuel being pumped out of the open spark plug hole could ignite, causing severe injury!**

4 If no spark occurs, the following checks should be made:
5 Unscrew a spark plug cap from a plug wire and check the cap resistance with an ohmmeter **(see illustration)**. If the resistance is infinite, replace it with a new one. Repeat this check on the other plug cap.
6 Make sure all electrical connectors are clean and tight. Refer to the wiring diagrams at the end of this book and check all wires for shorts, opens and correct installation.
7 Check the battery voltage with a voltmeter and the specific gravity with a hydrometer (see Chapters 1 and 9). If the voltage is less than 12-volts or if the specific gravity is low, recharge the battery.
8 Check the ignition fuse and the fuse connections. If the fuse is blown, replace it with a new one; if the connections are loose or corroded, clean or repair them.
9 Refer to Section 3 and check the ignition coil primary and secondary resistance.
10 Refer to Section 4 and check the pickup coil resistance.
11 If the preceding checks produce positive results but there is still no spark at the plug, have the IC igniter checked by a Kawasaki dealer service department or other repair shop equipped with the special tester required.

Engine starts but misfires

12 If the engine starts but misfires, make the following checks before deciding that the ignition system is at fault.
13 The ignition system must be able to produce a spark across a seven millimeter (1/4-inch) gap (minimum). A simple test fixture **(see illustration)** can be constructed to

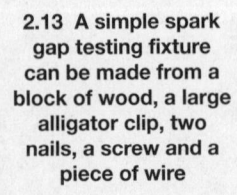

2.13 A simple spark gap testing fixture can be made from a block of wood, a large alligator clip, two nails, a screw and a piece of wire

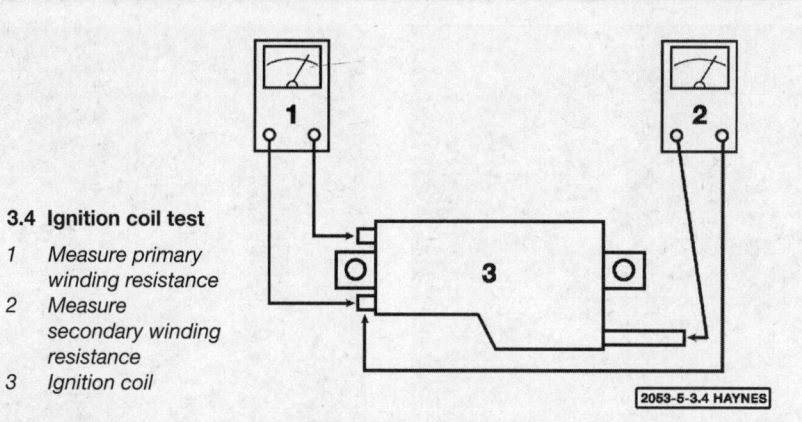

Ignition system 5•3

3.4 Ignition coil test
1. Measure primary winding resistance
2. Measure secondary winding resistance
3. Ignition coil

3.10a The EN450/500 ignition coils are mounted to the frame . . .

make sure the minimum spark gap can be jumped. Make sure the fixture electrodes are positioned seven millimeters apart.

14 Connect one of the spark plug wires to the protruding test fixture electrode, then attach the fixture's alligator clip to a good engine ground/earth.

15 Crank the engine over (it may start and run on the remaining cylinder) and see if well-defined, blue sparks occur between the test fixture electrodes. If the minimum spark gap test is positive, the ignition coil for that cylinder is functioning properly. Repeat the check on the spark plug wire that is connected to the other coil. If the spark will not jump the gap during either test, or if it is weak (orange colored), refer to Steps 5 through 11 of this Section and perform the component checks described.

3 Ignition coils - check, removal and installation

Check

1 In order to determine conclusively that the ignition coils are defective, they should be tested by an authorized Kawasaki dealer service department which is equipped with the special electrical tester required for this check.

2 However, the coils can be checked visually (for cracks and other damage) and the primary and secondary coil resistances can be measured with an ohmmeter. If the coils are undamaged, and if the resistances are as specified, they are probably capable of proper operation.

3 To check the coils for physical damage, they must be removed (see Step 9). To check the resistances, simply remove the fuel tank (see Chapter 4), unplug the primary circuit electrical connectors from the coil(s) and remove the spark plug wire from the plug that is connected to the coil being checked. Mark the locations of all wires before disconnecting them.

4 To check the coil primary resistance, attach one ohmmeter lead to one of the primary terminals and the other ohmmeter lead to the other primary terminal (see illustration).

5 Place the ohmmeter selector switch in the Rx1 position and compare the measured resistance to the value listed in this Chapter's Specifications.

6 If the coil primary resistance is as specified, check the coil secondary resistance by disconnecting the meter leads from the primary terminals and attaching one of them to the spark plug wire terminal and the other to either of the primary terminals (see illustration 3.4).

7 Place the ohmmeter selector switch in the Rx100 position and compare the measured resistance to the values listed in this Chapter's Specifications.

8 If the resistances are not as specified, unscrew the spark plug wire retainers from the coil, detach the wires and check the resistance again. If it is now within specifications, one or both of the wires are bad. If it's still not as specified, the coil is probably defective and should be replaced with a new one.

Removal and installation

9 To remove the coils, refer to Chapter 4 and remove the fuel tank, then disconnect the spark plug wires from the plugs. After labeling them with tape to aid in reinstallation, unplug the coil primary circuit electrical connectors.

10 Support the coil with one hand and remove the coil mounting screws (see illustrations), then remove the coil.

11 Installation is the reverse of removal. If a new coil is being installed, disconnect the spark plug wire terminal from the coil, disconnect the wire and transfer it to the new

3.10b . . . and the EX250 coils are mounted to brackets - note any ground wires and harness retainers secured by the coil bolts . . .

3.10c . . . label the coil according to right or left side and its wire colors . . .

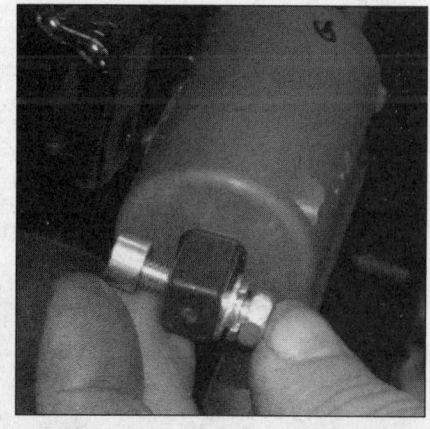

3.10d . . . and don't forget to reinstall the spacers (if equipped) and reconnect any ground wires that are secured by the coil mounting bolts

5•4 Ignition system

4.1 Follow the pickup coil wiring harness from this grommet (arrow) to the connector (apply silicone sealer to the grommet whenever it's removed and reinstalled) (EN450/500 shown)

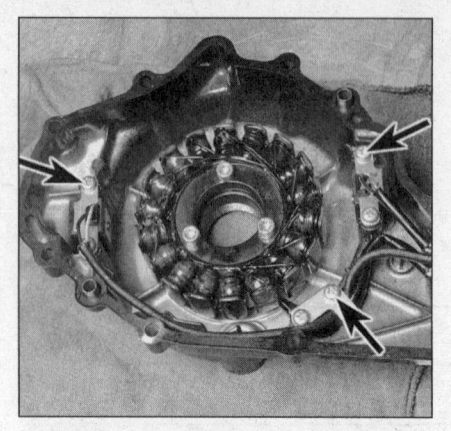

4.6a To remove the pickup coils (upper arrows), remove the mounting screws; also remove the screws that secure the harness clip (lower arrow) (early EN450/500 shown) . . .

4.6b . . . later models use a single pickup coil (EX250 shown)

coil. Make sure the primary circuit electrical connectors are attached to the proper terminals.

4 Pickup coils - check, removal and installation

Check

1 Follow the pickup coil wiring harness from the point where it leaves the alternator cover to the electrical connector, then disconnect the connector for the pickup coils **(see illustration)**.

2 Probe each pair of terminals in the pickup coil connector with an ohmmeter (the black and yellow wire terminals, then the blue and black/white wire terminals) and compare the resistance reading with the value listed in this Chapter's Specifications.

3 Set the ohmmeter on the highest resistance range. Measure the resistance between a good ground/earth and each terminal in the electrical connector. The meter should read infinity.

4 If the pickup coils fail either of the above tests, they must be replaced.

Removal

5 Remove the alternator cover (see Chapter 9).

6 Unscrew the pickup coil mounting screws and remove the pickup coil(s) **(see illustrations)**. Remove the wiring harness retainer, slip the grommet out of its slot and remove the pickup coils together with their wiring harness.

Installation

7 Position the pickup coils in the alternator cover and install the screws, tightening them securely. Apply a small amount of silicone sealant to the grommet on the wiring harness and seat the grommet securely in the notch in the alternator cover **(see illustration 4.1)**.

8 Install the alternator cover and connect the electrical connector.

5 IC igniter - removal, check and installation

Removal

1 If you're working on an EN450/500 model, remove the seat. If you're working on an EX250 model, remove the left side cover (see Chapter 8).

2 On EN450 models, disconnect its electrical connector and remove the two bolts which retain the igniter to the battery holder bracket. Lift out the igniter.

3 On EN500 and EX250 models, disconnect the electrical connector and slip the igniter off its mounting tabs **(see illustrations)**. Take the igniter out.

Check

4 A special tester is required to accurately measure the resistance values across the various terminals of the IC igniter. Take the unit to a Kawasaki dealer service department or other repair shop equipped with this tester.

Installation

5 Installation is the reverse of the removal steps.

5.3a The IC igniter is mounted behind the battery, on the fender front portion (EN500 models) . . .

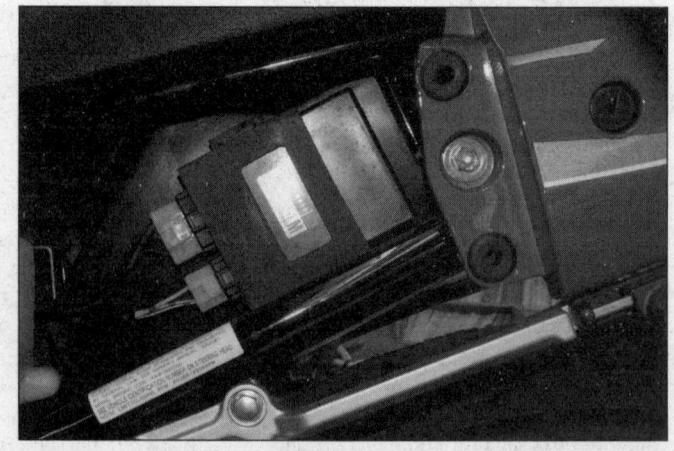

5.3b . . . and on EX250 models, it's mounted to the frame beneath the left side cover

Chapter 6
Suspension, steering and final drive

Contents

Drive belt/chain - adjustment	See Chapter 1
Drive belt/chain and sprockets - removal, inspection and installation	11
Fork oil - replacement	See Chapter 1
Forks - disassembly, inspection and reassembly	4
Forks - removal and installation	3
General information	1
Handlebars - removal and installation	2
Rear shock absorber(s) - removal and installation	6
Rear suspension linkage (EX250 models) - removal, inspecton and installation	7
Rear wheel coupling/rubber damper - check and replacement	12
Steering head bearings - check and adjustment	See Chapter 1
Steering head bearings - replacement	5
Suspension - check	See Chapter 1
Suspension adjustments	13
Swingarm - removal and installation	9
Swingarm bearings - check	8
Swingarm bearings - replacement	10

Degrees of difficulty

Easy, suitable for novice with little experience	**Fairly easy,** suitable for beginner with some experience	**Fairly difficult,** suitable for competent DIY mechanic	**Difficult,** suitable for experienced DIY mechanic	**Very difficult,** suitable for expert DIY or professional

Specifications

Front suspension
Fork oil type, amount and level .... See Chapter 1
Fork spring length
  EN450 models
    Standard .... 442 mm (17.4 inches)
    Minimum .... 433 mm (17.04 inches)
  EN500 models
    Through 1996
      Standard .... 372.9 mm (14.68 inches)
      Minimum .... 365 mm (14.37 inches)
    1997 and later
      Standard .... 302.9 mm (11.9 inches)
      Minimum .... 297 mm (11.7 inches)
  EX250 models
    1986 and 1987 (long spring)
      Standard .... 274.4 mm (10.803 inches)
      Minimum .... 269 mm (10.590 inches)
    1986 and 1987 (short spring)
      Standard .... 265.2 mm (10.441 inches)
      Minimum .... 260 mm (10.236 inches)
    1988 and later
      Standard .... 463.8 mm (18.259 inches)
      Minimum .... 455 mm (17.913 inches)
Front fork air pressure (early EN450 models only)
  Standard .... 0 psi (0 Bars)
  Maximum .... 36 psi (2.51 Bars)

Rear spring preload standard setting

EN450 models	1
EN500 models	2
EX250 models (1986 and 1987 only)	Spring free length minus 5 mm (0.2 inch)

Final drive belt sprockets (EN450/500)

Tooth height
- EN450 engine sprocket
  - Standard .... 6.60 to 6.73 mm (0.260 to 0.265 inch)
  - Minimum .... 6.3 mm (0.248 inch)
- EN450 rear sprocket .... Not specified
- EN500 engine sprocket
  - Standard .... 6.42 to 6.49 mm (0.253 to 0.255 inch)
  - Minimum .... 6.1 mm (0.240 inch)
- EN500 rear sprocket
  - Standard .... 6.62 to 6.70 mm (0.260 to 0.264 inch)
  - Minimum .... 6.3 mm (0.248 inch)

Rear sprocket diameter
- Standard .... 300.23 to 300.28 mm (11.820 to 11.822 inches)
- Minimum .... 299.63 mm (11.796 inches)

Torque specifications

Handlebar bracket bolts
- EN450 models .... 19 Nm (162 in-lbs)
- EN500 models .... 23 Nm (16.5 ft-lbs)
- EX250 models .... 23 Nm (16.5 ft-lbs)

Handlebar bracket nuts (1997 and later EN500) .... 34 Nm (25 ft-lbs)
Handlebar-to-bracket bolts (EX250) .... 23 Nm (16.5 ft-lbs)

Damper rod bolts (1)
- EN450/500
  - 1985 through 1996 .... 20 Nm (14.5 ft-lbs)
  - 1997 and later .... 29 Nm (22 ft-lbs)
- EX250 .... 20 Nm (14.5 ft-lbs)

Steering stem bolt
- EN450/500
  - 1985 through 1996 .... 42 Nm (31 ft-lbs)
  - 1997 and later .... 44 Nm (33 ft-lbs)
- EX250 .... 47 Nm (35 ft-lbs)

Steering stem adjusting nut
- EN450/500
  - Initial torque .... 39 Nm (29 ft-lbs)
  - Final torque .... Hand tighten (approximately 4.9 Nm/43 in-lbs)
- EX250
  - Initial torque .... 20 Nm (174 in-lbs)
  - Final torque .... Hand tighten (until steering turns lightly with no play)

Fork upper triple clamp bolts .... 20 Nm (174 in-lbs)
Fork lower triple clamp bolts
- EN450/500
  - 1985 through 1996 .... 25 Nm (18 ft-lbs)
  - 1997 and later .... 29 Nm (22 ft-lbs)
- EX250 .... 29 Nm (22 ft-lbs)

Rear shock absorber mounting bolts/nuts
- EN450 models .... 29 Nm (22 ft-lbs)
- EN500 models (through 1996)
  - Upper .... 25 Nm (18 ft-lbs)
  - Lower .... Not specified
- EN500 models (1997 and later)
  - Upper .... 25 Nm (18 ft-lbs)
  - Lower .... 34 Nm (25 ft-lbs)
- EX250 models .... 44 Nm (33 ft-lbs)

Suspension linkage pivot bolts/nuts (EX250) .... 44 Nm (33 ft-lbs)
Swingarm pivot shaft nut .... 88 Nm (65 ft-lbs)
Belt final drive
- Rear sprocket-to-wheel coupling nuts .... 69 Nm (51 ft-lbs)
- Engine sprocket holding plate bolts .... 9.8 Nm (87 in-lbs)

Suspension, steering and final drive 6•3

Chain final drive
   Rear sprocket-to-wheel coupling nuts
      EN500
         1997 through 2003 .... 74 Nm (54 ft-lbs)
         2004 and later .... 69 Nm (43 ft-lbs)
      EX250 .... 67 Nm (49 ft-lbs)
   Engine sprocket locknut (EN500 models)........................... 125 Nm (94 ft-lbs) (2)
   Engine sprocket bolts (EX250 models) .... 9.8 Nm (87 inch-lbs)

1. Use non-permanent thread locking agent on the threads.
2. Lubricate the shaft threads and the nut seating surface with engine oil.

2.1a On models through 1996, unbolt the upper bracket . . .

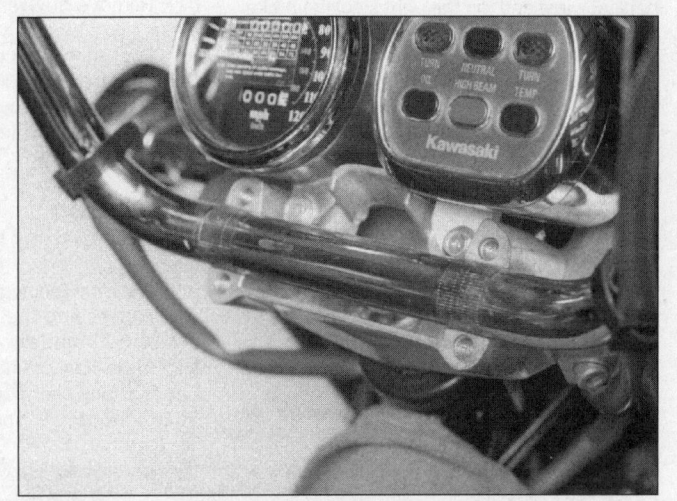

2.1b . . . and lift the handlebar off

1 General information

The front forks on these models are of the conventional coil spring, hydraulically-damped telescopic type. Early EN450 forks include an air pressure adjustment mechanism.

The rear suspension on EN450/500 models consists of two coil spring/shock absorbers and a square-section swingarm. EX250 models use a progressive rising rate suspension with a single coil spring/shock absorber.

The final drive on EN450 and EN500 A models uses a cogged belt. EN500 C models and EX250 models use a chain final drive. A rubber damper is installed between the rear wheel coupling and the wheel.

2 Handlebars - removal and installation

EN450/500 models

1 Models through 1996 use a one-piece handlebar, secured to the upper triple clamp by an upper and lower bracket. If the handlebars must be removed for access to other components, such as the forks or the steering head, simply remove the bolts and lift the handlebar(s) off **(see illustrations)**. 1997 and later models also use a one-piece handlebar with integral mounting studs. To remove this type, unscrew the mounting nuts from the underside of the upper triple clamp and lift the handlebars off.

EX250 models

2 These models use clip-on handlebars, secured to the upper triple clamp by a separate mounting bracket on each side of the bike. If the handlebars must be removed for access to other components, such as the forks or the steering head, simply remove the

6•4 Suspension, steering and final drive

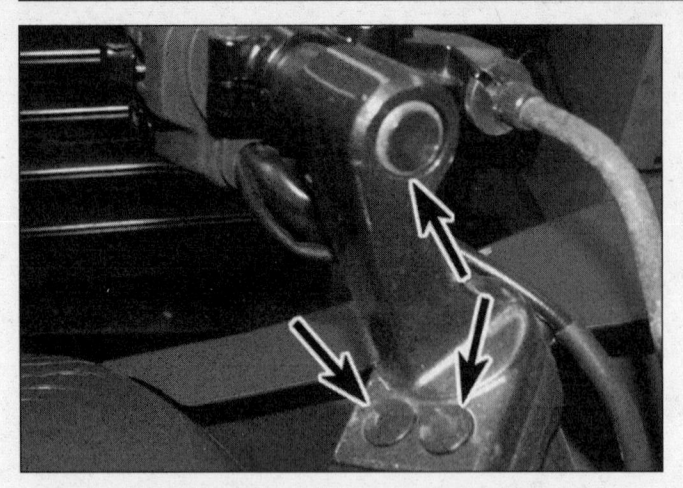

2.2 The EX250 handlebar bolt (upper arrow) and bracket bolts (lower arrows) are covered with trim plugs

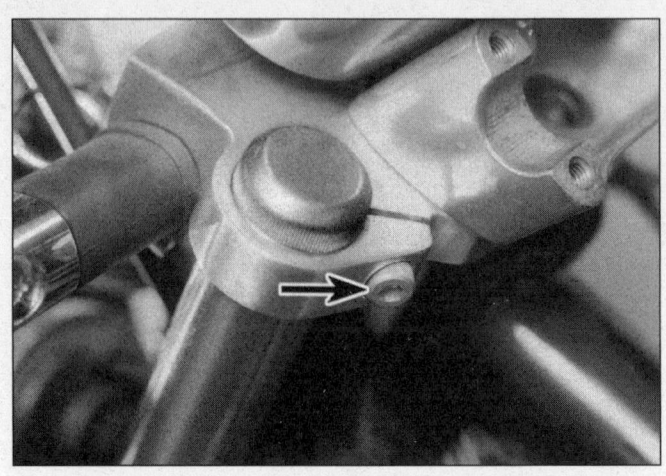

3.7 The front forks are held in the upper triple clamp by pinch bolts (arrow)

bolts and lift the handlebar(s) off **(see illustration)**.

All models

3 It's not necessary to disconnect the cables, wires or hoses, but it is a good idea to support the assembly with a piece of wire or rope, to avoid unnecessary strain on the cables, wires and (on the right side) the brake hose.
4 Check the handlebar(s) for cracks and distortion and replace it if any undesirable conditions are found.
5 Installation is the reverse of the removal steps. Tighten the bolts to the torque listed in this Chapter's Specifications.

3 Forks - removal and installation

Removal

1 Set the bike on its centerstand (if equipped).

2 Remove the fuel tank (see Chapter 4).
3 If you're removing the left fork leg, remove the brake caliper and hang it from the bike with a piece of rope or wire (see Chapter 7).
4 Remove the wheel (see Chapter 7).
5 Remove the front fender (see Chapter 8).
6 Remove any wiring harness clamps or straps from the fork tubes.
7 Loosen the fork upper triple clamp bolts **(see illustration)**. Loosen the lower triple clamp bolts, then twist the fork tubes and slide them downward and out of the triple clamps.

Installation

8 Slide each fork leg into the lower triple clamp.
9 Slide the fork legs up, installing the tops of the tubes into the upper triple clamp. On EN450/500 models, the end of each tube should be flush with the top surface of the upper triple clamp **(see illustration)**. On EX250 models, it should be about 12 mm (0.47 inch) above the triple clamp top surface.
10 The remainder of installation is the reverse of the removal procedure. Be sure to tighten the triple clamp bolts to the torque listed in this Chapter's Specifications. Tighten the caliper mounting bolts to the torque listed in the Chapter 7 Specifications.
11 Pump the front brake lever several times to bring the pads into contact with the discs.

4 Forks - disassembly, inspection and reassembly

Disassembly

1 Remove the forks following the procedure in Section 3. Work on one fork leg at a time to avoid mixing up the parts.
2 Remove the retaining ring, top plug, spacer, spring seat and fork spring (see Chapter 1). On 1986 and 1987 EX250 models,

3.9 EN450/500: When installed, the top of the inner fork tube should be flush with the upper triple clamp (arrow) (fork cap removed for clarity)

4.4a This is the Kawasaki tool that keeps the damper rod from turning - the corners of the tapered section bite into the round hole in the damper rod to hold it

Suspension, steering and final drive 6•5

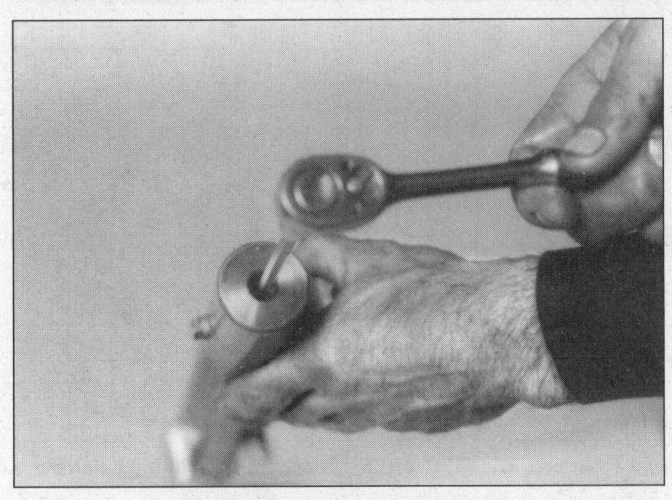

4.4b Hold the damper rod and remove the screw with an Allen wrench

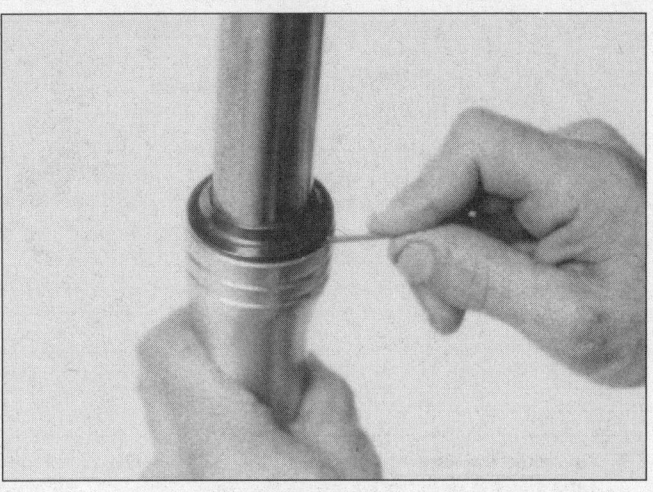

4.6 Pry the dust seal out of the outer tube with a small screwdriver

there's an upper spring (longer), spring seat and lower spring (shorter).

3 Invert the fork assembly over a container and allow the oil to drain out.

4 Prevent the damper rod from turning using a holding handle (available from Kawasaki or aftermarket tool suppliers) **(see illustration)**. Unscrew the Allen bolt at the bottom of the outer tube and retrieve the copper washer **(see illustration)**.

5 Pull out the damper rod and its spring. Don't remove the Teflon ring from the damper rod; the damper rod is sold as an assembly, so if the ring is worn, you'll need a new damper rod.

6 Pry the dust seal from the outer tube **(see illustration)**.

7 Pry the retaining ring from its groove in the outer tube **(see illustration)**.

8 Hold the outer tube and yank the inner tube upward, repeatedly (like a slide hammer), until the seal, washer and outer tube guide bushing pop loose.

9 Slide the seal, washer and outer tube guide bushing from the inner tube.

10 Invert the outer tube and remove the damper rod base **(see illustration)**.

Inspection

11 Clean all parts in solvent and blow them dry with compressed air, if available. Check the inner and outer fork tubes, the guide bushings and the damper rod for score marks, scratches, flaking of the chrome and excessive or abnormal wear. Look for dents in the tubes and replace them if any are found. Check the fork seal seat for nicks, gouges and scratches. If damage is evident, leaks will occur around the seal-to-outer tube junction. Replace worn or defective parts with new ones.

12 Have the fork inner tube checked for runout at a dealer service department or other repair shop.

⚠ *Warning: If it is bent, it should not be straightened; replace it with a new one.*

13 Measure the overall length of the long spring and check it for cracks and other damage. Compare the length to the minimum length listed in this Chapter's Specifications. If it's defective or sagged, replace both fork springs with new ones. Never replace only one spring.

Reassembly

14 If it's necessary to replace the inner guide bushing (the one that won't come off that's on the bottom of the inner tube), pry it apart at the slit and slide it off. Make sure the new one seats properly.

15 Place the rebound spring over the damper rod and slide the rod assembly into the inner fork tube until it protrudes from the lower end of the tube.

16 If you haven't already done so, install the damper rod base onto the end of the damper rod **(see illustration 4.10)**.

17 Insert the inner tube/damper rod assembly into the outer tube **(see illustration)** until the Allen-head bolt (with copper washer) can be threaded into the damper rod from the lower end of the outer tube **(see illustra-**

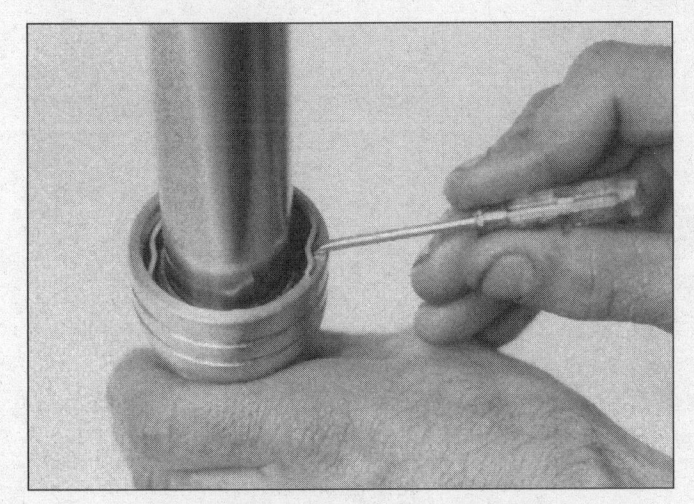

4.7 Pry the retaining ring out of its groove

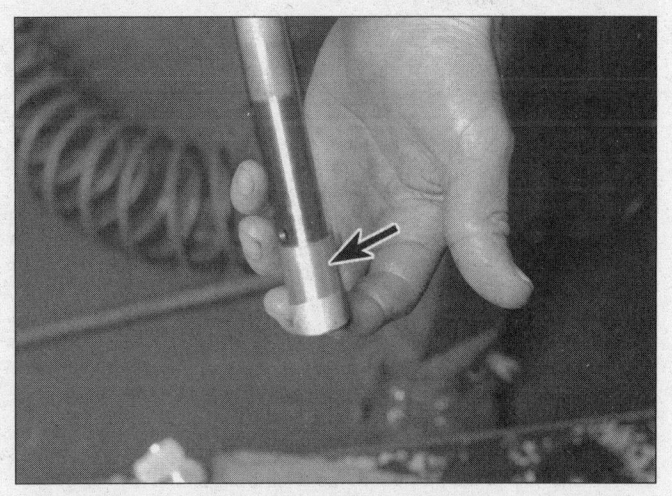

4.10 Dump the damper rod base (arrow) out of the fork tube and put it back on the damper rod

6•6 Suspension, steering and final drive

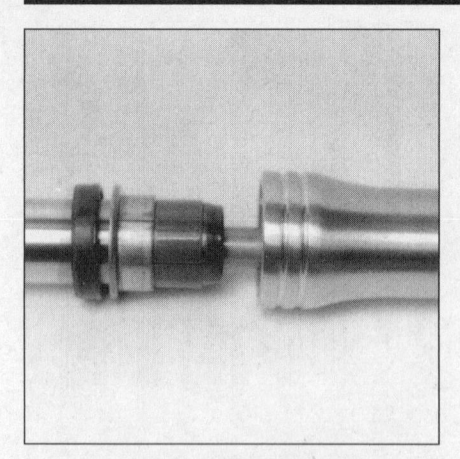

4.17a Install the assembled inner fork tube into the outer fork tube . . .

4.17b . . . place a new washer on the damper rod bolt . . .

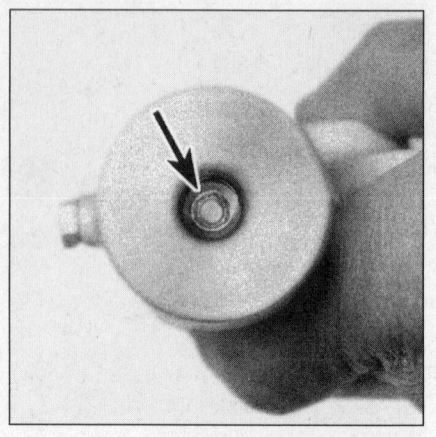

4.17c . . . and thread it into the damper rod (arrow)

tion). **Note:** *Apply a non-permanent thread locking compound to the threads of the bolt.* Keep the two tubes fairly horizontal so the damper rod base doesn't fall off. Using the tool described in Step 4, hold the damper rod and tighten the Allen bolt to the torque listed in this Chapter's Specifications.

18 Slide the outer guide bushing down the inner tube. On EN450 models, the slit in the bushing must point to the left or right - not to the front or rear. Using a special bushing driver (Kawasaki tool no. 57001-1219) or equivalent and a used guide bushing placed on top of the guide bushing being installed, drive the bushing into place until it is fully seated. If you don't have access to one of these tools, it is highly recommended that you take the assembly to a Kawasaki dealer service department or other motorcycle repair shop to have this done. It is possible, however, to drive the bushing into place using a section of tubing and an old guide bushing **(see illustration)**. Wrap tape around the ends of the tubing to prevent it from scratching the fork tube.

19 Slide the washer down the inner tube, into position over the guide bushing.

20 Lubricate the lips and the outer diameter of the fork seal with the recommended fork oil (see Chapter 1) and slide it down the inner tube, with the lips facing down. Drive the seal into place with a special seal driver (Kawasaki tool no. 57001-1091 or equivalent). If you don't have access to one of these, it is recommended that you take the assembly to a Kawasaki dealer service department or other motorcycle repair shop to have the seal driven in. If you are very careful, the seal can be driven in with a hammer and a drift punch. Work around the circumference of the seal, tapping gently on the outer edge of the seal until it's seated. Be careful - if you distort the seal, you'll have to disassemble the fork again and end up taking it to a dealer anyway!

21 Install the retaining ring, making sure the ring is completely seated in its groove **(see illustration)**.

22 Install the dust seal, making sure it seats completely.

23 Install the drain screw and a new gasket, if it was removed.

24 Compress the fork fully and add the recommended type and quantity of fork oil (see Chapter 1).

25 Install the fork spring, with the small-diameter end or the widely spaced coils at the bottom (depending on spring design) **(see illustrations)**. If you're working on a 1986 or 1987 EX250, install the spring seat and upper spring on top of the lower spring. Install the spring seat and spacer, then install the top plug and secure it with the retaining ring (see Chapter 1).

26 Install the fork by following the procedure outlined in Section 3. If you won't be installing the fork right away, store it in an upright position to prevent leakage.

4.18 If you don't have the special tool, a section of pipe can be used the same way the special tool would be used - as a slide hammer (be sure to tape the ends of the pipe so it doesn't scratch the fork tube)

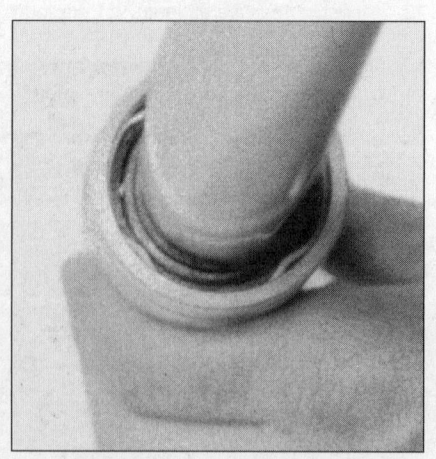

4.21 Install the retaining ring and make sure it seats in its groove

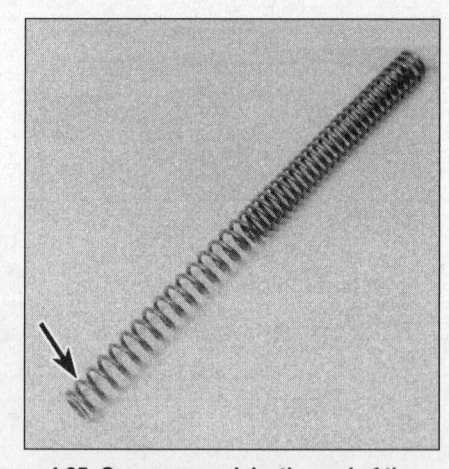

4.25 On some models, the end of the spring with widely spaced coils (arrow) goes downward (other models have a tapered end which must be positioned at the bottom)

Suspension, steering and final drive 6•7

5.4 Remove the bolts (arrows) and detach the cover from the front of the lower triple clamp (EN500 model shown)

5.8a Remove the steering stem bolt (EN450/500 shown) ...

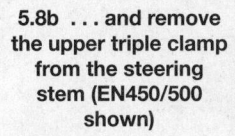

5.8b ... and remove the upper triple clamp from the steering stem (EN450/500 shown)

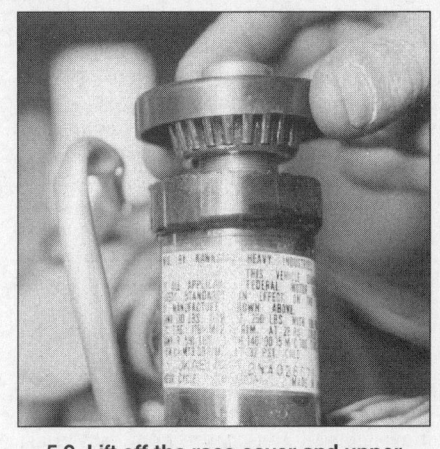

5.9 Lift off the race cover and upper bearing (EN450/500)

5 Steering head bearings - replacement

1 If the steering head bearing check/adjustment (see Chapter 1) does not remedy excessive play or roughness in the steering head bearings, the entire front end must be disassembled and the bearings and races replaced with new ones.
2 Refer to Chapter 4 and remove the fuel tank. If you're working on an EX250, remove the fairing (see Chapter 8).
3 Refer to Chapter 7 and remove the front wheel.
4 If you're working on an EN450/500, remove the cover from the front of the lower triple clamp (see illustration).
5 Refer to Section 3 and remove the front forks.
6 Refer to Chapter 9 and remove the front turn signals, headlight assembly, instruments and ignition switch.
7 Refer to Section 2 and remove the handlebars.
8 Remove the steering stem bolt (see illustration), then lift off the upper triple clamp (see illustration).

EN450/500 models
9 Remove the stem locknut. Using an adjustable spanner wrench, remove the stem adjusting nut while supporting the steering head from the bottom. Lift off the race cover and upper bearing (see illustration).
10 Remove the steering stem and lower triple clamp assembly together with the lower bearing (see illustration). If it's stuck, gently tap on the top of the steering stem with a plastic mallet or a hammer and a wood block.

5.10 Lower the steering stem out of the steering head (EN450/500)

6•8 Suspension, steering and final drive

5.11a On EX250 models, remove the washer and upper bearing race...

5.11b ...and the ball bearings

EX250 models

11 Remove the washer and upper race from the upper bearing, then remove the ball bearing (see illustrations).
12 Lower the steering stem and triple clamp just far enough to expose the lower ball bearings (see illustration). If it's stuck, gently tap on the top of the steering stem with a plastic mallet or a hammer and wood block. Note: *Ball bearings may fall out when you lower the steering stem. Position your hands so you can catch them.*

All models

13 Clean all the parts with solvent and dry them thoroughly, using compressed air, if available. If you do use compressed air, don't let the bearings spin as they're dried - it could ruin them. Wipe the old grease out of the frame steering head and bearing races.
14 Examine the races in the steering head for cracks, dents, and pits. If you're working on an EX250, check the lower race on the steering stem as well (see illustration). If even the slightest amount of wear or damage is evident, the races should be replaced with new ones.
15 To remove the races, drive them out of the steering head with Kawasaki tool no. 57001-1107 or equivalent. A slide hammer with the proper internal-jaw puller will also work. Since the races are an interference fit in the frame, installation will be easier if the new races are left overnight in a freezer. This will cause them to contract and slip into place in the frame with very little effort. When installing the races, use Kawasaki press shaft no. 57001-1075 and drivers no. 57001-1106 and 57001-1076, or tap them gently into place with a hammer and bearing driver or a large socket. Do not strike the bearing surface or the race will be damaged.
16 Check the bearings for wear. Look for cracks, dents, and pits in the races and flat spots on the bearings. Replace any defective parts with new ones. If a new bearing is required, replace both of them as a set.
17 To remove the lower bearing from the steering stem, use a bearing puller (Kawasaki tool no. 57001-135 or equivalent) (see illustration). Don't remove this bearing unless it, or the grease seal underneath, must be replaced.
18 Check the grease seal under the lower

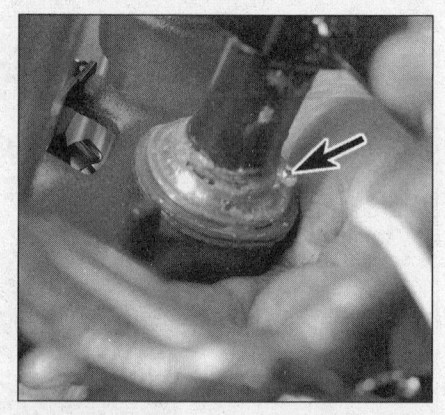

5.12 When you lower the steering stem on an EX250, some ball bearings (arrow) will fall out, so be ready to catch them

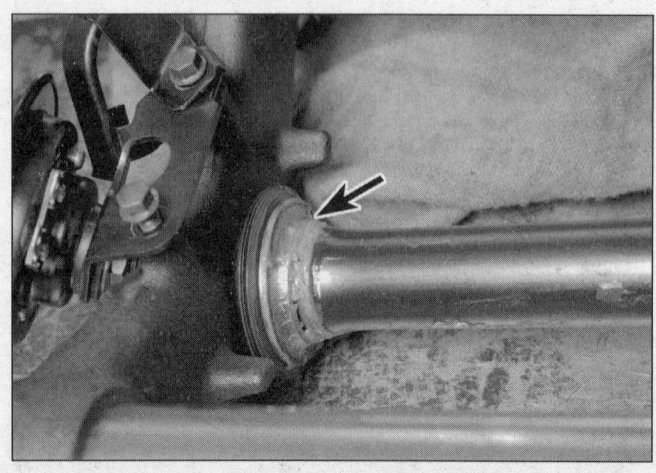

5.14 Don't remove the EX250 lower race (arrow) or the seal beneath it unless they need to be replaced

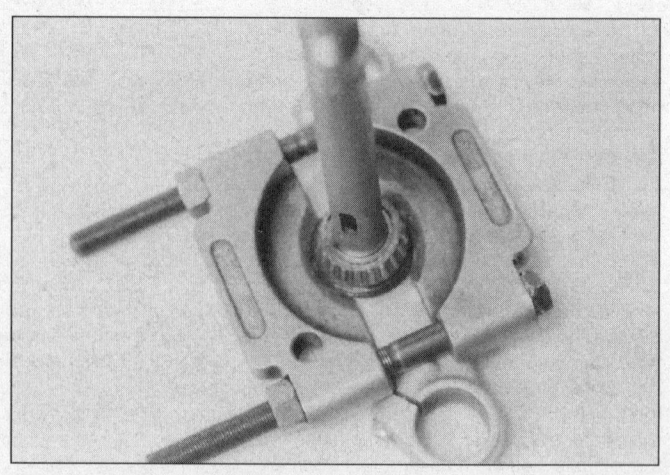

5.17 To remove the steering stem bearing, you'll need a bearing splitter like this one and a puller or hydraulic press (if you don't have the necessary tools, have it pressed off by a Kawasaki dealer or machine shop)

Suspension, steering and final drive 6•9

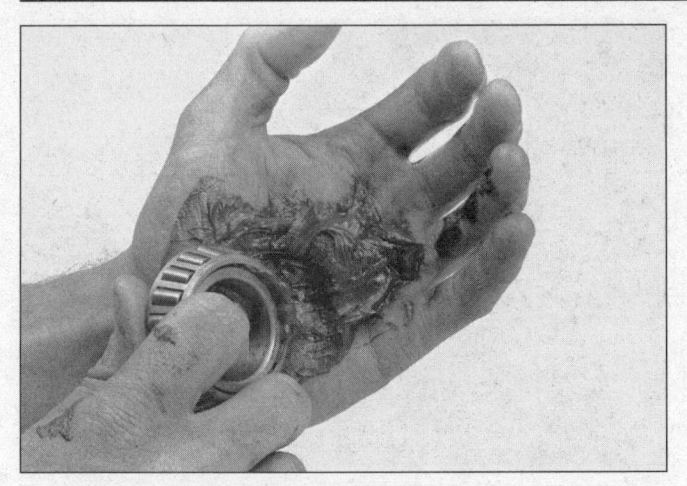

5.21 Work the grease completely into the rollers

5.23a On EX250 models, smear a thick layer of grease onto the lower race to hold the ball bearings in place

bearing and replace it with a new one if necessary.

19 Inspect the steering stem/lower triple clamp for cracks and other damage. Do not attempt to repair any steering components. Replace them with new parts if defects are found.

20 Check the bearing cover - if it's worn or deteriorated, replace it.

21 On EN450/500 models, pack the bearings with high-quality grease (preferably a moly-based grease) **(see illustration)**. Coat the outer races with grease also.

22 Install the grease seal and lower bearing onto the steering stem. Drive the lower bearing onto the steering stem using Kawasaki stem bearing driver no. 57001-137 and adapter no. 57001-1074. If you don't have access to these tools, a section of pipe with a diameter the same as the inner race of the bearing can be used. Drive the bearing on until it is fully seated.

23 If you're working on an EX250, apply a thick layer of grease to the lower race and stick the bearings to it **(see illustrations)**.

24 Insert the steering stem/lower triple clamp into the frame head. On EX250 models, grease the upper race and stick the bearings to it the same way as the lower ones **(see illustrations 5.23a and 5.23b)**. Install the upper bearing(s) and the race cover **(see illustration 5.9 or 5.11a)**.

25 Install the adjusting nut with its shoulder down (against the bearing). Using the adjustable spanner, tighten the nut while moving the lower triple clamp back and forth. Continue to tighten the nut (to approximately 29 ft-lbs/39 Nm) until the steering head becomes tight, then back off the nut until there is some play in the bearings. Now tighten the nut to the final torque listed in this Chapter's Specifications. The steering stem should turn freely and smoothly, but there should be no play in the bearings.

26 Install the locknut and tighten it securely, but don't allow the adjustment nut to turn (counterhold it with another wrench if necessary).

27 Install the upper triple clamp and bolt, but don't tighten the bolt yet.

28 Slide the forks through the lower triple clamp and into the upper triple clamp, to the proper height (see Section 3). Tighten the fork upper triple clamp bolts to the torque listed in this Chapter's Specifications.

29 Tighten the steering stem bolt to the torque listed in this Chapter's Specifications.

30 Tighten the fork lower triple clamp bolts to the torque listed in this Chapter's Specifications.

31 The remainder of installation is the reverse of the removal procedure.

6 Rear shock absorber(s) - removal and installation

Removal

1 Set the bike on its centerstand (if equipped). If the bike doesn't have a centerstand, support it in an upright position so it can't be knocked over during this procedure.

EN450/500 models

2 If you're working on an EN450 model, remove the mufflers (see Chapter 4). Remove the shock absorber upper and lower nuts and lift the shock off the motorcycle **(see illustration)**.

5.23b Stick the ball bearings into place in the grease (EX250)

6.2 Once the bolt is removed, the upper end of the shock absorber can be detached from its mounting bracket (EN450/500)

6•10 Suspension, steering and final drive

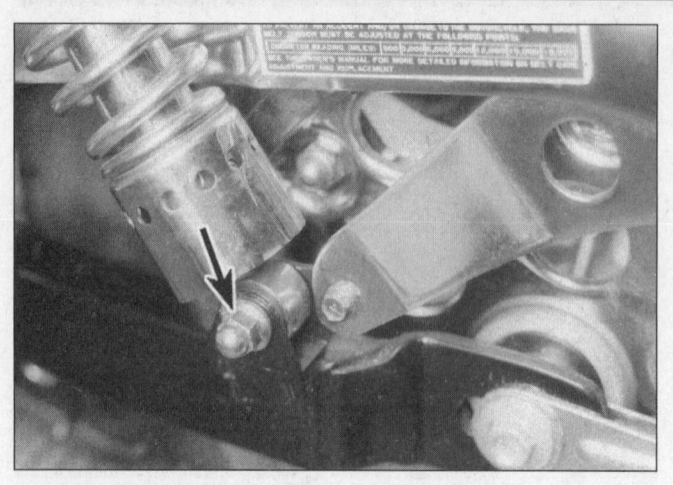

6.3 Remove the nut and bolt (arrow) from the lower end and remove the shock absorber (EN450/500)

6.6 Here's the EX250 rear shock absorber upper bolt

3 If you're working on an EN500 model, remove the rear side trim pieces, together with the rear turn signals (see Chapter 9). The forward bolt on the rear side trim also secures the top of the shock absorber. Remove the shock absorber lower bolt and lift the shock off the motorcycle **(see illustration)**.

EX250 models

4 Remove the seat, knee grip pads (1986 and 1987 models) and side covers (see Chapter 8).
5 Remove the coolant reservoir tank and IC igniter unit (see Chapters 3 and 5).
6 Loosen the shock absorber upper bolt and nut, but don't remove them yet **(see illustration)**.
7 Remove the lower bolt and nut from the shock absorber **(see illustration)**.
8 Remove the upper bolt and nut, then move the tie rods out of the way and lower the shock absorber away from the bike.

Installation

9 Installation is the reverse of the removal procedure. Tighten the shock absorber bolts/nuts (and tie rod bolt/nut on EX250 models) to the torque values listed in this Chapter's Specifications.

6.7 Rear suspension linkage details (EX250)

- A *Tie rod-to-swingarm bolts/nuts*
- B *Tie rod-to-rocker arm bots/nuts*
- C *Rocker arm-to-frame bolt/nut*
- D *Shock absorber lower bolt/nut*

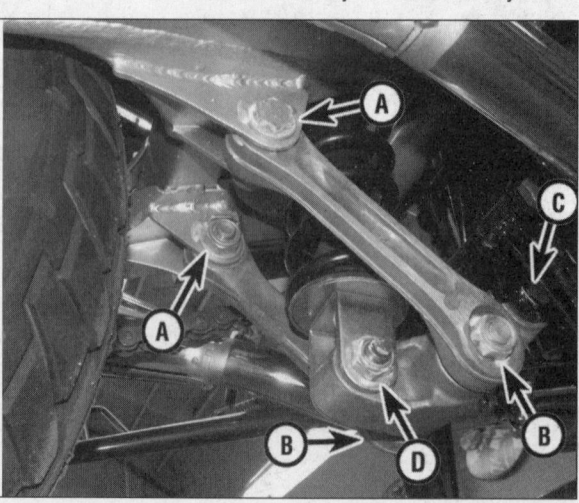

7 Rear suspension linkage (EX250 models) - removal, inspection and installation

Removal

1 Place the motorcycle on its centerstand.

Tie-rods

2 Remove the tie-rod lower bolt and nut, then the upper bolt and nut and take the tie-rods off **(see illustration 6.7)**.
3 Installation is the reverse of the removal steps. Tighten the bolts and nuts to the torque listed in this Chapter's Specifications.

Rocker arm

4 Remove the mufflers (see Chapter 4).
5 Support the motorcycle securely so it can't be knocked over, then raise the centerstand.
6 Support the swingarm with a jack. Remove the shock absorber lower bolt and tie-rod lower bolt.
7 Remove the nut from the rocker arm pivot shaft, then pull out the shaft and lower the rocker arm away from the motorcycle.

Inspection

8 Pry out the seals and slip the bushings out of the sleeves. Check the bushings and sleeves for wear or damage. If the bushings and sleeves are good, lubricate them with molybdenum disulfide grease and install the bushings.
9 If the seals are worn or appear to have been leaking, replace them. Press the seals in with a seal driver or socket the same diameter as the seals.
10 If the sleeves are worn or damaged, replace the rocker arm.

Installation

11 Installation is the reverse of the removal steps. Tighten the nuts and bolts to the torque listed in this Chapter's Specifications.

8 Swingarm bearings - check

1 Refer to Chapter 7 and remove the rear wheel, then refer to Section 6 and remove the rear shock absorbers.
2 Grasp the rear of the swingarm with one hand and place your other hand at the junction of the swingarm and the frame. Try to move the rear of the swingarm from side-to-side. Any wear (play) in the bearings should be felt as movement between the swingarm and the frame at the front. The swingarm will actually be felt to move forward and backward at the front (not from side-to-side). If any play is noted, the bearings should be replaced with new ones (see Section 10).
3 Next, move the swingarm up and down through its full travel. It should move freely, without any binding or rough spots. If it does not move freely, refer to Section 10 for servicing procedures.

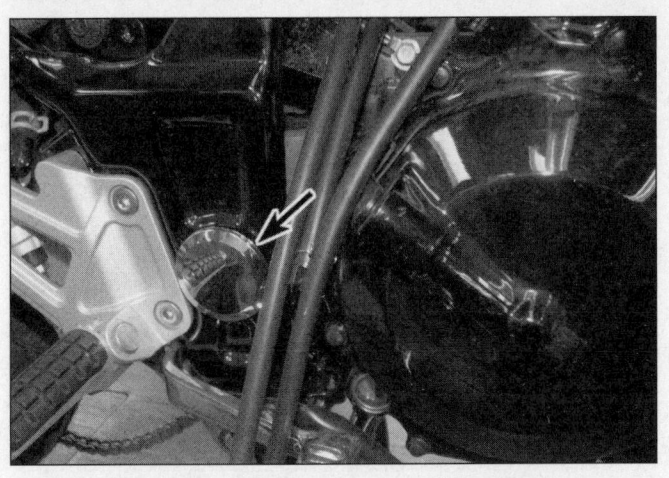

Suspension, steering and final drive 6•11

9.5a Pry off the trim cap (arrow) if equipped

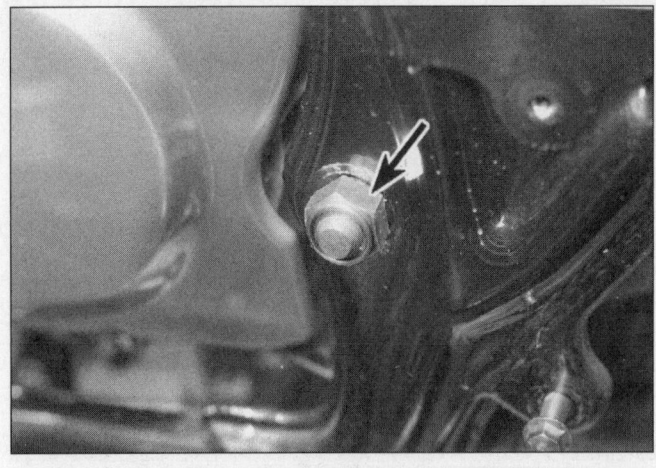

9.5b Remove the swingarm pivot shaft nut and withdraw the shaft

9 Swingarm - removal and installation

1 Raise the bike and set it on its centerstand (if equipped). If the bike doesn't have a centerstand, support it securely so it can't be knocked over during this procedure.
2 Remove the rear wheel (see Chapter 7).
3 If you're working on an EN450 or EX250 model, remove the mufflers (see Chapter 4).
4 If you're working on an EN450/500, detach the brake torque link from the swingarm. If you're working on an EX250, remove the rear brake caliper (see Chapter 7) and support it out of the way. Leave the brake hose connected.
5 Remove the cover (if equipped) from the swingarm pivot shaft nut and unscrew the nut **(see illustrations)**. Don't remove the pivot shaft yet. If you're working on an EX250, remove the nuts from the lower end of the shock absorber and upper end of the linkage tie-rod, but don't remove the bolts yet (see Sections 6 and 7).
6 If you're working on an EN450/500, support the swingarm with a jack and detach the shock absorbers (see Section 6). On EN450 models, you'll need to remove the shocks completely to get them off the swingarm studs.
7 Support the swingarm and pull the pivot shaft out. If you're working on an EX250, also remove the shock absorber bolt and linkage tie-rod bolt. Remove the swingarm. The bearing caps may fall out as this is done.
8 Remove the caps (if they didn't fall off), then pull out the sleeve and pry out the grease seals **(see illustrations)**. Check the pivot bearings in the swingarm for dryness or deterioration. If they're in need of lubrication or replacement, refer to Section 10.
9 Installation is the reverse of the removal procedure, with the following additions:
 a) Be sure the grease seals are in position before installing the pivot shaft.

 b) Tighten the pivot shaft nut and the shock absorber mounting bolts/nuts to the torque values listed in this Chapter's Specifications.
 c) Adjust the drive belt or chain as described in Chapter 1.

10 Swingarm bearings - replacement

HAYNES HiNT *Bearing replacement and the tools needed to do it are described in* **Tools and Workshop Tips** *at the end of this manual.*

1 Bearing replacement isn't complicated, but it requires a blind hole (expanding) puller, a slide hammer and a hydraulic press. The puller and slide hammer can be rented if you don't have them, and you may be able to devise a substitute for a hydraulic press, but compare the cost of having the bearings replaced by a Kawasaki dealer to that of renting the equipment before you proceed. It may be cheaper, and it will probably be easier, to have the bearings replaced by the dealer. You can save money by removing the swingarm from the bike yourself.
2 Remove the swingarm (see Section 9).
3 Slide the sleeve out **(see illustration 9.8b)**.
4 Pry out the seals **(see illustration 9.8c)**.
5 Remove the bearings with a blind hole (expanding) puller and slide hammer.
6 Press new bearings into the swingarm.

9.8a Remove the bearing caps . . .

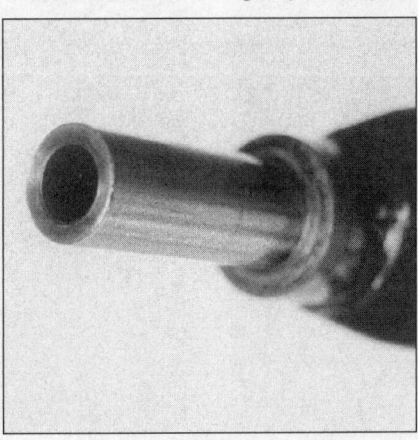

9.8b . . . slide out the sleeve . . .

9.8c . . . and pry out the grease seals for access to the bearings

6•12 Suspension, steering and final drive

11.2 Remove the mounting bolts (arrows) and take off the belt guard (EN450/500)

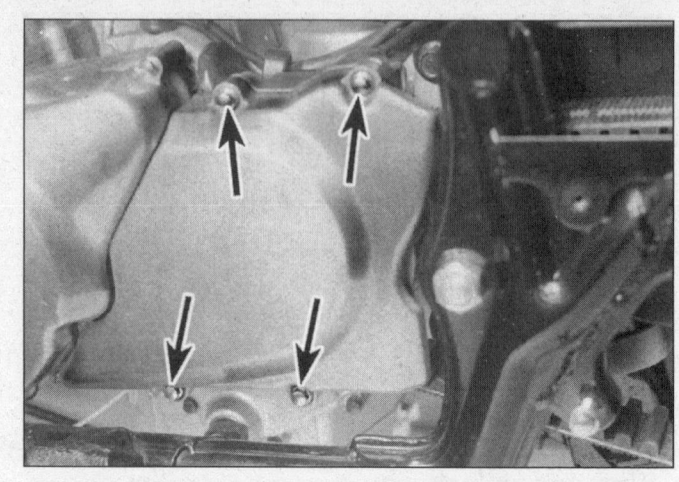

11.3 Remove the engine sprocket cover bolts (arrows) and take off the cover (EN450/500)

11 Drive belt/chain and sprockets - removal, inspection and installation

Removal
Drive belt
1 Remove the shift lever (see Chapter 2).
2 Remove the belt guard **(see illustration)**. Draw an arrow on the top of the belt pointing toward the front of the motorcycle to indicate the direction of belt rotation.
3 Remove the bolts securing the engine sprocket cover to the engine case **(see illustration)**. Slide the sprocket cover off.
4 Remove the rear wheel (see Chapter 7).
5 Remove two bolts that secure the engine sprocket holding plate, then remove the sprocket from the engine **(see illustration)**.
6 Remove the swingarm (see Section 9). Pull the swingarm back far enough to allow the belt to slip between the frame and the front of the swingarm.

11.5 Remove the holding plate bolts (arrows), then remove the holding plate and the sprocket (EN450/500)

Drive chain
7 Remove the engine sprocket cover **(see illustrations)**.
8 Have an assistant sit on the seat and

11.7a Remove the sprocket cover (EX250 shown) . . .

hold the rear brake on. If you're working on an EN500, bend back the tabs of the engine sprocket lockwasher and unscrew the sprocket nut. If you're working on an EX250, remove the bolts, align the teeth of the plate with the splines on the countershaft and slip

11.7b . . . locate the dowels and check the seal for leaks (arrows)

11.7c On EX250 models, note the routing of the wire harness (arrow)

Suspension, steering and final drive 6•13

11.8a Remove the sprocket plate bolts (arrows) . . .

11.8b . . . rotate the plate to align its teeth with the splines and slip it off

the plate off **(see illustrations)**.

9 Slip the sprocket off the transmission shaft, together with the drive chain **(see illustration)**. If there isn't enough slack in the chain, refer to the adjustment procedure in Chapter 1 and loosen it. **Note:** *The following steps deal with removal of the chain and rear sprocket. If you're just removing the engine sprocket to replace the oil seal behind it, ignore the steps that don't apply.*

10 Remove the rear wheel (see Chapter 6) and the swingarm (see Section 9).

11 Disengage the chain from the rear sprocket.

12 If necessary, remove the nuts that attach the rear sprocket to the coupling and take it off.

Inspection

Drive belt

13 Check the belt for wear (see Chapter 1). Replace it if it's worn or damaged.

14 Check the sprockets for damage and for worn teeth (see Chapter 1). Replace them if any undesirable conditions are found. If the sprockets must be replaced, install a new belt as well.

15 Measure the height of the sprocket teeth. Replace the sprockets and the belt if the teeth are worn to less than the value listed in this Chapter's Specifications.

16 Measure rear sprocket diameter. Replace the sprocket if it is worn to less than the value listed in this Chapter's Specifications.

Drive chain

Warning: *These motorcycles use an endless chain. On 2002 and earlier models, Kawasaki recommends against cutting the chain to install a master link. If the chain breaks in operation, it could cause loss of control of the motorcycle. The chain can be cut and reconnected on 2003 and later models, provided a chain breaker tool is used following the tool manufacturer's instructions.*

17 Soak the chain in kerosene or diesel fuel for approximately five or six minutes. Don't use other solvents, as they may wash out the lubricant contained inside the O-rings. Use a brush to work the solvent into the spaces between the links and plates. Blow the chain dry with compressed air.

Caution: *Don't allow the cleaning and drying process to take more than 10 minutes.*

18 Check the chain carefully for worn or damaged links. Replace the chain if wear or damage is found at any point.

19 Stretch the chain taut and measure its length between the number of pins listed in the Chapter 1 Specifications. Compare the measured length to the specified value and replace the chain if it's beyond the limit. If the chain needs to be replaced, check the sprockets as described below. If they're worn, replace them also. If a new chain is installed on worn sprockets, it will wear out quickly. Kawasaki recommends always replacing the chain and sprockets as a set.

20 Lubricate the chain with a lubricant compatible with O-ring chains. If this isn't available, use a heavy oil, such as SAE 90.

21 Check the teeth on the sprockets for wear. On the engine sprocket, wear will occur mostly on the forward side of each sprocket tooth. On the rear sprocket, wear will occur mostly on the rear side of each sprocket tooth. If the teeth are worn to points or have a hooked appearance, it's definitely time for new sprockets.

Installation

22 Installation is the reverse of the removal steps, with the following additions:

a) If you're working on a chain drive model, install the engine sprocket with the OUTSIDE mark away from the engine, and the rear sprocket with the tooth number mark away from the coupling. Use a new lockwasher on the engine sprocket.

b) Tighten the sprocket and suspension fasteners to the torque listed in this Chapter's Specifications.

c) Adjust the belt or chain slack (see Chapter 1).

d) Tighten the rear axle nut to the torque listed in the Chapter 7 Specifications.

11.9 Take the sprocket off - the raised center portion faces toward the bike

6•14 Suspension, steering and final drive

12 Rear wheel coupling/ rubber damper - check and replacement

1 Remove the rear wheel (see Chapter 7).
2 Lift the rear sprocket/rear wheel coupling from the wheel.
3 Remove the rubber damper **(see illustration)** and check it for cracks, hardening and general deterioration. Replace it with a new one if necessary.
4 Checking and replacement procedures for the coupling bearing are similar to those described for the wheel bearings. Refer to Chapter 7.
5 Installation is the reverse of the removal procedure.

Caution: Be sure not to forget the spacer (see illustration 12.3); if the axle nut is tightened without the spacer in position, the rear wheel bearings may be damaged.

12.3 Rear coupling details (belt drive shown; chain drive similar)
A Spacer
B Coupling
C Damper

13 Suspension adjustments

Front forks (early EN450 models)

1 The front forks on early EN450 models are equipped with air pressure valves. Later EN450 models and all EN500 and EX250 models have non-adjustable forks. The recommended air pressure setting is listed in this Chapter's Specifications.

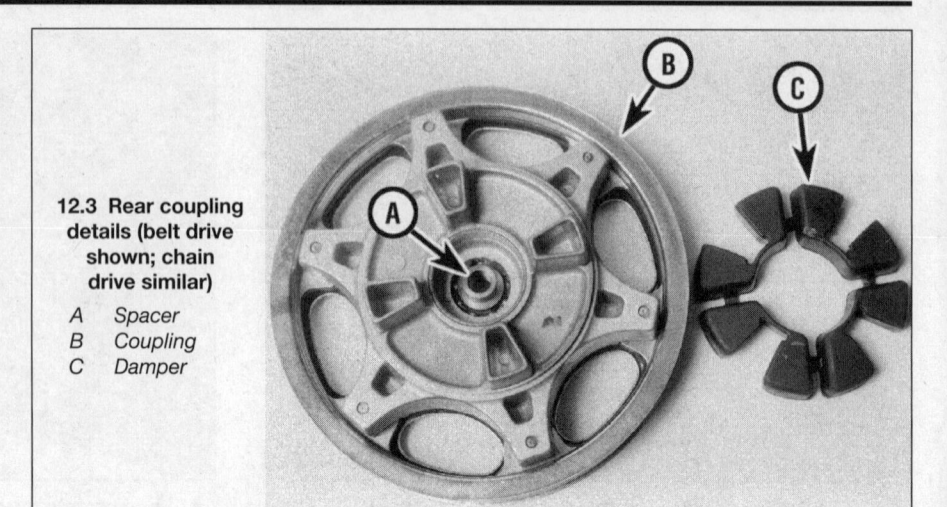

Warning: Never exceed the maximum pressure listed in this Chapter's Specifications. Never remove the fork springs and rely on air pressure alone to support the forks or unstable handling may occur. Ensure that the pressure is equal in both legs.

Rear spring preload adjustment

2 **Note:** *Spring preload is not adjustable on 1988 and later EX250 models.* The rear spring preload is adjusted by turning the adjusting sleeve at the bottom with the hook wrench included in the bike's tool kit. Compare preload with the values listed in this Chapter's Specifications and adjust as needed.

Warning: Always place both springs (EN450/500) on the same setting or unstable handling may occur.

Chapter 7
Brakes, wheels and tires

Contents

Brake caliper - removal, overhaul and installation	3	Brake system - general check	See Chapter 1
Brake disc - inspection, removal and installation	4	Brake system bleeding	8
Brake hoses and lines - inspection and replacement	7	Front wheel - removal, inspection and installation	11
Brake light switches - check and replacement	See Chapter 9	General information	1
Brake master cylinder - removal, overhaul and installation	5	Rear drum brake - removal, inspection and installation	6
Brake pads - replacement	2	Rear wheel - removal, inspection and installation	12
Brake pads and linings - wear check	See Chapter 1	Tires - general information	14
Brake pedal - removal and installation	9	Tires/wheels - general check	See Chapter 1
Brake pedal position and play - check and adjustment	See Chapter 1	Wheel bearings - inspection and maintenance	13
		Wheels - inspection, repair and alignment check	10

Degrees of difficulty

Easy, suitable for novice with little experience	Fairly easy, suitable for beginner with some experience	Fairly difficult, suitable for competent DIY mechanic	Difficult, suitable for experienced DIY mechanic	Very difficult, suitable for expert DIY or professional

Specifications

Brakes
Brake fluid type .... See Chapter 1
Brake pad minimum thickness .... See Chapter 1
Disc thickness
    All except 1986 and 1987 EX250 rear
        Standard .... 4.8 to 5.1 mm (0.189 to 0.200 inch)
        Minimum* .... 4.5 mm (0.177 inch)
    1986 and 1987 EX250 rear
        Standard .... 5.3 to 5.6 mm (0.189 to 0.200 inch)
        Minimum* .... 5.0 mm (0.197 inch)
* Refer to marks stamped into the disc (they supersede information printed here)
Disc runout (maximum)
    EN450 and EX250 models .... 0.15 mm (0.006 inch)
    EN500 models .... 0.2 mm (0.008 inch)
Brake pedal position and freeplay .... See Chapter 1
Rear drum brake lining thickness
    Standard
        EN450 models .... 5.0 mm (0.197 inch)
        EN500 models .... 4.8 to 5.1 mm (0.189 to 0.200 inch)
    Minimum
        EN450 models .... 2.5 mm (0.098 inch)
        EN500 models .... 2.0 mm (0.079 inch)
Brake drum diameter
    Standard .... 180.00 to 180.16 mm (7.087 to 7.093 inch)
    Maximum .... 180.75 mm (7.116 inch)
Brake cam diameter
    Standard .... 16.975 to 16.984 mm (0.668 to 0.669 inch)
    Minimum .... 16.88 mm (0.665 inch)
Cam hole diameter in brake panel
    Standard .... 17.00 to 17.07 mm (0.669 to 0.672 inch)
    Maximum .... 17.15 mm (0.675 inch)

7•2 Brakes, wheels and tires

Wheels and tires
Wheel runout
   Axial (side-to-side) .... 0.5 mm (0.020 inch)
   Radial (out-of-round)... 0.8 mm (0.031 inch)
Axle runout (front and rear)
   Standard .... 0.05 mm (0.002 inch) per 100 mm (3.94 inch) of axle length
   Limit .... 0.2 mm (0.007 inch) per 100 mm (3.94 inch) of axle length
Tire pressures.. See Chapter 1
Tire sizes
   Front
      EN450/500
         1985 through 1992.. 100/90-19 57S
         1993 and later... 100/90-19 M/C 57S
      EX250
         1986 through 2001.. 100/80-16 50S
         2002 through 2005.. 100/80-16 50S or 100/80-16 M/C 50S
         2006 and later... 100/80-16 M/C 50S
   Rear
      EN450 .... 140/90-15 70S
      EN500 .... 140/90-15M/C 70S
      EX250
         1986 and 1987 .... 120/80-16 60S
         1988 through 2001.. 120/80-16 64S
         2002 through 2005.. 130/80-16 64S or 130/80-16 M/C 64S
         2006 and later... 130/80-16 M/C 64S

Torque specifications
Caliper mounting bolts
   EN450 models... 29 Nm (22 ft-lbs)
   EN500 models
      Through 1996 .... 39 Nm (29 ft-lbs)
      1997 and later... 34 Nm (25 ft-lbs)
   EX250
      Front .... 32 Nm (24 ft-lbs)
      Rear .... 25 Nm (18 ft-lbs)
Banjo fitting bolts
   EN450/500
      Through 1995 .... 25 Nm (18 ft-lb)
      1996 and later... 34 Nm (25 ft-lbs)
   EX250 .... 25 Nm (18 ft-lb)
Brake disc-to-wheel bolts
   EN450/500
      Through 1995 .... 23 Nm (16.5 ft-lbs)
      1996 and later... 27 Nm (20 ft-lbs)
   EX250 .... 23 Nm (16.5 ft-lbs)
Master cylinder mounting bolts
   Front .... 8.8 Nm (78 in-lbs)
   Rear (EX250)
      Through 2005 .... 23 Nm (16.5 ft-lbs)
      2006 and later... 25 Nm (18 ft-lbs)
Front brake lever pivot pin locknut... 5.9 Nm (52 in-lbs)
Caliper bleed valve... 7.8 Nm (69 in-lbs)
Rear brake pedal pinch bolt .... 25 Nm (18 ft-lbs)
Rear brake fluid reservoir bolt (EX250).. 5.9 Nm (52 inch-lbs)
Front axle nut .... 88 Nm (65 ft-lbs)
Front axle clamp bolt
   EN450 models... 14 Nm (10 ft-lbs)
   EN500 models
      Through 1995 .... 16 Nm (138 in-lbs)
      1996 and later... 34 Nm (25 ft-lbs)
   EX250 .... Not applicable
Rear axle nut
   EN450/500
      Through 1995 .... 125 Nm (94 ft-lbs)
      1996 and later... 88 Nm (65 ft-lbs)
   EX250 .... 110 Nm (80 ft-lbs)

Brakes, wheels and tires 7•3

2.2 Remove the caliper mounting bolts (arrows) and support the caliper so it doesn't hang by the brake hose (single-piston caliper)

2.4a Slide the caliper bracket toward the pistons so it clears the inner pad ...

1 General information

The EN450/500 models covered by this manual are equipped with a hydraulic disc brake on the front and a mechanical drum brake on the rear. The front brake uses a single piston caliper.

The EX250 models covered by this manual use disc brakes at front and rear. Single-piston calipers are used at front and rear on 1986 and 1987 models. Dual-piston calipers are used at front and rear on 1988 and later models.

Most models are equipped with cast aluminum wheels, which require very little maintenance and allow tubeless tires to be used. 1996 and later EN500 models are equipped with wire-spoked wheels and require that tubes be used.

Caution: *Disc brake components rarely require disassembly. Do not disassemble components unless absolutely necessary. Do not use petroleum-based solvents on internal brake components. Solvents will cause seals to swell and distort. Use only brake system cleaner, clean brake fluid or alcohol for cleaning. Use care when working with brake fluid as it can injure your eyes and it will damage painted surfaces and plastic parts.*

2 Brake pads - replacement

Warning: *The dust created by the brake system is harmful to your health. Never blow it out with compressed air and don't inhale any of it. An approved filtering mask should be worn when working on the brakes.*

Note: *Pad replacement procedures are the same for front and rear calipers.*

1 Set the bike on its centerstand (if equipped).

Single-piston calipers

2 Remove the caliper mounting bolts **(see illustration)**. Slide the caliper and pads off the disc.

3 Support the caliper with rope or wire so it doesn't hang by the brake hose. It's a good idea to wrap the caliper with tape and rags to protect the caliper and wheel from scratches.

4 Remove the inner pad **(see illustration)**.

Caution: *If the caliper won't slide easily, do not hammer it or otherwise try to force it. Remove it for inspection and use a spreader tool.*

5 Remove the outer brake pad from the caliper **(see illustration)**.

6 Remove the anti-rattle spring **(see illustration)**. If it appears damaged, replace it.

7 Check the pad support clips on the caliper bracket. If they are missing or distorted, replace them.

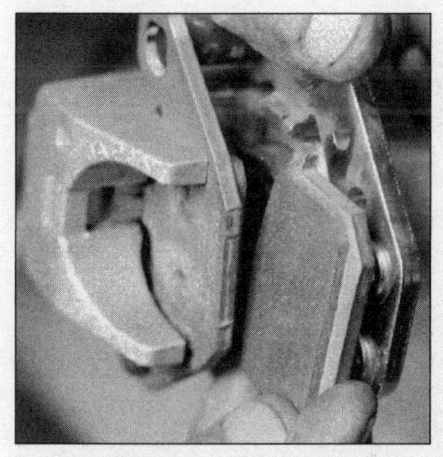

2.4b ... then remove the pad

2.5 Remove the outer pad

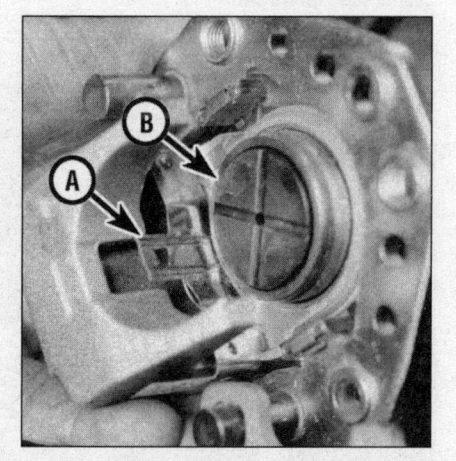

2.6 Remove the anti-rattle spring

A   Anti-rattle spring
B   Piston insert

7•4 Brakes, wheels and tires

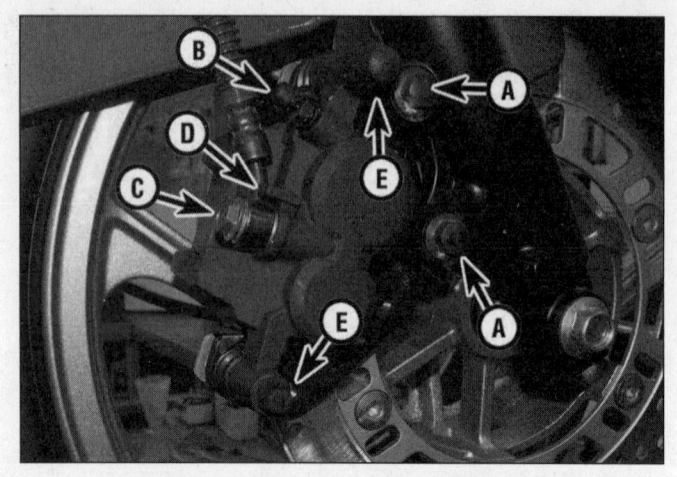

2.8a Front caliper details (dual-piston caliper)

A Mounting bolts
B Bleed valve
C Brake hose banjo fitting
D Brake hose stopper
E Slide pins and bushings

2.8b Rear caliper details (dual-piston caliper)

A Mounting bolts
B Bleed valve
C Brake hose banjo fitting
D Brake hose stopper
E Slide pins and bushings

Dual-piston calipers

8 Remove the caliper mounting bolts **(see illustrations)**. Push the caliper bracket in (toward the piston) as far it will go **(see illustration)**.

Caution: *If the caliper won't slide easily, do not hammer it or otherwise try to force it. Remove it for inspection and use a spreader tool.*

Slide the caliper and pads off the disc.

9 Support the caliper with rope or wire so it doesn't hang by the brake hose. It's a good idea to wrap the caliper with tape and rags to protect the caliper and wheel from scratches.

10 Remove the inner pad **(see illustration)**.

Caution: *If the caliper won't slide easily, do not hammer it or otherwise try to force it. Remove it for inspection and use a spreader tool.*

11 Remove the outer brake pad from the caliper **(see illustration)**.

12 Remove the anti-rattle spring **(see illustration)**. If it appears damaged, replace it.

13 Check the pad support clips on the caliper bracket **(see illustration 2.12)**. If they are missing or distorted, replace them.

All models

14 Check the condition of the brake disc (see Section 4). If it is in need of machining or replacement, follow the procedure in that Section to remove it. If it is okay, deglaze it with sandpaper or emery cloth, using a swirling motion.

15 Remove the cap from the master cylinder reservoir and siphon out some fluid. Push the piston into the caliper as far as possible, while checking the master cylinder reservoir to make sure it doesn't overflow. If you can't depress the piston with thumb pressure, try using a C-clamp. If the piston sticks, remove the caliper and overhaul it as described in Section 3.

16 Install the anti-rattle spring in the caliper.

2.8c Slide the caliper along the pins to create looseness in the pads

17 Install both pads in the caliper and pull the caliper bracket out, so the pins on the bracket engage with the holes in the pad backing plate.

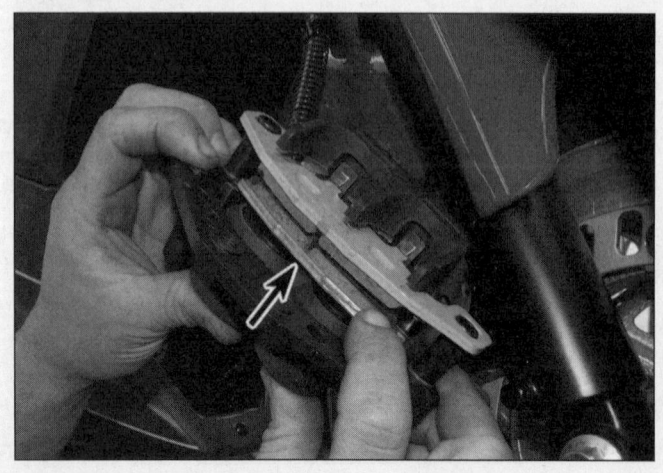

2.10 Remove the inner pad (arrow)

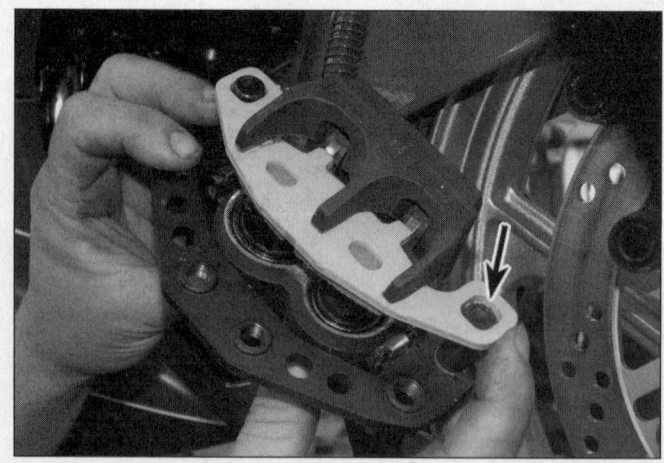

2.11 Lift one end of the outer pad off its post, then pivot the pad outward and lift it off the other post

Brakes, wheels and tires 7•5

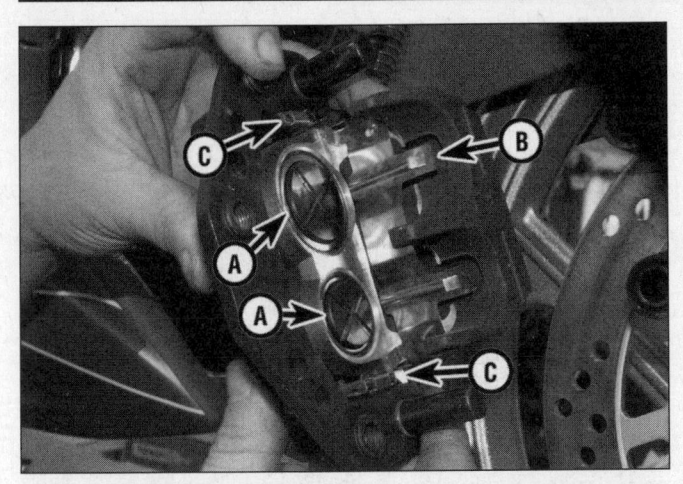

2.12 Remove the piston inserts (A) and pad spring (B) - remove the pad support clips (C) if they're worn or damaged

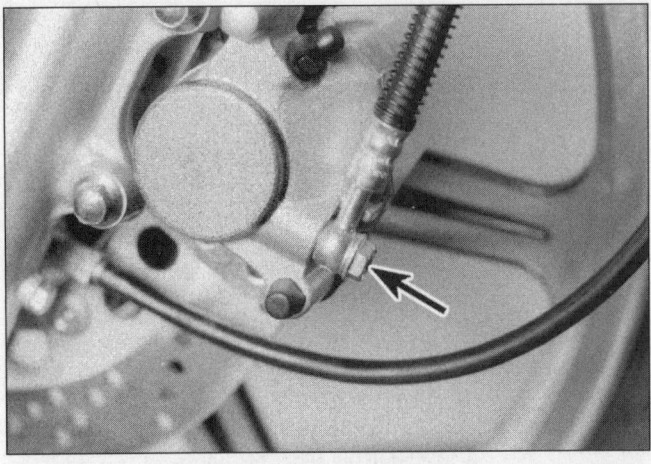

3.2 Remove the brake hose banjo fitting bolt - there's a sealing washer on each side of the fitting

18 Install the caliper, tightening the mounting bolts to the torque listed in this Chapter's Specifications.
19 Refill the master cylinder reservoir (see Chapter 1) and install the diaphragm and cap.
20 Operate the brake lever or pedal several times to bring the pads into contact with the disc. Check the operation of the brakes carefully before riding the motorcycle.

3 Brake caliper - removal, overhaul and installation

Warning: *If a caliper indicates the need for an overhaul (usually due to leaking fluid or sticky operation), all old brake fluid should be flushed from the system. Also, the dust created by the brake system is harmful to your health. Never blow it out with compressed air and don't inhale any of it. An approved filtering mask should be worn when working on the brakes. Do not, under any circumstances, use petroleum-based solvents to clean brake parts. Use clean brake fluid, brake cleaner or denatured alcohol only!*

Note: *If you are removing the caliper only to replace or inspect the brake pads, don't disconnect the hose from the caliper.*

Removal

1 Place the bike on its centerstand (if equipped).

HAYNES HINT *If you're planning to overhaul the caliper and don't have a source of compressed air to blow out the piston, use the bike's hydraulic system instead. To do this, remove the pads (see Section 2) and squeeze the brake lever to force the piston out of the cylinder. Note that brake fluid will run out of the caliper if* you remove the piston in this manner. Try to keep it off of the bike by holding the caliper over a pan. Be sure to wipe any spilled fluid off painted or plastic surfaces immediately and clean the area with soap and water.

2 Remove the brake hose banjo fitting bolt and separate the hose from the caliper **(see illustrations 2.8a, 2.8b and the accompanying illustration)**. Discard the sealing washers. Plug the end of the hose or wrap a plastic bag, secured with a rubber band, tightly around it to prevent excessive fluid loss and contamination.
3 Unscrew the mounting bolts and remove the caliper.

Overhaul

4 Remove the brake pads and anti-rattle spring from the caliper (see Section 2, if necessary).
5 Remove the caliper piston insert(s) (see Section 2).
6 Clean the exterior of the caliper with denatured alcohol or brake system cleaner.
7 Remove the caliper bracket and the slider pin boots from the caliper.
8 If you didn't force out the piston with the bike's hydraulic system in Step 1, place a few rags between the piston and the caliper frame to act as a cushion, then use compressed air, directed into the fluid inlet, to remove the piston. Use only enough air pressure to ease the piston out of the bore. If a piston is blown out, even with the cushion in place, it may be damaged.

Warning: *Never place your fingers in front of the piston in an attempt to catch or protect it when applying compressed air, as serious injury could occur.*

9 Using a wood or plastic tool, remove the dust seal **(see illustration)**. Metal tools may cause bore damage.
10 Using a wood or plastic tool, remove the piston seal from the groove in the caliper bore. If you're working on a dual-piston caliper, remove the dust seal and piston seal

3.9 The dust seal should be removed with a plastic or wooden tool to avoid damage to the bore and seal groove (a pencil works well) - remove the piston seal the same way

from the other bore.
11 Clean the piston(s) and the bore(s) with denatured alcohol, clean brake fluid or brake system cleaner and blow dry them with filtered, unlubricated compressed air. Inspect the surface of the piston for nicks and burrs and loss of plating. Check the caliper bore, too. If surface defects are present, the caliper must be replaced. If the caliper is in bad shape, the master cylinder should also be checked.
12 Temporarily reinstall the caliper bracket. Make sure it slides smoothly in-and-out of the caliper. If it doesn't, check the slider pins for burrs or excessive wear. Also check the slider pin bores in the caliper for wear and scoring. Replace the caliper bracket, the caliper, or both if necessary.
13 Lubricate the new piston seal with clean brake fluid and install it in its groove in the caliper bore. Make sure it seats completely and isn't twisted.
14 Lubricate the new dust seal with clean brake fluid and install it in its groove, making sure it seats correctly.
15 Lubricate the piston with clean brake

7•6 Brakes, wheels and tires

3.16 Install the slider pin boots

3.17 Apply a thin coat of the specified grease to the slider pins on the caliper bracket

fluid and install it in the caliper bore. Using your thumbs, push the piston all the way in, making sure it doesn't get cocked in the bore. If you're working on a dual-piston caliper, install the dust seal, piston seal and piston in the other bore.

16 Install the slider pin boots **(see illustration)**.

17 Apply a thin coat of PBC (poly butyl cuprysil) grease, or silicone grease designed for high-temperature brake applications, to the slider pins on the caliper bracket **(see illustration)**. Install the caliper bracket to the caliper and seat the boots over the lips on the bracket.

Installation

18 Install the piston insert(s) (see Section 2).
19 Install the anti-rattle spring and the brake pads (see Section 2).
20 Install the caliper, tightening the mounting bolts to the torque listed in this Chapter's Specifications.
21 Connect the brake hose to the caliper, using a new sealing washer on each side of the fitting. Tighten the banjo fitting bolt to the torque listed in this Chapter's Specifications.
22 Fill the master cylinder with the recommended brake fluid (see Chapter 1) and bleed the system (see Section 8). Check for leaks.
23 Check the operation of the brakes carefully before riding the motorcycle.

4 Brake disc - inspection, removal and installation

Inspection

1 Set the bike on its centerstand (if equipped).
2 Visually inspect the surface of the disc for score marks and other damage. Light scratches are normal after use and won't affect brake operation, but deep grooves and heavy score marks will reduce braking efficiency and accelerate pad wear. If the disc is badly grooved it must be machined or replaced.
3 To check disc runout, mount a dial indicator to a fork leg with the plunger on the indicator touching the surface of the disc about 1/2-inch from the outer edge. Slowly turn the wheel (have an assistant sit on the seat to raise the front wheel off the ground) and watch the indicator needle, comparing your reading with the limit listed in this Chapter's Specifications. If the runout is greater than allowed, check the hub bearings for play (see Chapter 1). If the bearings are worn, replace them and repeat this check. If the disc runout is still excessive, it will have to be replaced.
4 The disc must not be machined or allowed to wear down to a thickness less than the minimum allowable thickness listed in this Chapter's Specifications. The thickness of the disc can be checked with a micrometer. If the thickness of the disc is less than the minimum allowable, it must be replaced. The minimum thickness is also stamped into the disc **(see illustration)**.

Removal

5 Remove the wheel (see Section 11).

Caution: Don't lay the wheel down and allow it to rest on the disc - the disc could become warped.

6 Mark the relationship of the disc to the wheel, so it can be installed in the same position. Remove the Allen bolts that retain the disc to the wheel **(see illustration)**. Loosen the bolts a little at a time, in a criss-cross

4.4 The minimum allowable thickness is stamped into the disc

4.6 Loosen the disc retaining bolts a little at a time to prevent distortion

Brakes, wheels and tires 7•7

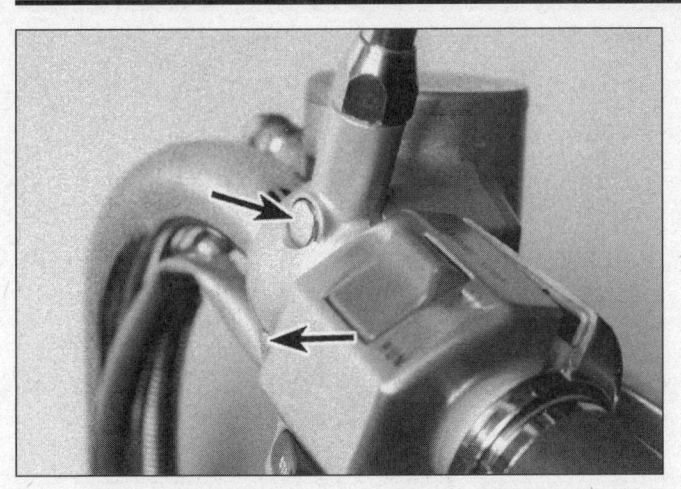

5.6 On EN500 models, the master cylinder mounting bolts are located beneath trim covers (arrows)

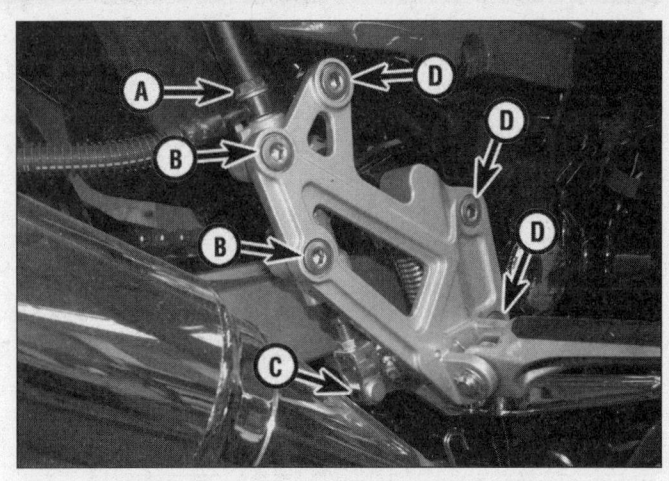

5.8 Rear master cylinder mounting details

A   Brake hose union bolt
B   Master cylinder mounting bolts
C   Cotter pin and clevis pin
D   Footpeg/brake pedal bracket bolts

pattern, to avoid distorting the disc.

7   Take note of any paper shims that may be present where the disc mates to the wheel. If there are any, mark their position and be sure to include them when installing the disc.

Installation

8   Position the disc on the wheel, aligning the previously applied matchmarks (if you're reinstalling the original disc). Make sure the arrow (stamped on the disc) marking the direction of rotation is pointing in the proper direction.

9   Apply a non-hardening thread locking compound to the threads of the bolts. Install the bolts, tightening them a little at a time, in a criss-cross pattern, until the torque listed in this Chapter's Specifications is reached. Clean off all grease from the brake disc using acetone or brake system cleaner.

10   Install the wheel.

11   Operate the brake lever several times to bring the pads into contact with the disc. Check the operation of the brakes carefully before riding the motorcycle.

5   Brake master cylinder - removal, overhaul and installation

1   If the master cylinder is leaking fluid, or if the lever does not produce a firm feel when the brake is applied, and bleeding the brakes does not help, master cylinder overhaul is recommended. Before disassembling the master cylinder, read through the entire procedure and make sure that you have the correct rebuild kit. Also, you will need some new, clean brake fluid of the recommended type, some clean rags and internal snap-ring pliers.

Caution 1: To prevent damage to the paint from spilled brake fluid, always

cover the fuel tank when working on the master cylinder.

Caution 2: Disassembly, overhaul and reassembly of the brake master cylinder must be done in a spotlessly clean work area to avoid contamination and possible failure of the brake hydraulic system components.

Removal

Front master cylinder

2   Loosen, but do not remove, the screws holding the reservoir cap in place.

3   Pull back the rubber boot (if equipped), loosen the banjo fitting bolt and separate the brake hose from the master cylinder.

4   Wrap the end of the hose in a clean rag and suspend the hose in an upright position or bend it down carefully and place the open end in a clean container. The objective is to prevent excess loss of brake fluid, fluid spills and system contamination.

5   Remove the locknut from the underside of the lever pivot bolt, then unscrew the bolt.

6   Remove the master cylinder mount-

ing bolts (see illustration) and separate the master cylinder from the handlebar.

Caution: Do not tip the master cylinder upside down or brake fluid will run out.

7   Disconnect the electrical connectors from the brake light switch.

Rear master cylinder

8   Remove the cotter pin and pull the clevis pin out of the brake pedal pushrod (see illustration).

9   If you're removing the master cylinder for overhaul, loosen the banjo fitting bolt on the brake hose (see illustration 5.8). Don't remove the bolt yet.

10   Unbolt the master cylinder reservoir and master cylinder (see illustration 5.8 and the accompanying illustration). Lift the cylinder and reservoir out.

11   If necessary, remove the banjo fitting bolt and disconnect the brake hose from the master cylinder body.

12   If necessary, loosen the hose clamps and disconnect the reservoir hose from the cylinder body and reservoir (see illustration).

5.10 The rear brake fluid reservoir is secured by a bolt (arrow)

5.12 The reservoir hose is secured by a clamp (arrow)

7•8 Brakes, wheels and tires

6.3 The brake shoes are mounted on a panel that fits into the rear wheel

6.4 Fold the shoes off the panel to remove them

Overhaul

13 Detach the reservoir cap and the rubber diaphragm, then drain the brake fluid into a suitable container. Wipe any remaining fluid out of the reservoir with a clean rag.

14 Carefully remove the rubber dust boot from the end of the piston.

15 On EN450 models, extract the washer, piston and cup assembly and the spring. On EN500 and EX250 models, remove the snap-ring and slide out the piston, the cup seals and the spring. Lay the parts out in the proper order to prevent confusion during reassembly.

16 Clean all of the parts with brake system cleaner (available at auto parts stores), denatured alcohol or clean brake fluid.

Caution: *Do not, under any circumstances, use a petroleum-based solvent to clean brake parts.*

If compressed air is available, use it to dry the parts thoroughly (make sure it's filtered and unlubricated). Check the master cylinder bore for corrosion, scratches, nicks and score marks. If damage is evident, the master cylinder must be replaced with a new one. If the master cylinder is in poor condition, then the caliper should be checked as well. Make sure the ports in the bottom of the master cylinder are clear. If the small relief port is clogged, the brakes will drag.

17 Remove the old cup seals from the piston and spring and install the new ones. If a new piston is included in the rebuild kit, use it regardless of the condition of the old one.

Note: *The secondary cups on EN500 models can't be removed. If they're worn or damaged, replace the piston assembly.*

18 Before reassembling the master cylinder, soak the piston and the rubber cup seals in clean brake fluid for ten to fifteen minutes. Lubricate the master cylinder bore with clean brake fluid, then carefully insert the piston and related parts in the reverse order of disassembly. Make sure the lips on the cup seals do not turn inside out when they are slipped into the bore.

19 On EN450 models, install the washer and rubber dust boot (make sure its lip locates correctly). On EN500 and EX250 models, depress the piston, then install the snap-ring (make sure the snap-ring is properly seated in the groove with the sharp edge facing out). Install the rubber dust boot (make sure the lip is seated properly in the piston groove).

Installation

Front master cylinder

20 Attach the master cylinder to the handlebar with the clamp. On EN450 models, the protrusion on the clamp must face to the right. Tighten the bolts to the torque listed in this Chapter's Specifications. **Note:** *Tighten the upper bolt first, then the lower bolt. There will be a gap at the bottom between the clamp and master cylinder body. Don't try to close the gap by overtightening the bolts or the clamp will break.*

21 Install the brake lever and tighten the pivot bolt locknut.

22 Connect the brake hose to the master cylinder, using new sealing washers. Tighten the banjo fitting bolt to the torque listed in this Chapter's Specifications. Refer to Section 8 and bleed the air from the system.

Rear master cylinder

23 If you removed the reservoir hose, connect it to the reservoir and master cylinder.

24 Place the master cylinder and reservoir in position and install the mounting bolts. Tighten them to the torque listed in this Chapter's Specifications.

25 Connect the brake hose to the master cylinder and caliper (if it was disconnected). Use new sealing washers on each side of both fittings. Make sure the metal portion of the brake hose is correctly positioned in the locating notch on the master cylinder. Tighten the union bolts to the torque listed in this Chapter's Specifications.

26 Bleed the rear brake and check brake pedal height (see Section 8 and Chapter 1).

6 Rear drum brake - removal, inspection and installation

Warning: *The dust collected by the brake system is harmful to your health. Never blow it out with compressed air and don't inhale any of it. An approved filtering mask should be worn when working on the brakes.*

Removal

1 Before you start, inspect the rear brake wear indicator (see Chapter 1).

2 Remove the rear wheel (see Section 12).

3 Lift the brake panel out of the wheel **(see illustration)**.

4 Fold the shoes toward each other to release the spring tension **(see illustration)**. Remove the shoes and springs from the brake panel.

Inspection

5 Check the linings for wear, damage, and signs of contamination from road dirt or water. If the linings are visibly defective, replace them.

6 Measure the thickness of the lining material (just the lining material, not the metal backing) and compare with the value listed in this Chapter's Specifications. Replace the shoes if the material is worn to less than the minimum.

7 Check the ends of the shoes where they contact the brake cam and pivot post. Replace the shoes if there's visible wear.

8 Check the brake cam and pivot post for wear and damage. If necessary, make match marks on the cam and cam lever, then remove the pinch bolt, lever, wear indicator pointer, seal, spring and cam.

9 Check the brake drum (inside the wheel) for wear or damage. Measure the diameter at several points with a brake drum micrometer

Brakes, wheels and tires 7•9

7.3a Unbolt the front brake hose bracket from the lower triple clamp (arrow) (EN450/500 shown; EX250 similar)

7.3b On EX250 models, free the rear brake hose from its retainers (arrows)

(or have this done by a Kawasaki dealer). If the measurements are uneven (indicating that the drum is out-of-round) or if there are scratches deep enough to snag a fingernail, have the drum turned (skimmed) by a dealer to correct the surface. If the drum has to be machined beyond the wear limit to remove the defects, replace it.

10 Check the brake cam for looseness in the brake panel hole. If it feels loose, measure the diameter of the cam and hole and compare them with those listed in this Chapter's Specifications. Replace worn parts.

Installation

11 Apply high temperature brake grease to the ends of the springs, the cam and the anchor pin.
12 Hook the springs to the shoes. Position the shoes in a V on the brake panel, then fold them down into position **(see illustration 6.4)**. Make sure the ends of the shoes fit correctly in the cam and on the pivot post.
13 The remainder of installation is the reverse of the removal steps.
14 Check the position of the brake pedal (see Chapter 1) and adjust it if necessary. Check the operation of the brakes carefully before riding the motorcycle.

8.5 Remove the bleed valve cap and fit a length of tubing over it; place the other end in a clean glass jar and place a wrench on the bleed valve

7 Brake hoses and lines - inspection and replacement

Inspection

1 Once a week, or if the motorcycle is used less frequently, before every ride, check the condition of the brake hose(s).
2 Twist and flex the rubber hose while looking for cracks, bulges and seeping fluid. Check extra carefully around the areas where the hose connects to the banjo fittings, as these are common areas for hose failure.

Replacement

3 The brake hose has banjo fittings on each end. Cover the surrounding area with plenty of rags and unscrew the banjo bolts on either end of the hose. On front hoses, remove the bolt that secures the hose to the lower triple clamp **(see illustration)**. On rear hoses, free the hose from the retainer that attaches it to the swingarm and caliper brace **(see illustration)**. Detach the hose from the clips and remove the hose.
4 Position the new hose, making sure it isn't twisted or otherwise strained, between the two components. Install the banjo bolts, using new sealing washers on both sides of the fittings, and tighten them to the torque listed in this Chapter's Specifications.
5 Flush the old brake fluid from the system, refill the system with the recommended fluid (see Chapter 1) and bleed the air from the system (see Section 8). Check the operation of the brakes carefully before riding the motorcycle.

8 Brake system bleeding

1 Bleeding the brake is simply the process of removing all the air bubbles from the brake fluid reservoir, the hose and the brake caliper. Bleeding is necessary whenever a brake system hydraulic connection is loosened, when a component or hose is replaced, or when the master cylinder or caliper is overhauled. Leaks in the system may also allow air to enter, but leaking brake fluid will reveal their presence and warn you of the need for repair.
2 To bleed the brake, you will need some new, clean brake fluid of the recommended type (see Chapter 1), a length of clear vinyl or plastic tubing, a small container partially filled with clean brake fluid, some rags and a wrench to fit the brake caliper bleed valve.
3 Cover the fuel tank and other painted components to prevent damage in the event that brake fluid is spilled.
4 Remove the reservoir cap and slowly pump the brake lever a few times, until no air bubbles can be seen floating up from the holes at the bottom of the reservoir. Doing this bleeds the air from the master cylinder end of the line. Reinstall the reservoir cap.
5 Attach one end of the clear vinyl or plastic tubing to the brake caliper bleeder valve and submerge the other end in the brake fluid in the container **(see illustration)**.

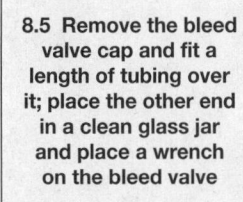

7•10 Brakes, wheels and tires

9.2 Unhook the brake pedal spring (arrow) (EN450/500)

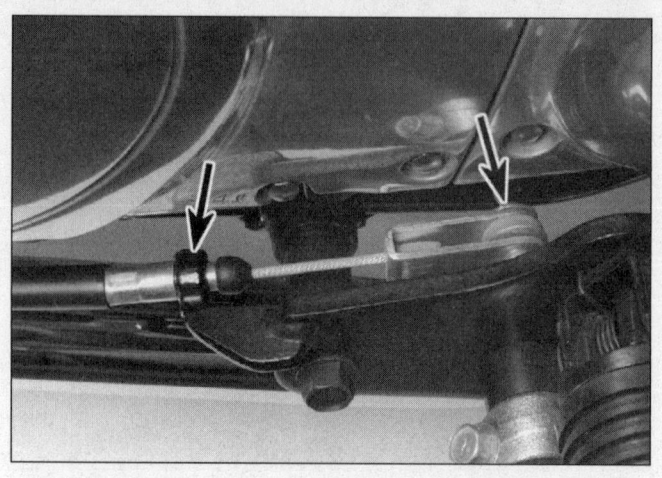

9.4 Remove the clevis pin (right arrow) and detach the cable from the bracket (left arrow) (EN450/500)

6 Remove the reservoir cap and check the fluid level. Do not allow the fluid level to drop below the lower mark during the bleeding process.

7 Carefully pump the brake lever three or four times and hold it while opening the caliper bleeder valve. When the valve is opened, brake fluid will flow out of the caliper into the clear tubing and the lever will move toward the handlebar.

8 Retighten the bleeder valve, then release the brake lever gradually. Repeat the process until no air bubbles are visible in the brake fluid leaving the caliper and the lever is firm when applied. Remember to add fluid to the reservoir as the level drops. Use only new, clean brake fluid of the recommended type. Never reuse the fluid lost during bleeding; it absorbs moisture from the air, which can lead to brake failure.

9 Replace the reservoir cap, wipe up any spilled brake fluid and check the entire system for leaks. **Note:** *If bleeding is difficult, it may be necessary to let the brake fluid in the system stabilize for a few hours (it may be aerated). Repeat the bleeding procedure when the tiny bubbles in the system have settled out.*

9 Brake pedal - removal and installation

1 Place the motorcycle on its centerstand (if equipped).

Pedal and cable (EN450/500)

2 Unhook the brake pedal spring **(see illustration)**.

3 Fully unscrew the brake free play adjusting nut from the wheel end of the brake cable and disengage the cable's threaded rod from the brake cam lever.

4 Remove the cotter pin and clevis pin at the brake pedal **(see illustration)**. Detach the cable from the brake pedal and the bracket and take it out.

5 Look for punch marks on the brake pedal and shaft that indicate their relationship with each other **(see illustration)**. If you don't see marks, make your own. Remove the pedal pinch bolt and take the pedal off.

Pedal (EX250)

6 Unbolt the brake pedal bracket **(see illustration 5.8)**.

7 Lift the bracket out and turn it around for access, then disconnect the brake light switch spring and brake pedal spring **(see illustration)**. Remove the clevis pin and cotter pin that secure the pedal to the rear master cylinder, then remove the pedal bolt and washer and take the pedal off.

All models

8 Installation is the reverse of the removal steps, with the following additions:

   a) Lubricate the pedal shaft with multi-purpose grease.
   b) Tighten the pedal pinch bolt to the torque listed in this Chapter's Specifications.

9.5 Look for punch marks on the pedal and shaft (arrows); make your own if they aren't visible (EN450/500)

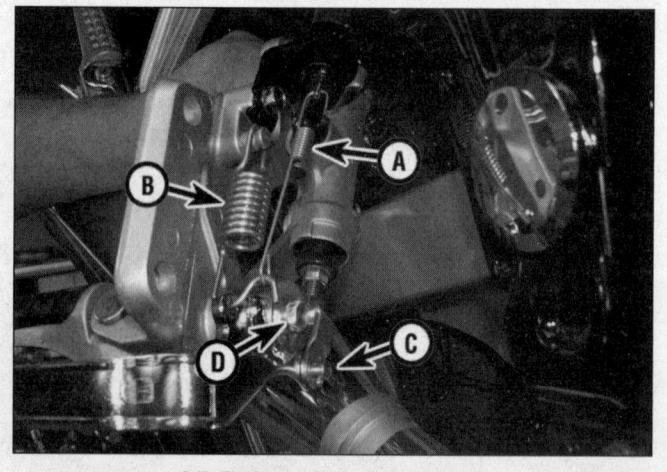

9.7 Brake pedal details (EX250)

A Brake light switch spring
B Brake pedal spring
C Cotter pin and clevis pin
D Pedal bolt and washer

Brakes, wheels and tires 7•11

11.2a Remove the nut from the left end of the axle - here's the EN450/500 . . .

11.2b . . . and this is the EX250

c) On EN450/500 models, lubricate the inner brake cable with engine oil.
d) Check brake pedal height and free play and adjust as necessary (see Chapter 1).

10 Wheels - inspection, repair and alignment check

Inspection and repair

1 Place the motorcycle on the centerstand (if equipped), then clean the wheels thoroughly to remove mud and dirt that may interfere with the inspection procedure or mask defects. Make a general check of the wheels and tires as described in Chapter 1.
2 With the motorcycle on the centerstand and the wheel in the air, attach a dial indicator to the fork slider or the swingarm and position the pointer against the side of the rim. Spin the wheel slowly and check the side-to-side (axial) runout of the rim, then compare your readings with the value listed in this Chapter's Specifications. In order to accurately check radial runout with the dial indicator, the wheel would have to be removed from the machine and the tire removed from the wheel. With the axle clamped in a vise, the wheel can be rotated to check the runout.
3 An easier, though slightly less accurate, method is to attach a stiff wire pointer to the fork slider or the swingarm and position the end a fraction of an inch from the wheel (where the wheel and tire join). If the wheel is true, the distance from the pointer to the rim will be constant as the wheel is rotated. Repeat the procedure to check the runout of the rear wheel. **Note:** *If wheel runout is excessive, refer to Section 13 and check the wheel bearings very carefully before replacing the wheel.*
4 The wheels should also be visually inspected for cracks, flat spots on the rim and other damage. Since tubeless tires are involved, look very closely for dents in the area where the tire bead contacts the rim. Dents in this area may prevent complete sealing of the tire against the rim, which leads to deflation of the tire over a period of time.
5 If damage is evident, or if runout in either direction is excessive, the wheel will have to be replaced with a new one. Never attempt to repair a damaged cast aluminum wheel.

Alignment check

6 Misalignment of the wheels, which may be due to a cocked rear wheel or a bent frame or triple clamps, can cause strange and possibly serious handling problems. If the frame or triple clamps are at fault, repair by a frame specialist or replacement with new parts are the only alternatives.
7 To check the alignment you will need an assistant, a length of string or a perfectly straight piece of wood and a ruler graduated in 1/64 inch increments. A plumb bob or other suitable weight will also be required.
8 Place the motorcycle on the centerstand, then measure the width of both tires at their widest points. Subtract the smaller measurement from the larger measurement, then divide the difference by two. The result is the amount of offset that should exist between the front and rear tires on both sides.
9 If a string is used, have your assistant hold one end of it about half way between the floor and the rear axle, touching the rear sidewall of the tire.
10 Run the other end of the string forward and pull it tight so that it is roughly parallel to the floor. Slowly bring the string into contact with the front sidewall of the rear tire, then turn the front wheel until it is parallel with the string. Measure the distance from the front tire sidewall to the string.
11 Repeat the procedure on the other side of the motorcycle. The distance from the front tire sidewall to the string should be equal on both sides.
12 As was previously pointed out, a perfectly straight length of wood may be substituted for the string. The procedure is the same.
13 If the distance between the string and tire is greater on one side, or if the rear wheel appears to be cocked, refer to Chapter 6, *Swingarm bearings - check*, and make sure the swingarm is tight. Also refer to the chain adjustment procedure in Chapter 1 and make sure the adjusters are set evenly.
14 If the front-to-back alignment is correct, the wheels still may be out of alignment vertically.
15 Using the plumb bob, or other suitable weight, and a length of string, check the rear wheel to make sure it is vertical. To do this, hold the string against the tire upper sidewall and allow the weight to settle just off the floor. When the string touches both the upper and lower tire sidewalls and is perfectly straight, the wheel is vertical. If it is not, place thin spacers under one leg of the centerstand.
16 Once the rear wheel is vertical, check the front wheel in the same manner. If both wheels are not perfectly vertical, the frame and/or major suspension components are bent.

11 Front wheel - removal, inspection and installation

Removal

1 Place the motorcycle on the centerstand (if equipped). If the bike doesn't have a centerstand, support it securely so it can't be knocked over during this procedure. Raise the front wheel off the ground by placing a floor jack, with a wood block on the jack head, under the engine. If you're working on an EX250, unbolt the caliper, lift it off and support it so it doesn't hang by the brake hose (see Section 2 or 3 if necessary).
2 Remove the cotter pin (if equipped) from the axle nut on the left side, then unscrew the nut **(see illustrations)**.

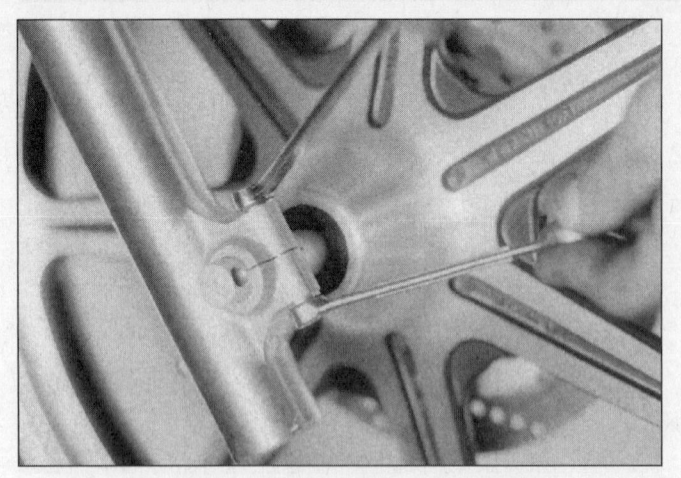

7•12 Brakes, wheels and tires

11.4 Loosen the axle clamp bolt (EN450/500)

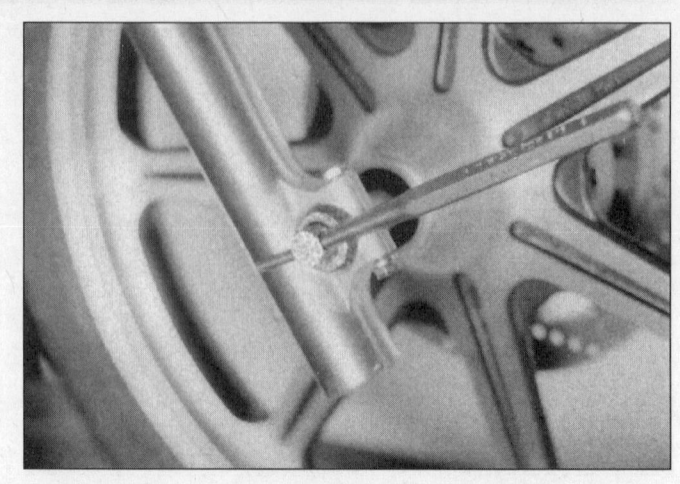

11.5a Insert a punch or similar tool into the hole in the axle . . .

3 Unscrew the speedometer cable from the drive unit on the right side (EN450/500) or left side (EX250) of the axle.
4 If you're working on an EN450/500, loosen the axle clamp bolt **(see illustration)**.
5 Support the wheel and pull the axle out from the right side. If you're working on an EN450/500, insert a punch or similar tool into the hole in the right side of the axle and pull it out **(see illustrations)**.
6 Carefully lower the wheel. On EN450/500 models, it may be necessary to tilt the wheel to one side to allow the brake disc to clear the caliper. Don't lose the spacer that fits into the right side of the hub **(see illustration)**.

Caution: Don't lay the wheel down and allow it to rest on the disc - the disc could become warped. Set the wheel on wood blocks so the disc doesn't support the weight of the wheel. If the axle is corroded, remove the corrosion with fine emery cloth.

Note: *Do not operate the front brake lever with the wheel removed. To prevent accidental operation of the brake, slip a piece of wood between the brake pads.*

11.5b . . . and use the tool to pull the axle out (EN450/500)

11.6 Remove the spacer from the wheel (arrow)

Inspection

7 Check the axle for straightness (see Section 12).
8 Check the condition of the wheel bearings (see Section 13).

Installation

9 Installation is the reverse of removal.

Apply a thin coat of grease to the seal lip, then slide the spacer into the right side of the hub. Position the speedometer drive unit in place in the left side of the hub (if it was removed), then slide the wheel into place. Make sure the notches in the speedometer drive assembly in the wheel line up with the lugs in the drive unit **(see illustrations)**. If the

11.9a Line up the lugs in the speedometer gear assembly with the notches in the speedometer drive (arrows) . . .

11.9b . . . and install the speedometer gear assembly on the wheel

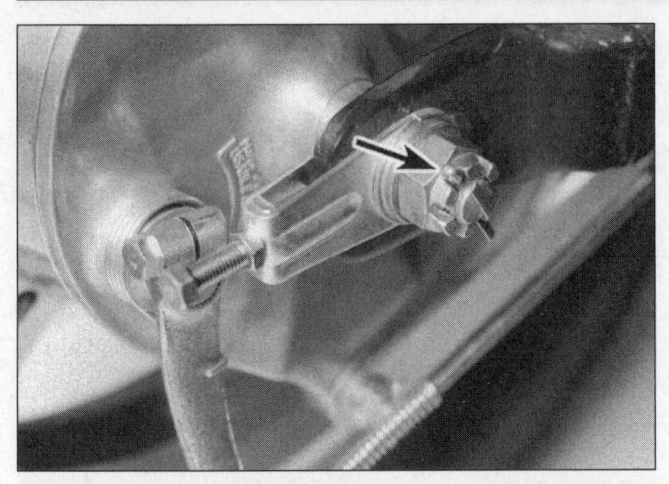

Brakes, wheels and tires 7•13

12.2a Remove the cotter pin from the axle nut (arrow); use a new one during installation - this is the EN450/500 belt drive installation . . .

12.2b . . . here's the EN500 with chain drive . . .

12.2c . . . and here's the EX250

disc will not slide between the brake pads, remove the wheel and carefully pry them apart with a piece of wood.

10 Slip the axle into place, then tighten the axle nut to the torque listed in this Chapter's Specifications. Tighten the right side axle clamp bolt to the torque listed in this Chapter's Specifications.

11 Apply the front brake, pump the forks up and down several times and check for binding and proper brake operation.

12 Rear wheel - removal, inspection and installation

Removal

1 Set the bike on its centerstand (if equipped). Remove the belt or chain guard.
2 Remove the cotter pin (split pin) from the axle nut and loosen the nut (see illustrations).
3 Fully loosen the drive belt or chain adjusters (see Chapter 1).
4 On drum brake models, unscrew the brake freeplay adjusting nut from the cable's threaded end (see illustrations 9.3a and 9.3b). Slide out the pin and disconnect the brake cable from the cam lever. Remove the cotter pin (split pin) from the torque link nut, then remove the nut and disconnect the torque link from the brake panel (see Section 6 if necessary).
5 On disc brake models, loosen the nut at the rear end of the torque link (see Section 2).
6 Push the rear wheel as far forward as possible. Lift the top of the drive belt or chain up off the rear sprocket and pull it to the left while rotating the wheel backwards (see illustration). This will disengage the belt from the sprocket.

⚠️ **Warning: Don't let your fingers slip between the belt or chain and the sprocket.**

7 Remove the axle nut and washer (see illustration). Note the location of the spacer on each side of the wheel.
8 Support the wheel and slide the axle

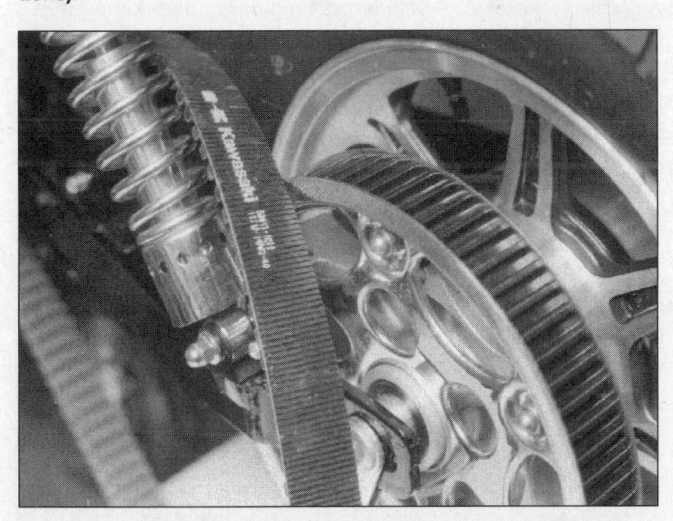

12.6 Slip the drive belt or chain off the sprocket

12.7 Note the location of the spacer (left arrow) on each side of the wheel, then remove the axle nut and the washer (right arrow) (belt drive shown; the washer is next to the axle nut on all models)

7•14 Brakes, wheels and tires

12.8 Rear axle and belt adjuster details (chain drive models similar)

1. Belt adjuster
2. Spacer
3. Axle
4. Spacer
5. Belt adjuster
6. Washer
7. Axle nut

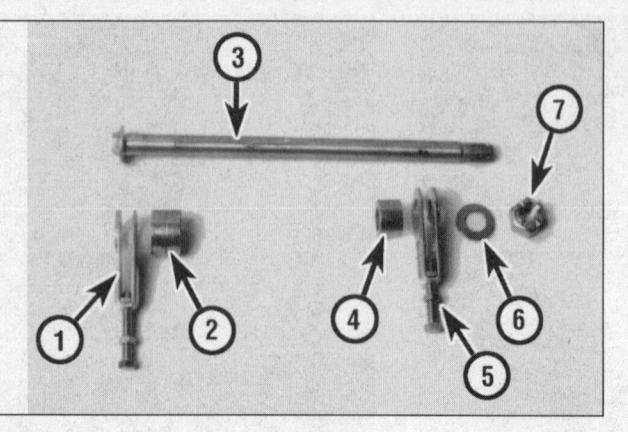

out. Lower the wheel and remove it from the swingarm, being careful not to lose the spacers on either side of the hub **(see illustration)**.

Caution: Don't lay the wheel down and allow it to rest on the sprocket - it could become warped.

Set the wheel on wood blocks so the pulley doesn't support the weight of the wheel.

Inspection

9 Before installing the wheel, check the axle for straightness. If the axle is corroded, first remove the corrosion with fine emery cloth. Set the axle on V-blocks and check it for runout using a dial indicator. If the axle exceeds the maximum allowable runout limit listed in this Chapter's Specifications, it must be replaced.

10 Check the condition of the wheel bearings (see Section 13).

Installation

11 Apply a thin coat of grease to the seal lips, then slide the spacers into their proper positions on the sides of the hub.

12 Place the axle, washer and drive belt adjuster in the left side of the swingarm so they're ready to go when the wheel is in position.

13 Slide the wheel and spacers into place.

14 Pull the belt up over the pulley, raise the wheel and install the axle drive belt adjuster, washer and axle nut. Don't tighten the axle nut at this time.

15 Adjust the belt slack (see Chapter 1) and tighten the adjuster locknuts.

16 Tighten the axle nut to the torque listed in this Chapter's Specifications. Install a new cotter pin (split pin), tightening the axle nut an additional amount, if necessary, to align the hole in the axle with the castellations on the nut.

17 Tighten the torque link nut to the torque listed in this Chapter's Specifications and install a new cotter pin (split pin).

18 The remainder of installation is the reverse of the removal steps.

19 Check the operation of the brakes carefully before riding the motorcycle.

13 Wheel bearings - inspection and maintenance

1 The front wheel uses two ball bearings, which are permanently lubricated and sealed on both sides. The rear wheel hub uses two ball bearings, which are sealed on the outer side. The drive belt pulley coupling uses one unsealed ball bearing.

2 Set the bike on its centerstand (if equipped). If the bike doesn't have a centerstand, support it securely so it can't be knocked over during this procedure. Remove the wheel (see Section 11 or 12).

3 Set the wheel on blocks so as not to allow the weight of the wheel to rest on the brake disc or pulley.

Front wheel bearings

4 Remove the speedometer gear housing and collar, brake disc (see Section 4), snap-ring and speedometer drive **(see illustrations 11.9a and 11.9b)**. If you're working on an EN450 model, remove the wheel cap.

5 Pry out the grease seal from the right side. Remove the remaining snap-ring.

6 Insert a brass drift from the right side of the hub and tap evenly around the inner race of the opposite bearing to remove it. Remove the bearing spacer, then remove the remaining bearing in the same way.

7 Thoroughly clean the inside of the hub with high-flash point solvent and blow it out with compressed air, if available.

8 Drive in the new bearings with a bearing driver or a socket the same diameter as the bearing outer race. Don't forget to install the spacer after you've installed the first bearing.

9 Install a new snap-ring on the right-hand side and make sure it seats securely in its groove.

10 Tap in a new grease seal evenly, using a bearing driver or a socket the same diameter as the seal, until it stops at the snap-ring.

11 The remainder of installation is the reverse of the removal steps. Use a new snap-ring for the speedometer drive.

Sprocket coupling bearing

12 Lift the coupling out of the rear wheel and remove the coupling collar **(see illustration)**.

13 Pry the grease seal out of the coupling to expose the bearing **(see illustration)**.

14 Tap against the back side of the bearing with a bearing driver or a socket to drive it out of the coupling **(see illustration)**.

13.12 Remove the coupling collar; don't forget to reinstall it during assembly

13.13 Pry the grease seal out to expose the bearing

Brakes, wheels and tires 7•15

13.14 Drive the bearing out from this side

13.17 Pack grease into the bearing until it's full

15 Thoroughly clean the bearing with solvent. Blow it dry with compressed air, if available, but don't spin the bearing with compressed air while it's dry. Hold the inner race with fingers and spin the outer race. If the bearing feels rough, loose, or makes noise (more than a slight whirring), replace it.
16 Drive the bearing into the coupling with a bearing driver or a socket the same diameter as the outer race.
17 Pack the bearing with grease **(see illustration)**.
18 Tap in a new grease seal with a brass or plastic mallet **(see illustration 13.13)**. Tap evenly so the seal doesn't tilt. If necessary, lay a block of wood across the seal so the hammer's force will be spread evenly.
19 Check the rubber damper in the rear wheel; if it shows signs of wear or deterioration it must be replaced.

Rear wheel bearings

20 If you haven't already done so, lift the sprocket coupling out of the hub.
21 Remove the snap-ring from the right-hand bearing **(see illustration)**.
22 Insert a brass drift into the hub and place it against the opposite bearing. Tap evenly around the inner race to drive the bearing from the hub. The bearing spacer will also come out.
23 Lay the wheel on its other side and remove the remaining bearing using the same technique.
24 Refer to Step 15 and inspect the bearings.
25 If the bearings check out okay and will be reused, wash them in solvent once again and dry them, then pack the bearings from the open side with medium weight, lithium-based multi-purpose grease.
26 Thoroughly clean the hub area of the wheel. Install the right-hand bearing into the recess in the hub, with the marked or shielded side facing out. Using a bearing driver or a socket large enough to contact the outer race of the bearing, drive it in until the snap-ring groove is visible. Install the snap-ring.
27 Turn the wheel over and install the bearing spacer and bearing, driving the bearing into place as described in Step 25.
28 Press a little grease into the bearing in the rear wheel coupling (if you haven't just repacked it). Install the coupling to the wheel, making sure the coupling collar is located in the inside of the inner race (between the wheel and the coupling).
29 The remainder of installation is the reverse of the removal steps.

14 Tires - general information

1 Models with spoked wheels are designed to take tubed tires. Models with cast wheels are designed to take tubeless tires only. Tire sizes are given in the Specifications at the beginning of this Chapter.
2 The force required to break the seal between the rim and the bead of the tire is substantial, especially on tubeless tires, and is usually beyond the capabilities of an individual working with normal tire irons.

13.21 Remove the snap-ring

3 Also, repair of a punctured tubeless tire and replacement on the wheel rim requires special tools, skills and experience that the average do-it-yourselfer lacks.
4 For these reasons, if a puncture or flat occurs with a tubeless tire, the wheel should be removed from the motorcycle and taken to a dealer service department or a motorcycle repair shop for repair or replacement of the tire.
5 Repair a punctured tubed tire by installing a new inner tube, and make sure that the item that caused the puncture is removed from the tire tread.
  The accompanying illustrations can be used as a guide for tire replacement in an emergency.

TIRE CHANGING SEQUENCE - TUBELESS TIRES

1. Deflate tire. After releasing beads, push tire bead into well of rim at point opposite valve. Insert lever next to valve and work bead over edge of rim.

2. Use two levers to work bead over edge of rim. Note use of rim protectors.

3. When first bead is clear, remove tire as shown.

4. Before installing, ensure that tire is suitable for wheel. Take note of any sidewall markings such as direction of rotation arrows.

5. Work first bead over the rim flange.

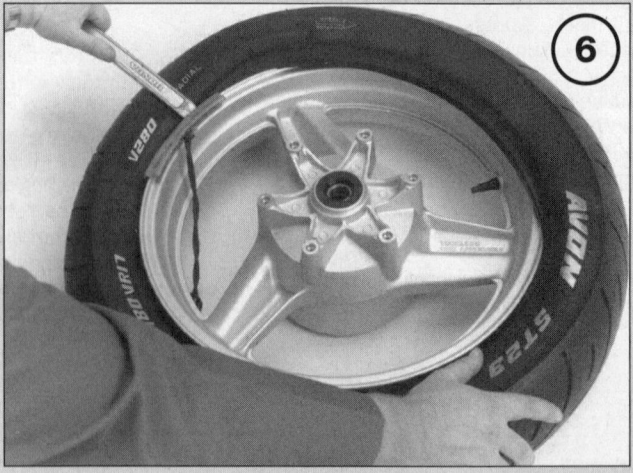

6. Use a tire lever to work the second bead over rim flange.

TIRE CHANGING SEQUENCE - TUBED TIRES

1. Deflate tire. After pushing tire beads away from rim flanges push tire bead into well of rim at point opposite valve. Insert tire lever adjacent to valve and work bead over edge of rim.

2. Use two levers to work bead over edge of rim. Note use of rim protectors.

3. Remove inner tube from tire.

4. When first bead is clear, remove tire as shown.

5. When fitting, partially inflate inner tube and insert in tire.

6. Work first bead over rim and feed valve through hole in rim. Partially screw on retaining nut to hold valve in place.

7. Check that inner tube is positioned correctly and work second bead over rim using tire levers. Start at a point opposite valve.

8. Work final area of bead over rim while pushing valve inwards to ensure that inner tube is not trapped.

Notes

Chapter 8
Frame and bodywork

Contents

Fairing (EX250 models) - removal and installation	12	Rear fender (EN500 models) - removal and installation	10
Footpegs and brackets - removal and installation	3	Rear fender (EX250 models) - removal and installation	11
Frame - inspection and repair	1	Rear view mirrors - removal and installation	5
Front fender - removal and installation	8	Seat - removal and installation	6
General information	1	Side and centerstand - maintenance	4
Rear fender (EN450 models) - removal and installation	9	Side covers - removal and installation	7

Degrees of difficulty

Easy, suitable for novice with little experience	**Fairly easy,** suitable for beginner with some experience	**Fairly difficult,** suitable for competent DIY mechanic	**Difficult,** suitable for experienced DIY mechanic	**Very difficult,** suitable for expert DIY or professional

1 General information

The machines covered by this manual use a backbone frame, constructed of steel tubing. This Chapter covers the procedures necessary to remove and install the side covers and other body parts. Since many service and repair operations on these motorcycles require removal of the side covers and/or other body parts, the procedures are grouped here and referred to from other Chapters.

2 Frame - inspection and repair

1 The frame should not require attention unless accident damage has occurred. In most cases, frame replacement is the only satisfactory remedy for such damage. A few frame specialists have the jigs and other equipment necessary for straightening the frame to the required standard of accuracy, but even then there is no simple way of assessing to what extent the frame may have been over-stressed.

2 After the machine has accumulated a lot of miles, the frame should be examined closely for signs of cracking or splitting at the

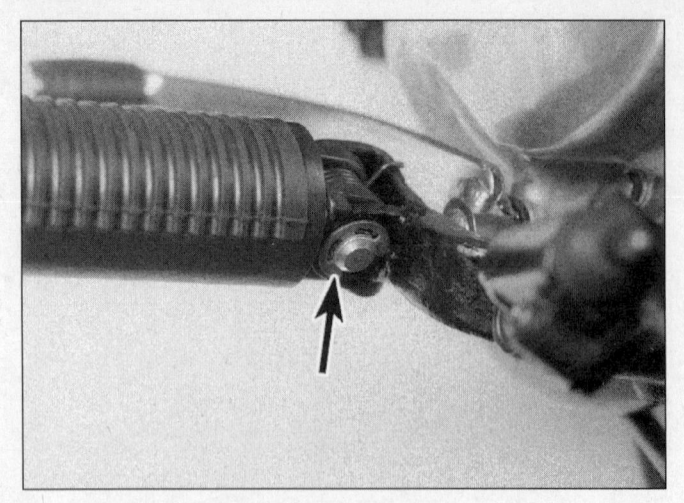

8•2 Frame and bodywork

3.1 Remove the circlip (arrow) to detach the footpeg from the bracket

3.2 Rear footpeg pivots are secured by a bolt and located by a dowel pin (arrow)

welded joints. Rust can also cause weakness at these joints. Loose engine mount bolts can cause ovaling or fracturing of the mounting tabs. Minor damage can often be repaired by welding, depending on the extent and nature of the damage.

3 Remember that a frame which is out of alignment will cause handling problems. If misalignment is suspected as the result of an accident, it will be necessary to strip the machine completely so the frame can be thoroughly checked.

3 Footpegs and brackets - removal and installation

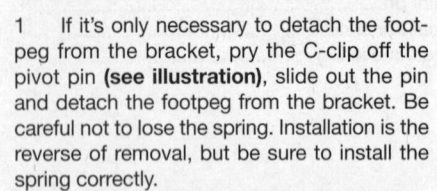

1 If it's only necessary to detach the footpeg from the bracket, pry the C-clip off the pivot pin **(see illustration)**, slide out the pin and detach the footpeg from the bracket. Be careful not to lose the spring. Installation is the reverse of removal, but be sure to install the spring correctly.

2 If it's necessary to remove the entire bracket from the frame, remove the bolts that secure the bracket to the frame, then detach the footpeg and bracket. The footpeg brackets on EX250 models are secured by Allen bolts **(see illustration 5.8 in Chapter 7)**. The right-side bracket supports the rear master cylinder and brake light switch. Rear footpegs on all models are secured by a bolt and located by a dowel pin **(see illustration)**.

3 Installation is the reverse of removal.

4 Side and centerstand - maintenance

1 The centerstand, used on EN450 and EX250 models, pivots on two bolts attached to the frame. Periodically, remove the pivot bolts and grease them thoroughly to avoid excessive wear.

2 Make sure the return spring is in good condition. A broken or weak spring is an obvious safety hazard.

3 The sidestand is bolted to the frame **(see illustration)**. An extension spring anchored to the bracket ensures that the stand is held in the retracted position.

4 Make sure the pivot bolt is tight and the extension spring is in good condition and not over stretched. An accident is almost certain to occur if the stand extends while the machine is in motion.

5 Rear view mirrors - removal and installation

1 To remove a mirror from an EN450/500, loosen its locknut. Unscrew the mirror from the bracket on the handlebar.

2 To remove an EX250 mirror, pry off the trim cap, then remove the Allen bolt and pull the mirror out of the fairing **(see illustrations)**.

3 Installation is the reverse of removal. Position the mirror.

6 Seat - removal and installation

EN450 models

1 Open the tool kit holder behind the seat.
2 Remove two mounting bolts and washers and lift the seat off.
3 Installation is the reverse of removal.

1995 and earlier EN500 models

4 Turn the seat lock clockwise to unlock it **(see illustration)**.
5 Unhook the seat at the front, then push it forward and unhook the center and rear. Lift the seat off.
6 To install the seat, engage the rear and center hooks securely in their brackets, then engage the front hook.

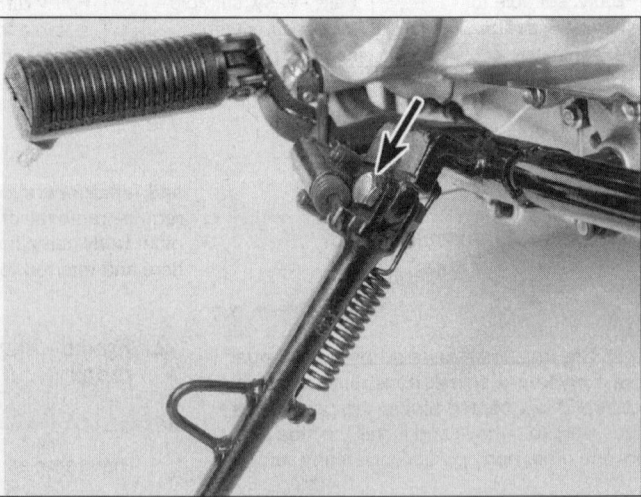

4.3 With the motorcycle securely supported, unhook the spring and remove the pivot bolt (arrow) to detach the sidestand

Frame and bodywork 8•3

5.2a Remove the trim cap and unscrew the mirror bolt . . .

5.2b . . . and lift the mirror off, noting how its locating pin fits in the fairing

6.4 On EN500 models, turn the seat lock to release the seat

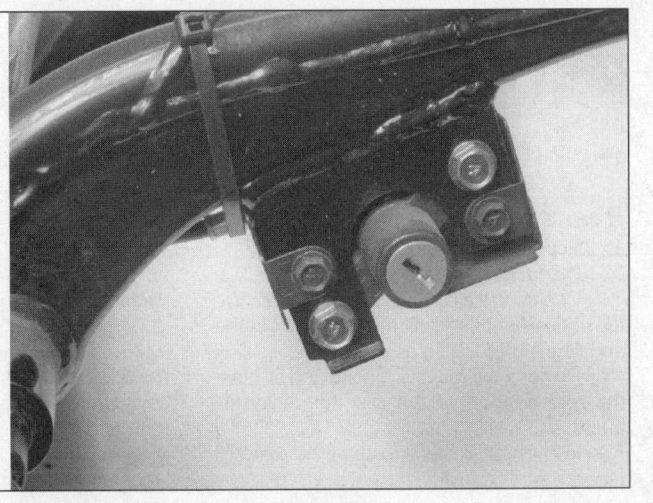

1996 and later EN500 models

7 Remove the mounting bolt at the rear of the seat. Pull the seat rearward to detach the hooks at the center and front. Lift the seat out.

EX250 models

8 Press down on the seat and turn the lock clockwise to disengage the latches from the hooks **(see illustration)**. Lift the seat up and to the rear, pulling the front tab from under the fuel tank bracket **(see illustration)**.

All models

9 Installation is the reverse of the removal steps.

7 Side covers - removal and installation

EN450/500 models

1 Remove the side cover mounting screw(s).
2 On front side covers, disengage the cover tabs and lift the covers off.
3 On rear side covers, carefully pull the securing lugs out of the grommets and lift the cover off.

Caution: *Don't use force. If the cover won't come off with a light pull, make sure all fasteners have been removed.*

4 Installation is the reverse of the removal procedure.

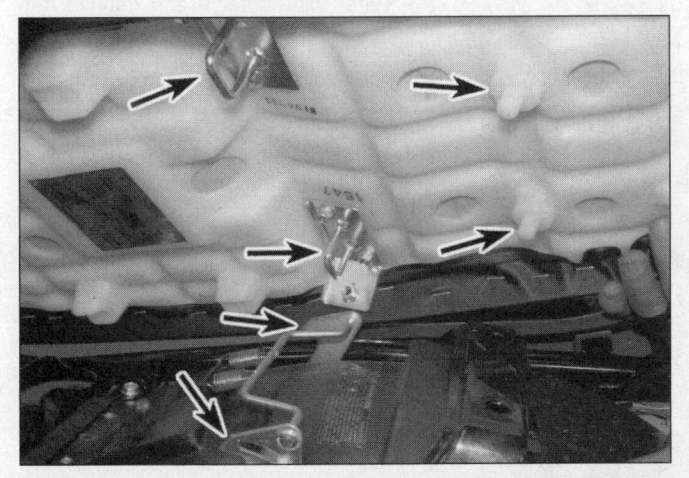

6.8a Unhook the latches from the hooks (left arrows) - the posts (right arrows) fit into grommets when the seat is installed . . .

6.8b . . . and the tab fits under the fuel tank bracket (arrow)

8•4 Frame and bodywork

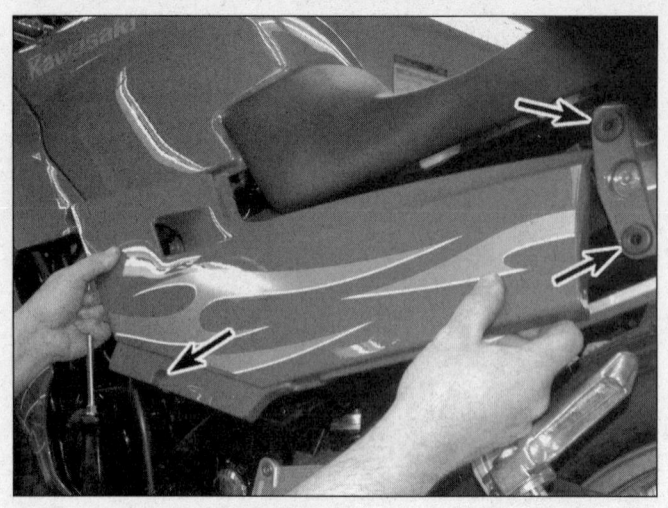

7.5 Remove the screw and pull the posts out of the grommets (arrows)

8.3 Remove the mounting bolts from inside the fender (arrows)

EX250 models
5   Remove the screw from the lower edge of the side cover. Pull the rear edge of the side cover to free the posts from the grommets, then lift it off the bike **(see illustration)**.

All models
6   Installation is the reverse of the removal steps.

8 Front fender - removal and installation

1   Set the bike on its centerstand (if equipped).
2   Disconnect the speedometer cable from the speedometer drive.
3   Remove the bolts from inside the fender **(see illustration)**.
4   Installation is the reverse of removal.

9 Rear fender (EN450 models) - removal and installation

Rear section
1   Set the bike on its centerstand.
2   Remove the seat (see Section 6).
3   Unplug the electrical connectors for the turn signal lights. Unbolt the seat back frame and take it off.
4   Remove the mounting bolts and remove the rear section of the rear fender/mudguard.
5   Installation is the reverse of the removal procedure.

Front section
6   Remove the rear section.
7   Remove the front section mounting bolts and lift the front section out.
8   Installation is the reverse of removal. Be sure to engage the tongue on the front fender section with the groove in the frame.

10 Rear fender (EN500 models) - removal and installation

Rear section
1   Remove the seat (see Section 6). Remove the seat back and side rails.
2   Disconnect the electrical connectors for the rear lights, then unbolt the seat bracket **(see illustration)**.
3   Unbolt the fender/mudguard rear section and remove it together with the taillight assembly.
4   Installation is the reverse of the removal procedure.

Front section
5   Remove the seat (see Section 6).
6   Remove the seat mounting base from the fender rear section.
7   Remove the side covers (see Section 7).
8   Refer to Chapter 9 and remove the junction box, turn signal relay, battery, starter relay and the mounting bolts for the IC igniter. Note carefully how the wiring harnesses and battery vent tube are routed.
9   Support the frame securely with a jack so the bike can't fall over, then remove the right rear shock absorber (see Chapter 6).
10   Remove the bracket that supports the fender front section **(see illustration)**. Note that one of the bolts secures the battery negative cable. Remove the fender front section to the right.
11   Installation is the reverse of removal, with the following additions:
   a) Fit the boss on the front of the fender section into the hole in the frame.

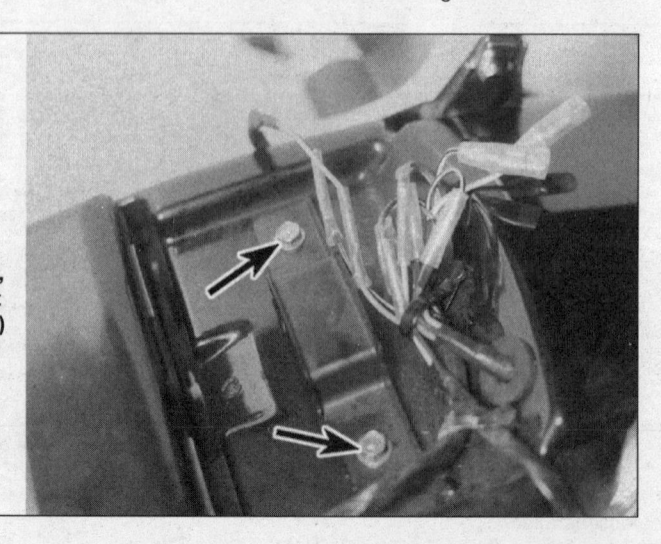

10.2 Unplug the electrical connectors, then remove the seat bracket bolts (arrows)

Frame and bodywork 8•5

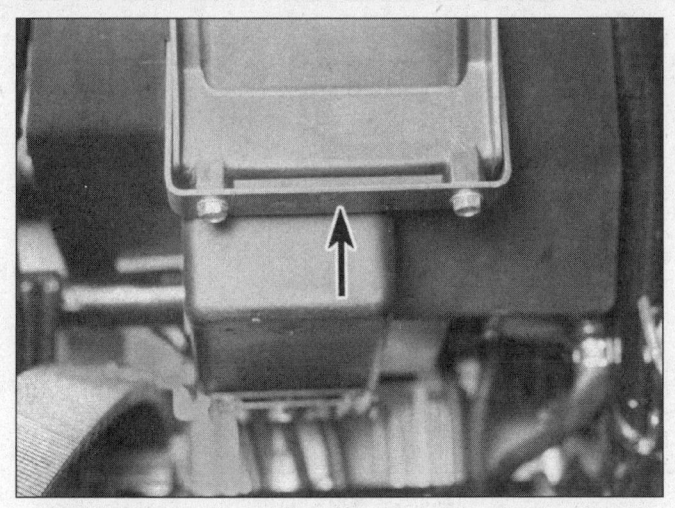

10.10 The bracket (arrow) is secured by four bolts, two at the bottom and one on each side

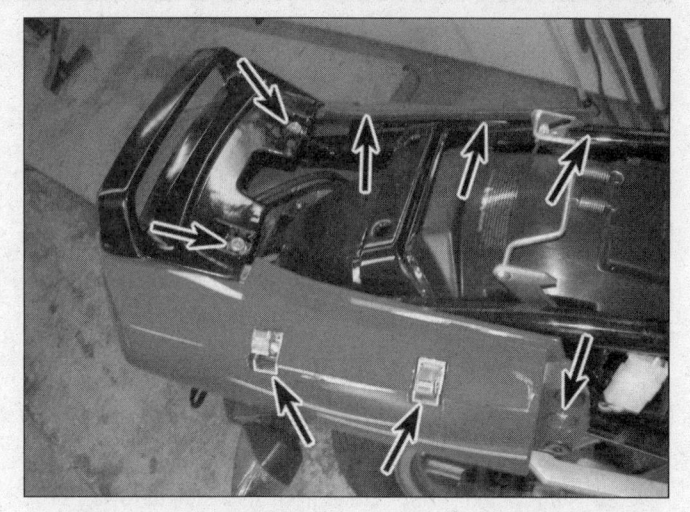

11.7 The tailpiece is secured by one bolt and two screws on each side (right side shown) and by two bolts at the rear (arrows)

b) *One left mounting bolt of the support bracket also secures the battery negative cable.*
c) *Be sure the wiring harnesses and battery vent tube are routed correctly.*

11 Rear fender (EX250 models) - removal and installation

Rear section

1 Disconnect the electrical connectors for the rear turn signals and license plate light.
2 Working under the fender, remove the four bolts that secure the rear section. Lower it away from the tailpiece and take it out.
3 Installation is the reverse of the removal steps.

Tailpiece

4 Remove the lower rear fender as described above.

5 Remove the seat and side covers (see Sections 6 and 7).
6 Locate the taillight connectors inside the tailpiece and disconnect them.
7 Remove the mounting screws (which also secure the cargo hooks) and mounting bolts **(see illustration)**. Carefully spread the tailpiece just enough to provide removal clearance and remove it to the rear.
8 Installation is the reverse of the removal steps.

Front section

9 Remove the lower rear fender and tailpiece as described above. Unhook the seat latch springs from the fender.
10 Remove the cooling system reservoir (see Chapter 3).
11 Remove the air cleaner retaining strap.
12 Remove the bolts that secure the battery housing to the fender.
13 Remove the ignition unit and regulator-rectifier (see Chapters 5 and 9).

14 Remove two mounting bolts from the upper front of the fender section and two from the underside. Pull the fender section rearward to clear the frame and lift it out.
15 Installation is the reverse of the removal steps.

12 Fairing (EX250 models) - removal and installation

Belly pan

1 A belly pan is used on 1988 and later models.
2 Support the belly pan so it won't fall, then remove the mounting screws **(see illustrations)**. Lower the pan free of the fairing.
3 Installation is the reverse of the removal steps.

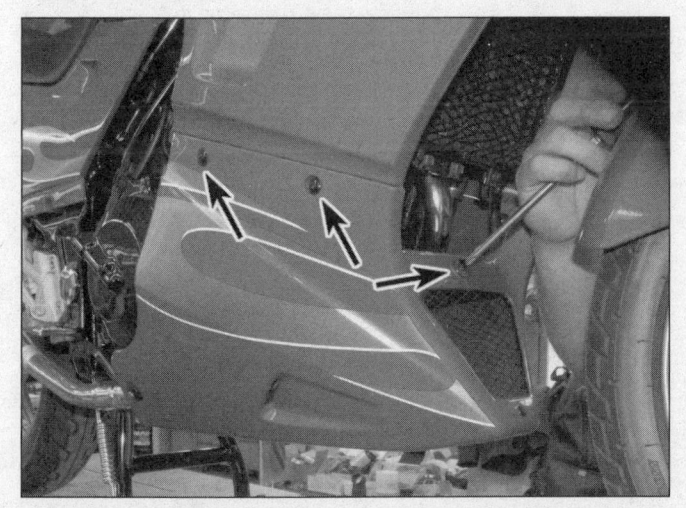

12.2a The belly pan is secured by two screws on each side (right side shown) and one in the center (arrows) ...

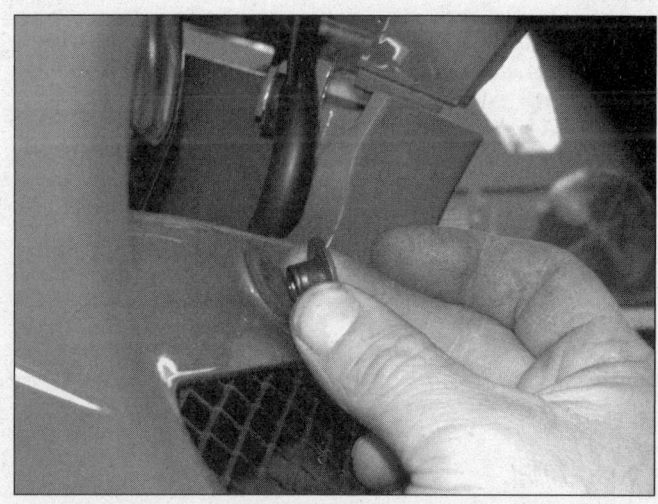

12.2b ... note the collars used on the screws

8•6 Frame and bodywork

12.5a Remove the fairing screws from each side (arrows) . . .

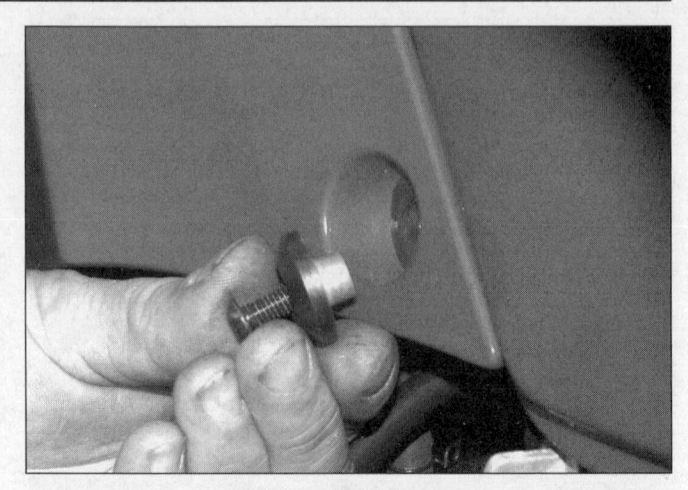

12.5b . . . and the collars

12.7 Support the fairing as you remove the second mirror

12.8 Pull the fairing forward off the posts and grommets (arrows)

Fairing

4 Remove the belly pan as described above. If you're working on a 1986 or 1987 model, remove the knee grip covers (see Step 10).
5 Remove the Allen bolts and special washers that secure the rear edge of the fairing **(see illustrations)**.
6 Working inside the fairing, disconnect the turn signal connectors on each side of the bike.
7 Remove one rear view mirror (see Section 5). Support the fairing and remove the other mirror **(see illustration)** (the fairing will drop as the mirror is removed).
8 Spread the fairing just enough to remove it. Pull it forward so the posts clear the grommets **(see illustration)** and lift the fairing off the bike.
9 Installation is the reverse of the removal steps.

Knee grip covers (1986 and 1987 models)

10 Remove the seat and the side covers (see Sections 6 and 7).
11 Remove the screws and collars from the rear of the cover, then carefully pull the cover off. The resistance that will be felt is the lug on the front part of the cover pulling out of its rubber grommet. Pull it out as straight as possible to avoid breaking it.
12 Installation is the reverse of removal.

Chapter 9
Electrical system

Contents

Alternator - removal and installation	33
Alternator - stator coil replacement	34
Alternator - unregulated output test	30
Alternator stator coils - continuity test	31
Battery - charging	4
Battery - inspection and maintenance	3
Battery electrolyte level/specific gravity check	See Chapter 1
Brake light switches - check and replacement	14
Charging system - regulated output test	29
Charging system testing - general information and precautions	28
Coolant temperature gauge/light and sender unit - check and replacement	See Chapter 3
Cooling fan and thermostatic switch - check and replacement	See Chapter 3
Electrical troubleshooting	2
Fuses - check and replacement	5
General information	1
Handlebar switches - check	20
Handlebar switches - removal and installation	21
Headlight aim - check and adjustment	10
Headlight assembly - removal and installation	9
Headlight bulb - replacement	8
Horn - check, replacement and adjustment	24
Ignition main (key) switch - check and replacement	19
Instrument and warning light bulbs - replacement	17
Instrument and warning light housings (EN500 and EX250 models) - removal and installation	15
Junction box (EN500 and EX250 models) - check	6
Lighting system - check	7
Meters and gauges - check and replacement	16
Neutral switch - check and replacement	22
Oil pressure switch - check and replacement	18
Sidestand switch - check and replacement	23
Starter clutch - removal and installation	35
Starter motor - disassembly, inspection and reassembly	27
Starter motor - removal and installation	26
Starter relay and starter circuit relay - check and replacement	25
Turn signal assemblies - removal and installation	12
Turn signal circuit - check	13
Turn signal, tail/brake light and license plate light bulbs - replacement	11
Voltage regulator/rectifier - check and replacement	32
Wiring diagrams	36

Degrees of difficulty

| **Easy,** suitable for novice with little experience | **Fairly easy,** suitable for beginner with some experience | **Fairly difficult,** suitable for competent DIY mechanic | **Difficult,** suitable for experienced DIY mechanic | **Very difficult,** suitable for expert DIY or professional |

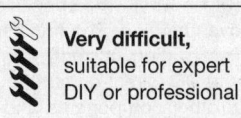

Specifications

Battery
Type
- EN450/500 .... 12 volt, 14Ah (amp hours)
- EX250 .... 12 volt, 8Ah (amp hours)

Specific gravity (fillable batteries only) .... See Chapter 1

Charging system
Charging system output .... 14 to 15 volts DC at 4000 rpm

Alternator output
- EN450/500 .... 60 volts AC at 4000 rpm
- EX250 .... 45 volts AC at 4000 rpm

Stator coil resistance
- EN450/500 .... 0.3 to 0.6 ohms
- EX250 .... 0.2 to 0.9 ohms

9•2 Electrical system

Starter motor
Brush length
  EN450 models
    Standard .... 12 mm (15/32 inch)
    Minimum .... 6.5 mm (17/64 inch)
  EN500 models
    Standard .... 12 to 12.5 mm (15/32 to 31/64 inch)
    Minimum .... 6 mm (15/64 inch)
  EX250 models
    Standard .... 11 mm (7/16 inch)
    Minimum .... 5 mm (3/16 inch)
Commutator diameter
  EN450/500
    Standard .... 28 mm (1-7/64 inch)
    Minimum .... 27 mm (1-1/16 inch)
  EX250
    Standard .... 23 mm (0.905 inch)
    Minimum .... 22 mm (0.866 inch)

Circuit fuse ratings
All except main fuse 10A
Main fuse 30A

Torque specifications
Alternator rotor bolt .... 69 Nm (51 ft-lbs)
Alternator stator screws .... 12 Nm (104 in-lbs)
Oil pressure switch .... 15 Nm (132 in-lbs)
Starter clutch bolts .... 34 Nm (25 ft-lbs)

1 General information

The machines covered by this manual are equipped with a 12-volt electrical system. The components include a crankshaft mounted permanent magnet alternator and a solid state voltage regulator/rectifier unit.

The regulator maintains the charging system output within the specified range to prevent overcharging. The rectifier converts the AC (alternating current) output of the alternator to DC (direct current) to power the lights and other components and to charge the battery.

The alternator consists of a multi-coil stator (bolted to the left-hand engine case) and a permanent magnet rotor.

An electric starter mounted to the engine case behind the cylinders is standard equipment. The starting system includes the motor, the battery, the solenoid, the starter circuit relay (part of the junction box) and the various wires and switches. If the engine stop switch and the main key switch are both in the On position, the circuit relay allows the starter motor to operate only if the transmission is in Neutral (Neutral switch on) or the clutch lever is pulled to the handlebar (clutch switch on) and the sidestand is up (sidestand switch on). **Note:** *Keep in mind that electrical parts, once purchased, can't be returned. To avoid unnecessary expense, make very sure the faulty component has been positively identified before buying a replacement part.*

2 Electrical troubleshooting

A typical electrical circuit consists of an electrical component, the switches, relays, etc. related to that component and the wiring and connectors that hook the component to both the battery and the frame. To aid in locating a problem in any electrical circuit, complete wiring diagrams of each model are included at the end of this Chapter.

Before tackling any troublesome electrical circuit, first study the appropriate diagrams thoroughly to get a complete picture of what makes up that individual circuit. Trouble spots, for instance, can often be narrowed down by noting if other components related to that circuit are operating properly or not. If several components or circuits fail at one time, chances are the fault lies in the fuse or ground connection, as several circuits often are routed through the same fuse and ground connections.

Electrical problems often stem from simple causes, such as loose or corroded connections or a blown fuse. Prior to any electrical troubleshooting, always visually check the condition of the fuse, wires and connections in the problem circuit.

If testing instruments are going to be utilized, use the diagrams to plan where you will make the necessary connections in order to accurately pinpoint the trouble spot.

The basic tools needed for electrical troubleshooting include a test light or voltmeter, a continuity tester (which includes a bulb, battery and set of test leads) and a jumper wire, preferably with a circuit breaker incorporated, which can be used to bypass electrical components. Specific checks described later in this Chapter may also require an ohmmeter.

Voltage checks should be performed if a circuit is not functioning properly. Connect one lead of a test light or voltmeter to either the negative battery terminal or a known good ground (earth). Connect the other lead to a connector in the circuit being tested, preferably nearest to the battery or fuse. If the bulb lights, voltage is reaching that point, which means the part of the circuit between that connector and the battery is problem-free. Continue checking the remainder of the circuit in the same manner. When you reach a point where no voltage is present, the problem lies between there and the last good test point. Most of the time the problem is due to a loose connection. Keep in mind that some circuits only receive voltage when the ignition key is in the On position.

One method of finding short circuits is to remove the fuse and connect a test light or voltmeter in its place to the fuse terminals. There should be no load in the circuit. Move the wiring harness from side-to-side while

Electrical system 9•3

watching the test light. If the bulb lights, there is a short to ground somewhere in that area, probably where insulation has rubbed off a wire. The same test can be performed on other components in the circuit, including the switch.

A ground/earth check should be done to see if a component is grounded (earthed) properly. Disconnect the battery and connect one lead of a self-powered test light (continuity tester) to a known good ground/earth. Connect the other lead to the wire or ground/earth connection being tested. If the bulb lights, the ground/earth is good. If the bulb does not light, the ground/earth is not good.

A continuity check is performed to see if a circuit, section of circuit or individual component is capable of passing electricity through it. Disconnect the battery and connect one lead of a self-powered test light (continuity tester) to one end of the circuit being tested and the other lead to the other end of the circuit. If the bulb lights, there is continuity, which means the circuit is passing electricity through it properly. Switches can be checked in the same way.

Remember that all electrical circuits are designed to conduct electricity from the battery, through the wires, switches, relays, etc. to the electrical component (light bulb, motor, etc.). From there it is directed to the frame (ground/earth) where it is passed back to the battery. Electrical problems are basically an interruption in the flow of electricity from the battery or back to it.

3 Battery - inspection and maintenance

3.3 On EX250 models, unhook the battery retaining strap

1 Most battery damage is caused by heat, vibration, and/or low electrolyte levels, so keep the battery securely mounted and make sure the charging system is functioning properly. On fillable batteries, refer to Chapter 1 for electrolyte level and specific gravity checking procedures.

2 If you haven't already done so, remove the seat (see Chapter 8). Check around the base inside of the battery for sediment, which is the result of sulfation caused by low electrolyte levels. These deposits will cause internal short circuits, which can quickly discharge the battery. Look for cracks in the case and replace the battery if either of these conditions is found.

Warning: *Always disconnect the negative cable first and reconnect it last to prevent sparks that could cause the battery to explode.*

3 Check the battery terminals and cable ends for tightness and corrosion. If corrosion is evident, remove the cables from the battery and clean the terminals and cable ends with a wire brush or knife and emery paper. If you need to remove a fillable battery, refer to Chapter 1. To remove a maintenance-free battery, unhook the retaining strap and lift it out of the carrier (see illustration). Reconnect the cables and apply a thin coat of petroleum jelly to the connections to slow further corrosion.

4 The battery case should be kept clean to prevent current leakage, which can discharge the battery over a period of time (especially when it sits unused). Wash the outside of the case with a solution of baking soda and water. Do not get any baking soda solution in the battery cells. Rinse the battery thoroughly, then dry it.

5 If acid has been spilled on the frame or battery box, neutralize it with the baking soda and water solution, dry it thoroughly, then touch up any damaged paint.

6 If the motorcycle sits unused for long periods of time, disconnect the cables from the battery terminals. Refer to Section 4 and charge the battery approximately once every month.

4 Battery - charging

1 If the machine sits idle for extended periods or if the charging system malfunctions, the battery can be charged from an external source. Charging procedures for the fillable battery used on early models are different from the procedures for maintenance-free batteries, which are used on later models.

Fillable batteries

2 To properly charge the battery, you will need a charger of the correct rating, a hydrometer, a clean rag and a syringe for adding distilled water to the battery cells.

3 The maximum charging rate for any battery is 1/10 of the rated amp/hour capacity. As an example, the maximum charging rate for a 14 amp/hour battery would be 1.4 amps. If the battery is charged at a higher rate, it could be damaged.

4 Do not allow the battery to be subjected to a so-called quick charge (high rate of charge over a short period of time) unless you are prepared to buy a new battery. The heat will warp the plates inside the battery until they touch each other, causing a short circuit.

5 When charging the battery, always remove it from the machine and be sure to check the electrolyte level before hooking up the charger. Add distilled water to any cells that are low.

6 Loosen the cell caps, hook up the battery charger leads (red to positive, black to negative), cover the top of the battery with a clean rag, then, and only then, plug in the battery charger.

Warning: *Remember, the gas escaping from a charging battery is explosive, so keep open flames and sparks well away from the area. If the gas ignites, the entire battery can explode and spray acid. Also, the electrolyte is extremely corrosive and will damage anything it comes in contact with.*

7 Allow the battery to charge until the specific gravity is as specified (refer to Chapter 1 for specific gravity checking procedures). The charger must be unplugged and disconnected from the battery when making specific gravity checks. If the battery overheats or gases excessively, the charging rate is too high. Either disconnect the charger or lower the charging rate to prevent damage to the battery.

8 If one or more of the cells do not show an increase in specific gravity after a long slow charge, or if the battery as a whole does not seem to want to take a charge, it is time for a new battery.

9 When the battery is fully charged, unplug the charger first, then disconnect the leads from the battery. Install the cell caps and wipe any electrolyte off the outside of the battery case.

Maintenance-free batteries

10 The battery should be charged at no more than the rate printed on the charging rate and time label affixed to the battery. Kawasaki recommends a special battery tes-

9•4 Electrical system

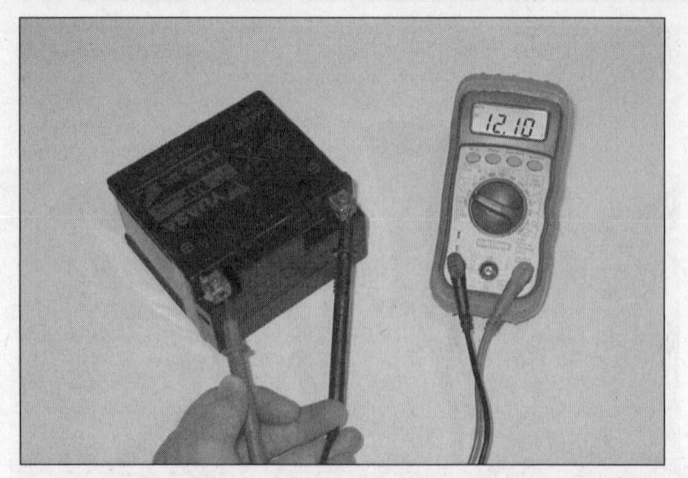

4.10 Check battery open circuit voltage with a voltmeter connected between the terminals

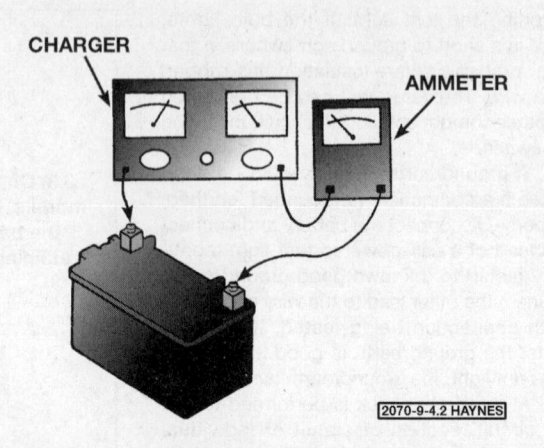

4.12 If the charger doesn't have an ammeter built in, connect one in series as shown; DO NOT connect the ammeter between the battery terminals or it will be ruined

5.2a Most of the EN500 fuses, including the spares, are located on the junction box

5.2b The EN500 main fuse is located on the starter relay . . .

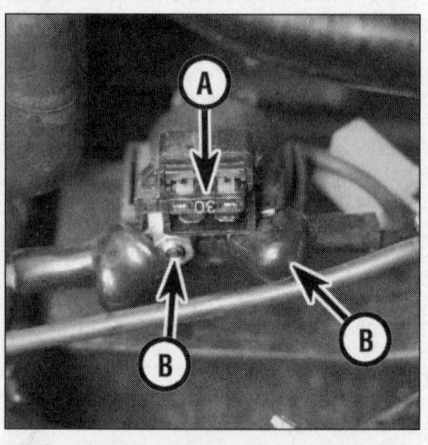

5.2c . . . remove the cover for access to the fuse

A Fuse
B Starter relay terminals

ter and charger that are unlikely to be available to the vehicle owner. To measure the charging rate, connect an ammeter in series with the battery charger **(see illustration)**.

11 Disconnect the battery cables (negative cable first), then connect a digital voltmeter between the battery terminals and measure the voltage.

12 If terminal voltage is 12.6 volts or higher, the battery is fully charged. If it's lower, recharge the battery **(see illustration)**.

13 A quick charge can be used in an emergency, provided the maximum charge rates and times are not exceeded (exceeding the maximum rate or time may buckle the plates inside the battery, rendering it useless). A quick charge should always be followed as soon as possible by a charge at the standard rate and time.

14 Hook up the battery charger leads (positive lead to battery positive terminal and negative lead to battery negative terminal), then, and only then, plug in the battery charger.

⚠ **Warning: The gas escaping from a charging battery is explosive, so keep open flames and sparks well away from the area. Also, the electrolyte is extremely corrosive and will damage anything it comes in contact with.**

15 Start charging at a high voltage setting (no more than 25 volts) and watch the ammeter for about 5 minutes. If the charging current doesn't increase, replace the battery with a new one.

16 When the charging current increases beyond the specified maximum, reduce the charging voltage to reduce the charging current to the rate listed on the battery's label. Do this periodically as the battery charges.

17 Allow the battery to charge for the specified time listed on the battery's label. If the battery overheats or gases excessively, the charging rate is too high. Either disconnect the charger or lower the charging rate to prevent damage to the battery.

18 After the specified time, unplug the charger first, then disconnect the leads from the battery.

19 Wait 30 minutes, then measure voltage between the battery terminals. If it's 12.6 volts or higher, the battery is fully charged. If it's between 12.0 and 12.6 volts, charge the battery again.

5 Fuses - check and replacement

1 On EN450 models, most of the fuses are located in a fuse box (dummy horn) below the headlight, on the opposite side from the real horn. The fuse box cover contains a spare fuse. The main fuse is located in a holder under the seat and its spare fuse is next to it.

2 On EN500 models, all of the fuses except the main fuse are located under the seat, on the junction box **(see illustration)**. The main fuse is located on the starter relay

Electrical system 9•5

5.3a On EX250 models, most of the fuses are beneath the cover on the junction box...

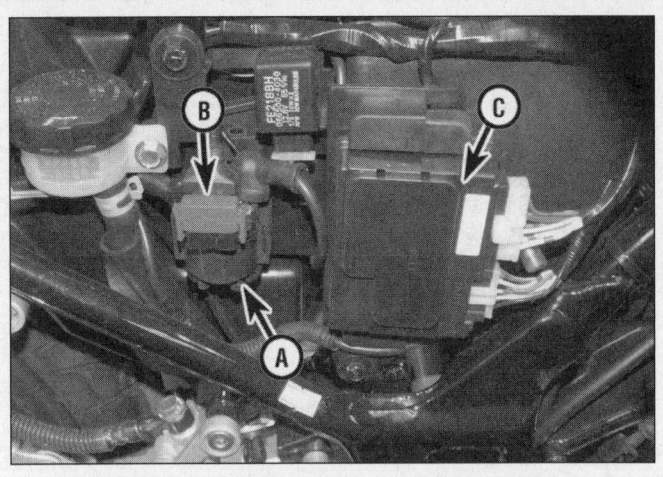

5.3b ... the main fuse is on the starter relay

A Starter relay
B Main fuse
C Junction box

(see illustrations). The fuses on the junction box are protected by a plastic cover, which snaps into place. This box contains fuses (and spares) which protect the fan, headlight, taillight and accessory circuit wiring and components from damage caused by short circuits.

3 On EX250 models, all of the fuses except the main fuse are located under the junction box. On early models, this is on the front portion of the rear fender, under the seat. On later models, it's on the right-hand side of the motorcycle behind the side cover (see Chapter 8 for side cover removal) (see illustration). The main fuse is located on the starter relay (see illustration).

4 If you have a test light, the fuses can be checked without removing them. Turn the ignition to the On position, connect one end of the test light to a good ground (earth), then probe each terminal on top of the fuse. If the fuse is good, there will be voltage available at both terminals. If the fuse is blown, there will only be voltage present at one of the terminals.

5 The 'plug-in' type fuses used on the EN500 and EX250 can be pulled from position. If you can't pull the fuse out with your fingertips, use a pair of needle-nose pliers. A blown fuse is easily identified by a break in the element (see illustration), but the best way to check for a blown fuse is with a test light. Check for power at the exposed terminal tips of each fuse. If power is present on one side of the fuse but not the other, the fuse is blown.

6 If a fuse blows, be sure to check the wiring harnesses very carefully for evidence of a short circuit. Look for bare wires and chafed, melted or burned insulation. If a fuse is replaced before the cause is located, the new fuse will blow immediately.

7 Never, under any circumstances, use a higher rated fuse or bridge the fuse block terminals, as damage to the electrical system - including melted wires, ruined components, and fire - could result.

8 Occasionally a fuse will blow or cause an open circuit for no obvious reason. Corrosion of the fuse ends and fuse block terminals may occur and cause poor fuse contact. If this happens, remove the corrosion with a wire brush or emery paper, then spray the fuse end and terminals with electrical contact cleaner.

6 Junction box (EN500 and EX250 models) - check

1 The junction box is used on EN500 and EX250 models only to house the starter circuit relay (not the starter relay) and the headlight relay (US and Canada only) (see illustration 5.3b or the accompanying illustration). Neither of these relays is replaceable individually. If one of them fails, the junction box must be replaced.

2 In addition to the relay checks, the fuse circuits and diode circuits should be checked also, to rule out the possibility of an open circuit condition or blown diode within the junction block as the cause of an electrical prob-

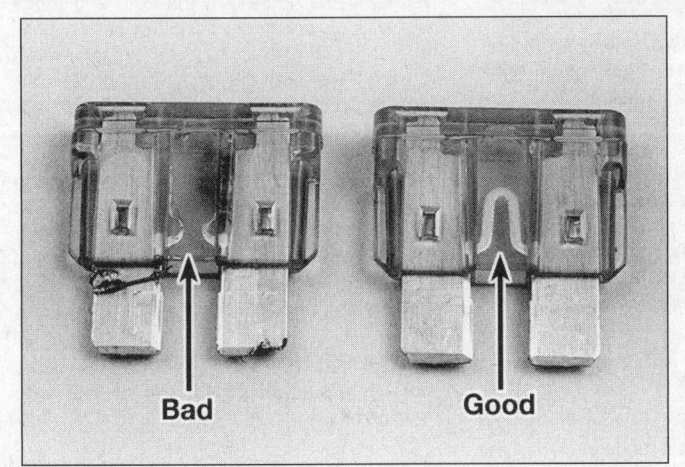

5.5 A blown "plug-in" type fuse can be identified by a broken element - be sure to replace a blown fuse with one of the same amperage rating

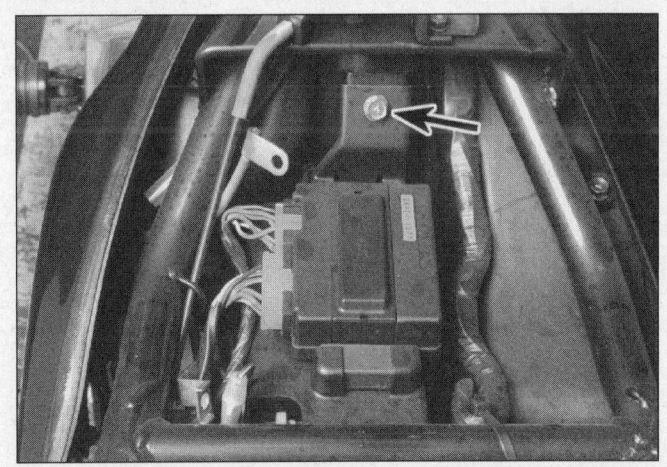

6.1 To remove the EN450/500 junction box, remove the mounting bolt (arrow), slide it out of its holder and disconnect the electrical connectors

9•6 Electrical system

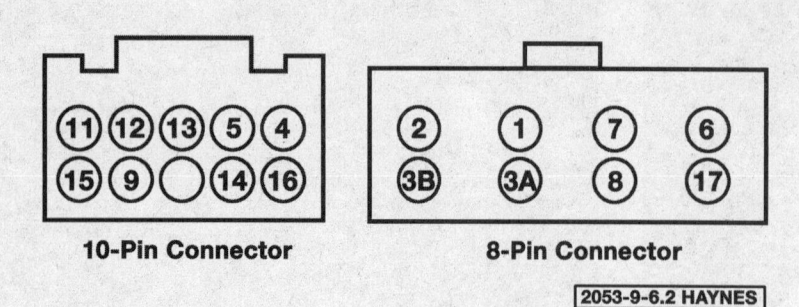

6.2 Junction box terminal pin numbers

lem. A terminal identification chart can be found in the accompanying illustration **(see illustration)**.

Fuse circuit check

3 Remove the junction box mounting bolt (if equipped) and slide it out of its holder **(see illustration 6.1 or 5.3b)**. Unplug the electrical connectors from the box.

4 If the terminals are dirty or bent, clean and straighten them. Check the continuity across the following terminals with an ohmmeter - some should have no resistance and others should have infinite resistance **(see illustration 6.2)**:

a) 1 to 2 - no resistance
b) 1 to 3A or 3B - no resistance
c) 6 to 7 - no resistance
d) 6 to 17 - no resistance
e) 1 to 7 - infinite resistance
f) 3A or 3B to 8 - infinite resistance
g) 8 to 17 - infinite resistance

5 If the resistance values are not as specified, replace the junction box.

Diode circuit check

6 Remove the junction box mounting bolt and slide it out of its holder (see illustration 6.1 or 5.3b). Unplug the electrical connectors from the box.

7 Using an ohmmeter, check the resistance across the following pairs of terminals, then write down the readings, as follows:

a) 13 and 8 (US and Canadian models only)
b) 13 and 9 (US and Canadian models only)
c) 12 and 14
d) 15 and 14
e) 16 and 14

8 Now, reverse the ohmmeter leads and check the resistances again, writing down the readings. The resistances should be low in one direction and at least ten times as high in the other direction. If the readings for any pair of terminals are low or high in both directions, a diode is defective and the junction box must be replaced.

Relay checks

9 Remove the junction box **(see illustration 6.1 or 5.3b)**. Unplug the electrical connectors from the box.

10 Using an ohmmeter, check the continuity across the terminals as follows:

a) 7 and 8 (US and Canadian models only)
b) 7 and 13 (US and Canadian models only)
c) 11 and 13
d) 12 and 13

The ohmmeter should indicate infinite resistance in all cases.

11 Energize each relay by applying battery voltage across the indicated terminals and check the continuity across the corresponding terminals listed below:

a) Battery positive to terminal 9 and negative to terminal 13 - no resistance between terminals 7 and 8
b) Battery positive to terminal 11 and negative to terminal 12 - no resistance between terminals 11 and 13

12 If the junction box fails any of these tests, it must be replaced.

7 Lighting system - check

1 The battery provides power for operation of the headlight, taillight, brake light, license plate light and instrument cluster lights. If none of the lights operate, always check battery voltage before proceeding. Low battery voltage indicates either a faulty battery, low battery electrolyte level or a defective charging system. Refer to Chapter 1 for battery checks and Sections 28 through 32 for charging system tests. Also, check the condition of the fuses and replace any blown fuses with new ones.

Headlight

2 If the headlight is out when the engine is running (US, Canadian models) or with the lighting switch On (UK models), check the fuse first with the key On (see Section 5), then unplug the electrical connector for the headlight and use jumper wires to connect the bulb directly to the battery terminals. If the light comes on, the problem lies in the wiring or one of the switches in the circuit. Refer to Sections 19 and 20 for the switch testing procedures, and also the wiring diagrams at the end of this Chapter. On US and Canadian EN500 and EX250 models also check the headlight relay in the junction box (see Section 6).

3 US and Canadian EN450 models use an additional relay in the system, called the reserve lighting unit. On these models, the headlight doesn't come on when the ignition switch is first turned on, but comes on when the starter button is pressed and stays on until the ignition is turned off. The light will go out whenever the starter is operated after the engine has stalled (this prevents excessive strain on the battery). This component is checked by process of elimination (if all other parts and circuits in the lighting system are good, the reserve lighting device is defective). For this reason, it's a good idea to have a Kawasaki dealer check the lighting system before replacing the reserve lighting device.

Taillight/license plate light

4 If the taillight fails to work, check the bulbs and the bulb terminals first, then check for battery voltage at the red wire in the taillight. If voltage is present, check the ground (earth) circuit for an open or poor connection.

5 If no voltage is indicated, check the wiring between the taillight and the main (key) switch, then check the switch.

Brake light

6 See Section 14 for the brake light circuit checking procedure.

Neutral indicator light

7 If the neutral light fails to operate when the transmission is in Neutral, check the fuses and the bulb (see Section 17 for bulb removal procedures). If the bulb and fuses are in good condition, check for battery voltage at the wire attached to the neutral switch on the left side of the engine. If battery voltage is present, refer to Section 22 for the neutral switch check and replacement procedures.

8 If no voltage is indicated, check the wires between the junction box and the bulb (EN450 models), the junction box and the switch (EN500 models and EX250) and between the switch and the bulb for open circuits and poor connections.

Oil pressure warning light

9 See Section 18 for the oil pressure warning light circuit check.

Coolant temperature warning light

10 See Chapter 3, Section 5 for the coolant temperature warning light circuit check.

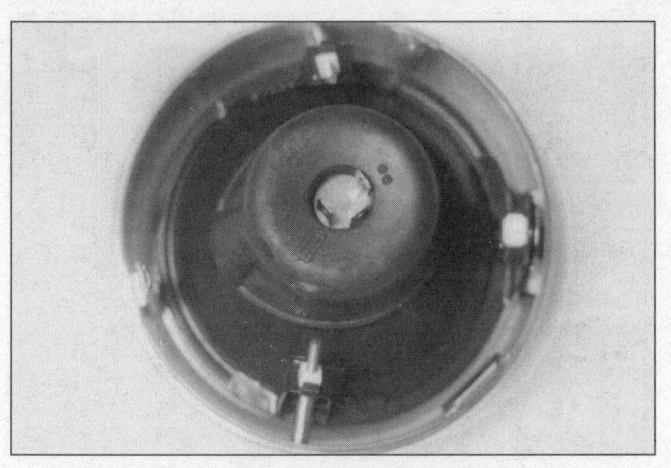

Electrical system 9•7

8.2 Pull up on the tab to lift the dust cover away from the headlight; be sure to push the dust cover all the way on after changing the bulb (EN450/500)

8.3 The bulb holder is held in place by this retaining clip

8 Headlight bulb - replacement

EN450/500 models

1 Remove the headlight assembly securing screw from each side of the housing, pull out the assembly and disconnect the electrical connector (see illustration).
2 Pull up the tab and remove the dust cover (see illustration).
3 Lift up the retaining clip and swing it out of the way (see illustration).

Warning: *If the headlight has just been on, let the bulb cool before you continue. It will be hot to enough to cause burns.*

4 Remove the bulb holder (see illustration).
5 When installing the new bulb, reverse the removal procedure. Be sure not to touch the bulb with your fingers - oil from your skin will cause the bulb to overheat and fail prematurely. If you do touch the bulb, wipe it off with a clean rag dampened with rubbing alcohol.

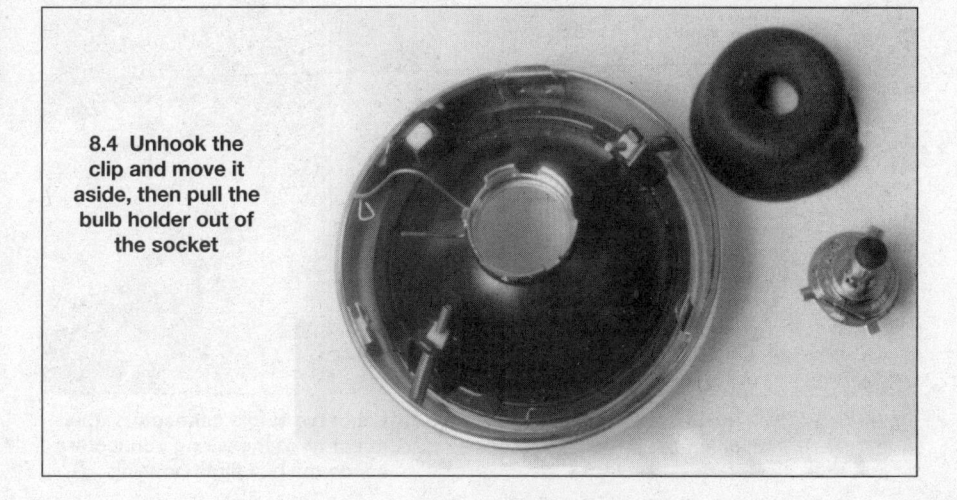

8.4 Unhook the clip and move it aside, then pull the bulb holder out of the socket

EX250 models

6 Reach behind the headlight and pull off the wiring connector (see illustrations).
7 Pull the dust cover out of the headlight

8.6a On EX250 models, grasp the electrical connector outer cover (arrow) . . .

8.6b . . . and pull it out of the dust cover

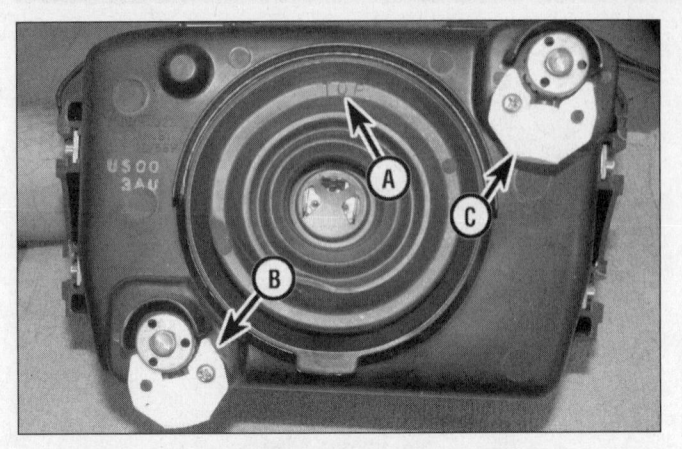

9•8 Electrical system

8.7 Pull off the dust cover, noting the TOP mark

A Top mark
B Vertical adjuster
C Horizontal adjuster

8.8 Release the clip (housing removed for clarity) . . .

8.9 . . . and pull the bulb out, noting the aligning tab

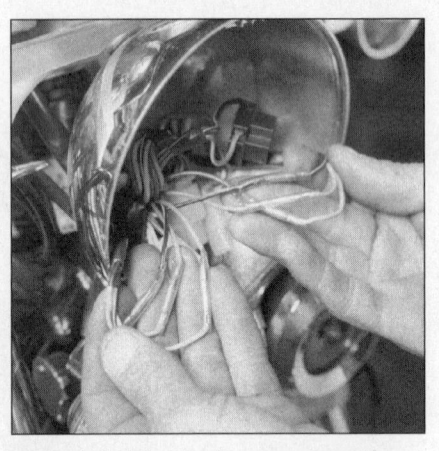

9.3a Label the single connectors, then disconnect all of the wiring connectors inside the headlight housing

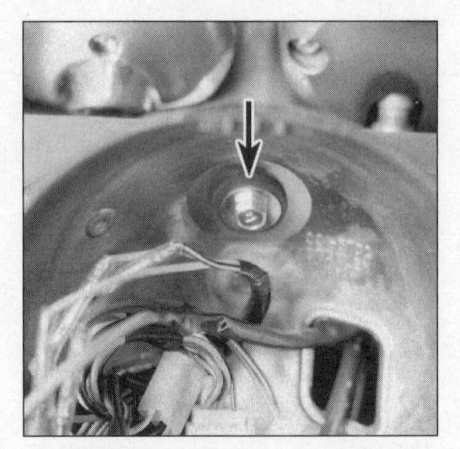

9.3b The headlight assembly on EN500 models is secured at the top by a bolt

housing, noting the position of the TOP mark (see illustration).

8 Unhook the retaining clip and pivot it out of the way (see illustration).

⚠ *Warning: If the headlight has just been on, let the bulb cool before you continue. It will be hot to enough to cause burns.*

9 Pull the bulb out of the housing, noting the position of the alignment tab (see illustration).
10 When installing the new bulb, reverse the removal procedure. Be sure not to touch the bulb with your fingers - oil from your skin will cause the bulb to overheat and fail prematurely. If you do touch the bulb, wipe it off with a clean rag dampened with rubbing alcohol.

9 Headlight assembly - removal and installation

1 Remove the headlight bulb holder housing (see Section 8).

EN450 models
2 Remove the nuts and bolts that secure the sides of the headlight assembly to the motorcycle.

EN500 models
3 Disconnect the electrical connectors inside the headlight housing and remove the headlight assembly mounting bolt (see illustrations).
4 Remove the steering stem cover (see Chapter 6).
5 Disconnect the wires from the horn and remove the horn bracket bolts (see illustration). Detach the headlight assembly from the horn bracket.
6 Installation is the reverse of removal. Be sure the Top mark on the lens is up. Adjust the headlight aim (see Section 10).

EX250 models
7 Remove the fairing (see Chapter 8).
8 Pull the wiring connector off the headlight housing (see illustrations 8.6a and 8.6b).
9 Remove the two bolts and mounting grommets on each side of the housing (see illustration). Take the housing off.
10 Installation is the reverse of the removal steps.

9.5 Remove the horn bracket bolts (arrow) (left bolt shown)

Electrical system 9•9

9.9 The EX250 headlight assembly is secured by two bolts on each side (arrows)

11.1a The tail/brake light lens is secured by two screws in the lens (arrows) or on the underside

10 Headlight aim - check and adjustment

1 An improperly adjusted headlight may cause problems for oncoming traffic or provide poor, unsafe illumination of the road ahead. Before adjusting the headlight, be sure to consult with local traffic laws and regulations.
2 The headlight beam can be adjusted both vertically and horizontally. Before performing the adjustment, make sure the fuel tank has at least a half tank of fuel, and have an assistant sit on the seat.
3 Insert a Phillips screwdriver into the horizontal adjuster screw, then turn the adjuster as necessary to center the beam. On EN450 models, the screw is on the right side of the headlight ring, just below the pivot. On EN500 and EX250 models, it's on the right side of the headlight ring.

EN450 models

4 To adjust the vertical position of the beam, remove the headlight bulb housing (see Section 9). Loosen the nuts and bolts on each side that secure the headlight bulb housing to the motorcycle, raise or lower the headlight assembly as needed and reinstall the headlight bulb housing.

EN500 models

5 Insert the screwdriver into the vertical adjuster screw and turn the adjuster as necessary to raise or lower the beam.

EX250 models

6 To make vertical adjustments, insert a screwdriver from below into the vertical adjuster and turn it (see illustration 8.7).
7 To make horizontal adjustments, use the horizontal adjuster on the right side of the headlight.

11 Turn signal, tail/brake light and license plate light bulbs - replacement

1 Remove the lens securing screw(s) and take off the lens (see illustrations).

2 Push the bulb in and turn it counter-clockwise to remove it. Check the socket terminals for corrosion and clean them if necessary. Line up the pins on the new bulb with the slots in the socket, push in and turn the bulb clockwise until it locks in place. It is a good idea to use a paper towel or dry cloth when handling the new bulb to prevent injury if the bulb should break and to increase bulb life.
3 Position the lens on the reflector and install the screws. Be careful not to overtighten them.

12 Turn signal assemblies - removal and installation

1 The turn signal assemblies can be removed individually in the event of damage or failure.
2 To remove a turn signal assembly, first follow the wiring harness from the turn signal to its electrical connectors. Mark the wires with pieces of numbered tape then unplug the electrical connectors.

11.1b Turn signal lenses are secured by one or two screws in the lens (arrow) . . .

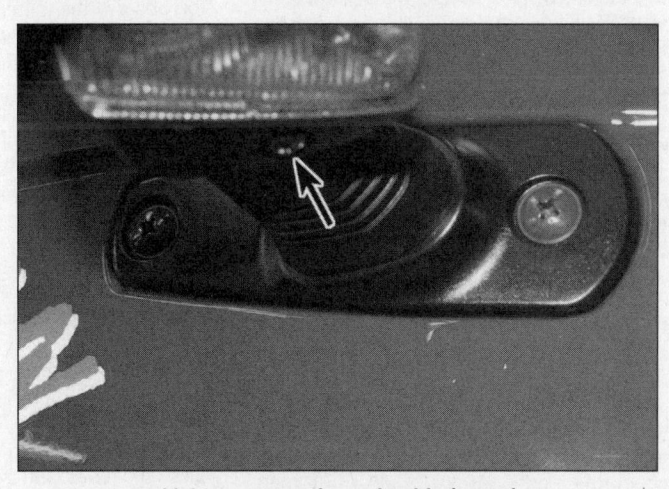

11.1c . . . or on the underside (arrow)

9•10 Electrical system

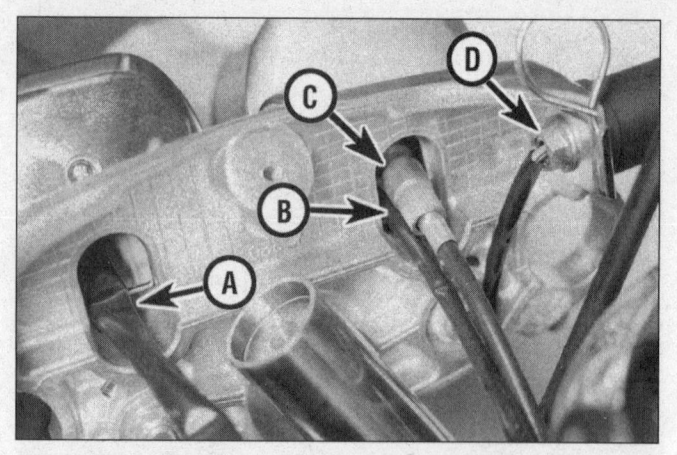

12.4 The turn signals on EN500 models are secured by a nut inside the triple clamp or seat back support bracket

A Warning light harness
B Speedometer harness
C Speedometer cable
D Turn signal assembly mounting nut

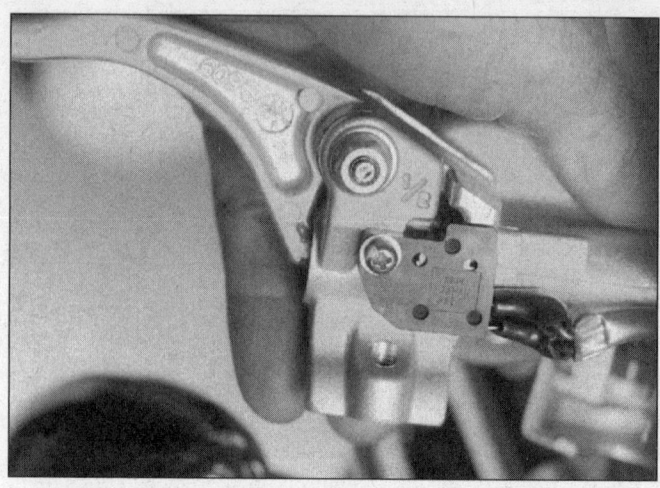

14.6 The brake light switch mounted on the brake lever is retained by a screw

3 If you're working on an EN450 model, remove the mounting screw and washer.

4 If you're working on an EN500 model, remove the upper triple clamp (see Chapter 6) or the rear seat back support bracket (see Chapter 8). Unscrew the nut that secures the turn signal to the triple clamp or bracket **(see illustration)**.

5 If you're working on an EX250, remove the mounting screws **(see illustration 11.1c)**.

6 Installation is the reverse of the removal procedure.

13 Turn signal circuit - check

1 The battery provides power for operation of the signal lights, so if they do not operate, always check the battery voltage and specific gravity first. Low battery voltage indicates either a faulty battery, low electrolyte level or a defective charging system. Refer to Chapter 1 for battery checks and Sections 28 through 32 for charging system tests. Also, check the fuses (see Section 5).

2 Most turn signal problems are the result of a burned out bulb or corroded socket. This is especially true when the turn signals function properly in one direction, but fail to flash in the other direction. Check the bulbs and the sockets (see Section 11).

3 If the bulbs and sockets check out okay, refer to the wiring diagrams at the end of this Chapter and check for power at the turn signal relay with the ignition On. On EN450 models, it's under the seat on the right side of the motorcycle. On EN500 models it's on the battery cover. On EX250 models it's next to the battery. If there's no power at the relay, check the junction box (EN500 and EX250 models) (see Section 6) and the switch (see Section 21).

4 If the junction box and switch are okay, check the wiring between the turn signal relay and the turn signal lights (see the wiring diagrams at the end of this Chapter).

5 If the wiring checks out okay, replace the turn signal relay.

6 The EN450 A1 through A4 models have self canceling turn signals. The circuit comprises the distance sensor in the speedometer and the turn signal control unit mounted on the electrical components plate under the seat. If a fault occurs in the self canceling function, and the turn signals function normally when operated manually, check the distance sensor, control unit, and their associated wiring to the handlebar switch.

7 The distance sensor can be checked by disconnecting its wiring at the connector (which can be accessed from the headlight housing) and connecting an ohmmeter across the red and green wires on the sensor side of the connector. Disconnect the speedometer drive cable at the wheel end and have an assistant turn the inner cable slowly while you observe the meter reading. If the sensor is functioning correctly, the ohmmeter should show continuity four times per cable revolution.

8 There is no test procedure for the turn signal control unit; if the fault cannot be traced to the distance sensor, switch or wiring, the control unit should be replaced.

14 Brake light switches - check and replacement

Circuit check

1 Before checking any electrical circuit, check the fuses (see Section 5).

2 Using a test light (or voltmeter) connected to a good ground (earth), check for voltage at the brown wire terminal in the electrical connector at the brake light switch. If there's no voltage present, check the brown wire between the switch and the main (key) switch (EN450 models) or between the switch and the junction box (EN500 models) (see the wiring diagrams at the end of this Chapter).

3 If voltage is available, touch the probe of the test light to the other terminal of the switch, then pull the brake lever or depress the brake pedal - if the test light doesn't light up, replace the switch.

4 If the test light does light, check the wiring between the switch and the brake lights (see the wiring diagrams at the end of this Chapter).

Switch replacement

Brake lever switch

5 Unplug the electrical connectors from the switch.

6 Remove the mounting screw **(see illustration)** and detach the switch from the brake lever bracket/front master cylinder.

7 Installation is the reverse of the removal procedure. The brake lever switch isn't adjustable.

Brake pedal switch

8 Locate the switch at the brake pedal, follow its wiring harness to the electrical connector and disconnect it.

9 Unhook the switch spring **(see illustrations)**.

10 Unscrew the adjuster nut all the way off the switch and take the switch out of the bracket.

11 Install the switch by reversing the removal procedure.

12 Adjust the switch by following the procedure described in Chapter 1.

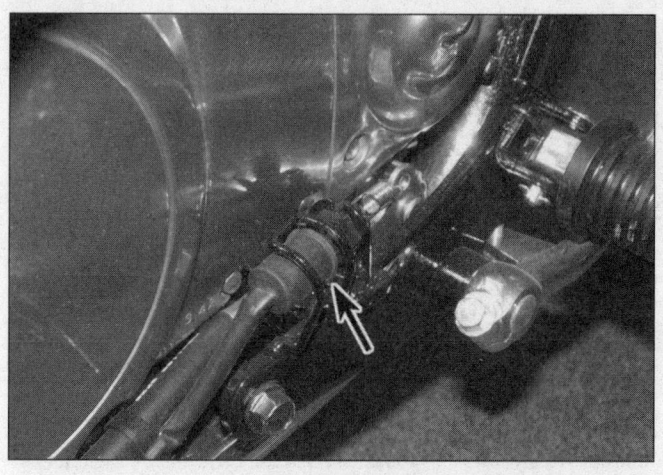

Electrical system 9•11

14.9a Here's the EN500 rear brake light switch (arrow)

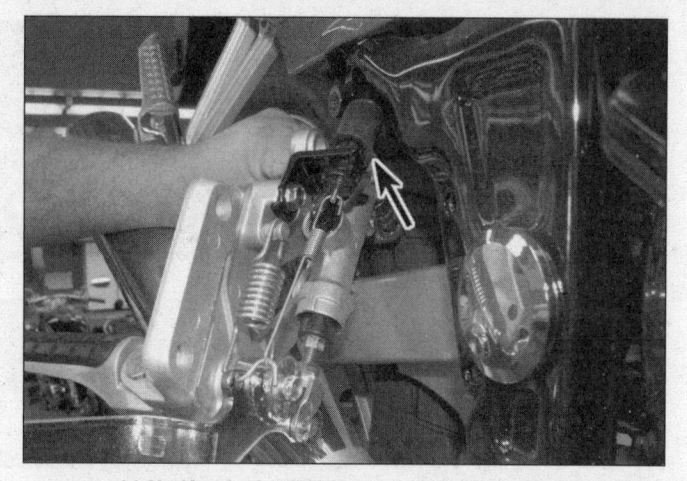

14.9b Here's the EX250 rear brake light switch

15.1 Instrument housing details (EX250)

A Mounting bolts
B Connectors
C Speedometer cable

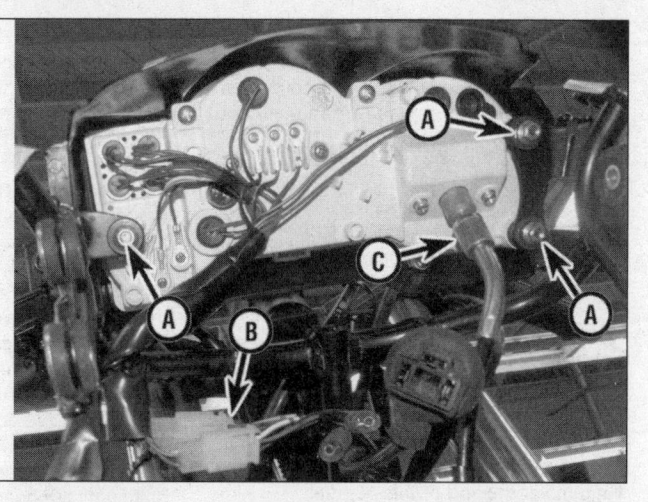

15.2 Instrument housing mounting bolts (EN500 models)

15 Instrument and warning light housings (EN500 and EX250 models) - removal and installation

1   Disconnect the electrical connectors from the temperature gauge (if equipped), speedometer and warning light harnesses (see illustration 12.4 and the accompanying illustration).
2   Disconnect the speedometer cable and remove the instrument mounting bolts (see illustration 15.1 and the accompanying illustration), then detach the housings from the bracket.

Caution: Keep the gauge(s) in an upright position while off the motorcycle or the gauges will be ruined.

3   Installation is the reverse of the removal procedure.

16 Meters and gauges - check and replacement

Check

Temperature gauge (if equipped)
1   Refer to Chapter 3 for the temperature gauge checking procedure.

Speedometer and tachometer (if equipped)
2   Special instruments are required to properly check the operation of these meters. Take the instrument cluster to a Kawasaki dealer service department or other qualified repair shop for diagnosis.

Gauge replacement

3   If you're working on an EN500 model, remove the handlebar (see Chapter 6). If you're working on an EX250, remove the fairing (see Chapter 8).
4   Remove the screws that secure the instrument housings (EN500) or cluster cover (EX250). Remove the gauge mounting fasteners and remove the gauge.

Caution: Always store gauges facing up or they will be ruined.

5   Installation is the reverse of the removal procedure.

Speedometer cable replacement

6   Disconnect the speedometer cable from the cluster (see illustration 12.4).
7   Disconnect the lower end of the speedometer cable from the drive at the front wheel (see illustration). Note carefully how the cable is routed, then remove it.
8   Installation is the reverse of the removal steps.

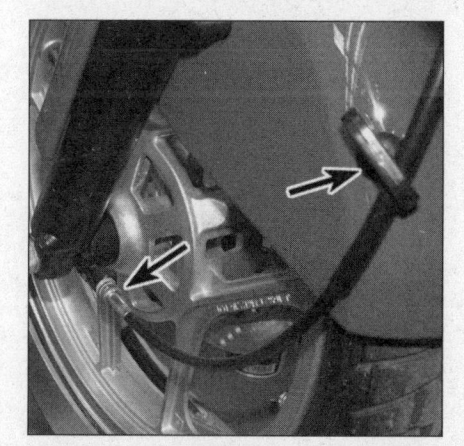

16.7 Unscrew the EX250 speedometer cable from the housing and free it from its retainer (arrows)

9•12 Electrical system

17.1 Pull the socket out of the instrument cluster, then pull the bulb out of the socket

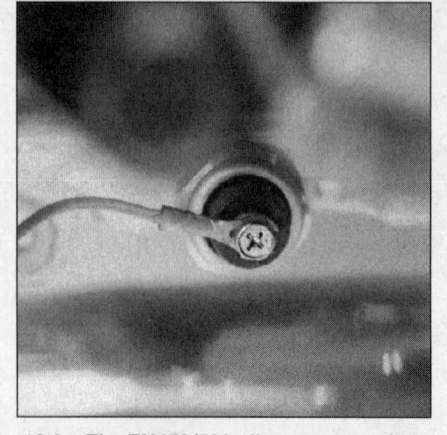

18.2a The EN450/500 oil pressure switch is mounted in the oil pan on the left side of the engine near the front

18.2b The EX250 oil pressure switch is at the left front corner of the engine (arrow)

17 Instrument and warning light bulbs - replacement

1 To replace a bulb, pull the appropriate rubber socket out of the back of the instrument housing, then pull the bulb out of the socket **(see illustration)**. If the socket contacts are dirty or corroded, they should be scraped clean and sprayed with electrical contact cleaner before new bulbs are installed.
2 Carefully push the new bulb into position, then push the socket into the instrument housing.

18 Oil pressure switch - check and replacement

1 If the oil pressure warning light fails to operate properly, check the oil level and make sure it is correct.
2 If the oil level is correct, disconnect the wire from the oil pressure switch **(see illustrations)**. Turn the main (key) switch On and ground the end of the wire. If the light comes on, the oil pressure switch is defective and must be replaced with a new one (only after draining the engine oil).
3 If the light does not come on, check the oil pressure warning light bulb, the wiring between the oil pressure switch and the light, and between the light and the main (key) switch (EN450 models) or between the light and the junction box (EN500 models) (see the wiring diagrams at the end of this Chapter).
4 To replace the switch, drain the engine oil (see Chapter 1) and unscrew the switch from the oil pan. Coat the threads of the new switch with a non-permanent thread locking agent (not sealant), then screw the unit into its hole, tightening it to the torque listed in this Chapter's Specifications.
5 Fill the crankcase with the recomended type and amount of oil (see Chapter 1) and check for leaks.

19 Ignition main (key) switch - check and replacement

Check
1 Disconnect the ignition switch electrical connector.
2 Using an ohmmeter, check the continuity of the terminal pairs shown in the wiring diagrams at the end of this manual.
3 If the switch fails any of the tests, replace it.

Replacement
4 On later EN500 models, unbolt the switch bracket from the frame **(see illustration)**. On all other models, remove bodywork components as necessary for access to the switch mounting screws.
5 If you haven't already done so, unplug the switch electrical connector.
6 The switch on EN450 and early EN500 models is held to the upper triple clamp with two shear-head bolts. Using a hammer and a sharp punch, knock the shear-head bolts in a counterclockwise direction to unscrew them **(see illustration)**. If they're too tight and won't turn, carefully drill holes through the centers of the bolts and unscrew them using a screw extractor (E-Z Out). Detach the switch from the upper triple clamp.
7 Hold the new switch in position and install the new shear-head bolts. Tighten the bolts until the heads break off.
8 The remainder of installation is the reverse of the removal steps.

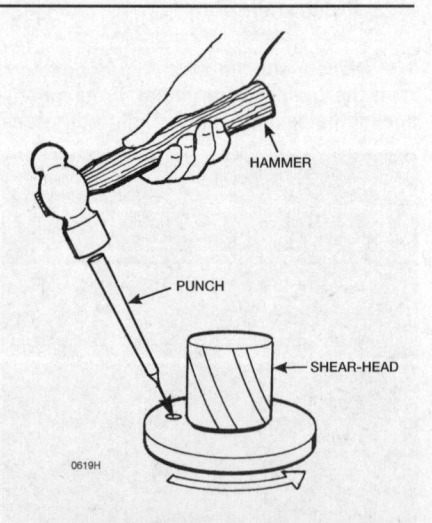

19.4 The ignition switch on later EN500 models is behind this plate on the right side of the frame

19.6 The shear-head bolts must be carefully drilled and removed with a screw extractor or knocked in a counterclockwise direction with a hammer and punch

Electrical system 9•13

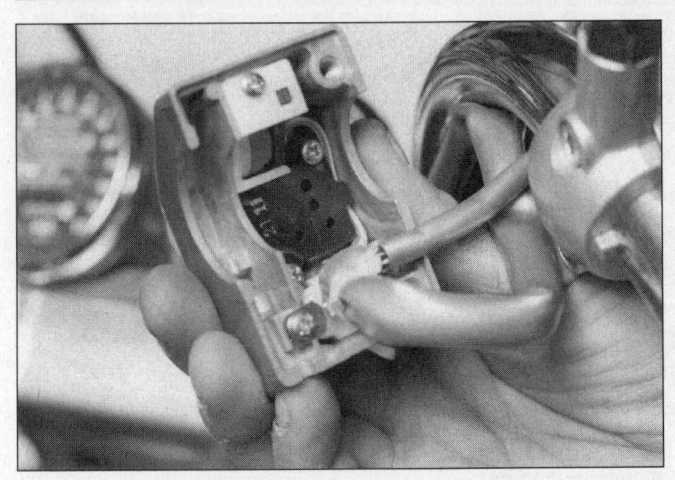

21.1 The handlebar switches are mounted inside the housings on the handlebar

21.3a There's an alignment hole for the switch housing in the handlebar (arrow) ...

20 Handlebar switches - check

1 Generally speaking, the switches are reliable and trouble-free. Most troubles, when they do occur, are caused by dirty or corroded contacts, but wear and breakage of internal parts is a possibility that should not be overlooked. If breakage does occur, the entire switch and related wiring harness will have to be replaced with a new one, since individual parts are not usually available.
2 The switches can be checked for continuity with an ohmmeter or a continuity test light. Always disconnect the battery ground/earth cable, which will prevent the possibility of a short circuit, before making the checks.
3 Trace the wiring harness of the switch in question and unplug the electrical connectors.
4 Using the ohmmeter or test light, check for continuity between the terminals of the switch harness with the switch in the various positions, referring to the wiring diagrams at the end of this manual.
5 If the continuity check indicates a problem exists, refer to Section 21, disassemble the switch and spray the switch contacts with electrical contact cleaner. If they are accessible, the contacts can be scraped clean with a knife or polished with crocus cloth. If switch components are damaged or broken, it will be obvious when the switch is disassembled.

21 Handlebar switches - removal and installation

1 The handlebar switches are composed of two halves that clamp around the bars. They are easily removed for cleaning or inspection by taking out the clamp screws and pulling the switch halves away from the handlebars **(see illustration)**.
2 To completely remove the switches, the mounting screws should be removed (see illustration 21.1) and the electrical connectors in the wiring harness should be unplugged.
3 When installing the switches, make sure the wiring harnesses are properly routed to avoid pinching or stretching the wires. If there's an alignment tab on the switch housing, make sure it engages with the hole in the handlebar **(see illustrations)**.

22 Neutral switch - check and replacement

Check

1 Remove the shift pedal and linkage (see Chapter 2).
2 Remove the engine sprocket cover (see Chapter 6).
3 Disconnect the wire from the neutral switch **(see illustrations)**. Connect one lead of an ohmmeter to a good ground and the other lead to the post on the switch.

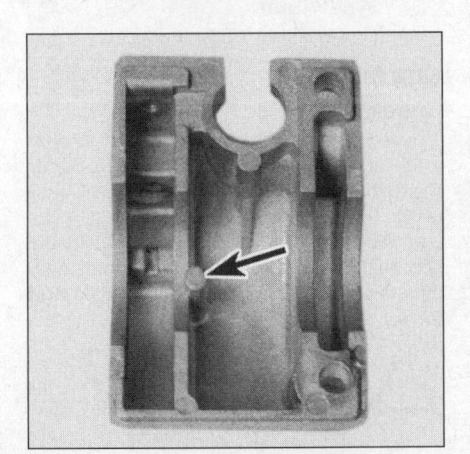

21.3b ... be sure the tab on the switch housing (arrow) fits into the hole when the housing is installed

22.3a Location of the EN450/500 neutral switch (arrow)

22.3b Here's the EX250 neutral switch (arrow)

9•14 Electrical system

23.7 The sidestand switch is mounted on the frame just forward of the sidestand

24.1a The horn on EN450 and early EN500 models is accessible from the front of the motorcycle - note the electrical connectors (arrow)

24.1b Here's the horn on later EN500 models

4   When the transmission is in neutral, the ohmmeter should read 0 ohms - in any other gear, the meter should read infinite resistance.
5   If the switch doesn't check out as described, replace it.

HAYNES HiNT *If the neutral light works intermittently, try removing the switch and reinstalling it temporarily without its sealing washer. If the light now works consistently, the switch plunger is worn and the switch should be replaced (don't just leave the old switch in position without the washer).*

Replacement

6   Unscrew the neutral switch from the case and remove the sealing washer.
7   Install the switch with a new sealing washer and tighten it securely.

23 Sidestand switch - check and replacement

Check

1   Place the bike on the centerstand (if equipped) or support it securely upright.
2   Follow the wiring harness from the switch to the connector, then disconnect the connector.
3   Connect the leads of an ohmmeter to the wire terminals on the switch side of the connector.
4   With the sidestand in the up position, there should be continuity through the switch (0 ohms). With the sidestand down, there should be no continuity (infinite resistance).
5   If the switch fails either of these tests, replace it.

Replacement

6   Support the bike and raise the sidestand.

24.1c Here's the EX250 horn

7   Remove the switch mounting screws **(see illustration)**. Follow the wiring harness to the electrical connector, unplug it and remove the switch.
8   Installation is the reverse of the removal procedure.

24 Horn - check, replacement and adjustment

Check

1   Unplug the electrical connectors from the horn **(see illustrations)**. Using two jumper wires, apply battery voltage directly to the terminals on the horn. If the horn sounds, check the switch (see Section 20) and the wiring between the switch and the horn (see the wiring diagrams at the end of this Chapter).
2   If the horn doesn't sound, replace it.

Replacement

3   Detach the electrical connectors and unbolt the horn bracket from the frame.

4   Detach the horn from the bracket and transfer the bracket to the new horn.
5   Installation is the reverse of removal.

25 Starter relay and starter circuit relay - check and replacement

Starter relay
Check

1   Remove the rear right side panel (EN450 models), left side panel (EN500 models) or right side panel (EX250 models) (see Chapter 8).
2   Disconnect the battery positive cable and the starter cable from the terminals on the starter relay **(see illustrations 5.2c and 6.1b)**.

⚠ *Warning: Don't let the battery positive cable make contact with anything, as it would be a direct short to ground.*

3   Connect the leads of an ohmmeter to the terminals of the starter relay.
4   Turn the ignition switch to On and the

Electrical system 9•15

25.9 The mounting tabs fit into slots in the relay holder (arrows) - EN500 models

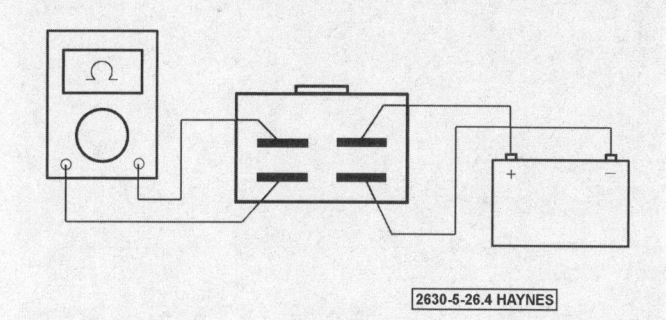

25.11 The ohmmeter should show continuity between the two terminals indicated when a battery is connected between the other two terminals - when the battery is disconnected, there should be no continuity (EN450 models)

26.3 Pull back the covers and disconnect the starter wires (arrows)

26.4a Remove the alternator cover bolts (arrows) (EN450/500) ...

engine stop switch to Run. Place the transmission in Neutral.
5 Press the starter button - the relay should click and the ohmmeter should indicate 0 ohms.
6 If the meter doesn't read 0 ohms or the relay doesn't click, replace it.

Replacement

7 Disconnect the cable from the negative terminal of the battery.
8 Detach the battery positive cable, the starter cable and electrical connector from the relay.
9 Pull the relay holder off its mounting tabs **(see illustration 5.2c and the accompanying illustration)**.
10 Installation is the reverse of removal. Reconnect the negative battery cable after all the other electrical connections are made.

Starter circuit relay

11 On EN450 models, the relay is a small cylindrical unit mounted in an upright position, next to the main starter relay. To check its operation, disconnect its wire connector plug and remove the relay from the motor-

cycle. Connect a 12V battery and ohmmeter across the relay terminals shown **(see illustration)**. With the battery connected, the meter should indicate 0 ohms (continuity), and with the battery disconnected, high resistance (no continuity) should be indicated.
12 On EN500 and EX250 models, the starter circuit relay is incorporated in the junction box; refer to the tests described in Section 6.

26 Starter motor - removal and installation

Removal

1 Disconnect the cable from the negative terminal of the battery.

EN450/500 models

2 Remove the fuel tank and carburetors (see Chapter 4).
3 Remove the nuts retaining the starter wires to the starter **(see illustration)**.

4 Remove the alternator cover bolts and pull off the cover **(see illustrations)**. **Note:** *The alternator magnets will hold the cover on. Pull firmly to remove it, but don't pry it off. If it won't come off with a firm two-hand pull, make sure you've removed all of the cover bolts.*

26.4b ... and pull off the cover (pull firmly to overcome the pull of the rotor magnets, but don't force it)

9•16 Electrical system

26.5 Remove the starter chain cover bolts (arrows)

26.6 Remove the starter mounting bolts (arrows)

26.9a Remove the bolts from the front of the alternator cover (arrows) . . .

26.9b . . . and from the rear (arrows) . . .

5 Remove the starter chain cover **(see illustration)**.
6 Remove the starter mounting bolts **(see illustration)**.

EX250 models
7 Drain the cooling system and detach the coolant tubes from the water pump (see Chapters 1 and 3).
8 Remove the shift linkage lever, pedal and adjusting rod (see Chapter 2B).
9 Remove the alternator cover and starter reduction gear **(see illustrations)**.
10 Disconnect the starter cable and remove the mounting bolts **(see illustration)**.

All models
11 Lift the starter up a little bit and pull it out, disengaging the starter sprocket from the chain on EN450/500 models **(see illustration)**.
12 Check the condition of the O-ring on the end of the starter and replace it if necessary.

26.9c . . . then take the cover off and locate the dowels (arrows)

26.9d Remove the starter reduction gear

Electrical system 9•17

26.10 Here are the EX250 starter mounting bolts (arrows)

26.11 Lift the starter and disengage it from the chain

Installation

13 Apply a little engine oil to the O-ring and install the starter by reversing the removal procedure.

27 Starter motor – disassembly, inspection and reassembly

1 Remove the starter motor (see Section 26).

Disassembly

2 Mark the position of the housing to each end cover. Remove the two through-bolts and detach the end and reduction covers.
3 Pull the armature out of the housing (toward the reduction gear side).
4 Remove the brush plate from the housing **(see illustration)**.
5 Remove the nut and push the terminal bolt through the housing. Remove the two brushes with the plastic holder from the housing **(see illustration)**.

27.4 Remove the brush plate from the housing (EN450 model shown)

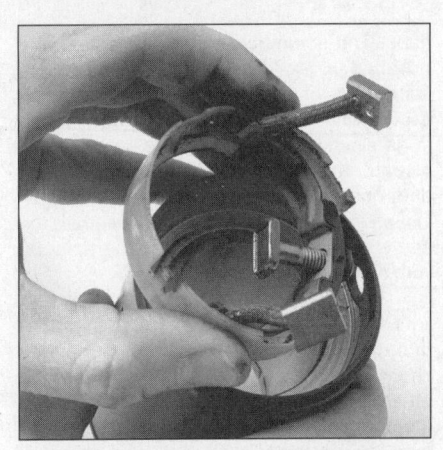

27.5 Push the terminal bolt through the housing and remove the plastic brush holder (EN450 model shown)

Inspection

6 The parts of the starter motor that most likely will require attention are the brushes. Measure the length of the brushes and compare the results to the brush length listed in this Chapter's Specifications **(see illustration)**. If any of the brushes are worn beyond the specified limits, replace the brush holder assembly with a new one. If the brushes are not worn excessively, cracked, chipped, or otherwise damaged, they may be reused.
7 Inspect the commutator **(see illustration)** for scoring, scratches and discolor-

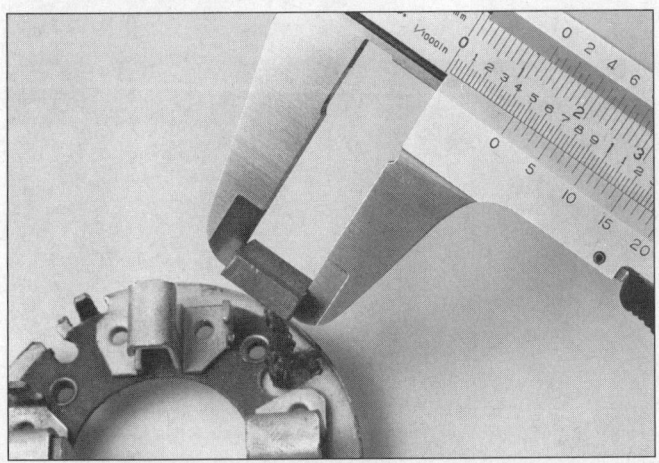

27.6 Measure the length of the brushes and compare the length of the shortest brush with the length listed in this Chapter's Specifications

27.7 Check the commutator for cracks and discoloring, then measure the diameter and compare it with the minimum diameter listed in this Chapter's Specifications

9•18 Electrical system

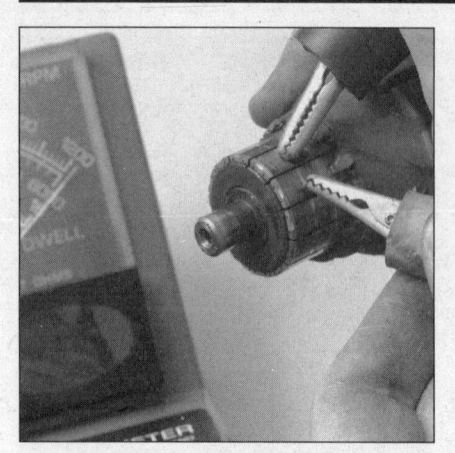

27.8a Continuity should exist between the commutator bars

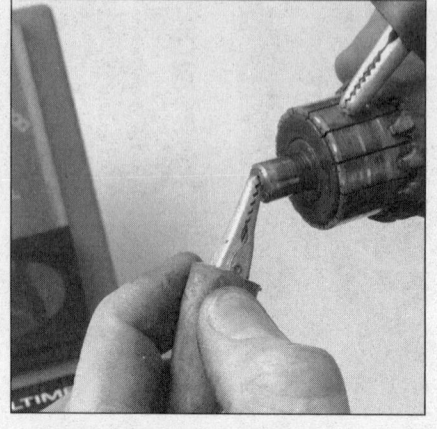

27.8b There should be no continuity between the commutator bars and the armature shaft

27.9 There should be almost no resistance (0 ohms) between the brushes and the brush plate (EN450 model shown)

ation. The commutator can be cleaned and polished with crocus cloth, but do not use sandpaper or emery paper. After cleaning, wipe away any residue with a cloth soaked in an electrical system cleaner or denatured alcohol. Measure the commutator diameter and compare it to the diameter listed in this Chapter's Specifications. If it is less than the service limit, the motor must be replaced with a new one.

8 Using an ohmmeter or a continuity test light, check for continuity between the commutator bars **(see illustration)**. Continuity should exist between each bar and all of the others. Also, check for continuity between the commutator bars and the armature shaft **(see illustration)**. There should be no continuity between the commutator bars and the shaft. If the checks indicate otherwise, the armature is defective.

9 Check for continuity between the brush plate and the brushes **(see illustration)**. The meter should read close to 0 ohms. If it doesn't, the brush plate has an open and must be replaced.

10 Using the highest range on the ohm-meter, measure the resistance between the brush holders and the brush plate **(see illustration)**. The reading should be infinite. If there is any reading at all, replace the brush plate.

11 Check the starter reduction gears for worn, cracked, chipped and broken teeth. If the gears are damaged or worn, replace the starter motor.

Reassembly

12 Install the plastic brush holder into the housing. Make sure the terminal bolt and washers are assembled correctly **(see illustration)**. Tighten the terminal nut securely.

13 Detach the brush springs from the brush plate (this will make armature installation much easier). Install the brush plate into the housing, routing the brush leads into the notches in the plate **(see illustration)**. Make sure the tongue on the brush plate fits into the notch in the housing.

14 Install the brushes into their holders and slide the armature into place. Install the brush springs **(see illustrations)**.

15 Install any washers that were present on the end of the armature shaft. Install the end and reduction covers, aligning the protrusions with the notches. Install the two through-bolts and tighten them securely.

28 Charging system testing - general information and precautions

1 If the performance of the charging system is suspect, the system as a whole should be checked first, followed by testing of the individual components (the alternator and the voltage regulator/rectifier). **Note:** *Before beginning the checks, make sure the battery is fully charged and that all system connections are clean and tight.*

2 Checking the output of the charging system and the performance of the various components within the charging system requires the use of special electrical test equipment. A voltmeter or a multimeter is the absolute minimum equipment required. In addition, an ohmmeter is generally required for checking the remainder of the system.

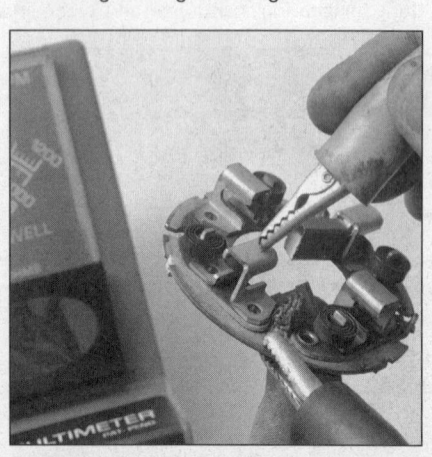

27.10 There should be no continuity between the brush plate and the brush holders (the resistance should be infinite) (EN450 model shown)

27.12 Install the washers on the starter terminal as shown (EN450 model shown)

27.13 When installing the brush plate, make sure the brush leads fit into the notches in the plate (arrow) - also, make sure the tongue on the plate fits into the notch in the housing (arrows)

Electrical system 9•19

27.14a Install each brush spring on the post in this position (EN450 model shown) . . .

27.14b . . . then pull the end of the spring 1/2 turn clockwise and seat the end of it in the groove in the end of the brush (EN450 model shown)

3 When making the checks, follow the procedures carefully to prevent incorrect connections or short circuits, as irreparable damage to electrical system components may result if short circuits occur. Because of the special tools and expertise required, it is recommended that the job of checking the charging system be left to a dealer service department or a reputable motorcycle repair shop.

29 Charging system - regulated output test

Caution: *Never disconnect the battery cables from the battery while the engine is running. If the battery is disconnected, the alternator and regulator/rectifier will be damaged.*

1 To check the charging system output, you will need a voltmeter or a multimeter with a voltmeter function.
2 The battery must be fully charged (charge it from an external source if necessary) and the engine must be at normal operating temperature to obtain an accurate reading.
3 Locate the regulator/rectifier **(see illustrations)** and follow its wiring harness to the connector.
4 Attach the positive (red) voltmeter lead to the white/red wire terminal and the negative lead to the black/yellow wire terminal (EN450/500) or black wire terminal (EX250). **Caution:** *The white/red wire is connected directly to the battery at all times, so don't allow the voltmeter to short this terminal to ground (don't let the voltmeter negative lead touch metal). The voltmeter selector switch (if so equipped) must be in a DC volt range greater than 15 volts.*
5 Start the engine. Run it at varying speeds up to 4,000 rpm, with headlight off and with it on (for US and Canadian models, disconnect the black/yellow wire at the headlight to turn it off with the engine running).
6 The charging system output should be within the range listed in this Chapter's Specifications.
7 If the output is as specified, the alternator is functioning properly. If the charging system as a whole is not performing as it should, refer to Section 32 and check the voltage regulator/rectifier.
8 Low voltage output may be the result of damaged windings in the alternator stator coils, loss of magnetism in the alternator rotor or wiring problems. Make sure all electrical connections are clean and tight, then refer to Sections 30 and 31 for specific alternator tests.

30 Alternator - unregulated output test

1 Follow the wiring harness from the alternator housing to the connector, then disconnect the connector.
2 Connect a voltmeter with a 250-volt AC scale to two of the yellow wire terminals in the alternator connector (at this point, you're measuring the alternator output before it has been rectified from alternating current to direct current, so the voltmeter must be able to measure AC).

29.3a The EN450/500 regulator/rectifier is located behind the right front side cover

29.3b The regulator/rectifier on 1988 and later EX250 models is behind the right side cover

9•20 Electrical system

3 Run the engine at 4,000 rpm and note the voltage reading.
4 Take three different measurements between different pairs of wires. In all cases, the voltage should be as listed in this Chapter's Specifications.
 a) If the voltage reading is correct but the regulated output voltage (checked in Section 29) is not, the rectifier/regulator is probably defective. Refer to Section 32 for test procedures.
 b) If the voltage reading is low, the alternator may be defective. Test the stator coils as described in Section 31. If the stator coils test out OK, the rotor magnets have probably lost magnetism. This can be caused by dropping or hitting the alternator, by leaving the alternator near another source of magnetism, or by age.

31 Alternator stator coils - continuity test

1 If charging system output is low or non-existent, the alternator stator coil windings and leads should be checked for proper continuity. The test can be made with the stator in place on the machine.
2 Using an ohmmeter (preferred) or a continuity test light, check for continuity between each of the wires coming from the alternator stator (the same connector that was disconnected in Section 30 for the output test). Continuity should exist between any one wire and each of the others (resistance values are listed in this Chapter's Specifications).
3 Check for continuity between each of the wires and the engine. No continuity should exist between any of the wires and the engine.
4 If there is no continuity between any two of the wires, or if there is continuity between the wires and an engine ground/earth, an open circuit or a short exists within the stator coils. Since repair of the stator is not feasible, it must be replaced with a new one.

32 Voltage regulator/rectifier - check and replacement

1 Remove the right front side cover (EN450/500) or right side cover (EX250) (see Chapter 8).
2 Locate the regulator/rectifier, follow its harness to the connector, then detach the electrical connector (see illustration 29.3a or 29.3b).
3 Using an ohmmeter set on R X 1000, connect the positive lead to the white/red wire and the negative lead to each yellow wire in turn and write the readings down. Switch the ohmmeter leads (negative to white/red and positive to each yellow in turn) and note the readings. The resistance should be low during one set of three measurements and at least 10 times as high during the other three measurements.
4 Repeat Step 3, using the black wire and each yellow wire (12 measurements total). Again, the readings should be low in one direction and at least 10 times as high in the other direction. If the meter readings are not as specified, replace the regulator/rectifier.
5 This check, combined with the tests outlined in Sections 29 through 31, should diagnose most charging system problems. If the voltage regulator/rectifier passes the tests described in Steps 3 and 4, and the stator coil passes the test in Section 31, take the regulator/rectifier to a dealer service department or other repair shop for further checks, or substitute a known good unit and recheck the charging system output.

33 Alternator - removal and installation

Removal
1 Disconnect the cable from the negative terminal of the battery.
2 Remove the starter (see Section 26).

33.3 The EN450/500 alternator rotor bolt has left-hand threads (turn it clockwise to loosen it); the EX250 rotor bolt has standard threads (turn counterclockwise to loosen)

3 Prevent the alternator rotor from turning by holding it with Kawasaki tool no. 57001-308, a strap wrench or a pin spanner wrench. Alternatively, shift the transmission into gear and apply the rear brake hard with the rear tire in firm contact with the ground. Remove the rotor bolt (see illustration 26.9c and the accompanying illustration).

Caution: On EN450/500 models, the bolt has left-hand threads (loosens in a clockwise direction).

4 Hold the rotor from turning again, and using a rotor puller, remove the rotor from the crankshaft (see illustrations).

Caution: Use a rotor puller to remove the rotor. Improvised tools may damage the rotor. Aftermarket rotor pullers are readily available from motorcycle dealers.

5 If you're going to replace the rotor, remove the starter clutch (see Section 35).

Installation
6 Clean all dirt from the crankshaft and the inside of the rotor with high flash point solvent.
7 Position the rotor on the engine and install the bolt, tightening it to the torque listed in this Chapter's Specifications.

33.4a This special tool is used to remove the EN450/500 alternator rotor . . .

33.4b . . . here's the special tool for EX250 models

Electrical system 9•21

34.2 The stator coils are secured in the housing by three Allen screws (arrows)

35.3a Remove the washer and starter sprocket (EN450/500) or gear (EX250) from the end of the crankshaft...

8 The remainder of installation is the reverse of the removal steps. Before you install the housing, make sure the magnets haven't picked up any pieces of metal that could damage the alternator.

34 Alternator - stator coil replacement

1 Remove the alternator cover (see Section 26).
2 Remove the stator screws **(see illustration)**, remove the wiring harness retainer and lift the stator coils out of the alternator housing.
3 Installation is the reverse of the removal steps. Tighten the stator screws to the torque listed in this Chapter's Specifications.

35 Starter clutch - removal and installation

1 The starter clutch is mounted on the back of the alternator rotor.

35.3b ... if the gear or sprocket comes off with the rotor ...

Removal

2 Remove the alternator rotor (see Section 33).
3 If the washer and starter clutch sprocket or gear didn't come off the crankshaft with the alternator rotor, remove them **(see illustrations)**.

35.3c ... pull it out of the rotor and remove the washer

4 Pull the rollers out of the starter clutch, then remove the spring caps and springs **(see illustrations)**.

Inspection

5 Check all parts for wear and damage. Replace any worn or damaged parts.

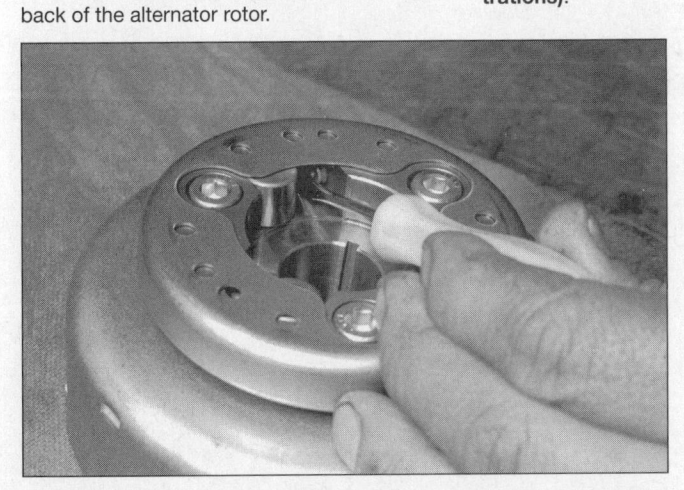

35.4a Compress the spring caps with a small screwdriver and remove the rollers, caps and springs

35.4b Starter clutch details

9•22 Electrical system

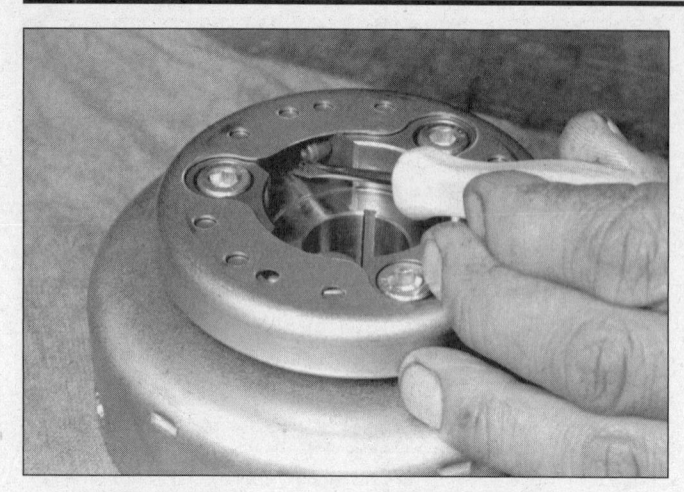

35.8a Press the springs and caps into the holes...

35.8b ...then install the rollers and release the caps

6   If you're going to replace the starter clutch housing or rotor, remove the three Allen bolts and separate the starter clutch from the rotor.

Installation

7   If you removed the starter clutch from the rotor, bolt it back on. Use a non-permanent thread locking agent on the threads of the Allen bolts and tighten them to the torque listed in this Chapter's Specifications.

8   Place the spring caps on the springs. Place the springs in their holes, compress them with a screwdriver and install the rollers **(see illustrations)**.

9   Install the alternator rotor on the engine (see Section 33).

36 Wiring diagrams

Prior to troubleshooting a circuit, check the fuses to make sure they're in good condition. Make sure the battery is fully charged and check the cable connections.

When checking a circuit, make sure all connectors are clean, with no broken or loose terminals or wires. When unplugging a connector, don't pull on the wires - pull only on the connector housings themselves.

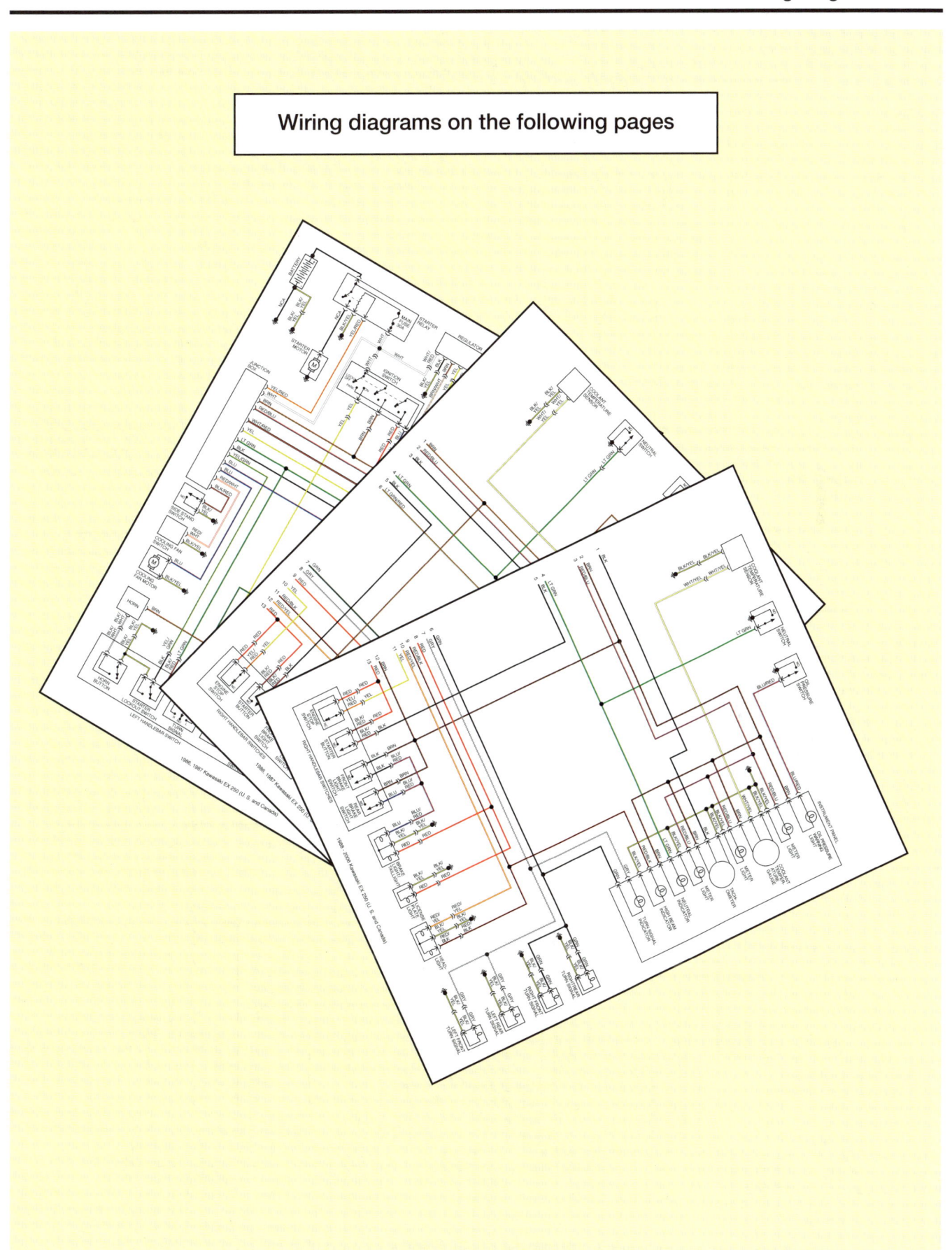

Wiring diagrams 9•23

Wiring diagrams on the following pages

9•24 Wiring diagrams

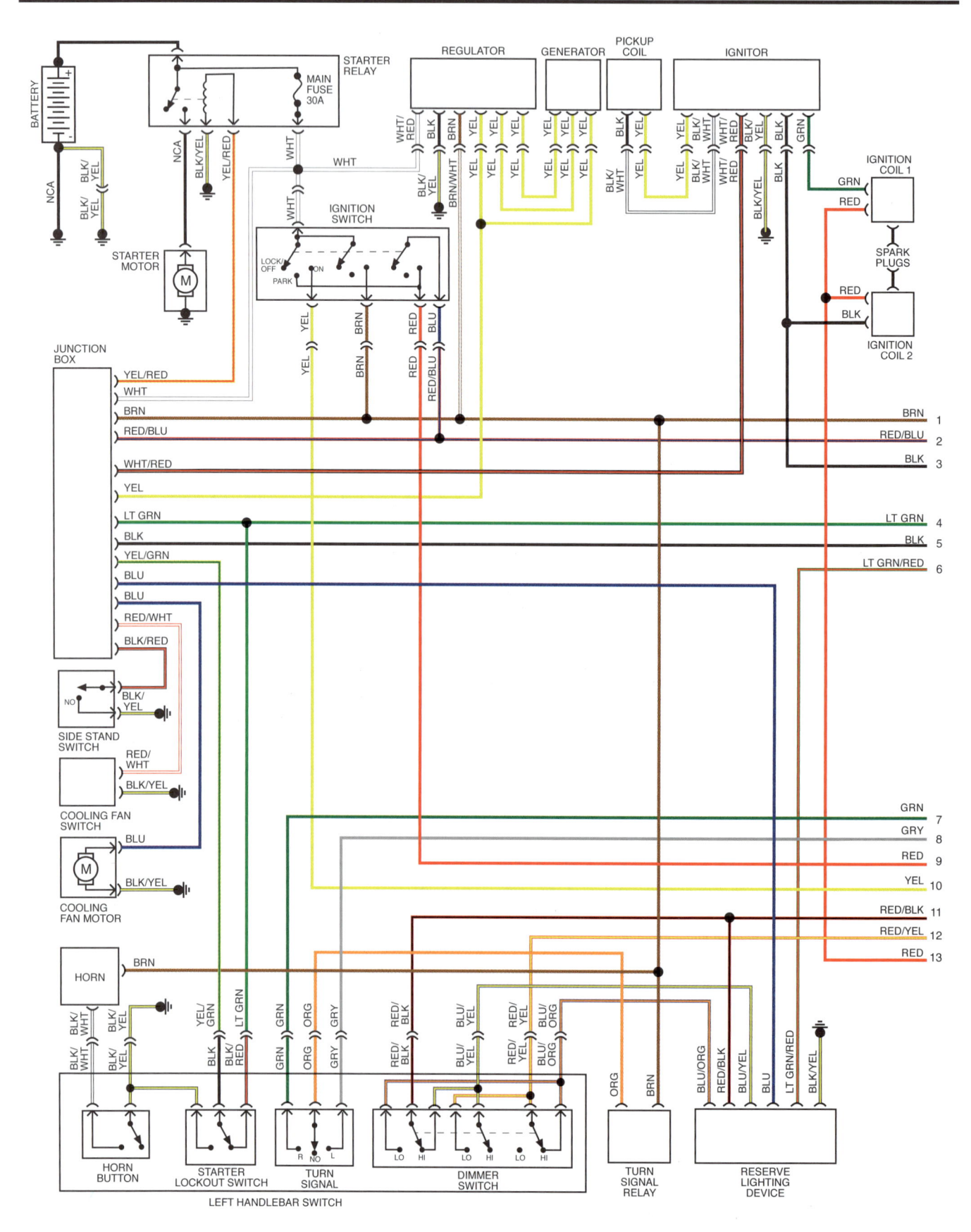

1986, 1987 Kawasaki EX 250 (U. S. and Canada) (1 of 2)

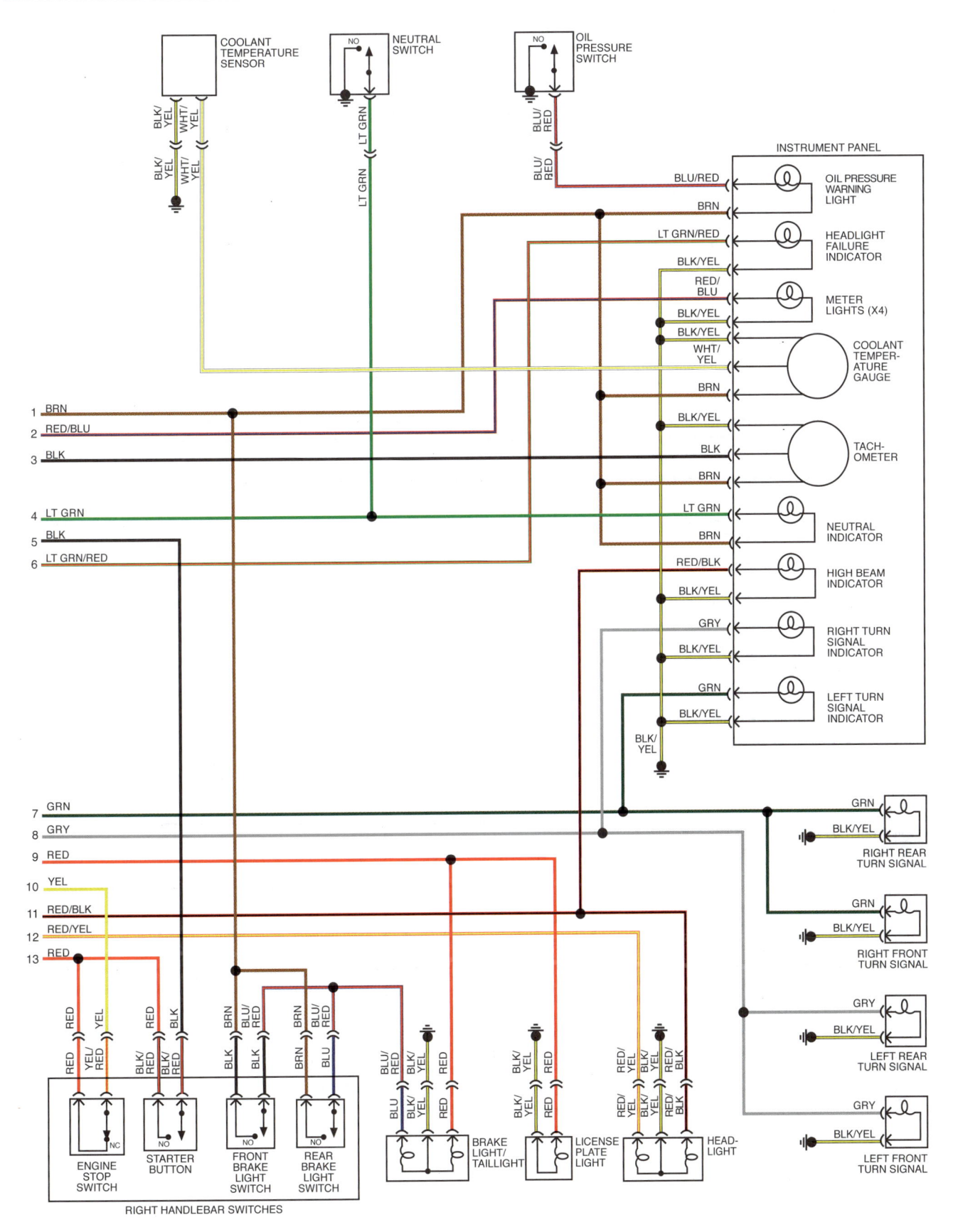

Wiring diagrams

1986, 1987 Kawasaki EX 250 (U. S. and Canada) (2 of 2)

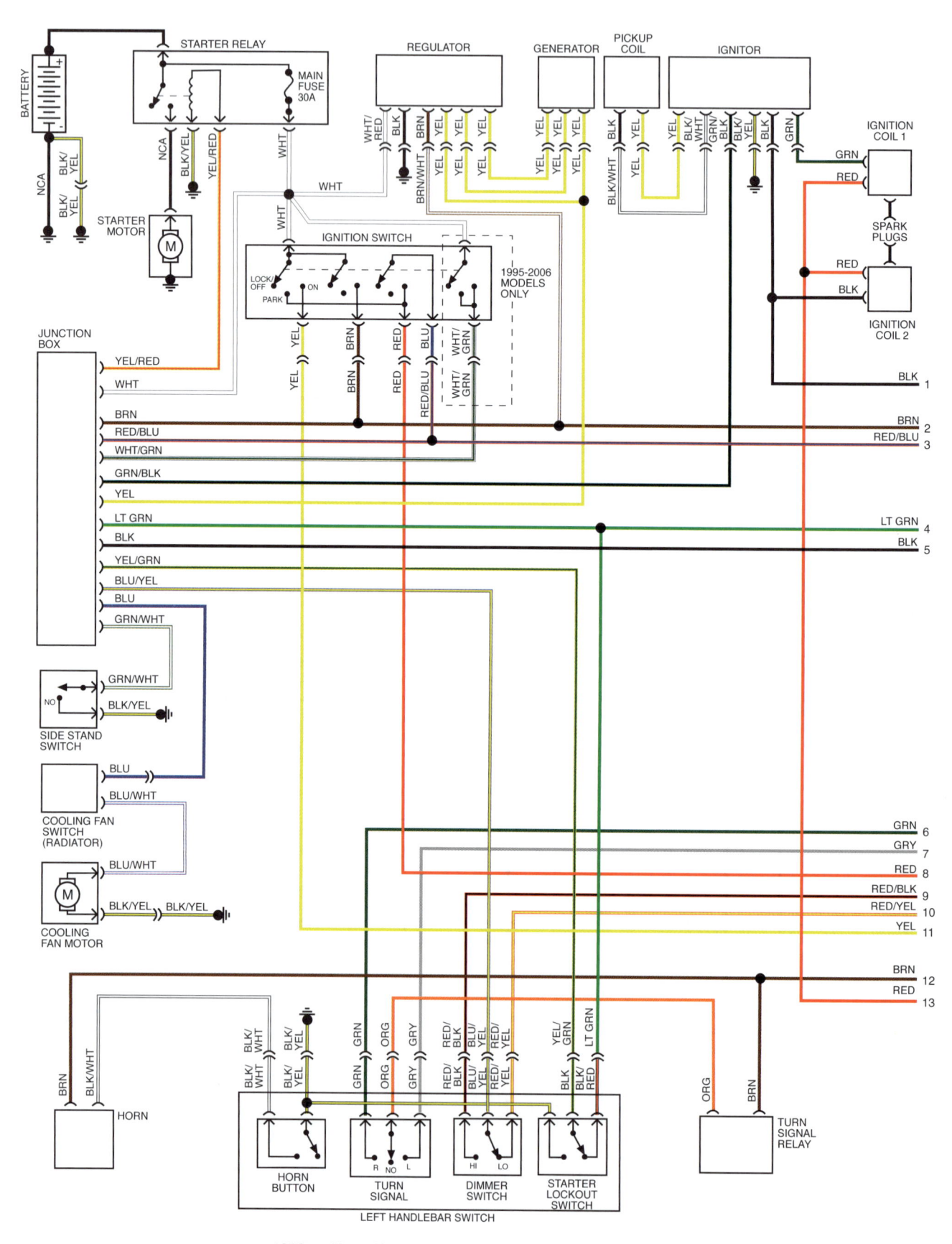

9•26 Wiring diagrams

1988 and later Kawasaki EX 250 (U. S. and Canada) (1 of 2)

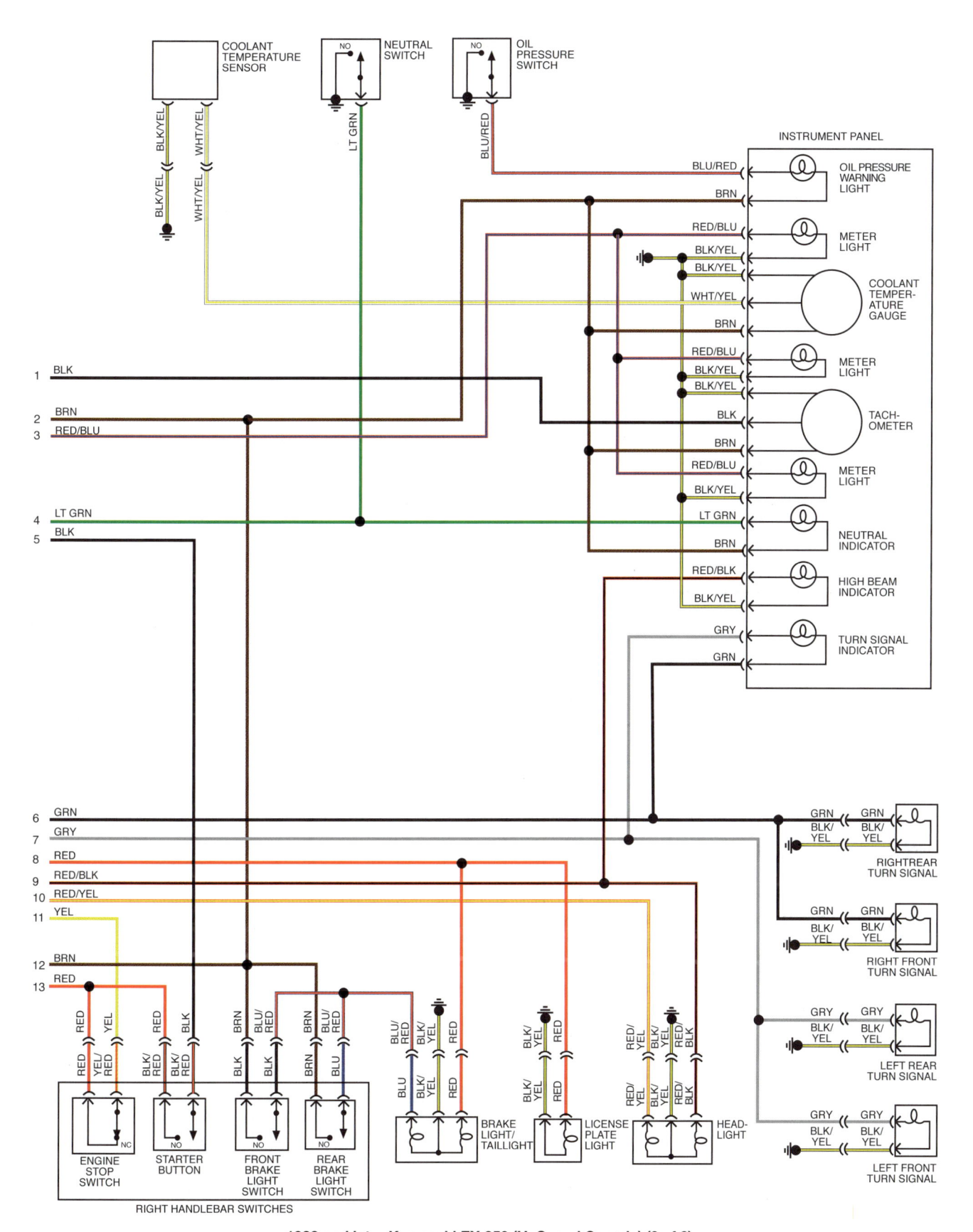

Wiring diagrams 9•27

1988 and later Kawasaki EX 250 (U. S. and Canada) (2 of 2)

9•28 Wiring diagrams

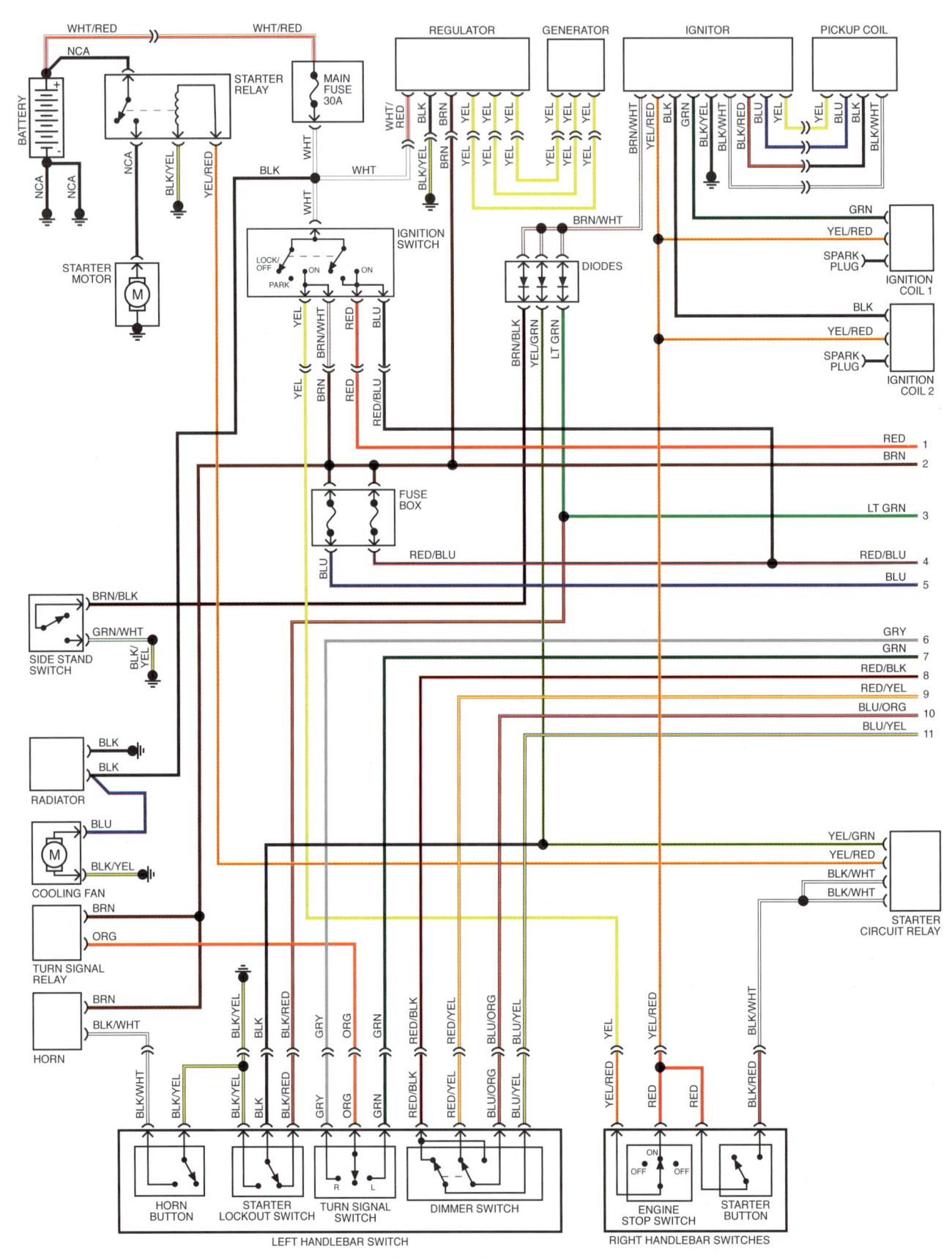

Kawasaki EN 450 (1 of 2)

Wiring diagrams 9•29

Kawasaki EN 450 (2 of 2)

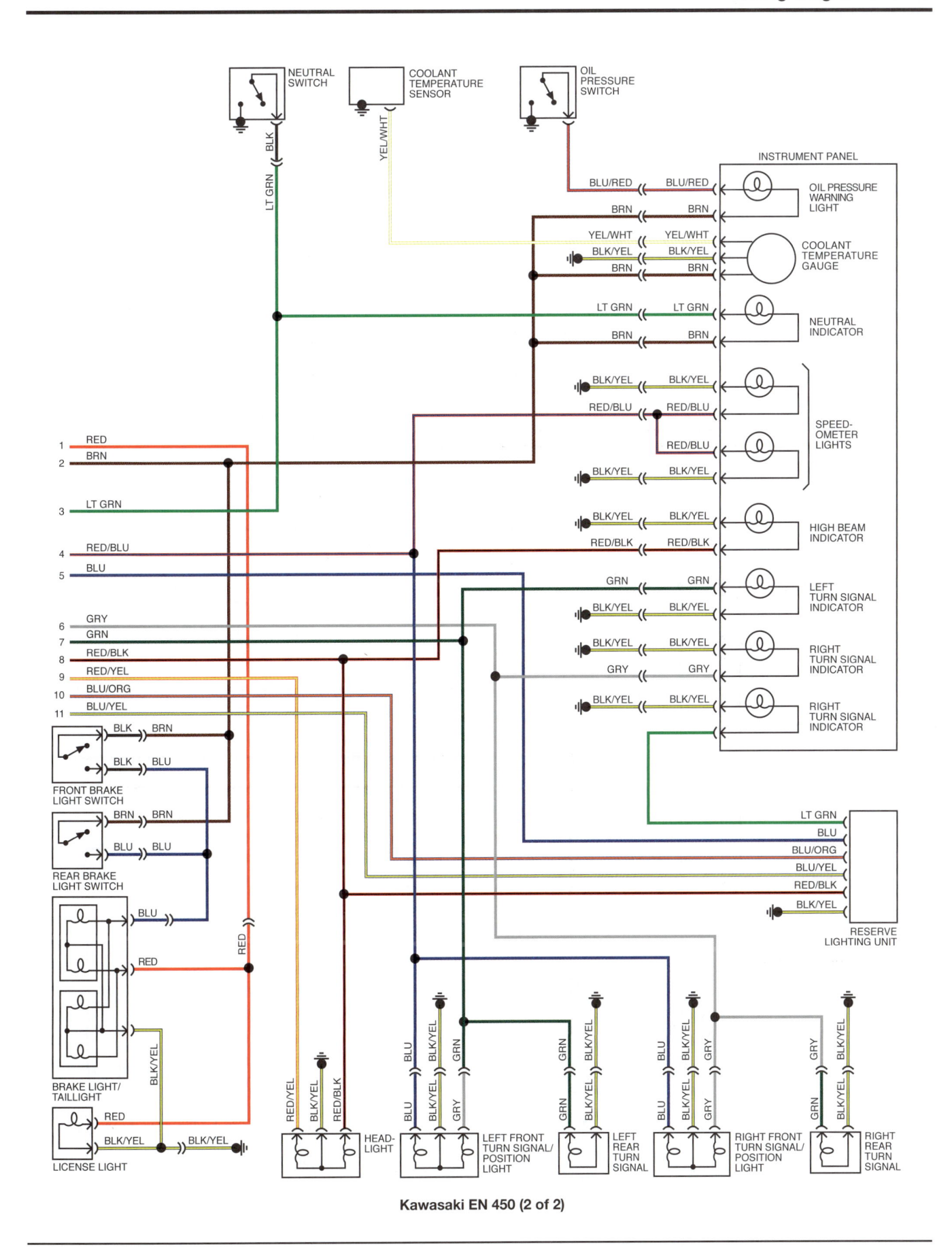

9•30 Wiring diagrams

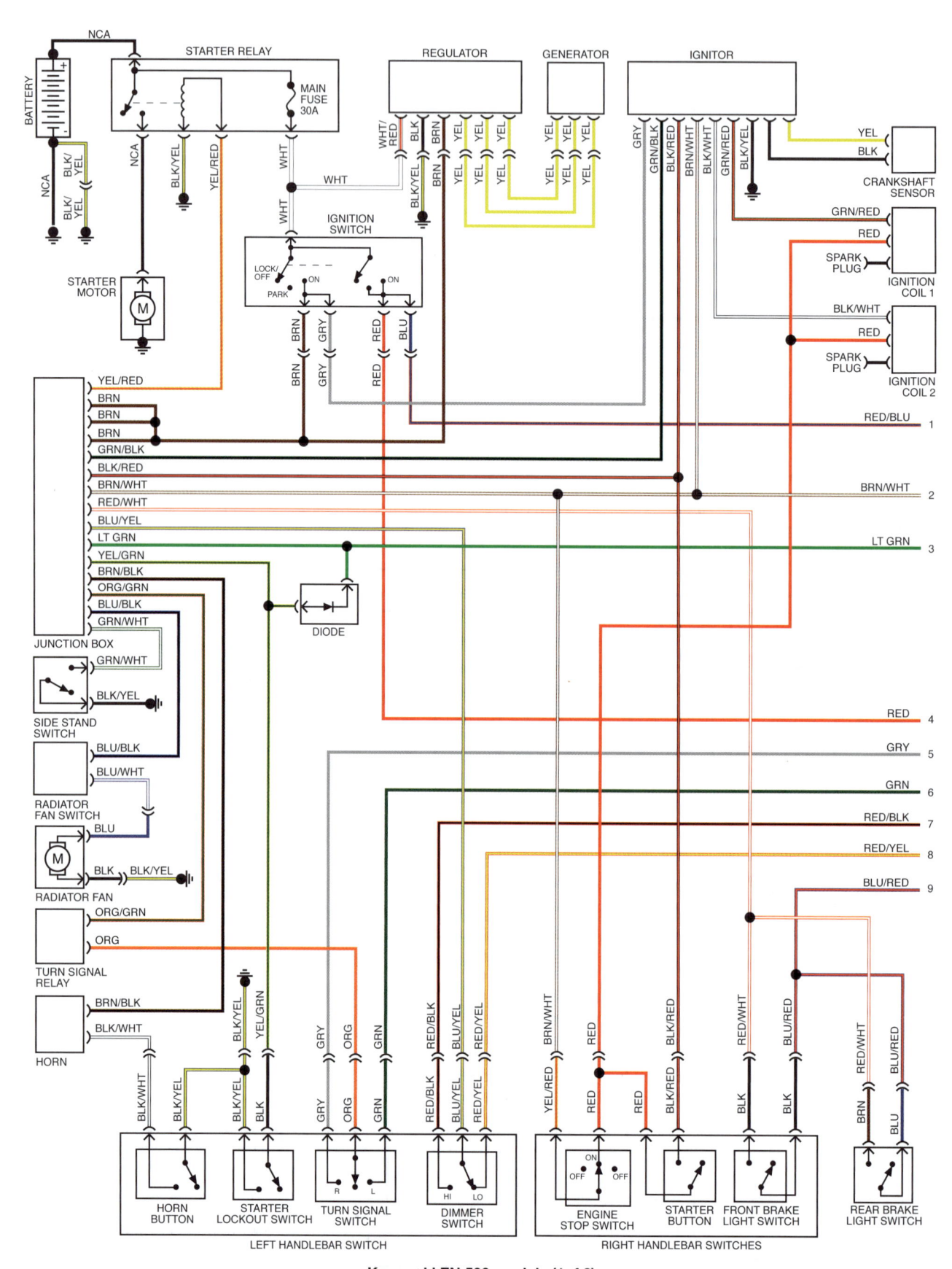

Kawasaki EN 500 models (1 of 2)

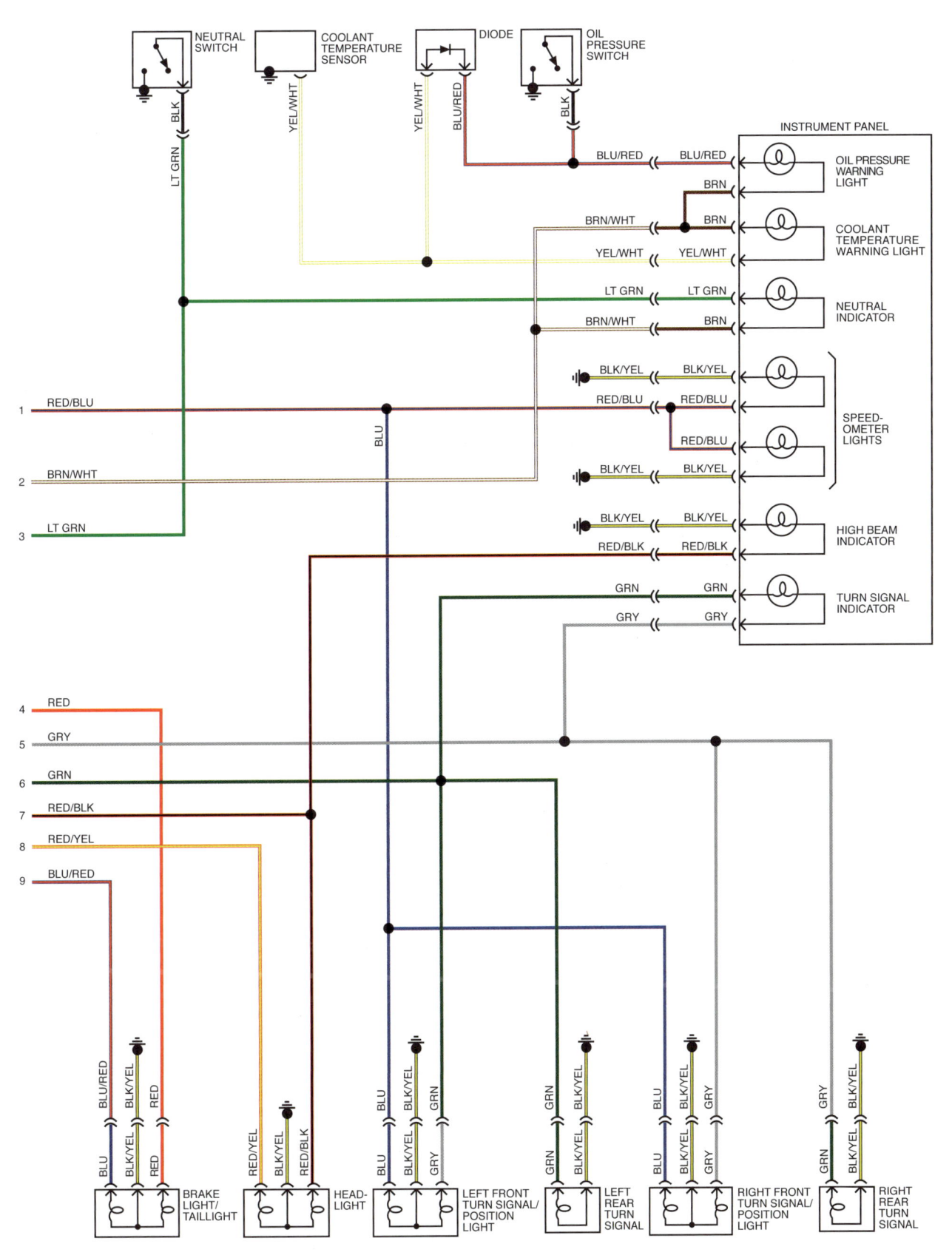

Wiring diagrams 9•31

Kawasaki EN 500 models (2 of 2)

Notes

Reference REF•1

Dimensions and Weights	**REF•1**	Troubleshooting	**REF•27**
Tools and Workshop Tips	**REF•4**	Troubleshooting Equipment	**REF•36**
Conversion Factors	**REF•22**	Security	**REF•40**
Motorcycle Chemicals and Lubricants	**REF•23**	Technical Terms Explained	**REF•43**
Storage	**REF•24**	Index	**REF•51**

Dimensions and weights

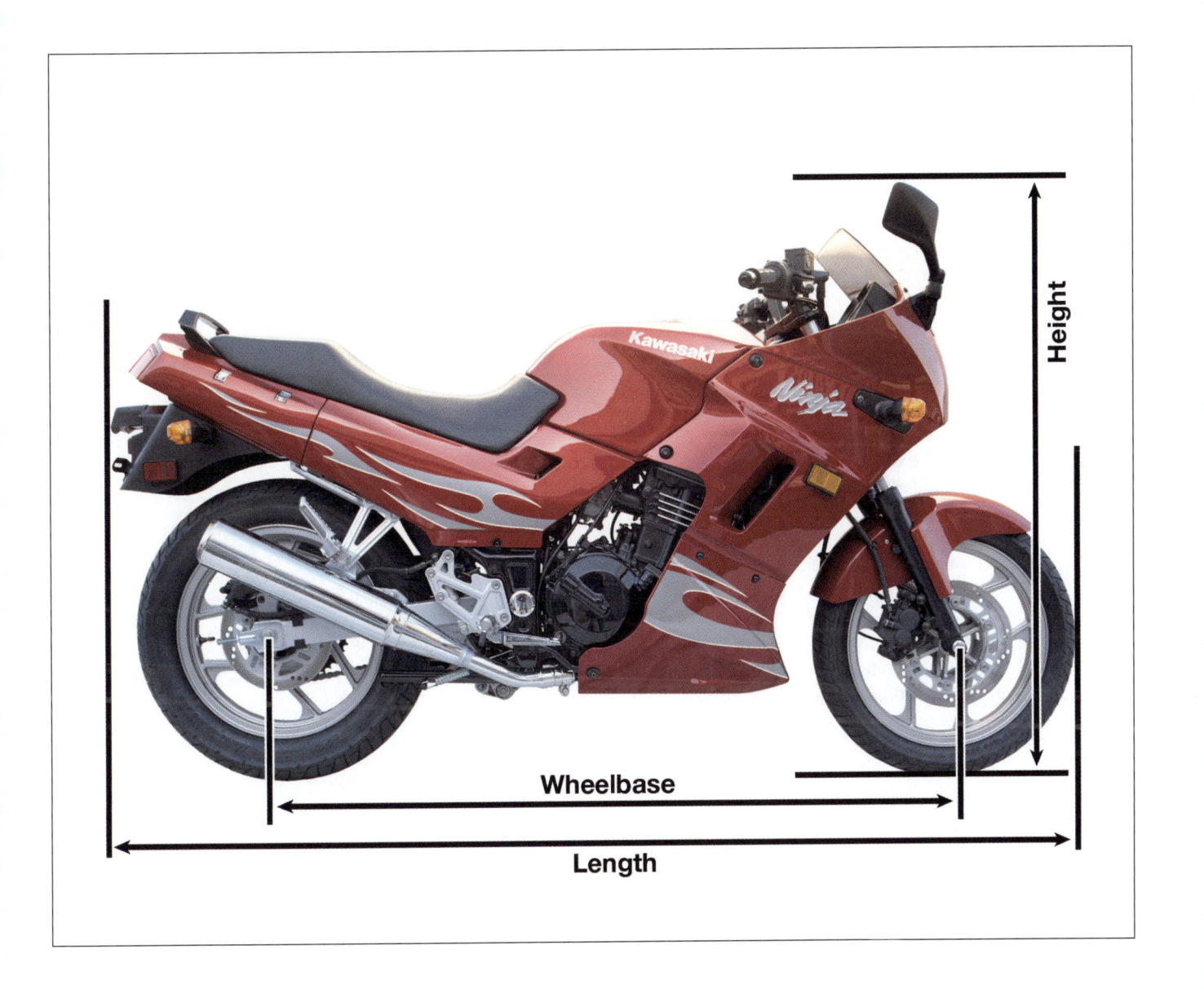

Reference

EN450/500 models

Frame and suspension

Wheelbase
- EN450 .... 1485 mm (58.46 inches)
- EN500 A .... 1555 mm (61.22 inches)
- EN500 C .... 1595 mm (62.8 inches)

Overall length
- EN450
  - US .... 2205 mm (86.81 inches)
  - UK .... 2210 mm (87.00 inches)
- EN500 A
  - Greece, Italy, Netherlands, Sweden, Germany..... 2290 mm (90.157 inches)
  - All other A models.............................. 2265 mm (89.17 inches)
- EN500 C .... 2320 mm (91.3 inches)

Overall width
- EN450 .... 820 mm (32.28 inches)
- EN500 A .... 840 mm (33.07 inches)
- EN500 C .... 830 mm (32.7 inches)

Overall height
- EN450 .... 1220 mm (48.03 inches)
- EN500 A .... 1230 mm (48.42 inches)
- EN500 C .... 1125 mm (44.3 inches)

Seat height
- EN450 .... 745 mm (29.33 inches)
- EN500 A .... 730 mmm (28.74 inches)
- EN500 C .... 715 mm (31.5 inches)

Dry weight
- EN450
  - US except California........................... 180 kg (396 lbs)
  - California.. 180.5 kg (397.1 lbs)
  - UK .... 181 kg (398.2 lbs)
- EN500 A
  - Except California................................ 186 kg (409.2 lbs)
  - California.. 186.5 kg (410.3 lbs)
- EN500 C
  - Except California................................ 199.0 kg (438 lbs)
  - California.. 199.5 kg (440 lbs)

Front suspension.. Telescopic fork
Rear suspension... Twin shocks/coil springs
Front brake .... Hydraulic disc
Rear brake .... Mechanical drum

Fuel tank capacity
- EN450, EN500 A .... 11.0 liters (2.9 US gal, 2.51 Imp gal)
- EN500 C .... 15.0 liters (3.9 US gal, 3.3 Imp gal)

Engine
Type	Liquid cooled, 4-stroke, DOHC parallel twin
Displacement	
EN450	454 cc (27.68 cubic inches)
EN500	498 cc (30.36 cubic inches)
Ignition system	Transistorized
Fuel system	
EN450, EN500 A	Two 34 mm Keihin carburetors
EN500 C	Two 32 mm Keihin carburetors
Clutch	Wet, multiplate
Transmission	5-speed, constant mesh

EX250 models

Frame and suspension
Wheelbase	1400 mm (55.12 inches)
Overall length	
1986 and 1987	1985 mm (78.15 inches)
1988 and later	2035 mm (80.12 inches)
Overall width	
1986 and 1987	695 mm (27.36 inches)
1988 and later	710 mm (27.95 inches)
Overall height	
1986 and 1987	1075 mm (43.32 inches)
1988 and later	1095 mm (43.11 inches)
Seat height	745 mm (29.33 inches)
Dry weight	
California	138.5 kg (304.7 lbs)
All others	138 kg (303.6 lbs)
Front suspension	Telescopic fork
Rear suspension	Single shock/coil spring with Unitrak
Front brake	Hydraulic disc
Rear brake	Hydraulic disc
Fuel tank capacity	
1986 and 1987	12.6 liters (3.36 gallons, 2.77 Imp gal)
1988 and later	18.0 liters (4.75 gallons 3.96 Imp gal)

Engine
Type	Liquid cooled, 4-stroke, DOHC parallel twin
Displacement	248 cc (15.13 cubic inches)
Ignition system	Transistorized
Fuel system	
1986 and 1987	Two 32 mm Keihin carburetors
1988 and later	Two 30 mm Keihin carburetors
Clutch	Wet, multiplate
Transmission	6-speed, constant mesh

REF•4 Tools and Workshop Tips

Buying tools

A good set of tools is a fundamental requirement for servicing and repairing a motorcycle. Although there will be an initial expense in building up enough tools for servicing, this will soon be offset by the savings made by doing the job yourself. As experience and confidence grow, additional tools can be added to enable the repair and overhaul of the motorcycle. Many of the special tools are expensive and not often used so it may be preferable to rent them, or for a group of friends or motorcycle club to join in the purchase.

As a rule, it is better to buy more expensive, good quality tools. Cheaper tools are likely to wear out faster and need to be replaced more often, nullifying the original savings.

> **Warning:** To avoid the risk of a poor quality tool breaking in use, causing injury or damage to the component being worked on, always aim to purchase tools which meet the relevant national safety standards.

The following lists of tools do not represent the manufacturer's service tools, but serve as a guide to help the owner decide which tools are needed for this level of work. In addition, items such as an electric drill, hacksaw, files, soldering iron and a workbench equipped with a vise, may be needed. Although not classed as tools, a selection of bolts, screws, nuts, washers and pieces of tubing always come in useful.

For more information about tools, refer to the Haynes *Motorcycle Workshop Practice Techbook* (Bk. No. 3470).

Manufacturer's service tools

Inevitably certain tasks require the use of a service tool. Where possible an alternative tool or method of approach is recommended, but sometimes there is no option if personal injury or damage to the component is to be avoided. Where required, service tools are referred to in the relevant procedure.

Service tools can usually only be purchased from a motorcycle dealer and are identified by a part number. Some of the commonly-used tools, such as rotor pullers, are available in aftermarket form from mail-order motorcycle tool and accessory suppliers.

Maintenance and minor repair tools

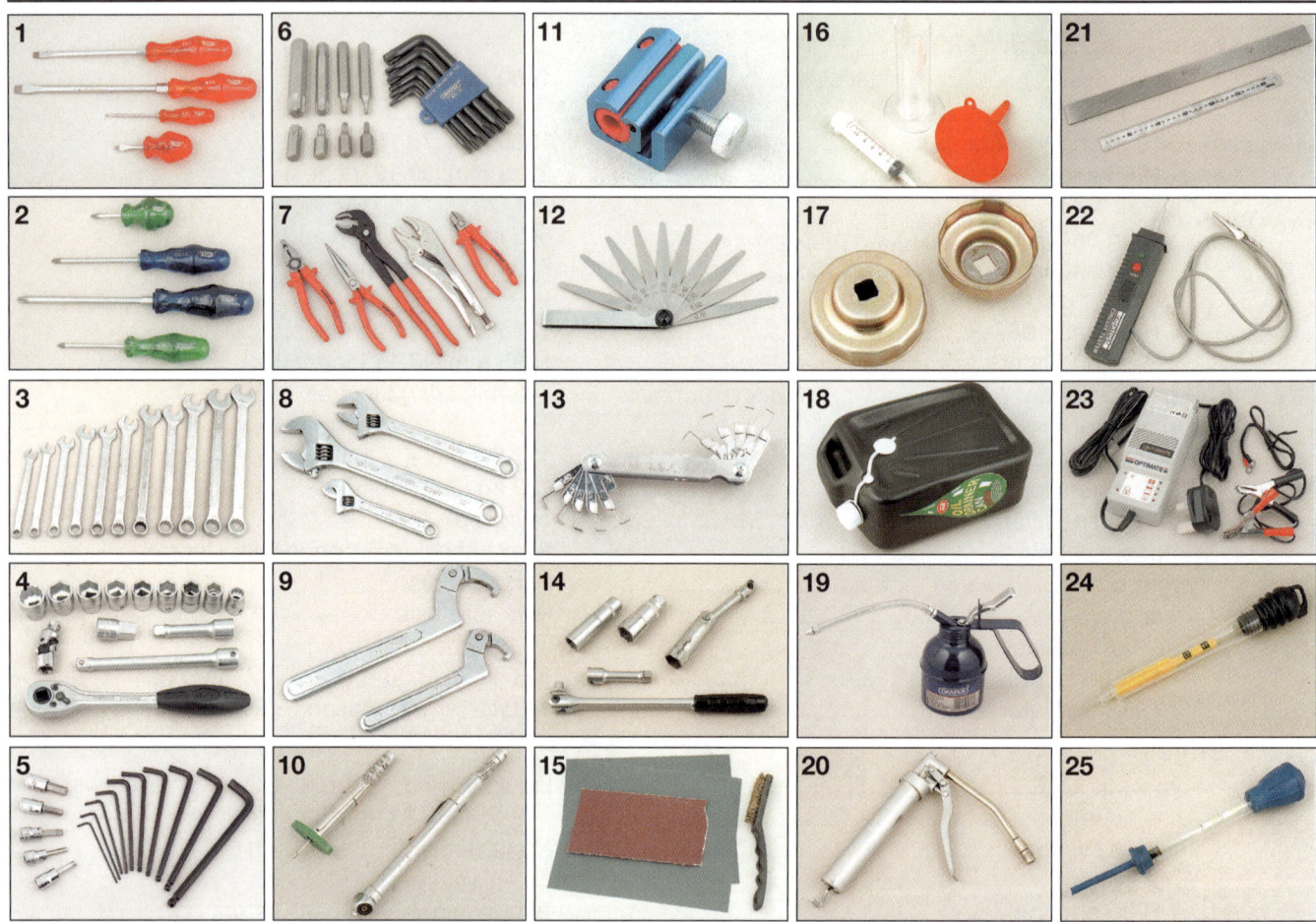

1. Set of flat-bladed screwdrivers
2. Set of Phillips head screwdrivers
3. Combination open-end and box wrenches
4. Socket set (3/8 inch or 1/2 inch drive)
5. Set of Allen keys or bits
6. Set of Torx keys or bits
7. Pliers, cutters and self-locking grips (vise grips)
8. Adjustable wrenches
9. C-spanners
10. Tread depth gauge and tire pressure gauge
11. Cable oiler clamp
12. Feeler gauges
13. Spark plug gap measuring tool
14. Spark plug wrench or deep plug sockets
15. Wire brush and emery paper
16. Calibrated syringe, measuring cup and funnel
17. Oil filter adapters
18. Oil drainer can or tray
19. Pump type oil can
20. Grease gun
21. Straight-edge and steel rule
22. Continuity tester
23. Battery charger
24. Hydrometer (for battery specific gravity check)
25. Anti-freeze tester (for liquid-cooled engines)

Tools and Workshop Tips REF•5

Repair and overhaul tools

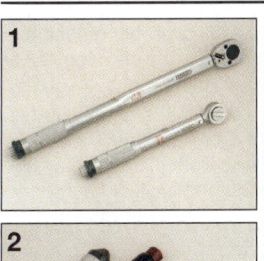

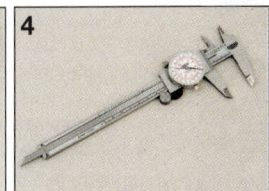

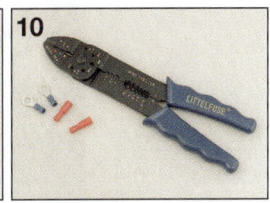

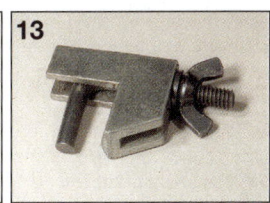

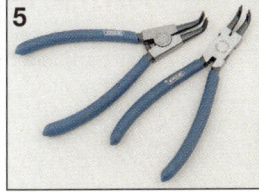

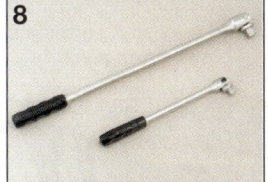

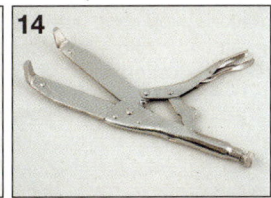

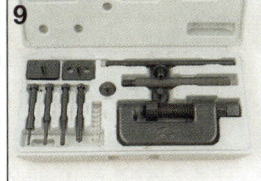

1. Torque wrench (small and mid-ranges)
2. Conventional, plastic or soft-faced hammers
3. Impact driver set
4. Vernier caliper
5. Snap-ring pliers (internal and external, or combination)
6. Set of cold chisels and punches
7. Selection of pullers
8. Breaker bars
9. Chain breaking/riveting tool set
10. Wire stripper and crimper tool
11. Multimeter (measures amps, volts and ohms)
12. Stroboscope (for dynamic timing checks)
13. Hose clamp (wingnut type shown)
14. Clutch holding tool
15. One-man brake/clutch bleeder kit

Special tools

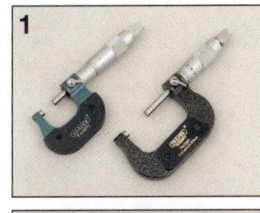

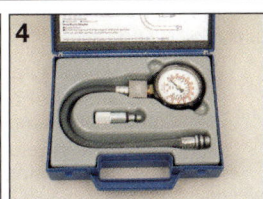

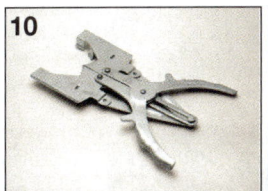

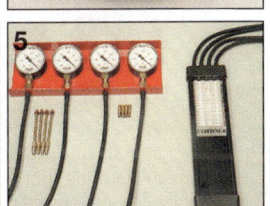

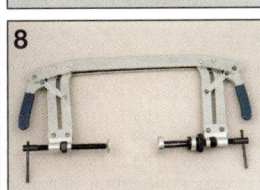

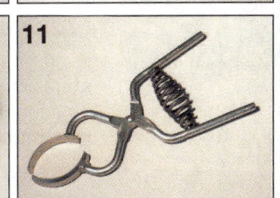

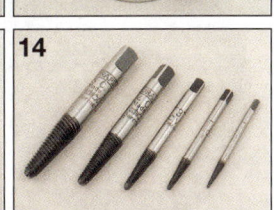

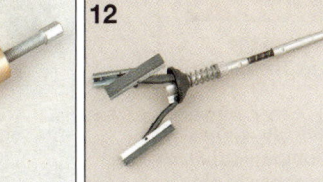

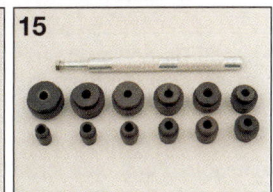

1. Micrometers (external type)
2. Telescoping gauges
3. Dial gauge
4. Cylinder compression gauge
5. Vacuum gauges (left) or manometer (right)
6. Oil pressure gauge
7. Plastigage kit
8. Valve spring compressor (4-stroke engines)
9. Piston pin drawbolt tool
10. Piston ring removal and installation tool
11. Piston ring clamp
12. Cylinder bore hone (stone type shown)
13. Stud extractor
14. Screw extractor set
15. Bearing driver set

Tools and Workshop Tips

1 Workshop equipment and facilities

The workbench

● Work is made much easier by raising the bike up on a ramp - components are much more accessible if raised to waist level. The hydraulic or pneumatic types seen in the dealer's workshop are a sound investment if you undertake a lot of repairs or overhauls **(see illustration 1.1)**.

1.1 Hydraulic motorcycle ramp

● If raised off ground level, the bike must be supported on the ramp to avoid it falling. Most ramps incorporate a front wheel locating clamp which can be adjusted to suit different diameter wheels. When tightening the clamp, take care not to mark the wheel rim or damage the tire - use wood blocks on each side to prevent this.

● Secure the bike to the ramp using tie-downs **(see illustration 1.2)**. If the bike has only a sidestand, and hence leans at a dangerous angle when raised, support the bike on an auxiliary stand.

1.2 Tie-downs are used around the passenger footrests to secure the bike

● Auxiliary (paddock) stands are widely available from mail order companies or motorcycle dealers and attach either to the wheel axle or swingarm pivot **(see illustration 1.3)**. If the motorcycle has a centerstand, you can support it under the crankcase to prevent it toppling while either wheel is removed **(see illustration 1.4)**.

1.3 This auxiliary stand attaches to the swingarm pivot

1.4 Always use a block of wood between the engine and jack head when supporting the engine in this way

Fumes and fire

● Refer to the Safety first! page at the beginning of the manual for full details. Make sure your workshop is equipped with a fire extinguisher suitable for fuel-related fires (Class B fire - flammable liquids) - it is not sufficient to have a water-filled extinguisher.

● Always ensure adequate ventilation is available. Unless an exhaust gas extraction system is available for use, ensure that the engine is run outside of the workshop.

● If working on the fuel system, make sure the workshop is ventilated to avoid a build-up of fumes. This applies equally to fume build-up when charging a battery. Do not smoke or allow anyone else to smoke in the workshop.

Fluids

● If you need to drain fuel from the tank, store it in an approved container marked as suitable for the storage of gasoline **(see illustration 1.5)**. Do not store fuel in glass jars or bottles.

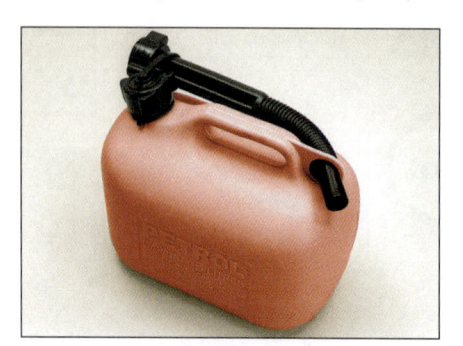

● Use proprietary engine degreasers or solvents which have a high flash-point, such as kerosene, for cleaning off oil, grease and dirt - never use gasoline for cleaning. Wear rubber gloves when handling solvent and engine degreaser. The fumes from certain solvents can be dangerous - always work in a well-ventilated area.

Dust, eye and hand protection

● Protect your lungs from inhalation of dust particles by wearing a filtering mask over the nose and mouth. Many frictional materials still contain asbestos which is dangerous to your health. Protect your eyes from spouts of liquid and sprung components by wearing a pair of protective

1.5 Use an approved can only for storing gasoline

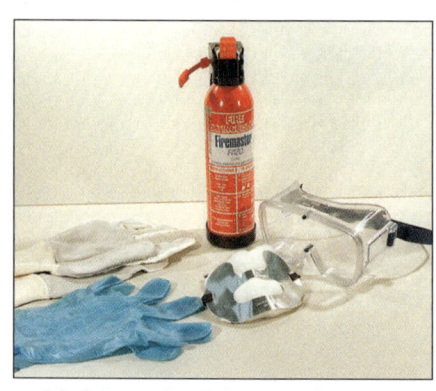

1.6 A fire extinguisher, goggles, mask and protective gloves should be at hand in the workshop

goggles **(see illustration 1.6)**.

● Protect your hands from contact with solvents, fuel and oils by wearing rubber gloves. Alternatively apply a barrier cream to your hands before starting work. If handling hot components or fluids, wear suitable gloves to protect your hands from scalding and burns.

What to do with old fluids

● Old cleaning solvent, fuel, coolant and oils should not be poured down domestic drains or onto the ground. Package the fluid up in old oil containers, label it accordingly, and take it to a garage or disposal facility. Contact your local disposal company for location of such sites.

Note: It is illegal to dump oil down the drain. Check with your local auto parts store, disposal facility or environmental agency to see if they accept the oil for recycling.

Tools and Workshop Tips REF•7

2 Fasteners - screws, bolts and nuts

Fastener types and applications

Bolts and screws

● Fastener head types are either of hexagonal, Torx or splined design, with internal and external versions of each type **(see illustrations 2.1 and 2.2)**; splined head fasteners are not in common use on motorcycles. The conventional slotted or Phillips head design is used for certain screws. Bolt or screw length is always measured from the underside of the head to the end of the item **(see illustration 2.11)**.

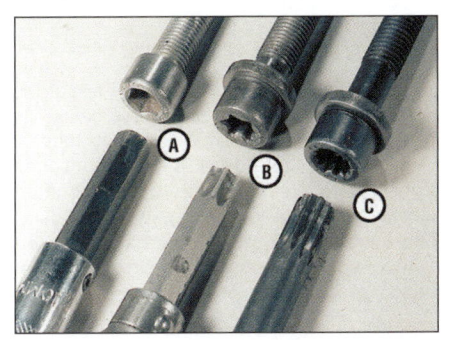

2.1 Internal hexagon/Allen (A), Torx (B) and splined (C) fasteners, with corresponding bits

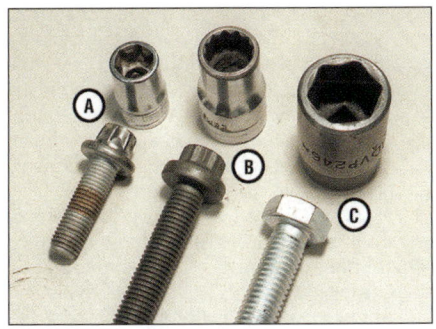

2.2 External Torx (A), splined (B) and hexagon (C) fasteners, with corresponding sockets

● Certain fasteners on the motorcycle have a tensile marking on their heads, the higher the marking the stronger the fastener. High tensile fasteners generally carry a 10 or higher marking. Never replace a high tensile fastener with one of a lower tensile strength.

Washers (see illustration 2.3)

● Plain washers are used between a fastener head and a component to prevent damage to the component or to spread the load when torque is applied. Plain washers can also be used as spacers or shims in certain assemblies. Copper or aluminum plain washers are often used as sealing washers on drain plugs.

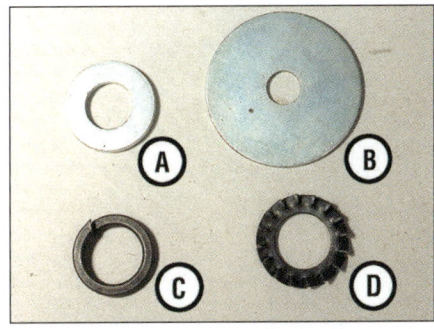

2.3 Plain washer (A), penny washer (B), spring washer (C) and serrated washer (D)

● The split-ring spring washer works by applying axial tension between the fastener head and component. If flattened, it is fatigued and must be replaced. If a plain (flat) washer is used on the fastener, position the spring washer between the fastener and the plain washer.

● Serrated star type washers dig into the fastener and component faces, preventing loosening. They are often used on electrical ground connections to the frame.

● Cone type washers (sometimes called Belleville) are conical and when tightened apply axial tension between the fastener head and component. They must be installed with the dished side against the component and often carry an OUTSIDE marking on their outer face. If flattened, they are fatigued and must be replaced.

● Tab washers are used to lock plain nuts or bolts on a shaft. A portion of the tab washer is bent up hard against one flat of the nut or bolt to prevent it loosening. Due to the tab washer being deformed in use, a new tab washer should be used every time it is removed.

● Wave washers are used to take up endfloat on a shaft. They provide light springing and prevent excessive side-to-side play of a component. Can be found on rocker arm shafts.

Nuts and cotter pins

● Conventional plain nuts are usually six-sided **(see illustration 2.4)**. They are sized by thread diameter and pitch. High tensile nuts carry a number on one end to denote their tensile strength.

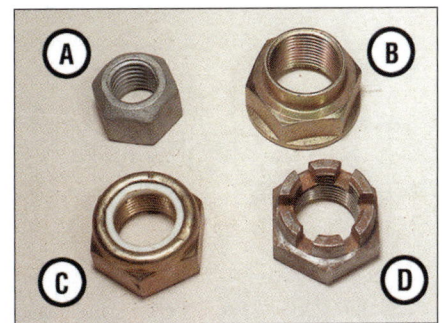

2.4 Plain nut (A), shouldered locknut (B), nylon insert nut (C) and castellated nut (D)

● Self-locking nuts either have a nylon insert, or two spring metal tabs, or a shoulder which is staked into a groove in the shaft - their advantage over conventional plain nuts is a resistance to loosening due to vibration. The nylon insert type can be used a number of times, but must be replaced when the friction of the nylon insert is reduced, i.e. when the nut spins freely on the shaft. The spring tab type can be reused unless the tabs are damaged. The shouldered type must be replaced every time it is removed.

● Cotter pins are used to lock a castellated nut to a shaft or to prevent loosening of a plain nut. Common applications are wheel axles and brake torque arms. Because the cotter pin arms are deformed to lock around the nut a new cotter pin must always be used on installation - always use the correct size cotter pin which will fit snugly in the shaft hole. Make sure the cotter pin arms are correctly located around the nut **(see illustrations 2.5 and 2.6)**.

2.5 Bend cotter pin arms as shown (arrows) to secure a castellated nut

2.6 Bend cotter pin arms as shown to secure a plain nut

Caution: If the castellated nut slots do not align with the shaft hole after tightening to the torque setting, tighten the nut until the next slot aligns with the hole - never loosen the nut to align its slot.

● R-pins (shaped like the letter R), or slip pins as they are sometimes called, are sprung and can be reused if they are otherwise in good condition. Always install R-pins with their closed end facing forwards **(see illustration 2.7)**.

REF•8 Tools and Workshop Tips

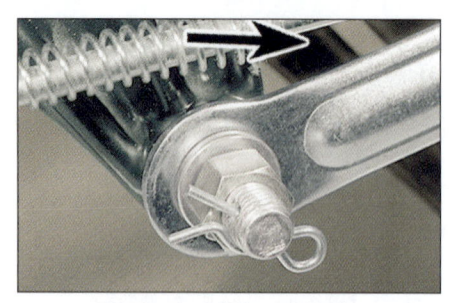

2.7 Correct fitting of R-pin. Arrow indicates forward direction

Snap-rings (see illustration 2.8)

● Snap-rings (sometimes called circlips) are used to retain components on a shaft or in a housing and have corresponding external or internal ears to permit removal. Parallel-sided (machined) snap-rings can be installed either way round in their groove, whereas stamped snap-rings (which have a chamfered edge on one face) must be installed with the chamfer facing away from the direction of thrust load **(see illustration 2.9)**.

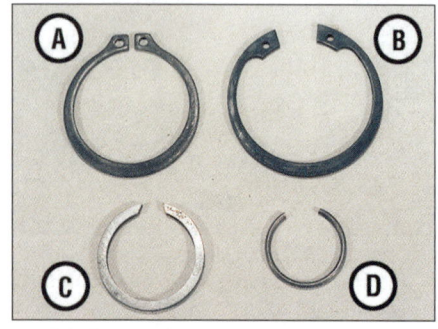

2.8 External stamped snap-ring (A), internal stamped snap-ring (B), machined snap-ring (C) and wire snap-ring (D)

● Always use snap-ring pliers to remove and install snap-rings; expand or compress them just enough to remove them. After installation, rotate the snap-ring in its groove to ensure it is securely seated. If installing a snap-ring on a splined shaft, always align its opening with a shaft channel to ensure the snap-ring ends are well supported and unlikely to catch **(see illustration 2.10)**.

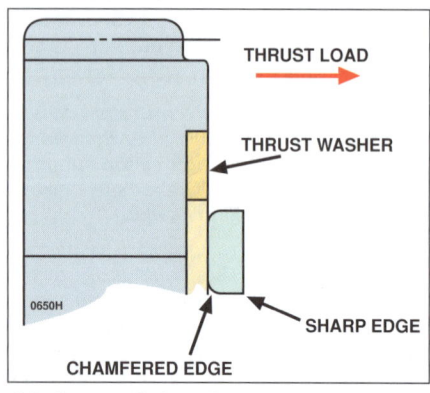

2.9 Correct fitting of a stamped snap-ring

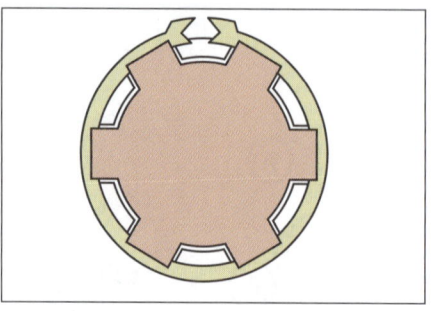

2.10 Align snap-ring opening with shaft channel

● Snap-rings can wear due to the thrust of components and become loose in their grooves, with the subsequent danger of becoming dislodged in operation. For this reason, replacement is advised every time a snap-ring is disturbed.

● Wire snap-rings are commonly used as piston pin retaining clips. If a removal tang is provided, long-nosed pliers can be used to dislodge them, otherwise careful use of a small flat-bladed screwdriver is necessary. Wire snap-rings should be replaced every time they are disturbed.

Thread diameter and pitch

● Diameter of a male thread (screw, bolt or stud) is the outside diameter of the threaded portion **(see illustration 2.11)**. Most motorcycle manufacturers use the ISO (International Standards Organization) metric system expressed in millimeters. For example, M6 refers to a 6 mm diameter thread. Sizing is the same for nuts, except that the thread diameter is measured across the valleys of the nut.

● Pitch is the distance between the peaks of the thread **(see illustration 2.11)**. It is expressed in millimeters, thus a common bolt size may be expressed as 6.0 x 1.0 mm (6 mm thread diameter and 1 mm pitch). Generally pitch increases in proportion to thread diameter, although there are always exceptions.

● Thread diameter and pitch are related for conventional fastener applications and the accompanying table can be used as a guide. Additionally, the AF (Across Flats), wrench or socket size dimension of the bolt or nut **(see illustration 2.11)** is linked to thread and pitch specification. Thread pitch can be measured with a thread gauge **(see illustration 2.12)**.

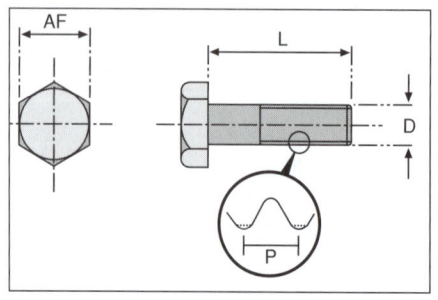

2.11 Fastener length (L), thread diameter (D), thread pitch (P) and head size (AF)

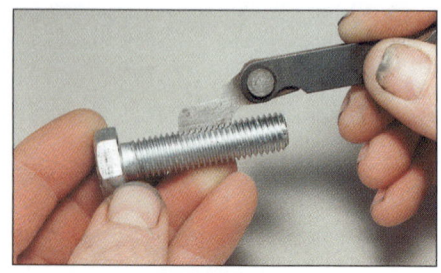

2.12 Using a thread gauge to measure pitch

AF size	Thread diameter x pitch (mm)
8 mm	M5 x 0.8
8 mm	M6 x 1.0
10 mm	M6 x 1.0
12 mm	M8 x 1.25
14 mm	M10 x 1.25
17 mm	M12 x 1.25

● The threads of most fasteners are of the right-hand type, ie they are turned clockwise to tighten and counterclockwise to loosen. The reverse situation applies to left-hand thread fasteners, which are turned counterclockwise to tighten and clockwise to loosen. Left-hand threads are used where rotation of a component might loosen a conventional right-hand thread fastener.

Seized fasteners

● Corrosion of external fasteners due to water or reaction between two dissimilar metals can occur over a period of time. It will build up sooner in wet conditions or in countries where salt is used on the roads during the winter. If a fastener is severely corroded it is likely that normal methods of removal will fail and result in its head being ruined. When you attempt removal, the fastener thread should be heard to crack free and unscrew easily - if it doesn't, stop there before damaging something.

● A smart tap on the head of the fastener will often succeed in breaking free corrosion which has occurred in the threads **(see illustration 2.13)**.

● An aerosol penetrating fluid (such as WD-40) applied the night beforehand may work its way down into the thread and ease removal. Depending on the location, you may be able to make up a modeling-clay well around the fastener head and fill it with penetrating fluid.

2.13 A sharp tap on the head of a fastener will often break free a corroded thread

Tools and Workshop Tips REF•9

● If you are working on an engine internal component, corrosion will most likely not be a problem due to the well lubricated environment. However, components can be very tight and an impact driver is a useful tool in freeing them **(see illustration 2.14)**.

2.14 Using an impact driver to free a fastener

● Where corrosion has occurred between dissimilar metals (e.g. steel and aluminum alloy), the application of heat to the fastener head will create a disproportionate expansion rate between the two metals and break the seizure caused by the corrosion. Whether heat can be applied depends on the location of the fastener - any surrounding components likely to be damaged must first be removed **(see illustration 2.15)**. Heat can be applied using a paint stripper heat gun or clothes iron, or by immersing the component in boiling water - wear protective gloves to prevent scalding or burns to the hands.

2.15 Using heat to free a seized fastener

● As a last resort, it is possible to use a hammer and cold chisel to work the fastener head unscrewed **(see illustration 2.16)**. This will damage the fastener, but more importantly extreme care must be taken not to damage the surrounding component.

> **Caution: Remember that the component being secured is generally of more value than the bolt, nut or screw - when the fastener is freed, do not unscrew it with force, instead work the fastener back and forth when resistance is felt to prevent thread damage.**

2.16 Using a hammer and chisel to free a seized fastener

Broken fasteners and damaged heads

● If the shank of a broken bolt or screw is accessible you can grip it with self-locking grips. The knurled wheel type stud extractor tool or self-gripping stud puller tool is particularly useful for removing the long studs which screw into the cylinder mouth surface of the crankcase or bolts and screws from which the head has broken off **(see illustration 2.17)**. Studs can also be removed by locking two nuts together on the threaded end of the stud and using a wrench on the lower nut **(see illustration 2.18)**.

2.17 Using a stud extractor tool to remove a broken crankcase stud

2.18 Two nuts can be locked together to unscrew a stud from a component

● A bolt or screw which has broken off below or level with the casing must be extracted using a screw extractor set. Centerpunch the fastener to centralize the drill bit, then drill a hole in the fastener **(see illustration 2.19)**. Select a drill bit which is approximately half

2.19 When using a screw extractor, first drill a hole in the fastener . . .

to three-quarters the diameter of the fastener and drill to a depth which will accommodate the extractor. Use the largest size extractor possible, but avoid leaving too small a wall thickness otherwise the extractor will merely force the fastener walls outwards wedging it in the casing thread.

● If a spiral type extractor is used, thread it counterclockwise into the fastener. As it is screwed in, it will grip the fastener and unscrew it from the casing **(see illustration 2.20)**.

2.20 . . . then thread the extractor counterclockwise into the fastener

● If a taper type extractor is used, tap it into the fastener so that it is firmly wedged in place. Unscrew the extractor (counter-clockwise) to draw the fastener out.

> ⚠️ **Warning: Stud extractors are very hard and may break off in the fastener if care is not taken - ask a machine shop about spark erosion if this happens.**

● Alternatively, the broken bolt/screw can be drilled out and the hole retapped for an oversize bolt/screw or a diamond-section thread insert. It is essential that the drilling is carried out squarely and to the correct depth, otherwise the casing may be ruined - if in doubt, entrust the work to a machine shop.

● Bolts and nuts with rounded corners cause the correct size wrench or socket to slip when force is applied. Of the types of wrench/socket available always use a six-point type rather than an eight or twelve-point type - better grip

REF•10 Tools and Workshop Tips

2.21 Comparison of surface drive box wrench (left) with 12-point type (right)

is obtained. Surface drive wrenches grip the middle of the hex flats, rather than the corners, and are thus good in cases of damaged heads **(see illustration 2.21)**.

● Slotted-head or Phillips-head screws are often damaged by the use of the wrong size screwdriver. Allen-head and Torx-head screws are much less likely to sustain damage. If enough of the screw head is exposed you can use a hacksaw to cut a slot in its head and then use a conventional flat-bladed screwdriver to remove it. Alternatively use a hammer and cold chisel to tap the head of the fastener around to loosen it. Always replace damaged fasteners with new ones, preferably Torx or Allen-head type.

HAYNES HiNT

A dab of valve grinding compound between the screw head and screwdriver tip will often give a good grip.

Thread repair

● Threads (particularly those in aluminum alloy components) can be damaged by overtightening, being assembled with dirt in the threads, or from a component working loose and vibrating. Eventually the thread will fail completely, and it will be impossible to tighten the fastener.

● If a thread is damaged or clogged with old locking compound it can be renovated with a thread repair tool (thread chaser) **(see illustrations 2.22 and 2.23)**; special thread

2.22 A thread repair tool being used to correct an internal thread

2.23 A thread repair tool being used to correct an external thread

chasers are available for spark plug hole threads. The tool will not cut a new thread, but clean and true the original thread. Make sure that you use the correct diameter and pitch tool. Similarly, external threads can be cleaned up with a die or a thread restorer file **(see illustration 2.24)**.

2.24 Using a thread restorer file

● It is possible to drill out the old thread and retap the component to the next thread size. This will work where there is enough surrounding material and a new bolt or screw can be obtained. Sometimes, however, this is not possible - such as where the bolt/screw passes through another component which must also be suitably modified, also in cases where a spark plug or oil drain plug cannot be obtained in a larger diameter thread size.

● The diamond-section thread insert (often known by its popular trade name of Heli-Coil) is a simple and effective method of replacing the thread and retaining the original size. A kit can be purchased which contains the tap, insert and installing tool **(see illustration 2.25)**. Drill out the damaged thread with the size drill specified **(see illustration 2.26)**. Carefully retap the thread **(see illustration 2.27)**. Install the

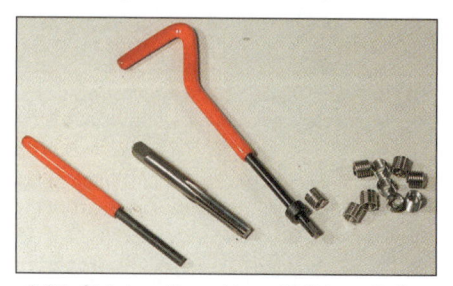

2.25 Obtain a thread insert kit to suit the thread diameter and pitch required

2.26 To install a thread insert, first drill out the original thread . . .

2.27 . . . tap a new thread . . .

2.28 . . . fit insert on the installing tool . . .

2.29 . . . and thread into the component . . .

2.30 . . . break off the tang when complete

insert on the installing tool and thread it slowly into place using a light downward pressure **(see illustrations 2.28 and 2.29)**. When positioned between a 1/4 and 1/2 turn below the surface withdraw the installing tool and use the break-off tool to press down on the tang, breaking it off **(see illustration 2.30)**.

● There are epoxy thread repair kits on the market which can rebuild stripped internal threads, although this repair should not be used on high load-bearing components.

Tools and Workshop Tips REF•11

Thread locking and sealing compounds

● Locking compounds are used in locations where the fastener is prone to loosening due to vibration or on important safety-related items which might cause loss of control of the motorcycle if they fail. It is also used where important fasteners cannot be secured by other means such as lockwashers or cotter pins.

● Before applying locking compound, make sure that the threads (internal and external) are clean and dry with all old compound removed. Select a compound to suit the component being secured - a non-permanent general locking and sealing type is suitable for most applications, but a high strength type is needed for permanent fixing of studs in castings. Apply a drop or two of the compound to the first few threads of the fastener, then thread it into place and tighten to the specified torque. Do not apply excessive thread locking compound otherwise the thread may be damaged on subsequent removal.

● Certain fasteners are impregnated with a dry film type coating of locking compound on their threads. Always replace this type of fastener if disturbed.

● Anti-seize compounds, such as copper-based greases, can be applied to protect threads from seizure due to extreme heat and corrosion. A common instance is spark plug threads and exhaust system fasteners.

3 Measuring tools and gauges

Feeler gauges

● Feeler gauges (or blades) are used for measuring small gaps and clearances **(see illustration 3.1)**. They can also be used to measure endfloat (sideplay) of a component on a shaft where access is not possible with a dial gauge.

● Feeler gauge sets should be treated with care and not bent or damaged. They are etched with their size on one face. Keep them clean and very lightly oiled to prevent corrosion build-up.

3.1 Feeler gauges are used for measuring small gaps and clearances - thickness is marked on one face of gauge

● When measuring a clearance, select a gauge which is a light sliding fit between the two components. You may need to use two gauges together to measure the clearance accurately.

Micrometers

● A micrometer is a precision tool capable of measuring to 0.01 or 0.001 of a millimeter. It should always be stored in its case and not in the general toolbox. It must be kept clean and never dropped, otherwise its frame or measuring anvils could be distorted resulting in inaccurate readings.

● External micrometers are used for measuring outside diameters of components and have many more applications than internal micrometers. Micrometers are available in different size ranges, typically 0 to 25 mm, 25 to 50 mm, and upwards in 25 mm steps; some large micrometers have interchangeable anvils to allow a range of measurements to be taken. Generally the largest precision measurement you are likely to take on a motorcycle is the piston diameter.

● Internal micrometers (or bore micrometers) are used for measuring inside diameters, such as valve guides and cylinder bores. Telescoping gauges and small hole gauges are used in conjunction with an external micrometer, whereas the more expensive internal micrometers have their own measuring device.

External micrometer

Note: *The conventional analogue type instrument is described. Although much easier to read, digital micrometers are considerably more expensive.*

● Always check the calibration of the micrometer before use. With the anvils closed (0 to 25 mm type) or set over a test gauge

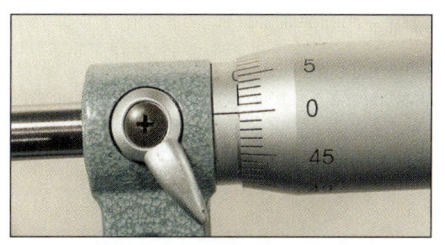

3.2 Check micrometer calibration before use

(for the larger types) the scale should read zero **(see illustration 3.2)**; make sure that the anvils (and test piece) are clean first. Any discrepancy can be adjusted by referring to the instructions supplied with the tool. Remember that the micrometer is a precision measuring tool - don't force the anvils closed, use the ratchet (4) on the end of the micrometer to close it. In this way, a measured force is always applied.

● To use, first make sure that the item being measured is clean. Place the anvil of the micrometer (1) against the item and use the thimble (2) to bring the spindle (3) lightly into contact with the other side of the item **(see illustration 3.3)**. Don't tighten the thimble down because this will damage the micrometer - instead use the ratchet (4) on the end of the micrometer. The ratchet mechanism applies a measured force preventing damage to the instrument.

● The micrometer is read by referring to the linear scale on the sleeve and the annular scale on the thimble. Read off the sleeve first to obtain the base measurement, then add the fine measurement from the thimble to obtain the overall reading. The linear scale on the sleeve represents the measuring range of the micrometer (eg 0 to 25 mm). The annular scale

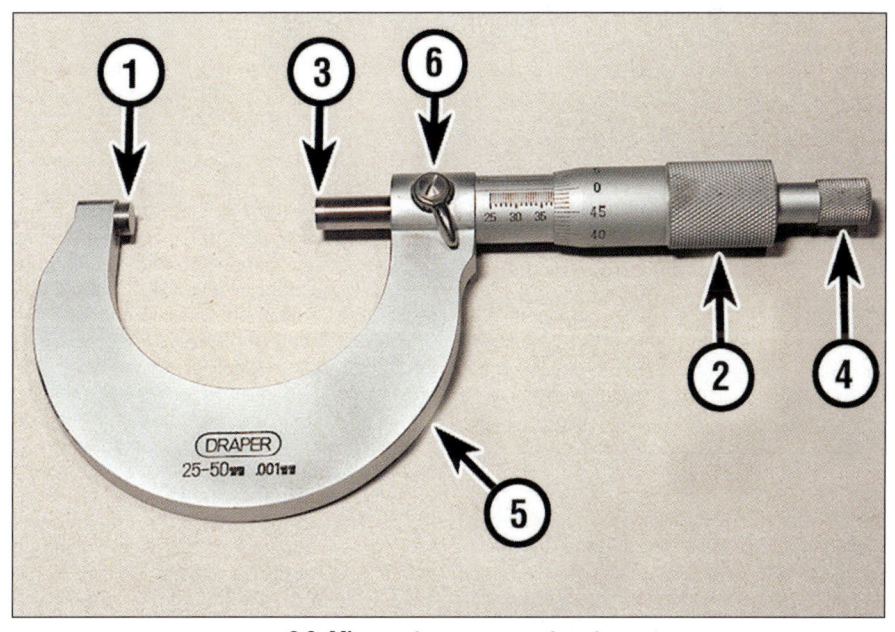

3.3 Micrometer component parts

| 1 Anvil | 3 Spindle | 5 Frame |
| 2 Thimble | 4 Ratchet | 6 Locking lever |

REF•12 Tools and Workshop Tips

on the thimble will be in graduations of 0.01 mm (or as marked on the frame) - one full revolution of the thimble will move 0.5 mm on the linear scale. Take the reading where the datum line on the sleeve intersects the thimble's scale. Always position the eye directly above the scale otherwise an inaccurate reading will result.

In the example shown the item measures 2.95 mm **(see illustration 3.4)**:

Linear scale	2.00 mm
Linear scale	0.50 mm
Annular scale	0.45 mm
Total figure	**2.95 mm**

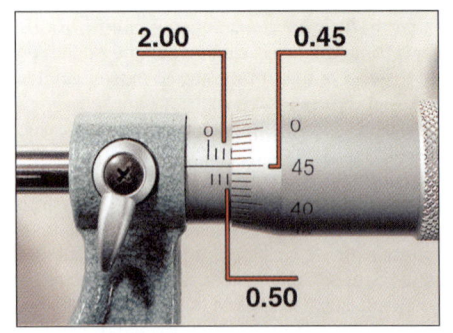

3.4 Micrometer reading of 2.95 mm

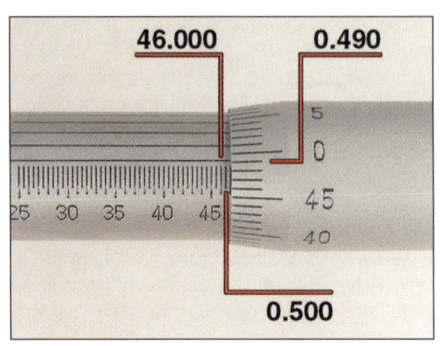

3.5 Micrometer reading of 46.99 mm on linear and annular scales . . .

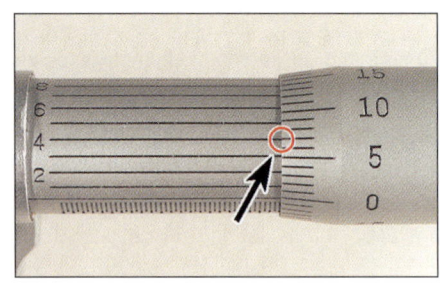

3.6 . . . and 0.004 mm on vernier scale

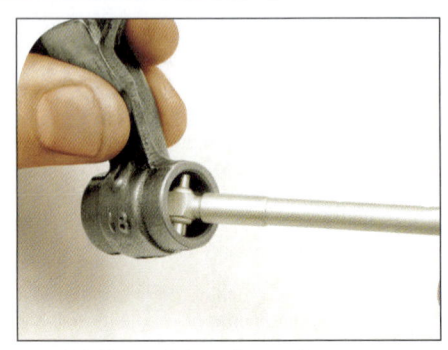

3.7 Expand the telescoping gauge in the bore, lock its position . . .

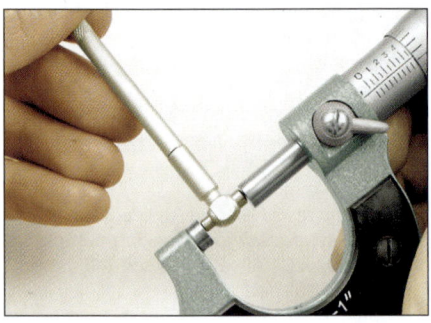

3.8 . . . then measure the gauge with a micrometer

3.9 Expand the small hole gauge in the bore, lock its position . . .

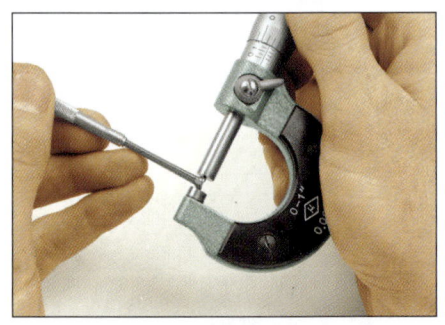

3.10 . . . then measure the gauge with a micrometer

Most micrometers have a locking lever (6) on the frame to hold the setting in place, allowing the item to be removed from the micrometer.
● Some micrometers have a vernier scale on their sleeve, providing an even finer measurement to be taken, in 0.001 increments of a millimeter. Take the sleeve and thimble measurement as described above, then check which graduation on the vernier scale aligns with that of the annular scale on the thimble **Note:** *The eye must be perpendicular to the scale when taking the vernier reading - if necessary rotate the body of the micrometer to ensure this.* Multiply the vernier scale figure by 0.001 and add it to the base and fine measurement figures.

In the example shown the item measures 46.994 mm **(see illustrations 3.5 and 3.6)**:

Linear scale (base)	46.000 mm
Linear scale (base)	00.500 mm
Annular scale (fine)	00.490 mm
Vernier scale	00.004 mm
Total figure	**46.994 mm**

Internal micrometer

● Internal micrometers are available for measuring bore diameters, but are expensive and unlikely to be available for home use. It is suggested that a set of telescoping gauges and small hole gauges, both of which must be used with an external micrometer, will suffice for taking internal measurements on a motorcycle.
● Telescoping gauges can be used to measure internal diameters of components. Select a gauge with the correct size range, make sure its ends are clean and insert it into the bore. Expand the gauge, then lock its position and withdraw it from the bore **(see illustration 3.7)**. Measure across the gauge ends with a micrometer **(see illustration 3.8)**.
● Very small diameter bores (such as valve guides) are measured with a small hole gauge. Once adjusted to a slip-fit inside the component, its position is locked and the gauge withdrawn for measurement with a micrometer **(see illustrations 3.9 and 3.10)**.

Vernier caliper

Note: *The conventional linear and dial gauge type instruments are described. Digital types are easier to read, but are far more expensive.*
● The vernier caliper does not provide the precision of a micrometer, but is versatile in being able to measure internal and external diameters. Some types also incorporate a depth gauge. It is ideal for measuring clutch plate friction material and spring free lengths.
● To use the conventional linear scale vernier, loosen off the vernier clamp screws (1) and set its jaws over (2), or inside (3), the item to be measured **(see illustration 3.11)**. Slide the jaw into contact, using the thumb-wheel (4) for fine movement of the sliding scale (5) then tighten the clamp screws (1). Read off the main scale (6) where the zero on the sliding scale (5) intersects it, taking the whole number to the left of the zero; this provides the base measurement. View along the sliding scale and select the division which lines up exactly with any of the divisions on the main scale, noting that the divisions usually represents 0.02 of a millimeter. Add this fine measurement to the base measurement to obtain the total reading.

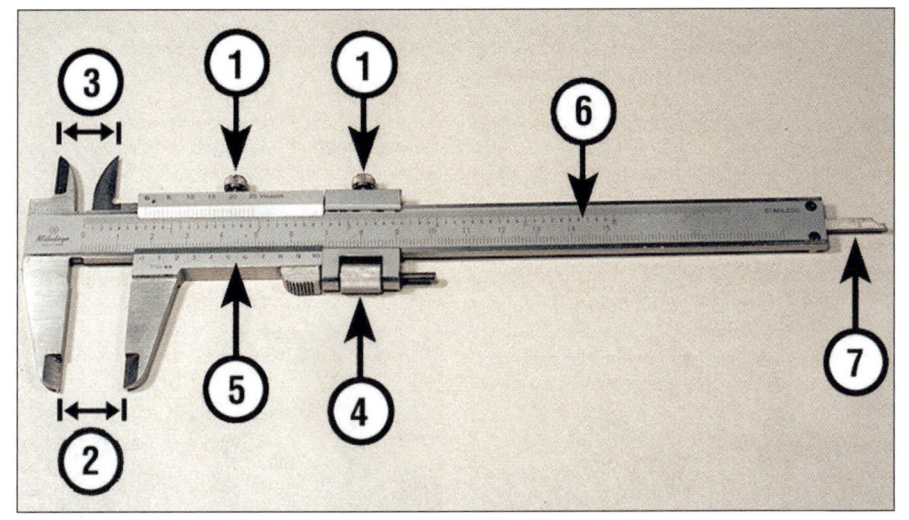

Tools and Workshop Tips REF•13

3.11 Vernier component parts (linear gauge)

1 Clamp screws
2 External jaws
3 Internal jaws
4 Thumbwheel
5 Sliding scale
6 Main scale
7 Depth gauge

In the example shown the item measures 55.92 mm **(see illustration 3.12)**:

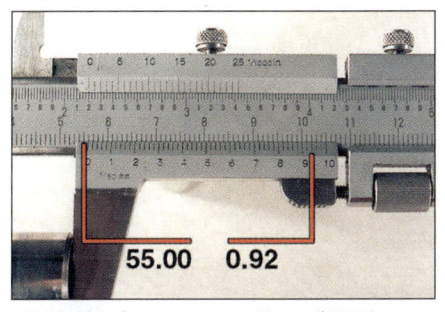

Base measurement	55.00 mm
Fine measurement	00.92 mm
Total figure	**55.92 mm**

● Some vernier calipers are equipped with a dial gauge for fine measurement. Before use, check that the jaws are clean, then close them fully and check that the dial gauge reads zero. If necessary adjust the gauge ring accordingly. Slacken the vernier clamp screw (1) and set its jaws over (2), or inside (3), the item to be measured **(see illustration 3.13)**. Slide the jaws into contact, using the thumbwheel (4) for fine movement. Read off the main scale (5) where the edge of the sliding scale (6) intersects it, taking the whole number to the left of the zero; this provides the base measurement. Read off the needle position on the dial gauge (7) scale to provide the fine measurement; each division represents 0.05 of a millimeter. Add this fine measurement to the base measurement to obtain the total reading.

In the example shown the item measures 55.95 mm **(see illustration 3.14)**:

Base measurement	55.00 mm
Fine measurement	00.95 mm
Total figure	**55.95 mm**

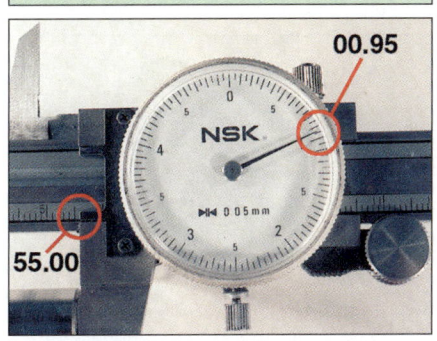

3.12 Vernier gauge reading of 55.92 mm

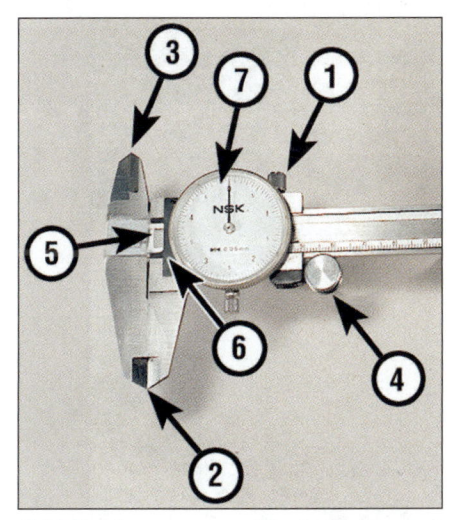

3.13 Vernier component parts (dial gauge)

1 Clamp screw
2 External jaws
3 Internal jaws
4 Thumbwheel
5 Main scale
6 Sliding scale
7 Dial gauge

3.14 Vernier gauge reading of 55.95 mm

Plastigage

● Plastigage is a plastic material which can be compressed between two surfaces to measure the oil clearance between them. The width of the compressed Plastigage is measured against a calibrated scale to determine the clearance.

● Common uses of Plastigage are for measuring the clearance between crankshaft journal and main bearing inserts, between crankshaft journal and big-end bearing inserts, and between camshaft and bearing surfaces. The following example describes big-end oil clearance measurement.

● Handle the Plastigage material carefully to prevent distortion. Using a sharp knife, cut a length which corresponds with the width of the bearing being measured and place it carefully across the journal so that it is parallel with the shaft **(see illustration 3.15)**. Carefully install both bearing shells and the connecting rod. Without rotating the rod on the journal tighten its bolts or nuts (as applicable) to the specified torque. The connecting rod and bearings are then disassembled and the crushed Plastigage examined.

3.15 Plastigage placed across shaft journal

● Using the scale provided in the Plastigage kit, measure the width of the material to determine the oil clearance **(see illustration 3.16)**. Always remove all traces of Plastigage after use using your fingernails.

Caution: Arriving at the correct clearance demands that the assembly is torqued correctly, according to the settings and sequence (where applicable) provided by the motorcycle manufacturer.

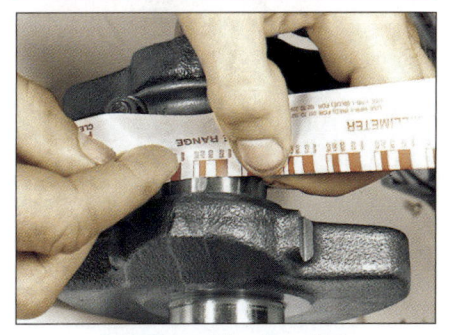

3.16 Measuring the width of the crushed Plastigage

REF•14 Tools and Workshop Tips

Dial gauge or DTI (Dial Test Indicator)

● A dial gauge can be used to accurately measure small amounts of movement. Typical uses are measuring shaft runout or shaft endfloat (sideplay) and setting piston position for ignition timing on two-strokes. A dial gauge set usually comes with a range of different probes and adapters and mounting equipment.

● The gauge needle must point to zero when at rest. Rotate the ring around its periphery to zero the gauge.

● Check that the gauge is capable of reading the extent of movement in the work. Most gauges have a small dial set in the face which records whole millimeters of movement as well as the fine scale around the face periphery which is calibrated in 0.01 mm divisions. Read off the small dial first to obtain the base measurement, then add the measurement from the fine scale to obtain the total reading.

Base measurement	1.00 mm
Fine measurement	0.48 mm
Total figure	**1.48 mm**

3.17 Dial gauge reading of 1.48 mm

In the example shown the gauge reads 1.48 mm **(see illustration 3.17)**:

● If measuring shaft runout, the shaft must be supported in vee-blocks and the gauge mounted on a stand perpendicular to the shaft. Rest the tip of the gauge against the center of the shaft and rotate the shaft slowly while watching the gauge reading **(see illustration 3.18)**. Take several measurements along the length of the shaft and record the maximum gauge reading as the amount of runout in the shaft. **Note:** *The reading obtained will be total runout at that point - some manufacturers specify that the runout figure is halved to compare with their specified runout limit.*

● Endfloat (sideplay) measurement requires that the gauge is mounted securely to the surrounding component with its probe touching the end of the shaft. Using hand pressure, push and pull on the shaft noting the maximum endfloat recorded on the gauge **(see illustration 3.19)**.

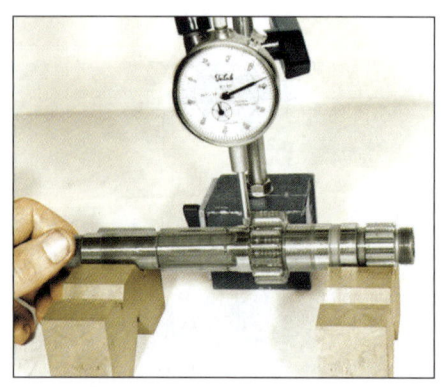

3.18 Using a dial gauge to measure shaft runout

3.19 Using a dial gauge to measure shaft endfloat

● A dial gauge with suitable adapters can be used to determine piston position BTDC on two-stroke engines for the purposes of ignition timing. The gauge, adapter and suitable length probe are installed in the place of the spark plug and the gauge zeroed at TDC. If the piston position is specified as 1.14 mm BTDC, rotate the engine back to 2.00 mm BTDC, then slowly forwards to 1.14 mm BTDC.

Cylinder compression gauges

● A compression gauge is used for measuring cylinder compression. Either the rubber-cone type or the threaded adapter type can be used. The latter is preferred to ensure a perfect seal against the cylinder head. A 0 to 300 psi (0 to 20 Bar) type gauge (for gasoline engines) will be suitable for motorcycles.

● The spark plug is removed and the gauge either held hard against the cylinder head (cone type) or the gauge adapter screwed into the cylinder head (threaded type) **(see illustration 3.20)**. Cylinder compression is measured with the engine turning over, but not running - carry out the compression test as described in *Troubleshooting Equipment*. The gauge will hold the reading until manually released.

3.20 Using a rubber-cone type cylinder compression gauge

Oil pressure gauge

● An oil pressure gauge is used for measuring engine oil pressure. Most gauges come with a set of adapters to fit the thread of the take-off point **(see illustration 3.21)**. If the take-off point specified by the motorcycle manufacturer is an external oil pipe union, make sure that the specified replacement union is used to prevent oil starvation.

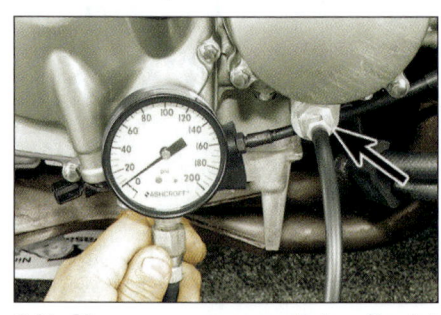

3.21 Oil pressure gauge and take-off point adapter (arrow)

● Oil pressure is measured with the engine running (at a specific rpm) and often the manufacturer will specify pressure limits for a cold and hot engine.

Straight-edge and surface plate

● If checking the gasket face of a component for warpage, place a steel rule or precision straight-edge across the gasket face and measure any gap between the straight-edge and component with feeler gauges **(see illustration 3.22)**. Check diagonally across the component and between mounting holes **(see illustration 3.23)**.

3.22 Use a straight-edge and feeler gauges to check for warpage

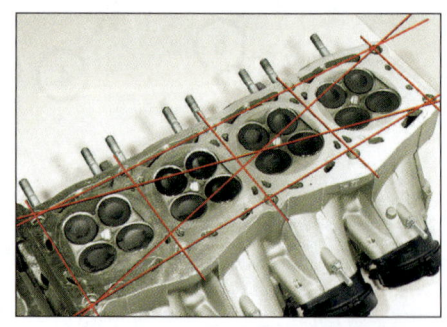

3.23 Check for warpage in these directions

Tools and Workshop Tips

- Checking individual components for warpage, such as clutch plain (metal) plates, requires a perfectly flat plate or piece of plate glass and feeler gauges.

4 Torque and leverage

What is torque?

- Torque describes the twisting force around a shaft. The amount of torque applied is determined by the distance from the center of the shaft to the end of the lever and the amount of force being applied to the end of the lever; distance multiplied by force equals torque.
- The manufacturer applies a measured torque to a bolt or nut to ensure that it will not loosen in use and to hold two components securely together without movement in the joint. The actual torque setting depends on the thread size, bolt or nut material and the composition of the components being held.
- Too little torque may cause the fastener to loosen due to vibration, whereas too much torque will distort the joint faces of the component or cause the fastener to shear off. Always stick to the specified torque setting.

Using a torque wrench

- Check the calibration of the torque wrench and make sure it has a suitable range for the job. Torque wrenches are available in Nm (Newton-meters), kgf m (kilograms-force meter), lbf ft (pounds-feet), lbf in (inch-pounds). Do not confuse lbf ft with lbf in.
- Adjust the tool to the desired torque on the scale (see illustration 4.1). If your torque wrench is not calibrated in the units specified, carefully convert the figure (see *Conversion Factors*). A manufacturer sometimes gives a torque setting as a range (8 to 10 Nm) rather than a single figure - in this case set the tool midway between the two settings. The same torque may be expressed as 9 Nm ± 1 Nm. Some torque wrenches have a method of locking the setting so that it isn't inadvertently altered during use.

- Install the bolts/nuts in their correct location and secure them lightly. Their threads must be clean and free of any old locking compound. Unless specified the threads and flange should be dry - oiled threads are necessary in certain circumstances and the manufacturer will take this into account in the specified torque figure. Similarly, the manufacturer may also specify the application of thread-locking compound.
- Tighten the fasteners in the specified sequence until the torque wrench clicks, indicating that the torque setting has been reached. Apply the torque again to double-check the setting. Where different thread diameter fasteners secure the component, as a rule tighten the larger diameter ones first.
- When the torque wrench has been finished with, release the lock (where applicable) and fully back off its setting to zero - do not leave the torque wrench tensioned. Also, do not use a torque wrench for loosening a fastener.

Angle-tightening

- Manufacturers often specify a figure in degrees for final tightening of a fastener. This usually follows tightening to a specific torque setting.
- A degree disc can be set and attached to the socket (see illustration 4.2) or a protractor can be used to mark the angle of movement on the bolt/nut head and the surrounding casting (see illustration 4.3).

4.2 Angle tightening can be accomplished with a torque-angle gauge . . .

4.3 . . . or by marking the angle on the surrounding component

4.1 Set the torque wrench index mark to the setting required, in this case 12 Nm

Loosening sequences

- Where more than one bolt/nut secures a component, loosen each fastener evenly a little at a time. In this way, not all the stress of the joint is held by one fastener and the components are not likely to distort.
- If a tightening sequence is provided, work in the REVERSE of this, but if not, work from the outside in, in a criss-cross sequence (see illustration 4.4).

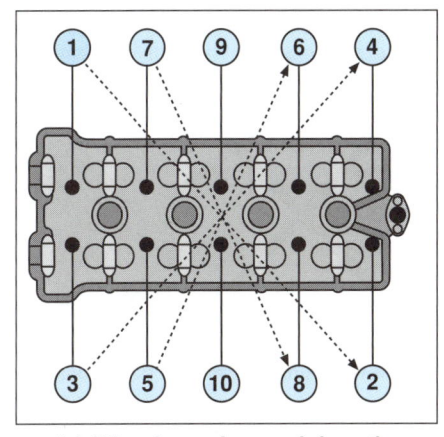

4.4 When loosening, work from the outside inwards

Tightening sequences

- If a component is held by more than one fastener it is important that the retaining bolts/nuts are tightened evenly to prevent uneven stress build-up and distortion of sealing faces. This is especially important on high-compression joints such as the cylinder head.
- A sequence is usually provided by the manufacturer, either in a diagram or actually marked in the casting. If not, always start in the center and work outwards in a criss-cross pattern (see illustration 4.5). Start off by securing all bolts/nuts finger-tight, then set the torque wrench and tighten each fastener by a small amount in sequence until the final torque is reached. By following this practice,

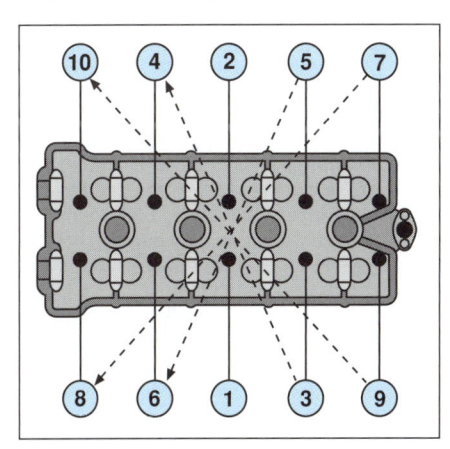

4.5 When tightening, work from the inside outwards

Tools and Workshop Tips

the joint will be held evenly and will not be distorted. Important joints, such as the cylinder head and big-end fasteners often have two- or three-stage torque settings.

Applying leverage

● Use tools at the correct angle. Position a socket or wrench on the bolt/nut so that you pull it towards you when loosening. If this can't be done, push the wrench without curling your fingers around it **(see illustration 4.6)** - the wrench may slip or the fastener loosen suddenly, resulting in your fingers being crushed against a component.

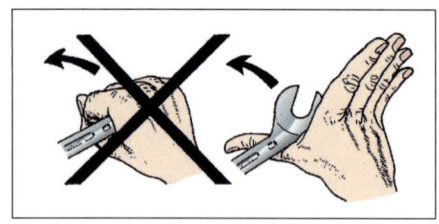

4.6 If you can't pull on the wrench to loosen a fastener, push with your hand open

● Additional leverage is gained by extending the length of the lever. The best way to do this is to use a breaker bar instead of the regular length tool, or to slip a length of tubing over the end of the wrench or socket.
● If additional leverage will not work, the fastener head is either damaged or firmly corroded in place (see *Fasteners*).

5 Bearings

Bearing removal and installation

Drivers and sockets

● Before removing a bearing, always inspect the casing to see which way it must be driven out - some casings will have retaining plates or a cast step. Also check for any identifying markings on the bearing and, if installed to a certain depth, measure this at this stage. Some roller bearings are sealed on one side - take note of the original installed position.
● Bearings can be driven out of a casing using a bearing driver tool (with the correct size head) or a socket of the correct diameter. Select the driver head or socket so that it contacts the outer race of the bearing, not the balls/rollers or inner race. Always support the casing around the bearing housing with wood blocks, otherwise there is a risk of fracture. The bearing is driven out with a few blows on the driver or socket from a heavy mallet. Unless access is severely restricted (as with wheel bearings), a pin-punch is not recommended unless it is moved around the bearing to keep it square in its housing.

● The same equipment can be used to install bearings. Make sure the bearing housing is supported on wood blocks and line up the bearing in its housing. Install the bearing as noted on removal - generally they are installed with their marked side facing outwards. Tap the bearing squarely into its housing using a driver or socket which bears only on the bearing's outer race - contact with the bearing balls/rollers or inner race will destroy it **(see illustrations 5.1 and 5.2)**.
● Check that the bearing inner race and balls/rollers rotate freely.

5.1 Using a bearing driver against the bearing's outer race

5.2 Using a large socket against the bearing's outer race

Pullers and slide-hammers

● Where a bearing is pressed on a shaft a puller will be required to extract it **(see illustration 5.3)**. Make sure that the puller clamp or legs fit securely behind the bearing and are unlikely to slip out. If pulling a bearing

5.3 This bearing puller clamps behind the bearing and pressure is applied to the shaft end to draw the bearing off

off a gear shaft for example, you may have to locate the puller behind a gear pinion if there is no access to the race and draw the gear pinion off the shaft as well **(see illustration 5.4)**.

Caution: Ensure that the puller's center bolt locates securely against the end of the shaft and will not slip when pressure is applied. Also ensure that puller does not damage the shaft end.

5.4 Where no access is available to the rear of the bearing, it is sometimes possible to draw off the adjacent component

● Operate the puller so that its center bolt exerts pressure on the shaft end and draws the bearing off the shaft.
● When installing the bearing on the shaft, tap only on the bearing's inner race - contact with the balls/rollers or outer race will destroy the bearing. Use a socket or length of tubing as a drift which fits over the shaft end **(see illustration 5.5)**.

5.5 When installing a bearing on a shaft use a piece of tubing which bears only on the bearing's inner race

● Where a bearing locates in a blind hole in a casing, it cannot be driven or pulled out as described above. A slide-hammer with knife-edged bearing puller attachment will be required. The puller attachment passes through the bearing and when tightened expands to fit firmly behind the bearing **(see illustration 5.6)**. By operating the slide-hammer part of the tool the bearing is jarred out of its housing **(see illustration 5.7)**.
● It is possible, if the bearing is of reasonable weight, for it to drop out of its housing if the casing is heated as described opposite. If

Tools and Workshop Tips REF•17

5.6 Expand the bearing puller so that it locks behind the bearing . . .

5.7 . . . attach the slide hammer to the bearing puller

this method is attempted, first prepare a work surface which will enable the casing to be tapped face down to help dislodge the bearing - a wood surface is ideal since it will not damage the casing's gasket surface. Wearing protective gloves, tap the heated casing several times against the work surface to dislodge the bearing under its own weight **(see illustration 5.8)**.

5.8 Tapping a casing face down on wood blocks can often dislodge a bearing

● Bearings can be installed in blind holes using the driver or socket method described above.

Drawbolts

● Where a bearing or bushing is set in the eye of a component, such as a suspension linkage arm or connecting rod small-end, removal by drift may damage the component. Furthermore, a rubber bushing in a shock absorber eye cannot successfully be driven out of position. If access is available to a hydraulic press, the task is straightforward. If not, a drawbolt can be fabricated to extract the bearing or bushing.

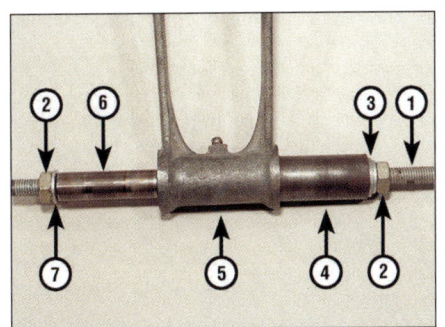

5.9 Drawbolt component parts assembled on a suspension arm

1 Bolt or length of threaded bar
2 Nuts
3 Washer (external diameter greater than tubing internal diameter)
4 Tubing (internal diameter sufficient to accommodate bearing)
5 Suspension arm with bearing
6 Tubing (external diameter slightly smaller than bearing)
7 Washer (external diameter slightly smaller than bearing)

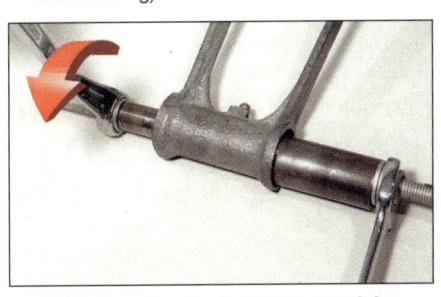

5.10 Drawing the bearing out of the suspension arm

● To extract the bearing/bushing you will need a long bolt with nut (or piece of threaded bar with two nuts), a piece of tubing which has an internal diameter larger than the bearing/bushing, another piece of tubing which has an external diameter slightly smaller than the bearing/bushing, and a selection of washers **(see illustrations 5.9 and 5.10)**. Note that the pieces of tubing must be of the same length, or longer, than the bearing/bushing.

● The same kit (without the pieces of tubing) can be used to draw the new bearing/bushing back into place **(see illustration 5.11)**.

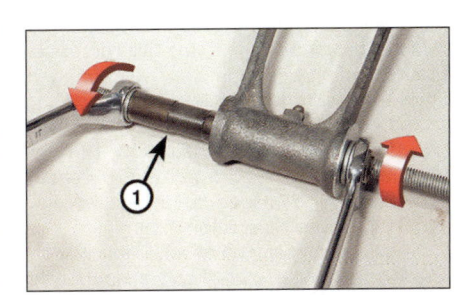

5.11 Installing a new bearing (1) in the suspension arm

Temperature change

● If the bearing's outer race is a tight fit in the casing, the aluminum casing can be heated to release its grip on the bearing. Aluminum will expand at a greater rate than the steel bearing outer race. There are several ways to do this, but avoid any localized extreme heat (such as a blow torch) - aluminum alloy has a low melting point.

● Approved methods of heating a casing are using a domestic oven (heated to 100°C/200°F) or immersing the casing in boiling water **(see illustration 5.12)**. Low temperature range localized heat sources such as a paint stripper heat gun or clothes iron can also be used **(see illustration 5.13)**. Alternatively, soak a rag in boiling water, wring it out and wrap it around the bearing housing.

> ⚠ **Warning: All of these methods require care in use to prevent scalding and burns to the hands. Wear protective gloves when handling hot components.**

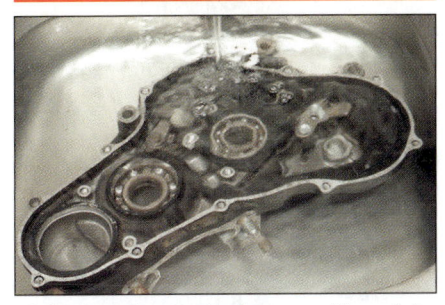

5.12 A casing can be immersed in a sink of boiling water to aid bearing removal

5.13 Using a localized heat source to aid bearing removal

● If heating the whole casing note that plastic components, such as the neutral switch, may suffer - remove them beforehand.

● After heating, remove the bearing as described above. You may find that the expansion is sufficient for the bearing to fall out of the casing under its own weight or with a light tap on the driver or socket.

● If necessary, the casing can be heated to aid bearing installation, and this is sometimes the recommended procedure if the motorcycle manufacturer has designed the housing and bearing fit with this intention.

REF•18 Tools and Workshop Tips

• Installation of bearings can be eased by placing them in a freezer the night before installation. The steel bearing will contract slightly, allowing easy insertion in its housing. This is often useful when installing steering head outer races in the frame.

Bearing types and markings

• Plain shell bearings, ball bearings, needle roller bearings and tapered roller bearings will all be found on motorcycles **(see illustrations 5.14 and 5.15)**. The ball and roller types are usually caged between an inner and outer race, but uncaged variations may be found.

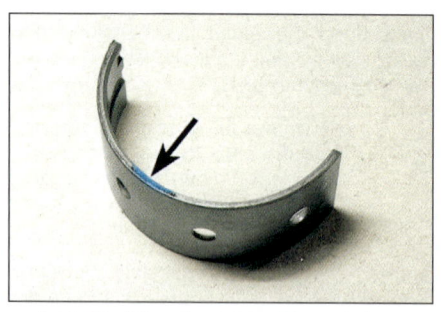

5.14 Shell bearings are either plain or grooved. They are usually identified by color code (arrow)

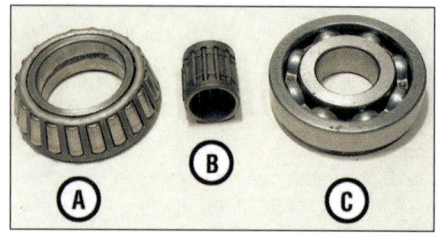

5.15 Tapered roller bearing (A), needle roller bearing (B) and ball journal bearing (C)

• Shell bearings (often called inserts) are usually found at the crankshaft main and connecting rod big-end where they are good at coping with high loads. They are made of a phosphor-bronze material and are impregnated with self-lubricating properties.

• Ball bearings and needle roller bearings consist of a steel inner and outer race with the balls or rollers between the races. They require constant lubrication by oil or grease and are good at coping with axial loads. Taper roller bearings consist of rollers set in a tapered cage set on the inner race; the outer race is separate. They are good at coping with axial loads and prevent movement along the shaft - a typical application is in the steering head.

• Bearing manufacturers produce bearings to ISO size standards and stamp one face of the bearing to indicate its internal and external diameter, load capacity and type **(see illustration 5.16)**.

• Metal bushings are usually of phosphor-bronze material. Rubber bushings are used in suspension mounting eyes. Fiber bushings have also been used in suspension pivots.

5.16 Typical bearing marking

Bearing troubleshooting

• If a bearing outer race has spun in its housing, the housing material will be damaged. You can use a bearing locking compound to bond the outer race in place if damage is not too severe.

• Shell bearings will fail due to damage of their working surface, as a result of lack of lubrication, corrosion or abrasive particles in the oil **(see illustration 5.17)**. Small particles of dirt in the oil may embed in the bearing material whereas larger particles will score the bearing and shaft journal. If a number of short journeys are made, insufficient heat will be generated to drive off condensation which has built up on the bearings.

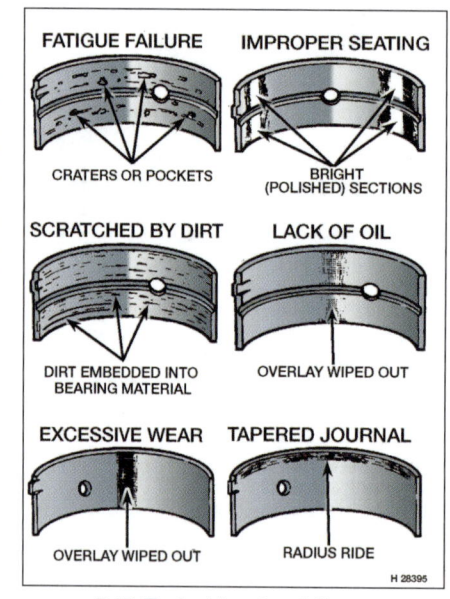

5.17 Typical bearing failures

• Ball and roller bearings will fail due to lack of lubrication or damage to the balls or rollers. Tapered-roller bearings can be damaged by overloading them. Unless the bearing is sealed on both sides, wash it in kerosene to remove all old grease then allow it to dry. Make a visual inspection looking to dented balls or rollers, damaged cages and worn or pitted races **(see illustration 5.18)**.

• A ball bearing can be checked for wear by listening to it when spun. Apply a film of light oil to the bearing and hold it close to the ear - hold the outer race with one hand and spin the inner race with the other hand **(see illustration 5.19)**. The bearing should be almost silent when spun; if it grates or rattles it is worn.

5.18 Example of ball journal bearing with damaged balls and cages

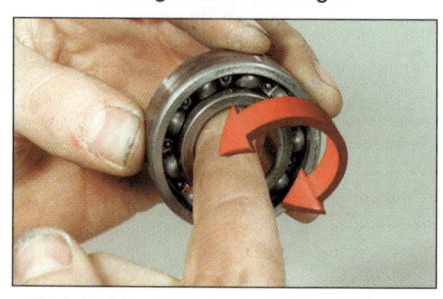

5.19 Hold outer race and listen to inner race when spun

6 Oil seals

Oil seal removal and installation

• Oil seals should be replaced every time a component is dismantled. This is because the seal lips will become set to the sealing surface and will not necessarily reseal.

• Oil seals can be pried out of position using a large flat-bladed screwdriver **(see illustration 6.1)**. In the case of crankcase seals, check first that the seal is not lipped on the inside, preventing its removal with the crankcases joined.

6.1 Pry out oil seals with a large flat-bladed screwdriver

• New seals are usually installed with their marked face (containing the seal reference code) outwards and the spring side towards the fluid being retained. In certain cases, such as a two-stroke engine crankshaft seal, a double lipped seal may be used due to there being fluid or gas on each side of the joint.

Tools and Workshop Tips   REF•19

• Use a bearing driver or socket which bears only on the outer hard edge of the seal to install it in the casing - tapping on the inner edge will damage the sealing lip.

Oil seal types and markings

• Oil seals are usually of the single-lipped type. Double-lipped seals are found where a liquid or gas is on both sides of the joint.

• Oil seals can harden and lose their sealing ability if the motorcycle has been in storage for a long period - replacement is the only solution.

• Oil seal manufacturers also conform to the ISO markings for seal size - these are molded into the outer face of the seal **(see illustration 6.2)**.

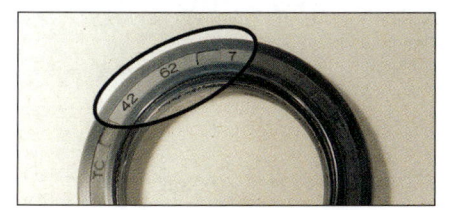

6.2 These oil seal markings indicate inside diameter, outside diameter and seal thickness

7 Gaskets and sealants

Types of gasket and sealant

• Gaskets are used to seal the mating surfaces between components and keep lubricants, fluids, vacuum or pressure contained within the assembly. Aluminum gaskets are sometimes found at the cylinder joints, but most gaskets are paper-based. If the mating surfaces of the components being joined are undamaged the gasket can be installed dry, although a dab of sealant or grease will be useful to hold it in place during assembly.

• RTV (Room Temperature Vulcanizing) silicone rubber sealants cure when exposed to moisture in the atmosphere. These sealants are good at filling pits or irregular gasket faces, but will tend to be forced out of the joint under very high torque. They can be used to replace a paper gasket, but first make sure that the width of the paper gasket is not essential to the shimming of internal components. RTV sealants should not be used on components containing gasoline.

• Non-hardening, semi-hardening and hard setting liquid gasket compounds can be used with a gasket or between a metal-to-metal joint. Select the sealant to suit the application: universal non-hardening sealant can be used on virtually all joints; semi-hardening on joint faces which are rough or damaged; hard setting sealant on joints which require a permanent bond and are subjected to high temperature and pressure. **Note:** *Check first if the paper gasket has a bead of sealant impregnated in its surface before applying additional sealant.*

• When choosing a sealant, make sure it is suitable for the application, particularly if being applied in a high-temperature area or in the vicinity of fuel. Certain manufacturers produce sealants in either clear, silver or black colors to match the finish of the engine. This has a particular application on motorcycles where much of the engine is exposed.

• Do not over-apply sealant. That which is squeezed out on the outside of the joint can be wiped off, whereas an excess of sealant on the inside can break off and clog oilways.

Breaking a sealed joint

• Age, heat, pressure and the use of hard setting sealant can cause two components to stick together so tightly that they are difficult to separate using finger pressure alone. Do not resort to using levers unless there is a pry point provided for this purpose **(see illustration 7.1)** or else the gasket surfaces will be damaged.

• Use a soft-faced hammer **(see illustration 7.2)** or a wood block and conventional hammer to strike the component near the mating surface. Avoid hammering against cast extremities since they may break off. If this method fails, try using a wood wedge between the two components.

Caution: If the joint will not separate, double-check that you have removed all the fasteners.

7.1 If a pry point is provided, apply gentle pressure with a flat-bladed screwdriver

7.2 Tap around the joint with a soft-faced mallet if necessary - don't strike cooling fins

Removal of old gasket and sealant

• Paper gaskets will most likely come away complete, leaving only a few traces stuck

HAYNES HiNT

Most components have one or two hollow locating dowels between the two gasket faces. If a dowel cannot be removed, do not resort to gripping it with pliers - it will almost certainly be distorted. Install a close-fitting socket or Phillips screwdriver into the dowel and then grip the outer edge of the dowel to free it.

on the sealing faces of the components. It is imperative that all traces are removed to ensure correct sealing of the new gasket.

• Very carefully scrape all traces of gasket away making sure that the sealing surfaces are not gouged or scored by the scraper **(see illustrations 7.3, 7.4 and 7.5)**. Stubborn deposits can be removed by spraying with an aerosol gasket remover. Final preparation of

7.3 Paper gaskets can be scraped off with a gasket scraper tool . . .

7.4 . . . a knife blade . . .

7.5 . . . or a household scraper

REF•20 Tools and Workshop Tips

7.6 Fine abrasive paper is wrapped around a flat file to clean up the gasket face

7.7 A kitchen scourer can be used on stubborn deposits

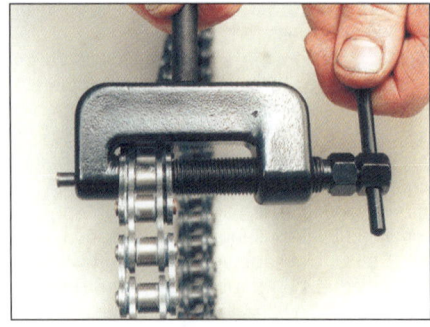

8.1 Tighten the chain breaker to push the pin out of the link . . .

8.2 . . . withdraw the pin, remove the tool . . .

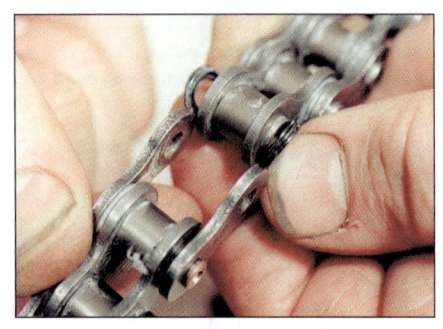

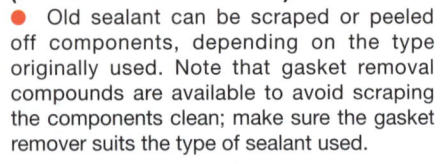

8.3 . . . and separate the chain link

8.4 Insert the new soft link, with O-rings, through the chain ends . . .

8.5 . . . install the O-rings over the pin ends . . .

8.6 . . . followed by the sideplate

8.7 Push the sideplate into position using a clamp

the gasket surface can be made with very fine abrasive paper or a plastic kitchen scourer **(see illustrations 7.6 and 7.7)**.
● Old sealant can be scraped or peeled off components, depending on the type originally used. Note that gasket removal compounds are available to avoid scraping the components clean; make sure the gasket remover suits the type of sealant used.

8 Chains

Breaking and joining final drive chains

● Drive chains for all but small bikes are continuous and do not have a clip-type connecting link. The chain must be broken using a chain breaker tool and the new chain securely riveted together using a new soft rivet-type link. Never use a clip-type connecting link instead of a rivet-type link, except in an emergency. Various chain breaking and riveting tools are available, either as separate tools or combined as illustrated in the accompanying photographs - read the instructions supplied with the tool carefully.

> **Warning: The need to rivet the new link pins correctly cannot be overstressed - loss of control of the motorcycle is very likely to result if the chain breaks in use.**

● Rotate the chain and look for the soft link. The soft link pins look like they have been deeply center-punched instead of peened over like all the other pins **(see illustration 8.9)** and its sideplate may be a different color. Position the soft link midway between the sprockets and assemble the chain breaker tool over one of the soft link pins **(see illustration 8.1)**. Operate the tool to push the pin out through the chain **(see illustration 8.2)**. On an O-ring chain, remove the O-rings **(see illustration 8.3)**. Carry out the same procedure on the other soft link pin.

> **Caution: Certain soft link pins (particularly on the larger chains) may require their ends to be filed or ground off before they can be pressed out using the tool.**

● Check that you have the correct size and strength (standard or heavy duty) new soft link - do not reuse the old link. Look for the size marking on the chain sideplates **(see illustration 8.10)**.
● Position the chain ends so that they are engaged over the rear sprocket. On an O-ring chain, install a new O-ring over each pin of the link and insert the link through the two chain ends **(see illustration 8.4)**. Install a new O-ring over the end of each pin, followed by the sideplate (with the chain manufacturer's marking facing outwards) **(see illustrations 8.5 and 8.6)**. On an unsealed chain, insert the link through the two chain ends, then install the sideplate with the chain manufacturer's marking facing outwards.
● Note that it may not be possible to install the sideplate using finger pressure alone. If using a joining tool, assemble it so that the plates of the tool clamp the link and press the sideplate over the pins **(see illustration 8.7)**. Otherwise, use two small sockets placed over

Tools and Workshop Tips REF•21

8.8 Assemble the chain riveting tool over one pin at a time and tighten it fully

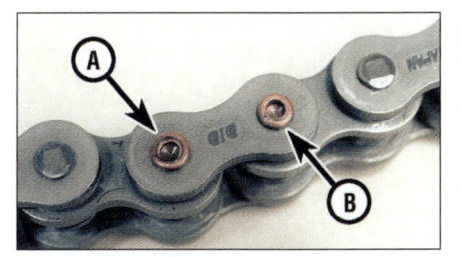

8.9 Pin end correctly riveted (A), pin end unriveted (B)

the rivet ends and two pieces of the wood between a C-clamp. Operate the clamp to press the sideplate over the pins.
● Assemble the joining tool over one pin (following the manufacturer's instructions) and tighten the tool down to spread the pin end securely **(see illustrations 8.8 and 8.9)**. Do the same on the other pin.

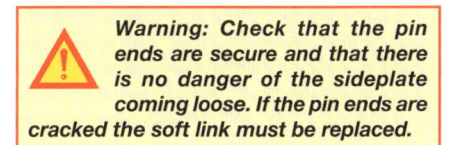

> ⚠ **Warning: Check that the pin ends are secure and that there is no danger of the sideplate coming loose. If the pin ends are cracked the soft link must be replaced.**

Final drive chain sizing
● Chains are sized using a three digit number, followed by a suffix to denote the chain type **(see illustration 8.10)**. Chain type is either standard or heavy duty (thicker sideplates), and also unsealed or O-ring/X-ring type.
● The first digit of the number relates to the pitch of the chain, ie the distance from the center of one pin to the center of the next pin **(see illustration 8.11)**. Pitch is expressed in eighths of an inch, as follows:

8.10 Typical chain size and type marking

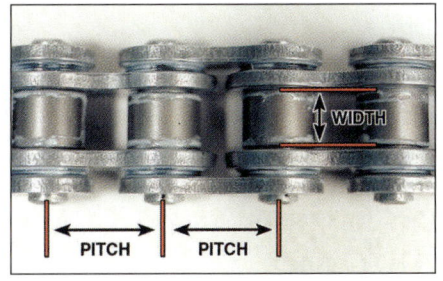

8.11 Chain dimensions

> Sizes commencing with a 4 (for example 428) have a pitch of 1/2 inch (12.7 mm)
> Sizes commencing with a 5 (for example 520) have a pitch of 5/8 inch (15.9 mm)
> Sizes commencing with a 6 (for example 630) have a pitch of 3/4 inch (19.1 mm)

● The second and third digits of the chain size relate to the width of the rollers, for example the 525 shown has 5/16 inch (7.94 mm) rollers **(see illustration 8.11)**.

9 Hoses

Clamping to prevent flow
● Small-bore flexible hoses can be clamped to prevent fluid flow while a component is worked on. Whichever method is used, ensure that the hose material is not permanently distorted or damaged by the clamp.
a) A brake hose clamp available from auto parts stores **(see illustration 9.1)**.
b) A wingnut type hose clamp **(see illustration 9.2)**.
c) Two sockets placed on each side of the hose and held with straight-jawed self-locking pliers **(see illustration 9.3)**.
d) Thick card stock on each side of the hose held between straight-jawed self-locking pliers **(see illustration 9.4)**.

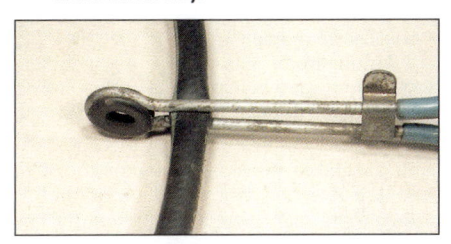

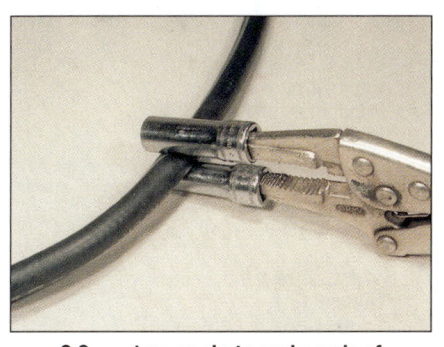

9.1 Hoses can be clamped with an automotive brake hose clamp . . .

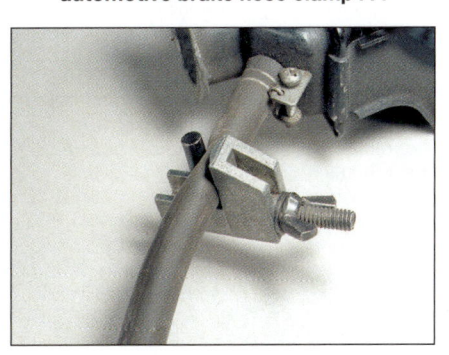

9.2 . . . a wingnut type hose clamp . . .

9.3 . . . two sockets and a pair of self-locking grips . . .

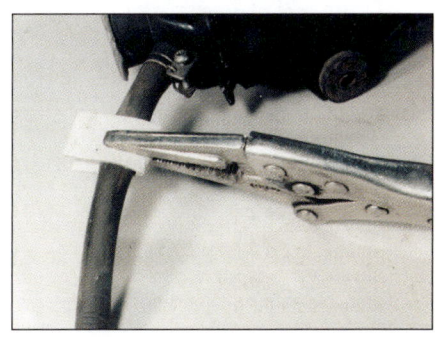

9.4 . . . or thick card and self-locking grips

Freeing and fitting hoses
● Always make sure the hose clamp is moved well clear of the hose end. Grip the hose with your hand and rotate it while pulling it off the union. If the hose has hardened due to age and will not move, slit it with a sharp knife and peel its ends off the union **(see illustration 9.5)**.
● Resist the temptation to use grease or soap on the unions to aid installation; although it helps the hose slip over the union it will equally aid the escape of fluid from the joint. It is preferable to soften the hose ends in hot water and wet the inside surface of the hose with water or a fluid which will evaporate.

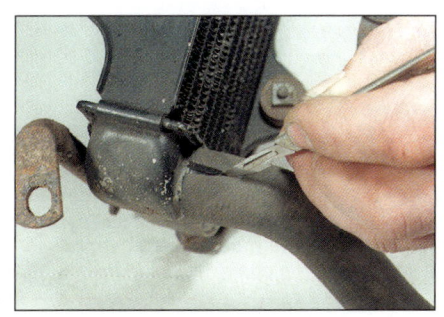

9.5 Cutting a coolant hose free with a sharp knife

Conversion Factors

Length (distance)
Inches (in)	X 25.4	= Millimeters (mm)	X 0.0394	= Inches (in)
Feet (ft)	X 0.305	= Meters (m)	X 3.281	= Feet (ft)
Miles	X 1.609	= Kilometers (km)	X 0.621	= Miles

Volume (capacity)
Cubic inches (cu in; in^3)	X 16.387	= Cubic centimeters (cc; cm^3)	X 0.061	= Cubic inches (cu in; in^3)
Imperial pints (Imp pt)	X 0.568	= Liters (l)	X 1.76	= Imperial pints (Imp pt)
Imperial quarts (Imp qt)	X 1.137	= Liters (l)	X 0.88	= Imperial quarts (Imp qt)
Imperial quarts (Imp qt)	X 1.201	= US quarts (US qt)	X 0.833	= Imperial quarts (Imp qt)
US quarts (US qt)	X 0.946	= Liters (l)	X 1.057	= US quarts (US qt)
Imperial gallons (Imp gal)	X 4.546	= Liters (l)	X 0.22	= Imperial gallons (Imp gal)
Imperial gallons (Imp gal)	X 1.201	= US gallons (US gal)	X 0.833	= Imperial gallons (Imp gal)
US gallons (US gal)	X 3.785	= Liters (l)	X 0.264	= US gallons (US gal)

Mass (weight)
Ounces (oz)	X 28.35	= Grams (g)	X 0.035	= Ounces (oz)
Pounds (lb)	X 0.454	= Kilograms (kg)	X 2.205	= Pounds (lb)

Force
Ounces-force (ozf; oz)	X 0.278	= Newtons (N)	X 3.6	= Ounces-force (ozf; oz)
Pounds-force (lbf; lb)	X 4.448	= Newtons (N)	X 0.225	= Pounds-force (lbf; lb)
Newtons (N)	X 0.1	= Kilograms-force (kgf; kg)	X 9.81	= Newtons (N)

Pressure
Pounds-force per square inch (psi; lbf/in^2; lb/in^2)	X 0.070	= Kilograms-force per square centimeter (kgf/cm^2; kg/cm^2)	X 14.223	= Pounds-force per square inch (psi; lbf/in^2; lb/in^2)
Pounds-force per square inch (psi; lbf/in^2; lb/in^2)	X 0.068	= Atmospheres (atm)	X 14.696	= Pounds-force per square inch (psi; lbf/in^2; lb/in^2)
Pounds-force per square inch (psi; lbf/in^2; lb/in^2)	X 0.069	= Bars	X 14.5	= Pounds-force per square inch (psi; lbf/in^2; lb/in^2)
Pounds-force per square inch (psi; lbf/in^2; lb/in^2)	X 6.895	= Kilopascals (kPa)	X 0.145	= Pounds-force per square inch (psi; lbf/in^2; lb/in^2)
Kilopascals (kPa)	X 0.01	= Kilograms-force per square centimeter (kgf/cm^2; kg/cm^2)	X 98.1	= Kilopascals (kPa)

Torque (moment of force)
Pounds-force inches (lbf in; lb in)	X 1.152	= Kilograms-force centimeter (kgf cm; kg cm)	X 0.868	= Pounds-force inches (lbf in; lb in)
Pounds-force inches (lbf in; lb in)	X 0.113	= Newton meters (Nm)	X 8.85	= Pounds-force inches (lbf in; lb in)
Pounds-force inches (lbf in; lb in)	X 0.083	= Pounds-force feet (lbf ft; lb ft)	X 12	= Pounds-force inches (lbf in; lb in)
Pounds-force feet (lbf ft; lb ft)	X 0.138	= Kilograms-force meters (kgf m; kg m)	X 7.233	= Pounds-force feet (lbf ft; lb ft)
Pounds-force feet (lbf ft; lb ft)	X 1.356	= Newton meters (Nm)	X 0.738	= Pounds-force feet (lbf ft; lb ft)
Newton meters (Nm)	X 0.102	= Kilograms-force meters (kgf m; kg m)	X 9.804	= Newton meters (Nm)

Vacuum
Inches mercury (in. Hg)	X 3.377	= Kilopascals (kPa)	X 0.2961	= Inches mercury
Inches mercury (in. Hg)	X 25.4	= Millimeters mercury (mm Hg)	X 0.0394	= Inches mercury

Power
Horsepower (hp)	X 745.7	= Watts (W)	X 0.0013	= Horsepower (hp)

Velocity (speed)
Miles per hour (miles/hr; mph)	X 1.609	= Kilometers per hour (km/hr; kph)	X 0.621	= Miles per hour (miles/hr; mph)

Fuel consumption*
Miles per gallon, Imperial (mpg)	X 0.354	= Kilometers per liter (km/l)	X 2.825	= Miles per gallon, Imperial (mpg)
Miles per gallon, US (mpg)	X 0.425	= Kilometers per liter (km/l)	X 2.352	= Miles per gallon, US (mpg)

Temperature
Degrees Fahrenheit = (°C x 1.8) + 32   Degrees Celsius (Degrees Centigrade; °C) = (°F - 32) x 0.56

It is common practice to convert from miles per gallon (mpg) to liters/100 kilometers (l/100km), where mpg (Imperial) x l/100 km = 282 and mpg (US) x l/100 km = 235

Motorcycle Chemicals and Lubricants

A number of chemicals and lubricants are available for use in motorcycle maintenance and repair. They include a wide variety of products ranging from cleaning solvents and degreasers to lubricants and protective sprays for rubber, plastic and vinyl.

- **Contact point/spark plug cleaner** is a solvent used to clean oily film and dirt from points, grim from electrical connectors and oil deposits from spark plugs. It is oil free and leaves no residue. It can also be used to remove gum and varnish from carburetor jets and other orifices.

- **Carburetor cleaner** is similar to contact point/spark plug cleaner but it usually has a stronger solvent and may leave a slight oily residue. It is not recommended for cleaning electrical components or connections.

- **Brake system cleaner** is used to remove brake dust, grease and brake fluid from the brake system, where clean surfaces are absolutely necessary. It leaves no residue and often eliminates brake squeal caused by contaminants.

- **Silicone-based lubricants** are used to protect rubber parts such as hoses and grommets, and are used as lubricants for hinges and locks.

- **Multi-purpose grease** is an all purpose lubricant used wherever grease is more practical than a liquid lubricant such as oil. Some multi-purpose grease is colored white and specially formulated to be more resistant to water than ordinary grease.

- **Gear oil** (sometimes called gear lube) is a specially designed oil used in transmissions and final drive units, as well as other areas where high friction, high temperature lubrication is required. It is available in a number of viscosities (weights) for various applications.

- **Motor oil** is the lubricant formulated for use in engines. It normally contains a wide variety of additives to prevent corrosion and reduce foaming and wear. Motor oil comes in various weights (viscosity ratings) from 0 to 50. The recommended weight of the oil depends on the season, temperature and the demands on the engine. Light oil is used in cold climates and under light load conditions. Heavy oil is used in hot climates and where high loads are encountered. Multi-viscosity oils are designed to have characteristics of both light and heavy oils and are available in a number of weights from 0W-20 to 20W-50.

- **Gasoline additives** perform several functions, depending on their chemical makeup. They usually contain solvents that help dissolve gum and varnish that build up on carburetor and inlet parts. They also serve to break down carbon deposits that form on the inside surfaces of the combustion chambers. Some additives contain upper cylinder lubricants for valves and piston rings.

- **Brake and clutch fluid** is a specially formulated hydraulic fluid that can withstand the heat and pressure encountered in break/clutch systems. Care must be taken that this fluid does not come in contact with painted surfaces or plastics. An opened container should always be resealed to prevent contamination by water or dirt.

- **Chain lubricants** are formulated especially for use on motorcycle final drive chains. A good chain lube should adhere well and have good penetrating qualities to be effective as a lubricant inside the chain and on the side plates, pins and rollers. Most chain lubes are either the foaming type or quick drying type and are usually marketed as sprays. Take care to use a lubricant marked as being suitable for O-ring chains.

- **Degreasers** are heavy duty solvents used to remove grease and grime that may accumulate on the engine and frame components. They can be sprayed or brushed on and, depending on the type, are rinsed with either water or solvent.

- **Solvents** are used alone or in combination with degreasers to clean parts and assemblies during repair and overhaul. The home mechanic should use only solvents that are non-flammable and that do not produce irritating fumes.

- **Gasket sealing compounds** may be used in conjunction with gaskets, to improve their sealing capabilities, or alone, to seal metal-to-metal joints. Many gasket sealers can withstand extreme heat, some are impervious to gasoline and lubricants, while others are capable of filling and sealing large cavities. Depending on the intended use, gasket sealers either dry hard or stay relatively soft and pliable. They are usually applied by hand, with a brush or are sprayed on the gasket sealing surfaces.

- **Thread locking compound** is an adhesive locking compound that prevents threaded fasteners from loosening because of vibration. It is available in a variety of types for different applications.

- **Moisture dispersants** are usually sprays that can be used to dry out electrical components such as the fuse block and wiring connectors. Some types an also be used as treatment for rubber and as a lubricant for hinges, cables and locks.

- **Waxes and polishes** are used to help protect painted and plated surfaces from the weather. Different types of pain may require the use of different types of wax polish. Some polishes utilize a chemical or abrasive cleaner to help remove the top layer of oxidized (dull) paint on older vehicles. In recent years, many non-wax polishes (that contain a wide variety of chemicals such as polymers and silicones) have been introduced. These non-wax polishes are usually easier to apply and last longer than conventional waxes and polishes.

REF•24 Storage

Preparing for storage

Before you start

If repairs or an overhaul is needed, see that this is carried out now rather than left until you want to ride the bike again.

Give the bike a good wash and scrub all dirt from its underside. Make sure the bike dries completely before preparing for storage.

Engine

● Remove the spark plug(s) and lubricate the cylinder bores with approximately a teaspoon of motor oil using a spout-type oil can **(see illustration 1)**. Reinstall the spark plug(s). Crank the engine over a couple of times to coat the piston rings and bores with oil. If the bike has a kickstart, use this to turn the engine over. If not, flick the kill switch to the OFF position and crank the engine over on the starter **(see illustration 2)**. If the nature of the ignition system prevents the starter operating with the kill switch in the OFF position, remove the spark plugs and fit them back in their caps; ensure that the plugs are grounded against the cylinder head when the starter is operated **(see illustration 3)**.

Warning: It is important that the plugs are grounded away from the spark plug holes otherwise there is a risk of atomized fuel from the cylinders igniting.

HAYNES HiNT *On a single cylinder four-stroke engine, you can seal the combustion chamber completely by positioning the piston at TDC on the compression stroke.*

● Drain the carburetor(s) otherwise there is a risk of jets becoming blocked by gum deposits from the fuel **(see illustration 4)**.

● If the bike is going into long-term storage, consider adding a fuel stabilizer to the fuel in the tank. If the tank is drained completely, corrosion of its internal surfaces may occur if left unprotected for a long period. The tank can be treated with a rust preventative especially for this purpose. Alternatively, remove the tank and pour half a liter of motor oil into it, install the filler cap and shake the tank to coat its internals with oil before draining off the excess. The same effect can also be achieved by spraying WD40 or a similar water-dispersant around the inside of the tank via its flexible nozzle.

● Make sure the cooling system contains the correct mix of antifreeze. Antifreeze also contains important corrosion inhibitors.

● The air intakes and exhaust can be sealed off by covering or plugging the openings. Ensure that you do not seal in any condensation; run the engine until it is hot, then switch off and allow to cool. Tape a

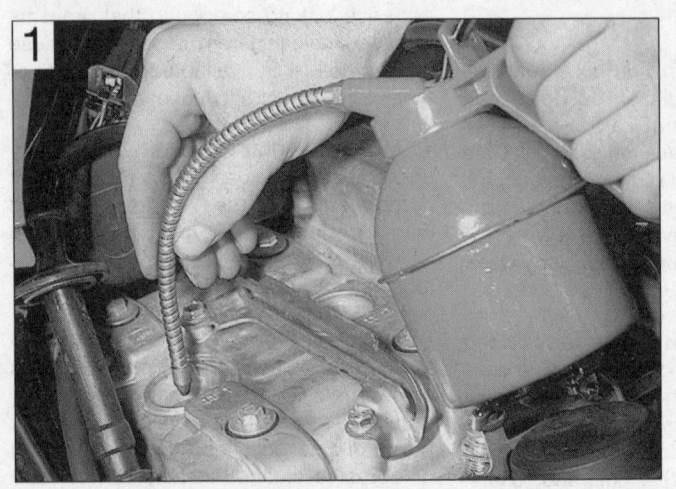

1 Squirt a drop of motor oil into each cylinder

2 Flick the kill switch to OFF . . .

3 . . . and ensure that the metal bodies of the plugs (arrows) are grounded against the cylinder head

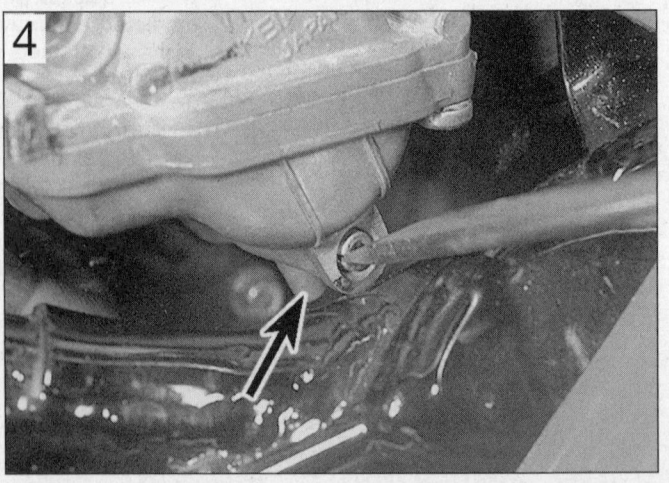

4 Connect a hose to the carburetor float chamber drain stub (arrow) and unscrew the drain screw

Storage REF•25

Exhausts can be sealed off with a plastic bag

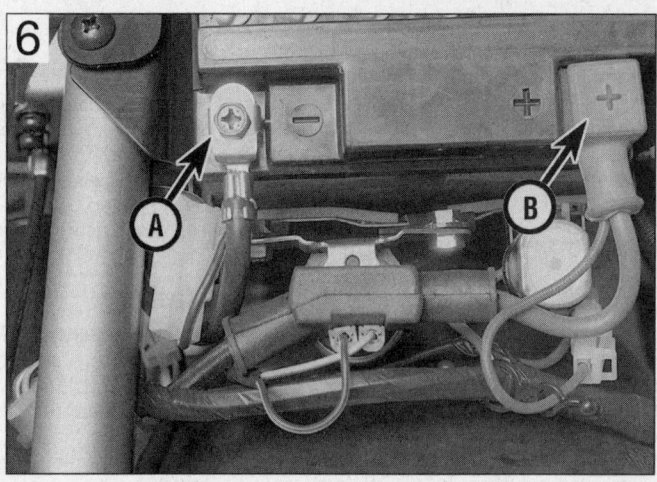

Disconnect the negative lead (A) first, followed by the positive lead (B)

piece of thick plastic over the silencer end(s) **(see illustration 5)**. Note that some advocate pouring a tablespoon of motor oil into the silencer(s) before sealing them off.

Battery

● Remove it from the bike - in extreme cases of cold the battery may freeze and crack its case **(see illustration 6)**.
● Check the electrolyte level and top up if necessary (conventional refillable batteries). Clean the terminals.
● Store the battery off the motorcycle and away from any sources of fire. Position a wooden block under the battery if it is to sit on the ground.
● Give the battery a trickle charge for a few hours every month **(see illustration 7)**.

Tires

● Place the bike on its centerstand or an auxiliary stand which will support the motorcycle in an upright position. Position wood blocks under the tires to keep them off the ground and to provide insulation from damp. If the bike is being put into long-term

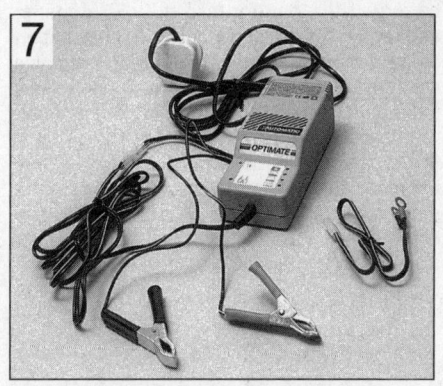

Use a suitable battery charger - this kit also assesses battery condition

storage, ideally both tires should be off the ground; not only will this protect the tires, but will also ensure that no load is placed on the steering head or wheel bearings.
● Deflate each tire by 5 to 10 psi, no more or the beads may unseat from the rim, making subsequent inflation difficult on tubeless tires.

Pivots and controls

● Lubricate all lever, pedal, stand and footrest pivot points. If grease nipples are fitted to the rear suspension components, apply lubricant to the pivots.
● Lubricate all control cables.

Cycle components

● Apply a wax protectant to all painted and plastic components. Wipe off any excess, but don't polish to a shine. Where fitted, clean the screen with soap and water.
● Coat metal parts with Vaseline (petroleum jelly). When applying this to the fork tubes, do not compress the forks otherwise the seals will rot from contact with the Vaseline.
● Apply a vinyl cleaner to the seat.

Storage conditions

● Aim to store the bike in a shed or garage which does not leak and is free from damp.
● Drape an old blanket or bedspread over the bike to protect it from dust and direct contact with sunlight (which will fade paint). Beware of tight-fitting plastic covers which may allow condensation to form and settle on the bike.

Getting back on the road

Engine and transmission

● Change the oil and replace the oil filter. If this was done prior to storage, check that the oil hasn't emulsified - a thick whitish substance which occurs through condensation.
● Remove the spark plugs. Using a spout-type oil can, squirt a few drops of oil into the cylinder(s). This will provide initial lubrication as the piston rings and bores comes back into contact. Service the spark plugs, or buy new ones, and install them in the engine.

● Check that the clutch isn't stuck on. The plates can stick together if left standing for some time, preventing clutch operation. Engage a gear and try rocking the bike back and forth with the clutch lever held against the handlebar. If this doesn't work on cable-operated clutches, hold the clutch lever back against the handlebar with a strong rubber band or cable tie for a couple of hours **(see illustration 8)**.
● If the air intakes or silencer end(s) were blocked off, remove the plug or cover used.
● If the fuel tank was coated with a rust

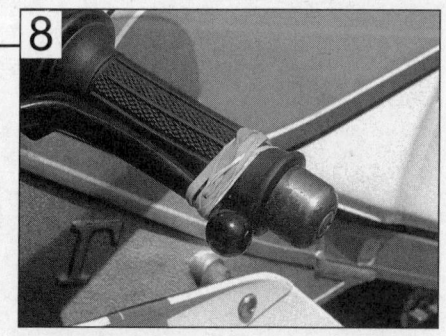

Hold the clutch lever back against the handlebar with rubber bands or a cable tie

REF•26 Storage

preventative, oil or a stabilizer added to the fuel, drain and flush the tank and dispose of the fuel sensibly. If no action was taken with the fuel tank prior to storage, it is advised that the old fuel is disposed of since it will go bad over a period of time. Refill the fuel tank with fresh fuel.

Frame and running gear

- Oil all pivot points and cables.
- Check the tire pressures. They will definitely need inflating if pressures were reduced for storage.
- Lubricate the final drive chain (where applicable).
- Remove any protective coating applied to the fork tubes (stanchions) since this may well destroy the fork seals. If the fork tubes weren't protected and have picked up rust spots, remove them with very fine abrasive paper and refinish with metal polish.
- Check that both brakes operate correctly. Apply each brake hard and check that it's not possible to move the motorcycle forwards, then check that the brake frees off again once released. Brake caliper pistons can stick due to corrosion around the piston head, or on the sliding caliper types, due to corrosion of the slider pins. If the brake doesn't free after repeated operation, take the caliper off for examination. Similarly drum brakes can stick due to a seized operating cam, cable or rod linkage.
- If the motorcycle has been in long-term storage, replace the brake fluid and clutch fluid (where applicable).
- Depending on where the bike has been stored, the wiring, cables and hoses may have been nibbled by rodents. Make a visual check and investigate disturbed wiring loom tape.

Battery

- If the battery has been previously removed and given top up charges it can simply be reconnected. Remember to connect the positive cable first and the negative cable last.
- On conventional refillable batteries, if the battery has not received any attention, remove it from the motorcycle and check its electrolyte level. Top up if necessary then charge the battery. If the battery fails to hold a charge and a visual check show heavy white sulfation of the plates, the battery is probably defective and must be replaced. This is particularly likely if the battery is old. Confirm battery condition with a specific gravity check.
- On sealed (MF) batteries, if the battery has not received any attention, remove it from the motorcycle and charge it according to the information on the battery case - if the battery fails to hold a charge it must be replaced.

Starting procedure

- If a kickstart is fitted, turn the engine over a couple of times with the ignition OFF to distribute oil around the engine. If no kickstart is fitted, flick the engine kill switch OFF and the ignition ON and crank the engine over a couple of times to work oil around the upper cylinder components. If the nature of the ignition system is such that the starter won't work with the kill switch OFF, remove the spark plugs, fit them back into their caps and ground their bodies on the cylinder head. Reinstall the spark plugs afterwards.
- Switch the kill switch to RUN, operate the choke and start the engine. If the engine won't start don't continue cranking the engine - not only will this flatten the battery, but the starter motor will overheat. Switch the ignition off and try again later. If the engine refuses to start, go through the troubleshooting procedures in this manual. **Note:** *If the bike has been in storage for a long time, old fuel or a carburetor blockage may be the problem. Gum deposits in carburetors can block jets - if a carburetor cleaner doesn't prove successful the carburetors must be dismantled for cleaning.*
- Once the engine has started, check that the lights, turn signals and horn work properly.
- Treat the bike gently for the first ride and check all fluid levels on completion. Settle the bike back into the maintenance schedule.

Troubleshooting REF•27

This Section provides an easy reference-guide to the more common faults that are likely to afflict your machine. Obviously, the opportunities are almost limitless for faults to occur as a result of obscure failures, and to try and cover all eventualities would require a book. Indeed, a number have been written on the subject.

Successful troubleshooting is not a mysterious 'black art' but the application of a bit of knowledge combined with a systematic and logical approach to the problem. Approach any troubleshooting by first accurately identifying the symptom and then checking through the list of possible causes, starting with the simplest or most obvious and progressing in stages to the most complex. Take nothing for granted, but above all apply liberal quantities of common sense.

The main symptom of a fault is given in the text as a major heading below which are listed the various systems or areas which may contain the fault. Details of each possible cause for a fault and the remedial action to be taken are given. Further information should be sought in the relevant Chapter.

1 Engine doesn't start or is difficult to start
- [ ] Starter motor doesn't rotate
- [ ] Starter motor rotates but engine does not turn over
- [ ] Starter works but engine won't turn over (seized)
- [ ] No fuel flow
- [ ] Engine flooded
- [ ] No spark or weak spark
- [ ] Compression low
- [ ] Stalls after starting
- [ ] Rough idle

2 Poor running at low speed
- [ ] Spark weak
- [ ] Fuel/air mixture incorrect
- [ ] Compression low
- [ ] Poor acceleration

3 Poor running or no power at high speed
- [ ] Firing incorrect
- [ ] Fuel/air mixture incorrect
- [ ] Compression low
- [ ] Knocking or pinging
- [ ] Miscellaneous causes

4 Overheating
- [ ] Engine overheats
- [ ] Firing incorrect
- [ ] Fuel/air mixture incorrect
- [ ] Compression too high
- [ ] Engine load excessive
- [ ] Lubrication inadequate
- [ ] Miscellaneous causes

5 Clutch problems
- [ ] Clutch slipping
- [ ] Clutch not disengaging completely

6 Gearchanging problems
- [ ] Doesn't go into gear, or lever doesn't return
- [ ] Jumps out of gear
- [ ] Overselects

7 Abnormal engine noise
- [ ] Knocking or pinging
- [ ] Piston slap or rattling
- [ ] Valve noise
- [ ] Other noise

8 Abnormal driveline noise
- [ ] Clutch noise
- [ ] Transmission noise
- [ ] Final drive noise

9 Abnormal frame and suspension noise
- [ ] Front end noise
- [ ] Shock absorber noise
- [ ] Brake noise

10 Oil pressure warning light comes on
- [ ] Engine lubrication system
- [ ] Electrical system

11 Excessive exhaust smoke
- [ ] White smoke
- [ ] Black smoke

12 Poor handling or stability
- [ ] Handlebar hard to turn
- [ ] Handlebar shakes or vibrates excessively
- [ ] Handlebar pulls to one side
- [ ] Poor shock absorbing qualities

13 Braking problems
- [ ] Brakes are spongy, don't hold
- [ ] Brake lever or pedal pulsates
- [ ] Brakes drag

14 Electrical problems
- [ ] Battery dead or weak
- [ ] Battery overcharged

REF•28 Troubleshooting

1 Engine doesn't start or is difficult to start

Starter motor doesn't rotate
- [ ] Engine kill switch OFF.
- [ ] Fuse blown. Check main fuse and starter circuit fuse (Chapter 9).
- [ ] Battery voltage low. Check and recharge battery (Chapter 9).
- [ ] Starter motor defective. Make sure the wiring to the starter is secure. Make sure the starter relay clicks when the start button is pushed. If the relay clicks, then the fault is in the wiring or motor.
- [ ] Starter relay faulty. Check it according to the procedure in Chap-ter 9.
- [ ] Starter switch not contacting. The contacts could be wet, corroded or dirty. Disassemble and clean the switch (Chapter 9).
- [ ] Wiring open or shorted. Check all wiring connections and harnesses to make sure that they are dry, tight and not corroded. Also check for broken or frayed wires that can cause a short to ground (see wiring diagram, Chapter 9).
- [ ] Ignition (main) switch defective. Check the switch according to the procedure in Chapter 9. Replace the switch with a new one if it is defective.
- [ ] Engine kill switch defective. Check for wet, dirty or corroded contacts. Clean or replace the switch as necessary (Chapter 9).
- [ ] Faulty neutral, side stand or clutch switch. Check the wiring to each switch and the switch itself according to the procedures in Chapter 9.

Starter motor rotates but engine does not turn over
- [ ] Starter motor clutch defective. Inspect and repair or replace (Chapter 2).
- [ ] Damaged idler or starter gears. Inspect and replace the damaged parts (Chapter 2).

Starter works but engine won't turn over (seized)
- [ ] Seized engine caused by one or more internally damaged components. Failure due to wear, abuse or lack of lubrication. Damage can include seized valves, followers/rocker arms, camshafts, pistons, crankshaft, connecting rod bearings, or transmission gears or bearings. Refer to Chapter 2 for engine disassembly.

No fuel flow
- [ ] No fuel in tank.
- [ ] Fuel tank breather hose obstructed.
- [ ] Fuel filter is blocked (see Chapter 1).

Engine flooded
- [ ] Starting technique incorrect. Under normal circumstances the machine should start with little or no throttle. When the engine is cold, the choke should be operated and the engine started without opening the throttle. When the engine is at operating temperature, only a very slight amount of throttle should be necessary.

No spark or weak spark
- [ ] Ignition switch OFF.
- [ ] Engine kill switch turned to the OFF position.
- [ ] Battery voltage low. Check and recharge the battery as necessary (Chapter 9).
- [ ] Spark plugs dirty, defective or worn out. Locate reason for fouled plugs using spark plug condition chart and follow the plug maintenance procedures (Chapter 1).
- [ ] Spark plug caps or secondary (HT) wiring faulty. Check condition. Replace either or both components if cracks or deterioration are evident (Chapter 5).
- [ ] Spark plug caps not making good contact. Make sure that the plug caps fit snugly over the plug ends.
- [ ] Ignition HT coils defective. Check the coils, referring to Chapter 5.
- [ ] IC igniter unit defective. Refer to Chapter 5 for details.
- [ ] Pick-up coil defective. Check the unit, referring to Chapter 5 for details.
- [ ] Ignition or kill switch shorted. This is usually caused by water, corrosion, damage or excessive wear. The switches can be disassembled and cleaned with electrical contact cleaner. If cleaning does not help, replace the switches (Chapter 9).
- [ ] Wiring shorted or broken between:

    a) Ignition (main) switch and engine kill switch (or blown fuse)
    b) IC igniter unit and engine kill switch
    c) IC igniter unit and ignition HT coils
    d) Ignition HT coils and spark plugs
    e) IC igniter unit and ignition pick-up coil.

- [ ] Make sure that all wiring connections are clean, dry and tight. Look for chafed and broken wires (Chapters 5 and 9).

Compression low
- [ ] Spark plugs loose. Remove the plugs and inspect their threads. Reinstall and tighten to the specified torque (Chapter 1).
- [ ] Cylinder head not sufficiently tightened down. If the cylinder head is suspected of being loose, then there's a chance that the gasket or head is damaged if the problem has persisted for any length of time. The head bolts should be tightened to the proper torque in the correct sequence (Chapter 2).
- [ ] Improper valve clearance. This means that the valve is not closing completely and compression pressure is leaking past the valve. Check and adjust the valve clearances (Chapter 1).
- [ ] Cylinder and/or piston worn. Excessive wear will cause compression pressure to leak past the rings. This is usually accompanied by worn rings as well. A top-end overhaul is necessary (Chapter 2).
- [ ] Piston rings worn, weak, broken, or sticking. Broken or sticking piston rings usually indicate a lubrication or fuelling problem that causes excess carbon deposits or seizures to form on the pistons and rings. Top-end overhaul is necessary (Chapter 2).
- [ ] Piston ring-to-groove clearance excessive. This is caused by excessive wear of the piston ring lands. Piston replacement is necessary (Chapter 2).
- [ ] Cylinder head gasket damaged. If a head is allowed to become loose, or if excessive carbon build-up on the piston crown and combustion chamber causes extremely high compression, the head gasket may leak. Retorquing the head is not always sufficient to restore the seal, so gasket replacement is necessary (Chapter 2).
- [ ] Cylinder head warped. This is caused by overheating or improperly tightened head bolts. Machine shop resurfacing or head replacement is necessary (Chapter 2).
- [ ] Valve spring broken or weak. Caused by component failure or wear; the springs must be replaced (Chapter 2).
- [ ] Valve not seating properly. This is caused by a bent valve (from over-revving or improper valve adjustment), burned valve or seat (improper fuelling) or an accumulation of carbon deposits on the seat (from fuelling or lubrication problems). The valves must be cleaned and/or replaced and the seats serviced if possible (Chapter 2).

Troubleshooting REF•29

1 Engine doesn't start or is difficult to start (continued)

Stalls after starting

- ☐ Improper choke action (carbureted models). Make sure the choke linkage shaft is getting a full stroke and staying in the out position (Chapter 4).
- ☐ Ignition malfunction. See Chapter 5.
- ☐ Carburetor or fuel injection malfunction. See Chapter 4.
- ☐ Fuel contaminated. The fuel can be contaminated with either dirt or water, or can change chemically if the machine is allowed to sit for several months or more. Drain the tank (Chapter 4).
- ☐ Intake air leak. Check for loose intake manifold retaining clips and damaged/disconnected vacuum hoses (Chapter 4).
- ☐ Engine idle speed incorrect. Turn idle adjusting screw until the engine idles at the specified rpm (Chapter 1).

Rough idle

- ☐ Ignition malfunction. See Chapter 5.
- ☐ Idle speed incorrect. See Chapter 1.
- ☐ Carburetors not synchronized (twin carburetor models). Adjust them with vacuum gauge or manometer set as described in Chapter 4.
- ☐ Carburetor or fuel injection malfunction. See Chapter 4.
- ☐ Fuel contaminated. The fuel can be contaminated with either dirt or water, or can change chemically if the machine is allowed to sit for several months or more. Drain the tank (Chapter 4).
- ☐ Intake air leak. Check for loose intake manifold retaining clips and damaged/disconnected vacuum hoses. Replace the intake ducts if they are split or deteriorated (Chapter 4).
- ☐ Air filter clogged. Replace the air filter element (Chapter 1).

2 Poor running at low speeds

Spark weak

- ☐ Battery voltage low. Check and recharge battery (Chapter 9).
- ☐ Spark plugs fouled, defective or worn out. Refer to Chapter 1 for spark plug maintenance.
- ☐ Spark plug cap or HT wiring defective. Refer to Chapters 1 and 5 for details on the ignition system.
- ☐ Spark plug caps not making contact.
- ☐ Incorrect spark plugs. Wrong type, heat range or cap configuration. Check and install correct plugs listed in Chapter 1.
- ☐ IC igniter unit or ECM faulty. See Chapter 5.
- ☐ Pick-up coil defective. See Chapter 5.
- ☐ Ignition coils defective. See Chapter 5.

Fuel/air mixture incorrect

- ☐ Pilot screws incorrectly set (Chapter 4)
- ☐ Pilot jet or air passage blocked. Remove and overhaul the carburetors (Chapter 4).
- ☐ Air filter clogged, poorly sealed or missing (Chapter 1).
- ☐ Air filter housing poorly sealed. Look for cracks, holes or loose clamps and replace or repair defective parts.
- ☐ Fuel tank breather hose obstructed.
- ☐ Intake air leak. Check for loose intake manifold retaining clips and damaged/disconnected vacuum hoses. Replace the intake ducts if they are split or deteriorated (Chapter 4).

Compression low

- ☐ Spark plugs loose. Remove the plugs and inspect their threads. Reinstall and tighten to the specified torque (Chapter 1).
- ☐ Cylinder head not sufficiently tightened down. If the cylinder head is suspected of being loose, then there's a chance that the gasket and head are damaged if the problem has persisted for any length of time. The head bolts should be tightened to the proper torque in the correct sequence (Chapter 2).
- ☐ Improper valve clearance. This means that the valve is not closing completely and compression pressure is leaking past the valve. Check and adjust the valve clearances (Chapter 1).
- ☐ Cylinder and/or piston worn. Excessive wear will cause compression pressure to leak past the rings. This is usually accompanied by worn rings as well. A top-end overhaul is necessary (Chapter 2).
- ☐ Piston rings worn, weak, broken, or sticking. Broken or sticking piston rings usually indicate a lubrication or fuelling problem that causes excess carbon deposits or seizures to form on the pistons and rings. Top-end overhaul is necessary (Chapter 2).
- ☐ Piston ring-to-groove clearance excessive. This is caused by excessive wear of the piston ring lands. Piston replacement is necessary (Chapter 2).
- ☐ Cylinder head gasket damaged. If a head is allowed to become loose, or if excessive carbon build-up on the piston crown and combustion chamber causes extremely high compression, the head gasket may leak. Retorquing the head is not always sufficient to restore the seal, so gasket replacement is necessary (Chapter 2).
- ☐ Cylinder head warped. This is caused by overheating or improperly tightened head bolts. Machine shop resurfacing or head replacement is necessary (Chapter 2).
- ☐ Valve spring broken or weak. Caused by component failure or wear; the springs must be replaced (Chapter 2).
- ☐ Valve not seating properly. This is caused by a bent valve (from over-revving or improper valve adjustment), burned valve or seat (improper fuelling) or an accumulation of carbon deposits on the seat (from fuelling, lubrication problems). The valves must be cleaned and/or replaced and the seats serviced if possible (Chapter 2).

Poor acceleration

- ☐ Fuel system fault. Remove and overhaul the carburetors or check the fuel injection system (Chapter 4).
- ☐ Engine oil viscosity too high. Using a heavier oil than that recommended in Chapter 1 can damage the oil pump or lubrication system and cause drag on the engine.
- ☐ Brakes dragging. Usually caused by debris which has entered the brake piston seals, or from a warped disc or drum or bent axle. Repair as necessary (Chapter 7).

3 Poor running or no power at high speed

Firing incorrect
- [ ] Air filter restricted. Clean or replace filter (Chapter 1).
- [ ] Spark plugs fouled, defective or worn out. See Chapter 1 for spark plug maintenance.
- [ ] Spark plug caps or HT wiring defective. See Chapters 1 and 5 for details of the ignition system.
- [ ] Spark plug caps not in good contact. See Chapter 5.
- [ ] Incorrect spark plugs. Wrong type, heat range or cap configuration. Check and install correct plugs listed in Chapter 1.
- [ ] IC igniter unit or ECM defective. See Chapter 5.
- [ ] Pick-up coil defective. See Chapter 5.
- [ ] Ignition coils defective. See Chapter 5.

Fuel/air mixture incorrect
- [ ] Fuel system fault. Remove and overhaul the carburetors or check the fuel injection system (Chapter 4).
- [ ] Air filter clogged, poorly sealed, or missing (Chapter 1).
- [ ] Air filter housing poorly sealed. Look for cracks, holes or loose clamps, and replace or repair defective parts.
- [ ] Fuel tank breather hose obstructed.
- [ ] Intake air leak. Check for loose intake manifold retaining clips and damaged/disconnected vacuum hoses. Replace the intake ducts if they are split or deteriorated (Chapter 4).

Compression low
- [ ] Spark plugs loose. Remove the plugs and inspect their threads. Reinstall and tighten to the specified torque (Chapter 1).
- [ ] Cylinder head not sufficiently tightened down. If the cylinder head is suspected of being loose, then there's a chance that the gasket and head are damaged if the problem has persisted for any length of time. The head bolts should be tightened to the proper torque in the correct sequence (Chapter 2).
- [ ] Improper valve clearance. This means that the valve is not closing completely and compression pressure is leaking past the valve. Check and adjust the valve clearances (Chapter 1).
- [ ] Cylinder and/or piston worn. Excessive wear will cause compression pressure to leak past the rings. This is usually accompanied by worn rings as well. A top-end overhaul is necessary (Chapter 2).
- [ ] Piston rings worn, weak, broken, or sticking. Broken or sticking piston rings usually indicate a lubrication or fueling problem that causes excess carbon deposits or seizures to form on the pistons and rings. Top-end overhaul is necessary (Chapter 2).
- [ ] Piston ring-to-groove clearance excessive. This is caused by excessive wear of the piston ring lands. Piston replacement is necessary (Chapter 2).
- [ ] Cylinder head gasket damaged. If a head is allowed to become loose, or if excessive carbon build-up on the piston crown and combustion chamber causes extremely high compression, the head gasket may leak. Retorquing the head is not always sufficient to restore the seal, so gasket replacement is necessary (Chapter 2).
- [ ] Cylinder head warped. This is caused by overheating or improperly tightened head bolts. Machine shop resurfacing or head replacement is necessary (Chapter 2).
- [ ] Valve spring broken or weak. Caused by component failure or wear; the springs must be replaced (Chapter 2).
- [ ] Valve not seating properly. This is caused by a bent valve (from over-revving or improper valve adjustment), burned valve or seat (improper fuelling) or an accumulation of carbon deposits on the seat (from fuelling or lubrication problems). The valves must be cleaned and/or replaced and the seats serviced if possible (Chapter 2).

Knocking or pinging
- [ ] Carbon build-up in combustion chamber. Use of a fuel additive that will dissolve the adhesive bonding the carbon particles to the crown and chamber is the easiest way to remove the build-up. Otherwise, the cylinder head will have to be removed and decarbonized (Chapter 2).
- [ ] Incorrect or poor quality fuel. Old or improper grades of fuel can cause detonation. This causes the piston to rattle, thus the knocking or pinging sound. Drain old fuel and always use the recommended fuel grade.
- [ ] Spark plug heat range incorrect. Uncontrolled detonation indicates the plug heat range is too hot. The plug in effect becomes a glow plug, raising cylinder temperatures. Install the proper heat range plug (Chapter 1).
- [ ] Improper air/fuel mixture. This will cause the cylinders to run hot, which leads to detonation. An intake air leak can cause this imbalance. See Chapter 4.

Miscellaneous causes
- [ ] Throttle valve doesn't open fully. Adjust the throttle grip freeplay (Chapter 1).
- [ ] Clutch slipping. May be caused by loose or worn clutch components. Refer to Chapter 2 for clutch overhaul procedures.
- [ ] Engine oil viscosity too high. Using a heavier oil than the one recommended in Chapter 1 can damage the oil pump or lubrication system and cause drag on the engine.
- [ ] Brakes dragging. Usually caused by debris which has entered the brake piston seals, or from a warped disc, out-of-round drum or bent axle. Repair as necessary.

Troubleshooting REF•31

4 Overheating

Engine overheats

- ☐ Coolant level low. Check and add coolant (Chapter 1).
- ☐ Leak in cooling system. Check cooling system hoses and radiator for leaks and other damage. Repair or replace parts as necessary (Chapter 3).
- ☐ Thermostat sticking open or closed. Check and replace as described in Chapter 3.
- ☐ Faulty pressure cap. Remove the cap and have it pressure tested (Chapter 3).
- ☐ Coolant passages clogged. Have the entire system drained and flushed, then refill with fresh coolant.
- ☐ Water pump defective. Remove the pump and check the components (Chapter 3).
- ☐ Clogged radiator fins. Clean them by blowing compressed air through the fins from the backside.
- ☐ Cooling fan or fan switch fault (Chapter 3).

Firing incorrect

- ☐ Spark plugs fouled, defective or worn out. See Chapter 1 for spark plug maintenance.
- ☐ Incorrect spark plugs.
- ☐ IC igniter unit or ECM defective. See Chapter 5.
- ☐ Pick-up coil faulty. See Chapter 5.
- ☐ Faulty ignition coils. See Chapter 5.

Fuel/air mixture incorrect

- ☐ Fuel system fault. Remove and overhaul the carburetors or check the fuel injection system (Chapter 4).
- ☐ Air filter clogged, poorly sealed, or missing (Chapter 1).
- ☐ Air filter housing poorly sealed. Look for cracks, holes or loose clamps, and replace or repair defective parts.
- ☐ Fuel tank breather hose obstructed.
- ☐ Intake air leak. Check for loose intake manifold retaining clips and damaged/disconnected vacuum hoses. Replace the intake manifold(s) if they are split or deteriorated (Chapter 4).

Compression too high

- ☐ Carbon build-up in combustion chamber. Use of a fuel additive that will dissolve the adhesive bonding the carbon particles to the piston crown and chamber is the easiest way to remove the build-up. Otherwise, the cylinder head will have to be removed and decarbonized (Chapter 2).
- ☐ Improperly machined head surface or installation of incorrect gasket during engine assembly.

Engine load excessive

- ☐ Clutch slipping. Can be caused by damaged, loose or worn clutch components. Refer to Chapter 2 for overhaul procedures.
- ☐ Engine oil level too high. The addition of too much oil will cause pressurization of the crankcase and inefficient engine operation. Check Specifications and drain to proper level (Chapter 1).
- ☐ Engine oil viscosity too high. Using a heavier oil than the one recommended in Chapter 1 can damage the oil pump or lubrication system as well as cause drag on the engine.
- ☐ Brakes dragging. Usually caused by debris which has entered the brake piston seals, or from a warped disc or drum or bent axle. Repair as necessary.

Lubrication inadequate

- ☐ Engine oil level too low. Friction caused by intermittent lack of lubrication or from oil that is overworked can cause overheating. The oil provides a definite cooling function in the engine. Check the oil level (Chapter 1).
- ☐ Poor quality engine oil or incorrect viscosity or type. Oil is rated not only according to viscosity but also according to type. Some oils are not rated high enough for use in this engine. Check the Specifications section and change to the correct oil (Chapter 1).

Miscellaneous causes

- ☐ Modification to exhaust system. Most aftermarket exhaust systems cause the engine to run leaner, which makes it run hotter.

5 Clutch problems

Clutch slipping

- ☐ Clutch cable freeplay incorrectly adjusted (cable clutch models) (Chapter 1).
- ☐ Friction plates worn or warped. Overhaul the clutch assembly (Chapter 2).
- ☐ Plain plates warped (Chapter 2).
- ☐ Clutch springs broken or weak. Old or heat-damaged (from slipping clutch) springs should be replaced with new ones (Chapter 2).
- ☐ Clutch pushrod bent. Check and, if necessary, replace (Chapter 2).
- ☐ Clutch center or housing unevenly worn. This causes improper engagement of the plates. Replace the damaged or worn parts (Chapter 2).
- ☐ Wrong type of oil used. Make sure oil with anti-friction additives (such as molybdenum disulfide) is NOT used in an engine/transmission with a wet clutch.

Clutch not disengaging completely

- ☐ Clutch cable freeplay incorrectly adjusted (Chapter 1).
- ☐ Air in clutch hydraulic system (hydraulic clutch models). Bleed the system (Chapter 2).
- ☐ Worn master or slave cylinder (hydraulic clutch models). Inspect and repair or replace as necessary (Chapter 2).
- ☐ Clutch plates warped or damaged. This will cause clutch drag, which in turn will cause the machine to creep. Overhaul the clutch assembly (Chapter 2).
- ☐ Clutch spring tension uneven. Usually caused by a sagged or broken spring. Check and replace the springs as a set (Chapter 2).
- ☐ Engine oil deteriorated. Old, thin, worn out oil will not provide proper lubrication for the plates, causing the clutch to drag. Replace the oil and filter (Chapter 1).
- ☐ Engine oil viscosity too high. Using a heavier oil than recommended in Chapter 1 can cause the plates to stick together, putting a drag on the engine. Change to the correct weight oil (Chapter 1).
- ☐ Clutch housing bearing seized. Lack of lubrication, severe wear or damage can cause the bearing to seize on the input shaft. Overhaul of the clutch, and perhaps transmission, may be necessary to repair the damage (Chapter 2).
- ☐ Loose clutch center nut. Causes housing and center misalignment putting a drag on the engine. Engagement adjustment continually varies. Overhaul the clutch assembly (Chapter 2).

6 Gearchanging problems

Doesn't go into gear or lever doesn't return
- [ ] Clutch not disengaging. See above.
- [ ] Shift fork(s) bent or seized. Often caused by dropping the machine or from lack of lubrication. Overhaul the transmission (Chapter 2).
- [ ] Gear(s) stuck on shaft. Most often caused by a lack of lubrication or excessive wear in transmission bearings and bushings. Overhaul the transmission (Chapter 2).
- [ ] Gear shift drum binding. Caused by lubrication failure or excessive wear. Replace the drum and bearing (Chapter 2).
- [ ] Gear shift lever pawl spring weak or broken (Chapter 2).
- [ ] Gear shift lever broken. Splines stripped out of lever or shaft, caused by allowing the lever to get loose or from dropping the machine. Replace necessary parts (Chapter 2).
- [ ] Gear shift mechanism stopper arm broken or worn. Full engagement and rotary movement of shift drum results. Replace the arm (Chapter 2).
- [ ] Stopper arm spring broken. Allows arm to float, causing sporadic shift operation. Replace spring (Chapter 2).

Jumps out of gear
- [ ] Shift fork(s) worn. Overhaul the transmission (Chapter 2).
- [ ] Gear groove(s) worn. Overhaul the transmission (Chapter 2).
- [ ] Gear dogs or dog slots worn or damaged. The gears should be inspected and replaced. No attempt should be made to service the worn parts.

Overselects
- [ ] Stopper arm spring weak or broken (Chapter 2).
- [ ] Return spring post broken or distorted (Chapter 2).

7 Abnormal engine noise

Knocking or pinging
- [ ] Carbon build-up in combustion chamber. Use of a fuel additive that will dissolve the adhesive bonding the carbon particles to the piston crown and chamber is the easiest way to remove the build-up. Otherwise, the cylinder head will have to be removed and decarbonized (Chapter 2).
- [ ] Incorrect or poor quality fuel. Old or improper fuel can cause detonation. This causes the pistons to rattle, thus the knocking or pinging sound. Drain the old fuel and always use the recommended grade fuel (Chapter 4).
- [ ] Spark plug heat range incorrect. Uncontrolled detonation indicates that the plug heat range is too hot. The plug in effect becomes a glow plug, raising cylinder temperatures. Install the proper heat range plug (Chapter 1).
- [ ] Improper air/fuel mixture. This will cause the cylinders to run hot and lead to detonation. Blocked carburetor jets or an air leak can cause this imbalance. See Chapter 4.

Piston slap or rattling
- [ ] Cylinder-to-piston clearance excessive. Caused by improper assembly. Inspect and overhaul top-end parts (Chapter 2).
- [ ] Connecting rod bent. Caused by over-revving, trying to start a badly flooded engine or from ingesting a foreign object into the combustion chamber. Replace the damaged parts (Chapter 2).
- [ ] Piston pin or piston pin bore worn or seized from wear or lack of lubrication. Replace damaged parts (Chapter 2).
- [ ] Piston ring(s) worn, broken or sticking. Overhaul the top-end (Chapter 2).
- [ ] Piston seizure damage. Usually from lack of lubrication or overheating. Replace the pistons and cylinders, as necessary (Chapter 2).
- [ ] Connecting rod bearing clearance excessive. Caused by excessive wear or lack of lubrication. Replace worn parts.

Valve noise
- [ ] Incorrect valve clearances. Adjust the clearances by referring to Chapter 1.
- [ ] Valve spring broken or weak. Check and replace weak valve springs (Chapter 2).
- [ ] Camshaft or cylinder head worn or damaged. Lack of lubrication at high rpm is usually the cause of damage. Insufficient oil or failure to change the oil at the recommended intervals are the chief causes. Since there are no replaceable bearings in the head, the head itself will have to be replaced if there is excessive wear or damage (Chapter 2).

Other noise
- [ ] Cylinder head gasket leaking.
- [ ] Exhaust pipe leaking at cylinder head connection. Caused by improper fit of pipe(s) or loose exhaust nuts. All exhaust fasteners should be tightened evenly and carefully. Failure to do this will lead to a leak.
- [ ] Crankshaft runout excessive. Caused by a bent crankshaft (from over-revving) or damage from an upper cylinder component failure. Can also be attributed to dropping the machine on either of the crankshaft ends.
- [ ] Engine mounting bolts loose. Tighten all engine mount bolts (Chapter 2).
- [ ] Crankshaft bearings worn (Chapter 2).
- [ ] Cam chain, tensioner or guides worn. Replace according to the procedure in Chapter 2.

Troubleshooting REF•33

8 Abnormal driveline noise

Clutch noise
- [ ] Clutch outer drum/friction plate clearance excessive (Chapter 2).
- [ ] Loose or damaged clutch pressure plate and/or bolts (Chapter 2).

Transmission noise
- [ ] Bearings worn. Also includes the possibility that the shafts are worn. Overhaul the transmission (Chapter 2).
- [ ] Gears worn or chipped (Chapter 2).
- [ ] Metal chips jammed in gear teeth. Probably pieces from a broken clutch, gear or shift mechanism that were picked up by the gears. This will cause early bearing failure (Chapter 2).
- [ ] Engine oil level too low. Causes a howl from transmission. Also affects engine power and clutch operation (Chapter 1).

Final drive noise
- [ ] Chain or drive belt not adjusted properly (Chapter 1).
- [ ] Front or rear sprocket loose. Tighten fasteners (Chapter 6).
- [ ] Sprockets worn. Replace sprockets (Chapter 6).
- [ ] Rear sprocket warped. Replace sprockets (Chapter 6).
- [ ] Differential worn or damaged. Have it repaired or replace it (Chapter 7).

9 Abnormal frame and suspension noise

Front end noise
- [ ] Low fluid level or improper viscosity oil in forks. This can sound like spurting and is usually accompanied by irregular fork action (Chapter 6).
- [ ] Spring weak or broken. Makes a clicking or scraping sound. Fork oil, when drained, will have a lot of metal particles in it (Chapter 6).
- [ ] Steering head bearings loose or damaged. Clicks when braking. Check and adjust or replace as necessary (Chapters 1 and 6).
- [ ] Triple clamps loose. Make sure all clamp bolts are tightened to the specified torque (Chapter 6).
- [ ] Fork tube bent. Good possibility if machine has been dropped. Replace tube with a new one (Chapter 6).
- [ ] Front axle bolt or axle pinch bolts loose. Tighten them to the specified torque (Chapter 7).
- [ ] Loose or worn wheel bearings. Check and replace as needed (Chapter 7).

Shock absorber noise
- [ ] Fluid level incorrect. Indicates a leak caused by defective seal. Shock will be covered with oil. Replace shock or seek advice on repair from a dealer (Chapter 6).
- [ ] Defective shock absorber with internal damage. This is in the body of the shock and can't be remedied. The shock must be replaced with a new one (Chapter 6).
- [ ] Bent or damaged shock body. Replace the shock with a new one (Chapter 6).
- [ ] Loose or worn suspension linkage components (EX250 models). Check and replace as necessary (Chapter 6).

Brake noise
- [ ] Squeal caused by dust on brake pads. Usually found in combination with glazed pads. Clean using brake cleaning solvent (Chapter 7).
- [ ] Contamination of brake pads. Oil, brake fluid or dirt causing brake to chatter or squeal. Clean or replace pads (Chapter 7).
- [ ] Pads glazed. Caused by excessive heat from prolonged use or from contamination. Do not use sandpaper/emery cloth or any other abrasive to roughen the pad surfaces as abrasives will stay in the pad material and damage the disc. A very fine flat file can be used, but pad replacement is suggested as a cure (Chapter 7).
- [ ] Disc warped. Can cause a chattering, clicking or intermittent squeal. Usually accompanied by a pulsating lever and uneven braking. Replace the disc (Chapter 7).
- [ ] Loose or worn wheel bearings. Check and replace as needed (Chapter 7).

10 Oil pressure warning light comes on

Engine lubrication system
- [ ] Engine oil pump defective, blocked oil strainer screen or failed relief valve. Carry out oil pressure check (Chapter 1).
- [ ] Engine oil level low. Inspect for leak or other problem causing low oil level and add recommended oil (Chapter 1).
- [ ] Engine oil viscosity too low. Very old, thin oil or an improper weight of oil used in the engine. Change to correct oil (Chapter 1).
- [ ] Camshaft or journals worn. Excessive wear causing drop in oil pressure. Replace cam and/or cylinder head. Abnormal wear could be caused by oil starvation at high rpm from low oil level or improper weight or type of oil (Chapter 1).
- [ ] Crankshaft and/or bearings worn. Same problems as above. Check and replace crankshaft and/or bearings (Chapter 2).

Electrical system
- [ ] Oil pressure switch defective. Check the switch according to the procedure in Chapter 9. Replace it if it is defective.
- [ ] Oil pressure indicator light circuit defective. Check for pinched, shorted, disconnected or damaged wiring (Chapter 9).

11 Excessive exhaust smoke

White smoke
- [ ] Piston oil ring worn. The ring may be broken or damaged, causing oil from the crankcase to be pulled past the piston into the combustion chamber. Replace the rings with new ones (Chapter 2).
- [ ] Cylinders worn, cracked, or scored. Caused by overheating or oil starvation. Install a new cylinder block (Chapter 2).
- [ ] Valve oil seal damaged or worn. Replace oil seals with new ones (Chapter 2).
- [ ] Valve guide worn. Perform a complete valve job (Chapter 2).
- [ ] Engine oil level too high, which causes the oil to be forced past the rings. Drain oil to the proper level (Chapter 1).
- [ ] Head gasket broken between oil return and cylinder. Causes oil to be pulled into the combustion chamber. Replace the head gasket and check the head for warpage (Chapter 2).
- [ ] Abnormal crankcase pressurization, which forces oil past the rings. Clogged breather is usually the cause.

Black smoke
- [ ] Air filter clogged. Clean or replace the element (Chapter 1).
- [ ] Carburetor flooding. Remove and overhaul the carburetor(s) (Chapter 4).
- [ ] Main jet too large. Remove and overhaul the carburetor(s) (Chapter 4).
- [ ] Choke cable stuck (Chapter 4).
- [ ] Fuel level too high. Check the fuel level (Chapter 4).
- [ ] Fuel injector problem (Chapter 4).

12 Poor handling or stability

Handlebar hard to turn
- [ ] Steering head bearing adjuster nut too tight. Check adjustment as described in Chapter 1.
- [ ] Bearings damaged. Roughness can be felt as the bars are turned from side-to-side. Replace bearings and races (Chapter 6).
- [ ] Races dented or worn. Denting results from wear in only one position (e.g., straight ahead), from a collision or hitting a pothole or from dropping the machine. Replace races and bearings (Chapter 6).
- [ ] Steering stem lubrication inadequate. Causes are grease getting hard from age or being washed out by high pressure car washes. Disassemble steering head and repack bearings (Chapter 6).
- [ ] Steering stem bent. Caused by a collision, hitting a pothole or by dropping the machine. Replace damaged part. Don't try to straighten the steering stem (Chapter 6).
- [ ] Front tire air pressure too low (Chapter 1).

Handlebar shakes or vibrates excessively
- [ ] Tires worn or out of balance (Chapter 7).
- [ ] Swingarm bearings worn. Replace worn bearings (Chapter 6).
- [ ] Wheel rim(s) warped or damaged. Inspect wheels for runout (Chapter 7).
- [ ] Spokes loose (see Chapter 1).
- [ ] Wheel bearings worn. Worn front or rear wheel bearings can cause poor tracking. Worn front bearings will cause wobble (Chapter 7).
- [ ] Handlebar clamp bolts loose (Chapter 6).
- [ ] Fork yoke bolts loose. Tighten them to the specified torque (Chapter 6).
- [ ] Engine mounting bolts loose. Will cause excessive vibration with increased engine rpm (Chapter 2).

Handlebar pulls to one side
- [ ] Frame bent. Definitely suspect this if the machine has been dropped. May or may not be accompanied by cracking near the bend. Replace the frame (Chapter 8).
- [ ] Wheels out of alignment. Caused by improper location of axle spacers or from bent steering stem or frame (Chapters 6 and 8).
- [ ] Swingarm bent or twisted. Caused by age (metal fatigue) or impact damage. Replace the arm (Chapter 6).
- [ ] Steering stem bent. Caused by impact damage or by dropping the motorcycle. Replace the steering stem (Chapter 6).
- [ ] Fork tube bent. Disassemble the forks and replace the damaged parts (Chapter 6).
- [ ] Fork oil level uneven. Check and add or drain as necessary (Chapter 1).

Poor shock absorbing qualities
Too hard:
    a) Fork oil level excessive (Chapter 1).
    b) Fork oil viscosity too high. Use a lighter oil (see the Specifications in Chapter 1).
    c) Fork tube bent. Causes a harsh, sticking feeling (Chapter 6).
    d) Shock shaft or body bent or damaged (Chapter 6).
    e) Fork internal damage (Chapter 6).
    f) Shock internal damage.
    g) Tire pressure too high (Chapter 1).
Too soft:
    a) Fork or shock oil insufficient and/or leaking (Chapter 1).
    b) Fork oil level too low (Chapter 6).
    c) Fork oil viscosity too light (Chapter 6).
    d) Fork springs weak or broken (Chapter 6).
    e) Shock internal damage or leakage (Chapter 6).

Troubleshooting REF•35

13 Braking problems

Brakes are spongy, don't hold
- [ ] Air in brake line. Caused by inattention to master cylinder fluid level or by leakage. Locate problem and bleed brakes (Chapter 7).
- [ ] Pad or disc worn (Chapters 1 and 7).
- [ ] Brake fluid leak. See paragraph 1.
- [ ] Contaminated pads. Caused by contamination with oil, grease, brake fluid, etc. Clean or replace pads. Clean disc thoroughly with brake cleaner (Chapter 7).
- [ ] Brake fluid deteriorated. Fluid is old or contaminated. Drain system, replenish with new fluid and bleed the system (Chapter 7).
- [ ] Master cylinder internal parts worn or damaged causing fluid to bypass (Chapter 7).
- [ ] Master cylinder bore scratched by foreign material or broken spring. Repair or replace master cylinder (Chapter 7).
- [ ] Disc warped. Replace disc (Chapter 7).

Brake lever or pedal pulsates
- [ ] Disc warped. Replace disc (Chapter 7).
- [ ] Axle bent. Replace axle (Chapter 7).
- [ ] Brake caliper bolts loose (Chapter 7).
- [ ] Wheel warped or otherwise damaged (Chapter 7).
- [ ] Wheel bearings damaged or worn (Chapter 7).
- [ ] Brake drum out of round. Replace brake drum.

Brakes drag
- [ ] Master cylinder piston seized. Caused by wear or damage to piston or cylinder bore (Chapter 7).
- [ ] Lever binding. Check pivot and lubricate (Chapter 7).
- [ ] Brake caliper piston seized in bore. Caused by wear or ingestion of dirt past deteriorated seal (Chapter 7).
- [ ] Brake caliper mounting bracket pins corroded. Clean off corrosion and lubricate (Chapter 7).
- [ ] Brake pad or shoe damaged. Material separated from backing plate. Usually caused by faulty manufacturing process or from contact with chemicals. Replace pads or shoes (Chapter 7).
- [ ] Pads improperly installed (Chapter 7).
- [ ] Drum brake springs weak. Replace springs

14 Electrical problems

Battery dead or weak
- [ ] Battery faulty. Caused by sulfated plates which are shorted through sedimentation. Also, broken battery terminal making only occasional contact (Chapter 9).
- [ ] Battery cables making poor contact (Chapter 9).
- [ ] Load excessive. Caused by addition of high wattage lights or other electrical accessories.
- [ ] Ignition (main) switch defective. Switch either grounds internally or fails to shut off system. Replace the switch (Chapter 9).
- [ ] Regulator/rectifier defective (Chapter 9).
- [ ] Alternator stator coil open or shorted (Chapter 9).
- [ ] Wiring faulty. Wiring grounded or connections loose in ignition, charging or lighting circuits (Chapter 9).

Battery overcharged
- [ ] Regulator/rectifier defective. Overcharging is noticed when battery gets excessively warm (Chapter 9).
- [ ] Battery defective. Replace battery with a new one (Chapter 9).
- [ ] Battery amperage too low, wrong type or size. Install manufacturer's specified amp-hour battery to handle charging load (Chapter 9).

REF•36 Troubleshooting Equipment

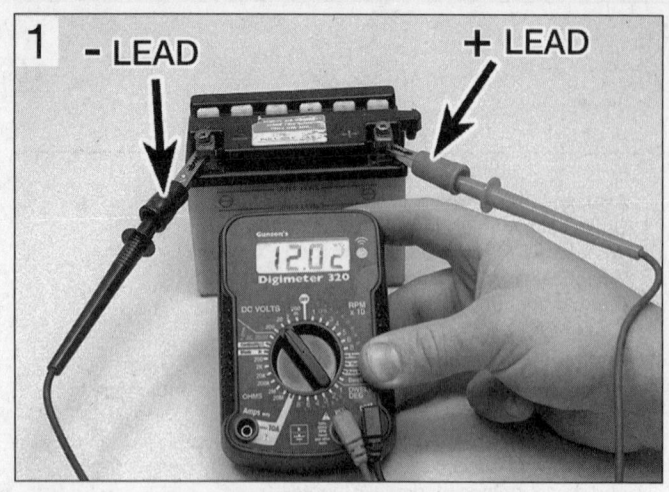

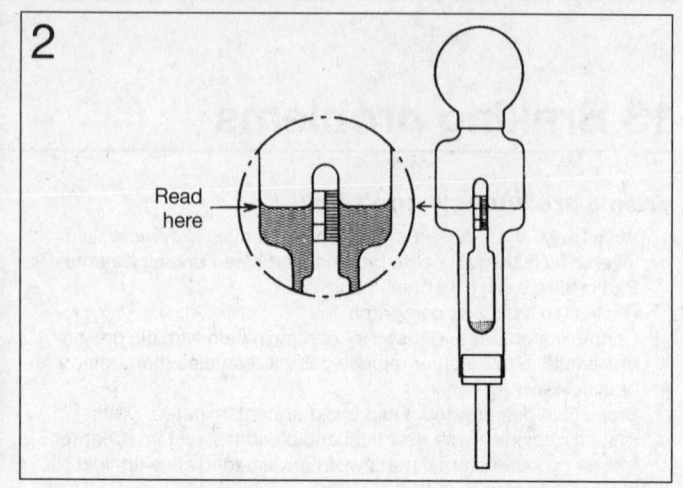

1 — LEAD   + LEAD

Measuring open-circuit battery voltage

2 Read here

Float-type hydrometer for measuring battery specific gravity

Checking engine compression

- Low compression will result in exhaust smoke, heavy oil consumption, poor starting and poor performance. A compression test will provide useful information about an engine's condition and if performed regularly, can give warning of trouble before any other symptoms become apparent.
- A compression gauge will be required, along with an adapter to suit the spark plug hole thread size. Note that the screw-in type gauge/adapter set up is preferable to the rubber cone type.
- Before carrying out the test, first check the valve clearances as described in Chapter 1.
- Compression testing procedures for the motorcycles covered in this manual are described in Chapter 2C.

Checking battery open-circuit voltage

> **Warning:** The gases produced by the battery are explosive - never smoke or create any sparks in the vicinity of the battery. Never allow the electrolyte to contact your skin or clothing - if it does, wash it off and seek immediate medical attention.

- Before any electrical fault is investigated the battery should be checked.
- You'll need a dc voltmeter or multimeter to check battery voltage. Check that the leads are inserted in the correct terminals on the meter, red lead to positive (+), black lead to negative (-). Incorrect connections can damage the meter.
- A sound, fully-charged 12 volt battery should produce between 12.3 and 12.6 volts across its terminals (12.8 volts for a maintenance-free battery). On machines with a 6 volt battery, voltage should be between 6.1 and 6.3 volts.

1 Set a multimeter to the 0 to 20 volts dc range and connect its probes across the battery terminals. Connect the meter's positive (+) probe, usually red, to the battery positive (+) terminal, followed by the meter's negative (-) probe, usually black, to the battery negative terminal (-) **(see illustration 1)**.

2 If battery voltage is low (below 10 volts on a 12 volt battery or below 4 volts on a six volt battery), charge the battery and test the voltage again. If the battery repeatedly goes flat, investigate the motorcycle's charging system.

Checking battery specific gravity (SG)

> **Warning:** The gases produced by the battery are explosive - never smoke or create any sparks in the vicinity of the battery. Never allow the electrolyte to contact your skin or clothing - if it does, wash it off and seek immediate medical attention.

- The specific gravity check gives an indication of a battery's state of charge.
- A hydrometer is used for measuring specific gravity. Make sure you purchase one which has a small enough hose to insert in the aperture of a motorcycle battery.
- Specific gravity is simply a measure of the electrolyte's density compared with that of water. Water has an SG of 1.000 and fully-charged battery electrolyte is about 26% heavier, at 1.260.
- Specific gravity checks are not possible on maintenance-free batteries. Testing the open-circuit voltage is the only means of determining their state of charge.

1 To measure SG, remove the battery from the motorcycle and remove the first cell cap. Draw some electrolyte into the hydrometer and note the reading **(see illustration 2)**. Return the electrolyte to the cell and install the cap.

2 The reading should be in the region of 1.260 to 1.280. If SG is below 1.200 the battery needs charging. Note that SG will vary with temperature; it should be measured at 20°C (68°F). Add 0.007 to the reading for every 10°C above 20°C, and subtract 0.007 from the reading for every 10°C below 20°C. Add 0.004 to the reading for every 10°F above 68°F, and subtract 0.004 from the reading for every 10°F below 68°F.

3 When the check is complete, rinse the hydrometer thoroughly with clean water.

Checking for continuity

- The term continuity describes the uninterrupted flow of electricity through an electrical circuit. A continuity check will determine whether an **open-circuit** situation exists.
- Continuity can be checked with an ohmmeter, multimeter, continuity tester or battery and bulb test circuit **(see illustrations 3, 4 and 5)**.
- All of these instruments are self-powered by a battery, therefore the checks are made with the ignition OFF.
- As a safety precaution, always disconnect the battery negative (-) lead before making checks, particularly if ignition switch checks are being made.
- If using a meter, select the appropriate

Troubleshooting Equipment REF•37

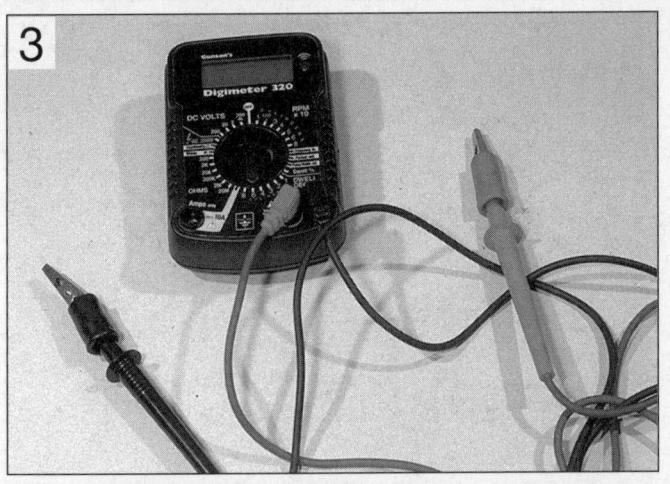

3 Digital multimeter can be used for all electrical tests

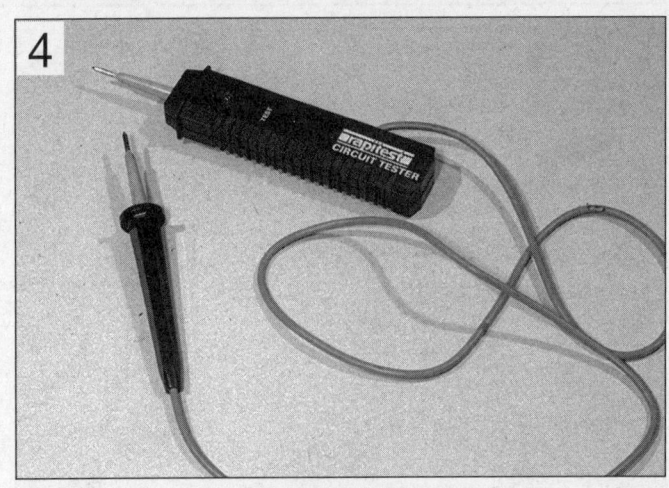

4 Battery-powered continuity tester

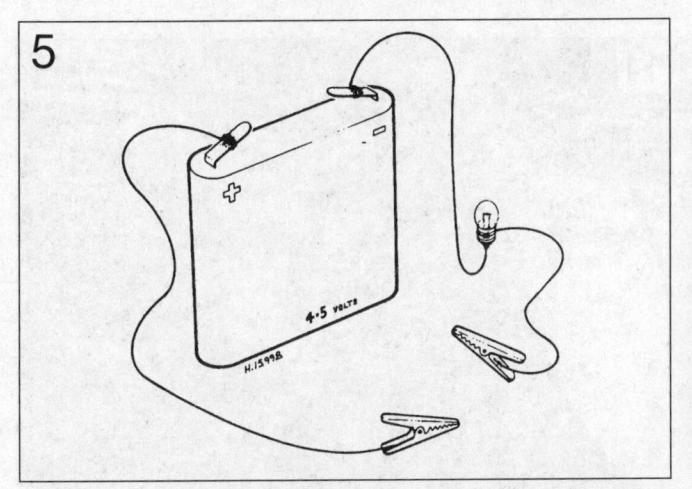

5 Battery and bulb test circuit

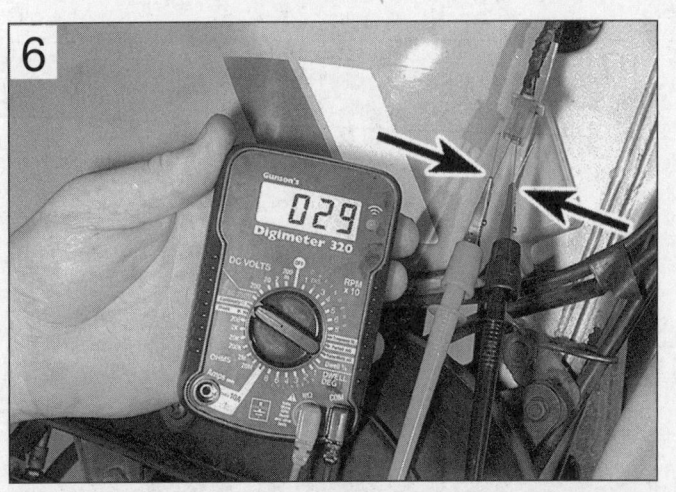

6 Continuity check of front brake light switch using a meter - note cotter pins used to access connector terminals

ohms scale and check that the meter reads infinity (∞). Touch the meter probes together and check that meter reads zero; where necessary adjust the meter so that it reads zero.
● After using a meter, always switch it OFF to conserve its battery.

Switch checks

1 If a switch is at fault, trace its wiring up to the wiring connectors. Separate the wire connectors and inspect them for security and condition. A build-up of dirt or corrosion here will most likely be the cause of the problem - clean up and apply a water dispersant such as WD40.
2 If using a test meter, set the meter to the ohms x 10 scale and connect its probes across the wires from the switch **(see illustration 6)**. Simple ON/OFF type switches, such as brake light switches, only have two wires whereas combination switches, like the ignition switch, have many internal links. Study the wiring diagram to ensure that you are connecting across the correct pair of wires. Continuity (low or no measurable resistance - 0 ohms) should be indicated with the switch ON and no continuity (high resistance) with it OFF.
3 Note that the polarity of the test probes doesn't matter for continuity checks, although care should be taken to follow specific test procedures if a diode or solid-state component is being checked.
4 A continuity tester or battery and bulb circuit can be used in the same way. Connect its probes as described above **(see illustration 7)**. The light should come on to indicate continuity in the ON switch position, but should extinguish in the OFF position.

Wiring checks

● Many electrical faults are caused by damaged wiring, often due to incorrect routing or chaffing on frame components.
● Loose, wet or corroded wire connectors can also be the cause of electrical problems, especially in exposed locations.

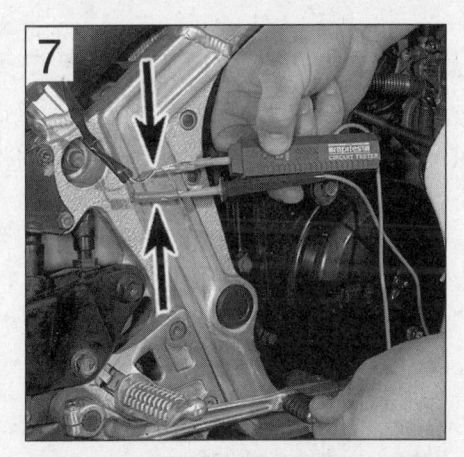

7 Continuity check of rear brake light switch using a continuity tester

REF•38 Troubleshooting Equipment

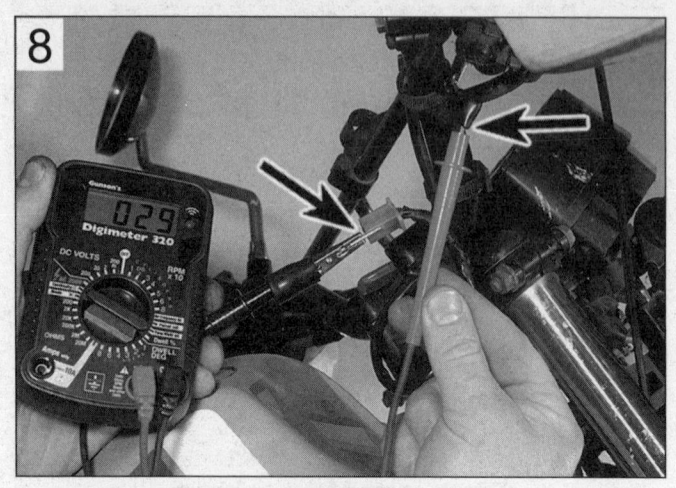

Continuity check of front brake light switch sub-harness

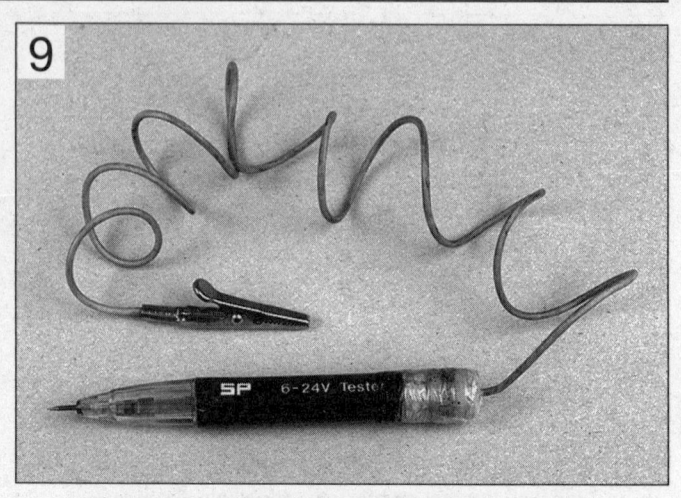

A simple test light can be used for voltage checks

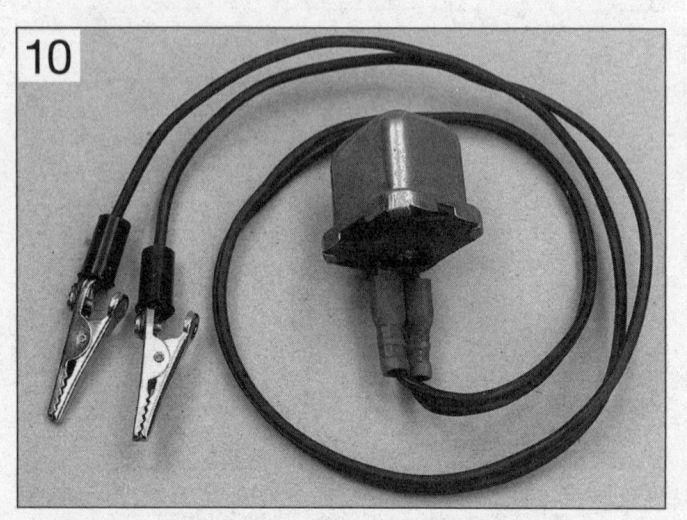

A buzzer is useful for voltage checks

Checking for voltage at the rear brake light power supply wire using a meter . . .

1 A continuity check can be made on a single length of wire by disconnecting it at each end and connecting a meter or continuity tester across both ends of the wire **(see illustration 8)**.

2 Continuity (low or no resistance - 0 ohms) should be indicated if the wire is good. If no continuity (high resistance) is shown, suspect a broken wire.

Checking for voltage

● A voltage check can determine whether current is reaching a component.
● Voltage can be checked with a dc voltmeter, multimeter set on the dc volts scale, test light or buzzer **(see illustrations 9 and 10)**. A meter has the advantage of being able to measure actual voltage.
● When using a meter, check that its leads are inserted in the correct terminals on the meter, red to positive (+), black to negative (-). Incorrect connections can damage the meter.
● A voltmeter (or multimeter set to the dc volts scale) should always be connected in parallel (across the load). Connecting it in series will destroy the meter.
● Voltage checks are made with the ignition ON.

1 First identify the relevant wiring circuit by referring to the wiring diagram at the end of this manual. If other electrical components share the same power supply (ie are fed from the same fuse), take note whether they are working correctly - this is useful information in deciding where to start checking the circuit.

2 If using a meter, check first that the meter leads are plugged into the correct terminals on the meter (see above). Set the meter to the dc volts function, at a range suitable for the battery voltage. Connect the meter red probe (+) to the power supply wire and the black probe to a good metal ground on the motor-cycle's frame or directly to the battery negative (-) terminal **(see illustration 11)**. Battery voltage should be shown on the meter with the ignition switched ON.

3 If using a test light or buzzer, connect its positive (+) probe to the power supply terminal and its negative (-) probe to a good ground on the motorcycle's frame or directly to the battery negative (-) terminal **(see illustration 12)**. With the ignition ON, the test light should illuminate or the buzzer sound.

4 If no voltage is indicated, work back towards the fuse continuing to check for voltage. When you reach a point where there is voltage, you know the problem lies between that point and your last check point.

Checking the ground

● Ground connections are made either

Troubleshooting Equipment REF•39

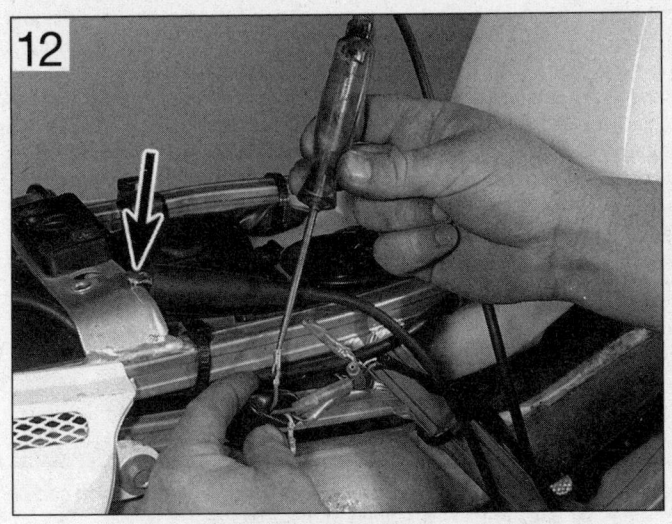

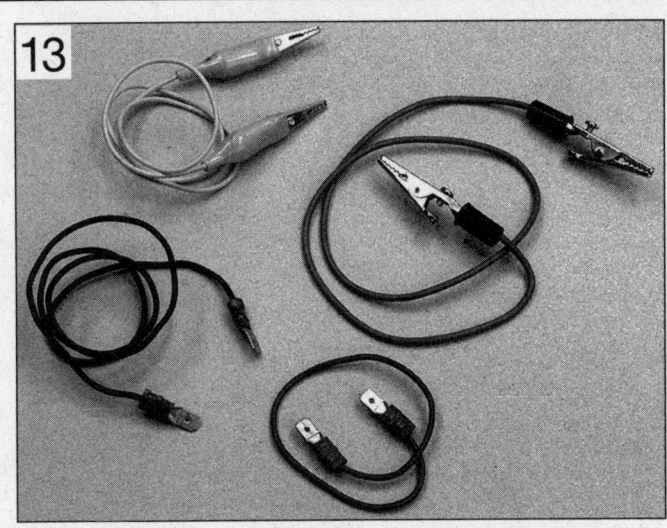

... or a test light - note the ground connection to the frame (arrow)

A selection of jumper wires for making ground checks

directly to the engine or frame (such as sensors, neutral switch etc. which only have a positive feed) or by a separate wire into the ground circuit of the wiring harness. Alternatively a short ground wire is sometimes run directly from the component to the motor-cycle's frame.

● Corrosion is often the cause of a poor ground connection.

● If total failure is experienced, check the security of the main ground lead from the negative (-) terminal of the battery and also the main ground point on the wiring harness. If corroded, dismantle the connection and clean all surfaces back to bare metal.

1 To check the ground on a component, use an insulated jumper wire to temporarily bypass its ground connection **(see illustration 13)**. Connect one end of the jumper wire between the ground terminal or metal body of the component and the other end to the motorcycle's frame.

2 If the circuit works with the jumper wire installed, the original ground circuit is faulty. Check the wiring for open-circuits or poor connections. Clean up direct ground connections, removing all traces of corrosion and remake the joint. Apply petroleum jelly to the joint to prevent future corrosion.

Tracing a short-circuit

● A short-circuit occurs where current shorts to ground bypassing the circuit components. This usually results in a blown fuse.

● A short-circuit is most likely to occur where the insulation has worn through due to wiring chafing on a component, allowing a direct path to ground on the frame.

1 Remove any body panels necessary to access the circuit wiring.

2 Check that all electrical switches in the circuit are OFF, then remove the circuit fuse and connect a test light, buzzer or voltmeter (set to the dc scale) across the fuse terminals. No voltage should be shown.

3 Move the wiring from side to side while observing the test light or meter. When the test light comes on, buzzer sounds or meter shows voltage, you have found the cause of the short. It will usually shown up as damaged or burned insulation.

4 Note that the same test can be performed on each component in the circuit, even the switch.

REF•40 Security

Introduction

In less time than it takes to read this introduction, a thief could steal your motorcycle. Returning only to find your bike has gone is one of the worst feelings in the world. Even if the motorcycle is insured against theft, once you've got over the initial shock, you will have the inconvenience of dealing with the police and your insurance company.

The motorcycle is an easy target for the professional thief and the joyrider alike and the official figures on motorcycle theft make for depressing reading; on average a motorcycle is stolen every 16 minutes in the UK!

Motorcycle thefts fall into two categories, those stolen 'to order' and those taken by opportunists. The thief stealing to order will be on the look out for a specific make and model and will go to extraordinary lengths to obtain that motorcycle. The opportunist thief on the other hand will look for easy targets which can be stolen with the minimum of effort and risk.

Whilst it is never going to be possible to make your machine 100% secure, it is estimated that around half of all stolen motorcycles are taken by opportunist thieves. Remember that the opportunist thief is always on the look out for the easy option: if there are two similar motorcycles parked side-by-side, they will target the one with the lowest level of security. By taking a few precautions, you can reduce the chances of your motorcycle being stolen.

Security equipment

There are many specialised motorcycle security devices available and the following text summarises their applications and their good and bad points.

Once you have decided on the type of security equipment which best suits your needs, we recommended that you read one of the many equipment tests regularly carried out by the motorcycle press. These tests compare the products from all the major manufacturers and give impartial ratings on their effectiveness, value-for-money and ease of use.

No one item of security equipment can provide complete protection. It is highly recommended that two or more of the items described below are combined to increase the security of your motorcycle (a lock and chain plus an alarm system is just about ideal). The more security measures fitted to the bike, the less likely it is to be stolen.

Lock and chain

Pros: *Very flexible to use; can be used to secure the motorcycle to almost any immovable object. On some locks and chains, the lock can be used on its own as a disc lock (see below).*

Cons: *Can be very heavy and awkward to carry on the motorcycle, although some types will be supplied with a carry bag which can be strapped to the pillion seat.*

● Heavy-duty chains and locks are an excellent security measure **(see illustration 1)**. Whenever the motorcycle is parked, use the lock and chain to secure the machine to a solid, immovable object such as a post or railings. This will prevent the machine from being ridden away or being lifted into the back of a van.

● When fitting the chain, always ensure the chain is routed around the motorcycle frame or swingarm **(see illustrations 2 and 3)**. Never merely pass the chain around one of the wheel rims; a thief may unbolt the wheel and lift the rest of the machine into a van, leaving you with just the wheel! Try to avoid having excess chain free, thus making it difficult to use cutting tools, and keep the chain and lock off the ground to prevent thieves attacking it with a cold chisel. Position the lock so that its lock barrel is facing downwards; this will make it harder for the thief to attack the lock mechanism.

1 Ensure the lock and chain you buy is of good quality and long enough to shackle your bike to a solid object

2 Pass the chain through the bike's frame, rather than just through a wheel . . .

3 . . . and loop it around a solid object

Security

U-locks

Pros: *Highly effective deterrent which can be used to secure the bike to a post or railings. Most U-locks come with a carrier which allows the lock to be easily carried on the bike.*

Cons: *Not as flexible to use as a lock and chain.*

- These are solid locks which are similar in use to a lock and chain. U-locks are lighter than a lock and chain but not so flexible to use. The length and shape of the lock shackle limit the objects to which the bike can be secured **(see illustration 4)**.

Disc locks

Pros: *Small, light and very easy to carry; most can be stored underneath the seat.*

Cons: *Does not prevent the motorcycle being lifted into a van. Can be very embarrassing if you forget to remove the lock before attempting to ride off!*

- Disc locks are designed to be attached to the front brake disc. The lock passes through one of the holes in the disc and prevents the wheel rotating by jamming against the fork/brake caliper **(see illustration 5)**. Some are equipped with an alarm siren which sounds if the disc lock is moved; this not only acts as a theft deterrent but also as a handy reminder if you try to move the bike with the lock still fitted.

- Combining the disc lock with a length of cable which can be looped around a post or railings provides an additional measure of security **(see illustration 6)**.

Alarms and immobilisers

Pros: *Once installed it is completely hassle-free to use. If the system is 'Thatcham' or 'Sold Secure-approved', insurance companies may give you a discount.*

Cons: *Can be expensive to buy and complex to install. No system will prevent the motorcycle from being lifted into a van and taken away.*

- Electronic alarms and immobilisers are available to suit a variety of budgets. There are three different types of system available: pure alarms, pure immobilisers, and the more expensive systems which are combined alarm/immobilisers **(see illustration 7)**.
- An alarm system is designed to emit an audible warning if the motorcycle is being tampered with.
- An immobiliser prevents the motorcycle being started and ridden away by disabling its electrical systems.
- When purchasing an alarm/immobiliser system, check the cost of installing the system unless you are able to do it yourself. If the motorcycle is not used regularly, another consideration is the current drain of the system. All alarm/immobiliser systems are powered by the motorcycle's battery; purchasing a system with a very low current drain could prevent the battery losing its charge whilst the motorcycle is not being used.

U-locks can be used to secure the bike to a solid object – ensure you purchase one which is long enough

A typical disc lock attached through one of the holes in the disc

A disc lock combined with a security cable provides additional protection

A typical alarm/immobiliser system

REF•42 Security

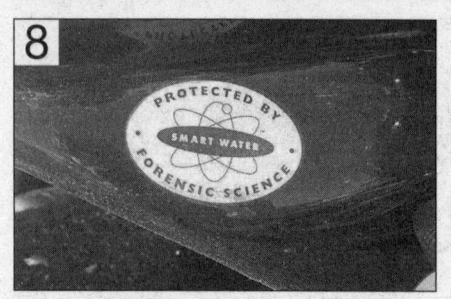

Indelible markings can be applied to most areas of the bike – always apply the manufacturer's sticker to warn off thieves

Chemically-etched code numbers can be applied to main body panels . . .

. . . again, always ensure that the kit manufacturer's sticker is applied in a prominent position

Security marking kits

Pros: *Very cheap and effective deterrent. Many insurance companies will give you a discount on your insurance premium if a recognised security marking kit is used on your motorcycle.*

Cons: *Does not prevent the motorcycle being stolen by joyriders.*

● There are many different types of security marking kits available. The idea is to mark as many parts of the motorcycle as possible with a unique security number **(see illustrations 8, 9 and 10)**. A form will be included with the kit to register your personal details and those of the motorcycle with the kit manufacturer. This register is made available to the police to help them trace the rightful owner of any motorcycle or components which they recover should all other forms of identification have been removed. Always apply the warning stickers provided with the kit to deter thieves.

Ground anchors, wheel clamps and security posts

Pros: *An excellent form of security which will deter all but the most determined of thieves.*

Cons: *Awkward to install and can be expensive.*

● Whilst the motorcycle is at home, it is a good idea to attach it securely to the floor or a solid wall, even if it is kept in a securely locked garage. Various types of ground anchors, security posts and wheel clamps are available for this purpose **(see illustration 11)**. These security devices are either bolted to a solid concrete or brick structure or can be cemented into the ground.

Permanent ground anchors provide an excellent level of security when the bike is at home

Security at home

A high percentage of motorcycle thefts are from the owner's home. Here are some things to consider whenever your motorcycle is at home:

✔ Where possible, always keep the motorcycle in a securely locked garage. Never rely solely on the standard lock on the garage door, these are usual hopelessly inadequate. Fit an additional locking mechanism to the door and consider having the garage alarmed. A security light, activated by a movement sensor, is also a good investment.

✔ Always secure the motorcycle to the ground or a wall, even if it is inside a securely locked garage.

✔ Do not regularly leave the motorcycle outside your home, try to keep it out of sight wherever possible. If a garage is not available, fit a motorcycle cover over the bike to disguise its true identity.

✔ It is not uncommon for thieves to follow a motorcyclist home to find out where the bike is kept. They will then return at a later date. Be aware of this whenever you are returning home on your motorcycle. If you suspect you are being followed, do not return home, instead ride to a garage or shop and stop as a precaution.

✔ When selling a motorcycle, do not provide your home address or the location where the bike is normally kept. Arrange to meet the buyer at a location away from your home. Thieves have been known to pose as potential buyers to find out where motorcycles are kept and then return later to steal them.

Security away from the home

As well as fitting security equipment to your motorcycle here are a few general rules to follow whenever you park your motorcycle.
✔ Park in a busy, public place.
✔ Use car parks which incorporate security features, such as CCTV.

✔ At night, park in a well-lit area, preferably directly underneath a street light.
✔ Engage the steering lock.
✔ Secure the motorcycle to a solid, immovable object such as a post or railings with an additional lock. If this is not possible, secure the bike to a friend's motorcycle. Some public parking places provide security loops for motorcycles.
✔ Never leave your helmet or luggage attached to the motorcycle. Take them with you at all times.

Technical Terms Explained REF•43

A

ABS (Anti-lock braking system) A system, usually electronically controlled, that senses incipient wheel lockup during braking and relieves hydraulic pressure at wheel which is about to skid.

Aftermarket Components suitable for the motorcycle, but not produced by the motorcycle manufacturer.

Allen key A hexagonal wrench which fits into a recessed hexagonal hole.

Alternating current (ac) Current produced by an alternator. Requires converting to direct current by a rectifier for charging purposes.

Alternator Converts mechanical energy from the engine into electrical energy to charge the battery and power the electrical system.

Ampere (amp) A unit of measurement for the flow of electrical current. Current = Volts ÷ Ohms.

Ampere-hour (Ah) Measure of battery capacity.

Angle-tightening A torque expressed in degrees. Often follows a conventional tightening torque for cylinder head or main bearing fasteners **(see illustration)**.

Angle-tightening cylinder head bolts

Antifreeze A substance (usually ethylene glycol) mixed with water, and added to the cooling system, to prevent freezing of the coolant in winter. Antifreeze also contains chemicals to inhibit corrosion and the formation of rust and other deposits that would tend to clog the radiator and coolant passages and reduce cooling efficiency.

Anti-dive System attached to the fork lower leg (slider) to prevent fork dive when braking hard.

Anti-seize compound A coating that reduces the risk of seizing on fasteners that are subjected to high temperatures, such as exhaust clamp bolts and nuts.

API American Petroleum Institute. A quality standard for 4-stroke motor oils.

Asbestos A natural fibrous mineral with great heat resistance, commonly used in the composition of brake friction materials. Asbestos is a health hazard and the dust created by brake systems should never be inhaled or ingested.

ATF Automatic Transmission Fluid. Often used in front forks.

ATU Automatic Timing Unit. Mechanical device for advancing the ignition timing on early engines.

ATV All Terrain Vehicle. Often called a Quad.

Axial play Side-to-side movement.

Axle A shaft on which a wheel revolves. Also known as a spindle.

B

Backlash The amount of movement between meshed components when one component is held still. Usually applies to gear teeth.

Ball bearing A bearing consisting of a hardened inner and outer race with hardened steel balls between the two races.

Bearings Used between two working surfaces to prevent wear of the components and a build-up of heat. Four types of bearing are commonly used on motorcycles: plain shell bearings, ball bearings, tapered roller bearings and needle roller bearings.

Bevel gears Used to turn the drive through 90°. Typical applications are shaft final drive and camshaft drive **(see illustration)**.

BHP Brake Horsepower. The British measure-ment for engine power output. Power output is now usually expressed in kilowatts (kW).

Bevel gears are used to turn the drive through 90°

Bias-belted tire Similar construction to radial tire, but with outer belt running at an angle to the wheel rim.

Big-end bearing The bearing in the end of the connecting rod that's attached to the crankshaft.

Bleeding The process of removing air from a hydraulic system via a bleed nipple or bleed screw.

Bottom-end A description of an engine's crankcase components and all components contained therein.

BTDC Before Top Dead Center in terms of piston position. Ignition timing is often expressed in terms of degrees or millimeters BTDC.

Bush A cylindrical metal or rubber component used between two moving parts.

Burr Rough edge left on a component after machining or as a result of excessive wear.

C

Cam chain The chain which takes drive from the crankshaft to the camshaft(s).

Canister The main component in an evap-orative emission control system (California market only); contains activated charcoal granules to trap vapors from the fuel system rather than allowing them to vent to the atmosphere.

Castellated Resembling the parapets along the top of a castle wall. For example, a castellated wheel axle or spindle nut.

Catalytic converter A device in the exhaust system of some machines which

Technical Terms Explained

Cush drive rubber segments dampen out transmission shocks

Cush drive Rubber damper segments fitted between the rear wheel and final drive sprocket to absorb transmission shocks (see illustration).

D

Degree disc Calibrated disc for measuring piston position. Expressed in degrees.

Dial gauge Clock-type gauge with adapters for measuring runout and piston position. Expressed in mm or inches.

Diaphragm The rubber membrane in a master cylinder or carburetor which seals the upper chamber.

Diaphragm spring A single sprung plate often used in clutches.

Direct current (dc) Current produced by a dc generator.

Decarbonization The process of removing carbon deposits - typically from the combustion chamber, valves and exhaust port/system.

Detonation Destructive and damaging explosion of fuel/air mixture in combustion chamber instead of controlled burning.

Diode An electrical valve which only allows current to flow in one direction. Commonly used in rectifiers and starter interlock systems.

Disc valve (or rotary valve) An induction system used on some two-stroke engines.

Double-overhead camshaft (DOHC) An engine that uses two overhead camshafts, one for the intake valves and one for the exhaust valves.

Drivebelt A toothed belt used to transmit drive to the rear wheel on some motorcycles. A drivebelt has also been used to drive the camshafts. Drivebelts are usually made of Kevlar.

Driveshaft Any shaft used to transmit motion. Commonly used when referring to the final driveshaft on shaft drive motorcycles.

converts certain pollutants in the exhaust gases into less harmful substances.

Charging system Description of the components which charge the battery, ie the alternator, rectifer and regulator.

Clearance The amount of space between two parts. For example, between a piston and a cylinder, between a bearing and a journal, etc.

Coil spring A spiral of elastic steel found in various sizes throughout a vehicle, for example as a springing medium in the suspension and in the valve train.

Compression Reduction in volume, and increase in pressure and temperature, of a gas, caused by squeezing it into a smaller space.

Compression damping Controls the speed the suspension compresses when hitting a bump.

Compression ratio The relationship between cylinder volume when the piston is at top dead center and cylinder volume when the piston is at bottom dead center.

Continuity The uninterrupted path in the flow of electricity. Little or no measurable resistance.

Continuity tester Self-powered bleeper or test light which indicates continuity.

Cp Candlepower. Bulb rating commonly found on US motorcycles.

Crossply tire Tire plies arranged in a criss-cross pattern. Usually four or six plies used, hence 4PR or 6PR in tire size codes.

E

ECU (Electronic Control Unit) A computer which controls (for instance) an ignition system, or an anti-lock braking system.

EGO Exhaust Gas Oxygen sensor. Some-times called a Lambda sensor.

Electrolyte The fluid in a lead-acid battery.

EMS (Engine Management System) A computer controlled system which manages the fuel injection and the ignition systems in an integrated fashion.

Endfloat The amount of lengthways movement between two parts. As applied to a crankshaft, the distance that the crankshaft can move side-to-side in the crankcase.

Endless chain A chain having no joining link. Common use for cam chains and final drive chains.

EP (Extreme Pressure) Oil type used in locations where high loads are applied, such as between gear teeth.

Evaporative emission control system Describes a charcoal filled canister which stores fuel vapors from the tank rather than allowing them to vent to the atmosphere. Usually only fitted to California models and referred to as an EVAP system.

Expansion chamber Section of two-stroke engine exhaust system so designed to improve engine efficiency and boost power.

F

Feeler blade or gauge A thin strip or blade of hardened steel, ground to an exact thickness, used to check or measure clearances between parts.

Final drive Description of the drive from the transmission to the rear wheel. Usually by chain or shaft, but sometimes by belt.

Firing order The order in which the engine cylinders fire, or deliver their power strokes, beginning with the number one cylinder.

Flooding Term used to describe a high fuel level in the carburetor float chambers,

Technical Terms Explained REF•45

leading to fuel overflow. Also refers to excess fuel in the combustion chamber due to incorrect starting technique.

Free length The no-load state of a component when measured. Clutch, valve and fork spring lengths are measured at rest, without any preload.

Freeplay The amount of travel before any action takes place. The looseness in a linkage, or an assembly of parts, between the initial application of force and actual movement. For example, the distance the rear brake pedal moves before the rear brake is actuated.

Fuel injection The fuel/air mixture is metered electronically and directed into the engine intake ports (indirect injection) or into the cylinders (direct injection). Sensors supply information on engine speed and conditions.

Fuel/air mixture The charge of fuel and air going into the engine. See Stoichiometric ratio.

Fuse An electrical device which protects a circuit against accidental overload. The typical fuse contains a soft piece of metal which is calibrated to melt at a predetermined current flow (expressed as amps) and break the circuit.

G

Gap The distance the spark must travel in jumping from the center electrode to the side electrode in a spark plug. Also refers to the distance between the ignition rotor and the pickup coil in an electronic ignition system.

Gasket Any thin, soft material - usually cork, cardboard, asbestos or soft metal - installed between two metal surfaces to ensure a good seal. For instance, the cylinder head gasket seals the joint between the block and the cylinder head.

Gauge An instrument panel display used to monitor engine conditions. A gauge with a movable pointer on a dial or a fixed scale is an analog gauge. A gauge with a numerical readout is called a digital gauge.

Gear ratios The drive ratio of a pair of gears in a gearbox, calculated on their number of teeth.

Glaze-busting see **Honing**

Grinding Process for renovating the valve face and valve seat contact area in the cylinder head.

Ground return The return path of an electrical circuit, utilizing the motorcycle's frame.

Gudgeon pin The shaft which connects the connecting rod small-end with the piston. Often called a piston pin or wrist pin.

H

Helical gears Gear teeth are slightly curved and produce less gear noise that straight-cut gears. Often used for primary drives.

Helicoil A thread insert repair system. Commonly used as a repair for stripped spark plug threads **(see illustration)**.

Installing a Helicoil thread insert in a cylinder head

Honing A process used to break down the glaze on a cylinder bore (also called glaze-busting). Can also be carried out to roughen a rebored cylinder to aid ring bedding-in.

HT (High Tension) Description of the electrical circuit from the secondary winding of the ignition coil to the spark plug.

Hydraulic A liquid filled system used to transmit pressure from one component to another. Common uses on motorcycles are brakes and clutches.

Hydrometer An instrument for measuring the specific gravity of a lead-acid battery.

Hygroscopic Water absorbing. In motorcycle applications, braking efficiency will be reduced if DOT 3 or 4 hydraulic fluid absorbs water from the air - care must be taken to keep new brake fluid in tightly sealed containers.

I

lbf ft Pounds-force feet. A unit of torque. Sometimes written as ft-lbs.

lbf in Pound-force inch. A unit of torque, applied to components where a very low torque is required. Sometimes written as inch-lbs.

IC Abbreviation for Integrated Circuit.

Ignition advance Means of increasing the timing of the spark at higher engine speeds. Done by mechanical means (ATU) on early engines or electronically by the ignition control unit on later engines.

Ignition timing The moment at which the spark plug fires, expressed in the number of crankshaft degrees before the piston reaches the top of its stroke, or in the number of millimeters before the piston reaches the top of its stroke.

Infinity (∞) Description of an open-circuit electrical state, where no continuity exists.

Inverted forks (upside down forks) The sliders or lower legs are held in the yokes and the fork tubes or stanchions are connected to the wheel axle (spindle). Less unsprung weight and stiffer construction than conventional forks.

J

JASO Japan Automobile Standards Organization. JASO MA is a standard for motorcycle oil equivalent to API SJ, but designed to prevent problems with wet-type motorcycle clutches.

Joule The unit of electrical energy.

Journal The bearing surface of a shaft.

K

Kickstart Mechanical means of turning the engine over for starting purposes.

Technical Terms Explained

Only usually fitted to mopeds, small capacity motorcycles and off-road motorcycles.

Kill switch Handebar-mounted switch for emergency ignition cut-out. Cuts the ignition circuit on all models, and additionally prevent starter motor operation on others.

km Symbol for kilometer.

kmh Abbreviation for kilometers per hour.

L

Lambda sensor A sensor fitted in the exhaust system to measure the exhaust gas oxygen content (excess air factor). Also called oxygen sensor.

Lapping see **Grinding**.

LCD Abbreviation for Liquid Crystal Display.

LED Abbreviation for Light Emitting Diode.

Liner A steel cylinder liner inserted in an aluminum alloy cylinder block.

Locknut A nut used to lock an adjustment nut, or other threaded component, in place.

Lockstops The lugs on the lower triple clamp (yoke) which abut those on the frame, preventing handlebar-to-fuel tank contact.

Lockwasher A form of washer designed to prevent an attaching nut from working loose.

LT Low Tension Description of the electrical circuit from the power supply to the primary winding of the ignition coil.

M

Main bearings The bearings between the crankshaft and crankcase.

Maintenance-free (MF) battery A sealed battery which cannot be topped up.

Manometer Mercury-filled calibrated tubes used to measure intake tract vacuum. Used to synchronize carburetors on multi-cylinder engines.

Tappet shims are measured with a micrometer

Micrometer A precision measuring instru-ment that measures component outside diameters **(see illustration)**.

MON (Motor Octane Number) A measure of a fuel's resistance to knock.

Monograde oil An oil with a single viscosity, eg SAE80W.

Monoshock A single suspension unit linking the swingarm or suspension linkage to the frame.

mph Abbreviation for miles per hour.

Multigrade oil Having a wide viscosity range (eg 10W40). The W stands for Winter, thus the viscosity ranges from SAE10 when cold to SAE40 when hot.

Multimeter An electrical test instrument with the capability to measure voltage, current and resistance. Some meters also incorporate a continuity tester and buzzer.

N

Needle roller bearing Inner race of caged needle rollers and hardened outer race. Examples of uncaged needle rollers can be found on some engines. Commonly used in rear suspension applications and in two-stroke engines.

Nm Newton meters.

NOx Oxides of Nitrogen. A common toxic pollutant emitted by gasoline engines at higher temperatures.

O

Octane The measure of a fuel's resistance to knock.

OE (Original Equipment) Relates to components fitted to a motorcycle as standard or replacement parts supplied by the motorcycle manufacturer.

Ohm The unit of electrical resistance. Ohms = Volts 4 Current.

Ohmmeter An instrument for measuring electrical resistance.

Oil cooler System for diverting engine oil outside of the engine to a radiator for cooling purposes.

Oil injection A system of two-stroke engine lubrication where oil is pump-fed to the engine in accordance with throttle position.

Open-circuit An electrical condition where there is a break in the flow of electricity - no continuity (high resistance).

O-ring A type of sealing ring made of a special rubber-like material; in use, the O-ring is compressed into a groove to provide the sealing action.

Oversize (OS) Term used for piston and ring size options fitted to a rebored cylinder.

Overhead cam (sohc) engine An engine with single camshaft located on top of the cylinder head.

Overhead valve (ohv) engine An engine with the valves located in the cylinder head, but with the camshaft located in the engine block or crankcase.

Oxygen sensor A device installed in the exhaust system which senses the oxygen content in the exhaust and converts this information into an electric current. Also called a Lambda sensor.

P

Plastigage A thin strip of plastic thread, available in different sizes, used for measuring clearances. For example, a strip of Plastigage is laid across a bearing journal. The parts are assembled and dismantled; the width of the crushed strip indicates the clearance between journal and bearing.

Polarity Either negative or positive ground, determined by which battery lead is connected to the frame (ground return). Modern motorcycles are usually negative ground.

Technical Terms Explained REF•47

Pre-ignition A situation where the fuel/air mixture ignites before the spark plug fires. Often due to a hot spot in the combustion chamber caused by carbon build-up. Engine has a tendency to 'run-on'.

Pre-load (suspension) The amount a spring is compressed when in the unloaded state. Preload can be applied by gas, spacer or mechanical adjuster.

Premix The method of engine lubrication on some gasoline two-stroke engines. Engine oil is mixed with the gasoline in the fuel tank in a specific ratio. The fuel/oil mix is sometimes referred to as "petrol".

Primary drive Description of the drive from the crankshaft to the clutch. Usually by gear or chain.

PS Pferdestärke - a German interpretation of BHP.

PSI Pounds-force per square inch. Imperial measurement of tire pressure and cylinder pressure measurement.

PTFE Polytetrafluroethylene. A low friction substance.

Pulse secondary air injection system A process of promoting the burning of excess fuel present in the exhaust gases by routing fresh air into the exhaust ports.

Q

Quartz halogen bulb Tungsten filament surrounded by a halogen gas. Typically used for the headlight **(see illustration)**.

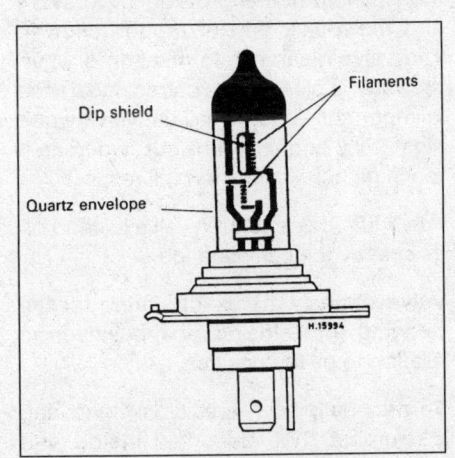

Quartz halogen headlight bulb construction

R

Rack-and-pinion A pinion gear on the end of a shaft that mates with a rack (think of a geared wheel opened up and laid flat). Sometimes used in clutch operating systems.

Radial play Up and down movement about a shaft.

Radial ply tires Tire plies run across the tire (from bead to bead) and around the circumference of the tire. Less resistant to tread distortion than other tire types.

Radiator A liquid-to-air heat transfer device designed to reduce the temperature of the coolant in a liquid cooled engine.

Rake A feature of steering geometry - the angle of the steering head in relation to the vertical **(see illustration)**.

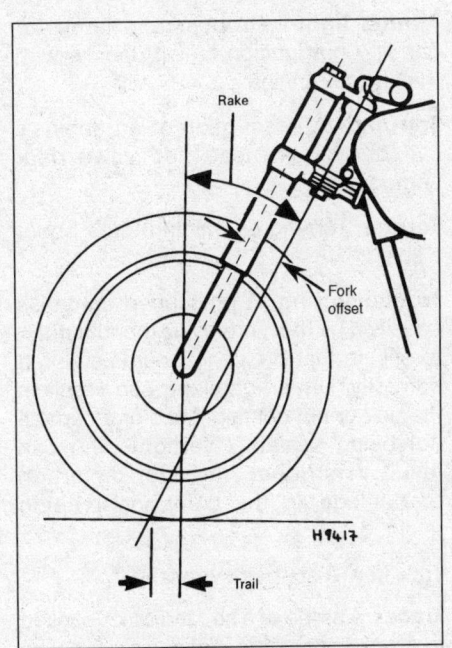

Steering geometry

Rebore Providing a new working surface to the cylinder bore by boring out the old surface. Necessitates the use of oversize piston and rings.

Rebound damping A means of controlling the oscillation of a suspension unit spring after it has been compressed. Resists the spring's natural tendency to bounce back after being compressed.

Rectifier Device for converting the ac output of an alternator into dc for battery charging.

Reed valve An induction system commonly used on two-stroke engines.

Regulator Device for maintaining the charging voltage from the generator or alternator within a specified range.

Relay A electrical device used to switch heavy current on and off by using a low current auxiliary circuit.

Resistance Measured in ohms. An electrical component's ability to pass electrical current.

RON (Research Octane Number) A measure of a fuel's resistance to knock.

rpm revolutions per minute.

Runout The amount of wobble (in-and-out movement) of a wheel or shaft as it's rotated. The amount a shaft rotates "out-of-true." The out-of-round condition of a rotating part.

S

SAE (Society of Automotive Engineers) A standard for the viscosity of a fluid.

Sealant A liquid or paste used to prevent leakage at a joint. Sometimes used in conjunction with a gasket.

Service limit Term for the point where a component is no longer useable and must be replaced.

Shaft drive A method of transmitting drive from the transmission to the rear wheel.

Shell bearings Plain bearings consisting of two shell halves. Most often used as big-end and main bearings in a four-stroke engine. Often called bearing inserts.

Shim Thin spacer, commonly used to adjust the clearance or relative positions between two parts. For example, shims inserted into or under tappets or followers to control valve clearances. Clearance is adjusted by changing the thickness of the shim.

Short-circuit An electrical condition where current shorts to ground bypassing the circuit components.

Technical Terms Explained

Skimming Process to correct warpage or repair a damaged surface, eg on brake discs or drums.

Slide-hammer A special puller that screws into or hooks onto a component such as a shaft or bearing; a heavy sliding handle on the shaft bottoms against the end of the shaft to knock the component free.

Small-end bearing The bearing in the upper end of the connecting rod at its joint with the gudgeon pin.

Snap-ring A ring-shaped clip used to prevent endwise movement of cylindrical parts and shafts. An internal snap-ring is installed in a groove in a housing; an external snap-ring fits into a groove on the outside of a cylindrical piece such as a shaft. Also known as a circlip.

Spalling Damage to camshaft lobes or bearing journals shown as pitting of the working surface.

Specific gravity (SG) The state of charge of the electrolyte in a lead-acid battery. A measure of the electrolyte's density compared with water.

Straight-cut gears Common type gear used on gearbox shafts and for oil pump and water pump drives.

Stanchion The inner sliding part of the front forks, held by the yokes. Often called a fork tube.

Stoichiometric ratio The optimum chemical air/fuel ratio for a gasoline engine, said to be 14.7 parts of air to 1 part of fuel.

Sulphuric acid The liquid (electrolyte) used in a lead-acid battery. Poisonous and extremely corrosive.

Surface grinding (lapping) Process to correct a warped gasket face, commonly used on cylinder heads.

T

Tapered-roller bearing Tapered inner race of caged needle rollers and separate tapered outer race. Examples of taper roller bearings can be found on steering heads.

Tappet A cylindrical component which transmits motion from the cam to the valve stem, either directly or via a pushrod and rocker arm. Also called a cam follower.

TCS Traction Control System. An electron-ically-controlled system which senses wheel spin and reduces engine speed accordingly.

TDC Top Dead Center denotes that the piston is at its highest point in the cylinder.

Thread-locking compound Solution applied to fastener threads to prevent loosening. Select type to suit application.

Thrust washer A washer positioned between two moving components on a shaft. For example, between gear pinions on gearshaft.

Timing chain See **Cam Chain**.

Timing light Stroboscopic lamp for carrying out ignition timing checks with the engine running.

Top-end A description of an engine's cylinder block, head and valve gear components.

Torque Turning or twisting force about a shaft.

Torque setting A prescribed tightness specified by the motorcycle manufacturer to ensure that the bolt or nut is secured correctly. Undertightening can result in the bolt or nut coming loose or a surface not being sealed. Overtightening can result in stripped threads, distortion or damage to the component being retained.

Torx key A six-point wrench.

Tracer A stripe of a second color applied to a wire insulator to distinguish that wire from another one with the same color insulator. For example, Br/W is often used to denote a brown insulator with a white tracer.

Trail A feature of steering geometry. Distance from the steering head axis to the tire's central contact point.

Triple clamps The cast components which extend from the steering head and support the fork stanchions or tubes. Often called fork yokes.

Turbocharger A centrifugal device, driven by exhaust gases, that pressurizes the intake air. Normally used to increase the power output from a given engine displacement.

TWI Abbreviation for Tire Wear Indicator. Indicates the location of the tread depth indicator bars on tires.

U

Universal joint or U-joint (UJ) A double-pivoted connection for transmitting power from a driving to a driven shaft through an angle. Typically found in shaft drive assemblies.

Unsprung weight Anything not supported by the bike's suspension (ie the wheel, tires, brakes, final drive and bottom (moving) part of the suspension).

V

Vacuum gauges Clock-type gauges for measuring intake tract vacuum. Used for carburetor synchronization on multi-cylinder engines.

Valve A device through which the flow of liquid, gas or vacuum may be stopped, started or regulated by a moveable part that opens, shuts or partially obstructs one or more ports or passageways. The intake and exhaust valves in the cylinder head are of the poppet type.

Valve clearance The clearance between the valve tip (the end of the valve stem) and the rocker arm or tappet/follower. The valve clearance is measured when the valve is closed. The correct clearance is important - if too small the valve won't close fully and will burn out, whereas if too large noisy operation will result.

Valve lift The amount a valve is lifted off its seat by the camshaft lobe.

Valve timing The exact setting for the opening and closing of the valves in relation to piston position.

Vernier caliper A precision measuring instrument that measures inside and outside dimensions. Not quite as accurate as a micrometer, but more convenient.

Technical Terms Explained REF•49

VIN Vehicle Identification Number. Term for the bike's engine and frame numbers.

Viscosity The thickness of a liquid or its resistance to flow.

Volt A unit for expressing electrical "pressure" in a circuit. Volts = current x ohms.

W

Water pump A mechanically-driven device for moving coolant around the engine.

Watt A unit for expressing electrical power. Watts = volts x current.

Wet liner arrangement

Wear limit see **Service limit**

Wet liner A liquid-cooled engine design where the pistons run in liners which are directly surrounded by coolant **(see illustration)**.

Wheelbase Distance from the center of the front wheel to the center of the rear wheel.

Wiring harness or loom Describes the electrical wires running the length of the motorcycle and enclosed in tape or plastic sheathing. Wiring coming off the main harness is usually referred to as a sub harness.

Woodruff key A key of semi-circular or square section used to locate a gear to a shaft. Often used to locate the alternator rotor on the crankshaft.

Wrist pin Another name for gudgeon or piston pin.

Index REF•51

Note: *References throughout this index are in the form, "Chapter number"•"Page number"*

A

About this manual, 0•7
Acknowledgements, 0•7
Adjustments, suspension, 6•14
Air filter element, servicing, 1•26
Air suction valves, check, 1•13
Air switching valve (US EN450/500 models), operational test, 4•14
Alignment, wheels, check, 7•11
Alternator
   removal and installation, 9•20
   stator coils
      replacement, 9•21
      continuity test, 9•20
      unregulated output test, 9•19

B

Balancer shaft
   inspection, 2C•26
   removal and installation
      EN450/500 models, 2A•20
      EX250 models, 2B•15
Battery
   charging, 9•3
   electrolyte level/specific gravity, check, 1•19
   inspection and maintenance, 9•3
Belt (drive) and sprockets, removal, inspection and installation, 6•12
Brake
   caliper, removal and installation, 7•5
   disc, inspection, removal and installation, 7•6
   fluid
      level check, 0•14
      type, 1•3
      replacement, 1•29
   hoses and lines, inspection and replacement, 7•9
   light switches, check and replacement, 9•10
   master cylinder, removal, overhaul and installation, 7•7
   pads
      and shoe linings, wear check, 1•17
      replacement, 7•3
   pedal
      position and play, check and adjustment (drum brakes), 1•17
      removal and installation, 7•10
   rear brake cam, lubrication (drum brakes), 1•29
   shoes, replacement, 7•8
   system bleeding, 7•9
   system, general check, 1•16
Brakes, wheels and tires, 7•1 through 7•18
Bulb replacement
   headlight, 9•7
   instruments and warning lights, 9•12
   turn signal, tail/brake light and license plate light, 9•9
Buying spare parts, 0•10

C

Cable replacement
   choke, 4•12
   throttle, 4•11
Caliper, disc brake, removal and installation, 7•5
Camshaft and rocker arms, inspection, 2C•9
Camshaft chain and guides, removal, inspection and installation
   EN450/500 models, 2A•20
   EX250 models, 2B•15
Camshaft chain tensioner, removal and installation
   EN450/500 models, 2A•5
   EX250 models, 2B•4
Camshafts, rocker arm shafts and rocker arms, removal, inspection and installation
   EN450/500 models, 2A•6
   EX250 models, 2B•5
Capacities, fluids and lubricants, 1•2, 1•3
Carburetors
   disassembly, cleaning and inspection, 4•6
   overhaul, general information, 4•5
   reassembly and fuel level adjustment, 4•9
   removal and installation, 4•5
   synchronization, check and adjustment, 1•14
Centerstand, maintenance, 8•2

Chain
   and sprockets, check and adjustment, 1•10
   and sprockets, wear check, 1•16
   lubrication, 1•10
Chain and sprockets, removal, inspection and installation, 6•12
Charging system
   alternator
      removal and installation, 9•20
      stator coils
         replacement, 9•21
         continuity test, 9•20
         unregulated output test, 9•19
   regulated output test, 9•19
   testing, general information and precautions, 9•18
   voltage regulator/rectifier, check and replacement, 9•20
Chemicals and lubricants, REF•23
Choke cable (EN450 and EX250 models), removal, installation and adjustment, 4•12
Clutch
   check and adjustment, 1•15
   housing, removal, inspection and installation, 2C•20
   inspection, 2C•17
   removal and installation
      EN450/500 models, 2A•14
      EX250 models, 2B•10
Clutch cable, replacement
   EN450/500 models, 2A•16
   EX250 models, 2B•11
Clutch housing, crankshaft and main bearings, removal, inspection, main bearing selection and installation, 2C•20
Coils, check, removal and installation
   ignition, 5•3
   pickup, 5•4
Connecting rods and bearings, removal, inspection, bearing selection and installation, 2C•24
Conversion factors, REF•22
Coolant
   reservoir, removal and installation, 3•2
   temperature gauge/light and sender unit, check and replacement, 3•4
   tubes, removal and installation, 3•8
   type, 1•3

Index

Coolant
level check, 0•13
replacement, 1•30
Cooling fan and thermostatic switch, check and replacement, 3•2
Cooling system, 3•1 through 3•10
Cooling system, check, 1•28
Coupling/rubber damper, rear wheel, check and replacement, 6•14
Crankcase components, inspection and servicing, 2C•19
Crankcase, disassembly and reassembly
EN450/500 models, 2A•17
EX250 models, 2B•13
Cylinder block
inspection, 2C•14
removal and installation
EN450/500 models, 2A•11
EX250 models, 2B•8
Cylinder compression, check, 2C•7
Cylinder head and valves, disassembly, inspection and reassembly, 2C•11
Cylinder head, removal and installation
EN450/500 models, 2A•8
EX250 models, 2B•7

D

Daily (pre-ride) checks, 0•12
brake fluid level check, 0•14
coolant level check, 0•13
engine/transmission oil level check, 0•12
legal and safety checks, 0•15
suspension, steering and final drive checks, 0•15
tire checks, 0•16
Diagnosis, REF•27
Diagnostic equipment, REF•36
Dimensions and weights, REF•1
Disc brake
caliper, removal and installation, 7•5
disc, inspection, removal and installation, 7•6
pads, replacement, 7•3
Drive belt, and sprockets, check and adjustment, 1•10
Drive belt/chain and sprockets, removal, inspection and installation, 6•12
Drive chain
and sprockets
check and adjustment, 1•10
wear check, 1•16
lubricant type, 1•3
lubrication, 1•10
Drum brake shoes, replacement, 7•8

E

Electrical system, 9•1 through 9•22
Electrical troubleshooting, 9•2
Electrolyte level/specific gravity, check, 1•19
Engine and frame numbers, 0•8
Engine and transmission, oil type and viscosity, 1•2

Engine coolant, level check, 0•13
Engine disassembly and reassembly, general information, 2C•9
Engine oil/filter, change, 1•25
Engine, clutch and transmission, EN450/500 models, 2A•1 through 2A•26
balancer shaft, removal and installation, 2A•20
camshaft chain tensioner, removal and installation, 2A•5
camshafts, rocker arm shafts and rocker arms, removal, inspection and installation, 2A•6
clutch cable, replacement, 2A•16
clutch, removal and installation, 2A•14
crankcase, disassembly and reassembly, 2A•17
cylinder block, removal and installation, 2A•11
cylinder head, removal and installation, 2A•8
engine, removal and installation, 2A•3
external shift mechanism, removal, inspection and installation, 2A•16
major engine repair, general note, 2A•3
oil pan, removal and installation, 2A•12
oil pressure relief valve, removal, inspection and installation, 2A•14
oil pump, removal and installation, 2A•13
operations possible with the engine in the frame, 2A•3
operations requiring engine removal, 2A•3
primary chain, camshaft chain and guides, removal, inspection and installation, 2A•20
shift drum and forks, removal, inspection and installation, 2A•26
transmission shafts, disassembly and reassembly, 2A•22
transmission shafts, removal and installation, 2A•21
valve cover, removal and installation, 2A•4
Engine, clutch and transmission, EX250 models, 2B•1 through 2B•18
balancer shaft, removal and installation, 2B•15
camshaft chain and guides, removal, inspection and installation, 2B•15
camshaft chain tensioner, removal and installation, 2B•4
camshafts, rocker arm shafts and rocker arms, removal, inspection and installation, 2B•5
clutch cable, replacement, 2B•11
clutch, removal and installation, 2B•10
crankcase, disassembly and reassembly, 2B•13
cylinder block, removal and installation, 2B•8
cylinder head, removal and installation, 2B•7
engine, removal and installation, 2B•3
external shift mechanism, removal, inspection and installation, 2B•11
major engine repair, general note, 2B•2
oil pressure relief valve, removal, inspection and installation, 2B•10

oil pump, removal and installation, 2B•9
operations possible with the engine in the frame, 2B•2
operations requiring engine removal, 2B•2
shift drum and forks, removal, inspection and installation, 2B•17
transmission shafts, removal and installation, 2B•17
valve cover, removal and installation, 2B•3
Engine, general overhaul procedures, 2C•1 through 2C•30
balancer shaft, inspection, 2C•26
camshaft and rocker arms, inspection, 2C•9
clutch housing, crankshaft and main bearings, removal, inspection, main bearing selection and installation, 2C•20
clutch, inspection, 2C•17
connecting rods and bearings, removal, inspection, bearing selection and installation, 2C•24
crankcase components, inspection and servicing, 2C•19
cylinder block, inspection, 2C•14
cylinder compression, check, 2C•7
cylinder head and valves, disassembly, inspection and reassembly, 2C•11
engine disassembly and reassembly, general information, 2C•9
external shift mechanism, inspection, 2C•19
intial start•up after overhaul, 2C•28
main and connecting rod bearings, general note, 2C•20
major engine repair, general note, 2C•7
oil pressure check, 2C•8
piston rings, installation, 2C•16
pistons, removal, inspection and installation, 2C•14
primary chain, camshaft chain and guides, inspection, 2C•27
recommended break•in procedure, 2C•28
shift drum and forks, inspection, 2C•28
transmission gears and shafts, inspection, 2C•27
Engine, removal and installation
EN450/500 models, 2A•3
EX250 models, 2B•3
Engine/transmission oil level check, 0•12
Evaporative emission control system (California models only), check, 1•15
Exhaust system
check, 1•28
removal and installation, 4•13
External shift mechanism
inspection, 2C•19
removal, inspection and installation
EN450/500 models, 2A•16
EX250 models, 2B•11

F

Fairing (EX250 models), removal and installation, 8•5
Fasteners, check, 1•29

Index

Fault finding, REF•27
Fender, removal and installation
 front, 8•4
 rear
  EN450 models, 8•4
  EN500 models, 8•4
  EX250 models, 8•5
Filter replacement, engine oil, 1•25
Fluid level checks
 battery electrolyte, 1•19
 brake fluid, 0•14
 engine coolant, 0•13
 engine/transmission oil, 0•12
Fluids and lubricants, recommended, 1•2
Footpegs and brackets, removal and installation, 8•2
Fork oil
 replacement, 1•31
 type, 1•3
Forks
 disassembly, inspection and reassembly, 6•4
 removal and installation, 6•4
Frame and bodywork, 8•1 through 8•6
Frame numbers, 0•8
Frame, inspection and repair, 8•1
Front wheel, removal, inspection and installation, 7•11
Fuel
 carburetors
  disassembly, cleaning and inspection, 4•6
  overhaul, general information, 4•5
  reassembly and fuel level adjustment, 4•9
  removal and installation, 4•5
 hoses, replacement, 1•32
 idle fuel/air mixture adjustment, general information, 4•4
 system, check and filter cleaning, 1•28
 tank
  cleaning and repair, 4•4
  removal and installation, 4•3
Fuel and exhaust systems, 4•1 through 4•14
Fuses, check and replacement, 9•4

G

Gauges, check and replacement, 9•11
General engine overhaul procedures, 2C•1 through 2C•30
 balancer shaft, inspection, 2C•26
 camshaft and rocker arms, inspection, 2C•9
 clutch housing, crankshaft and main bearings, removal, inspection, main bearing selection and installation, 2C•20
 clutch, inspection, 2C•17
 connecting rods and bearings, removal, inspection, bearing selection and installation, 2C•24
 crankcase components, inspection and servicing, 2C•19
 cylinder block, inspection, 2C•14
 cylinder compression, check, 2C•7
 cylinder head and valves, disassembly, inspection and reassembly, 2C•11
 engine disassembly and reassembly, general information, 2C•9
 external shift mechanism, inspection, 2C•19
 intial start•up after overhaul, 2C•28
 main and connecting rod bearings, general note, 2C•20
 major engine repair, general note, 2C•7
 oil pressure check, 2C•8
 piston rings, installation, 2C•16
 pistons, removal, inspection and installation, 2C•14
 primary chain, camshaft chain and guides, inspection, 2C•27
 recommended break•in procedure, 2C•28
 shift drum and forks, inspection, 2C•28
 transmission gears and shafts, inspection, 2C•27
Glossary, REF•43

H

Handlebar switches
 check, 9•13
 removal and installation, 9•13
Handlebars, removal and installation, 6•3
Headlight
 aim, check and adjustment, 9•9
 assembly, removal and installation, 9•8
 bulb, replacement, 9•7
Horn, check, replacement and adjustment, 9•14

I

IC igniter, removal, check and installation, 5•4
Identification numbers, 0•8
Idle fuel/air mixture adjustment, general information, 4•4
Idle speed, check and adjustment, 1•13
Ignition main (key) switch, check and replacement, 9•12
Ignition system, 5•1 through 5•4
 check, 5•2
 coils, check, removal and installation, 5•3
 IC igniter, removal, check and installation, 5•4
 pickup coils, check, removal and installation, 5•4
Instrument and warning light
 bulbs, replacement, 9•12
 housings (EN500 and EX250 models), removal and installation, 9•11
Intial start•up after overhaul, 2C•28
Introduction, 0•4

J

Junction box (EN500 and EX250 models), check, 9•5

L

Legal and safety checks, 0•15
Lighting system, check, 9•6
Linings, brake pads and shoes, wear check, 1•17
Linkage, rear suspension (EX250 models), removal, inspection and installation, 6•10
Lubricants and chemicals, REF•23
Lubricants and fluids, recommended, 1•2
Lubrication, general, 1•18

M

Main and connecting rod bearings, general note, 2C•20
Maintenance points
 EN450/500 models, 1•4, 1•5
 EX250 models, 1•6, 1•7
Maintenance schedule
 all except US and Canadian models, 1•9
 US and Canadian models, 1•8
Maintenance, routine, 1•1 through 1•32
Major engine repair, general note, 2C•7
 EN450/500 models, 2A•3
 EX250 models, 2B•2
Master cylinder, removal, overhaul and installation, 7•7
Meters and gauges, check and replacement, 9•11
Mirrors, removal and installation, 8•2
Motorcycle chemicals and lubricants, REF•23

N

Neutral switch, check and replacement, 9•13

O

Oil pan, EN450/500 models, removal and installation, 2A•12
Oil pressure check, 2C•8
Oil pressure relief valve, removal, inspection and installation
 EN450/500 models, 2A•14
 EX250 models, 2B•10
Oil pressure switch, check and replacement, 9•12
Oil pump, removal and installation
 EN450/500 models, 2A•13
 EX250 models, 2B•9
Oil, engine/transmission, level check, 0•12
Operations possible with the engine in the frame
 EN450/500 models, 2A•3
 EX250 models, 2B•2
Operations requiring engine removal
 EN450/500 models, 2A•3
 EX250 models, 2B•2

Index

P

Pads
and shoe linings, brake, wear check, 1•17
disc brake, replacement, 7•3
Parts, replacement, buying, 0•10
**Pedal, rear brake, removal and
installation, 7•10**
**Pickup coils, check, removal and
installation, 5•4**
Piston rings, installation, 2C•16
**Pistons, removal, inspection and
installation, 2C•14**
Pre-ride checks, 0•12
**Primary chain, camshaft chain and guides
(EN450/500 models)**
inspection, 2C•27
removal, inspection and installation, 2A•20

R

Radiator
cap, check, 3•2
removal and installation, 3•6
**Rear brake cam, lubrication
(drum brakes), 1•29**
**Rear drum brake, removal, inspection and
installation, 7•8**
**Rear shock absorber(s), removal and
installation, 6•9**
Rear suspension
linkage (EX250 models), removal,
inspection and installation, 6•10
lubrication, 1•28
**Rear view mirrors, removal and
installation, 8•2**
**Rear wheel coupling/rubber damper, check
and replacement, 6•14**
**Rear wheel, removal, inspection and
installation, 7•13**
Recommended break•in procedure, 2C•28
Recommended lubricants and fluids, 1•2
Reference, REF•1 through REF•50
**Repair operations possible with the engine
in the frame**
EN450/500 models, 2A•3
EX250 models, 2B•2
**Repair operations requiring engine
removal**
EN450/500 models, 2A•3
EX250 models, 2B•2
Replacement parts, buying, 0•10
**Rotor, brake, inspection, removal and
installation, 7•6**
**Routine maintenance and servicing,
1•1 through 1•32**
Routine maintenance intervals
all except US and Canadian models, 1•9
US and Canadian models, 1•8

S

Safety first!, 0•11
Scheduled maintenance, 1•1 through 1•32
Seat, removal and installation, 8•2
Security, REF•40
Shift drum and forks
inspection, 2C•28
removal, inspection and installation
EN450/500 models, 2A•26
EX250 models, 2B•17
**Shock absorber(s), rear removal and
installation, 6•9**
Shoes, drum brake
wear check, 1•17
replacement, 7•8
Side and centerstand, maintenance, 8•2
Side covers, removal and installation, 8•3
**Sidestand switch, check and
replacement, 9•14**
Spark plugs
type and gap, 1•1
cleaning and regap, 1•12
torque specification, 1•2
**Starter clutch, removal and
installation, 9•21**
Starter motor
disassembly, inspection and
reassembly, 9•17
removal and installation, 9•15
**Starter relay and starter circuit relay, check
and replacement, 9•14**
Steering head bearings
check and adjustment, 1•20
lubrication, 1•29
replacement, 6•7
Storage, REF•24
Suspension
adjustments, 6•14
linkage, rear (EX250 models), removal,
inspection and installation, 6•10
check, 1•20
steering and final drive checks, 0•15
**Suspension, steering and final drive,
6•1 through 6•14**
Swingarm
bearings
check, 6•10
replacement, 6•11
removal and installation, 6•11
Switches, check
brake light switch, 9•10
handlebar switches, 9•13
neutral switch, 9•13
sidestand switch, 9•14

T

Technical terms explained, REF•43

The Green Meanies, 0•4
**Thermostat and housing, removal, check
and installation, 3•4**
**Throttle and choke operation/grip freeplay,
check and adjustment, 1•21**
**Throttle cables, removal, installation and
adjustment, 4•11**
Tire checks, 0•16
Tires, general information, 7•15
Tools and workshop tips, REF•4
Transmission
gears and shafts, inspection, 2C•27
oil type and viscosity, 1•2
shafts, disassembly and reassembly
EN450/500 models, 2A•22
EX250 models, 2B•17
shafts, removal and installation, 2B•16
EN450/500 models, 2A•21
EX250 models, 2B•17
Troubleshooting, REF•27
Troubleshooting equipment, REF•36
Turn signal
assemblies, removal and installation, 9•9
circuit, check, 9•10
tail/brake light and license plate light
bulbs, replacement, 9•9

V

**Valve clearances, check and
adjustment, 1•22**
Valve cover, removal and installation
EN450/500 models, 2A•4
EX250 models, 2B•3
**Valves/valve seats/valve guides,
servicing, 2C•11**
Vehicle identification numbers, 0•8
**Voltage regulator/rectifier, check and
replacement, 9•20**

W

Warning light bulbs, replacement, 9•12
**Water pump, check, removal, inspection
and installation, 3•6**
Weights and dimensions, REF•1
Wheel bearings
inspection and maintenance, 7•14
lubricant type, 1•3
Wheel, removal, inspection and installation
front, 7•11
rear, 7•13
Wheels
and tires, general check, 1•18
inspection, repair and alignment
check, 7•11
Wiring diagrams, 9•22
Workshop tips, REF•4